Hannah 11:30-2pm

Fodor's

Pest market—at end
of shopping street

Andrassy at
Franz List square

BUDAPEST
FIRST EDITION

Where to Stay and Eat
for All Budgets

Must-See Sights
and Local Secrets

Ratings You Can Trust

Paris

Rue des Rosiers

Fodor's Travel Publications   New York, Toronto, London, Sydney, Auckland
www.fodors.com

FODOR'S BUDAPEST

Editor: Douglas Stallings

Editorial Production: Tom Holton
Editorial Contributors: Collin Campbell, Betsy Maury, Paul Olchváry, Kristen Schweizer, Jordan Simon, Julie Tomasz
Maps: David Lindroth, *cartographer;* Bob Blake and Rebecca Baer, *map editors*
Design: Fabrizio La Rocca, *creative director;* Moon Sun Kim, *cover designer;* Guido Caroti, *art director;* Melanie Marin, *senior photo editor*
Production/Manufacturing: Angela L. McLean
Cover Photo (Széchenyi thermal baths): Angelo Cavalli/age fotostock

SPECIAL SALES

This book is available for special discounts for bulk purchases for sales promotions or premiums. Special editions, including personalized covers, excerpts of existing books, and corporate imprints, can be created in large quantities for special needs. For more information, write to Special Markets/Premium Sales, 1745 Broadway, MD 6-2, New York, New York 10019, or e-mail specialmarkets@randomhouse.com.

AN IMPORTANT TIP & AN INVITATION

Although all prices, opening times, and other details in this book are based on information supplied to us at press time, changes occur all the time in the travel world, and Fodor's cannot accept responsibility for facts that become outdated or for inadvertent errors or omissions. So **always confirm information when it matters,** especially if you're making a detour to visit a specific place. Your experiences—positive and negative—matter to us. If we have missed or misstated something, **please write to us.** We follow up on all suggestions. Contact the Budapest editor at editors@fodors.com or c/o Fodor's at 1745 Broadway, New York, New York 10019.

PRINTED IN THE UNITED STATES OF AMERICA

10 9 8 7 6 5 4 3 2 1

DESTINATION BUDAPEST

B udapest, an old-world city with a flourishing urban pulse, is one
of the most exciting and attractive capitals of the newly expanded
European Union. Having endured centuries of wars and revolution, and decades of steady decay under the neglect of Soviet rule,
Budapest is an embraceably real and resilient city. It's a city that blooms
and fades simultaneously in front of your eyes: beautifully restored art
nouveau buildings and landmark city squares gleam in resurrected
majesty, while on inner-city streets graying stone facades riddled with
bullet holes crumble with quiet dignity. And as trams and cars stream
across the Danube's bridges in modern, urban rush-hour bustle, Budapest's deeply artistic history and spirit resonate in streets named after
poets and composers. Good roads and transportation links from Budapest make excursions around the rest of Hungary easy—to cobblestone
villages and hilltop castles in the Danube Bend; to the charming towns
and wine regions of Tokaj, Eger, Pécs, and Lake Balaton; and to the
Great Plain, where traditional life continues much as it has for centuries,
often on horseback. All this, and the generosity of the Magyar soul,
sustains visitors to this city and land of vital spirit and beauty.

Tim Jarrell, Publisher

CONTENTS

ON THE ROAD WITH FODOR'S

A trip takes you out of yourself. Concerns of life at home completely disappear, driven away by more immediate thoughts—about, say, what marvels will beguile the next day, or where you'll have dinner. That's where Fodor's comes in. We make sure that you know all your options, so that you don't miss something that's around the next bend just because you didn't know it was there. Because the best memories of your trip might well have nothing to do with what you came to Budapest to see, we guide you to sights large and small all over the region. You might set out to see Castle Hill, but back at home you find yourself unable to forget the soaring white atrium of the Museum of Applied Arts or your first taste of *szilva pálinka* (plum brandy). With Fodor's at your side, serendipitous discoveries are never far away.

Our success in showing you every corner of Budapest is a credit to our extraordinary writers. Although there's no substitute for travel advice from a good friend who knows your style, our contributors are the next best thing—the kind of people you would poll for travel advice if you knew them.

Betsy Maury, a former senior editor with the U.S. publisher Bantam Doubleday Dell, moved to Budapest in 1999 and has made the Magyar capital her home ever since. Her enthusiasm for the national cuisine—as well as a love of Hungarian wines—keeps her busy exploring the cosmopolitan city in search of interesting restaurants. She travels widely throughout Central Europe working as a freelance writer. Betsy authored several chapters in this guide, including "Where to Eat," "Spas & Sports," "Shopping," and "Pécs."

Paul Olchváry, a senior copywriter at Princeton University Press, lived in Hungary throughout the 1990s, initially in Pécs and later, from 1992, in Budapest. A native of Western New York, he has translated eight books from Hungarian to English, including Károly Pap's *Azarel* (Steerforth). He is currently completing a novel and a book of literary nonfiction; his stories and essays appeared regularly for years in the Budapest monthly *2000*. While in Hungary, in addition to translating, he taught English at a university and reported on politics under a fellowship with the U.S. Embassy. He's also worked as a newspaper reporter. Paul wrote "Exploring Budapest," "The Danube Bend," "Northern Hungary," "Books & Films," and "Language."

Kristen Schweizer has lived in Budapest since 1999 and has worked as a journalist for the *Budapest Business Journal*, Reuters, the Associated Press, and the International Federation of Red Cross/Red Crescent societies. Her writing has focused on topics including European Union accession, refugees, and organized crime. She has quit and restarted Hungarian more times than she cares to remember, but the most important lessons came from locals at the dog park. Her favorite things about Budapest are the thermal baths, Bohemian pubs, and any desserts with túró. Kristen wrote the "Nightlife & the Arts," "Sopron," "Lake Balaton," and "The Great Plain" chapters for this book.

Jordan Simon served as food and wine editor of *Mountain Sports & Living* (formerly *Snow Country*), *Ski Impact,* and *Vermont Vacations*; he's been the wine editor at several other magazines. He oversaw the creation and development of *Wine Country International* magazine, as founding Editor-in-Chief of Wine Country Network. The author of numerous guidebooks and co-author of *Celestial Seasonings Cookbook: Cooking with Tea,* he has written extensively on gastronomy for many national magazines. He serves as a corporate wine-tasting consultant (for restaurant groups such as Toscorp and alumni associations such as Boston Latin and Trinity Schools) and as a judge for numerous food and wine competitions (San

Francisco International Wine Competition, et al.). He contributed the essay in Hungarian wine.

Julie Tomasz was a founding editor of *The Budapest Sun* in the early 1990s and is a veteran Fodor's contributor, having worked as an editor in the New York office as well as a writer and updater in countries around the globe. Born in New York to refugees who fled Hungary after the 1956 Revolution, she later moved to Budapest for several years and remains hopelessly in love with it, returning frequently. She currently lives in London, where she writes travel articles and fiction. Her travel pieces have appeared in publications including *Travel Holiday* and *The Times of London*. Julie contributed chapters on "Where to Eat," "Smart Travel Tips," and several sections in the front matter.

ABOUT THIS BOOK

There's no doubt that the best source for travel advice is a like-minded friend who's just been where you're headed. But with or without that friend, you'll have a better trip with a Fodor's guide in hand. Once you've learned to find your way around its pages, you'll be in great shape to find your way around your destination.

SELECTION

Our goal is to cover the best properties, sights, and activities in their category, as well as the most interesting communities to visit. We make a point of including local food-lovers' hot spots as well as neighborhood options, and we avoid all that's touristy unless it's really worth your time. You can go on the assumption that everything you read about in this book is recommended wholeheartedly by our writers and editors. Flip to **On the Road with Fodor's** to learn more about who they are. It goes without saying that no property mentioned in the book has paid to be included.

RATINGS

Orange stars ★ denote sights and properties that our editors and writers consider the very best in the area covered by the entire book. These, the best of the best, are listed in the **Fodor's Choice** section in the front of the book. Black stars ★ highlight the sights and properties we deem **Highly Recommended,** the don't-miss sights within any region. Fodor's Choice and Highly Recommended options in each region are usually listed on the title page of the chapter covering that region. Use the index to find complete descriptions. In cities, sights pinpointed with numbered map bullets ❶ in the margins tend to be more important than those without bullets.

SPECIAL SPOTS

Pleasures & Pastimes focuses on types of experiences that reveal the spirit of the destination. Watch for **Off the Beaten Path** sights. Some are out of the way, some are quirky, and all are worth your while. If the munchies hit while you're exploring, look for **Need a Break?** suggestions.

TIME IT RIGHT

Wondering when to go? Check **On the Calendar** up front and chapters' **Timing** sections for weather and crowd overviews and best days and times to visit.

SEE IT ALL

Use Fodor's exclusive **Great Itineraries** as a model for your trip. (For a good overview of the entire destination, follow those that begin the book, or mix regional itineraries from several chapters.) In cities, **Good Walks** guide you to important sights in each neighborhood; ☞ indicates the starting points of walks and itineraries in the text and on the map.

BUDGET WELL

Hotel and restaurant price categories from ¢ to $$$$ are defined in the opening pages of each chapter—expect to find a balanced selection for every budget. For attractions, we always give standard adult admission fees; reductions are usually available for children, students, and senior citizens. Look in Discounts & Deals in Smart Travel Tips for information on destination-wide ticket schemes. Want to pay with plastic? AE, DC, MC, V following restaurant and hotel listings indicate whether American Express, Diners Club, MasterCard, or Visa are accepted.

BASIC INFO	Smart Travel Tips lists travel essentials for the entire area covered by the book; city- and region-specific basics end each chapter. To find the best way to get around, see the transportation section; see individual modes of travel ("Car Travel," "Train Travel") for details. We assume you'll check Web sites or call for particulars.
ON THE MAPS	Maps throughout the book show you what's where and help you find your way around. Black and orange numbered bullets ❶❶ in the text correlate to bullets on maps.
BACKGROUND	In general, we give background information within the chapters in the course of explaining sights as well as in CloseUp boxes and in Understanding Budapest & Hungary at the end of the book. To get in the mood, review the suggestions in Books & Movies. The Language section can be invaluable.
FIND IT FAST	Within the Exploring Budapest chapter, sights are grouped by neighborhood. Where to Eat and Where to Stay are also organized by neighborhood—Where to Eat is further divided by cuisine type. The Nightlife & the Arts and Thermal Spas & Outdoor Activities chapters are arranged alphabetically by entertainment type. Within Shopping, a description of the city's main shopping districts is followed by a list of specialty shops grouped according to their focus. The remaining chapters focus on side-trips from Budapest. The Danube Bend contains cities that can be seen easily as day-trips from Budapest. Lake Balaton covers the resort towns on Hungary's biggest lake, which is a major tourist destination for both Hungarians and visitors alike. Chapters on Sopron, Pécs, the Great Plain, and Northern Hungary, cover destinations throughout the country that can be reached in about a half day of travel, but most of these will require an overnight visit, so we've given you ample recommendations for hotels and other accommodations. All these chapters are subdivided by town, and the towns are covered in logical geographical order. Heads at the top of each page help you find what you need within a chapter.
DON'T FORGET	Restaurants are open for lunch and dinner daily unless we state otherwise; we mention dress only when there's a specific requirement and reservations only when they're essential or not accepted—it's always best to book ahead. Hotels have private baths, phone, TVs, and air-conditioning and operate on the European Plan (a.k.a. EP, meaning without meals). We always list facilities but not whether you'll be charged extra to use them, so when pricing accommodations, find out what's included.

SYMBOLS

Many Listings

★ Fodor's Choice
★ Highly recommended
⊠ Physical address
⊹ Directions
🕮 Mailing address
☎ Telephone
🖷 Fax
⊕ On the Web
✑ E-mail
🎫 Admission fee
🕓 Open/closed times
► Start of walk/itinerary
Ⓜ Metro stations
▭ Credit cards

Outdoors

🏌 Golf
🏕 Camping

Hotels & Restaurants

🏨 Hotel
🛏 Number of rooms
♿ Facilities
🍴 Meal plans
✕ Restaurant
🍸 Reservations
👔 Dress code
🚭 Smoking
🍷 BYOB
✕🏨 Hotel with restaurant that warrants a visit

Other

🐣 Family-friendly
☎ Contact information
⇨ See also
⊠ Branch address
☞ Take note

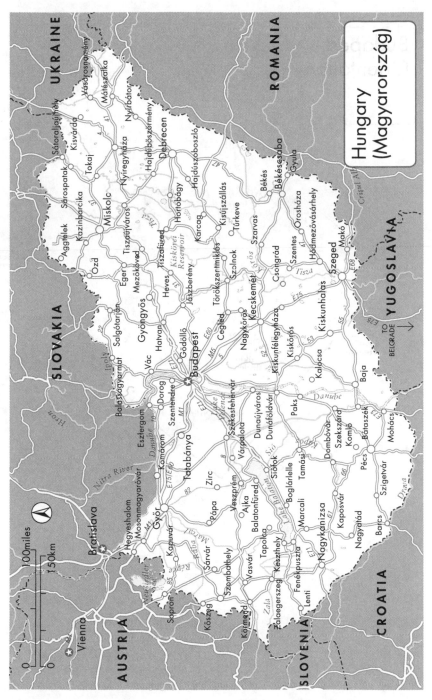

Hungary (Magyarország)

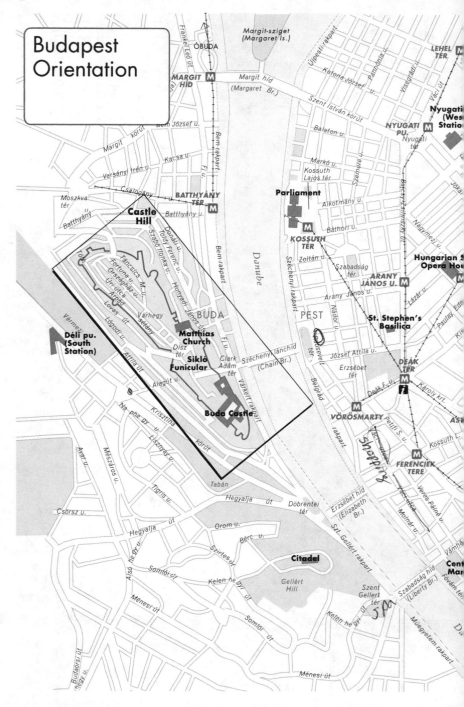

Budapest Orientation

OKTOGON Cafes

SPA

SZÉCHENYI FÜRDŐ

Lehel tér

Ferdinand híd

Ripp-Rónai u.

Dózsa György u.

HŐSÖK TERE

Vajda hunyad Vár

Olof Palme sétány

550 yards
500 meters

ati pu.
est
tion)

Podmaniczky utca

Szinyei Merse u.

Bajza u.

BAJZA U.

Benczúr u.

Varosliget
(City Park)

Ajtósi Dürer sor

Szondi u.

Rózsa u.

Aradi u.

Felső erdősor

KODÁLY KÖRÖND

Varosligeti fasor

Damjanich u.

Dózsa György út

Teréz körút

Jókai u.

VÖRÖSMARTY U.

Andrássy út

Vörösmarty u.

Dembinszky u.

Rottenbiller utca

István u.

OKTOGON

Liszt Ferenc tér

n State
House

OPERA

Erzsébet körút

Hársfa u.

Thököly út

Verseny u.

Ede u.

Király u.

Dob utca

Wesselényi utca

Klauzál u.

Rákóczi út

Fiumei út

KELETI PU.

Baross tér

Kerepesi út

BLAHA LUJZA TÉR

Erkel Ferenc Színház

Dohány utca

Rákóczi út

Szentkirály

József körút

Somogyi Béla u.

Népszínház u.

Köztársaság tér

Kerepesi temető (cemetery)

ASTORIA

h L. u.

Múzeum krt.

Puskin u.

Bérkocsis u.

Déri Miksa u.

Telekt László tér

Luther u.

Bródy Sándor u.

Mátyás tér

Dankó u.

Hungarian
National Museum

Múzeum u.

Krúdy u.

József u.

KÁLVIN TÉR

Baross utca

Baross utca

Diószeghy Sámuel u.

Central Market

Lónyai u.

Ráday u.

Üllői út

Nap u.

Práter u.

Szigony u.

FERENC KÖRÚT

Ferenc körút

Tömő u.

Üllői út

KLINIKÁK

Koranyi S. u.

Mester u.

Mány Kálmán u.

Koranyi S. u.

Boráros tér

Danube

Petőfi híd

KEY	
i	*Tourist Information*
→→	*Rail Lines*

Pest Neighborhoods

Around Andrássy út. Home to the Opera House, Millennium Underground, and Heroes' Square, the city's grandest boulevard (a UNESCO World Heritage Sight) echoes with Old World grandeur while buzzing with new restaurants, hotels, and shops. Aristocratic mansions line the leafier Heroes' Square end while the other end is full of city-center vitality. Liszt Ferenc tér is a hub of restaurant and bar activity.

Around Astoria. The famed Nagy Zsinagóga is this area's crowning sight, marking the gateway to Budapest's historic Jewish quarter. Astoria itself is the intersection of the little ring road with Kossuth Lajos utca/Rákókzci út, a major artery full of shops.

Around Blaha Lujza tér. Traffic is heavy at this busy intersection, and the area still has a reputation of seediness after hours. You'll find loads of less-touristy shops and restaurants around here.

Around Boráros tér. The narrow, dirty streets of District IX in southern Pest have long been one of the seediest, poorest parts of the city, but this is changing due to a major revitalization effort. Hungary's National Theater was relocated here from central Pest, and the new Holocaust Memorial Center recently opened. Numerous nightspots, of course, are already thriving.

Around Deák Ferenc tér. Deák tér is the hub of Budapest's three metro lines and the overall epicenter of downtown Pest. The Duna korzó, Váci utca, Andrássy út, and Szent István Bazilika are all within walking distance.

Around Ferenciek tere. The narrower streets of Pest's "inner city" (belváros) run south from around Ferenciek tere. This is one of Budapest's main university areas, with many cafés and nightspots frequented by students.

Around Kálvin tér. This busy square at the southern end of Pest's student area is the nexus of Districts V, VIII, and IX, buzzing with traffic and urban life. The Nemzeti Múzeum and Vásárcsarnok are here, as are numerous hotels, restaurants, and a thriving nightlife scene, especially along newly revitalized Ráday utca.

Around Keleti Train Station. Gritty and urban, this area teems with traffic, travelers, and city life, and it can get a bit dodgy after dark. Köztársaság tér and Budapest's "other" opera house, the Erkel, are here.

Around Király utca. Running parallel to Andrássy út, less-heralded Király utca is seeing more and more new shops, restaurants, and bars opening up along its sidewalks and narrow, atmospheric side streets.

Around Nyugati Train Station. Bustling with travelers, the area around the Western Train Station has always been one of Pest's busy business and shopping districts. The sprawling West End City Centre shopping mall is just behind it.

Around Váci utca. The area immediately surrounding Budapest's most famous and unabashedly overpriced shopping street has long been the heart of the city's tourist zone. Starting at Vörösmarty tér, it runs south all the way to the Vásárcsarnok, passing three bridges along the way. Running parallel is the Duna korzó and its stretch of Danube-front luxury hotels. The more recently pedestrianized stretch of Váci utca south of the Erzsébet Bridge runs through the less touristy university area.

City Park. In addition to some well-situated greenery, the square-kilometer that is City Park packs in several of Budapest's important children's sights: the zoo, circus, and amusement park. Here, too, however, are the popular Széchenyi thermal baths and lovely Vajdahunyad Castle, not to mention a pair of Budapest's best restaurants: Gundel and Robinson's.

Duna Plaza. One of Budapest's main shopping malls is in northern District XIII, on the outskirts of central Budapest.

Parliament. One of Pest's best squares, Kossuth tér is home to the Parliament building and Néprajzi Múzeum. All around is the banking and legislative center of Budapest, a neighborhood full of beautifully restored facades and increasingly coveted real estate. A host of antiques dealers have set up shop between Parliament and Szent István körút, and all around are good restaurants and a few well-situated hotels.

St. Stephen's Basilica. Resonating with the bells of Budapest's largest church, this neighborhood is full of Pest atmosphere and has numerous good restaurants, bars, and shops. Andrássy út begins just behind the basilica, and Deák tér is nearby.

Buda Neighborhoods

Around Batthyány tér. On the Danube directly across from Parliament, Batthyány tér offers glorious views as you come up from the metro and suburban rail station here. Parallel to the river, Fő utca can see heavy traffic but has some pretty squares and churches, and well-known Turkish baths. A few riverbank hotels are nearby.

Around Déli Train Station. This is the last metro stop in Buda. Buzzing with cars, buses, and trams, Alkotás utca and the nearby area are full of everyday shops and businesses. All trains to Lake Balaton leave from Déli Train Station.

Around Moszkva tér. Busy Moszkva tér is a major hub of Buda, with a shopping mall and lots of transport links, including the metro and the Várbusz, which serves nearby Castle Hill.

Buda Hills. The green, undulating areas of District XII and beyond give Buda its hilly reputation. Primarily residential (and pricey, at that), this is where people come to take walks and even ski in the winter. The Gyermek Vasút and Jánoshegy are recommended excursions.

Castle Hill. Budapest's undisputed "must-see" is Castle Hill, a hilltop district of cobblestoned streets and pastel facades, not to mention many of the city's top sights: the Royal Palace, the National Gallery, Mátyás templom, and Halászbástya, to name a few.

Gellért Hill & the Tabán. Several famed thermal-bath complexes and the views from Gellért Hill and its crowning fortress (citadella) are this area's main sights. Villas on and around Gellérthegy have always been prized real estate. Spreading below between Gellért and Castle hills is the Tabán, where just a few traditional buildings from its earlier days remain.

Margaret Island. Neither Buda nor Pest, this island in the Danube is an oasis of greenery between the city's two selves. It's primarily a park, with plenty of lawns and strolling paths. Two recommended hotels are at the northern end.

North Buda. The peaceful, leafy streets of Rozsa-domb (Rose Hill) are a prized residential area, "green" but still close to the more urban elements below. You'll find the Tomb of Gül Baba here.

Óbuda. Upriver from the main sights, Óbuda is on the outskirts of central Budapest. Much of it is a barrage of highways and concrete housing blocks, but its historic core is a gem of preserved buildings and charming restaurants. Numerous Roman ruins are also here.

South Buda. Behind Gellért Hill, Móricz-Zsigmond körtér is the hub of south Buda, with tram and bus links and plenty of car traffic. The area sees fewer tourists than other parts of Budapest, but this will likely change when a planned fourth metro line comes through.

Excursion Areas

The Danube Bend. Almost as many people take a day-trip to explore the picturesque Danube Bend as climb to the top of Castle Hill. Explore the venerable, cobblestoned artists' village of Szentendre; the 13th-century hilltop fortress of Visegrád; and Esztergom, Hungary's first capital (circa AD 1000) and home of its largest cathedral.

Lake Balaton. Central Europe's largest lake is landlocked Hungary's prized waterfront. Swimming beaches and watersports abound, but you can also explore typical old villages with thatched-roof, whitewashed cottages and indulge in the fruits of the north shore's hilltop vineyards.

Sopron. In Hungary's hilly green northwest corner, just an hour's drive from Vienna, this picturesque city's heart lies within Roman and medieval walls and contains many architectural and historical gems. Southeast of Sopron is the baroque Eszterházy Palace, where Joseph Haydn served as resident conductor for 30 years. Oft-overlooked Győr, to the east, is worthwhile for its baroque and neoclassical architecture, not to mention an impressive cathedral.

Pécs. This southwestern city rivals Budapest in its cultural and architectural offerings, all just on a smaller scale. In addition to being home of world-famous Zsolnay porcelain, Pécs has numerous art museums (including the best collection of Zsolnay porcelain in Hungary), a splendid cathedral, inviting cobblestone streets, and good restaurants and hotels. The nearby Villány region produces some of Hungary's best wines.

The Great Plain. The sandy, flat grasslands south and east of Budapest are home to shepherds tending their sheep and cattle and where the famous *csikós* (Hungarian cowboys), renowned for their equestrian skills, perform unique stunts on horseback. University-town Szeged, near the Serbian border, is famed for its paprika, and oft-overlooked Kecskemét has some excellent museums and more architectural treasures than you'd expect of a town in the very center of the country.

Northern Hungary. The baroque city of Eger and charming village of Tokaj are famous for their wines and abound with tasting opportunities. The tiny medieval mountain village of Hollókő is a protected UNESCO World Heritage site and an enchanting place to explore. In Aggtelek, the underground wonders of its extensive cave systems await.

If You Have 3 Days

Three days in Budapest will give you a solid take on the city's must-sees and must-dos and will allow you to start soaking in the flavor of the place and the people.

DAY 1: Start from the top by going up to Castle Hill, the undisputed first stop on everyone's itinerary. After admiring the views from where 13th-century Hungarian kings once stood, explore the museums in the wings of the Royal Palace. Later, stroll along the cobblestone streets among the colorful baroque, Gothic, and Renaissance facades, stopping in for a look at Matthias Church and taking in the postcard-perfect views from the Fishermen's Bastion. Don't forget to treat yourself to some *rétes* (streudel) and coffee at tiny Ruszwurm Cukrászda. Later, go for an after-dinner stroll along the Duna korzó in Pest—or perhaps an evening boat ride—to see the Chain Bridge and the whole palace lit up in golden lights.

DAY 2: You started with Buda, today it's Pest. Start with a look inside massive Szent István Bazilika (views from the cupola are worth the climb), then make your way down Andrássy út: World Heritage–classified address of the Opera House, Liszt Ferenc tér, House of Terror Museum, numerous sidewalk cafés, and a parade of elegant turn-of-the-20th-century stone mansions. At the other end is Hősök tere and its two art museums, from where you can take the Millennium Underground back to Vörösmarty tér. If you still have time and energy, a long walk down pedestrian-only, super-touristy Váci utca (the second half, past Ferenciek tere, is less brash) gets you to the vast Vásárcsarnok market hall, where you can stop for a snack and watch the hustle and bustle.

DAY 3: Spend the morning at the Gellért, Széchenyi, or another of the city's famous bath complexes, a quintessential Budapest experience. Later, take a tour of the Parliament building, visit the Néprajzi Múzeum across the way, and spend the afternoon browsing the antiques shops along Falk Miksa utca. In the evening, attend an opera or ballet at the splendid Opera House followed by an alfresco nightcap on Liszt Ferenc tér.

If You Have 7 Days

With an entire week to spend in Budapest, you'll be able to get a handle on the city's many sights in your first three days, which you should spend as outlined above, and then get a look at some of Hungary's other magnificent towns.

DAY 4: Spend your first three days as above. Today, explore the smaller, less commercial streets of Pest's atmospheric inner-city core, including the historic old Jewish quarter and its magnificently restored Nagy Zsinagóga, Europe's largest synagogue. Take an organized walking tour of this area for full effect. If you have time and energy, catch a bus out to Szobor Park for a blast from the Communist past. Later, hunker down in a typical Hungarian restaurant with live Gypsy music and make a night of it with a hearty traditional meal with all the trimmings.

DAY 5: Hop on a morning boat and take a scenic cruise upriver into the Danube Bend. Spend the day exploring the time-honored artists' village of Szentendre, the majestic fortress of Visegrád, and the cathedral town of Esztergom, Hungary's first capital in the year 1000. Return to Budapest by boat, bus, or train, depending on your pace and scheduling.

DAY 6: If you want to do some wine tasting, head northeast to Eger or Tokaj, two of the country's most famous wine regions. A baroque city with a castle, Eger is the better option for those who want to see more sights. It's best to spend the night either way so you can fully imbibe and enjoy an evening outside Budapest. An alternative northern option, sans wine tasting, is a day-trip to the UNESCO World Heritage village of Hollókő. Still another possibility is a day- or overnight trip to the northwestern city of Sopron on the Austrian border.

DAY 7: Once you've returned to Budapest, for the remainder of your last day you can take a walk or a bicycle ride on Margaret Island or go to Szobor Park if you weren't able to visit it on Day 4. Later, watch the sun set over Castle Hill from the Margaret Bridge or the Duna korzo.

If You Have 2 Weeks
With two weeks to spend in Hungary, you'll be able to thoroughly explore Budapest and its neighbors in the Danube Bend as well as some great places a bit farther afield. Spend the first six days as above, staying the last night in Eger, Tokaj, or Sopron.

DAY 7: Spend today exploring the surrounding countryside before going back to Budapest for the evening. If you stayed in Eger, try Tokaj, or vice versa. If you went to Sopron, consider a trip to the magnificent Eszterházy Palace, or stop over in Győr on your way back to Budapest. If you have a car and don't mind a day of travel, go directly south to Pécs and spend an extra half-day exploring the charming city.

DAYS 8 & 9: Get an early start from Budapest and go south to Pécs, exploring its beautiful town square, cathedral, and excellent museums. Spend the night here. See more of Pécs in the morning then tour some of the nearby Villány region's famous wineries, before spending another night back in Pécs.

DAY 10: If you have a car, make your way on scenic secondary roads through southern Transdanubia to Keszthely on the northwestern tip of Lake Balaton, visiting the spectacular Festetics mansion before moving east along the northern shore to Badacsony. On the way, you can make a stop in Szigliget and scale its castle hill to gaze at the sweeping Lake Balaton view. Check into a hotel in Badacsony, and if you have time and energy, climb the vineyard-carpeted slopes of Mount Badacsony and watch the sun set over the lake. Indulge in a big fish dinner with live Gypsy music and plenty of local wine.

DAY 11: Move on along the northern shore to Balatonfüred and Tihany, both of which have good lodging possibilities. Spend this day exploring one or both towns, cooling off with a swim in the lake. Spend the night.

DAY 12: Head back to Budapest. Use what's left of the day to see more sights or to regroup in another of the city's thermal baths. Later have a night on the town.

DAY 13: Get an early start and head south for a day on the Great Plain, strolling among the sights of lovely, often-overlooked Kecskemét before venturing out to the *puszta* (prairie) in Kiskunsági Nemzeti Park to experience the unique horsemanship stunts and demonstrations of Hungary's legendary cowboys, the csikós. Depending on how much you want to drive and how much of Budapest's nightlife you want to take in, you can either go back to Budapest for the night or spend it here in slow-paced Kecskemét.

DAY 14: If you're waking up in Budapest, you can use today for last-day shopping and sightseeing, possibly taking a daytrip to Hollókő if you haven't yet been. Be sure to have a farewell look at the nighttime view from the Danube promenade.

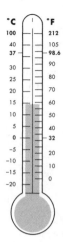

°C		°F
100		212
40		105
37		98.6
30		90
25		80
20		70
15		60
10		50
5		40
0		32
−5		20
−10		10
−15		0
−20		

July and August, peak vacation season for Hungarians as well as foreign tourists, can be extremely hot and humid; Budapest is stuffy and crowded with tour buses, and the entire Lake Balaton region is overrun with vacationers during this period. The Formula I race held annually in July or August maxes out Budapest's hotel capacity, not to mention doubles the room prices. If you want the city to yourself, however, and can handle some dreary weather, go in November or January. The ideal times to visit Budapest and Hungary are in the spring (May through June) and late summer into autumn (late August through October). The weather is milder, the crowds are smaller, and many of Hungary's major fairs and festivals take place during the spring and fall, including the Spring Festival (in Budapest and many other cities and towns) from late March to early April and the myriad wine-harvest festivals in late summer and early fall. Spring, too, is when the landscape starts to bloom, with fruit orchards blossoming as early as April, and crimson poppies blanketing seemingly all open spaces in May—visible from highways and trains and even the HÉV suburban railway to Szentendre. Summer in the countryside holds the unforgettable and quintessentially Hungarian sights of sweeping fields of swaying golden sunflowers and giant white storks summering in their bushy nests built on chimney tops. Hungary's Lake Balaton is the only area that gets boarded up during its extended low season, generally from mid- or late September until at least Easter, if not mid-May.

Climate

Hungary's climate is standard Continental. From November into March is typically lowest season for tourism, and with the shorter hours of daylight and cold, cloudy weather, Budapest can be quite grey and dreary. The city usually gets a few snow falls in December, January, and February, with more in the higher regions in the north. Being as shallow as it is, parts of Lake Balaton usually freeze in the coldest parts of winter, lending itself to good ice skating. July and August are hot (in the 80sF) and often humid, making the air in inner Budapest quite bad at times. May through June and September through October have the mildest temperatures and most pleasant weather, making them ideal times to visit.

🛈 Forecasts **Weather Channel Connection** ☎ 900/932−8437, 95¢ per minute from a Touch-Tone phone ⊕ www.weather.com.

BUDAPEST

Jan.	34F	1C	May	72F	22C	Sept.	73F	23C
	25	− 4		52	11		54	12
Feb.	39F	4C	June	79F	26C	Oct.	61F	16C
	28	− 2		59	15		45	7
Mar.	50F	10C	July	82F	28C	Nov.	46F	8C
	36	2		61	16		37	3
Apr.	63F	17C	Aug.	81F	27C	Dec.	39F	4C
	25	− 4		61	16		30	− 1

ON THE CALENDAR

The top seasonal events in Budapest and the rest of Hungary are listed below, and any one of them could provide the stuff of lasting memories. For contact information about most of these festivals, inquire at the Budapest Tourinform office or the local visitor information center. You can also plan ahead by checking the events calendars on various Hungarian tourism Web sites (see ⇨ Visitor Information *in* Smart Travel Tips).

ONGOING

Mid-September–June	The season at the **Hungarian State Opera House** opens in the early fall and continues through the early summer.

WINTER

December 1–24	Vendors selling handicrafts and other giftable items set up stalls on Vörösmarty tér and other squares throughout Budapest for the annual **Christmas markets**. There's entertainment, too.
December 30	To start celebrating early, the celebrated **100-member Gypsy Orchestra** plays their famous brand of traditional folk music at a massive concert in the Budapest Convention Center, with wine and refreshments.
December 30–January 1	Celebrating the **Budapest New Year,** free music and dance performances and general festivities take place around three squares in downtown Budapest: Nyugati tér, Oktogon, and Vörösmarty tér.
February	Banned for decades by the Communist regime, masquerade **Farsang Balls** are held throughout the carnival season in venues throughout Budapest.

SPRING

Mid-March–early April	Hungary's largest cultural festival, the **Budapest Spring Festival,** showcases the country's best performing artists in all disciplines (dance, theater, music, et al.), as well as visiting foreign artists. Other towns—including Kecskemét, Szentendre, Debrecen, Eger, and Pécs—also participate.
	Easter Sunday and Monday Villagers dressed in colorful traditional costumes hold egg-painting demonstrations and perform other local Easter customs during the **Hollókő Easter Festival** in this World Heritage–site village. There are also entertainment and market stalls.
May	The month-long **Balaton Festival** in Keszthely features high-caliber classical concerts and other festivities held in venues around town and outdoors on Kossuth Lajos utca.
Late May	Some 30 vintners introduce their wines with tastings and talks, plus music and dance programs, at the weekend-long **Tokaj Wine Festival** in Hungary's best-known wine region.

SUMMER

Mid-June–Mid-July	The monthlong **Sopron Festival Weeks** brings music, dance, and theater performances and art exhibits to the Fertőrákos cave theater and churches and venues around town.
Late June	A weekend of concerts, street performances, and costume contests is how the **Budapesti Búcsú** annually celebrates the departure of the last Soviet troops from Hungary in 1990.
Late June–late August	The **Szentendre Summer Days** festival offers open-air theater performances and jazz and classical concerts.
Early July	The **World Music Festival,** held on an outdoor stage in a Budapest park, has a few days of world music concerts by local and international artists.
July–mid-August	Budapest's oldest bridge finally gets a break from car traffic during the **Summer on the Chain Bridge** weeks, when it is open only to pedestrians and is transformed into a venue for open-air concerts.
July–August	During the Opera House's summer hiatus, the **BudaFest Summer Music Festival** presents opera, ballet, classical, and jazz performances in the Hilton Dominican Courtyard, in front of the Bazilika on St. Stephen's Square, and at the Opera House itself.
Mid-July–mid-August	Established in the 1930s, the annual **Szegedi Szabadtéri Játékok** (Open-Air Plays) offers a gala series of dramas, operas, operettas, classical concerts, and folk-dance performances by Hungarian and international artists, all performed outdoors before the imposing Dom Church. Tickets are always a hot commodity; plan far ahead.
Late July	A kind of multicultural Woodstock on the Danube, the massively popular annual **Sziget Festival** is held on an island in the river in northern Budapest. For a week, young people camp out and live on the island, where there is a virtually nonstop program of simultaneous rock concerts, films, and theater productions. Major Hungarian bands and international bands attend.
Late July	The last weekend in July you can join thousands of others in the annual **Balatoni-átúszás** (Cross-Balaton Swim), a 5.2-km (3-mi) swim from the north to south shore across Central Europe's largest lake.
Late July	Balatonfüred's **Anna Ball** is a traditional ball and beauty contest dating back almost 200 years.
Late July	From around the last week in July, the three-week **Festival Weeks in Baroque Eger** presents contemporary Hungarian dance and theater as well as classical concerts and opera.
Mid-August	Every year Budapest hosts an international **Formula 1** car race, flooding the city's hotels and restaurants with fast-car fans.

August 20	**St. Stephen's Day** is a major national holiday. Two highlights are the fireworks in Budapest and Debrecen's Flower Carnival, which features a festive parade of flower-covered floats and carriages.
Late August	The weeklong **Jewish Summer Festival**, held in late August and early September, features cantors, classical concerts, a kosher cabaret, films, and theater and dance performances, in Budapest and sometimes elsewhere.

FALL

September	The **Eger Harvest Festival** early in the month celebrates the grape harvest with a traditional parade and wine tastings.
Early September	The 10-day **Budapest International Wine and Champagne Festival** takes place on Castle Hill, showcasing Hungary's best wines in a festive atmosphere.
Early October	Tokaj's annual **Szüreti Hét** (Harvest Week) celebrates the autumn grape harvest with a parade, street ball, folk-art markets, and a plethora of wine-tasting opportunities from the local vintners' stands set up on and around the main square.
Mid-October	New directions in music and the arts are showcased in venues around the city during the two-week **Budapest Autumn Festival**.

PLEASURES & PASTIMES

Beaches & Water Sports Lake Balaton, the largest lake in Central Europe, is the most popular playground of this landlocked nation. If you're looking to relax in the sun and do a little windsurfing, swimming, or boating, settle in here for several days, basing yourself in either the northern shore's main town, Balatonfüred, or the more tranquil Tihany.

Hungarian Cuisine Through the lean postwar years the Hungarian kitchen lost none of its spice and sparkle. Meats, rich sauces, and creamy desserts predominate, but the more health-conscious will also find salads, even out of season. (Strict vegetarians should note, however, that even meatless dishes are often cooked with *zsír* [lard].) Lake Balaton is the major source of fish in Hungary, particularly for *fogas* (pike perch) and *süllő* (another kind of perch). Portions tend to be large, so don't plan to eat more than one main Hungarian meal a day. Desserts are lavish, and every inn seems to have its house *torta* (cake). In Budapest and other major cities, you'll find a good selection of restaurants, from the grander establishments that echo the imperial past of the Hapsburg era to trendy new international restaurants to cheap but cheerful spots favored by the working populace. In addition to trying out the standard *vendéglő* or *étterem* (restaurants), you can eat at a *bisztró étel bár* (sit-down snack bar), a *büfé* (snack counter), an *eszpresszó* (café), or a *söröző*pass up a visit to at least one *cukrászda* (pastry shop). Of course, if you find yourself longing for something non-Hungarian—anything from pizza to Indian, Turkish to Korean, Greek to American-style fast food—you can find it aplenty in Budapest.

Folk Art Hungary's centuries-old traditions of handmade, often regionally specific folk art are still beautifully alive. Intricately carved wooden boxes, vibrantly colorful embroidered tablecloths and shirts, matte black pottery pitchers, delicately woven lace collars, ceramic plates splashed with painted flowers and birds, and decorative heavy leather whips are among the favorite handcrafted pieces you can purchase. You'll find them in folk-art stores in Budapest and Szentendre, but you can purchase them directly from the artisans at crafts fairs and from peddlers on the streets. Dolls dressed in national costume are also popular souvenirs.

Grand Hotels Several of Budapest's once crumbling landmark buildings have been completely restored and made into deluxe five-star hotels. Staying in one of these museum-quality gems allows you to start your sightseeing right in your hotel lobby. And a room overlooking the Danube, from Buda or Pest, allows Budapest's magic to work on you even in bed. Bought back from the government over the years since the Iron Curtain fell, more and more of Hungary's magnificent, centuries-old castles and mansions are being restored and opened as country resorts; a night or two in one of these majestic old places makes for an unusual and romantic (but not always luxurious) lodging experience. Northern Hungary has some of the best.

Porcelain   Among the most sought-after items in Hungary are the exquisite hand-painted Herend and Zsolnay porcelain. Unfortunately, the prices on all makes of porcelain have risen considerably in the last few years. For guaranteed authenticity, make your purchases at the specific Herend and Zsolnay stores in Budapest and other major cities, or at the factories themselves in Herend and Pécs, respectively.

Spas & Thermal Baths   Several thousand years ago, the first settlers of the area that is now Budapest chose their home because of its abundance of hot springs. Centuries later, the Romans and the Turks built baths and developed cultures based on medicinal bathing. Now there are more than 1,000 medicinal hot springs bubbling up around the country. Budapest alone has some 14 historic working baths, which attract ailing patients with medical prescriptions for specific water cures as well as "recreational" bathers—locals and tourists alike—wanting to soak in the relaxing waters, try some of the many massages and treatments, and experience the architectural beauty of the bathhouses themselves. For most, a visit to a bath involves soaking in several thermal pools of varying temperatures and curative contents—perhaps throwing in a game of aquatic chess—relaxing in a steam room or sauna, and getting a brisk—if not brutal—massage. Many bath facilities are single-sex or have certain days set aside for men or women only, and most people walk around nude or with miniature loincloths, provided at the door. Men should be aware that some men-only baths have a strong gay clientele. Newer, modern spa hotels lack the charm and aesthetic appeal of their older peers but provide the latest treatments in sparkling facilities.

Wine, Beer & Spirits   Hungary tempts wine connoisseurs with its important wine regions, especially Villány, near Pécs, in the south; Eger and Tokaj in the north; and the northern shore of Lake Balaton. Szürkebarát (a pinot gris varietal) and especially Olaszrizling (a milder Rhine Riesling) are common white table wines; Tokay, one of the great wines of the world, can be heavy, dark, and sweet, and its most famous variety (Aszü) is drunk as an aperitif or a dessert wine. Good Tokay is expensive, especially by Hungarian standards, so it's usually reserved for special occasions. The red table wine of Hungary, Egri Bikavér (Bull's Blood of Eger, usually with *el toro* himself on the label), is a good buy and the safest bet with all foods. Villány produces superb reds and the best rosés; the most adventurous reds—with sometimes successful links to both Austrian and Californian wine making and viticulture—are from the Sopron area. Before- and after-dinner drinks tend toward schnapps, most notably *Barack-pálinka*, an apricot brandy. A plum brandy called *Kosher szilva-pálinka*, bottled under rabbinical supervision, is the very best of the brandies available in stores. *Vilmos körte-pálinka,* a pear variety, is almost as good. Unicum, Hungary's national liqueur, is a dark, thick, and potent herbal bitter that could be likened to Germany's Jägermeister. Its chubby green bottle makes it a good souvenir to take home. Major Hungarian beers are Dreher, Kőbányai, and Aranyászok, and several good foreign beers are produced in Hungary under license.

Nightlife

Budapest's nightlife is among the best in the new EU. It's varied, it's lively, and it's hopping into the wee hours. While dance clubs exist, you don't have to go to one to get your dancing groove on. Revellers moved by good, hip DJs usually have dance floors close by. Live music of all flavors is available somewhere every night, usually with little to no cover charge. Taking advantage of the major renovations going on throughout the city, a current trend is to open temporary nightspots in the courtyards of uninhabited buildings slated for demolition or massive overhaul. Also popular are the summer-only alfresco nightclubs sprawling over large park areas, with drinking and dancing under the stars and trees.

FODOR'S CHOICE

Fodor's Choice
★

The sights, restaurants, hotels, and other travel experiences on these pages are our editors' top picks—our Fodor's Choices. They're the best of their type in the area covered by the book—not to be missed and always worth your time. In the destination chapters that follow, you will find all the details.

LODGING

$$$$	**Four Seasons Hotel Gresham Palace Budapest,** Around Váci utca. A lavish, luxurious hotel created from a stunning art nouveau landmark. What more is there to say about Budapest's newest five-star hotel?
$$$$	**Kempinski Hotel Corvinus Budapest,** Around Deák Ferenc tér. Budapest's best business hotel may look cold and uninviting on the outside, but inside, the warm and spacious rooms will win you over.
$$$–$$$$	**Andrássy Hotel,** Around Andrássy út. The city's best boutique hotel was once a dreary orphanage. Now, it exudes style.
$$$–$$$$	**Corinthia Grand Hotel Royal,** Around Blaha Lujza tér. Like many of Budapest's best hotels, this one is a renovation of a late-19-century gem and has been restored to its former glory.
¢–$$	**Club Imola,** Balatonfüred. You'll appreciate the quiet seclusion of this small hotel in Balaton's busiest town.

BUDGET LODGING

$	**Count Degenfeld Castle Hotel,** Tarczal. A night in this meticulously kept palace hotel is one of Hungary's best bargains.
$	**Hotel Pest,** Around Andrássy út. An imaginatively restored 18th-century apartment house is now a convivial hotel, with an unbeatable location.
¢–$	**Club Hotel Badacsony,** Badacsony. One of the better large hotels near the shore of Lake Balaton has a heated pool open in winter.
¢–$	**Hotel Wollner,** Sopron. You can relax in the courtyard of this lovely 18th-century hotel that's been restored to its original splendor.
¢–$	**Kalmár Bed & Breakfast,** Gellért Hill & the Tabán. A rooming house in the Communist era, this 1900 mansion is now a family-run B&B and a great place to discover some of the old Buda ambience at reasonable prices.
¢–$	**Kastély Hotel,** Tihany. This mansion-turned-hotel, built in the 1930s, is right on the water.
¢	**Bock Pince Panzió,** Pécs. An inexpensive little pension that happens to be attached to one of Hungary's finest vineyards has an elegant restaurant to boot.

¢ | **Oliva Panzió,** Veszprém. You'll have to look carefully to find this little pension, but once you do, you'll be rewarded by a small hotel that's about as charming as they come.

¢ | **Pongrácz Manor,** Kecskemét. When you stay at this traditional Hungarian puszta hotel, it's as if you were bunking at a very sophisticated dude ranch.

RESTAURANTS

$$-$$$$ | **Café Kör,** St. Stephen's Basilica. This chic, upscale bistro is close by when you are touring St. Stephen's.

$$-$$$$ | **Ős Kaján,** Tolcsva. When you're in Tokaj, it's well worth the effort to seek out one of the country's best small restaurants.

$$-$$$ | **Aranysárkány,** Szentendre. During the busy summer season, you'll definitely need to call ahead to grab one of the eight tables in this small, excellent restaurant, which is also one of the few air-conditioned places in town.

$$-$$$ | **Vörös és Fehér,** Around Andrássy út. The food is good, but wine is the star at this excellent little bistro owned by the Budapest Wine Society.

$-$$$ | **Botond Restaurant,** Szeged. Szeged's best restaurant is the place to order the spicy fish soup for which the city is famous.

$-$$$ | **Café Pierrot,** Castle Hill. Your best bet for a lunch stop when touring the castle is this inviting café, which has an added advantage—free wireless Internet access for customers.

$-$$$ | **Kiskakkuk,** Parliament. The atmosphere is homey but a bit sophisticated, and the classic Hungarian poultry dishes are always a good bet.

$$ | **Náncsi Néni,** North Buda. Paprika pods may hang from the ceiling of this rustic restaurant, but the straightforward Hungarian staples are served with warmth and charm.

$-$$ | **Corvinus,** Sopron. The menu at this atmospheric restaurant on Sopron's main square is far-ranging, and everything is satisfying; the wonderful Renaissance-era setting doesn't hurt one's enjoyment of the food.

$-$$ | **Liberté Kávéház,** Kecskemét. You might even be able to imagine you were in Vienna if you stop here, but you're still on the Hungarian Great Plain.

$-$$ | **Menza,** Around Andrássy út. Hungarian comfort food gets reinvented in a retro-Communist atmosphere, minus the surly Communist-era service.

¢-$ | **Centrál Kávéház,** Around Váci utca. One of Budapest's most elegant cafés is also one of its most comfortable—it even has a no-smoking section.

$ **Soproni Borház,** Sopron. If you stop at this historic wine cellar restaurant, you'll have over 300 Hungarian vintages at your disposal; it's the best place for a tasting in northwestern Hungary.

MUSIC & THEATER IN BUDAPEST

Budapest Festival Orchestra. In a city with over 20 active symphonies, this is the best.

Liszt Ferenc Zeneakadémia, Around Andrássy út. The city's finest concert hall sells last-minute standing-room tickets for a song.

Magyar Állami Operaház, Around Andrássy út. The city's glittering opera house is the best place to see classical opera and dance.

Vígszínház, Around Nyugati Train Station. The best theater in Hungary stages plays as dazzling as the restored 19th-century venue, but they're all in Hungarian.

NIGHTLIFE IN BUDAPEST

BorBíróság, Around Kálvin tér. The city's best wine bar sells some 120 varieties by the glass.

Fészek Artists' Klub, Around Király utca. The large drinking garden (covered and heated in winter) has been the place bohemian Budapest imbibes for over 100 years.

Mélypont, Around Kálvin tér. It's like stepping back to the 1970s in this carefully styled, retro-Communist bar.

Piaf, Around Andrássy út. This late-night haunt near the opera house doesn't even open until 10 PM, but if you get past the doorman, you can drink and dance until dawn.

SHOPPING IN BUDAPEST

BomoArt, Around Váci utca. Though small, this shop sells one-of-a-kind, handmade paper diaries and stationery that are suitable for the grandest executive suite.

Budapest Bortársaság, Castle Hill. If you want to take home a viticultural souvenir, the Budapest Wine Society's shop has the largest selection in town.

Magma, Around Váci utca. Stop here for the best in hand-made jewelry, textiles, and housewares.

Mandarina Duck, Around Nyugati Train Station. These pricey Italian designer bags are actually worth the money.

Naray Tamás, Around Ferenciek tere. One of Hungary's best designers sells colorful couture that's a feast for the eyes.

Studio Agram, Parliament. Your best source in Budapest for the country's famous art deco pieces; and these are restored originals, not contemporary copies.

THERMAL BATHS & SPAS

Danubius Thermal Hotel Helia, Margaret Island. You don't even need to be a hotel guest to enjoy the services of Hungary's finest health spas.

Király Gyógyfürdő, Lower Buda. The oldest thermal baths in Budapest—popular on men's bathing days with the gay crowd—are also the most atmospheric.

Mandala Day Spa, Duna Plaza. Relaxation is the keyword at this pampering spa.

Mediterrán Elményfürdő, Debrecen. This enclosed thermal water park is the country's largest spa experience.

Széchenyi Gyógyfürdő, City Park. This indoor-outdoor thermal bathing complex is one of Europe's largest; on any given day a large portion of the city's populace seems to stop in for a dip.

CHURCHES & RELIGIOUS BUILDINGS

Mátyás templom, Castle Hill. Castle Hill's soaring Gothic church is colorfully ornate inside with lavishly frescoed Byzantine pillars.

Nagy Zsinagóga, Around Astoria. Europe's largest synagogue, this giant Byzantine-Moorish beauty underwent a massive restoration four decades after being ravaged by Hungarian and German Nazis during World War II.

Pécs Bazilika, Pécs. The four-spired cathedral is one of Europe's finest, particularly the gold- and silver-bedecked interior.

Püspöki katedra, Győr. The throne in this magnificent church was given by Empress Maria Theresa herself.

Szent István Bazilika, St. Stephen's Basilica. Inside this massive neo-Renaissance beauty, the capital's biggest church, is a rich collection of mosaics and statuary as well as the mummified right hand of Hungary's first king and patron saint.

ARCHITECTURAL HIGHLIGHTS

Bencés Apátság, Tihany. This ancient abbey stands on a hill outside of town, overlooking the entire Tihany Peninsula and Lake Balaton.

Eger Vár, Eger. The northern Hungarian stronghold is one of the country's most impressive.

Halászbástya, Castle Hill. The wondrous porch overlooking the Danube and Pest is the neo-Romanesque Fishermen's Bastion, a merry cluster of white stone towers, arches, and columns above a modern bronze statue of St. Stephen, Hungary's first king.

Margitsziget. An island of tranquility in the heart of Budapest, the capital's favorite place of respite offers not only lovely walks but swimming complexes, an outdoor theater, a Japanese garden, a hotel, and a petting zoo.

Rákóczi-pince, Tokaj. Hungary's most famous wine cellar is also the largest in all of Europe.

Storno Ház, Sopron. Directly on the town's main square, this is one of Sopron's finest Renaissance-era buildings.

Tűztorony, Sopron. This tower has sent the alarm about fires in the old city since Roman times.

Veszprém, Lake Balaton. This charming, small city is the center of Balaton's cultural life.

MUSEUMS

Magyar Fotográfia Múzeum, Debrecen. One of only a few museums in the country with a substantial photographic collection, this one is superb.

Magyar Nemzeti Galéria, Castle Hill. This grand and sweeping collection of Hungarian art includes everything from medieval ecclesiastical paintings and statues through the Gothic, Renaissance, and baroque art, to a wealth of 19th- and 20th-century works.

Néprajzi Múzeum, Parliament. A majestic 1890s structure across from the Parliament building—the lavish marble entrance hall alone is worth a visit—houses an impressive exhibit on Hungary's historic folk traditions.

Pick Szalámi és Szegedi Paprika Múzeum, Szeged. You'll know your salami after visiting this shrine to Hungary's favorite meat product and its favorite spice.

Szépművészeti Múzeum, City Park. Hungary's best collection of fine art includes esteemed works by Dutch and Spanish old masters, as well as exhibits of major Hungarian artists.

Zsolnay Múzeum, Pécs. See displays of one of Hungary's finest porcelain-makers here.

Finding out about your destination before you leave home means you won't squander time organizing everyday minutiae once you've arrived. You'll be more streetwise when you hit the ground as well, better prepared to explore the aspects of Budapest that drew you here in the first place. The organizations in this section can provide information to supplement this guide; contact them for up-to-the-minute details, and consult the A to Z sections that end the side-trips chapters for facts on the various topics as they relate to the areas around Budapest. Happy landings!

ADDRESSES

As in Paris, neighborhoods in Budapest are known and referred to locally not by name but by their district number, the equivalent to the Paris arrondissement. The standard format for street addresses is: first the district number—a Roman numeral designating one of Budapest's 22 districts, then the street name, then the street number. For the sake of clarity, in this book, the word "District" precedes the Roman numeral. For easier reference, we've also delineated and named neighborhoods (see ⇨ What's Where).

You will find few reminders among street names of the era of Communist rule, when streets and squares were named after Soviet heroes and concepts. If you look carefully at street signs, you may still find some with the old names crossed out with a triumphant red line. Today, many of Budapest's streets and squares are named after famous Hungarian composers, poets, and painters, reflecting the nation's strong regard for music and the arts.

Keep in mind that Hungary numbers building levels starting from zero (i.e., the ground floor is 0, next floor up is 1, etc.).

The following translations will help you in your navigating:

út (sometimes *útja*) means road

utca (u.) means street

tér (sometimes *tere*) means square

körút (krt.) means ring road

körtér and *körönd* mean circle
kerület (ker.) means district
emelet (em.) means floor
földszint (fsz.) means ground floor
Districts V, VI, and VII are in downtown
Pest; District I includes Castle Hill, the
main tourist district of Buda.

AIR TRAVEL
TO & FROM BUDAPEST

Malév Hungarian Airlines offers the only
nonstop service between the U.S. and
Budapest. These flights fill up very
quickly during the summer, so book
well in advance. Malév flies nonstop to
Budapest from New York–JFK as well
as from Toronto.

A wide variety of American and European
airlines offer connecting service from
North America, including Air France
(through Paris), Austrian Airlines (through
Vienna), British Airways (through London
Heathrow and Gatwick), Czech Airlines
(through Prague), KLM in partnership
with Northwest (through Amsterdam),
LOT (through Warsaw), and Lufthansa
(through Frankfurt, Berlin, or Munich).

If you are already in Europe or if you are
traveling from the U.K., there are many
more options for flying to Budapest on
low-cost carriers that have begun operating out of several of London's airports.
However, it is difficult for travelers from
North America to make connections between Heathrow (where most flights from
the U.S. land) and Gatwick, Stansted, or
Luton (where the majority of these cheap
flights originate). Most of these airlines
book tickets only on their Web sites.

BOOKING
When you book, remember that "direct"
flights are not nonstops. Connecting
flights usually require a change of plane.
Two airlines may operate a connecting
flight jointly through a codeshare arrangement, so ask whether your airline operates
every segment of the trip; you may find
that the carrier you prefer flies you only
part of the way. To find more booking tips
and to check prices and make online flight
reservations, log on to www.fodors.com.

CARRIERS
▶ Major Airlines that serve North America **Air
France** ☎ 1/483-8800 in Budapest, 800/237-2747
in the U.S., 0845/359-1000 in the U.K. ⊕ www.
airfrance.com. **Alitalia** ☎ 1/474-8874 in Budapest,
800/223-5730 in the U.S., 0870/544-8259 in the
U.K. ⊕ www.alitalia.com. **American** ☎ 1/266-6222
in Budapest, 800/433-7300 in the U.S., 0845/778-
9789 in the U.K. ⊕ www.aa.com. **Austrian Airlines**
☎ 1/327-9080 in Budapest, 800/843-0002 in the
U.S., 888/817-4444 in Canada, 0870/124-2625 in the
U.K. ⊕ www.austrianairlines.com. **British Airways**
☎ 1/411-5555 in Budapest, 800/247-9297 in the
U.S., 0870/850-9850 in the U.K. ⊕ www.
britishairways.com. **Czech Airlines** (CSA) ☎ 1/318-
3175 in Budapest, 800/223-2365 in the U.S., 0870/
444-3747 in the U.K. ⊕ www.czechairlines.com.
Delta ☎ 1/483-8800 in Budapest, 800/241-4141 in
the U.S., Canada, 0800/414-767 in the U.K. ⊕ www.
delta.com. **Finnair** ☎ 1/317-4022 in Budapest, 800/
950-5000 in the U.S., 0870/241-4411 in the U.K.
⊕ www.finnair.com. **KLM Royal Dutch Airlines**
☎ 1/373-7737 in Budapest, 800/447-4747 in the
U.S., 0870/507-4074 in the U.K. ⊕ www.klm.com.
LOT Polish Airlines ☎ 1/266-4771 in Budapest,
800/223-0593 in the U.S. outside NYC, 212/789-0970
in the U.S. from NYC, 0870/414-0088 in the U.K.
⊕ www.lot.com. **Lufthansa** ☎ 1/411-9900 in Budapest, 800/645-3880 in the U.S., 0870/837-7747 in
the U.K. ⊕ www.lufthansa.com. **Malév Hungarian
Airlines** ☎ 1/235-3888 in Budapest, 800/223-6884
in the U.S. outside NYC, 212/566-9944 in the U.S. in
NYC, 0870/909-0577 in the U.K. ⊕ www.malev.hu.
Northwest ☎ 800/447-4747 in the U.S., 0870/507-
4074 in the U.K. ⊕ www.nwa.com. **SAS Scandina-
vian Airlines** ☎ 1/266-2633 in Budapest, 800/221-
2350 in the U.S. & Canada, 0870/6072-7727 or 0208/
990-7159 in the U.K. ⊕ www.scandinavian.net.
Swiss International Airlines ☎ 1/328-5000 in
Budapest, 877/359-7947 in the U.S., 0845/601-0956
in the U.K. ⊕ www.swiss.com.
▶ European Airlines **Air Berlin** ☎ 0870/738-
8880 in the U.K., calls charged at 8p per minute)
⊕ www.airberlin.com flies between Budapest and
Berlin and Hamburg, in Germany. **Alpieagles** ☎ 39
041/599-7788 ⊕ www.alpieagles.com flies between
Budapest and Venice. **Easyjet** ☎ 0871/750-0100 in
U.K., calls charged at 10p per minute ⊕ www.
easyjet.com connects Budapest with London (Luton),
Berlin, and Dortmund. **Germanwings** ☎ 06800/
16015 toll-free in Hungary, 0208/321-7255 in the U.K.
⊕ www.germanwings.com serves Budapest from

Cologne and Stuttgart. **Skyeurope** ☎ 1/777-7000 in Budapest, 0207/365-0365 in U.K. ⊕ www. skyeurope.com flies between Budapest and Amsterdam, Dubrovnik, London (Stansted), Milan, Paris, Rome, Split, Venice, Warsaw, and Zurich. **Snowflake** ☎ 457/766-1005 ⊕ www.flysnowflake. net flies between Budapest and Stockholm. **Wizzair** ☎ 1/470-9499 in Budapest ⊕ www.wizzair.com flies between Budapest and Athens, Barcelona (Girona), Brussels (Charleroi), London (Luton), Paris (Beauvais), Prague, Rome (Ciampino), and Stockholm (Skavsta).

CHECK-IN & BOARDING

Always **find out your carrier's check-in policy.** Plan to arrive at the airport about two hours before your scheduled departure time for domestic flights and 2½ to 3 hours before international flights. You may need to arrive earlier if you're flying from one of the busier airports or during peak air-traffic times. Ferihegy Airport's main facility (Terminal 2) is small, modern, and easy to navigate. The older Terminal 1, closed to commercial traffic for years, is undergoing renovation and is due to reopen in May 2005 as the main gateway for budget airlines. Check-in counters for flights to North America open three hours before departure, but under normal circumstances arriving two hours ahead is plenty of time. For shorter-haul flights, arrive between one and two hours before departure. To avoid delays at airport-security checkpoints, try not to wear any metal. Jewelry, belt and other buckles, steel-toe shoes, barrettes, and underwire bras are among the items that can set off detectors.

Assuming that not everyone with a ticket will show up, airlines routinely overbook planes. When everyone does, airlines ask for volunteers to give up their seats. In return, these volunteers usually get a several-hundred-dollar flight voucher, which can be used toward the purchase of another ticket, and are rebooked on the next flight out. If there are not enough volunteers, the airline must choose who will be denied boarding. The first to get bumped are passengers who checked in late and those flying on discounted tickets, so get to the gate and check in as early as possible, especially during peak periods.

Always **bring a government-issued photo ID** to the airport; even when it's not required, a passport is best.

CUTTING COSTS

The least expensive airfares to Budapest must usually be purchased well in advance; flights on major airlines are usually cheaper if booked for round-trip travel. The flock of new budget airlines serving Hungary offer fantastic fares from major European hubs like London, Paris, and Amsterdam, most priced on a one-way basis (see ⇨ European Airlines, *above*). With a little geographical creativity and some flexibility, you can save yourself quite a bit of money. Most budget airlines offer cheaper tickets if you book online; tickets purchased over the phone usually involve a surcharge. When shopping around for fares, be sure to calculate in taxes if they're not included; they can often add over $100 to your final fare. Airlines generally allow you to change your return date for a fee; most low-fare tickets, however, are not changeable and are nonrefundable. Sometimes you can find better rates and have more schedule options if you fly in and out of Vienna, just a two- to three-hour bus or train journey from Budapest. It's smart to call a number of airlines and check the Internet; when you are quoted a good price, book it on the spot—the same fare may not be available the next day, or even the next hour. Always check different routings and look into using alternate airports. Also, price off-peak flights, which may be significantly less expensive than others. Travel agents, especially low-fare specialists (⇨ Discounts & Deals), are helpful.

Consolidators are another good source. They buy tickets for scheduled flights at reduced rates from the airlines, then sell them at prices that beat the best fare available directly from the airlines. (Many also offer reduced car-rental and hotel rates.) Sometimes you can even get your money back if you need to return the ticket. Carefully read the fine print detailing penalties for changes and cancellations, purchase the ticket with a credit card, and confirm your consolidator reservation with the airline.

EuropebyAir's Flight Pass system offers $99 one-way fares for country-hopping between many European cities, including direct flights connecting Budapest with Brussels and Venice. Taxes are not included and restrictions apply. Check their Web site for specifics.

🔃 **Consolidators AirlineConsolidator.com** ☎ 888/468-5385 ⊕ www.airlineconsolidator.com; for international tickets. **Best Fares** ☎ 800/880-1234 or 800/576-8255 ⊕ www.bestfares.com; $59.90 annual membership. **Cheap Tickets** ☎ 800/377-1000 or 800/652-4327 ⊕ www.cheaptickets.com. **Expedia** ☎ 800/397-3342 or 404/728-8787 ⊕ www.expedia.com. **Hotwire** ☎ 866/468-9473 or 920/330-9418 ⊕ www.hotwire.com. **Now Voyager Travel** ✉ 45 W. 21st St., Suite 5A New York, NY 10010 ☎ 212/459-1616 🖳 212/243-2711 ⊕ www.nowvoyagertravel.com. **Onetravel.com** ⊕ www.onetravel.com. **Orbitz** ☎ 888/656-4546 ⊕ www.orbitz.com. **Priceline.com** ⊕ www.priceline.com. **Travelocity** ☎ 888/709-5983, 877/282-2925 in Canada, 0870/876-3876 in the U.K. ⊕ www.travelocity.com.

🔃 **Discount Passes FlightPass,** EuropebyAir, ☎ 888/321-4737 ⊕ www.europebyair.com.

ENJOYING THE FLIGHT

State your seat preference when purchasing your ticket, and then repeat it when you confirm and when you check in. For more legroom, you can request one of the few emergency-aisle seats at check-in, if you're capable of moving obstacles comparable in weight to an airplane exit door (usually between 35 pounds and 60 pounds)—a Federal Aviation Administration requirement of passengers in these seats. Seats behind a bulkhead also offer more legroom, but they don't have underseat storage. Don't sit in the row in front of the emergency aisle or in front of a bulkhead, where seats may not recline.

Ask the airline whether a snack or meal is served on the flight. If you have dietary concerns, request special meals when booking. These can be vegetarian, low-cholesterol, or kosher, for example. It's a good idea to pack some healthful snacks

and a small (plastic) bottle of water in your carry-on bag. On long flights, try to maintain a normal routine, to help fight jet lag. At night, get some sleep. By day, eat light meals, drink water (not alcohol), and **move around the cabin** to stretch your legs. For additional jet-lag tips consult *Fodor's FYI: Travel Fit & Healthy* (available at bookstores everywhere).

Smoking policies vary from carrier to carrier. Most airlines prohibit smoking on all of their flights; others allow smoking only on certain routes or certain departures. With very rare exception, your flight to Budapest will not allow smoking on board, but ask your carrier about its policy.

FLYING TIMES

Travel time to Budapest can vary greatly depending on whether or not you can get a nonstop flight. A nonstop flight from NYC to Budapest is approximately 9 hours. Most trips from the U.S. require a change at Frankfurt, London, Paris, Prague, Zurich, Amsterdam, or Vienna and can take up to 15 hours. Direct flights from London to Budapest take between 2 and 3 hours. From Sydney you will have to fly first of all to London, Paris, or Amsterdam (23 hours total travel time).

HOW TO COMPLAIN

If your baggage goes astray or your flight goes awry, complain right away. Most carriers require that you **file a claim immediately.** The Aviation Consumer Protection Division of the Department of Transportation publishes *Fly-Rights,* which discusses airlines and consumer issues and is available online. You can also find articles and information on mytravelrights.com, the Web site of the nonprofit Consumer Travel Rights Center.

🔃 **Airline Complaints Aviation Consumer Protection Division** ✉ U.S. Department of Transportation, Office of Aviation Enforcement and Proceedings, C-75, Room 4107, 400 7th St. SW, Washington, DC 20590 ☎ 202/366-2220 ⊕ airconsumer.ost.dot.gov. **Federal Aviation Administration Consumer Hotline** ✉ for inquiries: FAA, 800 Independence Ave. SW, Washington, DC 20591 ☎ 800/322-7873 ⊕ www.faa.gov.

RECONFIRMING

Check the status of your flight before you leave for the airport. You can do this on your carrier's Web site, by linking to a flight-status checker (many Web booking services offer these), or by calling your carrier or travel agent. Always confirm international flights at least 72 hours ahead of the scheduled departure time. When you purchase your ticket, inquire whether it is necessary to reconfirm in advance. If so, under normal circumstances reconfirmation can be taken care of with a simple phone call to your airline's office.

AIRPORTS & TRANSFERS

Ferihegy Repülőtér, Hungary's only commercial airport with regularly scheduled service, is 24 km (15 mi) southeast of downtown Budapest. All non-Hungarian airlines operate from Terminal 2B; those of Malév, from Terminal 2A. At this writing, the older part of the airport, Terminal 1, was scheduled to undergo a renovation and reopen in May 2005 as the main terminal for low-cost airlines flying to European destinations.
⨻ Airport Information Ferihegy Repülőtér ☎ 1/ 296-9696, 1/296-7000 flight information.

AIRPORT TRANSFERS

Many hotels offer their guests car or minibus transportation to and from Ferihegy, but all of them—except the Hilton on Castle Hill—charge for the service. You should arrange for a pickup in advance. If you're taking a taxi, allow anywhere between just 25 minutes during nonpeak hours to an hour during rush hours (7 AM–9 AM from the airport, 4 PM–6 PM from the city).

Sadly, at the time of this writing taxis at the airport were largely prone to gross overcharging. If you must take a taxi, your best option is to call Főtaxi or Buda Taxi from a pay phone and order one. Főtaxi has a toll-free number, so you don't need to use a coin or phone card. Both companies are trustworthy and offer fixed-rates from and to the airport; destinations in Pest cost around 3,500 HUF, in Buda, 4,000 HUF. If you choose to take a taxi from among those waiting outside the ter-

minal, first look for one with the Főtaxi or Buda Taxi logo *AND* phone numbers printed clearly on the car. Avoid drivers who approach you before you are out of the arrivals lounge. No matter what, it is imperative that you agree on a price with the driver beforehand. A taxi ride to the center of Budapest should cost around 4,000 HUF. Always get a receipt.

Most travelers—locals and tourists alike—use the Airport Minibus, which provides convenient door-to-door service between the airport and any address in the city. To get to the airport, call to arrange a pickup at least 12 hours before your flight leaves; the call center is open between 6 AM and 10 PM and is very busy, so keep trying if your call doesn't go through. To get to the city, make arrangements at the Airport Minibus airport desk and wait nearby until the driver calls out your address; the wait is usually about 10 minutes. Service to or from either terminal costs 2,100 HUF per person; the discounted round-trip fare is 3,600 HUF. Credit cards (AE, MC, V) are accepted. If you plan to buy a Budapest Card (see below) during your stay, you can purchase it at the minibus desk and immediately receive the card's 15% discount on your fare. Since it normally shuttles several people at once, remember to allow time for a few other pickups or drop-offs.
⨻ Taxis & Shuttles Airport Minibus ☎ 1/296- 8555. **Buda Taxi** ☎ 1/233-3333. **Fő Taxi** ☎ 1/222- 2222 or 06-80-222-222 toll-free in Hungary.

DUTY-FREE SHOPPING

Ferihegy's duty-free shops stay open to accommodate all scheduled flights. The selection is not as extensive as it is in major international airports, but the shops are particularly good for picking up "alcoholic" souvenirs such as Unicum, pálinka, and wines from Hungary's famous wine regions, such as Tokaj and Villány.

BOAT & FERRY TRAVEL

From late July through early September, two swift hydrofoils leave Vienna daily at 8 AM and 1 PM (once-a-day trips are scheduled mid-April–late July and

September–October). After a 5½-hour journey downriver, with a stop in Bratislava, the Slovak capital, and views of Hungary's largest church, the cathedral in Esztergom, the boats head into Budapest via its main artery, the Danube. The upriver journey takes about an hour longer. Combined hydrofoil-train and hydrofoil-bus trips are also available for those preferring one leg of their trip to be by land.

FARES & SCHEDULES

Schedules are available at the MAHART office and on its Web site, as well as at most hotels, travel agencies, and tourist information offices. Tickets (€75 one-way, €99 round-trip) are reserved through the MAHART Web site or by phone. They can be purchased by credit card via phone or the Web site, or they can be purchased in person at the check-in counter by cash or credit card (MC, V).

🚢 **Boat & Ferry Lines** MAHART PassNave ⊠ International Mooring Point, District V, Belgrád rakpart, Around Ferenciek tere, Budapest ☎ 1/484–4005 or 1/484–4025 🖷 1/266–4201 ⊠ Handelskai 265, Vienna, Austria ☎ 431/729-2161 or 431/729-2162 ⊕ www.mahartpassnave.hu.

BUSINESS HOURS

Banks are generally open weekdays until 3 or 4; most close by 2 on Friday.

Museums are usually open Tuesday through Sunday from 10 to 6 and are closed on Monday; most stop admitting people 30 minutes before closing time. Some have a free-admission day (see ⇨ What to See), but double-check, as the days tend to change.

Budapest's numerous malls tend to have the longest opening hours; mall stores are open weekdays from 10 to 9, weekends from 10 to 6 or 7. Department stores are open weekdays from 10 to 5 or 6, Saturday until 1. Grocery stores are generally open weekdays 7 AM to 6 or 7 PM, Saturday until 1 PM; "nonstops," or *éjjel-nappali*, are (theoretically) open 24 hours.

BUS TRAVEL

Most buses in Hungary are run by the state-owned Volánbusz company, which is in partnership with Eurolines, Europe's main coach line. Long-distance buses link Budapest's Népliget bus station with most cities in Hungary as well as major cities in Europe. Though inexpensive, these buses tend to be crowded, so if you travel by bus, buy your tickets as far in advance as possible, either at the station or at a Volánbusz travel agency. The Budapest–Vienna route is especially popular.

Buses to the eastern part of Hungary depart from the Stadion station. For the Danube Bend, buses leave from the bus terminal at Árpád Bridge.

Long-distance coaches are generally comfortable, but in warm weather it's worth inquiring about air-conditioning, as some don't have it. Smoking on board is prohibited on both domestic and international routes.

FARES & SCHEDULES

Schedule and fare information is available online in English on the Volánbusz Web site. Telephone inquiries in English are unlikely to work, so your best bet is to go in person to the bus station or, more conveniently, to the Volánbusz travel office in downtown Pest, which handles most, but not all, bus routes.

RESERVATIONS

Reservations cannot be made by phone, and a few domestic routes allow purchases only from the driver. For bus travel to another country, check-in commences 90 minutes before departure and closes 30 minutes before. For bus travel within the country, arrive at least 20 minutes before departure to buy a ticket (this is not possible for all routes, as tickets for some routes can only be purchased directly from the driver). If there's a crowd pressing to get on, feel free to wave your pre-purchased ticket about as you jostle your way aboard. Technically speaking, reserved seats must be occupied by no later than 10 minutes before departure time.

🚌 **Bus Stations & Ticket Offices** Árpád Bridge bus station ⊠ District III, Árboc u. 1–3, Óbuda ☎ 1/329-1450. Népliget bus station ⊠ District IX, Üllői út 131, Around Keleti station ☎ 1/219-8080 for information, 1/219-8020 international ticket office. Sta-

dion bus station ✉ District XIV, Hungária krt.
48–52 ☎ 1/251–0125. **Volánbusz Travel Agency**
✉ District V, Erzsébet tér 1, Around Deák tér ☎ 1/
318–2122 ⊕ www.volanbusz.hu.

BUS & TRAM TRAVEL WITHIN BUDAPEST

Trams (villamos) and buses (autóbusz) are abundant and convenient. Tickets are widely available in metro stations and—in theory only—at newsstands and rusting roadside automats; your best bet is to stock up at a metro station. Tickets must be validated on board by inserting them, downward-facing, into the little devices provided for that purpose, then pulling the knob; with newer devices, just insert the ticket. Hold on to whatever ticket you have; spot checks by aggressive undercover checkers (look for the red armbands) are numerous and often targeted at tourists. Trolley-bus stops are marked with red, rectangular signs that list the route stops; regular bus stops are marked with similar light blue signs. (The trolley buses and regular buses themselves are red and blue, respectively.) Tram stops are marked by light blue or yellow signs. When getting on a bus or tram, if the doors don't open automatically right away, press the green or red button next to the door to open it.

FARES & SCHEDULES

A one-fare ticket (145 HUF) is valid for only one ride in one direction on any form of public transportation, including the metro; a "transfer ticket" (250 HUF) allows you to make one transfer. You can also purchase a napijegy (day ticket, 1100 HUF), a three-day "tourist ticket" (2300 HUF), or a one-week ticket (2,700 HUF), all of which allow unlimited travel on all services within the city limits. Bulk ticket books in 10- and 20-piece (1,250 HUF and 2,450 HUF, respectively) units are also available; don't tear the tickets from their binding after validating them or else you'll run into trouble with the undercover checkers. Most lines run from 5 AM and stop operating at 11 PM, but there is all-night service on certain key routes. Consult the separate night-bus map posted in most metro stations for all-night service.

CAMERAS & PHOTOGRAPHY

In general, people are pleased to be photographed, but ask first. Never photograph Gypsies, however colorful their attire, without explicit permission and payment clearly agreed upon. Photographing anything military, assuming you'd want to, is usually prohibited. The *Kodak Guide to Shooting Great Travel Pictures* (available at bookstores everywhere) is loaded with tips.
🖪 Photo Help **Kodak Information Center** ☎ 800/242–2424 ⊕ www.kodak.com.

EQUIPMENT PRECAUTIONS

Don't pack film or equipment in checked luggage, where it is much more susceptible to damage. X-ray machines used to view checked luggage are extremely powerful and therefore are likely to ruin your film. Try to ask for hand inspection of film, which becomes clouded after repeated exposure to airport X-ray machines, and keep videotapes and computer disks away from metal detectors. Always keep film, tape, and computer disks out of the sun. Carry an extra supply of batteries, and be prepared to turn on your camera, camcorder, or laptop to prove to airport security personnel that the device is real.

FILM & DEVELOPING

Major brands of film are sold throughout Budapest, and 1-hour and 24-hour developing are widely available. Major processing chains with stores throughout Budapest include Sooters, Fotex, and Fotohall. Getting a 24-print color roll developed will cost around 2,500 HUF. Most stores can also put your images onto CDs in digital form.

VIDEOS

Due to differing television systems, VHS tapes and DVDs bought in Central and Eastern Europe (which use the SECAM standard) are not compatible with U.S. machines (which use the NTSC standard).

CAR RENTAL

You should not rent a car if you do not plan to leave Budapest itself because of traffic and parking concerns. However, a car can be quite convenient for traveling around the country.

Rental rates are high in Hungary. Daily rates for automatics begin around $50 to $60 plus 50¢ per kilometer (½ mi); personal, theft, and accident insurance (this is coverage beyond the ordinary CDW for theft and is not required but recommended) runs an additional $25 to $30 per day. Rates for manual-transmission cars, however, are lower. Rates tend to be significantly lower if you arrange your rental *from home* through the American offices. Locally based companies usually offer lower rates. Fox Autorent, for example, has "unlimited-mileage weekend + 1 day" specials, and rates include free delivery and pickup of the car anywhere in Budapest.

7 Major Agencies **Alamo** 🏠 800/522-9696 ⊕ www.alamo.com. **Avis** 🏠 800/331-1084, 800/ 879-2847 in Canada, 0870/606-0100 in the U.K., 02/ 9353-9000 in Australia, 09/526-2847 in New Zealand ⊕ www.avis.com. **Budget** 🏠 800/527-0700, 0870/156-5656 in the U.K. ⊕ www.budget. com. **Dollar** 🏠 800/800-6000, 0800/085-4578 in the U.K. ⊕ www.dollar.com. **Hertz** 🏠 800/654-3001, 800/263-0600 in Canada, 0870/844-8844 in the U.K., 02/9669-2444 in Australia, 09/256-8690 in New Zealand ⊕ www.hertz.com. **National Car Rental** 🏠 800/227-7368, 0870/600-6666 in the U.K. ⊕ www.nationalcar.com.

7 Local Offices of Major Agencies **Avis** ⊠ District V, Szervita tér 8, Around Deák Ferenc tér 🏠 1/318-4240 ⊕ www.avis.hu ⊠ Ferihegy Repülőtér, Terminal 2B 🏠 1/296-6421. **Budget** ⊠ District I, Hotel Mercure Buda, Krisztina krt. 41-43, Around Déli station 🏠 1/214-0420 ⊕ www.budget.hu ⊠ Ferihegy Repülőtér, Terminal 2B 🏠 1/296-8197. **Europcar** (also known in Hungary as EUrent) ⊠ District V, Deák Ferenc tér 3, Around Deák Ferenc tér 🏠 1/328-6464 ⊕ www.europcar.hu ⊠ Ferihegy Repülőtér, Terminal 2B 🏠 1/421-8370. **Hertz** (also known in Hungary as Mercur Rent-a-Car) ⊠ District XXII, Hertz u. 2 🏠 1/296-0999 ⊠ District V, Marriott hotel, Apáczai Csere János u. 4, Around Váci utca 🏠 1/266-4361 ⊠ Ferihegy Repülőtér, Terminal 2B 🏠 1/296-7171. **National Car Rental** (also known in Hungary as National Alamo Hungary) ⊠ District VIII, Üllői út 60-62, Around Ferenc körút 🏠 1/477-1080 ⊕ www.nationalcar.hu ⊠ Ferihegy Repülőtér, Terminal 2B 🏠 1/296-6610.

CUTTING COSTS

For a good deal, book through a travel agent who will shop around. Do look into wholesalers, companies that do not own fleets but rent in bulk from those that do and often offer better rates than traditional car-rental operations. Prices are best during off-peak periods. Rentals booked through wholesalers often must be paid for before you leave home.

7 Local Agencies **Fox Autorent** ⊠ District XI, Vegyész u. 17-25, South Buda 🏠 1/382-9000 ⊕ www. fox-autorent.com. **Recent Car** ⊠ District III, Hajógyári sziget 131, Óbuda 🏠 1/453-0003 ⊕ www. recentcar.hu.

7 Wholesalers **Auto Europe** 🏠 207/842-2000 or 800/223-5555 🖨 207/842-2222 ⊕ www. autoeurope.com. **Destination Europe Resources** (DER) ⊠ 9501 W. Devon Ave., Rosemont, IL 60018 🏠 800/782-2424 🖨 800/282-7474 ⊕ www.der. com. **Europe by Car** 🏠 212/581-3040 or 800/223-1516 🖨 212/246-1458 ⊕ www.europebycar.com. **Kemwel** 🏠 877/820-0668 or 800/678-0678 🖨 207/842-2147 ⊕ www.kemwel.com.

INSURANCE

When driving a rented car you are generally responsible for any damage to or loss of the vehicle. Collision policies that car-rental companies sell for European rentals typically do not cover stolen vehicles. Most agencies will recommend you take out both CDW (collision-damage waiver) and TP (theft protection) policies. Before you rent—and purchase collision or theft coverage—see what coverage you already have under the terms of your personal auto-insurance policy and credit cards.

REQUIREMENTS & RESTRICTIONS

You must be 21 to rent a car in Hungary; some agencies have an over-25 age limit on superior-model cars, and some charge extra for all models driven by those who are under 25. Most countries, including Hungary, require that you will have held your driver's license for at least a year before you can rent a car. Keep in mind that Hungarian law states that children under 16 may not travel in the front passenger seat, and that car seats are compulsory for infants and toddlers and must be placed in the backseat of the car. Always inform the rental agency about what borders you plan to cross with the car; most will require extra insurance and special paperwork (to prove you're not driving one of the many stolen cars crossing those borders) for trips into Romania, Serbia, Montenegro, Macedonia, Albania, and Bulgaria.

SURCHARGES

Before you pick up a car in one city and leave it in another, ask about drop-off charges or one-way service fees, which can be substantial. Also inquire about early-return policies; some rental agencies charge extra if you return the car before the time specified in your contract while others give you a refund for the days not used. To avoid a hefty refueling fee, fill the tank just before you turn in the car, but be aware that gas stations near the rental outlet may overcharge. It's almost never a deal to buy the tank of gas that's in the car when you rent it; the understanding is that you'll return it empty, but some fuel usually remains. Cars rented from the Budapest airport carry an 11% to 12% surcharge; be sure to ask if it is included in your initial price quote. If you are renting in the winter, inquire about additional "winter upkeep" charges. Additional insurance is sometimes required if you drive the car into certain countries, such as Romania, Bulgaria, and Serbia. Car seats can be rented with the car for about €9 per day. Some firms have a surcharge for drivers who are under 25; Hertz charges an extra €7 per day (to a maximum of €45 per rental) on all models.

CAR TRAVEL

Although driving in Budapest is a bad idea, getting around by car is the best way to see Hungary. It's a small country, so even driving from one end to the other is manageable.

In Hungary, visitors are technically required to have an International Driver's Permit (IDP). They are available from the American and Canadian automobile associations and, in the United Kingdom, from the Automobile Association and Royal Automobile Club. These international permits, valid only in conjunction with your regular driver's license, are universally rec-

ognized; having one may save you a problem with local authorities.

Many car rental agencies will accept an international license, but the formal permit is technically required. If you intend to drive across a border, ask about restrictions on driving into other countries. The minimum age required for renting is usually 21 or older, and some companies also have maximum ages; be sure to inquire when making your arrangements.

The main routes into Budapest are the M1 from Vienna (via Győr), the M3 from near Gyöngyös, the M5 from Kecskemét, and the M7 from the Balaton; the M3 and M5 are being upgraded and extended to Hungary's borders with Slovakia and Yugoslavia, respectively. Budapest, like any Western city, is plagued by traffic jams during the day, but motorists should have no problem later in the evening. Motorists not accustomed to sharing the city streets with trams should pay extra attention. You should be prepared to be flagged down numerous times by police conducting routine checks for drunk driving and stolen cars. Be sure all of your papers are in order and readily accessible; unfortunately, the police have been known to give foreigners a hard time.

EMERGENCY SERVICES

In case of a breakdown, your best friend is the telephone. Try contacting your rental agency or the national breakdown service. **F** Hungarian Automobile Club's breakdown service ☎ 188.

GASOLINE

Gas stations are plentiful in Hungary, and many on the main highways stay open all night, even on holidays. Major chains, such as MOL, Shell, and OMV, have Western-style full-facility stations with restrooms, brightly lit convenience stores, and 24-hour service. Lines are rarely long, and supplies are stable. Unleaded gasoline (*bleifrei* or *ólommentes*) is generally available at most stations and is usually the 95-octane-level choice. If your car requires unleaded gasoline, be sure to double-check that you're not reaching for the leaded before you pump.

PARKING

Gone are the "anything goes" days of parking in Budapest, when cars parked for free practically anywhere in the city, straddling curbs or angled in the middle of sidewalks. Now most streets in Budapest's main districts have restricted, fee-based parking; there are either parking meters that accept coins and give you a ticket to display on your dashboard (usually for a maximum of two hours) or attendants who approach your car as you park and charge you according to how many hours you intend to stay. Hourly rates average 200 HUF. In most cases, parking overnight (generally after 6 PM and before 8 AM) and Sunday in these areas is free. The number of parking garages in Budapest has increased dramatically in the last few years. A few central Pest ones in District V are at Szervita tér, Aranykéz utca 4–6, and underground at Szabadság tér. In general, though, lots and garages are easy to find by following the standard blue "P" signs marking their entrances.

Away from Budapest, smaller towns usually have free parking on the street and some hourly fee lots near main tourist zones. Throughout the country, no-parking zones are marked with the international "No Parking" sign: a white circle with a diagonal line through it.

ROAD CONDITIONS

There are four classes of roads: expressways (designated by the letter "M" and a single digit), main highways (a single digit), secondary roads (a two-digit number), and minor roads (a three-digit number). Highways, expressways, and secondary roads are generally in good condition. The conditions of minor roads vary considerably; keep in mind that tractors and horse-drawn carts may slow your route down in rural areas. In planning your driving route with a map, opt for the larger roadways whenever possible; you'll generally end up saving time even if there is a shorter but smaller road. It's not so much the condition of the smaller roads but the kind of traffic on them and the number of towns (where

the speed limit is 50 kph [30 mph]) they pass through that will slow you down. If you're in no hurry, however, explore the smaller roads!

At this writing, Hungary was continuing a massive upgrading and reconstruction of many of its expressways, gearing up for its role as the main bridge for trade between the Balkan countries and the former Soviet Union and Western Europe. To help fund the project, tolls are required on several routes. Toll roads include the M1, which runs west from Budapest toward Vienna; the M3, which runs northeast toward Slovakia; the M5, from Budapest to just south of Kecskemét (and eventually through Szeged to Serbia and Montenegro); and the M7, which goes south towards Lake Balaton.

ROAD MAPS

In Hungary, good maps are sold at most large gas stations. In Budapest, the Globe Térképbolt has an excellent supply of domestic and foreign maps. The English-language version of the utak.hu Web site is a good resource for trip planning and traffic information.

🚩 **Globe Térképbolt** Globe Map Store ⊠ District VI, Bajcsy-Zsilinszky út 37, Around Nyugati station ☎ 1/312–6001

RULES OF THE ROAD

Hungarians drive on the right and observe the usual Continental rules of the road (but they revel in passing). Unless otherwise noted, the speed limit is 50 kph (30 mph), on main roads 90 to 110 kph (55 to 65 mph), and on highways 130 kph (78 mph). Stay alert: speed-limit signs are few and far between. Developed areas are marked by a white rectangular sign with the town name written in black; slow down to 50 kph (or less if so marked) as soon as you pass one. You can speed up again once you pass a similar sign with the town name crossed out in red. Seat belts are compulsory (front-seat belts in lower speed zones, both front and back in higher speed zones), as is the use of headlights outside of cities or towns. Children under 16 may not travel in the front passenger seat; infants and toddlers must sit in a car seat in the backseat of the car. Holding a mobile phone while driving is illegal; headsets are OK. Drinking alcohol is prohibited—there is a zero-tolerance policy, and the penalties are very severe.

Speed traps are numerous, so it's best to observe the speed limit; fines start from the equivalent of $50, but they can easily get higher. In an effort to forestall bribe-taking, the time-honored practice of on-the-spot payment for violations was abolished in 2000, so police must now give accused speeders an invoice payable at post offices. (Remember this should you feel innocent and an officer suggests an on-the-spot "discount.") Spot checks are frequent as well, and police occasionally try to take advantage of foreigners, so always have your papers on hand.

Toll fares must be paid ahead of time in the form of a pre-paid sticker ("matrica") that is displayed on the upper left corner of your windshield; the toll stations electronically deduct the toll amount as you drive through. These stickers can be bought at all gas stations, but NOT at the tollbooths themselves. Be sure to ask for and keep the receipt. They come in 10-day, monthly, and yearly increments, but a more convenient four-day version is likely to be available by 2005. In the summer, spot-checks are frequent. If you're not in a hurry, you can also always take the free route that was replaced by the toll road.

CHILDREN IN BUDAPEST

Budapest has numerous sights and events of interest to children, including the Budapest Zoo and amusement park in City Park, the wave pools at some of the bath complexes, boat trips on the Danube, bicycling on Margaret Island, not to mention omnipresent ice cream stands and shops. Puppet shows in Hungarian are held regularly at the Budapest Puppet Theater on Andrássy út. Places that are especially appealing to children are indicated by a rubber-duckie icon (🐤) in the margin.

If you are renting a car, don't forget to arrange for a car seat when you reserve. For general advice about traveling with children, consult *Fodor's FYI: Travel with Your Baby* (available in bookstores everywhere).

FLYING

If your children are two or older, ask about children's airfares. As a general rule, infants under two not occupying a seat fly at greatly reduced fares or even for free. But if you want to guarantee a seat for an infant, you have to pay full fare. Consider flying during off-peak days and times; most airlines will grant an infant a seat without a ticket if there are available seats. When booking, confirm carry-on allowances if you're traveling with infants. In general, for babies charged 10% to 50% of the adult fare you are allowed one carry-on bag and a collapsible stroller; if the flight is full, the stroller may have to be checked or you may be limited to less.

Experts agree that it's a good idea to use safety seats aloft for children weighing less than 40 pounds. Airlines set their own policies: if you use a safety seat, U.S. carriers usually require that the child be ticketed, even if he or she is young enough to ride free, because the seats must be strapped into regular seats. And even if you pay the full adult fare for the seat, it may be worth it, especially on longer trips. Do **check your airline's policy about using safety seats during takeoff and landing.** Safety seats are not allowed everywhere in the plane, so get your seat assignments as early as possible.

When reserving, request children's meals or a freestanding bassinet (not available at all airlines) if you need them. But note that bulkhead seats, where you must sit to use the bassinet, may lack an overhead bin or storage space on the floor.

FOOD

Most Hungarian restaurants have french fries (*hasábburgonya*) on the menu, as well as breaded fried chicken or pork cutlets (*rántott hús*) that if necessary can be sliced up and passed off as chicken fingers. Ice cream and sweets of all kinds are never far away. For better or worse, you'll have no trouble finding McDonald's and Burger King in all main cities.

Iguana (see ⇨ Where to Eat), a festive Mexican restaurant popular with expats, serves American-style breakfasts on weekends and has a small play area near the bar, where children can entertain themselves while parents sip their coffees (or margaritas) nearby. The ample weekend brunches at the Corinthia Grand Hotel Royal, InterContinental Hotel, and Sofitel Atrium Hotel have something for everyone on their menus, plus toys and games for the kids. **Champs Sport Pub** (⊠ District VII, Dohány u. 20, Around Blaha Lujza tér ☎ 1/413–1655) has a playroom supervised by trained nannies. The room is free to children (over 3) of parents eating or otherwise imbibing on the premises; they also have a children's menu. The playroom is open weekdays 4–8 PM, weekends noon–8 PM, but call ahead to confirm.

LODGING

Most hotels in Hungary allow one child under a certain age (usually 12) to stay in their parents' room at no extra charge, but others charge for them as extra adults; be sure to find out the cutoff age for children's discounts. The Budapest Hilton on Castle Hill has an unusual policy allowing children of any age—even middle-aged adults—to stay for free in their parents' room.

SUPPLIES & EQUIPMENT

Disposable diapers (*pelenka*) are widely available in Budapest and most of the country. Large grocery stores and health and beauty shop chains (such as "DM" and "Azur") carry an adequate selection, and even smaller "non-stop" shops stock at least one kind. Western brands, such as Pampers, as well as less expensive local varieties are available. The average price of a 21-pack of diapers is 1700 HUF. Baby formula (*tápszer*) is sold in pharmacies and big grocery stores, where western brands like Nestlé are available. Jarred baby food,

including Gerber-brand, is also widely available.

COMPUTERS ON THE ROAD

Bring an adapter for your laptop plug. Adapters are inexpensive, and some models have several plugs suitable for different systems throughout the world. Some hotels lend adapters to guests for use during their stay.

At the airport, be prepared to turn on your laptop to prove to security personnel that the device is real. Security X-ray machines can be damaging to a laptop, and keep computer disks away from metal detectors.

CONSUMER PROTECTION

Whether you're shopping for gifts or purchasing travel services, **pay with a major credit card** whenever possible, so you can cancel payment or get reimbursed if there's a problem (and you can provide documentation). If you're doing business with a particular company for the first time, contact your local Better Business Bureau and the attorney general's offices in your state and (for U.S. businesses) the company's home state as well. Have any complaints been filed? Finally, if you're buying a package or tour, always consider travel insurance that includes default coverage (⇨ Insurance).

🗗 BBBs **Council of Better Business Bureaus** ⊠ 4200 Wilson Blvd., Suite 800, Arlington, VA 22203 ☎ 703/276–0100 🖶 703/525–8277 ⊕ www. bbb.org.

CUSTOMS & DUTIES

When shopping abroad, keep receipts for all purchases. Upon reentering the country, **be ready to show customs officials what you've bought.** Pack purchases together in an easily accessible place. If you think a duty is incorrect, appeal the assessment. If you object to the way your clearance was handled, note the inspector's badge number. In either case, first ask to see a supervisor. If the problem isn't resolved, write to the appropriate authorities, beginning with the port director at your point of entry.

IN AUSTRALIA

Australian residents who are 18 or older may bring home A$400 worth of souvenirs and gifts (including jewelry), 250 cigarettes or 250 grams of cigars or other tobacco products, and 1,125 ml of alcohol (including wine, beer, and spirits). Residents under 18 may bring back A$200 worth of goods. Members of the same family traveling together may pool their allowances. Prohibited items include meat products. Seeds, plants, and fruits need to be declared upon arrival.

⑦ Australian Customs Service ⬚ Regional Director, Box 8, Sydney, NSW 2001 ☎ 02/9213-2000 or 1300/363263, 02/9364-7222 or 1800/020-504 quarantine-inquiry line 🖷 02/9213-4043 ⊕ www.customs.gov.au.

IN CANADA

Canadian residents who have been out of Canada for at least seven days may bring in C$750 worth of goods duty-free. If you've been away fewer than seven days but more than 48 hours, the duty-free allowance drops to C$200. If your trip lasts 24 to 48 hours, the allowance is C$50. You may not pool allowances with family members. Goods claimed under the C$750 exemption may follow you by mail; those claimed under the lesser exemptions must accompany you. Alcohol and tobacco products may be included in the seven-day and 48-hour exemptions but not in the 24-hour exemption. If you meet the age requirements of the province or territory through which you reenter Canada, you may bring in, duty-free, 1.5 liters of wine *or* 1.14 liters (40 imperial ounces) of liquor *or* 24 12-ounce cans or bottles of beer or ale. Also, if you meet the local age requirement for tobacco products, you may bring in, duty-free, 200 cigarettes and 50 cigars. Check ahead of time with the Canada Customs and Revenue Agency or the Department of Agriculture for policies regarding meat products, seeds, plants, and fruits.

You may send an unlimited number of gifts (only one gift per recipient, however) worth up to C$60 each duty-free to Canada. Label the package UNSOLICITED GIFT—VALUE UNDER $60. Alcohol and tobacco are excluded.

⑦ Canada Customs and Revenue Agency ⬚ 2265 St. Laurent Blvd., Ottawa, Ontario K1G 4K3 ☎ 800/461-9999 in Canada, 204/983-3500, 506/636-5064 ⊕ www.ccra.gc.ca.

IN HUNGARY

You may import duty-free into Hungary 250 cigarettes or 50 cigars or the equivalent in tobacco, 1 liter of spirits, and 1 liter of wine. In addition to the above, you are permitted to import into Hungary gifts valued up to 29,500 HUF.

Objects considered to be of museum value—certain works of art or antiques marked *védett*—cannot be taken out of the country. Take care when you leave Hungary that you have the right documentation for exporting goods. Keep receipts of any major purchases. Upon leaving, you are entitled to a value-added tax (VAT) refund on new goods (i.e., not works of art, antiques, or objects of museum value) valued at 50,000 HUF or more (VAT inclusive). For details, see VAT Refunds, below.

⑦ Hungarian Customs & Finance Guard ⬚ District XIV, Hungária krt. 112-114, Budapest ☎ 1/470-4121 or 1/470-4122 ⊕ www.vam.hu.

IN NEW ZEALAND

All homeward-bound residents may bring back NZ$700 worth of souvenirs and gifts; passengers may not pool their allowances, and children can claim only the concession on goods intended for their own use. For those 17 or older, the duty-free allowance also includes 4.5 liters of wine or beer; one 1,125-ml bottle of spirits; and either 200 cigarettes, 250 grams of tobacco, 50 cigars, *or* a combination of the three up to 250 grams. Meat products, seeds, plants, and fruits must be declared upon arrival to the Agricultural Services Department.

⑦ New Zealand Customs ⬚ Head office: The Customhouse, 17-21 Whitmore St., Box 2218, Wellington ☎ 09/300-5399 or 0800/428-786 ⊕ www.customs.govt.nz.

IN THE U.K.

If you are a U.K. resident and your journey was wholly within the European Union, you probably won't have to pass through customs when you return to the United Kingdom. If you plan to bring back large quantities of alcohol or tobacco, check EU limits beforehand. In most cases, if you bring back more than 200 cigars, 3,200 cigarettes, 400 cigarillos, 10 liters of spirits, 110 liters of beer, 20 liters of fortified wine, and/or 90 liters of wine, you have to declare the goods upon return. Prohibited items include unpasteurized milk, regardless of country of origin.

⊞ HM Customs and Excise ⊠ Portcullis House, 21 Cowbridge Rd. E, Cardiff CF11 9SS ☎ 0845/010–9000 or 0208/929–0152 advice service, 0208/929–6731 or 0208/910–3602 complaints ⊕ www.hmce.gov.uk.

IN THE U.S.

U.S. residents who have been out of the country for at least 48 hours may bring home, for personal use, $800 worth of foreign goods duty-free, as long as they haven't used the $800 allowance or any part of it in the past 30 days. This exemption may include 1 liter of alcohol (for travelers 21 and older), 200 cigarettes, and 100 non-Cuban cigars. Family members from the same household who are traveling together may pool their $800 personal exemptions. For fewer than 48 hours, the duty-free allowance drops to $200, which may include 50 cigarettes, 10 non-Cuban cigars, and 150 ml of alcohol (or 150 ml of perfume containing alcohol). The $200 allowance cannot be combined with other individuals' exemptions, and if you exceed it, the full value of all the goods will be taxed. Antiques, which U.S. Customs and Border Protection defines as objects more than 100 years old, enter duty-free, as do original works of art done entirely by hand, including paintings, drawings, and sculptures. This doesn't apply to folk art or handicrafts, which are in general dutiable.

You may also send packages home duty-free, with a limit of one parcel per addressee per day (except alcohol or tobacco products or perfume worth more than $5). You can mail up to $200 worth of goods for personal use; label the package

PERSONAL USE and attach a list of its contents and their retail value. If the package contains your used personal belongings, mark it AMERICAN GOODS RETURNED to avoid paying duties. You may send up to $100 worth of goods as a gift; mark the package UNSOLICITED GIFT. Mailed items do not affect your duty-free allowance on your return.

To avoid paying duty on foreign-made high-ticket items you already own and will take on your trip, register them with Customs before you leave the country. Consider filing a Certificate of Registration for laptops, cameras, watches, and other digital devices identified with serial numbers or other permanent markings; you can keep the certificate for other trips. Otherwise, bring a sales receipt or insurance form to show that you owned the item before you left the United States.

For more about duties, restricted items, and other information about international travel, check out U.S. Customs and Border Protection's online brochure, *Know Before You Go.*

⊞ U.S. Customs & Border Protection ⊠ for inquiries and equipment registration, 1300 Pennsylvania Ave. NW, Washington, DC 20229 ⊕ www.cbp.gov ☎ 877/287–8667, 202/354–1000 ⊠ for complaints, Customer Satisfaction Unit, 1300 Pennsylvania Ave. NW, Room 5.2C, Washington, DC 20229.

DISABILITIES & ACCESSIBILITY

Provisions for travelers with disabilities in Hungary are extremely limited; probably the best solution is to travel with a companion who can help you. Although many hotels, especially those belonging to large international chains, offer some wheelchair-accessible rooms, special facilities at museums and restaurants and on public transportation are difficult to find. For advice and further information, contact MEOSZ in Budapest.

⊞ Local Resources Mozgáskorlátozottak Egyesületeinek Országos Szövetsége National Association of People with Mobility Impairments, or MEOSZ ⊠ San Marco u. 76, Budapest 1032 ☎ 1/250–9013 English-speaking or 1/388–5529 ⊕ www.meoszinfo.hu.

LODGING

Many hotels in Budapest have at least one room that is equipped to some degree for travelers with disabilities. Your best bets are newer hotels and international chains, but always ask, as standards vary drastically.

RESERVATIONS

When discussing accessibility with an operator or reservations agent, ask hard questions. Are there any stairs, inside *or* out? Are there grab bars next to the toilet *and* in the shower/tub? How wide is the doorway to the room? To the bathroom? For the most extensive facilities meeting the latest legal specifications, opt for newer accommodations. If you reserve through a toll-free number, consider also calling the hotel's local number to confirm the information from the central reservations office. Get confirmation in writing when you can.

SIGHTS & ATTRACTIONS

Most tourist attractions in the region pose significant problems. Many are historic structures without ramps or other means to improve accessibility. Streets are often cobblestone, and potholes are common.

TRANSPORTATION

Some inroads are being made into making Budapest's public transport system more accessible to people with mobility problems, but it's nowhere near enough yet. More information is available in English on the BKV public transport Web site. A better bet is to use MEOSZ's access-a-ride service (see ⇨ Local Resources, *above*), which charges by the kilometer and requires advance booking.

🚈 **BKV** ⊕ www.bkv.hu.

🚈 Complaints **Aviation Consumer Protection Division** (⇨ Air Travel) for airline-related problems. **Departmental Office of Civil Rights** ⊠ for general inquiries, U.S. Department of Transportation, S-30, 400 7th St. SW, Room 10215, Washington, DC 20590 ☎ 202/366-4648 🖷 202/366-9371 ⊕ www.dot. gov/ost/docr/index.htm. **Disability Rights Section** ⊠ NYAV, U.S. Department of Justice, Civil Rights Division, 950 Pennsylvania Ave. NW, Washington, DC 20530 ☎ ADA information line 202/514-0301, 800/ 514-0301, 202/514-0383 TTY, 800/514-0383 TTY

⊕ www.ada.gov. **U.S. Department of Transportation Hotline** ☎ for disability-related air-travel problems, 800/778-4838 or 800/455-9880 TTY.

TRAVEL AGENCIES

In the United States, the Americans with Disabilities Act requires that travel firms serve the needs of all travelers. Some agencies specialize in working with people with disabilities.

🚈 Travelers with Mobility Problems **Access Adventures/B. Roberts Travel** ⊠ 206 Chestnut Ridge Rd., Scottsville, NY 14624 ☎ 585/889-9096 ⊕ www.brobertstravel.com ✑ dltravel@prodigy. net, run by a former physical-rehabilitation counselor. **CareVacations** ⊠ No. 5, 5110-50 Ave., Leduc, Alberta, Canada, T9E 6V4 ☎ 780/986-6404 or 877/ 478-7827 🖷 780/986-8332 ⊕ www.carevacations. com, for group tours and cruise vacations. **Flying Wheels Travel** ⊠ 143 W. Bridge St., Box 382, Owatonna, MN 55060 ☎ 507/451-5005 🖷 507/451-1685 ⊕ www.flyingwheelstravel.com.

🚈 Travelers with Developmental Disabilities **New Directions** ⊠ 5276 Hollister Ave., Suite 207, Santa Barbara, CA 93111 ☎ 805/967-2841 or 888/967-2841 🖷 805/964-7344 ⊕ www.newdirectionstravel.com. **Sprout** ⊠ 893 Amsterdam Ave., New York, NY 10025 ☎ 212/222-9575 or 888/222-9575 🖷 212/222-9768 ⊕ www.gosprout.org.

DISCOUNTS & DEALS

In Budapest, the popular Budapest Card entitles holders to unlimited travel on public transportation; free admission to many museums and sights; and discounts on various services from participating businesses. The cost (at this writing) is 4,350 HUF for two days, 5,450 HUF for three days; one card is valid for an adult plus one child under 14. It is available at many tourist offices, hotels, travel agencies, and metro ticket counters. A similar pass called the Hungary Card gives discounts to museums, sights, and services across the entire country.

DISCOUNT RESERVATIONS

To save money, look into discount reservations services with Web sites and toll-free numbers, which use their buying power to get a better price on hotels, airline tickets (⇨ Air Travel), even car rentals. When booking a room, always

call the hotel's local toll-free number (if one is available) rather than the central reservations number—you'll often get a better price. Always ask about special packages or corporate rates.

When shopping for the best deal on hotels and car rentals, look for guaranteed exchange rates, which protect you against a falling dollar. With your rate locked in, you won't pay more, even if the price goes up in the local currency.

🔁 Hotel Rooms **Accommodations Express** ☎ 800/444-7666 or 800/277-1064 ⊕ www.acex.net. **Hotels. com** ☎ 800/246-8357 ⊕ www.hotels.com. **International Marketing & Travel Concepts** ☎ 800/790-4682 ⊕ www.imtc-travel.com. **Turbotrip.com** ☎ 800/473-7829 ⊕ www.turbotrip.com.

PACKAGE DEALS

Don't confuse packages and guided tours. When you buy a package, you travel on your own, just as though you had planned the trip yourself. Fly/drive packages, which combine airfare and car rental, are often a good deal. In cities, ask the local visitor's bureau about hotel and local transportation packages that include tickets to major museum exhibits or other special events. If you **buy a rail/drive pass,** you may save on train tickets and car rentals. All Eurailpass holders get a discount on Eurostar fares through the Channel Tunnel and often receive reduced rates for buses, hotels, ferries, sightseeing cruises, and car rentals.

ELECTRICITY

The electrical current in Hungary is 220 volts, 50 cycles alternating current (AC); wall outlets generally take plugs with two round prongs. To use electric-powered equipment purchased in the U.S. or Canada, **bring a converter and adapter.** However, if your appliances are dual-voltage, you'll need only an adapter. Don't use 110-volt outlets marked FOR SHAVERS ONLY for high-wattage appliances such as blow-dryers. Most laptops operate equally well on 110 and 220 volts and so require only an adapter.

EMBASSIES

🔁 Australia **Australian Consulate** ⊠ District XII, Királyhágó tér 8-9, Around Déli train station ☎ 1/457-9777.

🔁 Canada **Canadian Consulate** ⊠ District XII, Budakeszi út 32, Buda Hills ☎ 1/392-3360.
🔁 New Zealand **New Zealand Consulate** ⊠ District VI, Teréz krt. 38, Around Nyugati station ☎ 1/331-4908.
🔁 United Kingdom **British Embassy** ⊠ District V, Harmincad u. 6, Around Deák Ferenc tér ☎ 1/266-2888.
🔁 United States **U.S. Embassy** ⊠ District V, Szabadság tér 12, Parliament ☎ 1/475-4400 ⊕ www. usembassy.hu.

EMERGENCIES

If you need a doctor, ask your hotel or embassy for a recommendation, or contact American Clinics International, a private, American-standard clinic staffed by English-speaking doctors offering 24-hour emergency service. The clinic accepts major credit cards and has direct billing agreements with numerous international insurance companies. In an emergency, you can call for a general ambulance or call American Clinics International and they will arrange it for you.

Profident Dental Services is a private, English-speaking dental practice consisting of Western-trained dentists and hygienists, with service available until 10 PM, except Sundays. S.O.S. Dent, also a private English-speaking dental clinic offering 24-hour care.

Most pharmacies (*gyógyszertár*) close between 6 PM and 8 PM, but several stay open at night and on the weekend, offering 24-hour service, with a small surcharge for items that aren't officially stamped as urgent by a physician. You must ring the buzzer next to the night window and someone will respond over the intercom. Staff are unlikely to speak English, so try to get at least a rough translation of what you need before you go. A small extra fee (100 HUF–200 HUF) is added to the bill. Late-night pharmacies are usually located across from the train stations.

Unlike those in the U.S., Hungarian hospitals don't have dedicated general emergency rooms that one can just walk into. If you call an ambulance, the paramedics assess you and, based on your condition and location, take you to the relevant specific department of the hospital where you are immediately treated. Hungarian doctors are well-trained, and most speak English or German. State hospitals, however, are in poor condition and not recommended; the private Telki Hospital just outside of Budapest or one arranged by the American Clinic is the best option.

🔢 **Doctors & Dentists American Clinics International** ✉ Hattyúház, District I, Hattyú u. 14, 5th floor, Around Moszkva tér ☎ 1/224-9090 ⊕ www. americanclinics.com. **Profident Dental Services** ✉ District VII, Karoly Köröt u. 1, Around Deák Ferenc tér ☎ 1/342-6972. **S.O.S. Dent** ✉ District VI, Király u. 14, Around Király utca ☎ 1/267-9602.

🔢 **Emergency Services Ambulance** ☎ 104. **Police** ☎ 107 or 112.

🔢 **Hospitals Telki Hospital** ✉ Telki kórház fasor 1, Telki ☎ 26/372-300.

🔢 **24-Hour Pharmacies Second District** ✉ District II, Frankel Leó út 22, Around Batthyány tér ☎ 1/212-4311. **Sixth District** ✉ District VI, Teréz körút 41, Around Nyugati Train Station ☎ 1/311-4439. **Twelfth District** ✉ District XII, Alkotás u. 1/b, Around Déli Train Station ☎ 1/355-4691.

ENGLISH-LANGUAGE MEDIA

Several English-language weeklies exist to serve the needs of Budapest's large expatriate community. The *Budapest Sun* and the *Budapest Business Journal* are sold at major newsstands, hotels, and tourist points. The mini-guidebook *Budapest in Your Pocket* appears six times a year and is also widely available. *Where Budapest,* a free monthly magazine, is available at Tourinform offices and major hotels. *The Hungarian Quarterly,* an erudite English-language journal of Hungarian literature and cultural, historical, and political essays, provides a deeper look into Hungary's current intellectual and cultural soul.

BOOKS

The store Bestsellers sells almost entirely English-language books and publications, including Hungarian classics translated into English, popular British and American best-sellers, and newspapers and magazines. The Central European University Bookshop, in the Central European University, should be your first stop for books concerned with Central European politics

and history. Bamako, in the Vista travel agency, has a broad range of travel guides in English. The Red Bus Bookstore buys and sells used books in English.

🔢 **Bamako** ✉ District VI, Andrássy út 1, Around Andrássy út. **Bestsellers** ✉ District V, Október 6 u. 11, Szent István Bazilika ☎ 1/312-1295. **Central European University Bookshop** ✉ District V, Nádor u. 9, Szent István Bazilika ☎ 1/327-3096. **Red Bus Bookstore** ✉ District V Semmelweis u. 14, Around Deák Ferenc tér ☎ 1/337-7453.

RADIO & TELEVISION

Almost all hotel TVs have standard English-language satellite channels such as CNN, BBC World, and—of course—the globally ubiquitous MTV. Radio Budapest (available on shortwave-, satellite-, and Internet radio) has a number of daily programs in English, including 30-minute "Hungary Today," a current affairs news and culture show.

Radio Budapest (⊕ www.radiobudapest. radio.hu).

ETIQUETTE & BEHAVIOR

Hungarians are traditionally polite and well-mannered people. The language itself has two main forms of address: a polite form, used with elders and in formal or business situations, and an informal one, used with friends, peers, and family. It is customary and polite to greet people upon entering and exiting a store or restaurant rather than just walking in and out without a word. There's no need to seek someone out and force eye contact if no one is immediately available, just call out a greeting of *jo napot kivánok/jo estét* (good day/good evening) when you enter and *viszontlátásra* when you leave. You'll likely hear the same in response from the storekeeper. The same rule applies when approaching someone for, say, directions on the street. These greetings are the more formal versions and should cover all bases for your purposes.

There is a very large population of elderly people in Budapest and chivalry towards them is customary, even among young people. When riding public transportation, it is polite to give your seat to an elderly person, man or woman.

Excepting business situations, women and men double-kiss, once on each cheek, in greeting. Men generally shake hands with each other.

To apologize for bumping into someone, you can say *bocsánat* (sorry) or *elnézést* (excuse me). Thank you is *köszönöm*. To get a waiter's attention in a restaurant, you can say or call out *legyen szíves* (please) and hope for the best!

GAY & LESBIAN TRAVEL

Hungary is relatively open-minded, though even in Budapest the gay population keeps a fairly low profile. Some of Budapest's thermal baths are popular meeting places, as are the city's several gay bars and clubs, which you can find listed in English-language newspapers and the monthly magazine *Mások,* which is available only in Hungarian.

◪ Gay- & Lesbian-Friendly Travel Agencies **Different Roads Travel** ✉ 8383 Wilshire Blvd., Suite 520, Beverly Hills, CA 90211 ☏ 323/651-5557 or 800/429-8747 (Ext. 14 for both) ☖ 323/651-5454 ✐ lgernert@tzell.com. **Kennedy Travel** ✉ 130 W. 42nd St., Suite 401, New York, NY 10036 ☏ 212/840-8659, 800/237-7433 ☖ 212/730-2269 ⊕ www.kennedytravel.com. **Now, Voyager** ✉ 4406 18th St., San Francisco, CA 94114 ☏ 415/626-1169 or 800/255-6951 ☖ 415/626-8626 ⊕ www.nowvoyager.com. **Skylink Travel and Tour/Flying Dutchmen Travel** ✉ 1455 N. Dutton Ave., Suite A, Santa Rosa, CA 95401 ☏ 707/546-9888 or 800/225-5759 ☖ 707/636-0951; serving lesbian travelers. ◪ Web Sites **Budapest GayGuide.net** ⊕ www.gayguide.net/europe/hungary/budapest. **Budapest Gayvisitor** ⊕ www.budapestgayvisitor.hu.

HEALTH

You may gain weight, but there are few other serious health hazards for the traveler in Hungary. Tap water may taste bad but is generally drinkable; when it runs rusty out of the tap in an old building or the aroma of chlorine is overpowering, it might help to have some bottled water handy.

HOLIDAYS

January 1; March 15 (anniversary of 1848 Revolution); Easter Sunday and Easter Monday (in March, April, or May); May 1 (Labor Day); Pentecost Monday (also known as Whitsun Monday; Whitsunday is the seventh Sunday after Easter); August 20 (St. Stephen's and Constitution Day); October 23 (1956 Revolution Day); December 24–26.

INSURANCE

The most useful travel-insurance plan is a comprehensive policy that includes coverage for trip cancellation and interruption, default, trip delay, and medical expenses (with a waiver for preexisting conditions).

Without insurance you'll lose all or most of your money if you cancel your trip, regardless of the reason. Default insurance covers you if your tour operator, airline, or cruise line goes out of business—the chances of which have been increasing. Trip-delay covers expenses that arise because of bad weather or mechanical delays. Study the fine print when comparing policies.

If you're traveling internationally, a key component of travel insurance is coverage for medical bills incurred if you get sick on the road. Such expenses aren't generally covered by Medicare or private policies. U.K. residents can buy a travel-insurance policy valid for most vacations taken during the year in which it's purchased (but check preexisting-condition coverage). British and Australian citizens need extra medical coverage when traveling overseas.

Always **buy travel policies directly from the insurance company**; if you buy them from a cruise line, airline, or tour operator that goes out of business, you probably won't be covered for the agency or operator's default, a major risk. Before making any purchase, review your existing health and home-owner's policies to find what they cover away from home.

◪ Travel Insurers In the U.S.: **Access America** ✉ 2805 N. Parham Rd., Richmond, VA 23294 ☏ 800/284-8300 ☖ 804/673-1491 or 800/346-9265 ⊕ www.accessamerica.com. **Travel Guard International** ✉ 1145 Clark St., Stevens Point, WI 54481 ☏ 715/345-0505 or 800/826-1300 ☖ 800/955-8785 ⊕ www.travelguard.com. ◪ In the U.K.: **Association of British Insurers** ✉ 51 Gresham St., London EC2V 7HQ ☏ 020/

7600-3333 🖶 020/7696-8999 ⊕ www.abi.org.uk. In Canada: **RBC Insurance** ✉ 6880 Financial Dr., Mississauga, Ontario L5N 7Y5 ☎ 800/668-4342 or 905/816-2400 🖶 905/813-4704 ⊕ www.rbcinsurance.com. In Australia: **Insurance Council of Australia** ✉ Insurance Enquiries and Complaints, Level 12, Box 561, Collins St. W, Melbourne, VIC 8007 ☎ 1300/780808 or 03/9629-4109 🖶 03/9621-2060 ⊕ www.iecltd.com.au. In New Zealand: **Insurance Council of New Zealand** ✉ Level 7, 111-115 Customhouse Quay, Box 474, Wellington ☎ 04/472-5230 🖶 04/473-3011 ⊕ www.icnz.org.nz.

LANGUAGE

Hungarian (*Magyar*) tends to look and sound intimidating at first because it is not an Indo-European language. Generally, older people speak some German, and many younger people speak at least rudimentary English, which has become the most popular language to learn. It's a safe bet that anyone in the tourist trade will speak at least one of the two languages. Also note that when giving names, Hungarians put the family name before the given name, thus János Szabó (John Taylor) becomes Szabó János.

MAIL & SHIPPING

Airmail letters and postcards generally take seven days to travel between Hungary and the United States, sometimes more than twice as long, however, during the Christmas season. At this writing, postage for an airmail letter to the U.S. costs 210 HUF; an airmail letter to the U.K. and elsewhere in Western Europe costs 190 HUF; airmail postcards to the U.S. cost 150 HUF and to the U.K. and the rest of Western Europe, 130 HUF.

Budapest's main post office branch is downtown. The post offices near Budapest's Keleti (East) and Nyugati (West) train stations stay open until 9 PM on weekdays, the former just as long on weekends although the latter shuts its doors at 8 PM. The American Express office in Budapest has poste restante services—or "client mail," as they call it—for cardholders, but they will not accept packages.
🛈 **American Express** ⓓ District V, Deák Ferenc u. 10, H-1052 Budapest ☎ 1/235-4330. **Downtown Budapest post office branch** ✉ District V, Magyar

Posta 4. sz., Városház u. 18, H-1052 Budapest. **Keleti post office** ⓓ District VIII, Baross tér 11/C, H-1087 Budapest. **Nyugati post office** ✉ District VI, Teréz krt. 51, H-1052 Budapest.

OVERNIGHT SERVICES

Both DHL, FedEx, and UPS operate in Budapest. Overnight service is possible to the U.K. but not always to the U.S., which might take two days. Express service to Australia and New Zealand can take three to four days. All services are expensive (starting at around $50 for an overnight document to the U.K.).
🛈 **DHL** ☎ 0640/454-545 ⊕ www.dhl.hu. **UPS** ☎ 0640/262-000 ⊕ www.ups.com. **FedEx Hungary** ☎ 0629/551-900 or 0640/980-980 ⊕ www.fedex.com/hu.

MONEY MATTERS

The easiest way to handle money in Budapest is to withdraw forints directly from your home bank account at one of the city's many ATMs. Many banks will cash American Express and Visa traveler's checks, but stores and restaurants are unlikely to accept them as payment. American Express has a full-service office in Budapest. There are also several Citibank branches, offering full services to account holders. For information on taxes, *see* Taxes.

ATMS

ATMs are common in Budapest and more often than not are part of the Cirrus and Plus networks. You can withdraw forints only (automatically converted at the bank's official exchange rate) directly from your account. Instructions are in English. Some levy a 1% or $3 service charge; ask your bank about its surcharges before you travel. Outside of urban areas, machines are scarce and you should plan to carry enough cash to meet your needs.
🛈 **American Express** ✉ District V, Deák Ferenc u. 10, Around Deák Ferenc tér ☎ 1/235-4330 🖶 1/267-2028 ✉ District I, Dísz tér 8, Castle Hill. **Citibank** ✉ District V, Vörösmarty tér 4, Around Váci utca ☎ 1/288-2352 ✉ District V, Báthori u. 12, Parliament ☎ 1/301-2700.

CREDIT CARDS

All major credit cards are accepted in Hungary, but don't rely on them in smaller towns or less expensive accommodations and restaurants. The most commonly accepted cards are MasterCard and Visa.

Throughout this guide, the following abbreviations are used: **AE,** American Express; **DC,** Diners Club; **MC,** MasterCard; and **V,** Visa.

🎦 Lost Credit Cards American Express ☎ 336/ 393-1111 collect to the U.S. **Diners Club** ☎ 0680-488-888 in Budapest. **MasterCard** ☎ 0680-012-517 in Budapest. **Visa** ☎ 0680-011-272 in Budapest.

CURRENCY

Hungary joined the European Union in 2004, but it still uses the forint (HUF or Ft.). There are bills of 200, 500, 1,000, 2,000, 5,000, 10,000 and 20,000 forints and coins of 1, 2, 5, 10, 20, 50, and 100 forints.

CURRENCY EXCHANGE

At this writing, the exchange rate was approximately 188 HUF to the U.S. dollar, 156 HUF to the Canadian dollar, 348 HUF to the pound sterling, and 244 HUF to the euro. There is still a black market in hard currency, but changing money on the street is risky and illegal, and the bank rate almost always comes close. Stick with banks and official exchange offices. Banks may charge a commission, but their rates tend to be much better than those at exchange offices. If you're lured into an exchange office by an attractive advertised rate, be sure to read and ask about special conditions and service charges before putting any money down. There are also many cash-exchange machines in Budapest, into which you feed paper currency for forints, but this can feel too risky for those with a healthy distrust of machines. Most bank automats and cash-exchange machines are clustered around their respective bank branches throughout downtown Pest.

It can help to have some local currency before you leave. If your local bank doesn't offer this service, you can order some foreign currency before you leave from International Currency Express or Travelex.

🎦 Before You Go International Currency Express ✉ 427 N. Camden Dr., Suite F, Beverly Hills, CA

90210 ☎ 888/278-6628 orders 🖶 310/278-6410 ⊕ www.foreignmoney.com. **Travelex Currency Services** ☎ 800/287-7362 orders and retail locations ⊕ www.travelex.com.

TRAVELER'S CHECKS

Do you need traveler's checks? It depends on where you're headed. If you're going to rural areas and small towns, go with cash; traveler's checks are best used in cities. Lost or stolen checks can usually be replaced within 24 hours. To ensure a speedy refund, buy your own traveler's checks—don't let someone else pay for them: irregularities like this can cause delays. The person who bought the checks should make the call to request a refund. Banks in Hungary will exchange traveler's checks, but stores and businesses are not a given.

PACKING

Although fashion was all but nonexistent under 40 years of Communist rule, these days residents of Budapest, especially young people, are dressed in the latest Western trends. Don't worry about packing lots of formal clothing: a sports jacket for men and a dress or pants for women are appropriate for an evening out. Everywhere else, you'll feel comfortable in casual pants or jeans.

Hungary enjoys all the extremes of an inland climate, so plan accordingly. In the higher elevations winter can last until April, and even in summer the evenings will be on the cool side.

Many areas are best seen on foot, so take a pair of sturdy walking shoes and be prepared to use them. High heels will present considerable problems on the cobblestone streets of towns in Hungary.

In your carry-on luggage, pack an extra pair of eyeglasses or contact lenses and enough of any medication you take to last a few days longer than the entire trip. You may also ask your doctor to write a spare prescription using the drug's generic name, as brand names may vary from country to country. In luggage to be checked, **never pack prescription drugs, valuables, or undeveloped film.** And don't forget to carry with you the addresses of offices that handle refunds of lost traveler's checks. Check *Fodor's How to Pack* (available at online retailers and bookstores everywhere) for more tips.

To avoid customs and security delays, carry medications in their original packaging. Don't pack any sharp objects in your carry-on luggage, including knives of any size or material, scissors, nail clippers, and corkscrews, or anything else that might arouse suspicion.

To avoid having your checked luggage chosen for hand inspection, don't cram bags full. The U.S. Transportation Security Administration suggests packing shoes on top and placing personal items you don't want touched in clear plastic bags.

CHECKING LUGGAGE

You're allowed to carry aboard one bag and one personal article, such as a purse or a laptop computer. Make sure what you carry on fits under your seat or in the overhead bin. Get to the gate early, so you can board as soon as possible, before the overhead bins fill up.

Baggage allowances vary by carrier, destination, and ticket class. On international flights, you're usually allowed to check two bags weighing up to 70 pounds (32 kilograms) each, although a few airlines allow checked bags of up to 88 pounds (40 kilograms) in first class. Some international carriers don't allow more than 66 pounds (30 kilograms) per bag in business class and 44 pounds (20 kilograms) in economy. On domestic flights, the limit is usually 50 to 70 pounds (23 to 32 kilograms) per bag. In general, carry-on bags shouldn't exceed 40 pounds (18 kilograms). Most airlines won't accept bags that weigh more than 100 pounds (45 kilograms) on domestic or international flights. Expect to pay a fee for baggage that exceeds weight limits. Check baggage restrictions with your carrier before you pack.

Airline liability for baggage is limited to $2,500 per person on flights within the United States. On international flights it amounts to $9.07 per pound or $20 per

kilogram for checked baggage (roughly $640 per 70-pound bag), with a maximum of $634.90 per piece, and $400 per passenger for unchecked baggage. You can buy additional coverage at check-in for about $10 per $1,000 of coverage, but it often excludes a rather extensive list of items, shown on your airline ticket.

Before departure, itemize your bags' contents and their worth, and label the bags with your name, address, and phone number. (If you use your home address, cover it so potential thieves can't see it readily.) Include a label inside each bag and **pack a copy of your itinerary**. At check-in, make sure each bag is correctly tagged with the destination airport's three-letter code. Because some checked bags will be opened for hand inspection, the U.S. Transportation Security Administration recommends that you leave luggage unlocked or use the plastic locks offered at check-in. TSA screeners place an inspection notice inside searched bags, which are re-sealed with a special lock.

If your bag has been searched and contents are missing or damaged, file a claim with the TSA Consumer Response Center as soon as possible. If your bags arrive damaged or fail to arrive at all, file a written report with the airline before leaving the airport.

☎ Complaints U.S. Transportation Security Administration Contact Center ☎ 866/289–9673 ⊕ www.tsa.gov.

PASSPORTS & VISAS

When traveling internationally, carry your passport even if you don't need one (it's always the best form of ID) and **make two photocopies of the data page** (one for someone at home and another for you, carried separately from your passport). If you lose your passport, promptly call the nearest embassy or consulate and the local police.

U.S. passport applications for children under age 14 require consent from both parents or legal guardians; both parents must appear together to sign the application. If only one parent appears, he or she must submit a written statement from the other parent authorizing passport issuance for the child. A parent with sole authority must present evidence of it when applying; acceptable documentation includes the child's certified birth certificate listing only the applying parent, a court order specifically permitting this parent's travel with the child, or a death certificate for the nonapplying parent. Application forms and instructions are available on the Web site of the U.S. State Department's Bureau of Consular Affairs (⊕ travel.state.gov).

ENTERING HUNGARY

Only a valid passport is required of U.S., British, Canadian, and New Zealand citizens; Australian citizens must obtain a visa.

🚩 **Hungarian Embassies Abroad Australia** ✉ 17 Beale Crescent, Deakin ACT., Canberra 2600 ☎ 6126/282-3226. **Canada** ✉ 299 Waverley St., Ottawa, Ontario K2P 0V9 ☎ 613/230-2717. **New Zealand** Consulate General ⌂ Box 29-039, Wellington 6030 ☎ 4/973-7507. **United States** ✉ 3910 Shoemaker St. NW, Washington, DC 20008 ☎ 202/364-8218. **United Kingdom** ✉ 35b Eaton Pl., London SW1X 8BY ☎ 0207/201-3440.

PASSPORT OFFICES

The best time to apply for a passport or to renew is in fall and winter. Before any trip, check your passport's expiration date, and, if necessary, renew it as soon as possible.

🚩 **Australian Citizens Passports Australia** Australian Department of Foreign Affairs and Trade ☎ 131-232 ⊕ www.passports.gov.au.
🚩 **Canadian Citizens Passport Office** ✉ to mail in applications: 200 Promenade du Portage, Hull, Québec J8X 4B7 ☎ 819/994-3500 or 800/567-6868 ⊕ www.ppt.gc.ca.
🚩 **New Zealand Citizens New Zealand Passports Office** ☎ 0800/22-5050 or 04/474-8100 ⊕ www.passports.govt.nz.
🚩 **U.K. Citizens U.K. Passport Service** ☎ 0870/521-0410 ⊕ www.passport.gov.uk.
🚩 **U.S. Citizens National Passport Information Center** ☎ 877/487-2778, 888/874-7793 TDD/TTY ⊕ travel.state.gov.

RESTROOMS

While the restrooms at Budapest's Ferihegy Airport may sparkle and smell of soap, don't expect the same of those at Hungarian train and bus stations—which, by the way, usually have attendants on hand who collect a fee of about 50 HUF. Especially outside Budapest, public restrooms are often run-down and sometimes rank. Pay the attendant on the way in; you will receive toilet tissue in exchange. Since public restrooms are generally few and far between, you will sometimes find yourself entering cafés, bars, or restaurants primarily to use their toilets; when doing so, unless it happens to be a bustling fast-food place, you should probably order a little something.

SAFETY

Don't wear a money belt or a waist pack, both of which peg you as a tourist. Distribute your cash and any valuables (including your credit cards and passport) between a deep front pocket, an inside jacket or vest pocket, and a hidden money pouch. Do not reach for the money pouch once you're in public.

Crime rates are still relatively low in Budapest and the rest of Hungary, but travelers should beware of pickpockets in crowded areas, especially on public transportation, at railway stations, in western fast-food chains like McDonald's and Burger King, and in big hotels. In general, always keep your valuables with you—in open bars and restaurants, purses hung on or placed next to chairs are easy targets. Make sure your wallet is safe in a buttoned pocket, or watch your handbag. Although a typical rental car is less likely to be stolen, expensive German makes such as Audi, BMW, Volkswagen, and Mercedes are hot targets for car thieves. Never leave valuables in your car.

Hungary has relatively little violent crime, especially against tourists, but racially motivated attacks on arabic, black, and gypsy people do occur.

LOCAL SCAMS

The Hungarian word for "help" is *segítség,* pronounced sheh-geet-shayg. The word for "police" is *rendőr,* pronounced rend-er.

Male tourists are the target of Budapest's most prevalent and hardest-dying local scam, which generally happens in the Váci utca area: a pair of women (but sometimes more, sometimes only one) approaches the tourist in a casual, friendly way, sometimes acting as locals, sometimes pretending to be just visiting Budapest. They eventually suggest having a drink to continue the conversation and take the man to a colluding bar or café, where all is well until the bill arrives with outrageously high prices and his companions have conveniently left their wallets at home. When the victim protests, the waiter claims the group ordered some special expensive version of whatever drinks were had and soon several of the waiter's large, intimidating colleagues join the conversation while the women disappear. If your ego clouds your judgment enough so that you do end up sitting down somewhere with such new "friends," don't allow anyone to order anything without choosing it from a menu with prices, even if your companions offer to treat you—and don't assume the extra zeroes are just typos! Be sure to contact the police if you feel threatened. The U.S. embassy's Budapest-related Web site keeps an up-to-date list of several bars and cafés that are repeat offenders in these scams.

Note that Hungarian police will NEVER ask you for money, neither as a fine nor to "inspect" or count your currency; if they do, refuse and seek help—they may be con-artists impersonating officers. Also, at currency exchange offices—especially those around Váci utca and those open late at night—always confirm all rates and surcharges before commencing the transaction. Sometimes very high fees are hidden in the fine print not shown with the rates in the window.

If you do become a victim of a crime while in Hungary, you can contact White Ring (Fehér Gyűrű), a crime prevention and victim protection organization dedicated to helping foreigners with everything from free legal advice and counseling to help filing reports and replacing stolen documents. During peak tourist seasons, the main office of Tourinform has a police officer on-site to help visitors with crime and safety issues. **F** **Tourinform** ✉ District V, Sütő u. 2, Around Deák Ferenc tér ☎ 1/317-9800. **White Ring** ✉ District V, Szt. István krt. 1, Around Nyugati Train Station ☎ 1/472-1161 or 1/312-2287. **U.S. Embassy in Budapest** ⊕ www.usembassy.hu.

WOMEN IN BUDAPEST

If you carry a purse, choose one with a zipper and a thick strap that you can drape across your body; adjust the length so that the purse sits in front of you at or above hip level. (Don't wear a money belt or a waist pack.) Store only enough money in the purse to cover casual spending. Distribute the rest of your cash and any valuables between deep front pockets, inside jacket or vest pockets, and a concealed money pouch. It isn't wise for a woman to go alone to a bar or nightclub or to wander the streets late at night. When traveling by train at night, seek out compartments that are well populated.

SENIOR-CITIZEN TRAVEL

To qualify for age-related discounts, mention your senior-citizen status up front when booking hotel reservations (not when checking out) and before you're seated in restaurants (not when paying the bill). Be sure to have identification on hand. When renting a car, ask about promotional car-rental discounts, which can be cheaper than senior-citizen rates. **F** **Educational Programs Elderhostel** ✉ 11 Ave. de Lafayette, Boston, MA 02111-1746 ☎ 877/426-8056, 978/323-4141 international callers, 877/426-2167 TTY 🖷 877/426-2166 ⊕ www.elderhostel.org. **Interhostel** ✉ University of New Hampshire, 6 Garrison Ave., Durham, NH 03824 ☎ 603/862-1147 or 800/733-9753 🖷 603/862-1113 ⊕ www.learn.unh.edu.

SHOPPING

Bargaining is acceptable at flea markets, but otherwise Hungary is a land of set prices.

SMART SOUVENIRS

If you're short on space (and cash), you can buy a few tubes of **Piros Arany** (Red Gold), a zingy paprika paste found in almost every Hungarian household. It's available in all food stores, costs around $1, and is the size (and shape) of a tube of toothpaste. Also very Hungarian is **Unicum**, the potent secret-recipe herbal liqueur that people either love or hate. It comes in unusual round green bottles that make an interesting and eye-catching addition to any liquor cabinet or shelf. Bottles come in several sizes, including one smaller than a fist and a flattened flask-style container that fits in a pocket; there are also attractive gift-tins, some with Unicum-logo shot glasses. You can find Unicum in most food stores, as well as in the duty-free shop at the airport. **Coffee-table books** published in Hungary have gotten much better in quality over the years and are a nice way to bring back the myriad magical visual details of what you've experienced on your trip. You can find a good selection at most bookstores and at Bestsellers English-language bookstore.

WATCH OUT

So-called "védett" (protected) items cannot be taken out of the country, as they are considered to be national treasures. These items, usually works of art or antiques, are rarely sold in stores and are encountered only at high-level auctions. If you do find yourself the proud owner of such a piece, you'll be registered as such with the museum authorities when you buy it—and will likely need to find yourself a local wall to hang it on!

SIGHTSEEING TOURS

BOAT TOURS

Hour-long evening sightseeing cruises on the *Danube Legend* depart nightly at 8:15 from mid-March through April and in October and three times nightly (at 8:15, 9, and 10) from May through September. From November to mid-December, cruises only Fri. and Sat. at 6:30 PM. The 6:30 PM cruise also operates during the Christmas season: December 27–30 and New Year's Day. Guests receive headphones with recorded explanations of the sights (available in some 30 languages), as well as a free drink. Boats depart from Pier 6–7 at

Vigadó tér. It's wise to double-check the schedule to avoid missing the boat.

The *Duna-Bella* takes six two-hour Danube cruises a day, most of which include a one-hour walk on Margaret Island. Recorded commentary is provided through earphones. The tour is offered July through August eight times a day; May through June and in September six times a day; and mid-March through April and October through mid-December once a day. Boats depart from Pier 6–7 at Vigadó tér.

From early April to early September at noon every day boats leave from the dock at Vigadó tér on 1½-hour cruises between the railroad bridges north and south of the Árpád and Petőfi bridges, respectively. The trip, organized by MAHART Passnave, runs only on Friday, Saturday, Sunday, and holidays (once a day, at noon) in April; then there are regular daily services until early September. From late April to mid-June, there is an additional tour leaving every day at 7:30 PM. Tickets are 1,600 HUF. For an additional 2,800 HUF you can partake of a buffet meal while you cruise.

One-hour "Duna Corso" cruises commencing from Vigadó tér pier take in the sights between Margaret Bridge and the Gellért Hotel with commentary in four languages. Tours run every day from May to late September and depart at 11 AM and 1 PM, then hourly through 7 PM, with additional tours at 8:30 and 9:30. In low season (late March through late April and late September through late October) the last tour is at 5 PM. These tours are also run by MAHART Passnave and cost 2,400 HUF.

🚤 *Danube Legend* ⊠ District V, Vigadó tér, Pier 6–7, Around Váci utca ☎ 1/317–2203 reservations and information. *Duna-Bella* ⊠ District V, Vigadó tér, Pier 6–7, Around Around Váci utca ☎ 1/317–2203 reservations and information. **MAHART Passnave** ⊠ District V, Belgrád rakpart, Around Ferenciek tere ☎ 1/484–4013 ⊕ www.mahartpassnave.hu.

BUS TOURS

Program Centrum conducts two- and three-hour bus tours of the city that operate all year (no two-hour tour from November through March) and cost 5,000 HUF and 6,400 HUF, respectively. Starting from Erzsébet tér, tours take in parts of both Buda and Pest. The company can also provide private English-speaking guides on request. EUrama also offers a three-hour city bus tour (about 6,000 HUF per person). IBUSZ runs a variety of city-highlight tours, some including interior tours of Parliament or the Great Synagogue, some with extras such as post-tour wine tasting. All three agencies also offer full- and half-day bus excursion tours outside of Budapest. Budatours runs two-hour city tours on its open-top buses daily May through September for 4,800 HUF. All bus tours have commentary in English, but inquire whether it's recorded or live if it's important to you.

⚑ Budatours ⊠ District VI, Andrássy út 2, ☎ 1/374-7070 or 1/353-0558 ⊕ www.budatours.hu. **EUrama** ⊠ Hotel InterContinental, District V, Apáczai Csere János u. 12-14, Around Váci utca ☎ 1/327-6690 ⊕ www.eurama.hu. **IBUSZ** ⊠ District V, Ferenciek tere 10, Around Ferenciek tere ☎ 1/485-2765. **Program Centrum** ⊠ District V, Erzsébet tér 9-10, Around Deák Ferenc tér ☎ 1/317-7767 or 1/318-4446 ⊕ www.programcentrum.hu.

BICYCLE TOURS

For something different, you can try Yellow Zebra's four-hour English-language bicycle tour taking in the major sights of Buda and Pest (via designated bike lanes and less-trafficked streets). Tours meet at the yellow church on Deák tér and run daily from May through October at 11 AM, rain or shine—ponchos (and bicycles, of course) are provided free of charge.

⚑ Yellow Zebra Bike Tours ⊠ District V, Sütő u. 2 ☎ 1/266-8777 ⊕ www.yellowzebrabikes.com.

WALKING TOURS

Absolute Walking Tours has broken the mold for guided walking tours in Central Europe. The company offers not only historical and general interest tours but also creatively executed theme tours, such as the "Hammer & Sickle Tour" and a "Budapest Dark Side" night tour. The 3½-hour Budapest walk costs 4,000 HUF. No reservations are necessary; just show

up at one of the two designated starting points, rain or shine. From June through August, tours start at 9:30 AM and 1:30 PM in front of the yellow church on Deák tér, and at 10 AM and 2 PM from the steps of the Műcsarnok on Heroes' Square. From September through May tours go just once a day: 10:30 AM from Deák tér and 11 AM from Heroes' Square (in January call ahead as tours don't run every day; there are no tours on December 25 and 26). Private theme tours can be specially arranged.

Chosen Tours offers a three-hour combination bus and walking tour (5,000 HUF) called "Budapest Through Jewish Eyes," highlighting the sights and cultural life of the city's Jewish history. Tours run daily except Saturday and include free pickup and drop-off at central locations. Arrangements can also be made for off-season tours, as well as custom-designed tours.

⚑ Absolute Walking Tours ☎ 30/211-8861, 1/266-1729 ⊕ www.absolutetours.com. **Chosen Tours** ⊠ District XII, Pagony u. 40, Buda Hills ☎☎ 1/355-2202.

STUDENTS IN HUNGARY

In Hungary, as a general rule, only Hungarian citizens and students at Hungarian institutions qualify for student discounts on domestic travel fares and admission fees. The Vista Travel Center in Budapest has information on all aspects of student and youth travel throughout the country and abroad. You can purchase your International Student Identity Card here for about one-third the price you'd pay in the United States. Budapest's numerous youth hostels can also provide information on student- and budget-travel.

⚑ Vista Travel Center ⊠ District VI, Paulay Ede u. 7, Around Deák Ferenc tér ☎ 1/429-9780.

SUBWAY TRAVEL

Service on Budapest's subways is cheap, fast, and frequent (even the escalators are fast!); stations are easily located on maps and streets by the big letter "M" (for metro). *Bejárat* means entrance; *kijárat* means exit. Tickets valid on all forms of mass transportation within the boundaries of Budapest can be bought at hotels, metro stations, newsstands, and kiosks—

but metro stations are least likely to run out and therefore your best bet. Metro fares are the same as bus and tram fares (see ⇨ Bus & Tram Travel, *above*). Special metro-only tickets are also available in several varieties, but it's generally not worth the confusion and the minimal cost difference. **Tickets must be validated** in the time-clock machines in station entrances and should be kept until the end of the journey, as there are frequent checks by undercover inspectors; a fine for traveling without a ticket is 2,000 HUF plus the fare.

Line 1 (marked FÖLDALATTI), which starts downtown at Vörösmarty tér and follows Andrássy út out past Gundel restaurant and City Park, is an antique tourist attraction in itself, built in the 1890s for the Magyar Millennium; its yellow trains with tank treads still work. Lines 2 and 3 were built 90 years later. Line 2 (red) runs from the eastern suburbs, past the Keleti (East) Railway Station, through the city center, and under the Danube to the Déli (South) station. One of the stations, Moszkva tér is also the terminus for the Várbusz (Castle Bus). Line 3 (blue) runs from the southeastern suburbs to Deák tér, through the city center, and northward to the Nyugati (West) station and the northern suburbs. All three metro lines meet at the Deák tér station and run from 4:30 AM to shortly after 11 PM.

🚾 **BKV Customer Affairs Office** ✉ District VII, Akácfa u. 18, Around Blaha Lujza tér ☎ 1/461-6571 ⊕ www.bkv.hu.

TAXES

As a tourist in Hungary you will generally encounter two kinds of tax. Value-Added Tax (VAT) of 5% to 25% is included in the price of most consumer goods and services. An additional tourist tax is added to hotel bills in some parts of the country—it's 3% in Budapest.

VALUE-ADDED TAX

VAT in Hungary is also called ÁFA and ranges from 5% to 25% depending on the type of goods or service you are purchasing. Most general consumer goods are taxed at 15%; and most other services and products, including hotel fees, car rental costs, and gasoline, are taxed at a whopping 25%. Upon leaving, you are entitled to a value-added tax (VAT) refund on new goods (i.e., not works of art, antiques, or objects of museum value) valued at 50,000 HUF or more (VAT inclusive) purchased at one store on one day (i.e., on one invoice). The goods in question must leave the country within 90 days of their purchase, and the refund must be requested within 183 days of the purchase. Be sure to request a VAT refund form, VAT refund envelope, and detailed invoice from the store where you made your purchase; ask them for instructions, too, on how to proceed. Keep your credit card receipt, too, or the receipt from where you exchanged your money into forints if you paid in cash (ATM receipt, if applicable). Present these documents, along with the relevant goods purchased, to a customs officer before you leave Hungary (at the airport or train station). The documents will be stamped to prove the goods are leaving the country. You can then get a cash refund (in forints) at the VAT refund agency in the airport, or apply by mail later for a credit card refund. A service charge is subtracted on all refunds. If the goods in question are packed in your luggage, be sure to tell the check-in agent before you check your bags that you want to get a VAT refund on goods in your luggage. They will arrange access.

For more information, pick up a tax refund brochure from any tourist office or hotel. For further Hungarian customs information, inquire at the Hungarian Customs and Finance Guard office. If you have trouble communicating, ask Tourinform (1/438–8080) for help.

🚾 **V.A.T. Refunds Global Refund** ✉ 99 Main St., Suite 307, Nyack, NY 10960 ☎ 800/566-9828 📠 845/348-1549 ⊕ www.globalrefund.com.

TAXIS

There are plenty of honest taxi drivers in Budapest and a few too many dishonest ones. If you follow these guidelines you should be able to avoid being one of the many frustrated travelers taken for a ride. Whenever possible, do as locals do and order a taxi by telephone—even if you're on the street. Fő taxi now has a toll-free number, which can be called from any pay phone without using any coins. All the companies we list have English-speaking operators. Citytaxi and Fő taxi are especially good with English and handling foreigners. You will be asked for the address, your name, and a contact phone number; if you're at a pay phone, give them the number written on the phone if it's visible. The taxi usually appears in 5 to 10 minutes, and the driver will ask you to confirm your name. Most locals open the front door and hop in the passenger seat next to the driver. If you're at a restaurant, you can ask your waiter to call you a cab, but be sure to specify which company or companies you want. Don't be shy: this is common practice in Budapest.

Hailing a taxi on the street is tricky, as the available ones will tend to be the sharks trolling for tourists. If a gleaming, unmarked white Mercedes offers to take you, don't do it! The reliable ones are easy to spot (but most of them on the streets are occupied by telephone customers): their company logo and phone number will be displayed clearly all over the car—again, it's safest to wait for one of the companies listed below. All legitimate taxis must have a working meter; make sure it is running when you begin. If one is hailed on the street, the base fare is generally 300 HUF and then 200 HUF per kilometer thereafter, plus 45 HUF per minute not in motion. When ordering a taxi by phone, the per-kilometer rate falls to around 180 HUF per kilometer.

Be especially wary at the airport and train stations, where many visitors run into trouble. *Never* go along with someone who approaches you on the platform. See also ⇨ Airports & Transfers *in* Air Travel to & from Budapest, *above*) Outside the train station will be a line of taxis; look there for one of the reliable ones. If you don't find one, call from a pay phone.

Another tip: if you're on a tight budget, avoid taking official hotel taxis, as they tend to be very expensive. Visitors stranded on Castle Hill should avoid the Hilton taxicabs, shiny as they may be, for this reason.

🚖 BudaTaxi ☎ 1/233-3333. **Citytaxi** ☎ 1/211-1111. **Fő taxi** ☎ 1/222-2222, 06/80-222-222 toll-free. **Radio Taxi** ☎ 1/377-7777. **6x6 Taxi** ☎ 1/266-6666.

TELEPHONES

Within Hungary, most towns can be dialed directly: dial "06" and wait for the buzzing tone; then dial the local number. Cellular phone numbers are treated like long-distance domestic calls: dial "06" before the number (when giving their cellular phone numbers, most people include the 06 anyway). It is unnecessary to use the city code, 1, when dialing within Budapest

AREA & COUNTRY CODES

The country code for Hungary is 36. When dialing a Hungarian number from abroad, drop the initial "06" from the local area code. The country code is 1 for the United States and Canada, 61 for Australia, 64 for New Zealand, and 44 for the United Kingdom. The city code for Budapest is 1.

DIRECTORY & OPERATOR ASSISTANCE

Dial "198" for directory assistance for all of Hungary. There is usually someone on hand who can speak English. You can also consult *The Phone Book*, an English-language telephone directory full of important Budapest numbers as well as cultural and tourist information; it's provided in guest rooms of most major hotels, as well as at many restaurants and English-language bookstores. The slim but information-packed city guide *Budapest in Your Pocket* lists important phone numbers; it appears six times a year and can be bought at newsstands and hotels.

INTERNATIONAL CALLS

Direct calls to foreign countries can be made from Budapest and all major provincial towns by dialing "00" and waiting for the international dialing tone; on pay phones the initial charge is 60 HUF.

The country code for Hungary is 36. When dialing from outside the country, drop the initial 06 prefix for area codes outside of Budapest.

LONG-DISTANCE SERVICES

AT&T, MCI, and Sprint access codes make calling long-distance relatively convenient, but you may find the local access number blocked in many hotel rooms. First ask the hotel operator to connect you. If the hotel operator balks, ask for an international operator, or dial the international operator yourself. One way to improve your odds of getting connected to your long-distance carrier is to travel with more than one company's calling card (a hotel may block Sprint, for example, but not MCI). If all else fails, call from a pay phone.

Access Codes AT&T ☎ 06/800-01111. MCI ☎ 06/800-01411. Sprint ☎ 06/800-01877.

PUBLIC PHONES

On their way to extinction but still around, coin-operated pay phones accept 10-HUF, 20-HUF, 50-HUF, and 100-HUF coins; the minimum initial amount is 20 HUF. Given that these phones often swallow up change without allowing a call in exchange, however, it's best when possible to use gray card–operated telephones, which outnumber coin-operated phones in Budapest and the Balaton region. The cards—available at post offices and most newsstands and kiosks—come in units of 800 HUF and work by being inserted into the telephone's card slot. Another option is to purchase a prepaid calling card from any general shop or newsstand; it can be used for local as well as international phone calls and works with a toll-free access number, so you don't need coins to use it at a pay phone. Two common types are Matáv's "barangoló" card and the Neo card.

TIME

Hungary is on Central European Time (CET), one hour ahead of Greenwich Mean Time and six hours ahead of the Eastern time zone of the United States.

TIPPING

Taxi drivers and hairdressers expect 10% to 15% tips; porters should get 200 HUF to 400 HUF. Coatroom attendants receive 50 HUF to 100 HUF, as do gas-pump attendants if they wash your windows or check your tires; dressing-room attendants at thermal baths receive 50 HUF to 100 HUF for opening and closing your locker. Gratuities are not included automatically on bills at most restaurants; when the waiter arrives with the bill, you should immediately add a 10% to 15% tip to the amount, as it is not customary to leave the tip on the table. If a Gypsy band plays exclusively for your table, you should leave at least 500 HUF in a plate discreetly provided for that purpose.

TOURS & PACKAGES

Because everything is prearranged on a prepackaged tour or independent vacation, you spend less time planning—and often get it all at a good price.

BOOKING WITH AN AGENT

Travel agents are excellent resources. But it's a good idea to collect brochures from several agencies, as some agents' suggestions may be influenced by relationships with tour and package firms that reward them for volume sales. If you have a special interest, find an agent with expertise in that area; the American Society of Travel Agents (ASTA; ⇨ Travel Agencies) has a database of specialists worldwide. You can log on to the group's Web site to find an ASTA travel agent in your neighborhood.

Make sure your travel agent knows the accommodations and other services of the place being recommended. Ask about the hotel's location, room size, beds, and whether it has a pool, room service, or programs for children, if you care about these. Has your agent been there in person or sent others whom you can contact?

Do some homework on your own, too: local tourism boards can provide information about lesser-known and small-niche operators, some of which may sell only direct.

BUYER BEWARE

Each year consumers are stranded or lose their money when tour operators—even large ones with excellent reputations—go out of business. So check out the operator. Ask several travel agents about its reputation, and try to **book with a company that has a consumer-protection program.** (Look for information in the company's brochure.) In the United States, members of the United States Tour Operators Association are required to set aside funds ($1 million) to help eligible customers cover payments and travel arrangements in the event that the company defaults. It's also a good idea to choose a company that participates in the American Society of Travel Agents' Tour Operator Program; ASTA will act as mediator in any disputes between you and your tour operator.

Remember that the more your package or tour includes, the better you can predict the ultimate cost of your vacation. Make sure you know exactly what is covered, and beware of hidden costs. Are taxes, tips, and transfers included? Entertainment and excursions? These can add up.

⑦ Tour-Operator Recommendations American Society of Travel Agents (⇨ Travel Agencies). **National Tour Association** (NTA) ✉ 546 E. Main St., Lexington, KY 40508 ☎ 859/226-4444 or 800/682-8886 🖷 859/226-4404 ⊕ www.ntaonline.com. **United States Tour Operators Association** (USTOA) ✉ 275 Madison Ave., Suite 2014, New York, NY 10016 ☎ 212/599-6599 🖷 212/599-6744 ⊕ www. ustoa.com.

TRAIN TRAVEL
International trains are routed to two stations in Budapest. Keleti pályaudvar (East Station) receives most international rail traffic coming in from the west, including Vienna. Nyugati pályaudvar (West Station) handles a combination of international and domestic trains. Déli handles trains to the Lake Balaton region.

Snacks and drinks are often not available on trains, so pack a lunch for the road; train picnics are a way of life. For more information about rail travel, contact or visit MAV Passenger Service.

CUTTING COSTS
To save money, **look into rail passes.** But be aware that if you don't plan to cover many miles, you may come out ahead by buying individual tickets.

Only Hungarian citizens are entitled to student discounts on domestic train fares; all senior citizens (men over 60, women over 55), however, are eligible for a 20% discount.

For travel only within Hungary, there's a Hungarian Flexipass, which costs $76 for any 5 days of travel within a 15-day period, or $95 for 10 days within a one-month period. There are also MÁV's own seven- and 10-day *turista bérlet* (tourist pass; 12,600 HUF and 18,140 HUF, respectively, for second-class travel) available directly from the MÁV office.

The European East Pass, available outside of Europe, may be used on the national rail networks of Hungary, Austria, the Czech Republic, Poland, and Slovakia. The pass covers anywhere from five to 10 days of unlimited first- or second-class travel within a one-month period; a five-day first-class pass costs $226, second-class costs $160.

Hungary is also covered by the Eurailpass, which provides unlimited first-class rail travel, in all of the participating countries of Europe, for the duration of the pass. Purchase rail passes in the U.S. and Canada from Rail Europe from either ACP Rail, Euro Railways, or Rail Europe. Service charges can vary dramatically so be sure to shop around.

For further information on the Hungarian Flexipass, European East Pass, and Eurailpass, contact Euro Railways in the U.S. *see* Train Travel, *below.*

⑦ Rail Passes ACP Rail International ☎ 866/938-7245 ⊕ www.eurail-acprail.com. **Euro Railways** ☎ 866/768-8927 ⊕ www.eurorailways.com. **Rail Europe** ☎ 877/257-2887 in the U.S., 800/361-7245 in Canada ⊕ www.raileurope.com.

FARES & SCHEDULES
Domestic fares are calculated based on how many kilometers you travel, minus a series of complicated discounts for which foreigners are mostly not eligible. Information staff at the Budapest train stations and MAV Passenger Service office (with 24-hour telephone information) should, in theory, be able to help you with ticket information, as well as selling you your tick-

ets. If you have trouble communicating, however, you can ask for help at any tourist information office or travel agency listed below. MÁV's English-language Web site, called "ELVIRA," has current domestic schedule and fare information in English and is a good place to start.

Travel by train from Budapest to other large cities or to Lake Balaton is cheap and efficient. Avoid *személyvonat* (local trains), which are extremely slow; instead, take Intercity (IC) trains—which are especially clean and fast but require a *helyjegy* (seat reservation) for about 350 HUF—or *gyorsvonat* (express trains). On timetables, *vágány* (tracks) are abbreviated with a "v"; *indul* means departing, and *érkezik* means arriving. Trains get crowded during weekend travel in summer, especially to Lake Balaton; you're more likely to have elbow room if you pay a little extra for first-class tickets.

Å **MAV Passenger Service** ⊠ District VI, Andrássy út 35, Budapest ☎ 1/461-5500 international information, 1/461-5400 domestic information ⊕ www. elvira.hu.

Å **Train Stations** Keleti Pályaudvar (East Railway Station) ⊠ District VIII, Baross tér. **Nyugati Pályaudvar** (West Railway Station) ⊠ District V, Nyugati tér. **Déli Pályaudvar** (South Railway Station) ⊠ District XII, Alkotás u.

TRAVEL AGENCIES

A good travel agent puts your needs first. Look for an agency that has been in business at least five years, emphasizes customer service, and has someone on staff who specializes in your destination. In addition, **make sure the agency belongs to a professional trade organization.** The American Society of Travel Agents (ASTA)—the largest and most influential in the field with more than 20,000 members in some 140 countries—maintains and enforces a strict code of ethics and will step in to help mediate any agent-client disputes involving ASTA members if necessary. ASTA (whose motto is "Without a travel agent, you're on your own") also maintains a Web site that includes a directory of agents. (If a travel agency is also acting as your tour operator, *see* Buyer Beware *in* Tours & Packages.)

Local agencies in Budapest can help you book excursions, hotel rooms, and train and airline tickets for travel beyond the city.

Å **Local Agent Referrals American Society of Travel Agents (ASTA)** ⊠ 1101 King St., Suite 200, Alexandria, VA 22314 ☎ 703/739-2782 or 800/965-2782 24-hr hotline 📠 703/684-8319 ⊕ www. astanet.com. **Association of British Travel Agents** ⊠ 68-71 Newman St., London W1T 3AH ☎ 020/7637-2444 📠 020/7637-0713 ⊕ www.abta.com. **Association of Canadian Travel Agencies** ⊠ 130 Albert St., Suite 1705, Ottawa, Ontario K1P 5G4 ☎ 613/237-3657 📠 613/237-7052 ⊕ www.acta.ca. **Australian Federation of Travel Agents** ⊠ Level 3, 309 Pitt St., Sydney, NSW 2000 ☎ 02/9264-3299 or 1300/363-416 📠 02/9264-1085 ⊕ www.afta.com. au. **Travel Agents' Association of New Zealand** ⊠ Level 5, Tourism and Travel House, 79 Boulcott St., Box 1888, Wellington 6001 ☎ 04/499-0104 📠 04/499-0786 ⊕ www.taanz.org.nz.

Å **Travel Agencies in Budapest American Express** ⊠ District V, Deák Ferenc u. 10, Around Deák Ferenc tér ☎ 1/235-4330 📠 1/267-2028. **Getz International** ⊠ District V, Falk Miksa u. 5, Parliament ☎ 1/312-0645 or 1/312-0649 📠 1/312-1014. **IBUSZ Travel** central branch ⊠ District V, Ferenciek tere 10, Around Ferenciek tere ☎ 1/485-2700. **Vista Travel Center** main office ⊠ District VI, Andrássy út 1, Around Andrássy út ☎ 1/269-6032 or 1/269-6033 📠 1/269-6031 ⊠ District II, Mammut shopping mall, Lövőház u. 2-6, Around Moszkva tér ☎ 1/315-1105 ⊕ www.vista.hu.

VISITOR INFORMATION

Learn more about foreign destinations by checking government-issued travel advisories and country information. For a broader picture, consider information from more than one country.

Within Hungary, Tourinform has continued to expand and smarten up its act. It has numerous offices in Budapest and outposts throughout the country. Its toll-free tourist information telephone hotline operates 24 hours a day. For off-hours help in person, you can visit the Non-Stop Hotel Service travel agency, the only such office open 24 hours a day. The Tourism Office of Budapest has developed the Budapest Card, which entitles holders to unlimited travel on public transportation; free admission to many museums and sights; and discounts on various services from participating businesses. The cost at this writing was 4,350 HUF for two days, 5,450 HUF for three days; one card is valid for an adult plus one child under 14.

🚹 Before You Leave In the U.S. and Canada: **Hungarian National Tourist Office of New York** ✉ 150 E. 58th St., New York, NY 10155 ☎ 212/355-0240 📠 212/207-4103 ⊕ www.gotohungary.com.

In Canada: **Hungarian Consulate General Office** ✉ 121 Bloor St. E, Suite 1115, Toronto M4W3M5, Ontario ☎ 416/923-8981 📠 416/923-2732.

In the U.K.: **Hungarian National Tourist Board** ✉ c/o Embassy of the Republic of Hungary, Commercial Section, 46 Eaton Pl., London, SW1X 8AL ☎ 020/7823-1032 📠 020/7235-9840 ✍ htlondon@hungarytourism.hu.

🚹 Within Hungary **Non-Stop Hotel Service** ✉ District V, Apáczai Csere János u. 1, Around Váci utca ☎ 1/318-3925 or 1/266-8042 ⊕ www.nonstophotelservice.hu. **Tourinform** ✉ District V, Sütő u. 2, Around Deák Ferenc tér ☎ 1/438-8080, 80/630-800 24-hour toll-free hotline within Hungary, 30/303-0600 24-hr hotline from abroad ⊕ www.hungarytourism.hu. **Tourism Office of Budapest** ✉ District VI, Liszt Ferenc tér 11, Around Andrássy út ☎ 1/322-4098 ✉ District VI, Nyugati pályaudvar, Around Nyugati Train Station ☎ 1/302-8580 ✉ District I, Szentháromság tér, Castle Hill ☎ 1/488-0475 ⊕ www.budapestinfo.hu.

🚹 Government Advisories **U.S. Department of State** ✉ Overseas Citizens Services Office, 2100 Pennsylvania Ave. NW, 4th floor, Washington, DC 20520 ☎ 202/647-5225 interactive hotline or 888/407-4747 ⊕ www.travel.state.gov. **Consular Affairs Bureau of Canada** ☎ 800/267-6788 or 613/944-6788 ⊕ www.voyage.gc.ca. **U.K. Foreign and Commonwealth Office** ✉ Travel Advice Unit, Consular Division, Old Admiralty Building, London SW1A 2PA ☎ 0870/606-0290 or 020/7008-1500 ⊕ www.fco.gov.uk/travel. **Australian Department of Foreign Affairs and Trade** ☎ 300/139-281 travel advice, 02/6261-1299 Consular Travel Advice Faxback Service ⊕ www.dfat.gov.au. **New Zealand Ministry of Foreign Affairs and Trade** ☎ 04/439-8000 ⊕ www.mft.govt.nz.

WEB SITES

Several Web sites will be helpful to travelers going to Budapest. All the sites listed below have an English-language translation option, though you may have to click on an American or British flag to activate it. The Hungarian news agency's (MTI) English-language Web site has daily news plus a backlog of earlier articles. Web sites of the *Budapest Sun* and *Budapest Business Journal* have news articles and features, plus bits of current tourist information like a restaurant guide in *Budapest Sun*. The Mayor of Budapest's Web site has current city-related news features plus notes about upcoming cultural events and festivals, and general visitor information. Travellers Youth Hostels' Web site has tips and information for the globe-roaming budget set. The utak.hu Web site has some helpful maps and route planning information in English. Budapest In Your Pocket's Web site has some useful visitor information and articles for tourists; a more extensive print-version is available at newsstands. The Hungary Page has, well, just about everything.

🚹 Recommended Web Sites **Budapest Business Journal** ⊕ www.bbj.hu. **Budapest In Your Pocket** ⊕ www.inyourpocket.com. **Budapest Sun** ⊕ www.budapestsun.com. **The Hungary Page** ⊕ www.thehungarypage.com. **Office of the Mayor of Budapest** ⊕ www.budapest.hu. **MTI** ⊕ www.english.mti.hu. **Travellers Youth Hostels** ⊕ www.backpackers.hu. **Utak.hu** ⊕ www.utak.hu.

EXPLORING BUDAPEST

By Paul
Olchváry

SITUATED ON BOTH BANKS OF THE DANUBE, Budapest unites the colorful hills of Buda and the wide, businesslike boulevards of Pest. Though it was the site of a Roman outpost during the 1st century AD, the city was not officially created until 1873, when the towns of Óbuda, Pest, and Buda united. Since then, Budapest has been the cultural, political, intellectual, and commercial heart of Hungary; for the 20% of the nation's population who live in the capital, anywhere else is simply *vidék* ("the country").

Budapest has suffered many ravages in the course of its long history. It was totally destroyed by the Mongols in 1241, captured by the Turks in 1541, and nearly destroyed again by Soviet troops in 1945. But this bustling industrial and cultural center survived as the capital of the People's Republic of Hungary after the war—and then, as the 1980s drew to a close, it became renowned for "goulash socialism," a phrase used to describe the state's tolerance of an irrepressible entrepreneurial spirit. Budapest has undergone a radical makeover since the free elections of 1990. As more and more restaurants, bars, shops, and boutiques open their doors—and with fashion-conscious youths parading the streets—almost all traces of Communism have disappeared. But then look again: the elderly ladies selling flowers at the train station are a poignant reminder that some Hungarians have been left behind in this brave new world of competition.

Much of the charm of a visit to Budapest lies in unexpected glimpses into shadowy courtyards and in long vistas down sunlit cobbled streets. Although some 30,000 buildings were destroyed during World War II and in the 1956 Revolution, the past lingers on in the often crumbling architectural details of the antique structures that remain.

The principal sights of the city fall roughly into three areas, each of which can be comfortably covered on foot. The Budapest hills are best explored by public transportation. Note that, by tradition, the district number—a Roman numeral designating one of Budapest's 22 districts—precedes each address. For the sake of clarity, in this book, the word "District" precedes the number. Districts V, VI, and VII are in downtown Pest; District I includes Castle Hill, the main tourist district of Buda.

VÁRHEGY (CASTLE HILL)

Most of the major sights of Buda are on Várhegy (Castle Hill), a long, narrow plateau laced with cobblestone streets, clustered with beautifully preserved baroque, Gothic, and Renaissance houses and crowned by the magnificent Royal Palace. The area is theoretically banned to private cars (except for those of neighborhood residents and Hilton hotel guests), but the streets manage to be lined bumper to bumper with shiny new Opels, Suzukis, Mercedes, and Trabants all the same—sometimes the only visual element to verify you're not in a fairy tale. As in all of Budapest, thriving urban new has taken up residence in historic old; international corporate offices, diplomatic residences, restaurants, and boutiques occupy many of its landmark buildings. The most striking example, perhaps, is the Hilton hotel on Hess András tér, which has

FIGHTING OVER THE NEW FACE OF BUDAPEST

THOUGH POLITICIANS COME AND GO, their priciest building projects may outlive them by centuries. This helps explain why, in post–Cold War Budapest, architecture—or more specifically the issue of how to revive the city's frayed face as Communism has given way to resurgent nationalism—has been to Hungarian politics what sex scandals are to American politics.

The first building controversy surfaced soon after the first post-Communist government was elected in 1990. The government wanted Budapest to co-host the World Expo with Vienna in 1996. Huge sums were spent to give the proposed neighborhood—along the Danube near the Petőfi híd—a massive facelift. Critics alleged that the reckless spending was fueled by government-inspired nationalism. The first thing the socialist-liberal opposition did on being elected in 1994 was to scrap the expo plans.

Next came the question of how to replace the Nemzeti Színház (National Theater), which the Communist regime had demolished in 1965. In 1998, with a socialist-liberal government in office, construction began in earnest on the $75 million project. A huge hole was dug right in front of the city's main bus station, which was on Erzsébet tér at that time. However, the conservative opposition derided the costly plan, and in 1998, when Viktor Orbán became prime minister (his right-leaning government held power until 2002), the project on Erzsébet tér was cancelled. What was left was a huge crater that is today, surprisingly, an attractive park of sorts. In the end, the national theater was built, but not downtown at all. Rather, it was in the glum outskirts of downtown, where the Expo was to have been hosted, and the price tag was a more palatable $40 million.

The Orbán government's pet project was the so-called Terror Háza (House of Terror), a liberally funded plan to turn the former secret police headquarters on Andrássy út—a symbol of fascist- and Communist-era human rights abuses—into a museum reminding Hungarians of the "terror" imposed by past regimes. Critics—not least Orbán's socialist-liberal opposition—alleged that the museum, which finally did open in early 2002, did more to nurture people's aptitude for vengeance than for understanding and forgiveness. The museum director staunchly defends the venue, and he has become one of the most controversial personalities in modern-day Budapest.

Last but not least, there was the Sándor Palota, that grand old palace on Castle Hill, which the Orbán government planned to restore as a stately residence for Hungarian heads of government (i.e., Orbán himself), as had been the case between 1867 and 1944. This time the opposition accused the government of seeking to endow the office of head of government with too much pomp and circumstance. Having the PM live high above the rest of Budapest just seemed unseemly to them.

However, as politics would have it, Orbán's government was defeated in the 2002 elections, and the socialist-liberal coalition turned the palace into the Köztársásági Elnöki Hivatal (Presidential Office Building), a less controversial move. It's a move that has made most everyone happy.

ingeniously incorporated remains of Castle Hill's oldest church (a tower and one wall), built by Dominican friars in the 13th century.

Numbers in the text correspond to numbers in the margin and on the Castle Hill (Várhegy) map.

a good walk

Castle Hill's cobblestone streets and numerous museums are best explored on foot: plan to spend about a day here. Most of the transportation options for getting to Castle Hill deposit you on Szent György tér or Dísz tér, toward the southern end of Castle Hill and a short walk from most of its museums and grandest sights. It's impossible not to find Castle Hill, but it is possible to be confused about how to get on top of it. If you're already on the Buda side of the river, you can take the Castle bus—*Várbusz*—from the Moszkva tér metro station, northwest of Castle Hill.

If you're starting out from Pest, you can take a taxi or Bus 16 from Erzsébet tér or, the most scenic alternative, cross the Széchenyi Lánchíd (Chain Bridge) on foot to Clark Ádám tér and ride the *Sikló* (funicular) up Castle Hill.

Begin your exploration by walking slightly farther south to visit the **Királyi Palota ❶** at the southern end of the hill. Of the palace's wealth of museums, the Ludwig Múzeum, the Magyar Nemzeti Galéria, the Budapesti Történeti Múzeum, and Országos Széchenyi Könyvtár are all interesting. Stop to take a look at the **Statue of Prince Eugene of Savoy ❷** outside the entrance to Wing C before moving on. From here, you can cover the rest of the area by walking north along its handful of cobbled streets.

From Dísz tér, you can walk over to the **Köztársásági Elnöki Hivatal ❸** and the **Nemzeti Táncszínház ❹** theater on Szinház utca, then go up Tárnok utca, whose houses and open courtyards offer glimpses of how Hungarians have integrated contemporary life into Gothic, Renaissance, and baroque settings. Of particular interest are the houses at No. 16, now the Aranyhordó restaurant, and at No. 18, the 15th-century Arany Sas Patika (Golden Eagle Pharmacy Museum), with a naïf Madonna and child in an overhead niche. This tiny museum displays instruments, prescriptions, books, and other artifacts from 16th- and 17th-century pharmacies. Modern commerce is also integrated into Tárnok utca's historic homes; you'll encounter numerous folk souvenir shops and tiny boutiques lining the street. Tárnok utca funnels into **Szentháromság tér ❺** and the Trinity Column; this is also where you'll find the **Mátyás templom ❻** and, just behind it, the **Halászbástya ❼**.

After exploring them, double back to Dísz tér and set out northward again on **Úri utca ❽**, which runs parallel to Tárnok utca; this long street is lined with beautiful, genteel homes. The **Budavári Labirintus ❾**, at No. 9, is worth a stop, as is the amusing little Telefónia Museum, at No. 49. At the end of Úri utca you'll reach **Kapisztrán tér ❿**, where you'll find the **Hadtörténeti Múzeum ⓫**.

To take in a little explored, yet lovely, corner of Castle Hill, go beyond the museum to the northwest corner of the hill and walk along the castle wall (behind the museum) back toward Vienna Gate. Along this path you will find a little memorial to the Ottoman leader Vezir Abdurrahman Abdi Arnaut Pasa, who went down with his troops at the close of the long Turkish occupation of Hungary in 1686. The inscription reads, in part: "fell in battle near here on the afternoon of the last month of summer, 1686, in his 70th year. He was a heroic enemy, peace be with him."

Or else you can move on from the Hadtörténeti Múzeum toward Castle Hill's more notable sights by walking south again on Országház utca (Parliament Street), the main thoroughfare of 18th-century Buda; it takes its name from the building at No. 28, which was the seat of Parliament from 1790 to 1807. You'll end up back at Szentháromság tér, with just two streets remaining to explore.

You can stroll up little Fortuna utca, named for the 18th-century Fortuna Inn, which now houses the **Magyar Kereskedelmi és Vendéglátóipari Múzeum** ⑫. At the end of Fortuna utca you'll reach **Bécsi kapu tér** ⑬, opening to Moszkva tér just below. Head back on Táncsics Mihály, where you will find both the **Középkori Zsidó Imaház** ⑭ and the **Zenetörténeti Múzeum** ⑮. Next door, at No. 9, is the baroque house (formerly the Royal Mint) where rebel writer Táncsics Mihály was imprisoned in the dungeons and freed by the people on the Day of Revolution, March 15, 1848. Another famous prisoner, from 1837 to 1840, was Lajos Kossuth, who went on to become the most prominent figure of the Revolution. Continue down this street, and you'll find yourself in front of the Hilton hotel, back at Hess András tér, bordering Szentháromság tér.

Those whose feet haven't protested yet can finish off their tour of Castle Hill by strolling south back to Dísz tér on **Tóth Árpád sétány** ⑯, the romantic, tree-lined promenade along the Buda side of the hill.

TIMING   Castle Hill is small enough to cover in one day, but perusing its major museums and several tiny exhibits will require more time.

What to See

⑬ **Bécsi kapu tér** (Vienna Gate Square). Marking the northern entrance to Castle Hill, the stone gateway (rebuilt in 1936) called Vienna Gate opens toward Vienna—or, closer at hand, Moszkva tér a few short blocks below. The square named after it has some fine baroque and rococo houses but is dominated by the enormous neo-Romanesque (1913–17) headquarters of the **Országos Levéltár** (Hungarian National Archives), a cathedral-like shrine to paperwork. ⊠ *District I* Ⓜ *Várbusz (2nd stop after M2: Moszkva tér).*

⑨ **Budavári Labirintus** (Labyrinth of Buda Castle). Used as a wine cellar during the 16th and 17th centuries and then as an air-raid shelter during World War II, the labyrinth—entered at Úri utca 9 below an early-18th-century house—can be explored with a tour or, if you dare, on your own. There are some English-language brochures available. ⊠ *District I, Úri u. 9* ☎ *1/212–0207 Ext. 34* ⊜ *1,200 HUF* ☉ *Daily 9:30–7:30* Ⓜ *Várbusz (4th stop from M2: Moszkva tér).*

⑪ **Hadtörténeti Múzeum** (Museum of Military History). Fittingly, this museum is lodged in a former barracks, on the northwestern corner of Kapisztrán tér. The exhibits, which include collections of uniforms and

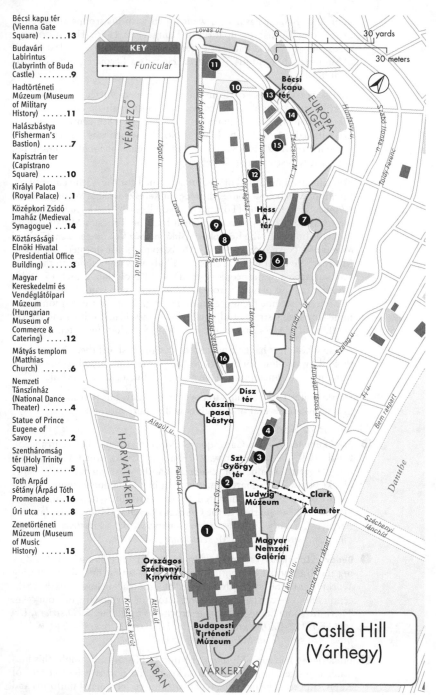

Castle Hill
(Várhegy)

military regalia, trace the military history of Hungary from the original Magyar conquest in the 9th century through the period of Ottoman rule to the mid-20th century. Families or couples can arrange an English-language group tour in advance for 2,500 HUF, and for larger groups it's 3,000 HUF. There is a charge to use a camera or video camera. ⊠ *District I, Tóth Árpád sétány 40* ☎ *1/356–9522* ⊕ *www.militaria.hu* ▣ *Museum free, photos 600 HUF, videos 1,200 HUF* ☉ *Apr.–Sept., Tues.–Sun. 10–6; Oct.–Mar., Tues.–Sun. 10–4* Ⓜ *Várbusz (3rd stop from M2: Moszkva tér).*

❼ Halászbástya (Fishermen's Bastion). The wondrous porch overlooking **FodorśChoice** the Danube and Pest is the neo-Romanesque Fishermen's Bastion, a merry ★ cluster of white stone towers, arches, and columns above a modern bronze statue of St. Stephen, Hungary's first king. Although you must now pay to wander over most of it during the day over much of the year (as has been the practice since 2000), the price is reasonable. Medieval fishwives once peddled their wares here, but now you see merchants selling souvenirs and crafts, musicians, and—less visible but always present—pickpockets. Buy your tickets at the booth beside the Tourinform office in the small, adjacent park. ⊠ *District I, East of Szentháromság tér* ▣ *300 HUF Mar.–Oct., 9 AM–11 PM daily; free Nov.–Feb.* ☉ *Daily 24 hrs* Ⓜ *Várbusz (4th stop from M2: Moszkva tér).*

❿ Kapisztrán tér (Capistrano Square). Castle Hill's northernmost square was named after St. John of Capistrano, an Italian friar who in 1456 recruited a crusading army to fight the Turks who were threatening Hungary. There's a statue of this honored Franciscan on the northwest corner; also here are the Museum of Military History and the remains of the 12th-century Gothic Mária Magdolna templom (Church of St. Mary Magdalene). Its *torony* (tower), completed in 1496, is the only part left standing; the rest of the church was destroyed by air raids during World War II. Ⓜ *Várbusz (3rd stop from M2: Moszkva tér).*

★ ❶ Királyi Palota (Royal Palace). A palace originally built on this spot in the 13th century for the kings of Hungary was reconstructed under the supervision of King Matthias during the 15th century. That, in turn, was demolished during the Turkish siege of Budapest in 1686. The Hapsburg empress Maria Theresa directed the building of a new palace in the 1700s. It was damaged during an unsuccessful attack by revolutionaries in 1849, but the Hapsburgs set about building again, completing work in 1905. Then, near the end of the Soviets' seven-week siege in February 1945, the entire Castle Hill district of palaces, mansions, and churches was reduced to rubble. Decades passed before reconstruction and whatever restoration was possible were completed. Archaeologists were able to recover both the original defensive walls and royal chambers, due in part to still surviving plans and texts from the reigns of Holy Roman Emperor Sigismund and King Matthias.

Freed from mounds of rubble, the foundation walls and medieval castle walls were completed, and the ramparts surrounding the medieval royal residence were re-created as close to their original shape and size as possible. If you want an idea of the Hungarian home-life of Franz

Josef and Sissi, however, you'll have to visit the baroque Gódóllő Palace. The Royal Palace today is used as a cultural center and museum complex.

The Royal Palace's baroque southern wing (Wing E) contains the **Budapesti Történeti Múzeum** (Budapest History Museum), displaying a fascinating permanent exhibit of modern Budapest history from Buda's liberation from the Turks in 1686 through the 1970s. Viewing the vintage 19th- and 20th-century photos and videos of the castle, the Széchenyi Lánchíd, and other Budapest monuments—and seeing them as the backdrop to the horrors of World War II and the 1956 Revolution—helps to put your later sightseeing in context; while you're browsing, peek out one of the windows overlooking the Danube and Pest and let it start seeping in.

Through historical documents, objects, and art, other permanent exhibits depict the medieval history of the Buda fortress and the capital as a whole. This is the best place to view remains of the medieval Royal Palace and other archaeological excavations. Some of the artifacts unearthed during excavations are in the vestibule in the basement; others are still among the remains of medieval structures. Down in the cellars are the original medieval vaults of the palace; portraits of King Matthias and his second wife, Beatrice of Aragon; and many late-14th-century statues that probably adorned the Renaissance palace. ⊠ *District I, Királyi Palota (Wing E), Szt. György tér 2* ☎ *1/224–3700* ⊕ *www.btm.hu* ✉ *800 HUF* ⊙ *Mar.–mid-May and mid-Sept.–Oct., Wed.–Mon. 10–6; mid-May–mid-Sept., daily 10–6; Nov.–Feb., Wed.–Mon. 10–4* Ⓜ *Várbusz (5th stop from M2: Moszkva tér).*

The collection at the **Ludwig Múzeum** includes more than 200 pieces of Hungarian and contemporary international art, including works by Picasso and Lichtenstein, and occupies the castle's northern wing. ⊠ *District I, Királyi Palota (Wing A), Dísz tér 17* ☎ *1/375–9175* ⊕ *www.ludwigmuseum.hu* ✉ *600 HUF; ground-floor exhibits free* ⊙ *Tues., Wed., and Fri.–Sun. 10–6, Thurs. 10–8* Ⓜ *Várbusz (5th stop from M2: Moszkva tér).*

Fodor'sChoice
★
The **Magyar Nemzeti Galéria** (Hungarian National Gallery), which is made up of the immense center block of the Royal Palace (Wings B, C, and D), exhibits Hungarian fine art, from medieval ecclesiastical paintings and statues through Gothic, Renaissance, and baroque art, to a rich collection of 19th- and 20th-century works. Especially notable are the works of the romantic painter Mihály Munkácsy, the impressionist Pál Szinyei Merse, and the surrealist Mihály Tivadar Kosztka Csontváry, whom Picasso much admired. There is also a large collection of modern Hungarian sculpture. Labels and commentary for both permanent and temporary exhibits are in English. If you contact the museum in advance, you can book a tour for up to five people with an English-speaking guide for 3,200 HUF (more for a larger group). There is a charge to use a camera or video camera. ⊠ *District I, Királyi Palota (entrance in Wing C), Dísz tér 17* ☎ *1/375–5567* ⊕ *www.mng.hu* ✉ *Museum free; special exhibits 600*

HUF; photos 1,500 HUF, videos 2,000 HUF ⊙ *Tues.–Sun. 10–6*
Ⓜ *Várbusz (5th stop from M2: Moszkva tér).*

The western wing (F) of the Royal Palace is the **Országos Széchenyi
Könyvtár** (Széchenyi National Library), which houses more than 2 million volumes. Its archives include well-preserved medieval codices,
manuscripts, and historic correspondence. This is not a lending library,
but the reading rooms are open to the public (though you must show a
passport); the most valuable materials can be viewed only on microfilm,
however. Temporary exhibits on rare books and documents, for example, are usually on display; the hours for these special exhibits vary, and
admission for smaller exhibits is sometimes free, though major exhibits
usually have a charge of around 500 HUF. Note that the entire library
closes for one month every summer, usually in July or August. ⊠ *District I, Királyi Palota (Wing F), Dísz tér 17* ☏ *1/224–3745, 1/224–3700
to arrange English-language tours* ⊕ *www.oszk.hu* ⊡ *Museum 600 HUF;
sometimes a separate fee for special exhibits* ⊙ *Reading rooms Mon.
1–9, Tues.–Fri. 9–9, Sat. 10–6; exhibits Mon. 1–6, Tues.–Sat. 10–6*
Ⓜ *Várbusz (5th stop from M2: Moszkva tér).*

🄔 **Középkori Zsidó Imaház** (Medieval Synagogue). The excavated one-room
medieval synagogue is now used as a museum. On display are objects
relating to the Jewish community, including religious inscriptions, frescoes, and tombstones dating to the 15th century. ⊠ *District I, Táncsics
Mihály u. 26* ☏ *1/224–3700 for general info. on Castle Hill museums,
including this one* ⊡ *300 HUF* ⊙ *May–Oct., Tues.–Sun. 10–5* Ⓜ *Várbusz (2nd stop from M2: Moszkva tér).*

🄷 **Köztársásági Elnöki Hivatal** (Presidential Office Building). This grand
palace, which is right between the National Dance Theater and the National Gallery, holds not just the President's office but also his official
residence during his five-year term (to which he can be reelected once).
Though the medieval palace on this site was razed during the Turkish
occupation, after the reconquest of Buda in 1686 two military barracks
sprang up here. In 1803 Count Vincze Sándor set out to build the gorgeous palace you can see today. Designed by János Ámon and Mihály
Pollack, the building has a facade beautified by Bavarian sculptor Anton
Kirchmayer's statues representing mythological and historical themes—
from the gods of Olympus to the knighting of Count Sándor. Between
1867 and 1944, the palace was home to Hungarian prime ministers. Heavily damaged in World War II, it was rebuilt in the late 1980s and was
remodeled once again, this time for its latest purpose, in 2002. Although plans originally called for the palace to be open to the public on
occasion, as of this writing it appears that it will not. ⊠ *District I, Szent
György tér* Ⓜ *Várbusz (5th stop from M2: Moszkva tér).*

🄬 **Magyar Kereskedelmi és Vendéglátóipari Múzeum** (Hungarian Museum of
Commerce & Catering). The 18th-century Fortuna Inn now serves visitors in a different way—as the Catering Museum. Displays in a permanent exhibit show the city as a tourist destination from 1870 to the
1930s; you can see, for example, what a room at the Gellért Hotel, still
operating today, would have looked like in 1918. The Commerce Mu-

seum, just across the courtyard, chronicles the history of Hungarian commerce from the late 19th century to 1947, when the new, Communist regime "liberated" the economy into socialism. The four-room exhibit includes everything from an antique chocolate-and-caramel vending machine to early shoe-polish advertisements. You can rent an English-language recorded tour for 300 HUF. ⊠ *District I, Fortuna u. 4* ☎ *1/ 212–1245* ᐃ *300 HUF* ⊗ *Wed.–Fri. 10–5, weekends 10–6* Ⓜ *Várbusz (get off at Szentháromság tér and walk toward M2: Moszkva tér).*

need a break?

Whether **Magyar Borok Háza** (House of Hungarian Wines; ⊠ District 1, Szentháromság tér 6, across the street from the Budapest Hilton ☎ 1/212–1030 or 1/212–1031) is more properly called a museum or simply a self-promoting venture by the Hungarian wine industry is open to question, but it's the best place in Budapest to *liberally* sample a comprehensive selection of the country's finest wines while still appearing to be a respectable traveller. A ticket (which costs 3,500 HUF) is good for a two-hour, self-guided tour through a cellar with more than 700 wines on display arranged by 22 wine regions and classical music in the background; you may pour as you wish from some 40 open bottles, but you may not get visibly smashed. It's open daily from noon to 8 PM.

❻ **Mátyás templom** (Matthias Church). The ornate white steeple of the **Fodor's**Choice Matthias Church is the highest point on Castle Hill. It was added in ★ the 15th century, above a 13th-century Gothic chapel. Officially the Buda Church of Our Lady, it has been known as the Matthias Church since the 15th century, in remembrance of the so-called "just king," who greatly added to and embellished it during his reign. Many of these changes were lost when the Turks converted it into a mosque. The intricate white stonework, mosaic roof decorations, and some of its geometric patterned columns seem to suggest Byzantine, yet it was substantially rebuilt again in the neo-baroque style, 87 years after the Turkish defeat in 1686. One fortunate survivor of all the changes was perhaps the finest example of Gothic stone carving in Hungary, the Assumption of the Blessed Virgin Mary, visible above the door on the side of the church that faces the Danube.

The **Szentháromság Kápolna** (Trinity Chapel) holds an *encolpion,* an enameled casket containing a miniature copy of the Gospel to be worn on the chest; it belonged to the 12th-century king Béla III and his wife, Anne of Chatillon. Their burial crowns and a cross, scepter, and rings found in their excavated graves are also displayed here. The church's **treasury** contains Renaissance and baroque chalices, monstrances, and vestments. High Mass is celebrated every Sunday at 10 AM, sometimes with full orchestra and choir—and often with major soloists; get here early if you want a seat. During the summer there are usually organ recitals on Friday at 8 PM. Tourists are asked to remain at the back of the church during weddings and services; at such times they can access the treasury (and a view of the church) through a separate entrance in the back, near the Budapest Hilton's parking garage. ⊠ *District I, Szentháromság tér 2* ☎ *1/355–5657* ⊗ *Church Mon.–Sat. 9–5 (often closed* *to the public on Sat. afternoons), Sun. 1–5; treasury daily 9–5* 🖼 *Church and treasury 550 HUF; treasure only 330 HUF* Ⓜ *Várbusz (4th stop from M2: Moszkva tér).*

❹ Nemzeti Táncszínház (National Dance Theater). This former Franciscan church was transformed into a more secular royal venue in 1787 under the supervision of courtier Farkas Kempelen. The first theatrical performance in Hungarian was held here in 1790. Heavily damaged during World War II, the theater was rebuilt and reopened in 1978. While the building retains its original late-baroque-style facade, the interior was renovated with marble and concrete. It is now used for performances of Hungarian contemporary dance, including ballet, as well as concerts. There is usually an art exhibit or a historical exhibition in its foyer—usually theater-related, such as a display of costumes. ✉ *District I, Színház u. 1–3* ☏ *1/201–4407* 🌐 *www.nemzetitancszinhaz.hu* 🖼 *Free* ⊙ *Daily 1–6* Ⓜ *Várbusz (5th stop from M2: Moszkva tér).*

❷ Statue of Prince Eugene of Savoy. In front of the Royal Palace, facing the Danube by the entrance to Wing C, stands an equestrian statue of Prince Eugene of Savoy, a commander of the army that liberated Hungary from the Turks at the end of the 17th century. From here there is a superb view across the river to Pest. ✉ *District I, Királyi Palota (by Wing C entrance), Dísz tér 17* Ⓜ *Várbusz (5th stop from M2: Moszkva tér).*

❺ Szentháromság tér (Holy Trinity Square). This square is named for its baroque Trinity Column, erected in 1712–13 as a gesture of thanksgiving by survivors of a plague. The column stands in front of the famous Gothic Matthias Church, its large pedestal a perfect seat from which to watch the wedding spectacles that take over the church on spring and summer weekends: from morning until night, frilly engaged pairs flow in one after the other and, after a brief transformation inside, back out onto the square. ✉ *District I* Ⓜ *Várbusz (4th stop from M2: Moszkva tér).*

★ ⑯ Tóth Árpád sétány (Árpád Tóth Promenade). This romantic, tree-lined promenade along the Buda side of the hill is often mistakenly overlooked by sightseers. Beginning at the Museum of Military History, the promenade takes you "behind the scenes" along the back sides of the matte-pastel baroque houses that face Úri utca, with their regal arched windows and wrought-iron gates. On a late spring afternoon, the fragrance of the cherry trees and the sweeping view of the quiet Buda neighborhoods below may be enough to revive even the most weary. ✉ *District I, from Kapisztrán tér to Szent György u.* Ⓜ *Várbusz (3rd stop from M2: Moszkva tér).*

❽ Úri utca (Úri Street). Running parallel to Tárnok utca, Úri utca has been less commercialized by boutiques and other shops. The longest and oldest street in the castle district, it is lined with many stately houses, all worth special attention for their delicately carved details. Both gateways of the baroque palace at Nos. 48–50—like those at Nos. 54–56—are articulated by Gothic niches from the 14th and 15th centuries.

The **Telefónia Múzeum** (Telephone Museum) is an endearing little museum entered through a central courtyard shared with the local district police station. Both the oldest and most recent products of telecommunication—from the 1882 wooden box with hose attachment to the latest digital marvels—can be observed and tested here. On weekends and holidays the entrance is on the opposite side of the building, at Országház u. 30. ⊠ *District I, Úri u. 49* ☎ *1/201–8188* 🖃 *200 HUF* ☉ *Tues.–Sun. 10–4* Ⓜ *Várbusz (3rd stop from M2: Moszkva tér).*

A short walk from Szentháromság tér, the **Ruszwurm** (⊠ Szentháromság u. 7 ☎ 1/375–5284) is Budapest's oldest surviving café, dating to the early 19th century. Known for its excellent pastries and reasonable prices, this elegant little gem has been a Castle Hill fixture since the 19th century. What's more, there's no smoking inside.

⑮ **Zenetörténeti Múzeum** (Museum of Music History). This handsome gray-and-pearl-stone 18th-century palace is where Beethoven is believed to have stayed in 1800 when he came to Buda to conduct his works. The museum housed here has been closed since 2003 and won't reopen until at least 2006; even then, it might be relocated. ⊠ *District I, Táncsics Mihály u. 7* ☎ *1/214–6770 Ext. 250* Ⓜ *Várbusz (2nd stop from M2: Moszkva tér).*

off the beaten path

TRAM NO. 56 TO THE BUDA HILLS – The spot below the four-sided clock on the center of Moszkva tér—the bustling square and public transportation hub below the northern end of Castle Hill—is second only to Pest's Deák tér in the realm of Budapest's meeting spots. Here you will find a less than pretty subway station but a great place to people-watch: a zestful mix of rushing commuters; illegal immigrants loitering about and waiting for employers to come by to take them to construction sites; men who sit for hours on one of the square's three-wide, concrete tree-pots; and many, many pigeons.

If you have at least an hour to spare, hop aboard Tram No. 56, which sets out from Moszkva tér for a lovely 17-minute ride into the heart of the Buda Hills—perhaps the most economical scenic excursion in all of Budapest at a cost of two public transport tickets (or nothing if you have a pass). The *Fogaskerekű vasút* (cogwheel railway) station, from where you can ride up into the hills all the way to the beginning point of the scenic *Gyermek vasut* (Children's Railway), is on your left at the third stop. Before long the greenery becomes lush on your left, and the stately, if worn, apartment houses give you a sense of what Buda must have been like a century or more ago. At the fifth stop (Nagyajtai utca) is a statue of Raoul Wallenberg in a small, shaded park to your right. From the seventh stop on, the lovely, forested Buda Hills are increasingly visible to your right; by the 12th stop it's as if the tram were passing through a forest; and, finally, the tram reaches its 13th and final stop, at Hüvösvölgy, which is also near the terminus of the Children's Railway. Here you might go for a hike from one of several nearby trailheads, or take a scenic ride on the Children's Railway. There's also a tavern-cum-pizzeria at the station itself, where you can grab a snack or other refreshment. Or, of course, you might simply ride back on down to Moszkva tér.

TABÁN & GELLÉRT-HEGY (GELLÉRT HILL)

Spreading below Castle Hill is the old quarter called Tabán (from the Turkish word for "armory"). A onetime suburb of Buda, it was known at the end of the 17th century as Little Serbia (*Rác*) because so many Serbian refugees settled here after fleeing from the Turks. It later became a district of vineyards and small taverns. Though most of the small houses characteristic of this district have been demolished—mainly in the interest of easing traffic—a few traditional buildings remain.

Gellért-hegy (Gellért Hill), 761 feet high, is the most beautiful natural formation on the Buda bank. It takes its name from St. Gellért (Gerard) of Csanad, a Venetian bishop who came to Hungary in the 11th century and, legend has it, was rolled off the top of the hill in a cart by pagans. The walk up can be tough, but take solace from the cluster of hot springs at its foot; these soothe and cure bathers at the Rác, Rudas, and Gellért baths.

Numbers in the text correspond to numbers in the margin and on the Central Budapest map.

a good walk

From the **Semmelweis Orvostörténeti Múzeum** ⑰, walk around the corner to Szarvas tér, where you will find the **Szarvas-ház** ⑱ at No. 1, and a few yards toward the river to the **Tabán plébánia-templom** ⑲. Walking south on Attila út and crossing to the other side of Hegyalja út will take you to the foot of Gellért Hill. You are now close to two Turkish baths, the **Rác Fürdő** (Rác Baths) ⑳ and, on the other side of the **Erzsébet híd** ㉑, the **Rudas Fürdő** (Rudas Baths) ㉒. You might need to take a soak after climbing the stairs to the top of the hill, a 30-minute walk, but keep in mind that both are closed at this writing until sometime in 2005, and even then the Rudas Baths are open only to men (the Rác baths are open to both men and women, but on alternating days). Here, overlooking Budapest, is the **Citadella** ㉓, with its panoramic views of Budapest and the nearby Liberation Monument. You can return the way you came, or go down the southeastern side of the hill to the **Gellért Szálloda és Thermál Fürdő** ㉔ at its southeastern foot. If you don't feel like walking to the Gellért baths, you can also take Bus 27 down the back of the hill to Móricz Zsigmond körtér and walk back toward the Gellért on busy Bartók Béla út, or take Tram 47, 49, 18, or 19 a couple of stops to Szent Gellért tér. This is your best bet if you want to soak your aching bones after the long walk, as the baths are open to both men and women on any day.

TIMING   The Citadella and Szabadság szobor are lit in golden lights every night, but the entire Gellért-hegy is at its scenic best every year on August 20, when it forms the backdrop to the spectacular St. Stephen's Day fireworks display. On a more practical note, should you wish to take advantage of the arca's inviting baths, remember that not all baths are open on Sundays or Saturday afternoons, and they all close by 6 or 7.

CloseUp

WHAT'S FREE

The permanent collections of several museums can be visited for free, though admission prices are charged for special exhibits. These include the **Hadtörténeti Múzeum, Ludwig Múzeum,** and **Magyar Nemzeti Galéria,** all of which are in Várhegy (Castle Hill); the **Semmelweis Orvostudoáyi Múzeum** in Tabán; the **Magyar Nemzeti Múzeum,** near the Small Ring Road; the **Ráth György Múzeum** and **Szépművészeti Múzeum,** both of which are just off Andrássy út; the Vajdahuyad

Vár in Varosliget (City Park); and the **Hercules Villa** and **Kassák Múzeum** in Óbuda.

There's never a charge for the exceptional view from the Citadella on Gellért Hill, and even the popular Halászbástaya is free during the off-season, from November through March.

You can tour the **Nagy Zsinagóga,** Europe's largest, for free.

What to See

★ ㉓ **Citadella.** The sweeping views of Budapest from this fortress atop the hill were once valued by the Austrian army, which used it as a lookout after the 1848–49 War of Independence. Some 60 cannons were housed in the citadel, though never used on the city's resentful populace. In the 1960s the Citadel was converted into a tourist site. It has cafés, a beer garden, wine cellars, and a hostel. In its inner wall is a small graphic exhibition (with some relics) of Budapest's 2,000-year history.

Visible from many parts of the city, the 130-foot-high **Szabadság szobor** (Liberation Monument), just below the southern edge of the Citadella, was originally planned as a memorial to a son of Hungary's then-ruler, Miklós Horthy, whose warplane had crashed in the Ukraine in 1942. However, by the time of its completion in 1947 (three years after Horthy was ousted), it had become a memorial to the Russian soldiers who fell in the 1944–45 siege of Budapest; and hence for decades it was associated chiefly with this. From afar it looks light, airy, and even liberating. A sturdy young girl, her hair and robe swirling in the wind, holds a palm branch high above her head. During much of the Communist era, and for a couple years after its close, she was further embellished with sculptures of giants slaying dragons, Red Army soldiers, and peasants rejoicing at the freedom that Soviet liberation promised (but failed) to bring to Hungary. Since 1992, her mood has lightened: in the Budapest city government's systematic purging of Communist symbols, the Red Combat infantrymen who had flanked the Liberation statue for decades were hacked off and carted away. A few are now on display among the other evicted statues in Szobor Park in the city's 22nd district. ⊠ District XI, Citadella sétány, Gellért-hegy & Tabán ☎ No phone ☞ Free ⊙ Fortress daily Ⓜ 47 or 49 tram.

need a break?

Erzsébet híd eszpresszó (✉ District I, Döbrentei tér 2–1, Gellérthegy & Tabán) may not Budapest's most elegant café-cum–beer garden, but it sure is popular. Near the foot of the bridge after which it is named and close to Tabán's major sights (and baths), this is a convenient and inviting place to sit down in the shade at one of the many tables out front on a warm sunny day for a beer, wine, espresso, mineral water, or soft drink. Despite the traffic roaring by, it is a longtime favorite with young Budapesters.

㉑ Erzsébet híd (Elizabeth Bridge). This bridge was named for Empress Elizabeth (1837–98), called Sissi, of whom the Hungarians were particularly fond. The beautiful but unhappy wife of Franz Joseph, she was stabbed to death in 1898 by an anarchist while boarding a boat on Lake Geneva. The bridge was built between 1897 and 1903; at the time, it was the longest single-span suspension bridge in Europe. Ⓜ *M3: Ferenciek tere.*

★ **㉔ Gellért Szálloda és Thermál Fürdő** (Gellért Hotel & Thermal Baths). At the foot of Gellért Hill are these beautiful art nouveau establishments. The Danubius Hotel Gellért is the oldest spa hotel in Hungary, with hot springs that have supplied curative baths for nearly 2,000 years. It is the most popular among tourists, both because you don't need reservations, as you do at most other hotel-based thermal spas, and also because there's a wealth of treatments—including chamomile steam baths, salt-vapor inhalations, and hot mud packs. Many of these treatments require a doctor's prescription; prescriptions from foreign doctors are accepted. Because most staff speak English, it's easy to communicate. Men and women have separate steam and sauna rooms; both the indoor pool and the outdoor wave pool are coed. ✉ *District XI, Gellért tér 1, at the foot of the hill, Gellért-hegy & Tabán* ☎ *1/466–6166 baths* 💶 *2,900 HUF, 3,200 HUF with a private cabin; treatments extra* ⊙ *Baths Apr.–Oct., daily 6 AM–6 PM; Nov.–Mar., weekdays 6 AM–6 PM, weekends 6 AM–4 PM* Ⓜ *M3: Kálvin tér, then 47 or 49 tram 2 stops across the Danube.*

㉓ Rác Fürdő (Rác Baths). These baths take their name from the Serbians who settled in this area after fleeing the Turks. It is said that King Matthias II used to visit via secret tunnels from his palace on Castle Hill. Such antiquity will not be obvious from without: the canary-yellow building was rebuilt by Miklós Ybl in the mid-19th century. However, the inside is a different story. The Ottoman-era octagonal pool and cupola were retained during reconstruction. The waters are high in sodium and thought to be medicinal; you can also get a massage. As of this writing, the Rác is closed for renovation until at least mid- to late 2005, as a hotel is slowly being built around it. When it does reopen, it will continue to function as a bath, but new fees and hours are yet to be determined. If past practice is continued, women could bathe on Monday, Wednesday, and Friday; men on Tuesday, Thursday, and Saturday. The Rác has long been popular with the gay community. ✉ *District I, Hadnagy u. 8–10, near Gellért-hegy Gellért-hegy & Tabán* ☎ *1/356–*

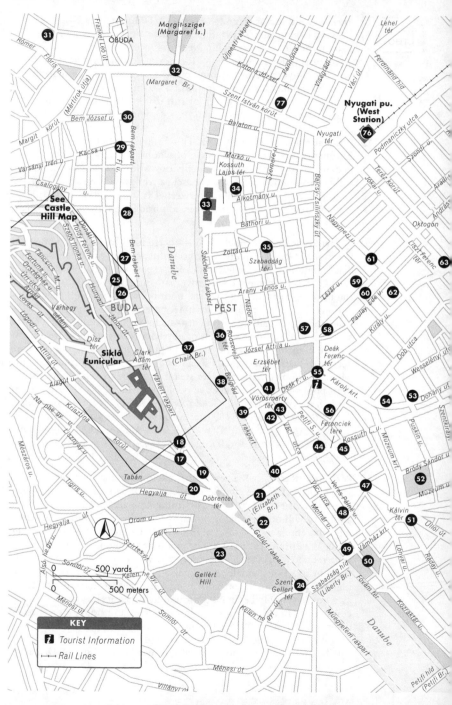

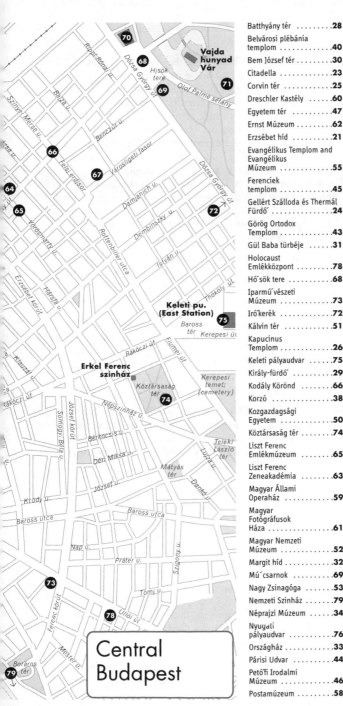

Central Budapest

1322 Ⓜ *M3: Ferenciek tere, then a 10-minute walk to Buda, across Erzsébet híd.*

㉒ **Rudas Fürdő** (Rudas Baths). This bath is on the riverbank, the original Turkish pool making its interior possibly the most dramatically beautiful of Budapest's baths. A high, domed roof admits pinpricks of bluish-green light into the dark, circular stone hall with its austere columns and arches. Fed by eight springs with a year-round temperature of 44°C (111°F), the Rudas's highly fluoridated waters have been known for 1,000 years. The facility is open to men only and does not have a large gay following; a less interesting outer swimming pool is open to both sexes. Massages are available. As of this writing, the facility was undergoing renovation and was due to reopen by early 2005. Fees and opening hours might change. ⊠ *District I, Döbrentei tér 9, at the northern foot of the hill, Gellért-hegy & Tabán* ☎ *1/356–1322* 🖫 *1,000 HUF for 1½ hrs weekdays (for 1 hr weekends)* ☉ *Weekdays 6 AM–6 PM, weekends 6 AM–noon* Ⓜ *M3: Ferenciek tere, then a 10-minute walk to Buda, across Erzsébet híd.*

⑰ **Semmelweis Orvostörténeti Múzeum** (Semmelweis Museum of Medical History). This splendid baroque house was the birthplace of Ignác Semmelweis (1818–65), the Hungarian physician who proved the contagiousness of puerperal (childbed) fever. It's now a museum that traces the history of healing. Semmelweis's grave is in the garden. Out front is a bust of József Antall, a former director of the museum who went on to serve as Hungary's first prime minister in the post-Communist era, from 1990 until he succumbed to cancer three years later. ⊠ *District I, Apród u. 1–3, Gellért-hegy & Tabán* ☎ *1/201–1577* 🖫 *Free* ☉ *Mar.–Oct., Tues.–Sun. 10:30–6; Nov.–Feb., Tues.–Sun. 10:30–4* Ⓜ *M3: Ferenciek tere, then a 15-minute walk to Buda, across Erzsébet híd.*

⑱ **Szarvas-ház** (Stag House). This Louis XVI–style building is named for the former Szarvas Café or, more accurately, for its extant trade sign, with an emblem of a stag not quite at bay, which can be seen above the arched entryway. The structure houses the Aranyszarvas restaurant, which preserves some of the mood of the old Tabán. ⊠ *District I, Szarvas tér 1, Gellért-hegy & Tabán* Ⓜ *M3: Ferenciek tere, then a 15-minute walk to Buda, across Erzsébet híd.*

off the beaten path | **SZOBOR PARK (STATUE PARK)** – After the collapse of the Iron Curtain, Hungarians were understandably keen to rid Budapest of the symbols of Soviet domination. The Communist statues and memorials that once dotted Budapest's streets and squares have been moved to this open-air "Disneyland of Communism." As well as the huge figures of Lenin and Marx, there are statues of the Hungarian worker shaking hands with his Soviet army comrade, and Hungarian puppet prime minister János Kádár. Somewhat tacky but amusing souvenirs are for sale, and songs from the Hungarian and Russian workers' movements play on a tinny speaker system. To get there, take a red Bus 7-173 to Etele tér, then the yellow Volán bus from Platform 2 (but ask here to be sure). ⊠ *District XXII, Balatoni út, corner of Szabadkai út, South Buda* ☎ *1/424–7500* ⊕ *www.szoborpark.hu* 🖫 *600 HUF* ☉ *Daily 10–dusk.*

⑲ Tabán plébánia-templom (Tabán Parish Church). In 1736 this church was built on the site of a Turkish mosque and subsequently renovated and reconstructed several times. Its present form—mustard-colored stone with a rotund, green clock tower—could be described as restrained baroque. ⊠ *District I, Attila u. 1, Gellért-hegy & Tabán* Ⓜ *M3: Ferenciek tere, then a 15-minute walk to Buda, across the Erzsébet híd.*

NORTH OF VÁRHEGY

Most of these sights are along Fő utca (Main Street), a long, straight thoroughfare that starts at the Chain Bridge and runs parallel to the Danube. It is lined on both sides with multistory late-18th-century houses—many darkened by soot and showing their age more than those you see in sparklingly restored Castle Hill. This northbound exploration can be done with the help of Bus 86, which covers the waterfront, or on foot, although this is a fairly large area.

Numbers in the text correspond to numbers in the margin and on the Exploring Budapest map.

a good walk

The walk begins along Fő utca. Stop first to take in the arresting beauty of the **Corvin tér ㉕**; just a block down Fő utca is the **Kapucinus Templom ㉖**, which was originally a Turkish mosque. Continue your walk up Fő utca, stopping at two other scenic squares, **Szilágyi Dezső tér ㉗** and **Batthyány tér ㉘**, with its head-on view of Parliament across the Danube. From there, continue north on Fő utca, passing (or stopping to bathe at) the famous Turkish **Király-fürdő㉙**. From **Bem József tér ㉚**, go one block north, turn left (away from the river) and walk up Fekete Sas utca, crossing busy Margit körút and turning right, one block past, up Mecset utca. This will take you up the hill to **Gül Baba türbéje ㉛**. From here, walk back to the river and cross the **Margit híd ㉜**. You might also wish to explore Margitsziget in the middle of the Danube (*see* Óbuda & Margitsziget, *below*).

TIMING Expect the walk from Bem József tér up the hill to Gül Baba türbéje to take about 25 minutes. Fő utca and Bem József tér can get congested during rush hours (from around 7:30 AM to 8:30 AM and 4:30 PM to 6 PM). But add 1½ hours for a good soak at the baths. Remember that museums are closed Monday and that the Király Baths are open to men and women on different days of the week.

What to See

㉘ Batthyány tér. There are tremendous views of Parliament from this square named after Count Lajos Batthyány, the prime minister shot dead in the 1848 revolution. The M2 subway, the HÉV electric railway from Szentendre, and various suburban and local buses converge on the square, and there's even a supermarket here. At No. 7 Batthyány tér is the beautiful, baroque twin-tower **Szent Anna-templom** (Church of St. Anne), dating from 1740–1762, its oval cupola adorned with frescoes and statuary. ⊠ *District I, Fő u. at Batthyány u., Around Batthyány tér* Ⓜ *M2: Batthyány tér.*

The **Angelika kávéház** (✉ District I, Batthyány tér 7, Around Batthyány tér ☎ 1/212–3784), in the rectory of the Church of St. Anne, quickly became a popular hangout for writers, poets, and other artists after its establishment in 1973. In the 18th century, it was a popular tavern. Elegant yet homey, rather touristy, and a bit smoky, it serves everything from traditional pastries to "red wine sylvan stewed fruit with bourbon-vanilla sauce and lime mousse" to gourmet appetizers, omelets, grilled meats, and stir-fries. You can sit inside on small velvety armchairs at round wooden tables, in one of several large rooms, or at one of the umbrella-shaded tables outdoors.

③⓪ Bem József tér. This square near the river is not particularly picturesque and can get heavy with traffic, but it houses the statue of its important namesake, Polish general József Bem, who offered his services to the 1848 revolutionaries in Vienna and then Hungary. Reorganizing the rebel forces in Transylvania, he was the war's most successful general. It was at this statue on October 23, 1956, that a great student demonstration in sympathy with the Poles' striving for liberal reforms exploded into the brave and tragic Hungarian uprising suppressed by the Red Army. ✉ District II, Fő u. at Bem József u., Around Batthyány tér Ⓜ M2: Batthyány tér.

②⑤ Corvin tér. This small, shady square on Fő utca is the site of a turn-of-the-20th-century building that houses the Hungarian Cultural Institute and, at No. 8, the Budai Vigadó concert hall. At the time of this writing, plans called for a new café to be built at the heart of this sleepy square, which may draw more visitors but will surely rob something of the tranquility that presently abounds. From Corvin tér you can see the spires of the Halászbástya (Fishermen's Bastion) up above, on Castle Hill. ✉ District I, Fő u. at Ponty u., Around Batthyány tér Ⓜ M2: Batthyány tér.

③① Gül Baba türbéje (Tomb of Gül Baba). Gül Baba, a 16th-century dervish and poet whose name means "father of roses" in Turkish, was buried in a tomb built of carved stone blocks with four oval windows. He fought in several wars waged by the Turks and fell during the siege of Buda in 1541. The tomb remains a place of pilgrimage; it is considered Europe's northernmost Muslim shrine and marks the spot where he was slain. Set at an elevation on Rózsadomb (Rose Hill), the tomb is near a good lookout for city views. ✉ District II, Mecset u. 14, North Buda ▨ 500 HUF ☉ May–Sept., Tues.–Sun. 10–6; Oct., Tues.–Sun. 10–4 Ⓜ M2: Batthyány tér or Moszkva tér.

GYERMEK VASÚT – The 12-km (7-mi) Children's Railway—so called because it's operated primarily by children—runs from Széchenyi-hegy to Hűvösvölgy. The sweeping views make the trip well worthwhile for children and adults alike. Departures are from Széchenyi-hegy. To get to Széchenyi-hegy, take Tram 56 from Moszkva tér, and change to the cog railway (public transport tickets valid) at the Fogaskerekű Vasút stop. Take the cog railway uphill to the last stop and then walk a few hundred yards down a short, partly forested road to the left, in the direction most others will be going. The railway terminates at Hűvösvölgy, where you can catch Tram 56 back to Moszkva tér. ⊠ *District XII, Szilágyi Erzsébet fasor and Pasaréti út, Buda Hills* ☎ *1/595–5420* ⊕ *www.gyermekvasut.com* 💲 *250 Ft one-way* ☉ *Late Apr.–Oct., weekdays 9–6, weekends 9–8; Nov.–late Apr., daily 9–5 (sometimes closed Tues.). Trains run hourly on weekdays, every 45 min on weekends* Ⓜ *M2: Moszkva tér.*

JÁNOSHEGY – A *libegő* (chairlift) will take you to János Hill—at 1,729 feet, the highest point in Budapest—where you can climb a lookout tower for the best view of the city. To get there, take Bus 158 from Moszkva tér to the last stop, Zugligeti út. *Chairlift* ⊠ *District XII, Zugligeti út 97, Buda Hills* ☎ *1/394–3764* 💲 *450 HUF one-way* ☉ *Mid-May–mid-Sept., daily 9–5; mid-Sept.–mid-May (depending on weather), daily 10–4; closed every other Mon.* Ⓜ *M2: Moszkva tér.*

㉖ Kapucinus templom (Capuchin Church). This church was converted from a Turkish mosque at the end of the 17th century. Damaged during the revolution in 1849, it acquired its current romantic-style exterior when it was rebuilt a few years later. ⊠ *District II, Fő u. 32, Around Batthyány tér* Ⓜ *M2: Batthyány tér.*

㉙ Király-fürdő (Király Baths). In 1565 Sokoli Mustapha, the Turkish pasha of Buda, ordered the construction of Turkish baths within the old city walls, to ensure that the Turks could still bathe in the event of siege. A stone cupola, crowned by a golden moon and crescent, arches over the steamy, dark pools indoors. It is open to men on Tuesday, Thursday, and Saturday; to women on Monday, Wednesday, and Friday. These baths are very popular with the gay male community. ⊠ *District II, Fő u. 84, Around Batthyány tér* ☎ *1/202–3688* 💲 *1,000 HUF for 1½ hrs* ☉ *Weekdays 9–8 for men (admission until 7), 7–6 for women (admission until 5); Sat. 6:30–noon* Ⓜ *M2: Batthyány tér.*

㉜ Margit híd (Margaret Bridge). At the southern end of the island, the Margaret Bridge is the closer of the two entrances for those coming from downtown Buda or Pest. Just north of the Chain Bridge, the bridge walkway provides gorgeous mid-river views of Castle Hill and Parliament. The original bridge was built during the 1840s by French engineer Ernest Gouin in collaboration with Gustave Eiffel. Toward the end of 1944, the bridge was blown up by the retreating Nazis while crowded with rush-hour traffic. It was rebuilt in the same unusual shape—forming an obtuse angle in midstream, with a short leg leading down to the island. ⊠ *Margitsziget* Ⓜ *M2: Batthyány tér or M1: Nyugati pu. (then tram 4 or 6).*

㉗ Szilágyi Dezső tér. This is another of the charming little squares punctuating Fő utca. At its center is the striking, neogothic **Budai Református Templom** (Buda Reformed Church), designed by Samu Pecz and built 1893–96; rising above the deep-red brickwork of its facade, both its steeple and what looks rather like a castle adjoining the steeple with several smaller spires—but is actually a massive dome above the main part of the church—are covered with colorful tilework from the famous Zsolnay factory in Pécs. The square is also home to the building where composer Béla Bartók lived, at No. 4. ⊠ *District I, Fő u. at Székely u.*, *Around Batthyány tér* Ⓜ *M2: Batthyány tér.*

DOWNTOWN PEST & THE SMALL RING ROAD

Budapest's urban heart is full of bona fide sights plus innumerable tiny streets and grand avenues where you can wander for hours admiring the city's stately old buildings—some freshly sparkling after their first painting in decades, others silently but still gracefully crumbling.

Dominated by the Parliament building, the district surrounding Kossuth tér is the legislative, diplomatic, and administrative nexus of Budapest; most of the ministries are here, as are the National Bank and Courts of Justice. Downriver, the romantic Danube promenade, the Duna korzó, extends along the stretch of riverfront across from Castle Hill. With Vörösmarty tér and pedestrian shopping street Váci utca just inland, this area forms Pest's tourist core. Going south, the korzó ends at Március 15 tér. One block in from the river, Ferenciek tere marks the beginning of the university area, spreading south of Kossuth Lajos utca. Here, the streets are narrower and the sounds of your footsteps echo off the elegantly aging stone buildings.

However, another stretch of Váci utca, pedestrianized in the 1990s and rivalling the older, more famous section with a rich array of antiques stores, bookshops, cafés, and restaurants continues on the other side of busy Szabad sajtó út all the way to the next bridge, Szabadság híd, and the indoor food market, the Vásárcsarnok. From here it's just a few blocks to yet another vibrant, Pest-side street revitalized in the 1990s, Ráday utca.

Pest is laid out in broad circular *körúts* ("ring roads" or boulevards). Vámház körút is the first sector of the 2½-km (1½-mi) Kis körút (Small Ring Road), which traces the route of the Old Town wall from Szabadság híd (Liberty Bridge) to Deák tér. Construction of the inner körút began in 1872 and was completed in 1880. Changing names as it curves, after Kálvin tér it becomes Múzeum körút (passing by the National Museum) and then Károly körút for its final stretch ending at Deák tér. Deák tér, the only place where all three subway lines converge, could be called the dead-center of downtown. East of Károly körút are the weathered streets of Budapest's former ghetto.

a good walk

After starting at Kossuth tér to see the **Országház** ㉝ and the **Néprajzi Múzeum** ㉞, it's worth walking a few blocks southeast to take in stately **Szabadság tér** ㉟ before heading back to the Danube and south to **Roosevelt tér** ㊱, which is at the foot of the **Széchenyi Lánchíd** ㊲. As this tour involves quite a bit of walking, you may want to take Tram 2 from Kossuth tér a few stops downriver to Roosevelt tér to save your energy. While time and/or energy may not allow it just now, at some point during your visit, a walk across the Chain Bridge is a must.

From Roosevelt tér go south, across the street, and join the **Korzó** ❸ along the river, strolling past the **Vigadó** ❸ at Vigadó tér, all the way to the **Belvárosi plébánia templom** ❹ at Március 15 tér, just under the Elizabeth Bridge. Double back up the korzó to Vigadó tér and walk in from the river on Vigadó utca to **Vörösmarty tér** ❹. Follow the crowds down pedestrian-only **Váci utca** ❹, and when you reach Régiposta utca, take a detour to the right to see the **Görög Ortodox templom** ❹. Return to Váci utca and continue south; at Ferenciek tere, look for the grand **Párisi Udvar** ❹ arcade. Across busy Kossuth Lajos utca, you will find the **Ferenciek templom** ❹. From here, stroll Petőfi Sándor utca, passing the Greek Orthodox temple, and continue along Károlyi Mihály utca past the **Petőfi Irodalmi Múzeum** ❹ and **Egyetem tér** ❹. Take a right on Szerb utca until you get to Veres Pálné utca, where you will find a 17th-century **Szerb Ortodox templom** ❹. Continuing down Szerb utca, you'll find yourself at the southern end of Váci utca, facing **Vásárcsarnok** ❹, the huge market hall. Or, from Ferenciek templom, you can get to the market hall just as easily—and cope with less traffic rumbling past you—by walking two blocks toward the river, to the continuation of pedestrian Vái utca, with its many boutiques, restaurants, and cafés. This will also get you to Szerb utca, where if you wish you can make a short detour to check out the Szerb Ortodox templom before heading on to the market hall.

Across Vámház körút is the campus of the **Közgazdasági Egyetem** ❺, the University of Economics, which was called Karl Marx University in the Communist days. From here you can either walk or take Tram 47 or 49 to **Kálvin tér** ❺. One block before Kálvin tér is Ráday utca, which in recent years has been transformed into a lovely, lively shopping and dining street; plans call for much of Ráday utca to be closed to all traffic by sometime in 2005.

Just north of Kálvin tér on Múzeum körút is the **Magyar Nemzeti Múzeum** ❺. The **Nagy Zsinagóga** ❺ is about ¾ km (⅓ mi) farther north along the Kis körút (Small Ring Road)—a longish walk or one short stop by tram; around the corner from the synagogue is the **Zsidó Múzeum** ❺. From here, more walking along the körút, or a tram ride to the last stop, brings you to Pest's main hub, Deák tér, where you'll find the **Evangelikus templom** ❺, Budapest's main Lutheran church. If you look to your left, by the way, as you walk or ride along Károly körút (the stretch of the Small Ring Road that gets you to Deák tér), you can't help but notice a rather bleak-looking, one-story row of storefronts that stretches for a long block. It is unclear whether this building left over from the Communist era is awaiting downtown revitalization or has deliberately been preserved to remind everyone of days (decades, regimes) gone by. In any case, it is something of an anomaly in this part of an otherwise spruced-up area, but one that exudes history nonetheless.

From Deák tér it's a short walk to the **Városház** ❺, Budapest's old city hall building. The **Szent István Bazilika** ❺ is an extra but rewarding 500-yard walk north on Bajcsy-Zsilinszky út.

TIMING   This is a particularly rich part of the city; the suggested walk will take the better part of a day, including time to visit the museums, stroll on the Korzó, and browse on Váci utca—not to mention time for lunch. Keep in mind that the museums are closed on Monday.

What to See

40 **Belvárosi plébánia templom** (Inner City Parish Church). Dating to the 12th century, this is the oldest ecclesiastical building in Pest. It's actually built on something even older—the remains of the Contra Aquincum, a third-century Roman fortress and tower, parts of which are visible next to the church. There is hardly any architectural style that cannot be found in some part or another, starting with a single Romanesque arch in its south tower. The single nave still has its original Gothic chancel and some 15th-century Gothic frescoes. Two side chapels contain beautifully carved Renaissance altar pieces and tabernacles of red marble from the early 16th century. During Budapest's years of Turkish occupation, the church served as a mosque—a *mihrab*, a Muslim prayer niche, is a reminder of this. During the 18th century, the church was given two baroque towers and its present facade. In 1808 it was enriched with a rococo pulpit, and still later a superb winged triptych was added to the main altar. From 1867 to 1875, Franz Liszt lived only a few steps away from the church, in a townhouse where he held regular "musical Sundays" at which Richard and Cosima Wagner were frequent guests and participants. Liszt's own musical Sunday mornings often began in this church. An admirer of its acoustics and organ, he conducted many masses here, including the first Budapest performance of his *Missa Choralis*, in 1872. ⊠ *District V, Március 15 tér 2, Around Váci utca* 🕾 *1/318–3108* Ⓜ *M3: Ferenciek tere.*

47 **Egyetem tér** (University Square). Budapest's University of Law sits here in the heart of the city's university neighborhood. On one corner is the cool gray-and-green marble **Egyetemi Templom** (University Church), one of Hungary's most beautiful baroque buildings. Built between 1725 and 1742, it has an especially splendid pulpit. ⊠ *District V, Around Ferenciek tere* Ⓜ *M3: Ferenciek tere.*

need a break?

Though billed as a café, **Centrál** (⊠ District V, Károlyi Mihály u. 9, Around Ferenciek tere 🕾 1/235–0599) is actually more a living museum. It enjoyed fame as an illustrious literary café during Budapest's late-19th- and early-20th-century golden age and, after years of neglect, was finally restored to its former glory a few years ago. Centrál's menu includes, with each main dish, a recommended wine by the glass—as well as a good selection of vegetarian dishes and desserts. And it has some of the most spotless toilets in all of Budapest.

55 **Evangélikus Templom & Evangélikus Múzeum** (Lutheran Church & Lutheran Museum). The neoclassical Lutheran Church sits in the center of it all on busy Deák tér. Classical concerts are regularly held here. The church's interior designer, János Krausz, flouted then-traditional church architecture by placing a single large interior beneath the huge vaulted roof structure. The adjoining school is now the Lutheran Museum, which traces the role of Protestantism in Hungarian history and contains Martin Luther's original will. ✉ *District V, Deák Ferenc tér 4, Around Deák Ferenc tér* ☎ *1/317–4173* 🎫 *Museum 300 HUF, including a tour of church* ⏲ *Museum Mar.–Oct., Tues.–Sun. 10–6; Nov.–Feb., Tues.–Sun. 10–5. Church can be seen only on a guided tour or during regular services (Sun. at 9, 11, and 6)* Ⓜ *M1, M2, M3: Deák Ferenc tér.*

㊺ **Ferenciek templom** (Franciscan Church). This pale yellow church was built in 1743. On the wall facing Kossuth Lajos utca is a bronze relief showing a scene from the devastating flood of 1838; the detail is so vivid that it almost makes you seasick. A faded arrow below the relief indicates the high-water mark of almost 4 feet. Next to it is the Nereids Fountain, a popular meeting place for students from the nearby Eötvös Loránd University. ✉ *District V, Felszabadulás tér, Around Ferenciek tere* Ⓜ *M3: Ferenciek tere.*

1

㊸ **Görög Ortodox templom** (Greek Orthodox Church). Built at the end of the 18th century in late-baroque style, the Greek Orthodox Church was remodeled a century later by Miklós Ybl, who designed the Opera House and many other important Budapest landmarks. The church retains some fine wood carvings and a dazzling collection of icons by late-18th-century Serbian master Miklós Jankovich. ✉ *District V, Petőfi tér 2/b, Around Váci utca* Ⓜ *M3: Ferenciek tere.*

(51) **Kálvin tér.** Calvin Square takes its name from the neoclassical Hungarian Reformed (Calvinist) church that tries to dominate this busy traffic hub; this is a hard task, what with a new office building arising across the square. The Kecskeméti Kapu, a main gate of Pest, once stood here, as well as a cattle market that was a notorious den of thieves. At the beginning of the 19th century, this was where Pest ended and the prairie began. ✉ *District V, Around Kálvin tér* Ⓜ *M3: Kálvin tér.*

㊿ **Közgazdagsági Egyetem** (University of Economics). Just below Szabadság híd (Liberty Bridge) on the waterfront, the monumental neo-Renaissance building was once the Customs House. Built in 1871–74 by Miklós Ybl, it is now also known as *közgáz* ("econ."), following a stint during the Communist era as Karl Marx University. ✉ *District V, Fővám tér, Around Kálvin tér* Ⓜ *M3: Kálvin tér.*

★ ㊳ **Korzó** (Promenade). The neighborhood to the south of Roosevelt tér has regained much of its past elegance—if not its architectural grandeur—with the erection of the Sofitel (formerly the Hyatt Regency), Inter-Continental, and Marriott luxury hotels. Traversing all three and continuing well beyond them is the riverside *korzó,* a pedestrian promenade lined with park benches and appealing outdoor cafés from which one can enjoy postcard-perfect views of Gellért Hill and Castle Hill directly across the Danube. Try to take a stroll in the evening, when the views are lit up in shimmering gold lights. ✉ *District V, from Eötvös tér to Március 15 tér, Around Váci utca* Ⓜ *M3: Ferenciek tere (or M1, M2, M3: Deák Ferenc tér).*

(52) **Magyar Nemzeti Múzeum** (Hungarian National Museum). Built between 1837 and 1847, the museum is a fine example of 19th-century classicism—simple, well proportioned, and surrounded by a large garden. In

front of this building on March 15, 1848, Sándor Petőfi recited his revolutionary poem, the "National Song" ("Nemzeti dal"), and the "12 Points," a list of political demands by young Hungarians calling on the people to rise up against the Hapsburgs. Celebrations of the national holiday commemorating the failed revolution are held on these steps every year on March 15. What used to be the museum's biggest attraction, the **Szent Korona** (Holy Crown), was moved to the Parliament building in early 2000 to mark the millenary of the coronation of Hungary's first king, St. Stephen. The museum still has worthwhile rarities, however, including a completely furnished Turkish tent; masterworks of cabinetmaking and woodcarving, including pews from churches in Nyírbátor and Transylvania; a piano that belonged to both Beethoven and Liszt; and, in the treasury, masterpieces of goldsmithing, among them the 11th-century Constantine Monomachos crown from Byzantium and the richly pictorial 16th-century chalice of Miklós Pálffy. Looking at it is like reading the "Prince Valiant" comic strip in gold. The epic Hungarian history exhibit chronicles, among other things, the end of Communism and the much-celebrated exodus of the Russian troops. ✉ *District IX, Múzeum krt. 14–16, Around Kálvin tér* ☎ *1/338–2122* ✎ *Free* ☼ *Tues.–Sun. 10–6* Ⓜ *M3: Kálvin tér.*

need a break? Just down the block from the National Museum (toward Deák tér), the **Múzeum Cukrászda** (✉ District IX, Múzeum körút 10, Around Astoria ☎ 1/338–4415) has long been a popular if somewhat cramped little café. You might try a slice of the heavenly *házi almás* (home-style apple cake), which has apple jam sandwiched between layers of sponge cake with just a touch of whipped cream on top.

㉝ Nagy Zsinagóga (Great Synagogue). Seating 3,000, Europe's largest synagogue was designed by Ludwig Förs and built between 1844 and 1859 in a Byzantine-Moorish style described as "consciously archaic Romantic-Eastern." Desecrated by German and Hungarian Nazis, it was painstakingly reconstructed with donations from all over the world; its doors reopened in the fall of 1996. While used for regular services during much of the year, it is generally not used in midwinter, as the space is too large to heat; between December and February, visiting hours are erratic. In the courtyard behind the synagogue, a weeping willow made of metal honors the victims of the Holocaust. Liszt and Saint-Saëns are among the great musicians who have played the synagogue's grand organ. ✉ *District VII, Dohány u. 2–8, Around Astoria* ☎ *1/342–8949* ✎ *Free* ☼ *Mon.–Thurs. 10–5, Fri. and Sun. 10–2* Ⓜ *M2: Astoria.*

㉞ Néprajzi Múzeum (Museum of Ethnography). The 1890s neoclassical temple formerly housed the Supreme Court. Now an impressive permanent exhibition, "The Folk Culture of the Hungarian People," explains all aspects of peasant life from the end of the 18th century until World War I; explanatory texts are provided in both English and Hungarian. Besides embroideries, pottery, and carvings—the authentic pieces you can't see at touristy folk shops—there are farming tools, furniture, and traditional costumes. The central room of the building alone is worth the entrance fee: a majestic hall with ornate marble staircases and pillars,

FodorsChoice ★

FodorsChoice ★

and towering stained-glass windows. ⊠ *District V, Kossuth tér 12, Parliament* ☎ *1/473–2400* ⊕ *www.neprajz.hu* ⊠ *500 HUF* ☺ *Tues.–Sun. 10–6* Ⓜ *M2: Kossuth tér.*

★ ㉝ **Országház** (Parliament). The most visible symbol of Budapest's left bank is the huge neo-Gothic Parliament. Mirrored in the Danube much the way Britain's Parliament is reflected by the Thames, it lies midway between the Margaret and Chain bridges and can be reached by the M2 subway and waterfront Tram 2. A fine example of historicizing, eclectic fin-de-siècle architecture, it was designed by the Hungarian architect Imre Steindl and built by a thousand workers between 1885 and 1902. The grace and dignity of its long facade and 24 slender towers, with spacious arcades and high windows balancing its vast central dome, lend this living landmark a refreshingly baroque spatial effect. The exterior is lined with 90 statues of great figures in Hungarian history; the corbels are ornamented by 242 allegorical statues. Inside are 691 rooms, 10 courtyards, and 29 staircases; some 88 pounds of gold were used for the staircases and halls. These halls are also a gallery of late-19th-century Hungarian art, with frescoes and canvases depicting Hungarian history, starting with Mihály Munkácsy's large painting of the Magyar Conquest of 896.

Since early 2000 Parliament's most sacred treasure has not been the Hungarian legislature but the newly exhibited **Szent Korona** (Holy Crown), which reposes with other royal relics under the cupola. The crown sits like a golden soufflé above a Byzantine band of holy scenes in enamel and pearls and other gems. It seems to date from the 12th century, so it could not be the crown that Pope Sylvester II presented to St. Stephen in the year 1000, when he was crowned the first king of Hungary. Nevertheless, it is known as the Crown of St. Stephen and has been regarded— even by Communist governments—as the legal symbol of Hungarian sovereignty and unbroken statehood. In 1945 the fleeing Hungarian army handed over the crown and its accompanying regalia to the Americans rather than have them fall into Soviet hands. They were restored to Hungary in 1978. The crown can be seen in the scope of daily tours of the Parliament building, which is the only way you can visit the Parliament, except during ceremonial events and when the legislature is in session (usually Monday and Tuesday from late summer to spring). Lines may be long, so it's best to call in advance for reservations. The building can also be visited as part of a four-hour city tour led by IBUSZ Travel at 10 and 11 AM daily for 9,900 HUF. ⊠ *District V, Kossuth tér, Parliament* ☎ *1/441–4412, 1/441–4415, or 1/441–4904 for info and tour reservations, 1/485–2722 for IBUSZ Travel* ☎ *1/441–4801* ⊕ *www.mkogy. hu* ⊠ *2,070 HUF* ☺ *Monday 8–11 AM, Tues.–Fri. 8–6, Sat. 8–4, Sun. 8–2; daily tours in English at 10 and 2, starting from Gate No. 10, just right of main stairs* Ⓜ *M2: Kossuth tér.*

㊹ **Párisi Udvar** (Paris Court). This glass-roof arcade was built in 1914 in richly ornamental neo-Gothic and eclectic styles. Nowadays it's filled with touristy boutiques. ⊠ *District VI, corner of Petőfi Sándor u. and Kossuth Lajos u., Around Ferenciek tere* Ⓜ *M3: Ferenciek tere.*

46 **Petőfi Irodalmi Múzeum** (Petőfi Literary Museum). Founded in 1954 as the national museum of 19th- and 20th-century Hungarian literature, this lovely venue—named after Hungary's famous poet of the 1848 Revolution, Sándor Petőfi—is well worth a visit regardless of what you know (or don't know) about Hungarian literature. For one thing, it's in the ravishing Károlyi Palota. Bestowed with a new facade and interior beginning in the late 18th century by its owners, the Károlyi family, the palace has some grand staircases and stunning rooms that were renovated in recent years. A ticket allows you to visit not only the literary exhibits, which include a fascinating collection of objects relating to the lives of some of Hungary's dearest writers and poets, but also other parts of the building. ✉ *District IX, Károly Mihályi u. 16, Around Ferenciek tere* ☎ *1/317–3611* 🌐 *www.pim.hu* 🎫 *280 HUF* ⏲ *Tues.–Sun. 10–6* Ⓜ *M3: Ferenciek tere.*

36 **Roosevelt tér.** This square opening onto the Danube is less closely connected with the U.S. president than with the progressive Hungarian statesman Count István Széchenyi, dubbed "the greatest Hungarian" even by his adversary Kossuth. The neo-Renaissance palace of the **Magyar Tudományos Akadémia** (Academy of Sciences) on the north side was built between 1862 and 1864, after Széchenyi's suicide. It is a fitting memorial, for in 1825, the statesman donated a year's income from all his estates to establish the academy. Another Széchenyi project, the Széchenyi Lánchíd, leads into the square; there stands a statue of Széchenyi near one of another statesman, Ferenc Deák, whose negotiations led to the establishment of the dual monarchy after Kossuth's 1848–49 revolution failed. Both men lived on this square. ✉ *District V, Around Váci utca* Ⓜ *M1, M2, M3: Dék Ferenc tér.*

★ 35 **Szabadságtér.** The sprawling Liberty Square is dominated by the long-time headquarters of **Magyar Televizió** (Hungarian Television), a former stock exchange with what look like four temples and two castles on its roof. Across from it is a solemn-looking neoclassical shrine, the **Nemzeti Bank** (National Bank). The bank's Postal Savings Bank branch, adjacent to the main building but visible from behind Szabadság tér on Hold utca, is another exuberant Art Nouveau masterpiece of architect Ödön Lechner, built in 1901 with colorful majolica mosaics, characteristically curvaceous windows, and pointed towers ending in swirling gold flourishes. In the square's center remains a gold hammer and sickle atop a white stone obelisk, one of the few monuments to the Russian "liberation" of Budapest in 1945. There were mutterings that it, too, would be pulled down, which prompted a Russian diplomatic protest; the monument, after all, marks a gravesite of fallen Soviet troops. With the Stars and Stripes flying out in front, and a high-security presence, the **American Embassy** is at Szabadság tér 12. ✉ *District V, Parliament* Ⓜ *M2: Kossuth tér or M3: Arany János utca.*

37 **Széchenyi Lánchíd** (Chain Bridge). This is the oldest and most beautiful of the seven road bridges that span the Danube in Budapest. Before it was built, the river could be crossed only by ferry or by a pontoon bridge that had to be removed when ice blocks began floating downstream in winter. It was constructed at the initiative of the great Hungarian re-

former and philanthropist Count István Széchenyi, using an 1839 design by the English civil engineer William Tierney Clark. This classical, almost poetically graceful and symmetrical suspension bridge was finished by the Scotsman Adam Clark (no relation to William Tierney Clark), who also built the 383-yard tunnel under Castle Hill, thus connecting the Danube quay with the rest of Buda. After it was destroyed by the Nazis, the bridge was rebuilt in its original form (though slightly widened for traffic) and was reopened in 1949, on the centenary of its inauguration. At the Buda end of the bridge is Clark Ádám tér (Adam Clark Square), where you can zip up to Castle Hill on the sometimes crowded **Sikló funicular.** ⊠ *District I, linking Clark Ádám tér with Roosevelt tér, Around Váci utca* 🎫 *Funicular 600 HUF uphill, 500 HUF downhill* ۞ *Funicular daily 7:30 AM–10 PM (closed every other Mon.)* Ⓜ *M2: Batthányi tér or M1, M2, M3: Deák Ferenc tér.*

❺❼
Fodor'sChoice
★
Szent István Bazilika (St. Stephen's Basilica). Handsome and massive, this is one of the chief landmarks of Pest and the city's largest church—it can hold 8,500 people. Its very Holy Roman front porch greets you with a tympanum bustling with statuary. The basilica's dome and the dome of Parliament are by far the most visible in the Pest skyline, and this is no accident: with the Magyar Millennium of 1896 in mind (the lavishly celebrated thousandth anniversary of the settling of the Carpathian Basin in 896), both domes were planned to be 315 feet high.

The millennium was not yet in sight when architect József Hild began building the basilica in neoclassical style in 1851, two years after the revolution was suppressed. After Hild's death, the project was taken over in 1867 by Miklós Ybl, the architect who did the most to transform modern Pest into a monumental metropolis. Wherever he could, Ybl shifted Hild's motifs toward the neo-Renaissance mode that Ybl favored. When the dome collapsed, partly damaging the walls, he made even more drastic changes. Ybl died in 1891, five years before the 1,000-year celebration, and the basilica was completed in neo-Renaissance style by József Kauser—but not until 1905.

Below the cupola is a rich collection of late-19th-century Hungarian art: mosaics, altarpieces, and statuary (what heady days the Magyar Millennium must have meant for local talents). There are 150 kinds of marble, all from Hungary except for the Carrara in the sanctuary's centerpiece: a white statue of King (St.) Stephen I, Hungary's first king and patron saint. Stephen's mummified right hand is preserved as a relic in the **Szent Jobb Kápolna** (Holy Right Chapel); press a button and it will be illuminated for two minutes. You can also climb the 364 stairs (or take the elevator) to the top of the cupola for a spectacular view of the city. Extensive renovation work here has, among other things, turned the cathedral from a sooty gray back to an almost bright tan. ⊠ *District V, Szt. István tér, Szent István Bazilika* ☎ *1/311–0839* 🎫 *Church free, Szt. Jobb chapel 150 HUF, cupola 500 HUF* ۞ *Church Mon.–Sat. 9–7, Sun. 1–5. Szt. Jobb Chapel Apr.–Oct., Mon.–Sat. 9–5, Sun. 1–5; Nov.–Mar., Mon. Sat. 10–4, Sun. 1–4. Cupola Apr. and Sept.–Oct., daily 10–5; May–Aug., daily 9–6* Ⓜ *M1, M2, M3: Deák Ferenc tér or M3: Arany János utca.*

48 **Szerb Ortodox templom.** Built in 1688, this lovely burnt-orange church, one of Budapest's oldest buildings, sits in a shaded garden surrounded by thick stone walls decorated with a large tile mosaic of St. George defeating the dragon. Its opening hours are somewhat erratic, but if the wrought-iron gates are open, wander in for a look at the beautiful hand-carved wooden pews. ⊠ *District V, Szerb utca, Around Váci utca* Ⓜ *M3: Kálvin tér.*

42 **Váci utca.** Immediately north of Elizabeth Bridge is Budapest's best-known shopping street and most unabashed tourist zone, Váci utca, a pedestrian precinct with electric 19th-century lampposts and smart shops with credit-card emblems on ornate doorways. No bargain basement, Váci utca gets its special flavor from the mix of native furriers, tailors, designers, folk-craft shops, china shops, bookstores, and internationally known boutiques. On Régi Posta utca, just off Vái utca, you'll find Hungary's first McDonald's, which opened in 1988. Váci utca's second half, south of Kossuth Lajos utca, was transformed into another pedestrian-only zone in the 1990s. While coming to resemble the northern side, this stretch of road still retains a flavorful, more soothing ambience of its own. On both halves of Váci utca, beware of inflated prices *and* pickpockets. ⊠ *District V, from Vörösmarty tér to Fővám tér, Around Váci utca* Ⓜ *M3: Ferenciek tere or M1: Vörösmarty tér.*

56 **Városház** (City Hall). The monumental former city council building, which used to be a hospital for wounded soldiers and then a resort for the elderly ("home" would be too cozy for so vast a hulk), is now Budapest's city hall. It's enormous enough to loom over the row of shops and businesses lining Károly körút in front of it but can only be entered through courtyards or side streets (it is most accessible from Gerlóczy utca). The Tuscan columns at the main entrance and the allegorical statuary of *Atlas, War,* and *Peace* are especially splendid. There was once a chapel in the center of the main facade, but now only its spire remains. ⊠ *District V, Városház u. 9–11, Around Deák Ferenc tér* ☎ *1/327–1000* 💲 *Free* ☉ *Weekdays 9–5* Ⓜ *M1, M2, M3: Deák Ferenc tér.*

49 **Vásárcsarnok** (Central Market Hall). The magnificent hall, a 19th-century iron-frame construction, was reopened in late 1994 after years of renovation (and disputes over who would foot the bill). Even during the leanest years of Communist shortages, the abundance of food came as a revelation to shoppers from East and West. Today, the cavernous, three-story market, which is near the southern end of Váci utca, once again teems with people browsing among stalls packed with salamis and red-paprika chains. Upstairs you can buy folk embroideries and souvenirs. ⊠ *District IX, Vámház krt. 1–3, Around Kálvin tér* ☎ *1/ 217–6067* ☉ *Mon. 6 AM–5 PM, Tues.–Fri. 6 AM–6 PM, Sat. 6 AM–2 PM* Ⓜ *M3: Kálvi tér.*

39 **Vigadó** (Concert Hall). Designed in a striking romantic style by Frigyes Feszl and inaugurated in 1865 with Franz Liszt conducting his own *St. Elizabeth Oratorio,* the concert hall is a curious mixture of Byzantine, Moorish, Romanesque, and Hungarian motifs, punctuated by dancing statues and sturdy pillars. Brahms, Debussy, and Casals are among the other phenomenal musicians who have graced its stage. Mahler's *Symphony No. 1* and many works by Bartók were first performed here. While you can go into the lobby on your own, the hall is open only for concerts. ⊠ *District V, Vigadó tér 2, Around Váci utca* ☏ *1/318–7932 box office* Ⓜ *M1: Vörösmarty tér.*

need a break?   If you only visit one café in Budapest, stop on Vörösmarty Square at **Gerbeaud** (⊠ District V, Vörösmarty tér 7, Around Váci utca ☏ 1/ 429–9000), a café and pastry shop founded in 1858 by Hungarian Henrik Kugler and a Swiss, Emil Gerbeaud. The decor (green-marble tables, Regency-style marble fireplaces) is as sumptuous as the tempting selection of cake and sweets. The Gerbeaud's piano was originally intentioned for the *Titanic* but was saved because it wasn't ready in time for the voyage.

★ ❹ **Vörösmarty tér.** Downtown revitalization since the early 1990s has decentralized things somewhat, but this large, handsome square at the northern end of Váci utca is still the heart of Pest's tourist life in many respects. Street musicians and sidewalk cafés make this one of the liveliest places in Budapest and a good spot to sit and relax. Grouped around a white-marble statue of the 19th-century poet and dramatist Mihály Vörösmarty are a cell phone shop, a department store, a travel agency, banks, and an airline office, not to mention an elegant former pissoir that today functions as a lovely kiosk displaying gold-painted historic scenes of the square's golden days. ⊠ *District V, at northern end of Váci utca, Around Váci utca* Ⓜ *M1: Vörösmarty tér.*

❺❹ **Zsidó Múzeum** (Jewish Museum). The four-room museum, around the corner from the Great Synagogue, has displays explaining the effect of the Holocaust on Hungarian and Transylvanian Jews. (There are labels in English.) In late 1993, burglars ransacked the museum and got away with approximately 80% of its priceless collection; several months later, the stolen objects were found in Romania and returned to their rightful home. ⊠ *District VII, Dohány u. 2, Around Astoria* ☏ *1/342–8949* 🎫 *1,000 HUF* ⊙ *Mid-Mar.–mid-Oct., Mon.–Thurs. 10–5, Fri. and Sun. 10–2; mid-Oct.–mid-Mar., weekdays 10–3, Sun. 10–1* Ⓜ *M2: Astoria.*

ALONG ANDRÁSSY ÚT

Behind St. Stephen's Basilica, at the crossroad along Bajcsy-Zsilinszky út, begins Budapest's grandest avenue, Andrássy út. For too many years, this broad boulevard bore the tongue-twisting name Népköztársaság útja (Avenue of the People's Republic) and, for a while before that, Stalin Avenue. In 1990, however, it reverted to its old name honoring Count Gyula Andrássy, a statesman who in 1867 became the first constitutional premier of Hungary. The boulevard that would eventually bear his name was begun in 1872, as Buda and Pest (and Óbuda) were about to be unified. Most of the mansions that line it were completed by 1884.

It took another dozen years before the first underground railway on the Continent was completed for—you guessed it—the Magyar Millennium in 1896. Though preceded by London's Underground (1863), Budapest's was the world's first electrified subway. Only slightly modernized but refurbished for the 1996 millecentenary, this "Little Metro" is still running a 4-km (2½-mi) stretch from Vörösmarty tér to the far end of City Park. Using tiny yellow trains with tanklike treads, and stopping at antique stations marked FÖLDALATTI (Underground) on their wrought-iron entranceways, Line 1 is a tourist attraction in itself. Six of its 10 stations are along Andrássy út.

a good walk

A walking tour of Andrássy út's sights is straightforward: begin at its downtown end, near Deák tér, and stroll its length (about 2 km [1 mi]) all the way to Hősök tere, at the entrance to Budapest's popular City Park. Of course, if your feet are weary, you can always hop on the Little Metro at one of its stations every few blocks and go one or more stops that way. The first third of the avenue, from Bajcsy-Zsilinszky út to the eight-sided intersection called Oktogon, is framed by rows of eclectic city palaces with balconies held up by stone giants. First stop is the mansion of the **Postamúzeum** ⑤. Continue until you reach the imposing **Magyar Állami Operaház** ⑤ and across the street the **Drechsler Kastély** ⑥. A block or two farther, on "Budapest's Broadway," Nagymező utca, you'll find theaters, nightclubs, and cabarets, is the **Magyar Fotográfusok Háza (Mai Manó Ház)** ⑥ photographic museum, to the left of Andrássy út; and a block-and-a-half to the right is the **Ernst Múzeum** ⑥, with its exhibits of modern art. Walk to the next block here and you'll find yourself on Király utca, a bustling narrow street rich in local flavor; walk even farther, and you'll be on Klauzál tér, the square at the heart of Budapest's wartime Jewish ghetto. Continuing down Andrássy, turn right onto Liszt Ferenc tér, a pedestrian street dominated by the **Liszt Ferenc Zeneakadémia** ⑥.

The Parisian-style boulevard of Andrássy alters when it crosses the Nagy körút (Outer Ring Road), at the Oktogon crossing. Four rows of trees and scores of flower beds make the thoroughfare look more like a garden promenade, but its cultural character lingers. Two blocks beyond the Oktogon, on your left, is the **Terror Háza** ⑥, a relatively new, state-of-the-art museum dedicated to victims of terror. Continue until you come to Vörösmarty utca, where a short detour right will take you to the **Liszt Ferenc Emlékmúzeum** ⑥. Farther up, past **Kodály körönd** ⑥, the rest of Andrássy út is dominated by widely spaced mansions surrounded by private gardens. At Kodály körönd take another detour, turning right onto Felső erdősor, then left onto Városligeti fasor, where you will find the **Ráth György Múzeum** ⑥, which focuses on Indian and Chinese art. Andrássy út ends at **Hősök tere** ⑥. Finish your tour by browsing through the **Műcsarnok** ⑥ and/or the **Szépművészeti Múzeum** ⑦, and then perhaps take a stroll into **Városliget** ⑦. Before exploring the park and its many attractions, however, you might want to turn back in the direction of the Oktogon for a moment and go left a couple blocks along Dózsa György út to a great big parking lot bordering the park; here you'll

A GOLDEN AGE FOR CAFÉS

D EPRIVING BUDAPEST OF ITS COFFEEHOUSES *would be like depriving it of its thermal baths. No, it would be worse. Without the cafés, Hungary's capital would be palpably less stimulating a place than it is; for the past, present, and future of this ravishing city is, in many respects, the past, present, and future of its coffeehouses. And this is why the extraordinary revival of Budapest's café scene since 1990 has helped breathe new life into the city after 40 years with a lackluster, state-owned service industry.*

At turn of the 20th century, Budapest had almost 600 coffeehouses. Writers wrote in them, intellectuals intellectualized in them, and whole families could be found in them enjoying not only coffee and pastries but also affordable meals. This golden age waned between the world wars until its final collapse, when the Communists, in the late 1940s, closed down or nationalized

the cafés, turning them into something much more mundane.

Budapest in 2005 may not quite be the coffeehouse powerhouse it was in 1900, but the café scene is incomparably more vibrant than it was under Communism. From the Gerbaud to the Művész and the Lukács, from the Angelika to the Ruszwurm, and from the Centrál to the Hauer, Budapest today is a city of beautifully restored, freshly founded, or simply revived cafés, all teeming with people. This is not to mention the many modern, hip cafés setting the standard for the future.

---

find the area's newest wonder, the **Írókerék** ⓦ. You can return to Deák tér on the Millenniumi Földalatti (Millennial Underground).

TIMING   As most museums are closed Monday, it's best to explore Andrássy út on other days, preferably weekdays or early Saturday, when stores are also open for browsing. During opera season, you can time your exploration to land you at the Operaház stairs just before 7 PM to watch the spectacle of operagoers flowing in for the evening's performance. City Park is best explored on a clear day.

What to See

⓺⓪ **Drechsler Kastély** (Drechsler Palace). Across the street from the Operaház is the French Renaissance–style Drechsler Palace. An early work by Ödön Lechner, Hungary's master of art nouveau, it was formerly the home of the National Ballet School. As of this writing, it was being remodeled to begin a new life as a hotel. ⊠ *District VI, Andrássy út 25, Around Andrássy út* Ⓜ *M1: Opera.*

⓺⓶ **Ernst Múzeum.** A block and-a-half to the right of Andrássy út, on Nagymező utca, this is Budapest's finest gallery of 20th-century and contemporary art and cultural objects of all sorts. The exhibits change monthly or bimonthly. This stretch of Nagymező utca has also some good cafés. Be careful crossing the street, though—the trolleys barrel down the road like wildfire. ⊠ *District VI, Nagymező u. 8, Around Andrássy út* ☎ *1/413-1310* 🎫 *450 HUF* ☉ *Tues.–Sat. 11–7.*

★ ⑱ **Hősök tere.** Andrássy út ends in grandeur at Heroes' Square, with Budapest's answer to Berlin's Brandenburg Gate. Cleaned and refurbished in 1996 for the millecentenary (1100th anniversary), the **Millenniumi Emlékmű** (Millennial Monument) is a semicircular twin colonnade with statues of Hungary's kings and leaders between its pillars. Set back in its open center, a 118-foot stone column is crowned by a dynamic statue of the archangel Gabriel, his outstretched arms bearing the ancient emblems of Hungary. At its base ride seven bronze horsemen: the Magyar chieftains, led by Árpád, whose tribes conquered the land in 896. Before the column lies a simple marble slab, the **Nemzeti Háborús Emlék Tábla** (National War Memorial), the nation's altar, at which every visiting foreign dignitary lays a ceremonial wreath. England's Queen Elizabeth upheld the tradition during her royal visit in May 1992. In 1991 Pope John Paul II conducted a mass here. Just a few months earlier, half a million Hungarians had convened to recall the memory of Imre Nagy, the reform-minded Communist prime minister who partially inspired the 1956 revolution. Little would anyone have guessed then that in 1995, palm trees—and Madonna—would spring up on this very square in a scene from the film *Evita* (set in Argentina, not Hungary), nor that Michael Jackson would do his part to consecrate the square with a music video. ⊠ *District VI, Városliget* Ⓜ *M1: Hősök tere.*

⑫ **Irőkerék** (Time Wheel). Against a lovely backdrop of tall plane trees and spruces at the edge of City Park just off Felvonulás tér—a huge parking lot along Dózsa György út that in decades past was used for Communist rallies—is the world's largest hourglass. Aimed at portraying time rather than measuring it, the Time Wheel was launched on May 1, 2004, to mark Hungary's accession to the European Union. Made of granite, stainless steel, and glass that allows you to watch (or imagine) a fine trickle of sand flow from top to bottom, it is 8 meters (26 feet) in diameter and weighs a whopping 60 tons. Once a year, on December 31, the top chamber empties out, and then the wheel is turned a half-circle along the track it is set in, always the same way, so the upper and lower chambers switch places, and the sand begins flowing once again. ⊠ *District XIV, Városliget, Around Andrássy út* Ⓜ *M1: Hősök tere.*

⑯ **Kodály körönd.** A handsome traffic circle with imposing statues of three Hungarian warriors—leavened by a fourth one of a poet—Kodály körönd is surrounded by plane and chestnut trees. Look carefully at the towered mansions on the north side of the circle—behind the soot you'll see the fading colors of ornate frescoes peeking through. The circle takes its name from the composer Zoltán Kodály, who lived just beyond it at Andrássy út 89. ⊠ *District VI, Andrássy út at Szinyei Merse u., Around Andrássy út* Ⓜ *M1: Kodály körönd.*

⑥⑤ Liszt Ferenc Emlékmúzeum (Franz Liszt Memorial Museum). Andrássy út No. 67 was the original location of the old Academy of Music and Franz Liszt's last home; entered around the corner, it now houses a museum. Several rooms display the original furniture and instruments from Liszt's time there; another room shows temporary exhibits. The museum hosts excellent, free classical concerts year-round, except August 1–20, when it is closed. ⊠ *District VI, Vörösmarty u. 35, Around Andrássy út* ☎ *1/ 322–9804* ⊕ *www.lisztmuseum.hu* 💲 *360 HUF* ⊙ *Weekdays 10–6, Sat. 9–5. Classical concerts (free with admission) Sept.–July, Sat. at 11* AM Ⓜ *M1: Vörösmarty utca.*

⑥③ Liszt Ferenc Zeneakadémia (Franz Liszt Academy of Music). This magnificent art nouveau building presides over the cafés and gardens of Liszt Ferenc tér. Along with the Vigadó, this is one of the city's main concert halls. On summer days, the sound of daytime rehearsals adds to the sweetness in the air along this pedestrian oasis of café society, just off buzzing Andrássy út. The academy itself has two auditoriums: a green-and-gold 1,200-seat main hall and a smaller hall for chamber music and solo recitals. Farther along the square is a dramatic statue of Liszt Ferenc (Franz Liszt) himself, hair blown back from his brow, seemingly in a flight of inspiration. Pianist Ernő (Ernst) Dohnányi and composers Béla Bartók and Zoltán Kodály were teachers here. ⊠ *District VI, Liszt Ferenc tér 8, Around Andrássy út* ☎ *1/462–4600* Ⓜ *M1: Oktogon.*

★ ⑤⑨ Magyar Állami Operaház (Hungarian State Opera House). Miklós Ybl's crowning achievement is the neo-Renaissance Opera House, built between 1875 and 1884. Badly damaged during the siege of 1944–1945, it was restored for its 1984 centenary. Two buxom marble sphinxes guard the driveway; the main entrance is flanked by Alajos Strobl's "romantic-realist" limestone statues of Liszt and of another 19th-century Hungarian composer, Ferenc Erkel, the father of Hungarian opera (his patriotic opera *Bánk bán* is still performed for national celebrations). (See also Strobl's magnificent sculpture "Mathias's Well" behind the ⇨ Királyi Palota, *in* Várhegy [Castle Hill] *above.*)

Inside, the spectacle begins even before the performance does. You glide up grand staircases and through wood-paneled corridors and gilt lime-green salons into a glittering jewel box of an auditorium. Its four tiers of boxes are held up by helmeted sphinxes beneath a frescoed ceiling by Károly Lotz. Lower down there are frescoes everywhere, with intertwined motifs of Apollo and Dionysus. In its early years, the Budapest Opera was conducted by Gustav Mahler (1888–91), and after World War II by Otto Klemperer (1947–50).

The best way to experience the Opera House's interior is to see a ballet or opera; and while performance quality varies, tickets are relatively affordable and easy to come by, at least for tourists. And descending from *La Bohème* into the Földalatti station beneath the Opera House was described by travel writer Stephen Brook in *The Double Eagle* as stepping "out of one period piece and into another." There are no performances in summer, except for the weeklong BudaFest international opera and ballet festival in mid-August. You cannot view the interior on your own, but 45-minute tours in English are usually conducted daily; buy tickets in the Opera Shop, by the sphinx at the Hajós utca entrance. (Large groups should call in advance.) ⊠ *District VI, Andrássy út 22, Around Andrássy út* ☎ *1/331–2550 Ext. 156 for tours, 1/331–8197 for other info* 🖅 *Tours 2,200 HUF* ⊙ *Tours daily at 3 and 4* Ⓜ *M1: Opera.*

⑥ Magyar Fotográfusok Háza (Mai Manó Ház) (Hungarian Photographers' House [Manó Mai House]). This ornate turn-of-the-20th-century building was built as a photography studio, where the wealthy bourgeoisie would come to be photographed by imperial and royal court photographer Manó Mai. Inside, ironwork and frescoes ornament the curving staircase leading up to the exhibition space, the largest of Budapest's three photo galleries. Right next door, by the way, is the impeccably fashionable little Mai Manó Café. ⊠ *District VI, Nagymező u. 20, Around Andrássy út* ☎ *1/473–2666* 🖅 *400 HUF* ⊙ *Weekdays 2–7, weekends 11–7* Ⓜ *M1: Opera.*

⑥⑨ Műcsarnok (Palace of Exhibitions). The city's largest hall for special exhibitions is a striking 1895 temple of culture with a colorful tympanum. Its program of events includes exhibitions of contemporary Hungarian and international art and a rich series of films, plays, and concerts. Admission is free on Tuesday. ⊠ *District XIV, Hősök tere, Városliget* ☎ *1/460–7000* ⊕ *www.mucsarnok.hu* 🖅 *600 HUF* ⊙ *Tues., Wed., Fri., and Sun. 10–6, Thurs. 10–8* Ⓜ *M1: Hősök tere.*

⑤⑧ Postamúzeum (Postal Museum). The best of Andrássy út's many marvelous stone mansions can be visited now, for the Postal Museum occupies an apartment with frescoes by Károly Lotz (whose work adorns St. Stephen's Basilica and the Opera House). Among the displays is an exhibition on the history of Hungarian mail, radio, and telecommunications. English-language pamphlets are available. Even if the exhibits don't thrill you, the venue, which was restored in 2001, is worth the visit. ⊠ *District VI, Andrássy út 3, Around Andrássy út* ☎ *1/269–6838* 🖅 *100 HUF* ⊙ *Tues.–Sun. 10–6* Ⓜ *M1: Bajcsy-Zsilinszky út.*

⑥⑦ Ráth György Múzeum (György Ráth Museum). Two blocks to the south of Andrássy út, this museum houses a rich collection of exotica from the Indian subcontinent as well as a several good examples of Chinese ceramics. The **Hopp Ferenc Kelet-Ázsiai Művészeti Múzeum** (Ferenc Hopp Museum of Eastern Asiatic Arts; ⊠ District VI, Andrássy út 103, Around Andrássy út? ☎ 1/322–8476), which is affiliated with the György Ráth, hosts changing exhibits. ⊠ *District VI, Városligeti fasor 12, Around Andrássy út* ☎ *1/342–3916* 🖅 *Ráth György: free; Ferenc Hopp 400 HUF* ⊙ *Tues.–Sun. 10–6* Ⓜ *M1: Bajza utca.*

need a break?

The **Művész Café** (⊠ District VI, Andrássy út 29, Around Andrássy út ☎ 1/352–1337) is perhaps the only surviving "writer's café" where you will occasionally see an actual writer at work. The combination of low lighting and striped, dark gold-green wallpaper gives it an elegant yet chic appeal. Sit at a table outside during summer to watch the world passing by on Andrássy út.

Several blocks beyond the Oktogon intersection and past the Terror Háza museum is **Lukács Cukrászda** (⊠ District VI, Andrássy út 70, Around Andrássy út ☎ 1/302–8747). With glass chandeliers, marble-topped tables, and ornate columns at one end of the spacious main room, this café—which has been here since 1912—is not only smashingly elegant, but it's even air-conditioned and offers live piano music weekday evenings. Try the Megyes-Mákos, a layer cake packed with sour cherries and poppy seeds.

⑳ Szépművészeti Múzeum (Museum of Fine Arts). Across Heroes' Square
Fodor's Choice from the Palace of Exhibitions and built by the same team of Albert
★ Schickedanz and Fülöp Herzog, the Museum of Fine Arts houses Hungary's best art collection, rich in Flemish and Dutch old masters. With seven fine El Grecos and five beautiful Goyas as well as paintings by Velázquez and Murillo, the collection of Spanish old masters is one of the best outside Spain. The Italian school is represented by Giorgione, Bellini, Correggio, Tintoretto, and Titian masterpieces and, above all, two superb Raphael paintings: *Eszterházy Madonna* and his immortal *Portrait of a Youth,* rescued after a world-famous art heist. Nineteenth-century French art includes works by Delacroix, Pissarro, Cézanne, Toulouse-Lautrec, Gauguin, Renoir, and Monet. There are also more than 100,000 drawings (including five by Rembrandt and three studies by Leonardo), Egyptian and Greco-Roman exhibitions, late-Gothic winged altars from northern Hungary and Transylvania, and works by all the leading figures of Hungarian art up to the present. A 20th-century collection was added to the museum's permanent exhibits in 1994, comprising an interesting series of statues, paintings, and drawings by Chagall, Le Corbusier, and others. Labels are in both Hungarian and English; there's also an English-language booklet for sale about the permanent collection. ⊠ *District XIV, Hősök tere, Around Andrássy út ☎ 1/ 469–7100 or 1/363–4654 ⊕ www.szepmuveszeti.hu ☞ Free, special exhibits 900 HUF ☺ Tues.–Sun. 10–5:30* Ⓜ *M1: Hősök tere.*

★ ⑭ **Terror Háza** (House of Terror). The most controversial museum in post-Communist Hungary was established at great cost, with the active support of the center-right government in power from 1998 to 2002. Many critics allege that its exhibits are less-than-objective, sensational attacks on those even loosely associated with the Communist-era dictatorship and place comparatively less emphasis on the terrors of the fascist era and the Holocaust in particular. The museum's much-maligned director has replied that the collection is dedicated to the victims of both regimes (fascist and Communist)—specifically noting that there is an exhibit on the atrocities against Jews before and during World War II—and that it was painstakingly researched and designed by experts. The building itself has a terrible history. Starting in 1939, it was headquarters of the Arrow Cross; from 1945 to 1956, the notorious Communist state security police, the ÁVO (later succeeded by the ÁVH), used it as its headquarters and as its interrogation-cum-torture center. A stunning visual and sensual experience—and a somewhat overbearing one, depending on one's frame of mind—this state-of-the-art, multimedia museum features everything from videos of sobbing victims telling their stories to a full-size Soviet tank. An English-language audio guide is available for 1,000 HUF per person above the ticket price; larger groups needing them for each member should call several days or more in advance to reserve, as the number of units is limited. ⊠ *District VI, Andrássy út 60, Around Andrássy út* ☏ *1/374–2600* ⊕ *www.terrorhaza.hu* ☞ *1,200 HUF* ⊙ *Tues.–Fri. 10–6, weekends 10–7:30* Ⓜ *M1: Vörösmarty utca.*

ⓒ ❼ **Városliget** (City Park). Heroes' Square is the gateway to a square kilometer (almost ½ square mi) of recreation, entertainment, beauty, and culture. A bridge behind the Millennial Monument leads across a boating basin that becomes an artificial ice-skating rink in winter; to the south of this lake stands a statue of George Washington, erected in 1906 with donations by Hungarian emigrants to the United States. You can soak or swim at the lovely, turn-of-the-20th-century Széchenyi Fürdő, jog along the park paths, or careen on Vidám Park's roller coaster. There's also the Petőfi Csarnok, a leisure-time youth center and major concert hall on the site of an old industrial exhibition. The Gundel restaurant charms diners with its turn-of-the-20th-century ambience. Fair-weather weekends, when the children's attractions are teeming with youngsters and parents and the Széchenyi Fürdő is brimming with bathers, are the best times for people-watchers to visit the park; if you go on a weekday, the main sights are rarely crowded. ⊠ *District XIV, Andrássy út, Városliget* ☞ *Park free, admission charged for attractions* ⊙ *Daily* Ⓜ *M1: Városliget.*

ⓒ The renovation of the once-depressing **Budapesti Állat-és Növénykert** (Budapest Zoo & Botanical Garden), which began in the late 1990s, was still underway as of this writing, but the place is already cheerier, especially for humans. The petting opportunities are aplenty, and a new monkey house allows endearing, seemingly clawless little simians to climb all over you (beware of pickpockets). Don't miss the elephant pavilion, decorated with Zsolnay majolica and glazed ceramic animals. Note that the last tickets are sold one hour before closing, and animal houses don't open until an hour after the zoo gates. ⊠ *District XIV, Városliget, Állatkerti krt. 6–12* ☏ *1/364–0109* ⊕ *www.zoobudapest.com* ☞ *1,300 HUF; tropical greenhouse and aquarium 300 HUF each* ⊙ *Jun.–Aug., Mon.–Thurs. 9–6, Fri.–Sun. 9–7; Mar.–Apr. and Sept.–Oct., daily 9–5; May, daily 9–6:30; Nov.–Feb., daily 9–4.*

ⓒ At the **Fővárosi Nagycirkusz** (Municipal Grand Circus), colorful performances by local acrobats, clowns, and animal trainers, as well as by international artists, are staged here in a small ring. ⊠ *District XIV, Városliget, Állatkerti krt. 7* ☏ *1/344–6008* ☞ *1,000–1,600 HUF* ⊙ *July–Aug., Wed. and Fri. at 3 and 7, Thurs. at 3, Sat. at 10:30, 3, and 7, Sun. at 10:30 and 3; Sept.–June, schedule varies.*

Széchenyi Fürdő (Széchenyi Baths), the largest medicinal bathing complex in Europe, is housed in a beautiful neo-baroque building in the middle of City Park. There are several thermal pools indoors as well as two outdoor pools, which remain open even in winter, when dense steam hangs thick over the hot water's surface—you can just barely make out the figures of elderly men, submerged shoulder deep, crowded around waterproof chessboards. To use the baths, you pay a deposit: a portion of which may be returned depending on how long you stay. Facilities include medical and underwater massage treatments, carbonated bath treatments, and mud wraps. ⊠ *District XIV, Városliget, Állatkerti krt. 11* ☎ *1/363–3210* ⊠ *2,200 HUF; changing room 400 HUF, cabin 700 HUF* ⊘ *May–Sept., daily 6 AM–7 PM; Oct.–Apr., weekdays 6 AM–7 PM, weekends 6 AM–5 PM.*

Beside the City Park's lake stands **Vajdahunyad Vár** (Vajdahunyad Castle), a fantastic medley of Hungary's historic and architectural past, starting with the Romanesque gateway of the cloister of Jak, in western Hungary. A Gothic castle whose Transylvanian turrets, Renaissance loggia, baroque portico, and Byzantine decorations are all guarded by a spooky modern (1903) bronze statue of the anonymous medieval "chronicler," who was the first recorder of Hungarian history. Designed for the millennial celebration in 1896, it was not completed until 1908. This hodgepodge houses the surprisingly interesting **Mezőgazdasági Múzeum** (Agricultural Museum), with intriguingly arranged sections on animal husbandry, forestry, horticulture, hunting, and fishing. ⊠ *District XIV, Városliget, Széchenyi Island* ☎ *1/363–2698* ⊠ *Free* ⊘ *Mar.–Sept., Tues.–Sun. 10–5; Oct.–Feb., Tues.–Sun. 10–4.*

Ⓒ Budapest's somewhat weary amusement park, **Vidám Park,** is next to the zoo and is crawling with happy children with their parents or grandparents in tow. Rides are affordable (some are for preschoolers). There are also game rooms and a scenic railway. In all, there are 35 different attractions, including Europe's longest wooden roller coaster and a merry-go-round dating to 1906 and beautifully restored in 1998. That said, both the Web site and brochures you'll get from tourism authorities or the rack in your hotel are a bit more glittery than the park itself. Next to the main park is a separate, smaller section for toddlers. There is a nominal admission charge, and then you buy individual tickets for rides; rides take one to three tickets. Kids under 120 cm (3.9 feet) tall get in for free. ⊠ *District XIV, Városliget, Állatkerti krt. 14–16* ☎ *1/343–9810 or 1/363–8310* ⊕ *www.vidampark.hu* ⊠ *300 HUF general admission, 250 HUF for a ride ticket, though most rides require two such tickets* ⊘ *July–Aug., Mon.–Thurs. and Sun. 10–8, Fri.–Sat. 10–10; May–June, weekdays 11–7, Sat. 10–10, Sun. 10–8; Apr. and Sept., weekdays noon–7, weekends 10–7:30; Mar. and Oct., weekdays 10–6, weekends 10–7.*

EASTERN PEST & THE LARGE RING ROAD

Pest's Large Ring Road (the Nagy körút) was laid out at the end of the 19th century in a wide semicircle, anchored to the Danube at both ends; an arm of the river was covered over to create this 114-foot-wide thoroughfare. The large apartment buildings on both sides also date from this era. Along with theaters, stores, and cafés, they form a boulevard unique in Europe for its "unified eclecticism," which blends several different historic styles into a harmonious whole. Its entire length of almost 4½ km (2¾ mi) from the Margaret Bridge to the Petőfi bridge is traversed by Trams 4 and 6, but strolling it in stretches is also a good way to experience the hustle and bustle of Budapest's busy, less-touristy urban thoroughfares full of people, cars, shops, and the city's unique urban flavor.

Beginning a few blocks from the Elizabeth Bridge, Kossuth Lajos utca is Budapest's busiest shopping street. Try to look above and beyond the store windows to the architecture and activity along Kossuth Lajos utca and its continuation, Rákóczi út, which begins when it crosses the Kis körút (Small Ring Road) at the busy intersection called Astoria. Most of Rákóczi út is lined with hotels, shops, and department stores, and it ends at the grandiose Keleti (East) Railway Station, on Baross tér.

Like its smaller counterpart, the Kis körút (Small Ring Road), the Large Ring Road comprises sectors of various names. Beginning with Ferenc körút at the Petőfi Bridge, it changes to József körút at the intersection marked by the Museum of Applied Arts, then to Erzsébet körút at Blaha Lujza tér. Teréz körút begins at the busy Oktogon crossing with Andrássy út and ends at the Nyugati (West) Railway Station, where Szent István takes over for the final stretch to the Margaret Bridge.

a good walk

Beginning with a visit to the **Iparművészeti Múzeum** ❼❸, near the southern end of the Large Ring Road, walk or take Tram 4 or 6 north (away from the Petőfi Bridge) to **Köztársaság tér** ❼❹. The neo-Renaissance **Keleti pályaudvar** ❼❺ is a one-metro-stop detour away from Blaha Lujza tér. Continuing in the same direction on the körút, go several stops on the tram to **Nyugati pályaudvar** ❼❻ and walk the remaining sector, Szent István körút, past the **Vígszínház** ❼❼ to Margaret Bridge. From the bridge, views of Margaret Island, to the north, and Parliament, Castle Hill, the Chain Bridge, and Gellért Hill, to the south, are gorgeous.

As an alternative, you might explore the newly revitalized neighborhood of Mester utca and environs along the Large Ring Road just one tram stop south of the Iparművészeti Múzeum. Walk or take Tram 4 or 6 south (toward Petőfi Bridge) three short blocks to Mester utca, on your left. This wide, lovely street, shaded by plane trees, has lots of small shops, grocery stores, and local flavor, including one of Budapest's best *rétes* (strudel) stands. Take the third street to your left, Páva utca, and go two blocks to the **Holocaust Emlékközpont** ❼❽. From here you're within a block of Üllői út, where you can take a left for a short walk back toward the museum. If you'd prefer to have a look at Hungary's stunning new national theater, the **Nemzeti Színház** ❼❾, go one tram stop farther, to Petőfi Bridge, and walk from Boráros tér, which is beside the bridge, some 20 minutes south along the Danube through a long, narrow, open park or take the HÉV electric railway from here one stop.

TIMING   As this area is packed with stores, it's best to explore during business hours—weekdays until around 5 PM and Saturday until 1 PM. Saturday will be most crowded. Keep in mind that the Iparművészeti Múzeum is closed Monday.

What to See

★ 🟢 **Holocaust Emlékközpont** (Holocaust Memorial Center). On the 60th anniversary of the closing off of Budapest's Jewish ghetto, April 15, 2004, Hungary's first major center for Holocaust research and exhibits opened in the presence of Hungarian statesmen and the Israeli president. The stone facade of this onetime synagogue looks like an awfully high, windowless castle wall; its entrance consists of two tall, massive iron doors. Much like the House of Terror along Andrássy út, it likewise commemorates the victims of past terrors, if not in quite such a multimediaish manner. The venue opened with an exhibit from the "Auschwitz Album," 150 moving photos from 235 on file here that were taken in 1944 of the deportation and internment of a group of Jews from a region of Hungary, today located in Ukraine, by two SS photographers. One display consists of ten flags representing the regions of Hungary from which Jews were deported; a separate display commemorates the Roma (Gypsy) victims of the Holocaust. During the three days of opening ceremonies, the names of 60,000 Hungarian Jews killed in the Holocaust were read aloud; this represented some 10% of the total. ⊠ *District IX, Páva u. 39, North of Blaha Lujza tér* 🕿 *1/216–6557* ⊕ *www.hdke. hu* 🖃 *Free* ⊙ *Tues.–Sun. 10–6* Ⓜ *M3: Üllői út.*

★ 🟢 **Iparművészeti Múzeum** (Museum of Applied & Decorative Arts). The templelike structure is indeed a shrine to Hungarian art nouveau, and in front of it, drawing pen in hand, sits a statue of its creator, Hungarian architect Ödön Lechner. Opened in the Magyar Millennial year of 1896, it was only the third museum of its kind in Europe. Its dome of deep green and golden tiles is crowned by a majolica lantern from the same source: the Zsolnay ceramic works in Pécs. Inside its central hall are playfully swirling whitewashed, double-decker, Moorish-style galleries and arcades. The museum, which collects and studies objects of interior decoration and use, has five departments: furniture, textiles, goldsmithing, ceramics, and everyday objects. ⊠ *District VIII, Üllői út 33–37, North of Blaha Lujza tér* 🕿 *1/456–5100* ⊕ *www.imm.hu* 🖃 *600 HUF* ⊙ *Tues.–Sun. 10–6* Ⓜ *M3: Üllői út.*

> **off the beaten path**
>
> **GÖDÖLLŐI KIRÁLYI KASTÉLY (ROYAL PALACE OF GÖDÖLLŐ)** – has been referred to as the Hungarian Versailles, though this baroque mansion and former royal residence does suffer by comparison. This is because the palace was used as a barracks by Soviet troops after 1945, and much of the palace was still under restoration at this writing. Still, those interested in Emperor Franz Josef I and his legendarily beautiful and charismatic wife, Elizabeth (known as Sissi), will find this a rewarding half-day excursion. Sissi's violet-colored rooms contain secret doors, which allowed her to avoid tiresome guests. To get there, go to the Örs Vezér tere—last stop on the red metro line—and take the HÉV suburban train to the Szabadság tere stop. The palace sits across the street. ⊠ *Grassalkovich Kastély, Gödöllő* 🕿 *28/430–864* 🖃 *1,300 HUF* ⊙ *Tues.–Sun. 10–6 (tickets until 5 PM)* Ⓜ *M2: Örs Vezér tere, then HÉV to Szabadság tere.*

⓻ Keleti pályaudvar (East Railway Station). The grandiose, imperial-looking station was built in 1884 and was considered Europe's most modern until well into the 20th century. Its neo-Renaissance facade, which resembles a gateway, is flanked by statues of two British inventors and railway pioneers, James Watt and George Stephenson. ⊠ *District VIII, Baross tér, Around Keleti Train Station* Ⓜ *M2: Keleti pu.*

⓻ Köztársaság tér. Surrounded by an extraordinary mix of faceless concrete monstrosities and lovely old buildings, the vast Square of the Republic has a serene, somewhat shaded park at its center. Its 20th-century historical significance stems from the fact that it was where the Communist Party of Budapest had its headquarters (today the Socialist Party offices), and saw heavy fighting in 1956. Here also is the city's second opera house, and Budapest's largest, the Erkel Ferenc színház (Ferenc Erkel Theater). ⊠ *District VIII, between Luther u. and Berzeriyi u., Around Keleti Train Station* Ⓜ *M2: Blaha Lujza tér or Keleti pu.*

⓻ Nemzeti Színház (National Theater). No area of downtown Budapest has undergone as much revitalization since the early 1990s as the corner of Eastern Pest that stretches from Petófi Bridge to Budapest's newest bridge, Lágymányosi híd, between the Danube and Mester utca. The key attraction here, the hugely expensive National Theater, was completed in 2000. Round and colonnaded in front and square in back, the massive building is a spectacular mix of modern and classical. The spacious square out front and to the side is something to behold. The large reflecting pool contains a toppled-over, life-size ancient theater facade (complete with six columns) and three eternal flames. The bow of a ship, which you can walk on, overlooks the pool. Elsewhere on the square, scattered about here and there, some on benches, others standing, are eight metal statues of famous, late Hungarian actors and actresses of the 20th century, each performing some legendary role. All this gives you a deep sense of Hungarian dramatic history, even if the details are privy only to Hungarians themselves. If you take the HÉV commuter railway, you get off a short distance beyond the theater, and you must walk back over a small bridge spanning the tracks. On the way, you'll pass by a structure that looks a lot like the Tower of Babel—and that's what it's called. As a friendly guard patrolling the theater's perimeter explained, the tower, which consists of concentric circles of yellow bricks, has stairs leading up to an exhibition space (otherwise closed to the public) that's used "a couple times a year." ⊠ *District IX, Bajor Gizi park 1, Around Boráros tér* ☎ *1/476–6800* ⊕ *www.nemzetiszinhaz.hu* Ⓜ *M3: Üllői út.*

⓻ Nyugati pályaudvar (West Railway Station). The iron-laced glass hall of the West Railway Station is in complete contrast to—and much more modern than—the newer East Railway Station. Built in the 1870s, it was designed by a team of architects from Gustav Eiffel's office in Paris. ⊠ *District XIII, Teréz krt., Around Nyugati Train Station* Ⓜ *M3: Nyugati pu.*

☾ No longer do you have to wait to take off from Ferihegy Airport nor do you have to climb Gellért-hegy for a bird's-eye view of Budapest. Simply hop aboard the city's very own **Helium Balloon** (⊠ District XIII, West End Shopping Center, Váci út 1–3, Around Nyugati Train Station ☎ 1/

238–7623), which floats 150 meters (487 feet) above Nyugati pályaud-var at the end of a metal cable for 30 minutes at a stretch. You can take the ride for 3,000 HUF; it's open from 10 to 10 daily in fair weather (i. e., when there is little or no wind), with rides leaving every 20 minutes.

★ ⑦ **Vígszínház** (Comedy Theater). This neo-baroque, late-19th-century, gemlike theater twinkles with just a tiny, playful anticipation of art nou-veau and sparkles inside and out since its 1994 refurbishment. The the-ater hosts primarily musicals, such as Hungarian adaptations of *Cats*, as well as dance performances and classical concerts. ⊠ *District XIII, Pannónia u. 1, Parliament* ☎ *1/329–2340 box office* ⊕ *www.vigszinhaz. hu* Ⓜ *M3: Nyugati pu.*

┌──────────┐
│ need a   │ A short walk from the Margaret Bridge toward the northern end of
│ break?   │ the Large Ring Road, the **Európa kávéház** (⊠ District XIII, Szent
└──────────┘ István krt. 7–9, Parliament ☎ 1/312–2362) is a turn-of-the-20th-
century style café that actually opened in the 1990s. Try the delectable *dobostorta*, with its many cream-filled layers and hard, caramel top; the apple pie deluxe; or the chestnut cake. Even the no-smoking back room is smoky, by the way, since only a huge open archway separates it from the front room, where smoking is allowed.

Just 1½ blocks from Blaha Lujza tér and the Large Ring Road, going away from the river, **Hauer Cukrászda** (⊠ District VIII, Rákóczi út 47–49, Around Blaha Lujza tér ☎ 1/323–1476) has been around since 1890. Last renovated in 2002, it is one of Budapest's most elegant such establishments. The best-looking sweets here include the tiramisu and the *borkrém-roládd* (wine-cream roll).

Rozi néni Rétesei (⊠ District IX, Mester utca, on the right between Liliom utca and Páva utca, Around Boráros tér) is worth the detour toward Mester utca simply to delight in the best, most filling strudels you can get at any sidewalk stand in town. Miss Rozi's Strudels has been operating here for many years. For 155 HUF you can choose between scrumptious strudels of the *túrós* (sweet curd-cheese), *kapros túrós* (sweet curd-cheese with dill), *almás* (apple), *szilvás* (plum), and *káposztás* (cabbage) varieties.

ÓBUDA & MARGITSZIGET (MARGARET ISLAND)

Until its unification with Buda and Pest in 1872 to form the city of Buda-pest, Óbuda (meaning Old Buda) was a separate town that used to be the main settlement; now it is usually thought of as a suburb. Although the vast new apartment blocks of Budapest's biggest housing project and busy roadways are what first strike the eye, the historic core of Óbuda has been preserved in its entirety. Margitsziget itself is an island in the middle of the Danube.

Numbers in the text correspond to numbers in the margin and on the Óbuda & Margaret Island map.

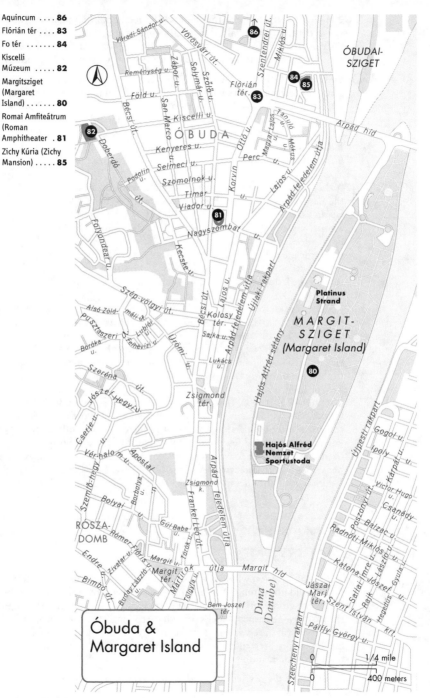

Óbuda &
Margaret Island

a good walk

Begin your tour on the Margit híd, entering **Margitsziget** ⑳ on its southern end. Stroll up the island, toward the Árpád híd, where you can catch the streetcar or just walk over to Óbuda. If you want to take a pass on Margitsziget, it's easy enough to get to Óbuda by car, bus, or streetcar via the Árpád Bridge from Pest or by the HÉV suburban railway from Batthyány tér to the Árpád Bridge. Once you're there, covering all the sights on foot involves large but manageable distances along major exhaust-permeated roadways. One way to tackle it is to take Tram 17 from its southern terminus at the Buda side of the Margaret Bridge. Óbuda really begins after the third stop; and the fourth stop marks a charming commercial subcenter of this part of town; after this, keep your eyes open to the right, as the tram soon passes by the ruins of the **Római amfiteátrum** ㉛. At the seventh stop, Szent Margit Kórház, get off and walk back a short distance to Kiscelli utca; from there, walk uphill to the **Kiscelli Múzeum** ㉜. Then walk back down the same street all the way past **Flórián tér** ㉝, continuing toward the Danube and making a left onto Hídfő utca or Szentlélek tér to enter **Fő tér** ㉞. On the south side of the square is the **Zichy Kúria** ㉟, a cultural center and museum. After exploring the square, walk a block or two southeast to the HÉV suburban railway stop and take the train just north to the museum complex at **Aquincum** ㊱ and the Hercules Villa, nearby.

TIMING A leisurely stroll from one end of Margitsziget to the other takes about 40 minutes, but it's nice to spend some extra time wandering. Margitsziget is most lively on a weekend, when the city's residents take full advantage of the island's green expanses; on a weekday, it's a much quieter place, and that can have its own rewards. It's best to begin touring Óbuda during the cooler, early hours of the day, as the heat on the area's busy roads can get overbearing. Avoid Monday, when museums are closed.

What to See

㊱ **Aquincum.** This complex comprises the reconstructed remains of a Roman settlement dating from the first century AD and the capital of the Roman province of Pannónia. Careful excavations have unearthed a varied selection of artifacts and mosaics, giving a tantalizing inkling of what life was like in the provinces of the Roman Empire. A gymnasium and a central heating system have been unearthed, along with the ruins of two baths and a shrine to Mithras, the Persian god of light, truth, and the sun. The **Aquincum múzeum** (Aquincum Museum) displays the dig's most notable finds: ceramics; a red-marble sarcophagus showing a triton and flying Eros on one side and on the other, Telesphorus, the angel of death, depicted as a hooded dwarf; and jewelry from a Roman lady's tomb. Near the main Aquincum ruins—but functioning as a separate museum, a fine third-century Roman dwelling, **Hercules Villa** (⊠ District III, Meggyfa u. 19–21) takes its name from the myth depicted on its beautiful mosaic floor. The ruin was unearthed between 1958 and 1967 and is now only open by request (inquire at the Aquincum Museum). ⊠ *District III, Szentendrei út 139, Óbuda* 🕾 *1/250–1650* 💷 *Aquincum Museum 700 HUF, Hercules Villa free* ⊙ *Aquincum Museum mid- to late Apr. and Oct., Tues.–Sun. 10–5; May–Sept., Tues.–Sun. 10–6 (grounds open an hour earlier than museum). Hercules Villa mid-April–Oct., Tues.–Sun. 10–5.*

⑧ Flórián tér (Flórián Square). The center of today's Óbuda is Flórián tér, where Roman ruins were first discovered when the foundations of a house were dug in 1778. Two centuries later, careful excavations were carried out during the reconstruction of the square, and today the restored ancient ruins lie in the center in mind-boggling contrast to the racing traffic and cement-block housing projects. In the middle of the large, grassy park stretching from the square toward Kiscelli utca is an eerie, black metal angel-like sculpture pointing one hand skyward and holding a wreath in the other. This is the **Memorial to the Victims of Road Accidents**. In case the title isn't enough, a wrecked car at the foot of the main statue and a list of annual highway death tolls from 1984 to the present further ensures that the point gets across, compliments of the National Police Headquarters' Accident Prevention Committee. ⊠ *District III, Vörösvári út at Pacsirtamező u., Óbuda.*

⑧ Fő tér (Main Square). Óbuda's old main square is its most picturesque part. There are several good restaurants and interesting museums in and around the baroque Zichy Mansion, which has become a neighborhood cultural center. Among the most popular offerings are the summer concerts in the courtyard and the evening jazz concerts. Toward the southern end of the square is the elaborate **Óbudai Szentháromság Szobor** (Óbuda Trinity Statue), built originally in 1740, razed in 1950, and rebuilt in 2000. ⊠ *District III, Kórház u. at Hídfő u., Óbuda.*

⑧ Kiscelli Múzeum (Kiscelli Museum). A short climb up the steep sidewalk of Remetehegy (Hermit Hill) will deposit you at this elegant, mustard-yellow baroque mansion. It was built between 1744 and 1760 as a Trinitarian monastery. Today, it holds an eclectic mix of paintings, sculptures, engravings, old clocks, antique furniture, and other items related to the history of Budapest. Included here is the printing press on which poet and revolutionary Sándor Petőfi printed his famous "Nemzeti Dal" ("National Song"), in 1848, inciting the Hungarian people to rise up against the Hapsburgs. There are concerts here every Sunday in July. ⊠ *District III, Kiscelli u. 108, Óbuda* ☏ *1/388–8560 or 1/250–0304* 🎟*600 HUF* ◷ *Nov.–Mar., Tues.–Sun. 10–4; Apr.–Oct., Tues.–Sun. 10–6.*

⟳ **⑧ Margitsziget** (Margaret Island). More than 2½ km (1½ mi) long and cov-
Fodor'sChoice ering nearly 200 acres, this island park is ideal for strolling, jogging,
★ sunbathing, or just loafing. In good weather, it draws a multitudinous cross-section of the city's population out to its gardens and sporting facilities. The outdoor pool complex of the Palatinus Baths, built in 1921, can attract tens of thousands of people on a summer day. Nearby are a tennis stadium, a youth athletic center, boathouses, sports grounds, and, most impressive of all, the Nemzeti Sportuszoda (National Sports Swimming Pool), designed by the architect Alfred Hajós (while still in his teens, Hajós won two gold medals in swimming at the first modern Olympic Games, held in Athens in 1896). In addition, walkers, joggers, bicyclists, and rollerbladers do laps around the island's perimeter and up and down the main road, closed to traffic except for Bus 26 (and a few official vehicles), which travels up and down the island and across the Margaret Bridge to and from Pest. The island's natural curative hot springs have given rise to the Danubius Grand and Thermal

hotels on the northern end of the island and are piped into two spa hotels on the mainland, the Aquincum on the Buda bank and the Hélia on the Pest side.

To experience Margaret Island's role in Budapest life fully, go on a Saturday or Sunday afternoon to join and/or watch people whiling away the day. Sunday is a particularly good choice for strategic sightseers, who can utilize the rest of the week to cover those city sights and areas that are closed on Sunday. On weekdays, you'll share the island only with joggers and children playing hooky from school.

The island was first mentioned almost 2,000 years ago as the summer residence of the commander of the Roman garrison at nearby Aquincum. Later known as Rabbit Island (Insula Leporum), it was a royal hunting ground during the Árpád dynasty. King Imre, who reigned from 1196 to 1204, held court here, and several convents and monasteries were built here during the Middle Ages. (During a walk round the island, you'll see the ruins of a few of these buildings.) It takes its current name from St. Margaret, the pious daughter of King Béla IV, who at the ripe old age of 10 retired to a Dominican nunnery here.

Through the center of the island runs the **Művész sétány** (Artists' Promenade), lined with busts of Hungarian visual artists, writers, and musicians. Shaded by giant plane trees, it's a perfect place to stroll. The promenade passes close to the **rose garden** (in the center of the island), a large grassy lawn surrounded by blooming flower beds planted with hundreds of kinds of flowers. It's a great spot to picnic or to watch a game of soccer or Ultimate Frisbee, both of which are regularly played here on weekend afternoons. Just east of the rose garden is a small, free would-be petting zoo, the **Margitsziget Vadaspark**, if the animals were allowed to be petted. A fenced-in compound houses a menagerie of goats, rabbits, donkeys, assorted fowl and ducks, and gargantuan peacocks that sit heavily on straining tree branches.

At the northern end of the island is a copy of the water-powered **Marosvásárhelyi zenélő kút** (Marosvásárhely Musical Fountain), which plays songs and chimes. The original was designed more than 150 years ago by a Transylvanian named Péter Bodor. It stands near a serene, artificial rock garden with Japanese dwarf trees and lily ponds. The stream coursing through it never freezes, for it comes from a natural hot spring causing it instead to give off thick steam in winter that enshrouds the garden in a mystical cloud. ✉ *Margitsziget* Ⓜ *M3: Árpád híd.*

㉛ Római amfiteátrum (Roman Amphitheater). Probably dating back to the second century AD, Óbuda's Roman military amphitheater once held some 16,000 people and, at 144 yards in diameter, was one of Europe's largest. A block of dwellings called the Round House was later built by the Romans above the amphitheater; massive stone walls found in the Round House's cellar were actually parts of the amphitheater. Below the amphitheater are the cells where prisoners and lions were held while awaiting confrontation. ✉ *District III, Pacsirtamező u. at Nagyszombat u., Óbuda.*

85 **Zichy Kúria** (Zichy Mansion). One wing of the Zichy Mansion is taken up by the **Óbudai Helytörténeti Gyüjtemény** (Óbuda Local History Collection). Permanent exhibitions here include traditional rooms from typical homes in the district of Békásmegyer and a popular exhibit covering the history of toys from 1860 to 1960. Another wing houses the **Kassák Múzeum,** which honors the literary and artistic works of a pioneer of the Hungarian avant-garde, Lajos Kassák. The museum entrances are deep inside the mansion's large courtyard, which hosts a popular series of summer concerts and evening jazz performances. ⊠ *District III, Fő tér 1, Óbuda* ☎ *1/250–1020, 368–1138 for Local History Collection, 1/368–7021 for Kassák Museum* ⊒ *Local History Collection 150 HUF, Kassák Museum free* ⊙ *Local History Collection mid-Mar.–mid-Oct., Tues.–Fri. 2–6, weekends 10–6; mid-Oct.–mid-Mar., Tues.–Fri. 2–5, weekends 10–5. Kassák Museum Tues.–Sun. 10–6.*

WHERE TO EAT

By Betsy
Maury

NOT LONG AGO dining out in Budapest offered few exciting choices. There were expensive grand dining rooms, tired Communist-era taverns, and a few foreign fast-food chains. Thankfully, dynamic dining options abound these days, and Budapest enjoys a lively restaurant scene. A typical night out can begin in a cozy Moroccan tapas bar and end up at a rustic Tuscan trattoria on a terrace overlooking the Danube. Young chefs trained abroad are having the biggest impact on the restaurant scene now, and in truth some of the best places to eat in Budapest aren't Hungarian. In addition to very good Italian restaurants, many of the most popular new places serve well-prepared, but not traditional, Hungarian-inspired cuisine.

Throughout the city, Hungarian chefs seem determined to bring their cuisine into a new era and are at once creating innovative dishes and seeking to prevent a few classics from disappearing from modern menus. In many of District V's newer establishments, for instance, menus include well-prepared Hungarian dishes that use new ingredients to complement traditional flavors. Pork, long a Hungarian staple, gets dressed up both with traditional *lecsó* (pepper, onion, and tomato ragout flavored with paprika) and is grilled—Florentine style—with rosemary. Some standbys, such as *gulyás leves* (goulash soup) and *paprikás csirke* (chicken paprikash) are on the menu at even the most stylish restaurants. Other Hungarian favorites like goose remain popular everywhere, and you'll find that a crispy goose leg (*sült libacomb*) served with sautéed red cabbage has a devoted following. Long-celebrated goose liver (*libamaj*) also survives on virtually every menu in the city. You'll find it prepared in one of many traditional Hungarian styles as well as in myriad new ways, like soaked in aged cognac and served with onion relish.

Dining aesthetics overall are better now in Budapest restaurants, too. Upscale bistros look and feel Parisian; trendy restaurants have low lighting and serve dishes using funky tableware. Service is markedly improved all over town, and while you're unlikely to find a waiter or waitress too chummy, professional service is now the norm in most good restaurants. Thankfully, the pace in Budapest restaurants remains decidedly European and therefore considerably slower than an average American establishment. Glasses of wine are finished before dessert is discussed, and you're allowed to linger in most restaurants for quite some time before paying the bill. In most cases, you will need to ask for the bill; it will not be brought spontaneously.

Downtown Pest & the Small Ring Road

★ **$$$$** ✗ **Fausto's.** Of all the excellent Italian restaurants now to be found in Budapest, this elegant one across from the main synagogue has been in business the longest. Its fans are unwavering on its consistently excellent cuisine, so this place is a good bet if you feel like a splurge. Authentic Italian delicacies like salmon carpaccio and homemade tagliatelli with rabbit ragout are lovingly prepared. The white-glove service is impeccable here and surprisingly friendly. ⊠ *District VII, Dohány utca 5, Around Deák Ferenc tér* ☎ *1/269–6806* ⚹ *Reservations essential* ▤ *AE, DC, MC, V* ⊗ *Closed Sun.* Ⓜ *M2: Astoria.*

Mealtimes Dinner hours in Budapest are typically from around 7 to 9 PM, although bustling downtown restaurants will serve until about 10. Lunch, the main meal for many, is served from noon to 2. Many restaurants are closed on Sunday.

Reservations Reservations for dinner are necessary in most of the nicer restaurants in Budapest. A day or two in advance is usually time enough to secure a good table. Reservations are mentioned in listings only when we feel you absolutely will not be able to get a table otherwise. You will nearly always find an English speaker at the restaurant who can competently book a table. Reservations are generally not necessary for lunch.

Smoking Budapest's smoking policy is typically European. Smokers are welcome everywhere, and many restaurants do not have designated sections. Some do, however, and you can request a non-smoking table at those places. Small restaurants and cafés can be quite smoky in the winter time.

What to Wear At most moderately priced and inexpensive restaurants, casual but neat dress is acceptable. In restaurant listings, we mention dress only when men are expected to wear a jacket or a jacket and tie.

Wine Hungarian wines make up the bulk of the offerings on most Budapest wine lists. While not cheap, most wines are affordable and nearly all are quite drinkable. Some visitors to Hungary find the local wines very good indeed. *Tokaj aszú,* Hungary's unique dessert wine, excites enthusiasts, and you shouldn't miss the chance to taste at least one glass while you're in Hungary. Most restaurants offer at least one white, one red, and one rosé by the glass (called a *pohár*). Wines to choose include whites and Rieslings from Lake Balaton, reds from Villány or Eger, rosés from Szekszárd, and Tokaj aszú from Tokaj. A popular aperitif in Hungary is *pezsgő* (sparking wine), which can be ordered dry (*száraz*) or sweet (*édes*).

Prices Although prices are steadily increasing, there are plenty of good, affordable restaurants offering Hungarian and international dishes. Even though prices in Budapest have increased tremendously in recent years, eating out can provide you with some of the best value for the money of any European capital. In almost all restaurants, an inexpensive prix-fixe lunch called a *napi menü* (daily menu) is available, usually for as little as 1,500 HUF. It includes soup or salad, a main course, and a dessert. Taxes (ÁFA) are included in menu prices but usually broken out on the final bill. There's a 25% tax on drinks and 15% tax on food. Service generally is not included, so an additional tip of 10% to 15% is customary in all restaurants. While rip-offs are less common in Budapest than they once were, it's best to scrutinize your bill in all establishments; restaurants in high-traffic tourist areas have been known to help themselves to a 10% tip before presenting you with the bill.

WHAT IT COSTS in Forints				
$$$$	$$$	$$	$	¢
AT DINNER over 3,500	2,500–3,500	1,500–2,500	800–1,500	under 800

Prices are per person for a main course at dinner and include 15% tax, but not service.

$$$–$$$$ ✕ **Óceán Bar & Grill.** Not long ago, fish entrées were scarce on Budapest menus and were limited to lake and river fish from the Hungarian countryside. So it was with great excitement that locals greeted this dedicated fish restaurant, which imports fish a few times a week—mostly from Scandinavia—and devotes about 85% of its menu to seafood. The Skagen toast starter is plump shrimp salad with dill and salmon roe on black bread. There's lots of salmon here, of course, but also halibut, monkfish, and tuna. For a real treat—and a splurge—chose a lobster from the tank and have it prepared to order. ⊠ *District V, Petőfi tér 3, Around Váci utca* ☎ *1/266–1826* ⊟ *AE, MC, V* Ⓜ *M1: Vórósmarty tér.*

$$–$$$$ ✕ **Papageno.** This tiny restaurant fills up quickly on weekdays with business people looking for well-prepared pasta and Italian dishes. Classy starters like duck breast carpaccio are followed by rich penne with Gorgonzola cheese or homemade gnocchi. Inventive salads are popular here, too, including a caprese salad with smoked chicken breast and basil. The menu is small but well-chosen, and there's a good offering of daily specials. Though it's possible to arrive here on the spur of the moment, it's best to reserve since the restaurant seats only 25. ⊠ *District V, Semmelweis utca 19, Around Deák Ferenc tér* ☎ *1/485–0161* ⊟ *MC, V* ⊘ *Closed Sun. No lunch Sat.* Ⓜ *M2: Astoria.*

$$–$$$ ✕ **Articsóka.** If Pest's urban jungle has got you down, this sunny restaurant will provide a welcome respite from city streets and traffic. The bright yellow interior is furnished with wrought-iron tables and lots of plants, so when you sit down to a candlelit table, you have the feeling you're dining somewhere in the Italian countryside. There's even a terrace upstairs for real alfresco dining when the weather is pleasant. The menu has Mediterranean influences and includes such delights as marinated sardines and *vitello tonnato*. The service is professional. ⊠ *District VI, Zichy Jenőutca 17, Around Andrássy út* ☎ *1/302–7757* ⊟ *AE, MC, V* ⚠ *Reservations essential* Ⓜ *M3: Arany János utca.*

$$–$$$ ✕ **Café Bouchon.** Friendly and attentive service is the hallmark in this French-inspired bistro in the edgy sixth district. Café tables, parquet floors, and a daily menu written on butcher's paper in the back all set the mood for a casual but sophisticated meal. Smoked duck breast salad and steak au poivre are classics on the menu, but the daily specials—usually seasonally inspired—are the real draw. ⊠ *District VI, Zichy Jenőutca 33, Around Andrássy út* ☎ *1/353–4094* ⊟ *No credit cards* ⊘ *Closed Sun.* Ⓜ *M3: Arany János utca.*

$$–$$$ ✕ **Cyrano.** This slick bistro just off Vörösmarty tér has an arty, contemporary bent, with wrought-iron chairs, green-marble floors, and long-stemmed azure glasses. The creative kitchen sends out elegantly presented

ON THE MENU

Csirke paprikás *(chicken paprikash).* This famous dish is made from cubed chicken breast or chicken legs covered in creamy paprika sauce.

Desszertek *(desserts).* Hungarian desserts can be cakes, pancakes, or fresh fruit in season.

Galuska *(semolina dumplings).* These thimble-sized dumplings are served with popular stews such as borjúpaprikás *(veal paprikash).*

Gesztenyepüré *(chestnut puree).* Chestnuts are ground with sugar, cream, and nutmeg to create this mound of light brown puree. It's usually served as a dessert in the winter.

Gulyásleves *(goulash soup).* While goulash is known outside of Hungary as a stew, it's mostly served in Hungary as a soup made of paprika-flavored beef broth, cubed beef, parsnips, and carrots.

Gundel palacsinta *(Gundel pancakes).* Made famous by Gundel restaurant, these light dessert crepes are stuffed with walnuts and served with chocolate sauce.

Halászlé *(spicy fish soup).* This soup is made from carp fillets and seasoned with spicy paprika.

Hortobágyi palacsinta *(Hortobagy pancakes).* These meat-stuffed pancakes get their name from a village in the Great Plain. The light pancakes are stuffed, rolled, and covered with a creamy paprika sauce. They are heavy and are usually served as an appetizer.

Lángos *(fried dough).* This popular but greasy street food is available at most Hungarian markets. It comes plain or with cheese, cabbage, or dill, and you can smear it with sour cream and garlic.

Lecsó *(a vegetable compote made of peppers, onions, tomato, and paprika).* Lecsó is a multi-purpose Hungarian vegetable dish, which can be served as a sauce on top of steaks, as an accompaniment to seared goose liver, or even mixed in with eggs for breakfast.

Libamaj *(goose liver).* One of the celebrated culinary treats in Hungary, goose liver is made into rich pâtés or seared whole and served with a light fruit sauce.

Pálinka *(fruit spirits).* This homegrown brandy is a popular drink to start off a Hungarian meal. Barack *(apricot)* and szliva *(plum)* are the two most widely available flavors.

Pogácsa *(scones).* These irresistible baked biscuits can be plain or savory and are available in most bake shops. Different flavors include sajtos *(cheese)* or tepertős *(spicy crackling).*

Rétes *(strudel).* Light pastry is filled with cheese, apples, raisins, or sour cherries and is a popular cake with coffee.

Sült libacomb *(crispy-fried goose leg).* A popular main course in many Hungarian restaurants, succulent goose legs are usually served with steamed red cabbage.

Téliszalámi *(Hungarian salami).* This delicious long-life salami from Szeged is made of 100% pork and has a very strong, smoky flavor. There are two big manufacturers, Pick and Herz.

Töltött káposzta *(stuffed cabbage).* Boiled cabbage is stuffed with meat and rice; this is a popular winter main course.

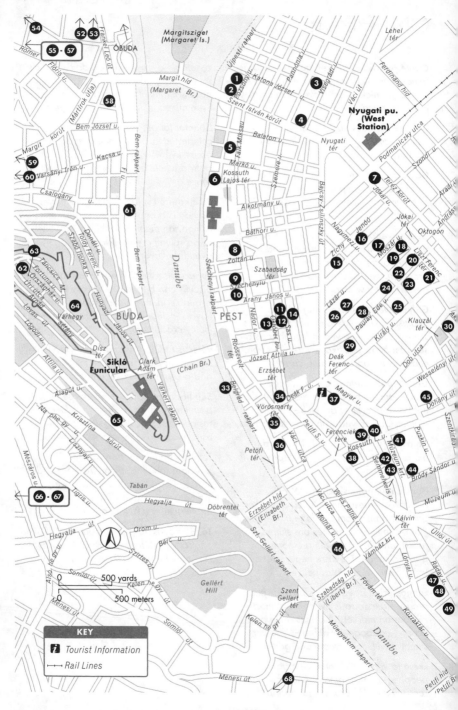

KEY

i   *Tourist Information*

↦ *Rail Lines*

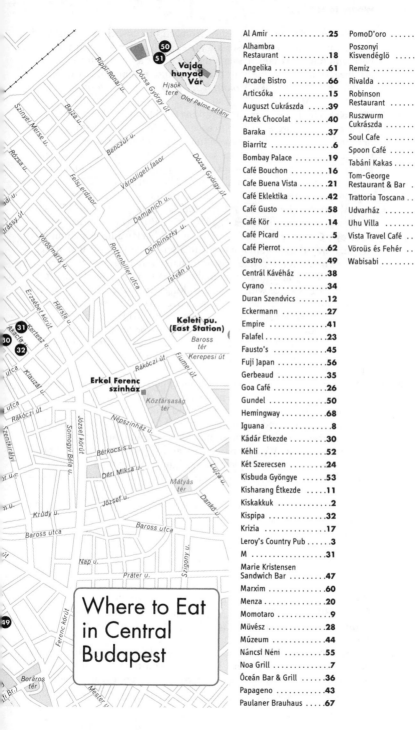

Where to Eat in Central Budapest

Hungarian and Continental dishes, from standards such as goulash and chicken paprikás to more esoteric tastes such as tender fried Camembert with blueberry jam. Though the prices are a bit high for what you get, the restaurant is in the heart of the Váci utca shopping district. ✉ *District V, Kristóf tér 7–8, Around Váci utca* ✍ *Reservations essential* 🖃 *AE, DC, MC, V.*

$$–$$$ ✗ **Empire.** This is one eating and drinking establishment that anyone nostalgic for Hapsburg-era magnificence shouldn't miss. Crystal chandeliers and antique furniture evoke a time of grand dining, especially once the live piano music begins. After sinking into one of the very comfortable leather chairs, you'll enjoy the insulation from the traffic outside on Kossuth Lajos street—and indeed the whole 21st century. Game dishes, such as wild boar cutlets with cherry sauce, are the noted specialty. ✉ *District V, Kossuth Lajos utca 19, Around Ferenciak tere* ☎ *1/317–3411* ✍ *Reservations essential* 🖃 *AE, DC, MC, V* Ⓜ *M3: Astoria.*

$$–$$$ ✗ **Leroy's Country Pub.** There's an air of laid-back California about this bright, modern restaurant not far from Nyugati pályaudvar with its big, wide-open bar, comfortable, worn-in chairs, and huge windows facing the street. The place can buzz at night, when trendy young Hungarians are sharing bar space with expats drinking exotic cocktails. The menu includes international pleasers, such as oven-roasted rosemary chicken, plus quite a few vegetarian options, including grilled eggplant, cream and mushroom risotto. The steaks, which can be ordered in sizes up to one kilo, are among the most reliable in Budapest. ✉ *District XIII, Visegrádi utca 50/a, Around Nyugati Train Station* ☎ *1/340–3316* 🖃 *AE, MC, V* Ⓜ *M3: Nyugati pu.*

$–$$ ✗ **Wabisabi.** For a real change of atmosphere, escape from the noisy 13th district into a zone of Zen-like calm at this vegan restaurant and tea house. There's a feeling of sanity and relaxation inside, where low tables, dim lights, and a soft-spoken staff look after your needs. The menu offers a variety of options, including pairings meant to bring you more into balance. Well-prepared tofu and vegetarian dishes and tasty soy shakes arm you for the next leg of sightseeing or shopping. ✉ *District XIII, Visegrádi utca 2, Around Nyugati Train Station* ☎ *1/412–0427* Ⓜ *M3: Nyugati pu.*

$ ✗ **Kádár Étkezde.** The walls are decorated with celebrities from years gone by and the tables are topped with old-fashioned spritzer bottles from which you serve yourself water. These are small tip-offs that this home-style family restaurant has been around for a while. But to its credit, there are generations of fans. Good old-fashioned Hungarian food is the thing here, including stuffed kohlrabi, *káposztás kocka* (cabbage pasta), and lots of boiled beef. Everyone orders the tasty raspberry *(málna)* drink. Tell the cashier at the door what you ate, and pay there. It's only open from 11:30 to 3:30. ✉ *District VII, Klauzá tér, Around Király utca* ☎ *No phone* 🖃 *No credit cards* ⊘ *Closed Sat.–Mon. No dinner* Ⓜ *M2: Blaha Lujza tér.*

¢–$ ✗ **Noa Grill.** This clean, spacious Israeli-owned fast food restaurant is the best choice for falafel or döner kebab in the bustling Nyugati area. And it's just about the only option for anything decent to eat after midnight. Pizzas are being freshly made at all hours, and there are two or three fresh salads to choose from. ⊠ *District VI, Terez Körút, Around Nyugati Train Station* ☎ *No phone* ▭ *No credit cards* Ⓜ *M3: Nyugati pu.*

Near St. Stephen's Basilica

$$–$$$$ ✕ **Café Kör.** The wrought-iron tables, vaulted ceilings, and crisp white
Fodor'sChoice tablecloths give this chic bistro a decidedly downtown feel. In the heart
★ of the busy fifth district, Café Kör is ideal for lunch or dinner when touring nearby St. Stephen's Basilica, although it's best to go early since the place enjoys a loyal local following. True to bistro aspirations, the daily specials are scribbled on the wall, in both Hungarian and English. Let the friendly waitstaff guide you—even if steamed leg of veal sounds a bit less than tempting, it's heavenly. Grilled ewe cheese salad is a favorite with regulars. ⊠ *District V, Sas utca 17, Szent István Bazilika* ☎ *1/311–0053* ⚑ *Reservations essential* ▭ *No credit cards* ◷ *Closed Sun.* Ⓜ *M3: Arany János utca.*

★ $$–$$$$ ✕ **Tom-George Restaurant & Bar.** Well-situated in the heart of downtown, Tom-George is Budapest's answer to urban chic. The spacious bar blends blond wood and wicker, giving the interior a relaxed yet sophisticated feel. Evenings find a young and stylish crowd choosing from the expansive cocktail menu. Minimalism at the table, though, belies exotic creativity in the kitchen. House specialties include Indian green curry chicken with naan, and lamb satay. Sushi—perhaps Budapest's best—is glamorously prepared in a corner of the dining room. Service is stylish and professional. ⊠ *District V, Október 6 utca 8, St. Stephen's Basilica* ☎ *1/266–3525* ⚑ *Reservations essential* ▭ *AE, V* Ⓜ *M3: Arany János utca.*

$$–$$$ ✕ **PomoD'oro.** Real Italian pizzas, made to order in a brick oven, attract a hungry business crowd during the week. Weekends find just as many people enjoying pastas like the priest strangler—homemade pasta in tomato ragout flambéed with Parmesan cheese. It makes quite a spectacular presentation. The seating here has rustic tables on many levels fenced in by wrought iron. Exposed bricks and hanging plants give the place a Tuscan patio feel. ⊠ *District V, Arany János utca 9, St. Stephen's Basilica* ☎ *1/302–6473* ▭ *AE, MC, V* Ⓜ *M3: Arany János utca.*

$$–$$$ ✕ **Spoon Café.** For a world-class view of Castle Hill, the Chain Bridge, and the Danube, step aboard this hip restaurant and café boat, moored in the heart of downtown Pest across from the Inter-Continental Hotel. Cocktail hour is crowded with tourists and residents alike, enjoying the spectacular view. Stylishly prepared international food like lemon chicken Caesar salad keeps the crowds happy. The food's even a bit better than you might expect, given the touristy locale. There are tempting choices here for vegetarians, like grilled goat cheese sandwiches and homemade pastas. Take notice of the bill, though, before you pay; unlike most other places in the city, service here is included. ⊠ *District V, Vigado tér St. Stephen's Basilica* ☎ *1/411–0933* ▭ *AE, MC, V* Ⓜ *M1: Vörösmarty tér.*

¢ ✕ **Duran Szendvics.** You feel almost like a kid in a candy store standing outside the window of this take-away sandwich shop at lunchtime. Beautiful rows of canapés are delicately piled with fluffy egg salad, ham with black caviar, pickled herring salad, and spicy pepperoni, each with a pretty sprig of curly parsley. Take a box of four, six, or eight and walk one block around the corner to the benches in front of St. Stephen's and enjoy a lovely picnic. It gets crowded at lunch, and the inventory is usually cleaned out by 4. ⊠ *District V, Október 6 utca 15, Szent István Bazilika* ☎ *1/332–9348* ▤ *No credit cards* ⊙ *Closed Sun. No dinner* Ⓜ *M3: Arany János utca.*

¢　✕ **Kisharang Étkezde.** There are only three tables and a counter at this tiny home-style restaurant not far from the Basilica. It gets a lunch crowd early and bustles well into the late afternoon with downtown professional types, closing right after early dinner (by 8 PM). Dishes Hungarian grandmothers make, including goose-dumpling soup and stuffed cabbage with pork, elicit smiles from most patrons. Daily specials generally come in two sizes, but even the biggest is cheaper than anything else in this area. ⊠ *District V, Október 6 utca 17, St. Stephen's Basilica* ☎ *1/269–3861* ▤ *No credit cards* ⊙ *No dinner weekends* Ⓜ *M3: Arany János utca.*

Parliament

$$–$$$　✕ **Biarritz.** This restaurant and café on a quiet residential street not far from Parliament originally opened its doors in 1938 to serve nearby politicians. Some 60 years later, it has reopened under the same name and today serves more or less the same clientele. The menu has strong French overtones and is known locally for its escargots, frogs' legs, and excellent steak au poivre. There are innovative Hungarian dishes as well, including larded pheasant with apple and quince. Lunch can be crowded. ⊠ *District V, Kossuth tér 18, Parliament* ☎ *1/311–4413* ▤ *AE, MC, V* Ⓜ *M2: Kossuth Lajos tér.*

$–$$$　✕ **Iguana.** People have been going to Iguana for its friendly service, big draft beers, and satisfying Mexican food for so long now that it's become almost a Budapest institution. Tex-Mex classics include whoop-ass chili and jalapeño poppers. It's a good place to go for a light bite and a beer as well as a full lunch or dinner. Jenő's favorite quesadilla is chock-full of chorizo, cheese, tomatoes, and guacamole and is perfect with a margarita. In summer, there's an easy-going mixed bar scene that spills out onto the street. ⊠ *District V, Zoltán utca 16, Parliament* ☎ *1/331–4352* ▤ *AE, MC, V* Ⓜ *M2: Kossuth Lajos tér.*

$–$$$　✕ **Kiskakukk.** The art deco facade of the Little Cuckoo restaurant evokes
Fodor's Choice　the history of this once-fashionable residential neighborhood. The set-
★　ting today is comfortable; wood-paneled walls and leather-upholstered chairs give the place a sophisticated, albeit homey, feel. All the classic Hungarian poultry dishes are well done, include goose and duck leg with cabbage, and there are a few refined dishes, too, such as veal medallions in cream sauce and lamb with rosemary. Service is friendly and attentive. ⊠ *District XIII, Pozsonyi utca 12, Parliament* ☎ *1/450–0829* ▤ *MC, V* Ⓜ *M3: Nyugati Pu.*

¢–$　✕ **Momotaro.** You'll find very few empty lunchtime tables at this bustling Asian restaurant not far from the Parliament. Big bowls of steaming *ramen* satisfy most diners, but scallion pizza and pork dumplings steamed in a bamboo pot have their fans. There's a big range of sautéed fresh vegetables available as well. The seating area isn't much, just a few low wooden tables and a counter, but turnover is quick most days. ⊠ *District V, Széchenyi utca 16, Parliament* ☎ *1/269–3802* ▤ *No credit cards* Ⓜ *M2: Kossuth Lajos tér.*

¢–$ ✗ **Poszonyi Kisvendéglő.** Rock-bottom prices ensure a crowd most days for lunch and dinner at this well-loved neighborhood *vendeglő* (restaurant serving home-cooking). Big bowls of *Jókai bableves* (bean soup) are sopped up with fresh white bread, and classics like *borjúpaprikás* (veal paprikash) are made the way Hungarian grandmothers used to make them—with plenty of lard. ✉ *District XIII Pozsonyi utca (corner of Radnóti Miklos u.)*, *Parliament* ☎ *1/329–2911* ⚄ *Reservations essential* ⊟ *No credit cards* Ⓜ *M3: Nyugati Pu.*

Around Andrássy út

$$$–$$$$ ✗ **Krizia.** Locals rate this Italian restaurant as one of the best in town for its homemade pastas like pumpkin ravioli and tagliatelli with asparagus and lemon. Other Italian classics like veal saltimbocca and carpaccio with *rucola* (arugula) and Parmesan are perennial favorites. The wine list here includes a reasonably priced selection of Italian vintages. The rustic cellar setting of brick, stucco, and wood is remarkably bright and intimate. ✉ *District VI, Moszár utca 12, Around Andrássy út* ☎ *1/331–8711* ⊟ *MC, V* ☉ *Closed Sun.* Ⓜ *M1: Oktogon.*

$$–$$$ ✗ **Alhambra Restaurant.** Tucked away on Jókai tér, across the street from busy Liszt Ferenc tér, this tiny Moroccan restaurant beckons visitors to the exotic world of North Africa. Low wooden tables, kilims on the wall, and an intricate interior balcony all evoke the feeling of a well-to-do Marrakesh *riad*. Tasty lamb and chicken tagines are served in the classic conical clay pots, and there's a big selection of couscous. Other dishes, such as grilled chicken breast with baked oranges and garlic-almond soup, make you feel like you're worlds away from Central Europe. ✉ *District VI, Jókai tér, Around Andrássy út* ☎ *1/354–1068* ⊟ *MC, V* ☉ *No lunch Sun.* Ⓜ *M1: Oktogon.*

$$–$$$ ✗ **Goa Café.** The airy, monochromatic design of this two-floor modern restaurant on Andrássy út has a decidedly Asian feel. Light-colored stone floors, rattan vases and placemats, and minimalist lighting all evoke Asia, though no specific place. The bar, which faces the streetside window, is a popular place for drinks. The kitchen turns out some high-quality fusion food, including blackened ahi tuna with wasabi soy dressing and Goan pork vindaloo, as well as some offbeat Mediterranean dishes, such as shiitake ravioli. You can order smaller salads and sandwiches at the bar all day. ✉ *District VI, Andrássy út 8, Around Andrássy út* ☎ *1/302–2570* ⊟ *AE, MC, V* Ⓜ *M1: Opera.*

$$–$$$ ✗ **Két Szerecsen.** Long a local favorite, Két Szerecsen keeps diners happy all day long with fresh and affordable soups, salads, and daily specials. The kitchen has a light touch with cold soups, especially the cucumber, dill, and gazpacho varieties. There's a small tapas menu with things like *tzatziki* (garlic cheese spread) topped with marinated olives, as well as daily quiches. The cozy, orange interior has café tables and copper lamps with vintage posters on the walls. It can get a bit smoky inside in the winter, but there's outdoor seating in the summer. It's open daily for breakfast. ✉ *District VI, Nagymező utca, Around Andrássy út* ☎ *1/343–1984* ⊟ *MC, V* Ⓜ *M1: Oktogon.*

$$–$$$ ✗ **Vörös és Fehér.** Hungarian wines are showcased in this modern yet
Fodor's Choice cozy bistro on bustling Andrássy út, close to the Opera and the Music
★ Academy. Owned by the Budapest Wine Society, this place takes wines

CloseUp
HUNGARY'S FAVORITE SPICE

AROUND THE WORLD, *Hungarian food is closely identified with bright-red paprika. Hungary's two most famous dishes, gulyás leves (goulash soup) and csirke paprikás (chicken paprikash), are brought to life with the rich, red spice. However, the peppers ground to make fragrant paprika—so closely associated with Hungarian cuisine—were only introduced to the country in the middle of the 19th century. Fame was assured, though, when in 1879 Auguste Escoffier brought the ground red powder from Szeged to the Grand Hotel in Monte Carlo and introduced it as a Hungarian spice. From that point on, paprika has been a vital ingredient to the national cuisine. It comes in many forms, from light and sweet to bold and fiery. Many Hungarian dishes, such as chicken paprikash, begin with paprika mixed with oil, onions, and flour, making a roux. Meat is cooked with the paprika roux and then mixed with cream to give the dish its light color and rich depth.*

Other dishes like goulash soup are flavored with paprika at the beginning of the cooking cycle and simmered over low heat for hours. While its rich flavor is only released in hot oil, many a Hungarian néni (great aunt) will warn novice chefs to use paprika judiciously. Removing the pan from heat when adding the delicate spice prevents paprika from burning and turning bitter.

Paprika is available in all Hungarian supermarkets. The varieties include különleges (special), the highest-quality version, which has a pleasantly spicy aroma and is very finely ground; édes (sweet), which has a rich color, mild aroma, and is somewhat coarsely ground; csipős (hot), which is light brown with yellowish tones, has a fiery flavor, and is coarsely ground; rózsa (rose), bright red in color, medium spicy, and medium-ground; and csemege (mild), which is light red in color, has a rich aroma, and is medium-ground.

---

seriously. Order a taster plate of olives or a hearty country pâté to pair with Hungary's best vintages, many available very reasonably by the glass. Main courses are seasonally inspired and the menu changes weekly. There's a good choice of vegetarian options, such as a trio of creams (dips) including smoked ewe cheese, paprika salsa, and Transylvanian eggplant caviar. ⊠ *District VI, Andrássy út 41, Around Andrássy út* ☎ *1/413–1545* ⊟ *MC, V* Ⓜ *M1: Opera.*

$$ ✕ **Bombay Palace.** This international chain set up Budapest's first Indian restaurant in 1994 and has enjoyed a loyal following ever since by providing first-class service and elegantly prepared Indian classics like lamb *vindaloo,* chicken *madras* (in coconut tomato sauce), and *saag paneer* (spinach with ewe cheese). There's a full range of fresh-baked Indian breads and lovely mango chutney to boot. All the dishes are brought to your table in small silver pots and served by obsequious waiters. ⊠ *District VI, Andrássy út. 44, Around Andrássy út* ☎ *1/332–8363* ⊟ *AE, MC, V* Ⓜ *M1: Oktogon.*

$–$$ ✕ **Kispipa.** If you find yourself wandering the streets of Andrássy, near Király utca, this old-time favorite is a good stop for lunch and a glimpse of old Pest. Don't be surprised if other patrons don't look at menus; most of them have been lunching here for decades. It's a somewhat shabby interior, but the wizened staff is authentic and really perfect for the place. Venison tarragon ragout soup is a crowd-pleaser, as is the *birka pörkölt* (mutton stew). ⊠ *District VII, Akácfa út 38, Around Király utca* ☎ 1/ 342–3969 ▭ *AE, MC, V* Ⓜ *M1: Oktogon.*

$–$$ ✗ **Menza.** This clever vision of a 1970s-style Communist-era cafeteria
Fodor'sChoice right in the heart of trendy Liszt Ferenc tér is a big hit. Details like retro
★ table settings, orange and olive green Formica, and the very worst in Communist lighting design miraculously come together to evoke warm childhood memories. Quirky dishes like homemade Hungarian soups served with cereal croutons get a giggle from most diners. Greasy childhood treats like *langós* (fried dough) get reinvented and stuffed with chicken and mushrooms. In spite of the groovy vibe, there's good old-fashioned Hungarian comfort food here and pretty attentive, non–Communist-era service. ⊠ *District VI, Liszt Ferenc tér 2, Around Andrássy út* ☎ *1/413–1482* ▭ *MC, V* Ⓜ *M1: Oktogon.*

$ ✗ **Al Amir.** When poking in shops along Király utca, treat yourself to the tastes of the Middle East in this long-standing Syrian restaurant, popular with Budapesters. Inside there's a painted mural of the Aleppo citadel with built-in running water. There are the usual *meze*—including hummus and eggplant dip—as well as a light lentil soup to start. Main courses are heavy on lamb, but the chicken is popular, too, and the *sistauk* (kebabs) come with homemade lemony mayonnaise. Save room for fresh honey-and-pistachio pastries and mint tea for dessert. If you're on the move, you can get a *shawarma* to go from the take-away shop in front. ⊠ *District VII, Király utca 17, Around Andrássy út* ☎ *1/352– 1422* ▭ *MC, V* Ⓜ *M1: Oktogon.*

$ ✗ **M.** A couple of upstarts opened this hole-in-the-wall restaurant a few years ago in the edgy seventh district not far from the popular kerts (summer bars). The entire restaurant is outfitted in brown paper bags, with things like windows and pictures frames drawn on. The daily Hungarian menu is limited to only three or four specials a night and if you don't get there early you won't have much choice; they run out of most things by 9. It's popular with students, who can be found there most evenings, drinking glasses of affordable red wine. ⊠ *District VII, Kertész utca 48, Around Andrássy út* ☎ *1/342–8991* ▭ *No credit cards* ☾ *No lunch* Ⓜ *M1: Oktogon.*

★ **$** ✗ **Vista Travel Café.** A favorite of Hungarian business lunchers, seasoned expats, and even backpackers, Vista is a curious but successful hybrid of brassiere, cybercafé, meeting place, and information center. The action in the kitchen can creak at times, but dual-language menus cheerfully warn you of that fact. Be patient; you can fill in the paper place-mat feedback forms while you wait for healthy, nutritious food to arrive. Highlights include the club sandwich, quiche Lorraine, pastas, and all-day breakfast menu. ⊠ *District VII, Paulay Ede utca 7, Around Andrássy út* ☎ *1/268–0888* ▭ *AE, DC, MC, V* Ⓜ *M1: Oktogon.*

¢–$ ✗ **Falafel.** This tiny take-away joint is one of Budapest's original salad bars and still one of the best. It is possible to get a seat upstairs but you have to be *very* lucky during the lunch hour, when the place is packed to the gills with health-conscious young professionals. Lots of Middle Eastern options like falafel and hummus are here, as well as fresh vegetables and legumes. A few holdovers from the good old days can be had, too, like frozen carrot and pea "salad" in a bath of mayonnaise. ⊠ *District VI, Paulay Ede utca 23, corner of Nagymező, Around Király utca* ☎ *1/351–1243* 🖃 *No credit cards* ⊘ *Closed weekends* Ⓜ *M1: Oktogon.*

Around Kálvin tér

★ **$$$–$$$$** ✕ **Baraka.** The gauzy beige curtains and giant vases of birds of paradise are offset by leather banquettes and light wood floors in this popular restaurant on quiet Magyar utca. The kitchen here is one of the best in the city thanks to chef David Seboek, a transplanted New Yorker who's helped redefine the Budapest dining scene. The menu shows Asian and French overtones and includes taste sensations that truly delight: boneless saddle of lamb in cardamom and orange sauce, and duck breast with ginger-apple soy sauce. The desserts don't disappoint either; the chocolate volcano is a spectacle of feather-light pastry and gooey chocolate filling. ⊠ *District V, Magyar utca 12–14, Around Kálvin tér* ☎ *1/483–1355* ⚑ *Reservations essential* 🖃 *AE, DC, MC, V* ⊘ *Closed Sun.* Ⓜ *M2: Astoria.*

$$–$$$ ✕ **Múzeum.** This old timer is a surprisingly affordable option for traditional cuisine served in turn-of-the-20th-century style. A beautifully frescoed ceiling and tables set with sterling silver and Zsolnay porcelain exude an elegant, if somewhat faded, grandeur. Hungarian classics here, such as *Hortobágyi palacsinta* (pancakes), and crispy goose leg with steamed cabbage, are accomplished, but the menu also includes a few ill-conceived fish dishes like sushi. Stick with pork or veal paired with a good red wine from Villány (Bock or Gere are always safe choices); the wine list is extensive and well-chosen ⊠ *District VIII, Múzeum krt. 11, Around Kálvin tér* ☎ *1/338–4221* 🍸 *Jacket and tie* 🖃 *MC, V* ⊘ *Closed Sun.* Ⓜ *M2: Kálvin tér.*

$$–$$$ ✕ **Soul Cafe.** Big club chairs and mustard-colored walls covered with framed textiles warm up this Mediterranean restaurant on up-and-coming Ráday utca. Grilled sandwiches and ample salads please vegetarians, and there's a good range of chicken and turkey dishes if you want to go non-veg. The zucchini cake with Camembert and sun-dried tomatoes wins just about everyone over. ⊠ *District IX, Ráday utca 11–13, Around Kálvin tér* ☎ *1/217–6986* 🖃 *MC, V* Ⓜ *M3: Kálvin tér.*

★ **$$–$$$** ✕ **Trattoria Toscana.** Visiting Italians tell us this popular trattoria feels pretty authentic, with its bustling waiters, rustic interior, and wooden tables filled with families on Sunday. An antipasti bar in front overflows with marinated artichokes, white bean salad, and other classic Tuscan treats and there's a well-worn brick pizza oven in back. The extensive menu boasts some of the best fish in town, including several sea bass options. The little understood mozzarella *ventigli* pasta with San Marzano tomatoes and fresh oregano (homemade cheese-filled ravioli with garlicky tomatoes and lots of oregano) is a dish to die for. ⊠ *District V, Belgrád Rakpart 13, Around Kálvin tér* ☎ *1/327–0045* ⚑ *Reservations essential* 🖃 *AE, DC, MC, V* Ⓜ *M3: Kálvin tér.*

$ ✕ **Castro.** The biggest surprise here may be that—despite the name—the specialty at this Communist-theme bar and restaurant is Serbian, not Cuban, food. Tasty *pleskavica* (spicy hamburgers) and *čevapčiči* (spicy meatballs) are served all day to a largely student crowd, who come mainly for the cheap draft beer. ⊠ *District IX, Ráday utca 25, Around Kálvin tér* ⊟ *No credit cards* Ⓜ *M3: Kálvin tér.*

¢ ✕ **Marie Kristensen Sandwich Bar.** Sandwiches are not a typical Hungarian lunch choice, but this Scandinavia-theme sandwich bar was a big hit with expats when it opened in the early 1990s. It's still a popular haunt for its fresh salad bar and innovative sandwiches. The "Norway Student" is tuna, bacon, and Camembert cheese; the "Viking" is tuna, egg salad, and smoked cheese. There's a small seating area in the back, but you can get everything to go or call for a delivery if you're not nearby. ⊠ *District IX, Ráday utca 7, Around Kálvin tér* ☎ *1/218–1673* ⊟ *No credit cards* ⊘ *Closed Sun.* Ⓜ *M3: Kálvin tér.*

North Buda & the Buda Hills

★ **$$$–$$$$** ✕ **Uhu Villa.** Once you find this elegant restaurant in a villa in the hills around Hűvösvölgy, you'll feel like you're in a distant relative's country estate, and you may even want to spend the night in the attached hotel. Whether in the intimate dining room or breezy terrace, you'll find some of the best Italian food in Budapest here. The sophisticated menu of antipasti, homemade pasta, and fish is selective; the chef relies on fresh ingredients found at local markets to make a new menu each day. Often, he turns up tableside to let you know what's good. ⊠ *District II, Keselý utca 1/a, Buda Hills* ☎ *1/275–1002* ⊕ *www.uhuvilla.hu* ⊟ *AE, MC, V* ⊘ *Closed Sun.*

$$–$$$$ ✕ **Fuji Japan.** An aura of Zen-like calm permeates this long-standing Japanese restaurant in the affluent Rószadomb district of Upper Buda. Comfortable club chairs and big windows make you feel miles away from the hustle and bustle of downtown Pest. Tables are set a comfortable distance apart so that you can watch the Japanese and Hungarian chefs work their craft in this full-service restaurant. Sushi and sashimi are expertly prepared, as are other Japanese specialties such as teriyaki tenderloin with sesame and mushroom tempura. There's even a separate dining room where you can eat at low tables, in traditional Japanese style. ⊠ *District II, Csatárka utca 54/b, Buda Hills* ☎ *1/325–7870* ⊟ *AE, DC, MC, V.*

$$$ ✕ **Udvarház.** The views from this Buda hilltop restaurant are unsurpassed. As you dine indoors at tables set with white linens or outdoors on the open terrace, your meals are accompanied by vistas of the Danube bridges and Parliament far below. Excellent fresh fish is prepared tableside; you could also try veal and goose liver in paprika sauce, served with salty cottage-cheese dumplings. Catering to the predominantly tourist crowd, folklore shows and live Gypsy music frequently enliven the scene. The buses up here are infrequent, so it's easier to take a car or taxi. ⊠ *District III, Hármashatárhegyi út 2, North Buda* ☎ *1/388–6921* ⊟ *AE, DC, MC, V* ⊘ *Closed Mon. Nov.–Mar. No lunch weekdays Nov.–Mar.*

$$
Fodor'sChoice
★
✕ **Náncsi Néni.** "Auntie Nancsi" has built a loyal following by serving up straightforward, home-style Hungarian cuisine in rustic surroundings. Chains of paprika and garlic dangle from the low wooden ceiling above tables set with red-and-white gingham tablecloths and fresh bread tucked into tiny baskets. Shelves along the walls are crammed with jars of home-pickled vegetables, which you can purchase to take home. The

menu includes turkey breast fillets stuffed with apples, peaches, mushrooms, cheese, and sour cream. There is a garden dining area open during warmer months, when reservations are essential. ⊠ *District III, Ördögárok út 80, North Buda* ☎ *1/397–2742* ⊟ *AE, DC, MC, V.*

Around Moskva tér & Castle Hill

☾ **$$$–$$$$** ✕ **Remiz.** The facade of this upscale restaurant in leafy Buda is fashioned out of an old tram depot that marks its history. The spacious restaurant includes a dining room to suit any season, including a *söröz* (beer cellar), a glass-enclosed room, a richly paneled dining room, and an outdoor terrace. There's a jungle gym and sandbox outside for kids, and that makes the terrace very popular in the summer. Buda families like the grilled meat cooked on a lava stone, including mouth-watering spare ribs. It's no surprise that the chocolate profiteroles are popular with children, not to mention their parents. ⊠ *District II, Budakeszi út 5, Around Moskva tér* ☎ *1/275–1396 or 1/200–3843* ⌕ *Reservations essential* ⊟ *AE, DC, MC, V.*

$$–$$$$ ✕ **Rivalda.** On summer nights, you can choose to dine outside in an 18th-century courtyard or in the restaurant's rather rococo interior—with poplin stage curtains, theatrical masks, and peach-colored walls. The food is a lighter take on Hungarian cuisine, with some excellent seafood dishes including cream of pumpkin bisque with smoked salmon, and fillet of pike perch. A terrific place for a celebration, whether intimate or with a group, Rivalda has a substantial vegetarian menu, still something of a rarity in Budapest. ⊠ *District I, Színház utca 5–9, Castle Hill* ☎ *1/489–0236* ⌕ *Reservations essential* ⊟ *AE, DC, MC, V.*

$–$$$ ✕ **Café Pierrot.** When touring the sights of Castle Hill tuck into this invit-
Fodor'sChoice ing café for a relaxing lunch. You may not want to leave once you hear
★ the soothing live jazz piano and see the charming interior—walls covered with paintings of harlequins and fresh flowers on the tables. The menu includes updated Hungarian favorites, as well as inventive pastas and sandwiches. With a free wireless Internet access available to customers, this is the best choice for a break in the Castle District. ⊠ *District I, Fortuna utca 14, Castle Hill* ☎ *1/375–6971* ⊟ *AE, DC, MC, V.*

$–$$ ✕ **Café Gusto.** Hidden away on a leafy street not far from the Margit bridge this tiny café turns out some of the best salads in town. The Italian-influenced menu is limited, but you won't find better carpaccio or tiramisu in Budapest. Otherwise, the always-crowded spot only offers cold salads and light seafood dishes. ⊠ *District II, Frankel Leó utca 12, Around Moskva tér* ☎ *1/316–3970* ⌕ *Reservations essential* ⊟ *No credit cards* ☉ *Closed Sun.*

$ ✕ **Marxim.** Relive the good old bad days of "goulash socialism" in this tongue-in-cheek tribute to Hungary's Communist past. Vintage propaganda posters cover the walls, and dining booths are even separated by barbed wire. The pizza here is perfectly serviceable, although the blaring techno and house music that sometimes plays in the background might be too revolutionary for some. As well as many standard pizzas, the menu includes theme pizzas, including the "Gulag Pizza," which is more nourishing than it sounds, as it includes just about everything: peppers, onions, salami, mushrooms. ⊠ *District II, Kis Rókus utca 23, Around Moskva tér* ☎ *1/316–0231* ⊟ *AE, DC, MC, V* ☉ *Closed Sun.*

Óbuda

$$–$$$ ✗ **Kéhli.** This pricey but laid-back, sepia-toned neighborhood tavern is on a hard-to-find street near the Óbuda end of the Árpád Bridge. Practically all the food here arrives in huge servings, which was just the way that Hungarian writer Gyula Krúdy (to whom the restaurant is dedicated) liked it, when he was a regular customer. Dishes like the hot pot with marrow bone and toast, or *lecsó* (a stew with a base of onions, peppers, tomatoes, and paprika) are great comfort food on a cool day. ⊠ *District III, Mókus utca 22, Óbuda* ☎ *1/250–4241 or 1/368–0613* ▤ *AE, DC, MC, V* ⊘ *No lunch weekdays.*

★ **$$–$$$** ✗ **Kisbuda Gyöngye.** Considered by many the finest restaurant in Óbuda, this intimate place is filled with antique furniture and decorated with an eclectic but elegant patchwork of carved, wooden cupboard doors and panels. The mood is set by the veteran pianist who can serenade guests in a dozen languages, but who is at his best with Hungarian ballads. Meat and game dishes stand out here. Try the tarragon ragout of game, or sample the goose wedding feast, a richly flavorful dish that includes a crispy goose leg with braised red cabbage, grilled goose liver, and lightly fried goose cracklings. ⊠ *District III, Kenyeres utca 34, Óbuda* ☎ *1/368–6402 or 1/368–9246* ⚄ *Reservations essential* ▤ *AE, DC, MC, V* ⊘ *Closed Sun.*

Gellért-hegy & the Tabán

$$–$$$$ ✗ **Hemingway.** It takes some brio to pull off a restaurant with the style of Ernest Hemingway, but when that restaurant is housed in what looks like a 19th-century hunting lodge—complete with wooden balcony and lake views—the odds for success start to look better. The menu includes several kinds of seafood cooked on Mediterranean lava stone. Fans of heroic consumption will also appreciate a cocktail menu with 100-some drinks, and a selection of after-dinner cigars. ⊠ *District XI, Kosztolányi Dezso tér 2, on Feneketlen Lake, South Buda* ☎ *1/489–0236* ⚄ *Reservations essential* ▤ *AE, DC, MC, V.*

★ **$$$** ✗ **Arcade Bistro.** Upscale residents of the 12th district pay regular patronage to this modern, sophisticated bistro on a leafy intersection not far from Déli Pályaudvar. The floor-to-ceiling waterfall smack in the middle of the dining room soothes as it keeps conversations discreet and complements the unfussy interior. Classy starters, such as first-rate caviar and breast of duck and ruccola (arugula) salad, prepare you for innovative game dishes and seasonal specialties. The smart and courteous staff will help you choose a wine from the refined list, all available by the glass. ⊠ *District XII, Kíss János Alt. utca 38, Around Déli Train Station* ☎ *1/225–1969* ▤ *MC, V* ⊘ *No dinner Sun.* Ⓜ *M2: Déli pu.*

$$–$$$ ✗ **Paulaner Brauhaus.** There's a lively mood at this German brewery and beerhall most nights, even though it's hidden away in a shopping mall. Big wooden tables fill three separate rooms, and there's space enough for impromptu dancing if the band gets you going. Solid Bavarian classics like *weisswürst* with honey mustard, and frankfurters with sauerkraut keep the crowd happy, and there's a wide selection of Paulaner beers on draft, including amber ales, pilsners, and light lagers. The classic *weissbier* is served in a huge mug with a lemon. ⊠ *District XII, Mom Park*

Shopping Center, Alkotás utca, Around Déli Train Station ☎ *1/224–2020* ☜ *Reservations essential* ▤ *AE, MC, V.*

$$ ✕ **Tabáni Kakas.** The owner of the Taban Rooster, a friendly no-frills *vendéglő* (restaurant with home cooking) usually stops by to play a few songs at the piano in the evening. Regulars love the place for its homey feel and well-prepared poultry dishes. Crispy duck leg, and goose soup with dumplings are standards, as is the tasty and filling pork dish known only as Rózsa Sándor's favorite (pork medallions with a garlicky tomato and paprika sauce). ✉ *District I, Attila út 27, Gellért-hegy & Tabán* ☎ *1/375–7165* ▤ *AE, MC, V.*

Városliget (City Park)

★ **$$$$** ✕ **Gundel.** This is probably Hungary's most celebrated restaurant, both for its history (opened in 1894) as well as its renovation in the 1990s by Hungarian-American restaurateur, George Lang. The gorgeous setting in the City Park includes an art nouveau bar designed by the brilliant Adam Tihany. Fin-de-siècle grandeur shines through in the glorious dining room, tastefully adorned with 19th- and 20th-century Hungarian paintings, and a 10-piece gypsy band adds an earnest nostalgia to the place. The food, sadly, is just a bit above average, though some classics such as goose liver pâté and Gundel pancakes are well executed. Nevertheless, a visit is a uniquely memorable experience. ✉ *District XIV, Várisoliget, Állatkerti út 2, Városliget* ☎ *1/321–3550* ☜ *Reservations essential* ⋒ *Jacket and tie* ▤ *AE, DC, MC, V* Ⓜ *M1: Hősök tere.*

$$$$ ✕ **Robinson Restaurant.** Robinson can certainly lay claim to one of the more exotic locations in Budapest dining—on wooden platforms atop an artificial lake, looking across to the delightful architectural folly of Vajdahunyad Castle. You can sit outside on the terrace during summer, or enjoy the warm pastel interior in colder months. Service is competent and the menu creative, with dishes such as crisp roast suckling pig with champagne-drenched cabbage or fresh fogas (pike perch) stuffed with spinach. ✉ *District XIV, Várisoliget, Városliget* ☎ *1/422–0222* ☜ *Reservations essential* ▤ *AE, DC, MC, V* Ⓜ *M1: Hősök tere.*

Cafés

The coffeehouse has a long tradition in Budapest. At the turn of the 20th century, there were more than 400 coffeehouses in the city, many of them patronized by struggling writers. Important journals and books were produced here, and the coffeehouse itself was a cornerstone of Budapest literary life. Though by no means vital to intellectual life today, the coffeehouse is still a popular institution. It is home to occasional writers but it's equally patronized by tourists, students, and grandmothers chatting over coffee and cake. In general, most *kávéházak* (coffeehouses) serve a wide range of coffees and a small list of spirits, wine, and beer. The more traditional ones serve a dizzying array of cakes, all made fresh daily. The modern ones serve cakes as well, but may also serve sandwiches, soups and light dishes. You will find both styles of grand turn-of-the-20th-century coffeehouses in Budapest, as well as quite a few modern cafés.

Angelika. This four-room café gets even bigger in the summer, when six small graduated terraces with awnings open up outside. You can buy lots of nice cakes here and a spectacular iced coffee with whipped cream. The terraces themselves have one of the best views of Parliament in the city. ⊠ *District I, Batthyány tér 7, Around Batthyány tér* ☎ *1/ 212–3784* ⊟ *No credit cards* Ⓜ *M2: Batthyány tér.*

Auguszt Cukrászda. This old-fashioned pastry shop has a loyal following for some of the lightest, most buttery pastries in Budapest. All the classic Hungarian cakes like *rétes* (strudel filled with sour cherries, apples, or cheese) and *Dobos Torta* (chocolate cream cake with caramel) can be enjoyed here. ⊠ *District V, Kossuth Lajos utca 14–16, Around Váci utca* ☎ *1/337–6379* ⊟ *No credit cards* ⊘ *Closed Sun.* Ⓜ *M2: Astoria.*

Aztek Chocolat. There are more than 20 kinds of coffee in this tiny café to give you a boost, and if the caffeine doesn't do it for you, opt for an original chocolate drink like cocoa with chili. (Remember the movie *Chocolat?*) Pretty pastries and hand-dipped chocolate are hard to resist. ⊠ *District V, Károly Körút 22, but enter through the courtyard of Semmelweis utca 19, Around Ferenciak tere* ☎ *1/266–7113* ⊟ *No credit cards* ⊘ *Closed Sun.* Ⓜ *M2: Astoria.*

Cafe Buena Vista. This stylish café in the heart of Liszt Ferenc tér is popular for coffee in the afternoon and cocktails in the evening. There's a good range of warm sandwiches and salads, most with a Mediterranean twist. ⊠ *District VI, Liszt Ferenc tér 4–5, Around Andrássy út* ☎ *1/ 344–6303* ⊟ *AE, MC, V* Ⓜ *M1: Oktogon.*

Café Eklektika. Temporary photo exhibitions and light jazz give this modern café an arty feel. Nearby music students are here during the day; by 6 the place has a mixed gay and straight crowd drinking cocktails. There's a fairly substantial menu served all day. ⊠ *District V, Semmelweis utca, Around Deák Ferenc tér* ☎ *No phone* ⊟ *No credit cards* ⊘ *No lunch weekends* Ⓜ *M1, M2, M3: Deák Ferenc tér.*

Café Picard. Antiques dealers and local artists can be found here most mornings chatting over short black coffees and croissants in this friendly café in the antiques district. Lunchtime finds the same crowd, plus a few shoppers enjoying homemade soups, tasty bruschetta sandwiches, and mixed cheese and salami plates. Some days, there are a few romantic lunchers, discreetly sipping champagne in the back booths. ⊠ *District V, Falk Miksa utca 10, Parliament* ☎ *1/473–0939* ⊟ *No credit cards* Ⓜ *M2: Kossuth Lajos tér.*

FodorśChoice
★ **Centrál Kávéház.** For an air of 19th-century grandeur in 21st-century comfort, go to this café. You can sit in a non-smoking section while admiring the old-fashioned moldings on the ceiling. Coffees are served on a silver tray with a glass of mineral water. The food menu includes pretty substantial dishes like *hortobágyi palacsinta* (meat pancakes with paprika sauce), and beef Stroganoff all day. ⊠ *District V, Károlyi Mihály utca 9, Around Váci utca* ☎ *1/235–0599* ⊟ *AE, MC, V* Ⓜ *M3: Ferenciek tere.*

Eckermann. The coffees are served in mugs with lots of milk at this popular spot directly across the street from Művész. You won't find much to eat on the menu, but you will find a few European intellectual types looking very serious. The café is attached to the Goethe Institute. ⊠ *District VI, Andrássy út 24, Around Andrássy út* ☎ *1/269–2542* ☱ *No credit cards* ☺ *Closed Sun.* Ⓜ *M1: Opera.*

Gerbeaud. It's hard to miss this grand coffeehouse, which has been selling its magnificent cakes at the north end of Vörösmarty tér since 1858. Accept that there are lots of tourists here at all times of the year. However, while the afternoon coffee and cake are pricey, the experience is pure Budapest. ⊠ *District V, Vörösmarty tér 7, Around Deák Ferenc tér* ☎ *1/429–9000* ☱ *AE, MC, V* Ⓜ *M1: Vörösmarty tér.*

Művész. While service at this grand coffeehouse can be less than cheery, its interior can't be beat for a faded-grandeur feel. In summer, the terrace spills out onto Andrássy út, and it's a premier place for people-watching. All the classic Hungarian cakes are here, as well as a moist, not-too-sweet *alma torta* (apple cake). ⊠ *District VI, Andrássy út 29, Around Andrássy út* ☎ *1/352–1337* ☱ *No credit cards* Ⓜ *M1: Opera.*

Ruszwurm Cukrászda. This tiny *cukrászda* (cake shop) on Castle Hill is Budapest's oldest. There are only a few tables inside and there's often a long wait for a coffee and cake. Peek inside at the gorgeous interior and you'll get an idea of this coffeeshop's enduring appeal. ⊠ *District I, Szentháromság utca 7 Várhegy* ☎ *1/375–5284* ☱ *No credit cards.*

WHERE TO STAY

SLEEP IN A PALACE
Four Seasons Hotel Gresham
Palace Budapest ⇨*p.79*

BEST BUDGET CHOICE
Kalmár Bed & Breakfast ⇨*p.78*

BEST BUSINESS HOTEL
Kempinski Hotel Corvinus Budapest ⇨*p.80*

BEST BOUTIQUE HOTEL
Andrássy Hotel ⇨*p.82*

MODERATELY PRICED MARVEL
Hotel Pest ⇨*p.84*

GRANDEUR, NO LONGER FADED
Corinthia Grand Hotel Royal ⇨*p.87*

By Julie Tomasz   **BUDAPEST HAS SEEN A STEADY INCREASE** in both the quantity and quality of its accommodations since 1989, when the country broke away from Communism, but the first years of the 21st century have seen an extraordinary number of new hotels opening their doors. Long gone are the old days when you had to settle for what was available. The advantage is shifting to the traveler, who will increasingly benefit from not only more sheer options but also from stiff competition keeping rates lower.

Luxury hotels are making a bit splash in Budapest. Where once the Hotel Kempinski single-handedly dominated, now there are many five-star properties from which to choose. Most are painstaking, multimillion dollar resurrections of faded glories, like the Le Méridien, Corinthia Grand Hotel Royal, and Four Seasons Budapest. Still to come is the legendary New York Palace, which was slated at this writing to re-open as a five-star hotel sometime in 2005. The word on the street is that the next big luxury overhaul will be the Drechsler Palace, across the boulevard from the Opera House and current home to the Hungarian National Ballet.

Numerous small and medium-size private hotels have opened on the streets of inner Pest, some in lovely old 18th- and 19th-century buildings refurbished to modern standards. Earlier it wasn't possible to stay so centrally without paying through the nose for a modern chain hotel or risking your safety in less expensive, but seedy, places. Indeed, the very definition of "central Pest" may need to be further calibrated, as the number of downtown properties grows.

In upper price ranges, you can expect top international-standard service, facilities, and amenities. Many of these high-priced hotels cater to business travelers, offering relatively new extras (to Hungary, at least) like wireless Internet hotspots and automated check-in and check-out. Perks like thicker mattresses and swankier bathrooms are more common. Generally, the older, less expensive properties can be a bit worn, with quintessential, brown and orange Communist-era decor, flimsy shower stalls instead of bathtubs, and low-riding single beds that are pushed together to make a double. There are plenty of exceptions, however, in newer and refurbished budget hotels—more of which are opening year by year—and family-run pensions and bed-and-breakfasts. Almost all of the least expensive hotels have basic TVs and telephones in the rooms, and most have at least a few air-conditioned rooms.

Regardless of the price range, Hungarian hotels still tend to count two single beds pushed together as a double bed. If it's important to you, be sure to specify you want a double mattress, often referred to as a *francia ágy* (French bed). Many properties keep a few so-called "bio" rooms aside for people with severe allergies. These rooms don't have the otherwise ubiquitous wall-to-wall carpeting and are specially fitted with hypo-allergenic linens and pillows. In theory, they are also non-smoking rooms.

Something important to keep in mind when planning your trip to Budapest is that every year for a week in mid-August the Formula 1 auto races descend upon the city, literally doubling the hotel rates and maxing out

Reservations Advance reservations are strongly advised in the summer, especially at the smaller, lower-priced hotels and during the week in August that Formula I racing descends upon Budapest. In winter it's not anywhere near as difficult to find a hotel room, even at the last minute, and prices are usually reduced by 20% to 30%. The best budget option is to book a private room or an entire apartment. Expect to pay between €20 and €30 for a double room. The number of rooms available can be limited in high season, so if you're booking your accommodation on the spot, it may be best arrive in Budapest early in the morning.

3

Prices All room rates indicated here are based on double-occupancy rack rates in high season. It's important to note, however, that these rates often double during the week Formula I racing comes to Budapest every year, usually in mid-August. On the other hand, most large hotels offer significant discounts, frequently including breakfast, for weekend bookings and during special sale periods throughout the year. If a property seems too expensive at first glance, it's worth looking into special rates by calling them as well as checking their Web site. Most hotels include all taxes as well as breakfast in their regular quoted rates. Luxury hotels usually do not included VAT of 15% and a tourist tax of 3% in the room rate, nor do they usually include breakfast. We note in the review when taxes are not included; each review indicates whether breakfast is included in the rates or not.

Assume that all hotels operate on the **European Plan** (EP, with no meals) unless we specify that they use the **Breakfast Plan** (BP, with a full breakfast) or **Continental Plan** (CP, with a Continental breakfast).

Most hotels allow children under 16 to stay in their parents' room for free, though age limits vary from property to property. For single rooms with bath, count on paying about 80% of the double-room rate. Most hotels in Budapest set their rates and expect payment in euros. With very few exceptions, credit cards are widely accepted.

WHAT IT COSTS In Euros and Forints				
$$$$	**$$$**	**$$**	**$**	**¢**
IN EUROS	over €225	€175–€225	€125–€175	€75–€125	under €75
IN FORINTS	over 56,000	44,000–56,000	31,000–44,000	18,500–31,000	under 18,500

Prices are for two people in a standard double room with a private bath and breakfast during peak season (May through October).

occupancy. If you're not a racing fan and can afford to be flexible, it's best to avoid this period in Budapest.

Addresses below are preceded by the district number (in Roman numerals) and include the Hungarian postal code. Districts V, VI, and VII are in downtown Pest; District I includes Castle Hill, the main tourist district of Buda.

BUDA HOTELS

Castle Hill and Around Batthyány tér

The fairytale surroundings of Castle Hill make it a delightful place to stay, and it doesn't even have to cost an arm and a leg anymore. The only downside is, because it's Budapest's number one tourist area, the district's restaurants and shops tend to be touristy and more expensive. Walking home is a strenuous uphill affair, but buses, taxis, and the *sikló* funicular can help out. Hotels on the Danube near Batthyány tér have great river views of Parliament and Pest, or of Castle Hill itself, and easy metro access to the rest of the city.

$$-$$$ 🏨 **art'otel.** Travelers bored with bland business-hotel decor may get more excited by this mod lodging's snazzy design. Everything—from the multimillion-dollar art collection on the walls to the whimsical red-and-white carpeting and even the cups and saucers—is the work of one man, American artist Donald Sultan. Encompassing one new building and four 18th-century baroque houses on the Buda riverfront, the art'otel adroitly blends old and new. Rooms are on the small side, but some have splendid views of Fisherman's Bastion and the Matthias Church. ✉ *District I, Bem rakpart 16–19, Around Batthyány tér H-1011* ☎ *1/487–9487* 🖷 *1/487–9488* ⊕ *www.artotel.de* 🛏 *155 rooms, 9 suites* 🔇 *Restaurant, room service, in-room data ports, in-room safes, minibars, cable TV, gym, hair salon, sauna, bar, shop, dry-cleaning, laundry service, concierge, Internet, meeting rooms, travel services, parking (fee), no-smoking rooms* 🖹 *AE, DC, MC, V* 🍴 *BP* Ⓜ *M2: Batthyány tér.*

★ 🏨 **Budapest Hilton.** You'll have to decide for yourself if this hotel, built
♨ **$$-$$$** in 1977 around the remains of a 17th-century Gothic chapel and adjacent to the Matthias Church, is a successful integration or not. The exterior certainly betrays the hotel's 1970s origins, but the modern and tasteful rooms and great views from Castle Hill will soothe the most delicate of aesthetic sensibilities. While the minimal fitness facilities leave much to be desired, the 24-hour business center and free airport shuttle service make the Hilton stand out among its peers. Rooms with the best Danube vistas cost more. Children, regardless of age, stay free when sharing a room with their parents. VAT and tourist tax are not included in the rates. ✉ *District I, Hess András tér 1–3, Castle Hill H-1014* ☎ *1/889–6600, 800/445–8667 in the U.S. and Canada* 🖷 *1/889–6644* ⊕ *www.budapest.hilton.com* 🛏 *295 rooms, 37 suites* 🔇 *2 restaurants, café, room service, in-room data ports, in-room safes, cable TV with video games, gym, hair salon, sauna, bar, wine shop, shops, babysitting, dry cleaning, laundry service, concierge, Internet, business ser-*

Apartment & Private Rooms

Apartments, available for short- and long-term rental, are often an economical alternative to staying in a hotel, with an increasing number of options available, as Hungarian entrepreneurs find uses for old family homes and inherited apartments. The Internet is teeming with apartment offers. A short-term rental in Budapest will probably cost from €40 to €60 a day in high season.

Accommodation can also be arranged in private rooms, sometimes with the option of breakfast. Since this usually involves sharing someone's home—your host is most often a kindly elderly Hungarian lady—it is an appealing possibility for those who want to meet the locals. The typical two-person, high-season rate for a private room is approximately €30 a night.

Both apartments and private rooms usually come with bed linens and towels. Payments generally need to be made in cash, but some bookings made through accommodation agencies allow use of credit cards.

IBUSZ Private Accommodation Service (✉ District V, Ferenciek tere 10, Around Ferenciek tere ☎ 1/485–2767 or 1/485–2768 🖷 1/337–1205 ⊕ www. ibusz.hu ✉ District V, Vörösmarty tér 6 ☎ 1/317–0532 🖷 1/317–1474), with offices throughout the city, rents out apartments in downtown Budapest, most consisting of two rooms plus a fully equipped kitchen and bathroom. Private rooms are also available. You can explore some of your options on the IBUSZ Web site. The main office, on Ferenciek tere, is closed on weekends and only open until 4 PM Monday through Thursday, until 3 PM Friday. **Non-Stop Hotel Service** (✉ District V, Apáczai Csere János u. 1, Around Váci utca ☎ 1/318–3925 or 1/266–8042 🖷 1/317–9099 ⊕ www.non-stophotelservice. hu) has the advantage of being the only accommodation service open 24 hours a day. The agency books apartments as well as rooms in private homes, and can also make hotel reservations. **Panaco Reservations** (☎ 1/430–0831 🖷 1/ 430–0833 ⊕ www.budapesthotels.com) is better known for its Web site, a thorough and professional Internet accommodation service with lots of helpful extra information about travelling in Budapest thrown in for good measure. **To-Ma Tours** (✉ District V, Október 6 u. 22, Around St. Stephen's Basilica ☎ 1/ 353–0819 🖷 1/269–5715 ⊕ www.tomatour.hu) arranges private apartments and rooms and is open on weekends.

Home Exchanges

If you would like to exchange your home for someone else's, join a home-exchange organization, which will send you its updated listings of available exchanges for a year and will include your own listing in at least one of them. It's up to you to make specific arrangements.

There are two major U.S.-based home exchange organizations. **HomeLink International** (✉ Box 47747, Tampa, FL 33647 ☎ 813/975–9825 or 800/ 638–3841 🖷 813/910–8144 ⊕ www.homelink.org); $110 yearly for a listing, online access, and catalog; $70 without catalog. Intervac U.S. (✉ 30 Corte San Fernando, Tiburon, CA 94920 ☎ 800/756–4663 🖶 415/435–7440 ⊕ www.intervacus.com); $125 yearly for a listing, online access, and a catalog; $65 without catalog.

Hostels

No matter what your age, you can save on lodging costs by staying at hostels. In some 4,500 locations in more than 70 countries around the world, Hostelling International (HI), the umbrella group for a number of national youth-hostel associations, offers single-sex, dorm-style beds and, at many hostels, rooms for couples and family accommodations. Membership in any HI national hostel association, open to travelers of all ages, allows you to stay in HI-affiliated hostels at member rates; one-year membership is about $28 for adults (C$35 for a two-year minimum membership in Canada, £14 in the U.K., A$52 in Australia, and NZ$40 in New Zealand); hostels charge about $10–$30 per night. Members have priority if the hostel is full; they're also eligible for discounts around the world, even on rail and bus travel in some countries.

In Hungary, most hostels are geared toward the college crowd. For further information, consult the free annual accommodations directory published by Tourinform or the listings in *Budapest in Your Pocket,* available at newsstands, or visit the Web site ⊕ Backpackers.hu. At the Internet-equipped **Back Pack Guesthouse** (✉ District XI, Takács Menyhért u. 33, South Buda ☎ 1/385–8946 ⊕ www.backpackbudapest.hu) rates range from 2,200 HUF for a bed in a 7- to 11-bed room to 2,800 HUF for a bed in a 4- to 5-bed room. You can get your own double for 6,600 HUF. The **Sirály Youth Hostel** (✉ District XIII, Margitsziget, Margaret Island ☎ 1/329–3952), situated in the relative peace, quiet, and clean air of an island-park on the Danube, charges 1,950 HUF per person for a bed in a 12-bed room.

For more information about hosteling, contact your local youth hostel office. **Hostelling International—USA** (✉ 8401 Colesville Rd., Suite 600, Silver Spring, MD 20910 ☎ 301/495–1240 🖶 301/495–6697 ⊕ www.hiusa.org). **Hostelling International—Canada** (✉ 205 Catherine St., Suite 400, Ottawa, Ontario K2P 1C3 ☎ 613/237–7884 or 800/663–5777 🖶 613/237–7868 ⊕ www.hihostels.ca). **YHA England and Wales** (✉ Trevelyan House, Dimple Rd., Matlock, Derbyshire DE4 3YH, U.K. ☎ 0870/870–8808, 0870/770–8868, or 0162/959–2600 🖶 0870/770–6127 ⊕ www.yha.org.uk). **YHA Australia** (✉ 422 Kent St., Sydney, NSW 2001 ☎ 02/9261–1111 🖶 02/9261–1969 ⊕ www.yha.com.au). **YHA New Zealand** (✉ Level 1, Moorhouse City, 166 Moorhouse Ave., Box 436, Christchurch ☎ 03/379–9970 or 0800/278–299 🖶 03/365–4476 ⊕ www.yha.org.nz).

---

vices, convention center, airport shuttle, travel services, some free parking, parking (fee), no-smoking floor 🖃 *AE, DC, MC, V* 🍴 *EP* Ⓜ *M2: Moszkva tér, then Várbusz.*

$ 🏨 **Burg Hotel.** You don't have to splurge on the Hilton to stay on Szentháromság tér. This prime piece of real estate opened in 2000, making it the third hotel on Castle Hill's most famous square. The only downside is having the peak-season crowds thronging under your window, but then the quiet nights are that much more magical. Rooms have green wall-to-wall carpeting, beige wallpaper, and blue-tiled bathrooms with either tubs or shower stalls. ⊠ *District I, Szentháromság tér 7–8, Castle Hill H-1014* ☎ *1/212–0269 or 1/212–0270* 🖷 *1/212–3970* ⊕ *www. burghotelbudapest.com* 🖙 *24 rooms, 2 suites* ⚲ *Minibars, cable TV, bar, Internet, travel services, parking (fee), no-smoking rooms* ⊟ *AE, DC, MC, V* 🍴 *BP* Ⓜ *M2: Moszkva tér, then Várbusz.*

★ $ 🏨 **Carlton Hotel.** The Carlton is proof that you can stay in the Castle Hill district—even nestled at the foot of the hill itself—without paying a fortune. Rooms on the upper floors offer lovely views over rooftops to Castle Hill, leaving one only to wish the smallish windows were larger. Request a newly refurbished room to avoid the adequate but stark gray furnishings of the earlier design. With downtown just a walk across the Chain Bridge away and the Castle Hill district rising in your backyard, it's hard to do better for location and price. A large buffet breakfast is served every morning. ⊠ *District I, Apor Péter u. 3, Castle Hill H-1011* ☎ *1/224–0999* 🖷 *1/224–0990* ⊕ *www.carltonhotel.hu* 🖙 *95 rooms* ⚲ *In-room data ports, in-room safes, minibars, cable TV, bar, dry cleaning, laundry service, Internet, business services, meeting room, parking (fee), some pets allowed (fee), no-smoking rooms* ⊟ *AE, DC, MC, V* 🍴 *BP* Ⓜ *M2: Batthyány tér.*

★ $ 🏨 **Hotel Kulturinov.** This inexpensive hotel can be found in rather noble quarters—one wing of a magnificent 1902 neo-baroque castle in the heart of the luxurious Castle District. The building's main tenants are the Hungarian Cultural Foundation and a large wine center, so part of the charm is navigating your way through the cavernous entry hall, up the sweeping staircase, and down the creaking hallway to finally reach the hotel's small reception desk. Rooms come with two or three beds and are very basic but peaceful; they have showers but no tubs. Children under 14 can share their parents' room for free. The neighborhood is simply magical. ⊠ *District I, Szentháromság tér 6, Castle Hill H-1014* ☎ *1/355–0122 or 1/375–1651* 🖷 *1/375–1886* ⊕ *www.mka.hu* 🖙 *16 rooms* ⚲ *Snack bar, some fans, minibars, cable TV, meeting rooms, parking (fee); no a/c* ⊟ *DC, MC, V* 🍴 *BP* Ⓜ *M2: Moszkva tér, then Várbusz or Bus 16.*

$ 🏨 **Hotel Victoria.** This small, family-run hotel has had a loyal following since it opened shortly after the Iron Curtain came down. Taking advantage of a choice Buda-side location on the Danube riverbank, each room has a small seating area in front of floor-to-ceiling windows looking across the river to Parliament. The reception staff is kind and able, and can direct you to the nearby restaurants where you can charge your meals to your room. Request a non-smoking room when reserving to avoid overlapping with a heavy smoker. Rates do not include 3% local tax. ⊠ *District I, Bem rakpart 11, Around Batthyány tér H-1011* ☎ *1/ 457–8080* 🖷 *1/457–8088* ⊕ *www.victoria.hu* 🖙 *27 rooms* ⚲ *In-room data ports, in-room safes, minibars, cable TV, sauna, bar, dry cleaning, laundry service, Internet, business services, meeting room, travel services, parking (fee)* ⊟ *AE, DC, MC, V* 🍴 *BP* Ⓜ *M2: Batthyány tér.*

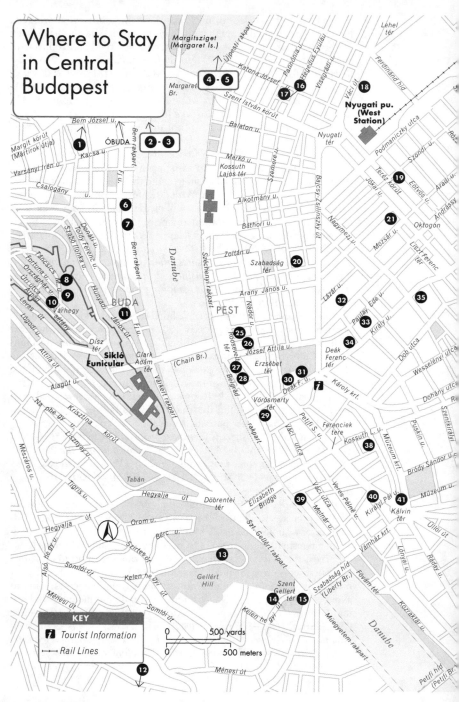

Where to Stay in Central Budapest

Margitsziget
(Margaret Is.)

Margaret
Br.

④ - ⑤

**Nyugati pu.
(West
Station)**

Bem József u.

ÓBUDA **② - ③**

①

Margit körút
(Mártírok útja)

Varsányi Irén u.

Csalogány u.

Kacsa u.

Bem rakpart

Fő u.

Szent István körút

Balaton u.

Markó u.

Kossuth
Lajos tér

Alkotmány u.

Báthori u.

Zoltán u.

Szabadság
tér **⑳**

Arany János u.

Katona József

Visegrádi u.

Pannónia u.

Hegedüs Gyula u.

⑰ **⑯**

Váci út

Nyugati
tér

Léhel
tér

Ferdinánd híd

Podmaniczky utca

Szondi u.

Teréz körút **⑲**

Jókai u.

Mozsár u.

Liszt Ferenc
tér

Eötvös u.

Aradi u.

Andrássy

Oktogon

㉑

Donáti u.
Toldi Ferenc u.
Szabó Ilonka u.

Táncsics
Fortuna u.
Országház u.
Úri utca
Anjou
Lovas út

⑧
⑨
⑩

Várhegy
sétány

BUDA

Hunyadi

Fő u.

Bem rakpart

⑥
⑦

Danube

Széchenyi rakpart

PEST

Nádor u.

Roosevelt
tér

㉕
㉖

József Attila u.

Erzsébet
tér

㉚ **㉛**

㉗
㉘

Belgrád

Deák F. u.

Deák
Ferenc
tér

Károly krt.

🛈

Bajcsy-Zsilinszky út

Nagymező u.

Lázár u. **㉜**

Paulay Ede u. **㉝**

Király u.

㉞

Dob utca

㉟

Wesselényi utca

Dohány utca

Szentkirály

Dísz
tér

⑪
János út
Várhegy

**Sikló
Funicular**

Clark
Ádám
tér

(Chain Br.)

Várkert rakpart

Alagút u.

Na phe gy u.

Krisztina

Mészáros u.

Tigris u.

Lisznyai u.

körút

Tabán

Hegyalja út

Döbrentei
tér

Hegyalja

Bérc u.

Alsó he gy u.

Somlói út

Szirtes út

Orom u.

Attila út

Lógodi u.

Vörösmarty
tér **㉙**

rakpart

Petőfi S. u.

Váci utca

Ferenciek
tere

Kossuth L. u.

㊳

Veres Pálné u.

Bródy Sándor u.

Múzeum krt.

Puskin u.

Múzeum u.

Elizabeth
Bridge

㊴

Molnár u.

Váci utca

㊵
Király P. u.
㊶

Kálvin
tér

Vámház krt.

Lónyai u.

Rádai u.

Üllői út

Szt. Gellért rakpart

⑬

Gellért
Hill

Somlói út

Kelen he gyi út

KEY

🛈 Tourist Information

⊢→ Rail Lines

0 _____ 500 yards
0 _____ 500 meters

Ménesi út

⑫

Szent
Gellért tér

⑭ **⑮**

Kelen he gyi u.

Szabadság híd
(Liberty Br.)

Fővám tér

Műegyetem rakpart

Danube

Köztelek u.

Petőfi híd
(Petőfi Br.)

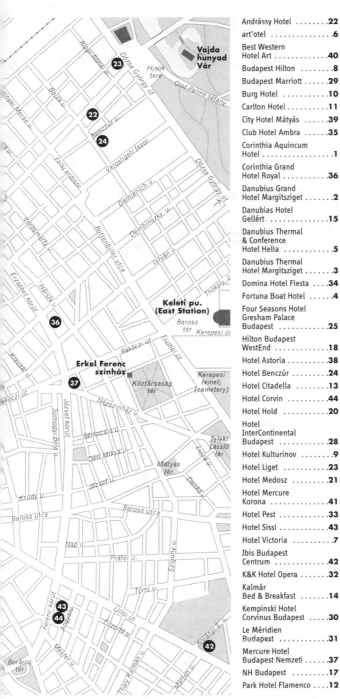

Gellért Hill and South Buda

In addition to offering easy access to the famed Gellert Hotel's thermal bath complex, the area around and south of Gellert Hill offers less hectic, greener surroundings from those of Pest, particularly as you move away from busy Bartók Béla út and the bridge traffic around Szent Gellért tér. The verdant slopes of Gellért Hill and its hilltop citadel and monument make for lovely views from hotel windows looking onto it. There is no metro in this part of Buda, but extensive tram and bus service make it still easily accessible.

★ **$$–$$$** 🏨 **Danubius Hotel Gellért.** Budapest's most renowned art nouveau hotel is undergoing an ongoing, incremental overhaul, as rooms are slowly refinished in the original Jugendstil style popular when it was built during World War I. Then, it was favored by Otto von Hapsburg, son of the last emperor. Request a refurbished room when you reserve for optimal comfort; unrenovated rooms are a good value, though, if you don't mind a little Iron-Curtain sternness. Regardless, enquire about options—and perhaps bargain—as rooms in this quirky building come in all shapes, sizes, and prices. Everyone staying here also has free access to the monumental and ornate thermal baths, with a dedicated elevator to whisk you directly to the premises. ⊠ *District XI, Szent Gellért tér 1, Gellért Hill & the Tabán H-1111* 🕾 *1/889–5500* 🖷 *1/889–5505* ⊕ *www.danubiusgroup.com* 🛏 *220 rooms, 14 suites* 🖧 *2 restaurants, café, room service, in-room data ports, in-room safes, minibars, cable TV, 3 outdoor pools, 10 indoor pools, hair salon, spa, Turkish bath, bar, shops, baby-sitting, dry cleaning, laundry service, concierge, Internet, business services, meeting rooms, travel services, parking (fee), no-smoking rooms; no a/c in some rooms* 🖃 *AE, DC, MC, V* 🍴 *BP* Ⓜ *Tram 18, 19, 47, 49 to Szt. Gellért tér.*

$ 🏨 **Park Hotel Flamenco.** This glass-and-concrete socialist-era leviathan looks out onto the supposedly bottomless Feneketlen Lake. Happily, once inside, you can almost forget the Stalinist architecture, due to the pleasant, contemporary furnishings. It's a bit out of the way (a good 20-minute tram ride will get you across the river into Pest), but the terrace restaurant has nice views of the lake and park surrounding it. ⊠ *District XI, Tas Vezér u. 7, South Buda H-1113* 🕾 *1/889–5600* 🖷 *1/889–5651* ⊕ *www.danubiusgroup.com* 🛏 *350 rooms, 8 suites* 🖧 *2 restaurants, in-room data ports, in-room safes, minibars, cable TV, indoor pool, 2 indoor tennis courts, health club, hair salon, sauna, bar, shop, dry cleaning, laundry service, concierge, Internet, business services, meeting rooms, travel services, parking (fee), some pets allowed (fee)* 🖃 *AE, DC, MC, V* 🍴 *BP* Ⓜ *Tram 19, 49 to Kosztolányi Dezső tér.*

¢–$ 🏨 **Kalmár Bed & Breakfast.** This treasure trove of elegant, old Budapest **Fodor'sChoice** is a 1900 yellow stone mansion on the lower slopes of Gellért Hill. Those ★ who appreciate original ambience over amenities will be pleased. While cheaper doubles on the ground floor are small and dark, there are also antique-filled suites and opulent, full-scale apartments that can accommodate two couples. Ask Eszter (who speaks English) to help you choose a room to fit your budget and standards. The Kalmár family has been running the house as a B&B since 1964, slowly buying back rooms and apartments that were partitioned during the Communist era. Breakfast is served on delicate matching porcelain. ✉ *District XI, Kelenhegyi út 7–9, Gellért Hill & the Tabán H-1118* ☎ *1/372-7530, 06–30–271–9312 English-speaking* 🖶 *1/385–2804* 🖥 *5 rooms, 2 suites, 2 apartments* ♻ *Minibars, cable TV* ⊟ *No credit cards* ℄ *BP* Ⓜ *Tram 18, 19, 47, 49 to Szt. Gellért tér.*

¢ 🖭 **Hotel Citadella.** Housed within the historical Citadella fort that crowns Gellért Hill, this hotel and hostel combination is geared towards low-maintenance, budget-minded travelers who don't mind an uphill hike at the end of their sightseeing day. Its origins as an army barracks still come through loud and clear: windows are small, and half the rooms share a WC. But the vaulted stone ceilings and marvelous views from many of the rooms make it unique in Budapest. Of the ten rooms with private bathrooms, two have a bathtub, the rest simple showers. ✉ *District XI, Citadella sétány, Gellért Hill H–1118* ☎ *1/466-5794* 🖶 *1/386–0505* ⊕ *www.citadella.hu* 🖥 *20 rooms, 10 with shared bath* ♻ *Restaurant, no a/c, no room phones, no room TVs, shop, some free parking, some pets allowed (fee)* ⊟ *No credit cards* ℄ *CP* Ⓜ *Bus 27 to Szirtes út.*

PEST HOTELS

Around Deák Ferenc tér

Budapest's poshest and priciest hotels line the Danube riverbank just south of the Chain Bridge. The area is hard to beat: central to major sights, restaurants, and business—Deák tér metro hub is nearby—and offering postcard-perfect views from your bedroom window.

$$$$ 🖭 **Four Seasons Hotel Gresham Palace Budapest.** It doesn't get much bet-
Fodor'sChoice ter than this: a centrally located, super-deluxe hotel in a museum-qual-
★ ity landmark with the prettiest views in town. No detail has been spared in restoring this stunning 1906 art nouveau palace to its original majesty: delicate wrought-iron vents in the hallways, exquisite gold mosaic tiles on the facade, stained-glass windows and cupolas. Three magnificent stairwells are so grand that you may not want to use the elevators. Rooms, some with balconies and vaulted ceilings, are similarly large and plush. Spanish-marble bathrooms—unlike any in Budapest—have both showers and deep soaking tubs. The lobby café is modeled after the building's original. ✉ *District V, Roosevelt tér 5–6, Around Váci utca H-1051* ☎ *1/268–6000* 🖶 *1/268–5000* ⊕ *www.fourseasons.com* 🖥 *165 rooms, 14 suites* ♻ *Restaurant, café, room service, in-room data ports, in-room safes, minibars, cable TV, indoor pool, gym, health club, sauna, spa, steam room, bar, lobby lounge, shops, baby-sitting, dry cleaning, laundry service, concierge, Internet, business services, convention center, travel services, parking (fee), no-smoking floors* ⊟ *AE, DC, MC, V* ℄ *EP* Ⓜ *M1: Vörösmarty tér.*

$$$$ 🖭 **Hotel InterContinental Budapest.** Its days as the socialist-era Fórum Hotel now firmly consigned to the past, the InterContinental appeals to the modern business traveler. Every room has a work desk, and some even have a printer. Additional executive-friendly perks include a 24-hour business center and wireless Internet in the lobby. The hotel is right next to

CloseUp

A SHORT HISTORY OF
THE GRESHAM PALACE

THE MASSIVE ART NOUVEAU *palace that is now the Four Seasons Hotel began its life near the turn of the 20th century as, of all things, the* headquarters of an insurance company. *The Gresham Life Assurance Company wanted to build a new foreign headquarters in Budapest and hired eminent architect Zsigmond Quittner and almost every prominent craftsman working in Hungary to create the building. The palace was to house both the company and British aristocrats, who found Budapest a useful meeting point away from the politically charged atmosphere of Vienna and Berlin. The palace kept them comfortably housed from its completion in 1906 until the beginning of World War II. In 1944 the building was damaged when the retreating German army blew up the nearby Chain Bridge. In 1948 the Communist government of Hungary* subdivided the palatial suites into tiny units to house both state offices and residential tenants; the building fell quickly into disrepair. By the 1970s it had been named a national protected landmark but continued its slow decline; passersby would collect the precious Zsolnay tiles that had crumbled off the facade. After the overthrow of the Communists in 1990, the City of Budapest took ownership of the palace and planned how to sell and redevelop it as a luxury hotel; long-term tenants, including the flamboyant actress Ida Turay, refused to vacate and filed lawsuits against the city, which finally won its case. The building was purchased by a private investment group which, along with Four Seasons, finally received permission to create the hotel. Construction commenced in 2000, and the hotel opened in June 2004.

the Chain Bridge in Pest, and 60% of the rooms have views across the Danube to Castle Hill (these are about €50 more expensive but worth it, considering the view). Rooms on higher floors ensure the least noise. All are decorated in pleasant pastels and furnished in the Biedermeier style typical of Central Europe. ⊠ *District V, Apáczai Csere János u. 12–14, Around Váci utca H-1052* ☎ *1/327–6333* 🖷 *1/327–6357* ⊕ *www.ichotelsgroup.com* 🖙 *398 rooms, 16 suites* ⚿ *2 restaurants, café, room service, in-room data ports, in-room safes, minibars, cable TV, indoor pool, health club, bar, business services, Internet, meeting rooms, car rental, parking (fee), no-smoking floors* ⊟ *AE, DC, MC, V* ⏀ *EP* Ⓜ *M1: Vörösmarty tér.*

$$$$ 🏨 **Kempinski Hotel Corvinus Budapest.** Budapest's best business hotel
Fodor'sChoice doesn't cater only to the international CEO set. Though rather cold and
★ futuristic-looking on the outside, the Kempinski has exceptionally spacious rooms and suites, with custom-made art deco fittings and furniture, as well as an emphasis on functional touches like three phones in every room. Large, sparkling bathrooms have tubs and separate shower stalls and come stocked with every toiletry. At this writing, a state-of-the-art spa was due to open in the first half of 2005. Rates do not include the buffet breakfast, which is said to be the best and most bountiful

in Budapest. ⊠ *District V, Erzsébet tér 7–8, Around Dék Ferenc tér H-1051* 🖼 *1/429–3777, 800/426–3135 in the U.S. and Canada* 🖨 *1/429–4777* ⊕ *www.kempinski-budapest.com* ⇝ *335 rooms, 30 suites* ♿ *3 restaurants, room service, in-room data ports, in-room safes, minibars, cable TV, indoor pool, gym, 2 hair salons, hot tub, sauna, spa, bar, lobby lounge, shops, dry cleaning, laundry service, concierge, Internet, business services, convention center, travel services, parking (fee), some pets allowed (fee), no-smoking floors* ▤ *AE, DC, MC, V* †◯| *EP* Ⓜ *M1, M2, M3: Deák tér.*

★ **$$$$** 🏨 **Le Méridien Budapest.** There could scarcely be more contrast between the stately Le Méridien and its pointedly modern neighbor, the Kempinski. The rooms of this entirely renovated, early-20th-century building are decorated in the French Empire style and are both comfortable and plush, with king-size beds in every double room and large bathrooms with separate shower stalls and bathtubs. Rooms on the higher floors are slightly smaller but come with an individual balcony. ⊠ *District V, Erzsébet tér 9–10, Around Dék Ferenc tér H-1051* 🖼 *1/429–5500, 800/543–4300 in U.S. and Canada* 🖨 *1/429–5555* ⊕ *www.lemeridien. com* ⇝ *218 rooms, 27 suites* ♿ *Restaurant, room service, in-room data ports, in-room safes, minibars, cable TV, indoor pool, gym, hot tub, massage, sauna, steam room, bar, lobby lounge, shops, baby-sitting, dry cleaning, laundry services, concierge, Internet, business services, convention center, travel services, parking (fee), no-smoking floors* ▤ *AE, DC, MC, V* †◯| *EP* Ⓜ *M1, M2, M3: Deák tér.*

$$$$ 🏨 **Sofitel Atrium Budapest.** The former Hyatt-Regency's spectacular 10-story atrium—a mix of glass-capsule elevators, cascading tropical greenery, towering California date palms, and an actual prop plane suspended over an open bar—is impressive albeit not at all representative of the city it's in. Quintessentially Budapest, however, are the postcard views across the Danube to Castle Hill. All rooms are decorated and furnished in muted blues and light woods, and many overlook the Danube or Roosevelt tér. These, of course, are more expensive than those with less commanding views. ⊠ *District V, Roosevelt tér 2, Around Váci utca H-1051* 🖼 *1/266–1234* 🖨 *1/266–9101* ⊕ *www.sofitel.com* ⇝ *330 rooms, 23 suites* ♿ *2 restaurants, café, room service, in-room data ports, in-room safes, minibars, cable TV, indoor pool, gym, hair salon, hot tub, sauna, spa, 2 bars, casino, shops, baby-sitting, dry cleaning, laundry service, concierge, business services, Internet, convention center, meeting rooms, travel services, parking (fee), no-smoking floor* ▤ *AE, DC, MC, V* †◯| *EP* Ⓜ *M1: Vörösmarty tér.*

$$ 🏨 **Starlight Suites.** The Chain Bridge, Danube promenade, St. Stephen's Basilica, and the heart of the banking and business districts are all within walking distance of this all-suites hotel, making it ideal for independent travelers and executives alike, who prefer to come and go on foot. Rooms are bright and spacious, with two TVs, microwaves, and separate sleeping and working areas. Some have bathtubs and some only showers. The staff is efficient and friendly, and, upon request, they will deliver breakfast to your room for free. A no-groups policy keeps the hotel staff free to focus on meeting each individual's needs. ⊠ *District V, Mérleg u. 6, St. Stephen's Basilica H-1051* 🖼 *1/484–3700* 🖨 *1/484–*

3711 ⊕ *www.starlighthotels.com* 🖙 *54 suites* ⅋ *Café, in-room data ports, in-room safes, minibars, microwaves, cable TV, gym, sauna, steam room, Internet, travel services, parking (fee)* ▤ *AE, DC, MC, V* ⭕ *CP* Ⓜ *M1, M2, M3: Deák tér.*

$–$$ ⊞ **Budapest Marriott.** North American–style hospitality on the Pest side of the Danube begins with the buffet of glazed pastries served daily in the lobby and the smiling, polished service at the front desk. Guest rooms have lushly patterned carpets, floral bedspreads, and etched glass. The hotel's prime Danube location makes for some breathtaking views. Gellért Hill, the Chain and Elizabeth bridges, and Castle Hill are visible from every guest room, as well as the lobby, ballroom, and even the impressive hotel fitness center. Regular rates do not include breakfast and taxes, but discounted weekend package rates with breakfast are often available. ⊠ *District V, Apáczai Csere János u. 4, Around Váci utca H-1052* 🕿 *1/266–7000, 800/228–9290 in the U.S. and Canada* 🖷 *1/266–5000* ⊕ *www.marriott.com* 🖙 *342 rooms, 20 suites* ⅋ *2 restaurants, room service, in-room data ports, in-room safes, minibars, cable TV with movies, health club, massage, squash, bar, shops, baby-sitting, dry cleaning, laundry service, concierge, concierge floors, Internet, business services, convention center, car rental, travel services, parking (fee), no-smoking rooms* ▤ *AE, DC, MC, V* ⭕ *EP* Ⓜ *M1: Vörösmarty tér.*

Around Andrássy út and Király utca

The city's grandest boulevard is thriving with new restaurants, hotels, and shops yet still maintains its Old World grandeur. The Opera House, Heroes' Square, hip Liszt Ferenc tér, and the theater district are just some of Andrássy út's local treasures, all navigable on foot or by the charming "little metro." The leafy side streets of the diplomatic district near Heroes' Square provide a gentler pace while the boulevard's other end is full of city-center buzz. Nearby and running parallel to Andrássy út is grittier, up-and-coming Király utca, full of dark, atmospheric sidestreets and blending into the city's old Jewish quarter. Restaurants and nightspots abound.

$$$–$$$$ ⊞ **Andrássy Hotel.** Budapest's best boutique hotel has come a long way
Fodor's Choice from its origins as a 1930s-era orphanage. Opened as a hotel in 2001,
★ it exudes grand style. In the bright art deco lobby, the sound of rushing water from a glass-window waterfall blends artfully into soft jazz music playing on the sound system, and hip young staff receive guests at the funky orange-lit front desk. Done up in terra-cotta, blue, and cream, rooms are large and well-appointed; most have lovely balconies overlooking the trees and mansions of the Andrássy út. With colorful, coordinated tilework, bathrooms follow the room design. The lack of health and fitness facilities is disappointing, but free access to a nearby center is available. A surcharge applies to children staying with their parents. ⊠ *District VI, Andrássy út 111, Around Andrássy út H-1063* 🕿 *1/462–2100* 🖷 *1/322–9445* ⊕ *www.andrassyhotel.com* 🖙 *62 rooms, 8 suites* ⅋ *Restaurant, room service, in-room data ports, in-room safes, minibars, cable TV, bar, dry cleaning, laundry service, concierge, Internet, business services, meeting rooms, travel services, parking (fee), no-smoking rooms* ▤ *AE, DC, MC, V* ⭕ *EP* Ⓜ *M1: Bajza utca.*

★ **$$$** ⛩ **K+K Hotel Opera.** Location, location, location: the K+K Hotel Opera has it all, around the corner from Budapest's beautiful opera house and just far enough away from busy Andrássy út to block out the noise of traffic. Sunflower-yellow walls and bamboo and wicker furniture give the rooms a cheerful look. Better, smiling staff are willing to go the extra mile, and a hearty breakfast buffet will set you up well for a day's sightseeing. ⊠ *District VI, Révay u. 24, Around Andrássy út H-1065* ☎ *1/ 269–0222* 🖷 *1/269–0230* ⊕ *www.kkhotels.com* ⟲ *204 rooms, 2 suites* ☖ *Restaurant, room service, some in-room data ports, in-room safes, minibars, cable TV, gym, massage, sauna, steam room, bar, baby-sitting, dry cleaning, laundry service, concierge, Internet, business services, meeting rooms, parking (fee), some pets allowed (fee), no-smoking floors* ▤ *AE, DC, MC, V* ⛁ *BP* Ⓜ *M1: Opera.*

$$ ⛩ **Domina Hotel Fiesta.** On a typical cobblestone street near Pest's old Jewish quarter, this young hotel provides modern comforts in a nicely restored turn-of-the-20th-century building. Rooms are larger than at other city-center hotels, with high ceilings and simple yellow and navy blue decor, but the bathrooms have flimsy shower stalls rather than tubs. Inner-facing rooms can be dark; for more natural light, request one of the street-facing rooms, which are quiet despite the car and bus traffic. Breakfast is served in the vaulted cellar restaurant. A pianist entertains in the lobby bar every evening. ⊠ *District VI, Király u. 20, Around Király utca H-1061* ☎ *1/328–3000* 🖷 *1/266–6024* ⊕ *www.ahotelfiesta.hu* ⟲ *112 rooms* ☖ *Restaurant, room service, in-room data ports, in-room safes, minibars, cable TV, gym, sauna, bar, shop, dry cleaning, laundry service, Internet, business services, meeting rooms, parking (fee), some pets allowed (fee), no-smoking floor* ▤ *AE, DC, MC, V* ⛁ *BP* Ⓜ *M1, M2, M3: Deák tér.*

$ ⛩ **Club Hotel Ambra.** This small hotel, which was built in 1998, is downtown in Pest's atmospheric old Jewish quarter. Standard "studio" rooms are slightly run down and have mismatched floral and checkerboard spreads and drapes. Large bathrooms, kitchens, and fresher furnishings make "superior" rooms worth the extra €10. Payment in cash gets you a 10% discount. ⊠ *District VII, Kisdiófa u. 13 Around Király utca H-1077* ☎ *1/ 321–1538 or 1/321–1540* 🖷 *1/321–1533* ⊕ *www.hotelambra.hu* ⟲ *21 rooms* ☖ *In-room safes, some kitchens, minibars, cable TV, hot tub, sauna, billiards, bar, laundry service, travel services, parking (fee), no smoking* ▤ *AE, DC, MC, V* ⛁ *BP* Ⓜ *M1: Opera.*

$ ⛩ **Hotel Liget.** With majestic Heroes' Square and the Museum of Fine Arts just across the street, and City Park—with the zoo, the Széchenyi Baths, and Gundel restaurant—a short walk away, the location couldn't be more ideal. The distance seems even shorter should you choose to borrow one of the free bicycles. Rooms are blandly modern, with green wall-to-wall carpeting and blond-wood furniture. Request an upper-floor room facing Dózsa György út for views of the museums. ⊠ *District VI, Dózsa György út 106, Around Andrássy út H-1068* ☎ *1/269–5300* 🖷 *1/ 269–5329* ⊕ *www.liget.hu* ⟲ *139 rooms* ☖ *Restaurant, room service, in-room data ports, some in-room safes, minibars, cable TV, sauna, bar, bicycles, dry cleaning, laundry service, Internet, meeting room, parking (fee), some free parking, some pets allowed (fee), no-smoking floors* ▤ *AE, DC, MC, V* ⛁ *BP* Ⓜ *M1: Hősök tere.*

$ ⊞ **Hotel Pest.** Echoes of true, old Pest are preserved in this once-crumbling—
Fodor'sChoice   now imaginatively refurbished—18th-century apartment building. In typ-
★   ical Budapest style, rooms open off an inner courtyard shared with the private building next door, where thick, green ivy spills over wrought-iron railings. In the guest rooms, daylight filters discretely through sheer curtains and homey brown wood window frames. Decor is a soothing mix of dark-wood and sage-colored textiles. Only some bathrooms have tubs, but all have heated towel racks. The breakfast room's stone walls are covered by a central glass skylight. Stepping out to the street through the heavy wood door, you will find yourself in the heart of inner Pest, just two blocks from the Opera House. ⊠ *District VI, Paulay Ede u. 31, Around Andrássy út H-1061* ☎ *1/343–1198* 🖷 *1/351–9164* ⊕ *www.hotelpest.hu* ⏎ *25 rooms* ⧉ *Minibars, cable TV, bar, laundry service, Internet, meeting room, travel services, parking (fee), no-smoking floor; no a/c in some rooms* ⊟ *AE, DC, MC, V* ⦿| *BP* Ⓜ *M1: Opera.*

¢–$ ⊞ **Hotel Benczúr.** The leafy lanes of Budapest's embassy district are where you will find this quiet, simply furnished hotel. Majestic Heroes' Square is but a short walk away, and your transport to the center is the antique underground railway line, the Földalatti. Renovated rooms in the Benczúr wing are basic, but much better than those crying out for refurbishment in the shabby older wing, the former Pedagógus Hotel. The front desk staff is knowledgable and capable. ⊠ *District VI, Benczúr u. 35, Andrássy út H-1068* ☎ *1/479–5650* 🖷 *1/342–1558* ⊕ *www. hotelbenczur.hu* ⏎ *153 rooms* ⧉ *Restaurant, café, some in-room data ports, some minibars, cable TV, bar, laundry service, Internet, meeting rooms, travel services, parking (fee), no-smoking rooms; no a/c in some rooms* ⊟ *MC, V* ⦿| *BP* Ⓜ *M1: Bajza u.*

¢   ⊞ **Hotel Medosz.** This unfortunate-looking cement-block building has a very fortunate location: a small square just off famous Andrássy út, within easy walking distance of the Opera House, Budapest's theater district, and the Millennium underground. Inside it's all Soviet-era-institutional: ancient-looking bathtubs, bare wood floors, and fraying draperies. However, the good-humored front desk service and low prices make the Medosz an attractive budget option. Some rooms, accessible only by two flights of stairs, are best left for the young and able-bodied. ⊠ *District V, Jókai tér 9, Around Andrássy út H-1061* ☎ *1/374– 3001 or 1/353–1700* 🖷 *1/332–4316* ⊕ *www.medoszhotel.hu* ⏎ *68 rooms* ⧉ *Café, cable TV, travel services; no a/c, no phones in some rooms* ⊟ *MC, V* ⦿| *BP* Ⓜ *M1: Oktogon.*

Around Nyugati Train Station

The area immediately around Nyugati train station is bustling nearly 24 hours a day with travelers' comings and goings. By foot or the frequently running 4/6 tram zipping along Szent István körút you are just minutes away from Buda and Margaret Island in one direction, and Andrássy út in the other. Areas north of Szent István körút are less touristed so they're a good place to stay for those who like to be slightly off the beaten track.

$$–$$$ ⊞ **Hilton Budapest WestEnd.** Once you get over the fact that you are staying in a shopping mall—the swanky West End City Centre—you should be very happy indeed at this modern glass tower. Despite its bustling location next to Nyugati train station, the public spaces and guest rooms are hushed and peaceful owing to exceptional sound-proofing and structural planning. Facilities and amenities are top-notch, worthy of any international-standard business hotel. The aubergine and teal room decor is at once funky and understated. Rooms overlook Nyugati train station, the mall roof garden, or busy Váci út. ⊠ *District VI Váci út 1–3, Around Nyugati Train Station H-1069* ☎ *1/288–5500, 800/445–8667 in the U.S.* 🖷 *1/288–5588* ⊕ *www.budapest-westend.hilton.com* ⇗ *223 rooms, 7 suites* ⚐ *Restaurant, café, room service, in-room data ports, in-room safes, minibars, cable TV, gym, bar, baby-sitting, dry cleaning, laundry service, concierge, Internet, business services, convention center, travel services, parking (fee), some pets allowed (fee), no-smoking floors* ⊟ *AE, DC, MC, V* ⅥⓄⅠ *EP* Ⓜ *M3: Nyugati pályaudvar.*

$$–$$$ 🖷 **Radisson SAS Béke Hotel Budapest.** If you are arriving in Budapest's Nyugati train station from Prague or Berlin, the Radisson could scarcely be better located, situated as it is within walking distance, on a bustling stretch of the Körút. Upon arrival at the Radisson, top-hat wearing bellmen will usher you through revolving doors into an impressive reception area, replete with sweeping marble staircase. The bland though comfortable and modern rooms are a faint disappointment after such grandeur, but snappy service and a great location compensate. ⊠ *District VI, Teréz krt. 43, Around Nyugati Train Station H-1067* ☎ *1/889–3900* 🖷 *1/889–3915* ⊕ *www.radissonsas.com* ⇗ *239 rooms, 8 suites* ⚐ *Restaurant, room service, in-room data ports, in-room safes, minibars, cable TV, indoor pool, gym, massage, sauna, 2 bars, baby-sitting, dry cleaning, laundry services, concierge, Internet, business services, meeting rooms, travel services, parking (fee), no-smoking floors* ⊟ *AE, DC, MC, V* ⅥⓄⅠ *EP* Ⓜ *M3: Nyugati pályaudvar.*

🖫 **$$–$$$** 🖷 **Sydney Apartment Hotel.** Although half the clientele here are business executives on longer-term stays, that shouldn't deter you from choosing these impeccably stylish, spacious apartments with such amenities as self-catering kitchens and one of the nicest indoor pools in town. The very helpful 24-hour front-office service can even arrange for groceries or local restaurant meals to be delivered to your kitchen. The extra space makes these apartments a good deal for families as well as business travelers on longer stays. ⊠ *District XIII, Hegedűs Gyula utca 52–54, Around Nyugati Train Station H-1133* ☎ *1/236–8888* 🖷 *1/236–8899* ⊕ *www.sydneyaparthotel.hu* ⇗ *21 rooms, 76 suites* ⚐ *In-room data ports, in-room safes, kitchens, minibars, cable TV, indoor pool, gym, hot tub, massage, sauna, steam room, dry cleaning, laundry facilities, laundry service, Internet, meeting rooms, travel services, parking (fee), some pets allowed (fee), no-smoking floor* ⊟ *AE, DC, MC, V* ⅥⓄⅠ *EP* Ⓜ *M3: Lehel tér.*

$$ 🖷 **Danubius Thermal & Conference Hotel Helia.** While this well-known spa hotel's upriver location offers a less hectic pace, it also positions you in an uninteresting neighborhood among depressing, Soviet-era housing blocks. SO, choose the Helia for what's inside. The spa facilities are the most spotlessly clean in Budapest, and an on-site medical clinic caters to English-speaking clients. Rooms are reasonably spacious and kitted out in IKEA-influenced, Scandinavian style. To make the most of the location, request a newly renovated room on the Danube side with a downriver view. All rates include unlimited use of the thermal bath and free parking. Town is a few stops south on Bus 79. ☒ *District XIII, Kárpát u. 62–64, Around Nyugati Train Station H-1133* ☏ *1/889–5800* 🖷 *1/889–5801* ⊕ *www.danubiusgroup.com* ⚲ *254 rooms, 8 suites* ⚫ *Restaurant, café, in-room data ports, some in-room safes, minibars, cable TV, 3 indoor pools, gym, health club, hair salon, hot tub, spa, Turkish bath, bar, shops, dry cleaning, laundry service, concierge, Internet, business services, convention center, travel services, free parking, some pets allowed (fee), no-smoking floors* ☰ *AE, DC, MC, V* ⦿ *BP* Ⓜ *M3: Dózsa György út.*

★ $$ ⌨ **NH Budapest.** Extra-thick mattresses, a pick-your-own pillow bar, and free ironing service are some of the welcome extras that set this new Spanish-owned business hotel apart. In the eight-story atrium lobby, an up-to-the-minute flight schedule monitoring any changes is streamed in from Ferihegy onto the television screen behind the front desk. Dark-wood and gray-tone rooms, though on the small side, are slick and professional, each with a whimsical cherry-red easy chair for relaxing, either postwork or post-sightseeing. The NH is central to sights and business, just behind the Vígszínház theater. ☒ *District XIII, Vígszínház u. 3, Around Nyugati Train Station H-1137* ☏ *1/814–0000* 🖷 *1/814–0100* ⊕ *www. nh-hotels.com* ⚲ *160 rooms* ⚫ *Restaurant, room service, in-room data ports, in-room safes, minibars, cable TV, gym, massage, sauna, bar, dry cleaning, laundry service, Internet, meeting rooms, travel services, parking (fee), some pets allowed (fee)* ☰ *AE, DC, MC, V* ⦿ *EP* Ⓜ *M3: Nyugati pályaudvar.*

$ ⌨ **Fortuna Boat Hotel.** For a change of pace, you can bed down on this retired 1967 vessel, which once plied the waters of the Danube and is now anchored near the Pest side of the Margaret Bridge. Snug cabins, each named after a different nautical persona (Jacques Cousteau, Captain Cook), open off narrow, wood-paneled corridors with tiny chandeliers. Furnishings are basic, and miniature bathrooms are almost too small to shower in. Request a Danube-facing room; the other side looks onto the cement and traffic of the Pest quay. Headroom is low and stairways are narrow, making this a poor choice for people with mobility issues (or for the merely tall). A 14-room hostel section is downstairs in the hold; these cheaper but tiny rooms have shared baths. ☒ *District XIII, Szent István Park, Lower quay, Around Nyugati Train Station H-1137* ☏ *1/288–8100* 🖷 *1/270–0351* ⊕ *www.fortunahajo.hu* ⚲ *58 rooms, 44 with private bath* ⚫ *Restaurant, room service, minibars, cable TV, bar, dry cleaning, laundry service, meeting rooms, travel services, free parking, no smoking* ☰ *AE, MC, V* ⦿ *BP* Ⓜ *M3: Lehel tér.*

Around Blaha Lujza tér and Ferenc körút

Less touristy than its other end, the area around this section of the "big" ring road thrums with real-life Budapest, full of traffic and grit and interesting less-trodden side streets. With a growing number of new boutiques, restaurants, and nightspots, it's undergoing a real renaissance, but parts can still be dodgy at night, especially east of the körút.

$$$–$$$$ 🏨 **Corinthia Grand Hotel Royal.** One of the newer five-star properties in
Fodor'sChoice Budapest—and with 414 rooms, the biggest—the Royal is back to its
★ 1896 origins when it opened as a luxury hotel for the Magyar Millen-
nium. Josephine Baker stayed here in 1928; her guestbook entry is dis-
played in a case the near the entrance. The expansive atrium lobby is
full of Italian marble and wrought-iron ornamentation. Guest rooms are
stylish with dark woods and jewel-tone upholsteries; bathrooms are all-
Italian, from marble floors to gleaming fixtures. Some rooms look in-
ward onto the lobby. Brasserie Royal's popular Sunday "V.I.K." (very
important kids) brunch caters to children. ⊠ *District VII, Erzsébet krt.*
43–49, Around Blaha Lujza tér H-1073 ☎ *1/479–4000* 🖷 *1/479–4333*
⊕ *www.corinthiahotels.com* ☞ *363 rooms, 51 suites* ⚒ *3 restaurants,*
café, room service, in-room data ports, in-room safes, minibars, cable
TV, indoor pool, hair salon, spa, bar, dry cleaning, laundry service, con-
cierge, Internet, business services, convention center, travel services,
parking (fee), no-smoking floors ☱ *AE, DC, MC, V* ꘏*EP* Ⓜ *M2: Blaha*
Lujza tér.

$ 🏨 **Hotel Corvin.** This small, Hungarian-owned property is tucked onto
a calm side street off busy Ferenc körút, a once seedy, now up-and-com-
ing area. Rooms come with two or three single beds and have simple,
floral pastel decor. Those overlooking the hotel's courtyard are quieter
than those opening onto the street. ⊠ *District IX, Angyal u. 31, Around*
Ferenc körút H-1094 ☎ *1/218–6566* 🖷 *1/218–6562* ⊕ *www.*
corvinhotelbudapest.hu ☞ *44 rooms, 3 suites* ⚒ *Dining room, cable*
TV, bar, meeting rooms, travel services, parking (fee), no-smoking floors
☱ *AE, DC, MC, V* ꘏*BP* Ⓜ *M3: Ferenc krt.*

$ 🏨 **Hotel Sissi.** This little hotel is next door to the Hotel Corvin in the
once edgy ninth district of Pest, near the Museum of Applied Arts. Tiny
rooms are decorated in cheery blue and yellow with Ikea-style blond-
wood furniture. Blue and white checked tiles in the bathrooms—some
with shower stalls, some with tubs—are a sweet touch. Those sensitive
to street noise may prefer a room facing the backyard. ⊠ *District IX,*
Angyal u. 33, Around Ferenc körút H-1094 ☎ *1/215–0082* 🖷 *1/216–*
6063 ⊕ *www.hotelsissi.hu* ☞ *44 rooms* ⚒ *Room service, in-room*
safes, minibars, cable TV, bar, laundry service, Internet, meeting room,
travel services, parking (fee), no-smoking floors ☱ *AE, DC, MC, V* ꘏*BP*
Ⓜ *M3: Ferenc körút.*

$ 🏨 **Mercure Hotel Budapest Nemzeti.** The eggshell blue baroque facade of
this turn-of-the-20th-century building is difficult to miss, even in this
busy part of Pest. The expansive lobby and public areas are festooned with
pillars, arches, and wrought-iron railings. The high-ceilinged rooms,
though not unpleasant, are small and comparatively plain, with outdated
floral bedspreads and fittings. Quadruple-glazed windows shield the front
rooms from the noise of the busy intersection below, but sound-proof win-
dows can't change the fact that this area can be a hangout for streetwalkers
at night. ⊠ *District XIII, József krt. 4, Around Blaha Lujza tér H-1088*
☎ *1/477–2000, 800/637–2873 in the U.S.* 🖷 *1/477–2001* ⊕ *www.*
mercure-nemzeti.hu ☞ *75 rooms, 1 suite* ⚒ *Restaurant, some in-room*
data ports, in-room safes, minibars, cable TV, bar, dry cleaning, laundry
facilities, Internet, meeting rooms, travel services, parking (fee), no-smok-
ing floors ☱ *AE, DC, MC, V* ꘏*EP* Ⓜ *M2: Blaha Lujza tér.*

Around Kálvin tér, Ferenciek tere, and Asztoria

This bustling downtown area can get clogged with traffic but myriad side streets offer quick escape. Home to loads of shops, restaurants, nightspots, and cafés, not to mention the Nemzeti Múzeum, and with excellent transport links, this area is a good place to stay for those who like to be in the thick of things.

$$ 🏨 **Hotel Mercure Korona.** The downside of a big chain hotel on one of Budapest's busiest squares is that rooms are tiny and traffic outside is fierce. The upside, however, is you are central to all the sights and experiences of bustling downtown Pest, including the National Museum and some of the city's hottest nightlife. Newly refurbished rooms are the nicest, decorated in a Scandinavian style with patterns in geometric beiges and browns. ✉ *District V, Kecskeméti u. 14, Around Kálvin tér H-1053* ☎ *1/486–8800* 🖨 *1/318–3867* ⊕ *www.mercure-korona.hu* 🛏 *424 rooms* ⚄ *Restaurant, tapas bar, room service, in-room data ports, in-room safes, minibars, cable TV, indoor pool, massage, sauna, bar, shops, baby-sitting, dry cleaning, laundry service, Internet, business services, meeting rooms, travel services, parking (fee), no-smoking floors* ⊟ *AE, DC, MC, V* ⦿ *EP* Ⓜ *M3: Kálvin tér.*

$ 🏨 **Best Western Hotel Art.** On a narrow inner-city street, the six-story Art offers great location at a cost: the lobby and guest rooms are tiny and dark; perhaps claustrophobia accounts for the reluctant front-desk service as well. With two windows rather than one, however, upper-floor corner rooms are more pleasant and worth requesting when you reserve. The area has numerous good restaurants and hopping nightlife. ✉ *District V, Királyi Pál u. 12, Around Kálvin tér H-1053* ☎ *1/266–2166* 🖨 *1/266–2170* ⊕ *www.bestwestern-ce.com* 🛏 *29 rooms, 3 suites* ⚄ *Restaurant, some in-room safes, minibars, cable TV, gym, sauna, bar, Internet, business services, meeting rooms, travel services, parking (fee), some pets allowed (fee), no-smoking floor* ⊟ *AE, DC, MC, V* ⦿ *BP* Ⓜ *M3: Kálvin tér.*

$ 🏨 **City Hotel Mátyás.** This low-frills hotel serves breakfast in one of the most famous (and touristy) restaurants in town, sharing neoclassical quarters with the Mátyás Pince eatery. Newer rooms are standard pastel-contemporary and have small bathrooms with shower stalls. The hotel's older section is still inhabited by some private tenants and is accessed by a tiny rickety elevator. Converted from apartments, these rooms are spacious and have soaring ceilings, but are best taken by those who find exposed heating units and other such quirks atmospheric rather than off-putting. Some rooms have stunning views over the Elizabeth Bridge, Belvárosi Church, and beyond to Castle Hill. ✉ *District V, Március 15 tér 7–8, Around Ferenciek tere H-1056* ☎ *1/338–4711* 🖨 *1/317–9086* ⊕ *www.taverna.hu/matyas* 🛏 *79 rooms, 6 suites* ⚄ *Restaurant, minibars, cable TV, laundry service, Internet, meeting rooms, travel services, parking (fee), no-smoking floor; no a/c in some rooms* ⊟ *AE, DC, MC, V* ⦿ *BP* Ⓜ *M3: Ferenciek tere.*

$ 🏨 **Hotel Astoria.** Constructed between 1912 and 1914, the Astoria has a fascinating and turbulent history. The first independent Hungarian government was formed here in 1918, but later the Nazi high command used the Astoria more or less as its headquarters, as did the Soviet forces during the ill-fated revolution of 1956. Nowadays, rooms are genteel, spacious, and comfortable, with renovations faithful to the original Empire-style decor. The Café Mirror, with its dripping chandeliers, is a wonderful place to relive the Mittel-European coffeehouse tradition. ⊠ *District V, Kossuth Lajos u. 19–21, Around Asztoria H-1053* ☎ *1/ 889–6000* 🖷 *1/889–6091* ⊕ *www.danubiusgroup.com* ⤴ *126 rooms, 5 suites* ⚒ *Restaurant, café, room service, in-room safes, minibars, cable TV, shop, baby-sitting, dry cleaning, laundry service, Internet, business services, meeting rooms, travel services, parking (fee), no-smoking rooms; no a/c in some rooms* ⊟ *AE, DC, MC, V* ⍾ *EP* Ⓜ *M2: Astoria.*

$ 🖭 **Ibis Budapest Centrum.** Near the National Museum and right on the hopping café and nightlife zone of Ráday utca, this nine-story chain hotel is good value for those who want to burn the candle at both ends. Small rooms done up in orange and turquoise are reminiscent of a U.S. circa-1970s motel and have shower stalls but no tubs. Friendly, willing front-desk staff double as bartenders at the attached lobby bar, where microwaved snacks are available around the clock. Request an inner-facing room to avoid street noise. ⊠ *District IX, Ráday u. 6, Around Kálvin tér H–1092* ☎ *1/456–4100* 🖷 *1/456–4116* ⊕ *www.ibis-centrum. hu* ⤴ *126 rooms* ⚒ *Dining room, snack bar, in-room data ports, in-room safes, cable TV, bar, Internet, travel services, parking (fee), no-smoking floors* ⊟ *AE, DC, MC, V* ⍾ *BP* Ⓜ *M3: Kálvin tér.*

Near Parliament

$ 🖭 **Hotel Hold.** A fantastic location on a lovely street behind the American embassy and across from the ornately mosaiced Hungarian National Bank gives this low-key little hotel its appeal. Parliament and the Basilica are a few minutes' walk away. Converted from private apartments in the turn-of-the-20th-century building, most guest rooms are quite small but have soaring ceilings and tall windows with translucent white curtains. Furnishings are flimsy but adequate; there's royal blue wall-to-wall carpeting throughout. Avoid the rooms on the ground floor, as they open directly onto the courtyard restaurant. Most bathrooms have showers only, no tubs. ⊠ *District V, Hold u. 5, Parliament H-1054* ☎ *1/ 472–0480* 🖷 *1/472–0484* ⊕ *www.hotelhold.hu* ⤴ *25 rooms, 3 suites* ⚒ *Restaurant, minibars, cable TV, Internet, travel services* ⊟ *AE, DC, MC, V* ⍾ *BP* Ⓜ *M3: Arany János u.*

MARGARET ISLAND HOTELS

Full of grass and trees, staying on Margaret Island in the Danube is a lovely change of pace to the typical city visit. Downtown is about 30 minutes away by bus, less by taxi, making it good for those who like to see the sights but not sleep in them. The island's thermal bath complexes are an added benefit.

★ $$$ 🖭 **Danubius Thermal Hotel Margitsziget.** Bubbling up from ancient thermal springs, curative waters fill the pools of this established spa hotel on the island's northern end. Rates include the use of spa facilities and also complex health and beauty treatments. Every guest room has a balcony, where you can sit and watch the sun set or rise. Buda-facing (sunset) rooms have the nicest views. Having been renovated in 2001, the shining, spacious lobby and contemporary guest rooms come as a pleasant surprise given the hotel's Iron Curtain cement-block exterior. ⊠ *District XIII, Margitsziget, Margaret Island H-1138* ☎ *1/889–4700* 🖷 *1/ 889–4988* ⊕ *www.danubiusgroup.com* ↩ *259 rooms, 8 suites* ⅃ *Restaurant, café, room service, in-room data ports, in-room safes, minibars, cable TV, indoor pools, outdoor pool, health club, hair salon, spa, shops, 2 bars, dry cleaning, laundry service, Internet, business services, meeting rooms, travel services, parking (fee), some pets allowed (fee), no-smoking floors* ☱ *AE, DC, MC, V* ⋈ *BP* Ⓜ *Bus 26 to northern end of Margaret Island.*

$$–$$$ 🏨 **Danubius Grand Hotel Margitsziget.** The older, more attractive next-door neighbor of the Thermal Hotel Margitsziget was built in 1873 by Opera House architect Miklós Ybl in neo-Renaissance style. Ceilings are high here, and rooms are decorated in Empire style, with red- or blue-upholstered antique-looking wood furnishings. Guests have free admission to the Thermal's spa facilities, directly accessed by a heated, underground walkway. ⊠ *District XIII, Margitsziget, Margaret Island H-1138* ☎ *1/ 889–4700* 🖷 *1/889–4988* ⊕ *www.danubiusgroup.com* ↩ *154 rooms, 10 suites* ⅃ *2 restaurants, café, room service, in-room safes, minibars, cable TV, bar, pub, shops, baby-sitting, dry cleaning, laundry service, Internet, business services, meeting rooms, travel services, parking (fee), some pets allowed (fee), no-smoking rooms* ☱ *AE, DC, MC, V* ⋈ *BP* Ⓜ *Bus 26 to northern end of Margaret Island.*

ÓBUDA HOTELS

$$$$ 🏨 **Corinthia Aquincum Hotel.** Capital of the Roman province of Pannonia in the first century AD, this part of Buda is more on the outskirts these days. With the HÉV railway just outside the Aquincum's door, it's well situated for easy trips to Szentendre, as well as into town; the ancient sights of Óbuda are just around the corner. Rooms in this huge property are fairly small for a hotel of this category, but they are sufficiently comfortable. The main draws are the sparkling spa and thermal baths, fed by ancient springs on Margaret Island, which is a short walk or bike ride across the nearby bridge. Although it's right on the Danube, the immediate surroundings are rather drab: a busy highway, the suburban railway, and the concrete Árpád Bridge. ⊠ *District III, Árpád fejedelem útja 94, Óbuda H–1036* ☎ *1/436–4100* 🖷 *1/436–4156* ⊕ *www. corinthiahotels.com* ↩ *302 rooms, 8 suites* ⅃ *Restaurant, room service, in-room data ports, minibars, cable TV, 3 indoor pools, gym, hair salon, hot tub, sauna, spa, steam room, 2 bars, shops, dry cleaning, laundry service, concierge, Internet, business services, meeting rooms, travel services, some free parking, some pets allowed (fee), no-smoking rooms* ☱ *AE, DC, MC, V* ⋈ *BP* Ⓜ *HÉV: Árpád híd.*

NIGHTLIFE
& THE ARTS

By Kristen
Schweizer

LIFE IN BUDAPEST HARDLY GOES AWAY when the sun goes down. In addition to particularly rich cultural offerings (the city has several classical orchestras and, in the Liszt Ferenc Music Academy, one of central Europe's greatest performance spaces), there are also a host of bars and clubs, where the cultural offerings are somewhat less than classical. Now that Communism has passed out the realm of realpolitic and into the realm of kitsch, there's even a small subdivision of bars with a retro-Communist theme.

Although heavily subsidized during the Communist years, most cultural groups have been able to find their own footing with private funding. Though tickets are not as cheap as they were in years gone by, you can still go to a concert or opera for a song—by Western standards, at least. The price of the most expensive opera box seat is still less than half what you'd pay in New York or London or Paris.

In the summer, everyone seems to practically live outdoors. Cafés on virtually every major square are open until the wee hours, and open-air pubs and beer gardens seem to pop up everywhere, particularly in Pest.

NIGHTLIFE

The streets of Budapest might seem mysteriously quiet late at night, but that doesn't mean Hungarians are home in bed. Quite the contrary. This is a nation of heavy drinkers and smokers who stay up late doing both nearly every night of the week, especially during the summer months—May to September—when it seems that everyone in the capital is sometimes spilled across the terraces and outdoor seating areas of Pest. While the city's nightlife is typically concentrated in Pest, where the majority of watering holes are located, Buda also boasts some excellent spots, although nighttime there is typically much quieter and concentrated in neighborhood pubs. The big nightlife destinations are mostly in Pest.

Budapest as a whole, however, seems to have every kind of drinking establishment you might imagine, from discos and bars to quiet indoor courtyards, live music joints, and artsy Bohemian spaces. Local pubs, where you can get mostly beer and wine, called *söröző* (beer joints) or a *borozó* (wine bars), are scattered across the city. Knowing a few words of basic Hungarian will help you, as these places cater more to locals than tourists.

Thursday night is a big party night in Budapest, especially in Pest, and is often busier than a weekend evening—a tradition begun by students who preferred to party on Thursday night after most of the week's classes were finished and before they headed to their parents' home in the countryside on Friday afternoon. Most nighttime spots in Budapest are open until 4 AM, with the exception of several outdoor terrace squares, where bars close around midnight or 1 AM. There are also numerous bars that stay open 24 hours.

Most nightspots and clubs have both bars and dance floors, and some also have pool tables. Although some places do accept credit cards, it is still much more common to pay in cash for your night on the town. As is the case in most cities, the life of a club or disco in Budapest can be somewhat ephemeral. We recommend places that are popular and seem to have some staying power. But for the very latest on the more transient "in" spots, consult the "Nightlife" section of the weekly *Budapest Sun,* or *Budapest in Your Pocket,* which is published six times a year.

A word of warning to the smoke-sensitive: although a 1999 law requiring smoke-free areas in many public establishments has had a discernible impact in restaurants, the bar scene is a firm reminder that Budapest remains a city of heavy smokers.

And finally, while it can seem the party never stops in Budapest, especially with late-night and non-stop bars, the city does have its share of seedy go-go clubs and "cabarets," some of which are known for scandalous billing and physical intimidation. To avoid such rip-offs, check the American Embassy in Budapest for places to avoid, which are posted at ⊕ www.budapest.usembassy.gov.

Bars & Pubs

Budapest has a wide selection of nightlife spots. Popular among creative types is a vast array of Bohemian pubs and cafés where you can find writers and artists debating politics, poetry, and art well into the night. But there are also a good many flashy—and not very expensive—cocktail and lounge bars, particularly on the pedestrianized Liszt Ferenc tér, a big outdoor square on the Pest side of the city with a handful of cafés that spill out onto the square; this is one of the best spots in the city to people-watch. Also rising in popularity is Ráday utca, a less touristy cobblestone street in Pest that is loaded with outdoor restaurants and cafés. Watch your bags and belongings in both areas—in fact in all bars in Budapest—as petty theft is common. Hungarian pubs typically stay open until 4 AM, although most pubs on Liszt Ferenc tér and Ráday utca close around 1 AM.

While local Hungarian beer is average at best, try the country's national drink, *Unicum,* a bitter liquor made from more than 50 herbs drunk both for pleasure and to ward off ailments. Also worth trying are different varieties of Hungarian fruit brandy called *pálinka.* But be warned: this strong brandy is not for the weak of stomach.

Becketts. Conveniently located near the center of Budapest, Becketts Irish pub attracts a mostly male ex-pat crowd and is a great place for lunch, an afternoon pint while you are watching a soccer match, or a rollicking good time in the evening when bands come on and the place fills up. ⊠ *District V, Bajcsy-Zsilinszky út 72, Around Nyugati Train Station* ☏ *1/311–1035* Ⓜ *M3: Nyugati.*

Cactus Juice. The interior is rustic American "Wild West." The pub serves lunch and dinner during the day but turns into a popular dance spot for Hungarians at night. It is usually open until dawn. ⊠ *District VI, Jókai tér 5, Around Andrássy út* ☏ *1/302–2116* Ⓜ *M1: Oktogon.*

Cafe Vian. Of all the see-and-be-seen cafés in Budapest, Vian is perhaps the most renowned, partly because of its unbeatable spot in Liszt Ferenc tér. It's a great place to while away the hours chatting and people-watch-

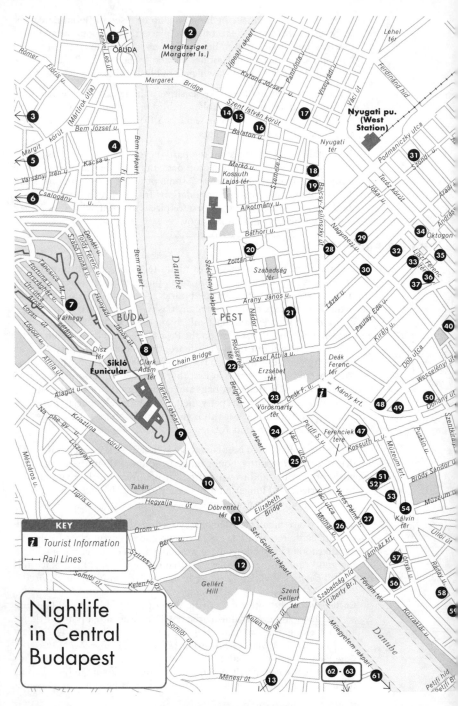

Nightlife in Central Budapest

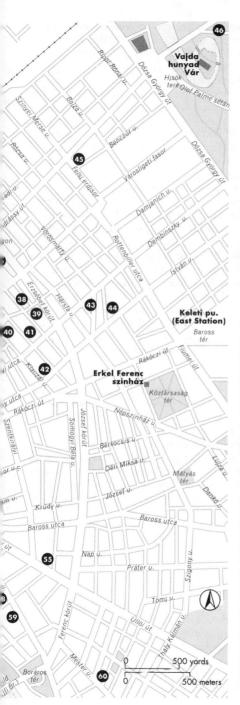

ing, either inside and surrounded by an ever-changing exhibit of modern art, or outside in the summer under a canopy. ⊠ *District VI, Liszt Ferenc tér 9, Around Andrássy út* ☎ *1/342–8991* Ⓜ *M1: Oktogon.*

Castro. A good mix of locals and ex-pats can be found at Castro any given night of the week. The popular Cuban-themed bar, with movie posters and artwork dotting the walls, tends to get extremely smoky but is well-positioned along Ráday utca. Castro also serves heavy, greaseladen Serbian food. Internet access is available on several computer terminals in the back, and you'll find outdoor seating along the street in warmer months. ⊠ *District IX, Ráday utca 35, Around Kálvin tér* ☎ *1/217–0269* Ⓜ *M3: Kálvin tér.*

Club Seven. Club Seven has more than one place to play, including an elegant cocktail bar separate from the main room, where an outgoing Hungarian crowd grooves to a mixture of live jazz, rock cover bands, and recorded dance music. And don't be put off by the surly bouncers. ⊠ *District VII, Akácfa u. 7, Around Blaha Lujza tér* ☎ *1/478–9030* Ⓜ *M2: Blaha Lujza.*

FodorśChoice ★ **Fészek Artists' Klub.** Bohemian Budapest is alive and well at Fészek, a huge club that dates back 100 years and attracts writers, artists, and other creative souls. A large enclosed drinking garden is covered with a canopy during the winter and heated with large outdoor lamps. A pizzeria is also outside, above the garden; a restaurant inside serves up delicious meals. Downstairs in the cellar, live musical acts from jazz to blues to hard rock can be heard most nights of the week, and the entire place is open 24 hours a day. ⊠ *District VII, Kertész ut. 36, Around Kiraly utca* ☎ *1/342–6548* Ⓜ *M1: Oktogon.*

Iguana. Aside from serving the only decent Mexican food in town, Iguana is a popular nightlife spot for ex-pats, where strong margaritas are quickly gulped down. The pub also hosts several outdoor street parties during the year, including the annual "Cinco de mayo" block party. ⊠ *District V, Zoltán u. 16, Parliament* ☎ *1/331–4352* Ⓜ *M2: Kossuth Lajos tér.*

★ **Lánchíd Söröző.** Next to Clark Ádá tér, a large square in Buda at the foot of the *Lánchíd* (Chain Bridge), this tiny pub attracts tourists and locals alike. The walls are covered in black-and-white photos from Budapest and Paris. Ask for owner Róbert Nagy, who speaks excellent English and loves to meet visitors from abroad. ⊠ *District 1, Fő utca 4, Around Batthyány tér* ☎ *1/214–3144.*

★ **Menza.** The name, which means "canteen" in Hungarian, refers to student cafeterias that were free of charge when the country was still under Communism. The Menza at this location boasts a funky, retro style in green, orange, and black colors, and it's a bit cheaper than most of the outdoor spots on Liszt Ferenc tér. ⊠ *District VI, Liszt Ferenc tér 2, Around Andrássy út* ☎ *1/413–1482* Ⓜ *M1: Oktogon.*

Negro. Conveniently situated on the square next to the Szent István Basilica, Negro is a sleek black and metal cocktail bar, upscale by Hungarian standards. Plenty of outdoor seating is available during the warmer months. ⊠ *District V, Szent István tér 11, St. Stephen's Basilica* ☎ *1/302–0136* Ⓜ *M3: Arany János.*

Oscar American Bar. Attracts a mixed Hungarian and international crowd, who venture over the Danube to what is, perhaps, Buda's most jumping neighborhood bar. Old-time Hollywood movie stills adorn its walls. ⊠ *District I, Ostrom u. 14, Around Moszkva tér* ☎ *1/212–8017* Ⓜ *M2: Moszkva tér.*

Picasso Point. Situated close to Budapest's opera and theater district, Picasso Point is a good pub where you can kick back for a few drinks. There's dancing in the basement at night with a DJ usually spinning the tunes. ⊠ *District VI, Hajós u. 31, Around Andrássy út* ☎ *1/312–1727* Ⓜ *M3: Arany János.*

Portside. This large underground warehouse with a nautical theme packs in a yuppie crowd on a near nightly basis. ⊠ *District VII, Dohány utca 7, Around Astoria* ☎ *1/351–8405* Ⓜ *M2: Astoria.*

★ **Pót Kulcs.** The name of this pub means "spare key," and this one attracts a hip, bohemian crowd. There is no sign outside, just a metal door bearing the name and address. Walk through the door and down the small pathway to find outdoor seating in warm months and a bit of respite from the smoky bar inside. At midnight on Friday and Saturday, gypsy bands play inside. Don't be surprised to smell marijuana wafting in the air. ⊠ *District VI, Csengery u. 65/b, Around Nyugati Train Station* ☎ *1/ 269–1050* Ⓜ *M3: Nyugati.*

Rigoletto. This bar packs them in weeknights as well as weekends, with a tempting two-for-one regular cocktail special. The music program is more varied—some nights live, mellow jazz; on weekends commercial disco. ⊠ *District XIII, Visegrádi u. 9, Around Nyugati Train Station* ☎ *1/237–0666* Ⓜ *M3: Nyugati.*

Sark. A short walk around the corner from Szimpla, this pub also caters to an artistic crowd. Interesting portraits of everyday people cover the walls while the cellar downstairs offers several *csó-csó* (foosball) tables, offering a chance to play a popular Hungarian bar sport. ⊠ *District VII, Klauzal u. 14, Around Kiraly utca* ☎ *1/328–0753* Ⓜ *M2: Blaha Lujza tér.*

Szimpla. This is another bohemian hot spot—just around the corner from Sark—where a host of local creative types gather in the large underground cellar, sprawled over an eclectic mix of furniture. Live jazz music is offered several nights a week in an extremely smoky environment. ⊠ *District VII, Kértesz u. 48, Around Kiraly utca* ☎ *30/275–7616* Ⓜ *M1: Oktogon.*

Dance Clubs & Discos

When Hungarians go out dancing, they typically stay out until dawn, evidenced by the variety of late-night dance clubs and discos around the capital city. Hungarians also party down in style, often donning their best outfits, with women in stiletto heels and men generous with hair gel. Some of the most lively nightlife in Budapest hinges around the electronica scene: trance, techno, drum 'n' bass, etc. Most dance clubs charge a cover which usually ranges between HUF 1,000 and HUF 1,500.

A38. A large ship permanently moored on the Buda side of the Danube has a restaurant upstairs and a large dance floor downstairs. Tuesday is jazz, Wednesday retro, Thursday reggae, Friday electronic, Saturday Latin. ⊠ *District XI, Near the Petőfi Híd, on the Buda side of the river, South Buda* ☎ *1/464–3940.*

★ **Cha-Cha-Cha.** This tiny, sweaty dance club in the Kálvin tér metro station packs in partygoers until dawn. DJs are featured Thursday through Saturday nights. It is often so crowded that people pour outside the club into the metro station walkway. ⊠ *District IX, Kálvin tér underpass, Around Kálvin tér* ☎ *1/215–0545* Ⓜ *M3: Kálvin tér.*

Citadella Dance Club. From the top of Budapest's beautiful Gellért Hill, you can gaze at the city's landscape through large windows while cutting a rug on the dance floor. Be warned that drinks are expensive and so are the taxis waiting outside to take you back down the hill. Unless you traipse back down to the tram/bus stops in front of the Gellért Hotel, public transportation is not available from here in the late-night hours. ⊠ *District XI, Citadella sétány 2, Gellért Hill & the Taban* ☎ *1/209–3271.*

Dokk Backstage. Budapest's version of a truly glitzy international disco is great for people-watching, especially if you wish to observe the get-rich-quick set and their trophy girlfriends at play. Dokk is more expensive than most dance and disco bars, with cocktails averaging around HUF 3,000 apiece. ⊠ *District III, Hajógyári sziget 122, Óbuda* ☎ *1/457–1023.*

Közgáz Pince Club. This large, underground dance club at the Budapest Economics University attracts a younger crowd. ⊠ *District IX, Fővám tér 8, Around Kálvin tér* ☎ *1/215–4359* Ⓜ *M3: Kálvin tér.*

Nincs Pardon (No excuse). There are plenty of reasons to come here and dance until dawn. Watch the steep steps coming into the underground dance club, though. Once you are past the bar, you'll find a series of several dance floors in back. ⊠ *District VII, Almássy tér 11, Around Blaha Lujza tér* ☎ *1/351–4351* Ⓜ *M2: Blaha Lujza tér.*

Fodor'sChoice **Piaf.** Next to Budapest's opera and theater district, Piaf is one of the city's
★ most interesting late-night clubs, with a piano bar and singer upstairs and a small dance floor underground. Watch for the small, red PIAF sign outside the bar, and ring the doorbell to get in, although your success sometimes depends on the mood of the doorkeeper. The entrance fee includes the first drink. Piaf is open from about 10 PM to 7 AM. ⊠ *District VI, Nagymező u. 20, Around Andrássy út* ☎ *1/312–3823* Ⓜ *M3: Arany János.*

Tracadero. It's billed as the only Latin disco in town, and weekends are the best nights to dance here. Occasional live acts include salsa and merengue shows. Be careful to enter the sign for Tracadero, as the place next door is for the "Nirvana Bar," a strip club known to be run by the mafia, which you should avoid. ⊠ *District V, Szent István körút 15, Around Nyugati Train Station* ☎ *1/311–4691* Ⓜ *M3: Nyugati.*

Retro-Communist

Although Communism is long gone in Hungary, the following spots either make their living off a nostalgia for the past or never got around to updating their interiors. Either way, time spent at one of the following is a trip down Budapest's memory lane.

★ **Bambi Eszpresszó.** This is the perfect place to sip Dreher, the popular Hungarian beer and watch older Hungarian men pass the day playing chess.

Sit inside the bare-bones establishment, on red plastic-covered chairs and peer out through white lace curtains that appear decades old, or outside on the terrace during warmer months. Rude service by the older Hungarian lady serving drinks is free of charge and adds to Bambi's character. ⊠ *District I, Frankel Leó u. 2–4, Around Battyány tér* ☎ *1/212– 3171* Ⓜ *M2: Batthyány tér.*

Jaffa. Named after an orange soda popular under Communism, Jaffa is laid-back cool, with a retro orange and black interior. Order a glass of Jaffa for yourself and decide. ⊠ *District IX, Ráday u. 39, Around Kálvin tér* ☎ *1/219–5285* Ⓜ *M3: Kálvin tér.*

Marxim. Across the street from Budapest's Millenáris Park, this bar and pizza parlor is a tribute to socialism, including graffiti-scrawled walls, chicken wire, and black and red paint smeared everywhere. Try the "Gulag Pizza," covered in spicy red paprika, ham, and corn; it also comes with a bottle of ketchup to pour on top—a popular condiment Hungarians slather on their pizza. ⊠ *District II, Kisrókus u. 23, Around Moszkva tér* ☎ *1/316–0231* Ⓜ *M2: Moszkva tér.*

Fodor's Choice ★ **Mélypont.** If you ever wondered what Hungarian interior design looked like under Communism, then look no further. A walk into this basement bar is a carefully stylized step back into 1970s Hungary, with decor mostly in black, orange, and lacquered wood. Old clocks, rugs, uncomfortable reclining chairs, and an espresso machine the size of a desk are all on hand to see. ⊠ *District V, Magyar utca 23, Around Kálvin tér* ☎ *No phone* Ⓜ *M3: Kálvin tér.*

Resti Kocsma. Hand-painted murals of socialist workers as well as old posters and pictures of Communist leaders adorn the walls of this basement restaurant/pub/Communist museum in the city center. A large, red-tiled star covers a sizable spot on the floor, and chains wind down the staircase from the street above. On Friday and Saturday nights, a DJ plays Hungarian hits from the 1970s, as the pub becomes a disco until 2 AM. ⊠ *District V, Deák Ferenc u. 2, Around Váci utca* ☎ *1/266–6210* Ⓜ *M1: Vörösmarty tér.*

Seasonal

Warm weather in Budapest means outdoor pubs and outdoor *kertek* (gardens), many of which offer live music and DJs on most nights. The kertek typically open in early May, when warm weather approaches, and close for the season around mid-September. Most places stay open daily until dawn.

Érzsébet Híd Eszpresszo. At the foot of the Érzsébet bridge in Buda, across from the Rudas baths, the Érzsébet Eszpresszo pub has a large outdoor terrace offering a beautiful view of the Danube River and the Pest landscape. ⊠ *District I, Döbrentei tér 1, Gellért Hill & the Taban* ☎ *1/212–2127.*

Rómkert. Directly across from the Érzsébet Eszpresszo, this outdoor pub in front of the Rudas baths specializes in cocktails. It's usually packed with yuppies and young Hungarian women, often wearing very little clothing. Rómkert is open daily and extremely crowded on weekends, when the crowd grinds to the dance music. ⊠ *District I, Döbrentei tér 9, Gellért Hill & the Taban* ☎ *No phone.*

CloseUp
BUDAPEST'S OWN WOODSTOCK

BUDAPEST IS THE HOME of Central Europe's annual Sziget Fesztival (Island Festival). The week-long event, which is held in late July or early August, is the region's largest outdoor music festival. The normally deserted Hajogyár Island in northern Budapest, a former shipyard, is taken over by 15 musical stages and 60 different venues for performing arts, classical music, blues, jazz, and poetry readings. Food and beer stands, amusement rides, and vendors hocking clothing, jewelry, and other items are also sprinkled over the island. A special area is dedicated to children's programs.

An estimated 300,000 people show up for the weeklong festival every year, and it has some 800 performances. But for a festival that has featured the likes of David Bowie, Lou Reed, Run DMC, Oasis, and Massive Attack, its beginnings were meager. Founded by Hungarian students,

the festival's first year in 1993, when it was called "Student Island," featured only local acts but attracted 43,000 people. A few years later, Pepsi snatched up sponsorship of the event and renamed it "Pepsi Island." Under Pepsi's leadership, Budapest was able to attract big names to the event for the first time.

In 2001, however, festival organizers endured a barrage of criticism by gay and lesbian groups after the organizers signed an agreement with the mayor to prohibit programs that included gay and lesbian themes at the event. The case went to court, and a local judge granted an injunction barring the agreement from taking effect on the grounds of discrimination. Festival organizers eventually apologized, and that year's festival went on as originally planned. Beginning in 2003, Pepsi stopped its sponsorship, so the event is now called the Sziget Fesztival.

Sark-kert. Sark-kert is the summer location of the Sark pub, which grills up Hungarian food on an outdoor barbecue nightly. Enjoy a tranquil evening under the stars on Margaret Island. From the Margit híd (Margaret Bridge) walk straight down the island following signs for the "Margaret Island Youth Hostel," Sark-kert is located adjacent to the hostel. ⊠ *District XIII, Margitsziget, Margaret Island* ☎ *No phone* Ⓜ *M3: Nyugati.*

West Balkan. A great outdoor dance spot in Budapest is a bit tricky to find. From the Buda side of the Lágymányos Bridge, walk south for about 10 to 15 minutes, following the Danube. You can also take a bicycle rickshaw from the bridge or from Zöldpardon. ⊠ *District XI, Kopaszi gát, South Buda* ☎ *No phone.*

Zöldpardon. The largest outdoor drinking garden in Budapest, which is located near the Buda side of the Petőfi Bridge, opens daily in the afternoons and stays open until dawn, serving breakfast and other food. Big-name Hungarian musical acts are featured on a regular basis, as well as DJs spinning house and drum 'n' bass music on a nightly basis. ⊠ *District XI, Goldmann György tér, South Buda* ☎ *No phone.*

Wine Bars

Budapest has literally hundreds of wine bars around the city, called *borozó*, but the majority are smoky little joints packed with older Hungarians from open until close. A borozó is perfectly safe to stop at and sample a slice of everyday Hungarian life; you can often get a small sampling of snacks to go with your wine. The places recommended here are good spots to try Hungarian wines, which, according to many wine experts, are among the top wines produced in Europe.

Fodor'sChoice
★ **BorBíróság** (Wine Court). Tucked behind the *Vásárcsarnok* (Central Market Hall) in downtown Budapest, this is just about the best place in Budapest to sample a range of quality Hungarian wines, unless you are planning a visit to the wine regions yourself. It's a bit pricey by Hungarian standards—a small glass of wine costs the equivalent of several dollars, on average. But the owners pride themselves on selecting the best 120 wines Hungary has to offer, and it's true. You can easily spend an entire afternoon or evening sampling different great wines here. Also check out the daily "Wine Happy Hour" from 4 to 5 PM, where every glass of wine is half-price. ⊠ *District IX, Csarnok tér 5, Around Kálvin tér* ☎ *1/219–0902* Ⓜ *M3: Kálvin tér.*

Egri Borozó. This borozó specializes in wine from the eastern Hungarian city of Eger. In the warmer months, you can order a small or large pint of the famed red *Bikavér* (Bull's Blood) while sitting on the terrace outside, or when the weather is less nice you can stay in the cellar-level bar. ⊠ *District V, Bajcsy-Zsilinszky út 72, Around Nyugati Train Station* ☎ *1/302–1724* Ⓜ *M3: Nyugati.*

Magyar Bortársaság (Hungarian Wine Society). Though technically not a wine bar, this shop has a wide selection of local vintages as well as locations in both Pest and Buda. It sells wine from every region of the country, and there are plenty of opportunities to try different wines at the free wine tastings each Saturday from 2 to 5. ⊠ *District 1, Batthyány utca 59, Around Moszkva tér* ☎ *1/212–2569* Ⓜ *M3: Moszkva tér* ⊠ *District IX, Ráday u. 7, Around Kálvin tér* ☎ *1/219–5647* Ⓜ *M3: Kálvin tér.*

Martino Gallery & Café. This cozy wine bar cum gallery looks like the living room of your artsy Parisian friend. The tiny space is filled with café tables and bookshelves; local artists exhibit their paintings on the wall. You can choose from a good selection of Hungarian wines as well as one of the best selections of French wines in Budapest. It's closed on Sundays. ⊠ *District V, Galamb u. 5, Around Ferenciek tere* ☎ *1/338–2880* Ⓜ *M3: Ferenciek tere.*

Sandaken Lisboa. The name might make you think this bar specializes in port, but in fact, only Hungarian wine is sold at this small wine bar along the pedestrianized Hajos utca, behind the Hungarian State Opera House. Take note, a bottle or glass of fine Hungarian wine is cheaper here than in a supermarket. ⊠ *District VI, Hajós u. 23, Around Andrássy út* ☎ *20/494–4545* Ⓜ *M1: Oktogon.*

Tokaji Borozó. This extremely smoky, underground wine bar offers Hungarian whites from the eastern Tokaj region plus snacks. It's usually filled with older Hungarians playing cards or chess, or debating politics. ⊠ *District V, Falk Miksa utca 32, Around Nyugati Train Station* ☎ *No phone* Ⓜ *M3: Nyugati, or M2: Kossuth Lajos tér.*

Vörös és Fehér Wine Bar & Restaurant. True wine lovers can choose from more than 150 types of Hungarian and international wines. Owned and operated by the Hungarian Wine Society, which also has popular wine shops in Budapest, "Red & White" is one of the best upscale wine bars and restaurants in Budapest. See also the review *in* Where to Eat. ✉ *District VI, Andrássy út 41, Around Andrássy út* ☎ *1/413–1545.*

Gay & Lesbian

Outward public affection among gays is pretty much under wraps in Budapest—even hand-holding is something rarely seen on the streets. The gay club scene, however, is quite lively, and many of the discos listed below are packed on weekends and a bit more mellow on weekdays. Virtually all gay bars and discos charge a cover of HUF 1,500 to HUF 2,500, or have a drink minimum. With the exception of Eklektika, Budapest's gay bars are mainly male-dominated, although Angyal, Capella, and Club Bohemian Alibi have some lesbian and straight clientele. Check out Web sites ⊕ www.gayguide.net and ⊕ www.gay.hu for the latest on gay clubs and happenings in the city. The major gay event is the annual Gay Pride Budapest festival and parade, which is held in early July.

Action Bar. Action is the perfect name for this bar in the city center, which features a popular dark room and video room, as well as go-go and erotic dance shows starting at midnight. The crowd is all-male, and this is mostly a pick-up scene, definitely not a place to go for a quiet drink. ✉ *District V, Magyar u. 42, Around Kálvin tér* ☎ *1/266–9148* Ⓜ *M3: Kálvin tér.*
Angyal Bar and Disco. Budapest's busiest gay dance club also attracts a mixed gay–straight crowd, who pack the floor to groove along to souped-up disco and happy house. It's closed Monday through Wednesday, and Saturday night is for men only. ✉ *District VII, Szövetség u. 33, Around Blaha Lujza tér* ☎ *1/351–6490* Ⓜ *M2: Blaha Lujza tér.*
Café Capella. Open Wednesday through Saturday, the club attracts a mixed gay–straight crowd clustered in this basement disco for frequent, glittery drag shows. There's also great music and lots of floor space to dance until dawn. ✉ *District V, Belgrád rakpart 23, Around Ferenciek tere* ☎ *1/318–6231.*
Chaos. This men-only bar is in a huge cellar with an industrial-looking, brick and metal motif. There's a small dance floor with a nightly DJ. Chaos also hosts a monthly leather-and-fetish sex party. ✉ *District VII, Dohány u. 38, Around Astoria* ☎ *1/344–4884* Ⓜ *M2: Astoria.*
Club Bohemian Alibi. One of the most popular gay bars in Budapest, Alibi is a basement club with three bars. Entertainment is provided by DJs and a midnight "Best Bohemian Transvestite" show that features singing, dancing, and occasional guest stars from the theater community. It also serves food until 11 PM. ✉ *District VIII, Üllői út 45, Around Ferenc Jozsef krt.* ☎ *20/314–1949* Ⓜ *M3: Ferenc Jozsef körút.*
Eklektika. A mixed straight and lesbian clientele frequents this quaint café with huge windows looking out on a historic neighborhood in Pest. Filled with 1960s and '70s furniture and relics, Eklektika also serves delicious food. The second Saturday of every month is a women-only

evening. ⊠ *District V, Semmelweis u. 21, Around Astoria* ☎ *1/266–1226* Ⓜ *M2: Astoria.*

Live Music Venues

Jazz & Blues

Fat Mo's. Established Hungarian jazz headliners and young up-and-comers play from Thursday through Saturday in the popular, though small, stylishly brick-walled cellar pub. The music is good, but the audience is mainly expats and tourists. ⊠ *District V, Nyári Pál u. 11, Around Ferenciek tere* ☎ *1/267–3199* Ⓜ *M3: Ferenciek tere.*

Jazz Garden. The basement jazz club/restaurant presents well-known Hungarian jazz musicians on a regular basis. ⊠ *District V, Veres Pálné u. 44/a, Around Ferenciek tere* ☎ *1/266–7364* Ⓜ *M3: Ferenciek tere.*

Long Jazz Club. A great place to see amateur live jazz acts on a nightly basis, the large cellar has ample seating and a bar. Outside the stage area is another bar and many places to sit while you listen to jazz recordings. ⊠ *District VII, Dohány u. 22–24, Around Astoria* ☎ *1/322–0006* Ⓜ *M2: Astoria.*

Old Man's Music Pub. One thing you can't fault this place for is consistency; it's packed even on Monday night. Of course, in Hungary that means you'll be inhaling a fair bit of second-hand smoke. If that doesn't ruin your fun, enjoy the live bluesy rock and jazz, as well as the friendly chaos behind the bar—while everyone squeezes onto the small dance floor. ⊠ *District VII, Akácfa u. 13, Around Blaha Lujza tér* ☎ *1/322–7645* Ⓜ *M2: Blaha Lujza tér.*

Trafó Bár Tango. In the basement of the Trafó House of Contemporary Arts, this bar features regular live jazz performances from some of Budapest's best jazz musicians including Mihály Dresch and Elemér Balázs. ⊠ *District IX, Liliom u. 41, Around Ferenc József krt.* ☎ *1/456–2040* Ⓜ *M3: Ferenc körút.*

Rock & Eclectic

Benczúr Klub. With a nice outdoor terrace in summer months, the Benczúr features local rock, folk, and jazz acts on a near-weekly basis indoors year-round. ⊠ *District VI, Benczúr u. 27, Around Andrássy út* ☎ *1/321–7334* Ⓜ *M1: Kodály Körönd.*

Pesti Est Cafe. While the upstairs is one of Liszt Ferenc tér's many indoor/outdoor pubs, downstairs you'll find a stage and bar that regularly features local rock and other eclectic acts. ⊠ *District VI, Liszt Ferenc tér 5, Around Andrássy út* ☎ *1/344–4381* Ⓜ *M1: Oktogon.*

Petőfi Csarnok. In City Park, this is a venue where local and mid-level international acts play regularly. However, the best time to drop in is in the summer, when the outdoor amphitheater is open, affording a pleasant switch from indoor drab interior. ⊠ *District XIV, Zichy Mihály út 14, City Park* ☎ *1/363–3730* Ⓜ *M1: Széchenyi Fürdő.*

Rocktogon. A large basement club features local rock, punk, and other acts every week. When there isn't a live act, the club regularly hosts DJs spinning dance and punk tunes into the wee hours of the night. ⊠ *District V, Mozsár u. 9, Around Andrássy út* ☎ *30/232–7914* Ⓜ *M1: Oktogon.*

Süss Fél Nap. Typically hosting a younger crowd, this is a good place to see up-and-coming rock, punk, techno, and electronic music acts. The colorful, busy interior is decorated with murals, paintings, and lots of tables, benches, and chairs. ⊠ *District V, Corner of Honvéd u. and Szent István körút, Around Nyugati Train Station* ☎ *1/374–3329* Ⓜ *M3: Nyugati.*

Wigwam. Although outside the city center, this is one of the few bars featuring live rock and heavy metal acts on a large stage. When the music's not live, you can twist and thrash on the dance floor while rock DJs spin the tunes. ⊠ *District XI, Fehévári út 202, South Buda* ☎ *1/208–5569.*

Casinos

There are literally hundreds of casinos in Budapest, but most are small establishments on side streets and are best avoided—as they are typically money laundering operations for the mafia. The casinos we list here are the largest in Budapest and are perfectly legal and safe to visit.

Casino Budapest Hilton. Inside the Hilton Hotel in the Castle District, this casino is among the most popular, with table games and slots. It's open daily from 7 PM to 2 AM. ⊠ *District 1, Budapest Hilton, Hess András tér 1–3, Castle District* ☎ *1/375–1001* Ⓜ *M2: Moszkva tér.*

Las Vegas Casino. The centrally located casino is inside the Sofitel Atrium. It's open daily from 2 PM to 5 AM and features 26 table games as well as slots. ⊠ *District V, Sofitel Atrium Budapest, Roosevelt tér 2, Around Váci utca* ☎ *1/317–6022* Ⓜ *M1: Vörösmarty tér.*

Tropicana. Next to Vörösmarty tér, the Tropicana is popular with locals as well as tourists. Sit outside during warmer months under palm trees. It's open daily from 2 PM to 5 AM. ⊠ *District V, Vigádó u. 2, Around Váci utca* ☎ *1/327–7250* Ⓜ *M1: Vörösmarty tér.*

Várkert Casino. An 1879 building designed by prolific architect Miklós Ybl—who also designed the State Opera House—the Várkert is the most visually striking of the city's casinos. It's open daily from 2 PM to 5 AM. ⊠ *District I, Miklós Ybl tér 9, Gellért Hill & the Taban* ☎ *1/202–4244.*

PERFORMING ARTS

Budapest is a city deeply-rooted in its love and appreciation for the performing arts. During the main season, which runs from September through June, you can find ballet, opera, classical music, and theater performances any night of the week. And compared to performances in many European cities, tickets to events in Budapest are dirt cheap.

The Hungarians have kept the arts in full swing, as nearly every theater and performing arts house that existed under socialism—and was heavily subsidized by the state—is still in operation today, even though many have since been privatized, and only a handful remain subsidized by the state or local governments. A night out at the opera or ballet is no casual affair. Hungarians dress for the occasion, and that usually means business or formal attire. Nor are the arts reserved only for older members of society. It is quite common to see teenagers and young adults donning their best outfits for the opera or the ballet.

Hungary is, perhaps, best known for modern classical music, having produced two of the most famous composers of the 20th century, Béla Bartók and Zoltán Kodály, both of whose works are widely played throughout the city by numerous orchestras. Budapest is also home to the world-renowned Liszt Ferenc Music Academy, named after Hungarian composer Franz Liszt, which has by far the city's finest classical concert hall.

The Hungarian State Opera House, a grandiose hall on the beautiful, tree-lined Andrássy út in the city center, is one of Budapest's most famous buildings, built in 1884 and celebrated at that time as the most modern opera house in all of Europe. It is home to the Hungarian State Opera and the National Ballet, which, in addition to their regular performance schedules, put on a special two-week Summer Opera & Ballet Festival in early August.

As for tradition, Hungarians celebrate their folk music history through a handful of folkloric dance ensembles, which perform regularly. You can even try your hand at learning a few steps at several community centers that teach the art.

For the latest on arts events, consult the entertainment listings of the English-language press. Detailed entertainment calendars map out all that's happening in Budapest's arts and culture world—from thrash bands in wild clubs to performances at the Opera House. Hotels and tourist offices will also provide you with a copy of the monthly publication, *Budapest Panorama* (⊕ www.budapestpanorama.com), which contains details of all cultural events. Check out also the English-language cultural events Web site: ⊕ www.ontheglobe.com.

FESTIVALS & EVENTS Some kind of festival always seems to be underway in Budapest. From music and theater to folk art and film, Hungarians have thought of every reason possible to hold a celebration.

Budapest International Wine & Champagne Festival. In mid-September, a wine exhibition in the Buda Castle features the country's best wine producers, including a wine auction. The arts component includes classical and jazz concerts each evening. ☎ 1/203–8507 ⊕ www.winefestival.hu.
Budapest Spring Festival. The most popular of Hungarian festivals is held for two weeks in mid-March and is the pride of Hungarian classical music. Spread across 50 to 60 venues around the city, the festival hosts renowned musicians and performers from across Europe and beyond and also includes various theater productions, performances, and film screenings. Tickets to events go fast, so it's wise to check out the festival's Web site and order online if you plan to be in Budapest in March. The Budapest Spring Festival event celebrated its 25th anniversary in March 2005. ☎ 1/486–3300 ⊕ www.festivalcity.hu.
Danube Carnival International Cultural Festival. Folk dancing, classical music, wind bands, world music, and contemporary dance performances are held at a variety of venues across the capital city for two weeks in mid-June. ☎ 1/201–6613 ⊕ www.dunaart.hu/carnival.

Danube Water Carnival. On the weekend in mid-June closest to the anniversary of the construction of Hungary's *Lánchíd* (Chain Bridge), the oldest and most stunning of the five bridges connecting Buda and Pest, a variety of aquatic events, competitions, and air shows take place along and above the Danube. Make sure to catch a glimpse of the Chain Bridge at night when it's lit up in all its glory. ⊕ *www.karneval.hu.*

Parliament Dome Concerts. On about six occasions annually, the Hungarian Virtuosi Chamber Orchestra, founded by graduates of the Liszt Ferenc Music Academy, gives performances in the Dome Hall of the Hungarian Parliament. Concerts start at 6 PM, with the option of a Parliament tour beginning at 5:15 PM. Tickets and dates are available at most ticket agencies in Budapest, including Ticket Express and the Liszt Ferenc Music Academy itself.

ℭ **Sziget Festival** (Island Festival). For one week at the end of July and into early August, one of Europe's biggest music festivals, hosting hundreds of local and international artists, is staged on Hajógyár Island, north of the Margit Bridge. Some 15 stages and numerous venues host nearly every musical genre as well as theater, film, art exhibitions, and sports competitions. ☎ *1/372–0684* ⊕ *www.sziget.hu.*

TICKETS   Tickets for arts events can be bought at the venues themselves, but many ticket offices across the city sell them without an extra charge. Prices are still very low, so mark-ups of even 30% shouldn't dent your wallet if you book through the concierge at your hotel. Inquire at Tourinform if you're not sure where to go. Ticket availability depends on the performance and season. It's usually possible to get tickets a few days before most shows, but performances by major international artists sell out early. Tickets to Budapest Spring Festival events also go particularly quickly. Virtually every performance and concert is listed on the Web site ⊕ www.koncertkalendarium.hu. A booklet copy is also available at Tourinform and other ticket agencies across the city.

Központi Jegyiroda (Central Ticket Office). This agency specializes in tickets to Hungarian theater productions. ⊠ *District VI, Andrássy út 15, Around Andrássy út* ☎ *1/267–1267.*

Liszt Ferenc Zeneakadémia. You can purchase tickets to all performances and classical music concerts held at the music academy through the ticket office. Given the large number of performances here, this is a major agency in Budapest for cultural tickets. ⊠ *District VI, Liszt Ferenc tér 8, Around Andrássy út* ☎ *1/342–0179* ⊕ *www.liszt.hu.*

Magyar Állami Operaház (Hungarian State Opera House). Tickets for the Hungarian State Opera, National Ballet, or the Erkel Theater can be purchased on-site. Given the number of major performances that take place at the opera house, this is a major source for tickets. ⊠ *District VI, Andrássy út 20, Around Andrássy út* ☎ *1/353–0170* ⊕ *www. opera.hu.*

Matáv Jegyiroda (Matáv Ticket Office). The Matáv Symphony Orchestra sells tickets to its own performances, as well as for the National Philharmonic, Budapest's Summer Opera & Ballet Festival, and other pop music and festival events around town. ⊠ *District VI, Nagymező u. 19, Around Andrássy út* ☎ *1/428–0791* ⊕ *www.ticket.axelero.hu.*

National Philharmonic Ticket Office. The Philharmonic's service sells tickets for classical music, ballet, and opera tickets, as well as tickets for major pop and rock shows. You can also stop in at the office and browse through the scores of free programs and fliers or scan the walls coated with upcoming concert posters. ⊠ *District VII, Madách u. 3, Around Deák Ferenc tér* ☎ *1/321–4199* ⊕ *www.filharmonikusok.hu.*

Ticket Express. The biggest agency in Budapest sells tickets to nearly every show or performance happening in Hungary, including theater, opera, musicals, and concerts. ⊠ *District VI, Andrássy út 18, Around Andrássy út* ☎ *1/312–0000* ⊕ *www.tex.hu.*

Major Performance Venues

Budapest has a wide range of performance venues, offering classical music, theater, ballet, and folk dancing performances. The best place to see a classical music concert is the Liszt Ferenc Music Academy, which regularly features Hungary's most talented musicians. The elegant Hungarian State Opera House is the venue for not just opera, but also ballet. The Trafó House of Contemporary Arts puts on dance productions nearly every night of the week.

Bartók Béla Emlékház (Bartók Béla Memorial House). The tiny recital room hosts intimate Friday-evening chamber music recitals by well-known ensembles from mid-March to June and September to mid-December. ⊠ *District II, Csalán út 29, Buda Hills* ☎ *1/394–4472* ⊕ *www. bartokmuseum.hu.*

Budapest Kongresszusi Központ (Budapest Convention Center). The city's largest-capacity (but least atmospheric) classical concert venue usually hosts the largest-selling events of the Spring Festival. ⊠ *District XII, Jagelló út 1–3, Gellért Hill & the Taban* ☎ *1/209–1990.*

Erkel Színház (Erkel Theater). The homely little sister of the Opera House, the Erkel is Budapest's other main opera and ballet venue. There are no regular performances in the summer, however. The unattractive, vast Soviet-style building never appears to be filled. ⊠ *District VIII, Köztársaság tér 30, Around Blaha Lujza tér* ☎ *1/333–0540* Ⓜ *M2: Blaha Lujza tér.*

Folklór Centrum. The center has been a major venue for folklore performances for more than 30 years. It hosts regular traditional folk concerts and dance performances from spring through fall. ⊠ *District XI, Fehérvári út 47, South Buda* ☎ *1/203–3868.*

★ **Fonó Budai Zeneház** (Fonó Buda Music House). Although it's a bit of a trek from the city center to Fonó, on the outskirts of Buda, it is a great place to see live folk acts. The music house has its own bar, several performance stages, and even its own folk music CD shop. Concerts are held on a near-nightly basis, and tickets are bought when you enter the music house. ⊠ *District XI, Sztregova u. 3, South Buda* ☎ *1/206–5300* ⊕ *www.fono.hu.*

IBS (International Buda Stage). Performances here include English- and Hungarian-language theater in addition to movies, dance, and concerts. English-only shows are typically once a month, although there is simultaneous translation into English during Hungarian-language events. ⊠ *District II, Tárogató út 2–4, Buda Hills* ☎ *1/391–2500* ⊕ *www. ibs-b.hu.*

CloseUp
BUDAPEST'S WINTER CARNIVAL

WHEN THE CHRISTMAS SEASON ENDS in Hungary, so starts another period of festivity, where designers and seamstresses across the capital are busy working in preparation for farsang (carnival), a winter celebration of sorts characterized by scores of elegant balls held in concert halls, museums, and hotels across the city. The farsang season peaks in mid-February, when the majestic Hungarian State Opera House Ball is held.

In the days of feudalism, all social classes were practically grounded by the fact the earth was frozen and covered with snow during winter months, and thus could not be worked. Royalty and landowning aristocracy capitalized on this fact to hold great wedding feasts and balls.

While farsang was suppressed under Communism, the carnivals in Budapest between the two world wars were considered some of the most brilliant in European history. Celebrities like the Duke and Duchess of Windsor, Charlie Chaplin, and Josephine Baker were some of the privileged who flocked to Budapest to enjoy the balls and private parties of the season. Of the more notable balls, the event held at Budapest's Gellért Hotel in early February is one of the more spectacular, as the famed hotel's massive thermal water bathing hall is host to the gala, which includes the traditional opening dance by debutantes, followed by Hungarian gypsy music and ballroom dancing. The most important and prestigious ball is held at the Hungarian State Opera House, with tickets costing several hundred dollars per person. The opera ball is the most fashionable, and many women turn out in one-of-a-kind fashions designed specifically for the event. Lavishly dressed dancers also perform for attendees.

Fodor'sChoice ★ **Liszt Ferenc Zeneakadémia.** (Franz Liszt Academy of Music). Usually referred to as the Music Academy, this is Budapest's premier classical concert venue, hosting orchestra and chamber music concerts in its splendid main hall. It's sometimes possible to grab a standing-room ticket just before a performance here. ⊠ *District VI, Liszt Ferenc tér 8, Around Andrássy út* ☎ *1/342–0179* Ⓜ *M1: Oktogon.*

Fodor'sChoice ★ **Magyar Állami Operaház** (Hungarian State Opera House). The glittering opera house is Budapest's main venue for opera and classical ballet, and presents an international repertoire of classical and modern works as well as such Hungarian favorites as Kodály's *Háry János.* Except during the two-week international opera and ballet festival in mid-August, the Opera House is closed during the summer. ⊠ *District VI, Andrássy út 22, Around Andrássy út* ☎ *1/353–0170* Ⓜ *M1: Opera.*

Millenáris Park (Millennium Park). Built for the year 2000, the park is a series of several buildings that feature film and dance, music, and theater performances. In warmer months a large stage for concerts is constructed outside in the park near several small, man-made lakes. ⊠ *District II, Fény u. 20–22, Around Moszkva tér* ☎ *1/438–5335* ⊕ *www.millenaris.hu* Ⓜ *M2: Moszkva tér.*

Nemzeti Színház (National Theater). After years of political bickering, cancelled contracts, and location changes, the National Theater finally opened in 2002 in a controversial spot on the outskirts of the city. The whole affair is still a sore subject with many Hungarians, including politicians and officials who claim a former Hungarian prime minister gave the design job to his friends—who had little architectural experience—and built the theater in a remote area of Pest in an effort to draw theatergoers and their money to a district that badly needed a facelift. That wish-list, however, is beginning to pay off as several new buildings are currently under construction around the new National Theater and others planned. The former location is colloquially referred to as the "National Ditch." There are nightly performances on at least one of two stages inside the theater. ⊠ *District IX, Bajor Gizi Park 1, Around Boraros tér* ☎ *1/476–6800* ⊕ *www.nemzetiszinhaz.hu.*

Nemzeti Táncszínház (National Dance Theater). The theater stages modern dance productions and ballet; it is also a venue for performance by popular folk bands. ⊠ *District I, Színház u. 19, Castle Hill* ☎ *1/201–4407* ⊕ *www.nemzetitancszinhaz.hu* Ⓜ *M2: Moszkva tér.*

Pesti Vigadó (Pest Concert Hall). Classical concerts are held regularly here, as well as occasional opera, operetta, and ballet series. ⊠ *District V, Vigadó tér 2, Around Váci utca* ☎ *1/317–5067* Ⓜ *M1: Vörösmarty tér.*

Thália Theater. This is the third site for performances by the Hungarian State Opera. This first is the state Opera House and the second is the Erkel Theater. ⊠ *District VI, Nagymező u. 22–24, Around Andrássy út* ☎ *1/312–4230* Ⓜ *M1: Oktogon.*

★ **Trafó Kortárs Művészetek Háza** (Trafó House of Contemporary Arts). A former electrical transformer station in Pest, the Trafó building today showcases contemporary and alternative dance performances by Hungarian and international companies. It also serves as the venue for one or two monthly musical concerts. ⊠ *District IX, Liliom u. 41, Around Ferenc József krt.* ☎ *1/456–2040* ⊕ *www.trafo.hu* Ⓜ *M2: Ferenc krt.*

Fodor'sChoice **Vígszínház** (Comedy Theater). Built in 1896, the sparkling Vígszínház ★ is the pride of the Hungarian theater world, seating over 1,000 people. The theater hosts modern European and American plays from playwrights such as Arthur Miller, Tennessee Williams, and Friedrich Dürrenmatt, but always in Hungarian. The theater is also a venue for musicals, such as Hungarian translations of *West Side Story* and a musical version of the *Jungle Book*. ⊠ *District XIII, Pannónia u. 1, Around Nyugati Train Station* ☎ *1/329–2340* Ⓜ *M3: Nyugati.*

Dance

Ballet

Ballet has a strong following in Hungary despite the fact that the National Ballet Theater, formerly across the street from the Hungarian State Opera House, was bought by foreign investors to turn into a hotel in the early 2000s. The best time to catch a performance is during Budapest's annual Summer Opera & Ballet Festival in early August.

Győri Balett (Győr Ballet). Founded in 1979, the Győr Ballet is the troupe to watch in Hungary and is by far the most talented of the major ballets countrywide. Although the Győr Ballet is based in Győr in western Hungary, it does perform premieres in Budapest several times a year. The company has also given shows throughout Europe, performed at the Olympic Games in Seoul, and staged the production of *Purim* in 2002 at the Joyce Theater in New York. ☎ 96/523–217 ⊕ *www.gyoribalett.hu.*

Magyar Fesztival Balett (Hungarian Festival Ballet). The company was formed in September 1996 as Europe's biggest private dance troupe. Since 2002, choreography has been accompanied by music from famed Hungarian composers Liszt Ferenc, Béla Bartók, and Zoltán Kodály. The company performs mainly at the National Dance Theater. ☎ 1/319–9855 ⊕ *www.magyarfesztivalbalett.hu.*

Magyar Nemzeti Balett (Hungarian National Ballet). Performing at the Hungarian State Opera House, or on occasion at the Erkel Theater, the company began in 1884. Though this ballet company has been called "lifeless" by some critics—and does not come out on top when compared to the Győr Ballet—they perform on a regular basis in Budapest. ☎ 1/353–0170 ⊕ *www.opera.hu.*

Pécsi Balett. (Pécs Ballet). The first modern ballet ensemble in Hungary began in the 1960s, on the basis of classical ballet mixed with pantomime, folk dance, and a language of gestures. The Pécs Ballet, although based outside Budapest, gives several major openings in the capital city throughout the year. ☎ 72/512–660 ⊕ *www.pnsz.hu.*

Folk Dancing

Many of Budapest's district cultural centers regularly hold traditional regional folk-dancing evenings, or *táncház* (dance houses), often with general instruction at the beginning. These sessions provide a less touristy way to taste Hungarian culture. Check out ⊕ www.tanchaz.hu for information on folk performers and the local scene.

Almássy téri Szabadidő központ (Almássy Square Recreation Center). The center holds numerous folk-dancing evenings, representing Hungarian as well as Greek and other ethnic cultures. ⊠ *District VII, Almássy tér 6, Around Blaha Lujza tér* ☎ 1/352–1572 Ⓜ *M2: Blaha Lujza tér.*

Belvárosi Ifjúsági ház (City Youth Center). Traditionally, the city's wildest táncház is held Saturday night at the Belvárosi, where the stomping and whirling go on way into the night. The center, like many such venues, closes from mid-July to mid-August. ⊠ *District V, Molnár u. 9, Around Ferenciek tere* ☎ 1/317–5928 Ⓜ *M3: Ferenciek tere.*

Marczibányi Téri Művelődési Központ (Marczibányi Square Cultural Center). A well-known Transylvanian folk ensemble, Tatros, hosts a weekly dance house at the center, from 8 until midnight on Wednesday night. ⊠ *District II, Marczibányi tér 5/a, Around Moszkva tér* ☎ 1/212–2820 Ⓜ *Around Moszkva tér.*

Modern Dance

The systematic changes in Hungary since the early 1990s have created a hunger for contemporary dance. Today, Hungarian dance companies have begun to take development into their own hands and are forming strategies for long-term survival. Finally given the room to flourish, modern-dance companies are thriving in Budapest and seeking out broader audiences throughout Hungary and abroad. Most of these companies perform at the National Dance Theater or Trafó House of Contemporary Arts.

The Artus Company. One of the most popular dance companies in Hungary, the Artus incorporates computers and video into dance performances. The company also began an "art laboratory" in the late 1990s, where 32 dancers, performers, choreographers, actors, costume designers, painters, sculptors, and architects work together on their projects in a 2,000-square-meter space. ☎ 30/279–6302 (mobile) ⊕ www.artus.hu.

Compagnie Pál Frenák. Choreographer Pál Frenák, a Hungarian who studied and lived in France for many years, bases his company in both Budapest and Paris, and has performances in Budapest every year. ☎ 30/966–2464 (mobile) ⊕ www.ciefrenak.org.

★ **Közép Europai Táncszínház** (Central European Dance Theater). This small, contemporary modern dance company incorporates traditional roots, rituals, and folklore into its performances, which are held four to five times monthly at its own theater. ⊠ District VII, Bethlen Gábor tér 3, Around Kiraly utca ☎ 1/342–7163 ⊕ www.cedt.hu Ⓜ M2: Keleti.

La Dance Company. A classically trained ballerina who performed with the Győr Ballet, the company's founder and choreographer, Andrea Ladányi, headed to Toronto, New York, and Los Angeles to train in modern dance. A former solo dancer for the Helsinki City Theater in Finland, Ladányi is one of Hungary's most acclaimed dancers. She founded La Dance in 1995, a small group of five dancers. ☎ 30/919–8843 (mobile).

Yvette Bozsik Company. After making a name for herself as a solo performer, Yvette Bozsik went on to perform her own choreographies and founded her own company in 1983. Based in the Katona József Theater (see ⇨ Theater, below), the company tours extensively throughout Europe, performing any number of the more than one dozen pieces Bozsik has choreographed for the troupe. ☎ 1/394–4386 ⊕ www.ybozsik.hu.

Classical Music

Budapest is a must-visit city for the classical music lover. Not only did Hungary produce Bartók, Kodály, and Liszt, but there are more than 20 active symphony orchestras just in Budapest. Hungarians are so deeply devoted in their love and appreciation of classical music that, aside from numerous top-notch music academies across the country, they put on a two-week Spring Festival each March that is the toast of classical music across Europe and beyond. More than any other performing art in Budapest, classical music is the most lauded by Hungarians.

Orchestras

The most noteworthy orchestras are the Budapest Festival Orchestra and Hungarian Radio Symphony. Most play at the Liszt Ferenc Music Academy, but for up-to-date information, pick up Fidelio, a free monthly booklet listing every classical music event available at ticket and Tourinform offices.

Fodor'sChoice **Budapest Festival Orchestra.** World-renowned conductor Iván Fischer, who ★ still heads the orchestra, formed the group with famed Hungarian conductor Zoltán Kocsis in 1983. The orchestra has won international accolades and is hands-down your best bet for classical music in Budapest. International soloists and conductors are often invited to perform with the orchestra. Its home has been the Liszt Ferenc Music Academy, but in early 2005 the orchestra moved to the brand-new National Concert Hall next to the National Theater. Tickets can be purchased at several locations around Budapest, including Ticket Express, the Liszt Ferenc Academy, or online. ✉ *Budapest Festival Foundation, District XII, Alkotás u. 39/c, South Buda* ☎ *1/355–4015* ⊕ *www.bfz.hu.*

Budapest Philharmonic Orchestra. The oldest Hungarian orchestra, the Budapest Philharmonic was founded in 1853 by Hungarian composer Ferenc Erkel. Its long and rich musical history and traditions have been formed by outstanding musicians including János Richter, Gustav Mahler, Johannes Brahms, Ernst von Dohnányi, and János Ferencsik. The Budapest Philharmonic is also famous for its first performances of works—some of them written originally for the orchestra—by Liszt, Brahms, Goldmark, Mahler, Bartók, Kodály and Dohnányi. Tickets can be purchased at the Hungarian State Opera House. ☎ *1/331–2250* ⊕ *www.bpo.hu.*

Danube Symphony Orchestra. Founded in 1961, this orchestra consists of about 60 professional musicians. Their repertoire covers almost every musical style from the baroque period to the 20th century. The orchestra performs at the Duna Palace. ✉ *Duna Palota, District V, Zrinyi u. 5, Parliament* ☎ *1/317–3142* Ⓜ *M2: Parliament.*

Hungarian National Philharmonic Orchestra. Formerly the Hungarian State Symphony Orchestra, it began performing in 1923. The orchestra, with 105 musicians, is currently directed by one of Hungary's most famous conductors, Zoltán Kocsis. The orchestra performs regularly at the Liszt Ferenc Music Academy, National Theater, Budapest Convention Center, and sometimes even in St. Stephen's Basilica. ☎ *1/411–6600* ⊕ *www.hunphilharmonic.org.hu.*

Hungarian Radio Symphony Orchestra. Considered one of the best in Europe and right up there with the Budapest Festival Orchestra, the Hungarian Radio Symphony has been bestowed much praise from critics worldwide, especially for its Beethoven concert series. Also well known for playing and recording Hungarian contemporary music, the orchestra has toured 45 countries in four continents thus far. The orchestra regularly plays at the Liszt Ferenc Music Academy and the Budapest Convention Center. ☎ *1/328–8779.*

Matáv Hungarian Symphony Orchestra. With the appointment of András Ligeti as music director in 1997, the symphony took on a new artistic conception and extended its diversity to include contemporary pieces, oratorios, and even youth concerts. The orchestra plays mainly at the Liszt Ferenc Music Academy. The orchestra's ticket office sells a wide selection of performance tickets (see ⇨ Tickets, *above*). ✉ *District VI, Nagymező u. 19, Around Andrássy út* ☎ *1/428–0791* ⊕ *www.orchestra. matav.hu* Ⓜ *M1: Oktogon.*

Church Concerts

Several of Budapest's most famous churches host concerts by pianists, orchestras, and sometimes singers, mostly during the summer months from May to September, for an average HUF 500 entry fee. We highly recommend visiting an orchestra concert in the Gothic Mátyás Templom in the Castle District, as it overlooks the entire city and the Danube River.

Budai Capuchin Templom (Buda Capuchin Church). The Capuchin Church holds monthly concerts on the last Thursday of every month starting at 7:30 PM. ⊠ *District 1, Fő u. 30–32, Around Batthyány tér* ☎ *No phone* Ⓜ *M2: Batthyány tér.*

Deák Tér Templom (Deak Square Church). After a years-long closure the yellow Deák Church re-opened in the summer of 2003 with a brand new facelift inside and out. In the city center in Pest, the church has organ music the first and last Sunday of the month during summer. The church dates back to 1809 and was used as a warehouse for military uniforms during World War II. ⊠ *District V, Deák tér 4, Around Deák tér* ☎ *1/ 317–4173* Ⓜ *M1; M2; M3: Deák tér.*

★ **Mátyás Templom.** (Matthias Church). The 13th-century Gothic chapel on Castle Hill is host to orchestra concerts every Saturday night from May through the end of September, usually starting at 8 PM. ⊠ *District 1, Szentháromság tér 2, Castle Hill* ☎ *1/355–5657* Ⓜ *Around Moszkva tér.*

Szent Anna Templom (St. Anne's Church). The historic baroque church, which was built in 1761, hosts a Friday night organ concert series throughout the year. Shows start at 8 PM. ⊠ *District I, Batthyány tér 7, Around Batthyány tér* ☎ *1/317–2754* Ⓜ *M2: Batthyány tér.*

Film

Budapest is a good destination for film-lovers. You'll find everything from shiny new multiplexes to a vast array of art-house theaters that continue to thrive. Hollywood, independent, foreign, low-budget, and Hungarian films can be seen around town any night of the week. Many of the English-language movies that come to Budapest are subtitled in Hungarian rather than dubbed; this applies less so, however, to independent and art films, as well as—paradoxically—some of the major blockbusters and children's movies, all of which are usually dubbed. Tickets are very inexpensive by Western standards (about HUF 600 to HUF 1,100). Consult the movie matrix in the *Budapest Sun* (⊕ www. budapestsun.com) or the Web site ⊕ www.xpatloop.com for a weekly list of what's showing.

Corvin Budapest Filmpalota. Inside a beautifully restored and historic building, the Corvin multiplex houses several theaters and is typically packed, showing Hollywood and foreign films as well as works from independent directors. The Corvin is also the site for the annual Hungarian Film Festival. ⊠ *District VIII, Corvin köz 1, Around Ferenc Jozsef krt.* ☎ *1/ 459–5050* Ⓜ *M3: Ferenc krt.*

Mammut Budai Moziközpont. In addition to loveseats in some of the theaters, Mammut has 10 large, modern movie screens, which mainly show Hollywood and other big-budget films in their original languages with Hungarian subtitles. ⊠ *District II, Lövöház u. 2–6, Around Moszkva tér* ☎ *1/345–8140* Ⓜ *M2: Moszkva tér.*

Müvesz. One of the most popular art cinemas in Budapest is centrally located and shows independent and foreign films on five screens. There's also a CD and art book shop in the foyer where you buy tickets. ✉ *District VI, Teréz körút 30, Around Andrássy út* ☎ *1/332–6726* Ⓜ *M1: Oktogon.*

Uránia. Hungary's national cinema, a showcase for Hungarian film, reopened after a major renovation in 2002. It is definitely worth a glimpse inside the beautifully restored Moorish interior. Aside from Hungarian films, the Uránia shows independent and foreign films, many of which are in English. ✉ *District VIII, Rákóczi út 21, Around Blaha Lujza tér* ☎ *1/486–3400* ⊕ *www.urania-nf.hu* Ⓜ *M2: Blaha Lujza tér.*

WestEnd Ster Century. The centrally located multiplex usually has several mainstream movies playing in their original languages with Hungarian subtitles. ✉ *District VI, Váci út 1–3, Around Nyugati Train Station* ☎ *1/238–7222* Ⓜ *M3: Nyugati.*

Folklore Performances

Folklore performances involve a large group of dancers who stage a grand folk-dancing show, as opposed to more local, neighborhood folk dance groups we list above. Folk performances are a tradition in Hungary dating back hundreds of years and are always accompanied by Hungarian or gypsy folk music. If you have time, it is worth checking out one of the ensembles listed below, as performers dress in traditional outfits, the women in peasant dresses with bright colors and men in white blouses and brown knickers.

Budapest Dance Ensemble. The group has performed since 1958 with the aim of reviving national folk traditions and bringing them to the stage. The group performs at the National Theater, at the edge of the city. ✉ *District I, Nemzeti Színház, Színház u. 19, Castle District* ☎ *1/201–4407* Ⓜ *Around Moszkva tér.*

Danube Folk Ensemble. Formed in 1957, the 30-member Danube troupe aims for a certain artistic vision through its performances, combining music and theater. Aside from presenting its own repertoire, the ensemble participates in various theater productions including musicals and rock operas. Like the Danube Symphony Orchestra, the ensemble performs at the Duna Palace. ✉ *District V, Duna Palota, Zrínyi u. 5, Parliament* ☎ *1/235–5500* Ⓜ *M2: Parliament.*

Hungarian State Folk Ensemble. The 30-member ensemble, formed in 1951, performs at the Budai Vigadó. Choreography is based on authentic dances that date back hundreds of years. It's considered to be one of the top folk groups worldwide, having performed in 44 countries. The ensemble gives between 90 and 100 shows in Budapest annually at their venue. ✉ *District 1, Budai Vigadó, Corvin tér 8, Around Batthyány tér* ☎ *1/201–3766* Ⓜ *Around Batthyány tér.*

Rajkó Folk Ensemble. This fiery group of 60 dancers uses both ballet and modern dance forms as well as combining folklore and operetta programs. They perform at the Budapest Bábszínház. ✉ *District VI, Andrássy út 69, Around Andrássy út* ☎ *1/303–6505* Ⓜ *M1: Oktogon.*

Opera

Magyar Állami Operaház. The National Opera Company has a solid reputation among listeners, and the group sometimes performs at various outdoor stages and festivals during the summer, and can be heard almost nightly on several local classical radio stations. At the Opera House, the company has performed works from the likes of Bártok, Bellini, and Donizetti. The main season runs from September to mid-June and includes about 50 major productions, including about five new opera premieres a year. The Hungarian State Opera House is one of the most famous landmarks of Budapest. ⊠ *District VI, Andrássy út 22, Around Andrássy út* ☎ *1/353–0170* ⊕ *www.opera.hu* Ⓜ *M1: Opera.*

Theater

Budapest's theater scene thrives from September to mid-August, with on-stage performances every night even in the remotest corner of the city. With nearly 100 small companies and theaters abound in Budapest alone, theater is one more important cornerstone of Hungarian art and culture.

Bárka Színház (Ark Theater). The company of actors, most of whom are in their early thirties, stage classics by Shakespeare and Chekhov, as well as Hungarian plays, all in Hungarian. ⊠ *Üllői út 82 Around Ferenc Jozsef krt.* ☎ *1/303–6505* ⊕ *www.barka.hu* Ⓜ *M3: Ferenc krt.*

Ⓒ **Budapest Bábszínház** (Budapest Puppet Theater). The company produces colorful shows that both children and adults can enjoy, even if they don't understand Hungarian. Watch for showings of *Cinderella* (*Hamupipőke*) and *Snow White and the Seven Dwarfs* (*Hófehérke*), part of the theater's regular repertoire. ⊠ *District VI, Andrássy út 69, Around Andrássy út* ☎ *1/342–2702* ⊕ *www.budapest-babszinhaz.hu* Ⓜ *M1: Oktogon.*

Katona József Theater. Funded by the City of Budapest, the Katona stages three premieres each year, usually adaptations of foreign classics, which have included plays by Dostoyevsky, Orwell, and Kleist. In operation since 1982, the company also regularly tours Europe. ⊠ *District V, Petőfi Sándor u. 6, Around Ferenciek tere* ☎ *1/318–6599* Ⓜ *M3: Ferenciek tere.*

Ⓒ **Kolibri Színház** (Humming Bird Theater). This children's theater company gives some 450 performances annually, including puppet shows, at its own theater. ⊠ *District VI, Jókai tér 10, Around Andrássy út* ☎ *1/311–0870* ⊕ *kolibri.szinhaz.hu* Ⓜ *M1: Oktogon.*

Madách Theater. The Madách features a regular bill of Hungarian-language plays and musicals, including popular adaptations of *Cats, Fiddler on the Roof,* and *A Christmas Carol.* Beginning in 2002, the Madách added an English-language version of Andrew Lloyd Webber's *Phantom of the Opera,* which is the theater's only English-language production. ⊠ *District VII, Erzsébet körút 31–33, Around Kiraly utca* ☎ *1/478–2000* ⊕ *www.madachszinhaz.hu* Ⓜ *M2: Blaha Lujza tér.*

Merlin Theater. Budapest's only full-time English-language theater is situated in downtown Pest. Extremely popular with the ex-pat community, the two-stage theater often hosts foreign actors, who perform along with locals. The Merlin celebrates its 15th anniversary in 2005. ⊠ *District V, Gerlóczy u. 4, Around Deák Ferenc tér* ☎ *1/317–9338* Ⓜ *M1; M2; M3: Deák Ferenc tér.*

Operetta Theater. Colorful Hungarian-language operettas, such as those by Lehár and Kálmán, are performed here. The libretto is displayed above the stage in English- and German-language subtitles. ⊠ *District VI, Nagymező u. 19, Around Andrássy út* ☎ *1/353–2172* Ⓜ *M1: Oktogon.*

Pesti Színház (Pest Theater). The chamber theater, a subsidiary of the Vígszínház (Comedy Theater), has its own resident company and stages several plays and musicals in English each season. ⊠ *District V, Váci u. 9, Around Váci utca* ☎ *1/266–5557* Ⓜ *M3: Ferenciek tere.*

Radnóti Színház (Radnóti Theater). This theater's company is a more literary stage, which aims to introduce works of Hungarian literature, including contemporary writers and poets. The company unveils four premieres each season. ⊠ *District VI, Nagymező u. 11, Around Andrássy út* ☎ *1/321–0600* Ⓜ *M1: Oktogon.*

Vidám Színpad (Comedy Stage). This small, yet popular, back-alley comedy theater occasionally puts on shows in English. ⊠ *District VI, Révay u. 18, Around Andrássy út* ☎ *1/301–2067* Ⓜ *M1: Opera.*

Late-Night Bites

After-hours food options in Budapest remain somewhat limited. Even with numerous gyro and Turkish food stands open 24 hours a day, it remains a challenge to find western, breakfast-type foods in a country that does not eat a western-style breakfast. But after a long night of clubbing or bar-hopping, you can expect several decent places to be open for some kind of late-night snack.

Buddha. This Thai noodle bar is conveniently across from the Radisson Hotel, and has several vegetarian offerings. It's open daily until 2 AM. ⊠ *District VI, Térez körút 46, Around Nyugati Train Station* ☎ *1/373–0881.*

Don Pepe Pizzeria. The cheap and fast pizzeria at Nyugati metro station also has pastas and salads on the menu. It's open daily until 6 AM. ⊠ *District V, Nyugati tér 8, Around Nyugati Train Station* ☎ *1/332–2954.*

Hepicentrum. This floating salad bar on a boat near the Buda side of the Margaret Bridge offers salads, pasta, and grilled meats 24 hours daily. ⊠ *District II, Bem Alsó Rakpart, Around Batthyány tér* ☎ *1/ 212–4866.*

Kádár Étkezde. This famous and popular greasy spoon, which is named after a former Communist leader, serves up Hungarian food until 3:30 AM daily. ⊠ *District VII, Klauzal u. 10, Around Kiraly utca* ☎ *1/321–3622.*

Nagyi Palacsintázója. Choose from more than 50 kinds of *palacsinta,* the Hungarian pancake that tastes and looks like a crepe and can be filled with everything imaginable. The place is dirt cheap and open 24 hours. ⊠ *District I, Batthyány tér 5, Around Batthyány tér* ☎ *1/212–4866.*

Noa Caffé. The best falafel in the city can be found at this Israeli café that serves gyros, kebabs, and other Middle Eastern food. It's open Sunday to Thursday until 2 AM, Friday and Saturday until 5 AM. ⊠ *District VI, Teréz körút 54, Around Nyugati Train Station* ☎ *1/354–1670.*

Pita House. Billing itself as a "Mediterranean pita bar," this small restaurant serves delicious falafel in a pita, or you can purchase fresh breads and homemade hummus from the bakery in back. Both the eatery and bakery are open until 3 AM. ⊠ *District II, Margit körút 105, Around Moszkva tér* ☎ *1/315–1479.*

SoHo Palacsintabár. More than 80 varieties of *palacsinta* (pancakes) are on hand 24 hours a day in the heart of the theater district in Pest. ⊠ *District VI, Nagymező u. 21, Around Andrássy út* ☎ *No phone.*

Stex Ház. Open daily until 6 AM, Stex features a variety of local and international cuisine and has various slot machines and pool tables to help you pass the time. ⊠ *District VII, József körút 55–57, Around Ferenc József krt.* ☎ *1/318–5716.*

Szent Jupát. The popular basement restaurant is open 24 hours a day, serving massive portions of Hungarian food to clog your arteries and send you rolling home to bed. ⊠ *District II, Retek u. 16, Around Moszkva tér* ☎ *1/212–2923.*

Szeráj. Extremely popular and always busy, Szeráj serves Turkish food in a cafeteria-style setting. It's open until 4 AM weekdays, until 5 AM weekends. ⊠ *District V, Szent István körút 13, Around Nyugati Train Station* ☎ *1/311–6690.*

THERMAL SPAS & OTHER ACTIVITIES

BEST OUTDOOR POOLS
Széchenyi Gyógyfürdő ⇨*p.120*

MOST ATMOSPHERIC THERMAL BATHS
Király Gyógyfürdő ⇨*p.119*

BEST HOTEL SPA
Danubius Thermal Hotel Helia ⇨*p.123*

BEST BET FOR RELAXATION
Mandala Day Spa ⇨*p.123*

Betsy Maury

WITH OVER 100 THERMAL SPRINGS bubbling up alongside the Danube River, Budapest is one of Europe's oldest spa destinations. The Romans were the first to develop public baths in Budapest at the site of Aquincum, which they called Ak-Ink, meaning plentiful water. Bathing culture really took root though during the Turkish occupation (1541–1686) when the Ottomans built large spa complexes like the Király, Rudás, and Rác (the Rudas and Rác are under renovation at this writing) in traditional Turkish style. These baths today are among the most important Ottoman ruins in Budapest.

In 1891 the Hungarian Balneological Society discovered the benefits of Budapest's mineral water and began to develop medicinal water treatments, further advancing bathing culture. The turn of the 20th century saw the building of grand thermal baths, including the Lukács, Széchenyi, and Gellért baths in beautiful Secessionist style. Budapest enjoyed yet another bathing hey day in the 1930s, when these baths were considered among the most fashionable in Europe.

Thermal baths remain a popular and egalitarian Hungarian institution, and taking the waters in Budapest is an activity not to be missed. Even in the depth of winter, spending an afternoon chin-deep in 36°C (97°F) water certainly will get the Central European chill out of one's bones. And sitting in a lounge chair amid art nouveau fountains at one of the outdoor thermal complexes in the summer is a pleasant way to cool off and also experience a bit of history. In any season, a soak in the thermal waters will leave you feeling relaxed and refreshed, ready for a big plate of *borjúpaprikás* (veal paprikash) and a nap.

The Turkish-era baths are the oldest and most atmospheric, with ancient domed cupolas positioned over a collection of small steaming pools of water. The grand complexes of Lukács, Gellért, and Széchenyi all have both indoor thermal baths and outdoor swimming pools and grounds for sitting and relaxing. Although Budapest's modern wellness hotels don't have the most character, they deliver perhaps the most luxurious day of spa-going, with thermal baths and swimming pools plus all the services—including massages, mud baths, and pedicures—of a well-staffed spa hotel.

THERMAL BATHS

At this writing, the Rác and Rudás baths were closed for substantial renovations. The Rác baths were not scheduled to reopen until late 2005; the Rudás baths might reopen as early as late 2004, but there was still some question regarding whether the Rudás baths would open as scheduled.

Fodor'sChoice ★ **Király Gyógyfürdő** (Király Baths). The Király baths don't have their own source of thermal water but they are the oldest in Budapest. The Turks built them here in 1565 inside the city walls and piped the water to this location so that in case of a siege, they would still be able to enjoy a good bath. Although they do show their age, you still get a feeling of the Orient in these baths, perhaps Budapest's most atmospheric. Men and women bathe on separate days in small pools underneath the Turkish cupola. They are popular with gay men on men's days. ⊠ *District II, Fő u. 84 Lower Buda* ☎ *1/202–3688* ⊕ *www.spasbudapest.com* 🖾 *1,100 HUF* ⊙ *Mon., Wed., Fri. 7–6 for women only; Tues., Thurs., Sat. 9–7 for men only.*

Lukács Gyógyfürdő (Lukács Baths). These thermal baths are popular with aging Hungarian film stars, who can be found lolling around the leafy outdoor mixed-sex pools on weekday afternoons. There's a full range of thermal baths in various temperatures here, with two swimming pools and lounge chairs to rest and recover in. White-coated medical attendants administering treatments to pensioners give the place a somewhat clinical feel. In addition to soaking, you can drink the mineral water, which is especially recommended for gastroenterological disorders. ⊠ *District II, Frankel Leó u. 25–29, Lower Buda* ☎ *1/326–1695* ⊕ *www.spasbudapest.com* 🖾 *1,400 HUF* ⊙ *Weekdays 6–6, weekends 6–4.*

Rudas Gyógyfürdő (Rudas Baths). The Rudas baths have been a favorite spot for Budapest men since the 16th century, when the Turks restored themselves and made their daily ablution along the marble floors. The central octagonal pool catches the light from the glass-tiled cupola and casts it around the surrounding six pools, capturing the feeling of an ancient Turkish *hamam*. The thermal waters are still only open to men, but the swimming pool is open to women as well on alternating days. At this writing the baths were closed for a substantial renovation but were expected to reopen by December 2004. At this writing, hours and admission prices have not yet been set. ⊠ *District I, Döbrentei tér 9 Gellért Hegy* ☎ *1/356–1322.*

FodorśChoice **Széchenyi Gyógyfürdő** (Széchenyi Baths). Over 2 million visitors to Buda-
★ pest have taken in the waters at this glorious indoor and outdoor thermal bath complex, one of Europe's largest. The turn-of-the-20th-century baths in the heart of City Park have that Old World feel, with yellow and white Secessionist-style architecture, beautiful grounds, and lots of fountains and loggias. There are a big swimming pool and two thermal baths outside, plus thermal pools, a cold shock pool, and the hottest steamroom in Budapest on the inside. On any given day, you will find wizened Hungarian men playing chess in one of the steaming thermal outdoor baths, which open all winter. ⊠ *District XVI, Állatkerti krt. 11, City Park* ☎ *1/363–3210* ⊕ *www.spasbudapest.com* 🖾 *1,900 HUF (1,300 HUF after 3 PM)* ⊙ *Weekdays 6 AM–7 PM, weekends 6–4.*

★ **Szent Gellért Gyógyfürdő** (Saint Gellért Baths). Budapest's most famous thermal baths were built in 1918 as part of the grand Gellért Hotel. They have long been a favorite in the city for their architectural beauty as well as their innovative outdoor wave pool, which was added in 1927 and is immensely popular to this day. The elegant art nouveau complex includes separate men's and women's thermal baths, mixed indoor and outdoor swimming pools, steam rooms, and saunas. There's a full range of treatments available here, including a well-established Thai massage center. Due to its popularity, these are probably the most crowded baths in Budapest, especially on summer weekends. ⊠ *District XI, Kelenhegyi út 4, Gellért Hill & the Tabán* ☎ *1/466–6166* ⊕ *www.spasbudapest.*

5

Arriving The entrance procedure to *gyógyfürdők* (thermal baths) in Budapest can be baffling to visitors. Some baths post prices and treatments in English, but it remains unclear what kind of ticket you need and what you're actually getting. Sadly, in most of the state-run baths there's not much help from the staff. Much of the information on the price list pertains to medical treatments offered at the spa for patients with prescriptions from their doctors. There's also a lengthy explanation of the refund policy, which entitles you to a refund of the ticket price if you stay less than the whole day. In general, buy a *belépő jegy* (entrance ticket), then choose a locker or cabin (cabins are slightly more expensive). An entrance ticket allows you to use both the thermal baths and the swimming pools. Most places issue small bits of paper as tickets. Hold on to these because you'll need them for the refund you can receive at the cashier's desk upon leaving.

Getting Ready Once you've paid, follow the directions to the locker room, where you will change. Once you have changed into your swimsuit—or disrobed completely if you're in a single-sex spa—the locker attendant will lock your cabin and give you a key. Make sure to tie this key around your wrist or attach it to your swimsuit. In the single-sex places you'll be given a sheet, or a cotton frock of some kind to wear when you walk between the locker room and the thermal bath. Signs are posted in all thermal baths to shower before entering the water.

What to Bring As a rule, bring shower shoes to all thermal baths and a towel to all but the big wellness hotels. Swimsuits are required in mixed company (at wellness hotels, at the Széchenyi and Lukács thermal baths, and at the swimming pool at the Gellért), and a bathing cap is required in most swimming pools. Keep some small change with you to tip locker attendants (100 HUF–200 HUF) and in case you want a beverage in between soaks. Check all your other valuables in a safe, which you can ask for when you buy your ticket. It's useful to bring your own shampoo, body lotion, and a comb for showering afterward, but most thermal baths have hair dryers.

Health Spas Visits to hotel wellness centers are more straightforward, and you will often find a cheerful, English-speaking receptionist who can guide you on the treatments offered. Most hotels accept credit cards as well. All thermal baths and wellness hotels have a medical doctor on staff because thermal waters are a recommended medical treatment for many conditions such as arthritis, rheumatism, and osteoporosis. If you wish to have a medical treatment, a checkup may be required. All other treatments, including massages and pedicures, should be booked in advance. In general, wellness hotels in Hungary feel more like medical facilities—with spotless, somewhat clinical interiors—than the soft-lighted spas in the U.S. There's no water-dripping music or incense burning, and the staff works in white coats. The treatments are first-rate, though, and guaranteed to bring an overall sense of relaxation and well-being.

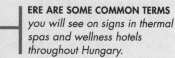

ON THE SPA MENU

HERE ARE SOME COMMON TERMS you will see on signs in thermal spas and wellness hotels throughout Hungary.

Caldarium. A hot water tub or tiled room of 40°C–50°C (104°F–122°F).

Gőzfürdő. Steamroom.

Gyógyfürdő. Any thermal bath that has naturally occurring water above 30°C (86°F). Most thermal baths contain minerals, which are listed at the entrance to the bath.

Hőlégfürdő. Sauna.

Iszapfürdő. Mud bath.

Kezelés. Treatment.

Kleopátra Fürdő. Cleopatra Bath. A bath of milk and essential oils, known to be a moisturizing skin treatment.

Kneipp cure. This body of treatments is based on the theories of Sebastian Kneipp, a German priest who believed in the importance of water and herbs in treating stress and exhaustion. Treatments are designed for the individual based on a medical exam and are offered at most wellness hotels. An average treatment uses alternating hot and cold stimuli to increase blood circulation followed by wrapping the body in herb infusions.

Laconium. A dry sauna of 55°C.

Masszázs. Massage. In general, massages are performed with light aromatic oil. Some, such as Thai massage, are performed with no oil.

Medence. Pool or basin—not a swimming pool.

Nyirokcsomó kezelés. Lymph drainage. This treatment restores balance to the lymph system and rids the body of accumulated toxins.

Öltöző. Changing room.

Páncélszekrény. Safe-deposit box.

Szakorvosi vizsgálatok. Medical examination, which is required for some treatments.

Száraz kefe masszázs. Dry brush massage. This massage is performed with a soft bristle brush. It helps exfoliate the skin and increase blood circulation.

Szekrény. Locker.

Thalasso. This general term refers to any treatment using seaweed or sea algae, known to help combat cellulite.

Uszoda. Swimming pool.

Víz alatti masszázs. Underwater massage. This massage is performed under jets of cold and warm water treating specific body parts.

com ☒ *2,900 HUF* ⊘ *Oct.–Apr., weekdays 7* AM–*5* PM, *weekends 7–7, May–Sept., daily 7–7.*

Spas & Wellness Hotels

Danubius Thermal Hotel Margitsziget. The location of this spa hotel couldn't be better for relaxation. It's at the northern end of Margaret Island, nestled among leafy walking paths and flower gardens and far away from the noise of downtown Pest. The full-service wellness hotel offers thermal baths and swimming pools plus all the things you need for a complete rehabilitation, including a fitness center, dentistry clinic, and cosmetic surgery department. The Thermal is connected by a passage way to the Danubius Grand Hotel, a slightly more elegant hotel in a historic building. ☒ *District XIII, Margitsziget, Margaret Island* ☎ *1/ 889–4700* ⊕ *www.danubiusgroup.com* ☒ *Weekdays 4,800 HUF, weekends 5,800 HUF* ⊘ *6:30* AM–*9:30* PM.

Fodor'sChoice ★ **Danubius Thermal & Conference Hotel Helia.** There's an exhaustive wellness program available at this spotless hotel not far from the Danube, and you don't need to be a guest to enjoy it. Aside from the thermal baths, sauna, steamroom, and 17-meter swimming pool, there are seven kinds of massage, hydrotherapy, electrotherapy, and mud treatments, plus on-site medical check-ups available as well, making this one of the most full-service places in town to take in the waters. The resident pedicurist has a loyal local clientele. There's also a fitness room with daily aerobics classes. ☒ *District XIII, Kárpát u. 62–64, Duna Plaza* ☎ *1/ 889–5800* ⊕ *www.danubiusgroup.com* ☒ *Weekdays, 3,000 HUF for morning session (7–3), 4,200 HUF for afternoon session (3–10); weekends, 4,800 HUF for the day* ⊘ *Daily 7* AM–*10* PM.

Spa Aphrodite Health & Wellness Center. Families flock to this luxury hotel wellness center on winter weekends for its thermal baths and swimming pool plus a pleasant seating area serving healthy meals all day. The layout provides spacious resting areas and comfortable lounge chairs nicely set apart, so it never feels too crowded here. The big swimming pool keeps the kids happy, and there's a full range of wellness treatments for adults, including several types of massage, a Dead Sea salt bath, and aromatherapy treatments. In addition, there are infrared saunas, steamrooms, a Thalaxion bath, a Jacuzzi, and a solarium. ☒ *District III, Corinthia Aquincum Hotel, Árpád fejedelem útja 94, Óbuda* ☎ *1/436–4130* ⊕ *www.corinthia. hu* ☒ *Weekdays, 2,000 HUF for morning session (7–10), 3,500 for the day; weekends, 4,200 HUF for the day* ⊘ *Daily 7* AM–*10* PM.

Fodor'sChoice ★ **Mandala Day Spa.** There are no thermal waters to take in at this day spa, but you'll find plenty here to relax you in this oasis of calm housed in an apartment complex in the 13th District. An attentive staff guides you to a service that's best for you and then hands you a fluffy robe and sends you inside for some herbal tea while you await your treatment. There's an Indonesian theme here, with soothing music, neutral-colored tiles, and plenty of comfortable rattan lounging chairs. Massages and mud baths are given in luxurious treatment rooms, and cosmetic treatments use high-end Clarins products. ☒ *District XIII, Ipoly u. 8 (in Kleopátra Ház, Duna Plaza* ☎ *1/801–2566* ⊕ *www.mandaladayspa. hu* ⊘ *Mon.–Thurs. 10–10, Fri. 9* AM–*10* PM, *Sat. 10–10, Sun. 10–6.*

SPORTS & THE OUTDOORS

Bicycling

Biking is a popular sport in Hungary, and Budapest has several places where you can rent the newest models.

Bringóhintó. This rental outfit on Margaret Island offers popular four-wheel pedaled contraptions called *bringóhintók*, as well as traditional two-wheelers; standard bikes cost about 1,200 HUF per half-hour or 1,800 HUF an hour. Bikes can be rented overnight with a 10,000 HUF deposit. ⊠ *District VIII, Hajós Alfréd sétány 1, across from Thermal Hotel, Margaret Island* ☎ *1/329–2072*.

Magyar Kerékpáros Túrázók Szövetsége (Bicycle Touring Association of Hungary). The organization can give you brochures and general information on bicycling conditions and suggested routes. ⒹDistrict V, *Bajcsy-Zsilinszky út 31, 2nd floor, Apt. 3* ☎ *1/332–7177*.

Yellow Zebra Bikes. The centrally located company offers bike tours of Budapest and also rents bikes for the day. Prices for a half-day are 2,000 HUF, a full day 3,000 HUF ⊠ *District V, Sütő u. 2, Around Deák Ferenc tér* ☎ *1/266–8777* ⊕ *www.yellowzebrabikes.com*.

Golf

Golf is a growing sport in Hungary, and the country now has several first-class courses, a couple of which are reasonably close to Budapest.

Old Lake Golf & Country Club. About 40 km (25 mi) from Budapest, this course is built on the grounds of an estate once owned by Count Ezsterházy. The course is well-kept, and there's a par-3 executive course as well as driving range. The golf course is attached to a hotel, which has a swimming pool and tennis courts. ⊠ *Remeteségpuszta, Tata* ☎ *34/ 587–620* ⊕ *www.oldlakegolf.com* ✉ *Weekdays, 6,000 HUF for 9 holes, 8,000 HUF for 8 holes; weekends, 9,000 for 9 holes, 13,000 HUF for 18 holes.*

★ **Pannonia Golf & Country Club.** This Austrian-owned, semiprivate club is also about 40 km (25 mi) outside of Budapest in the direction of Vienna. A top-class 18-hole golf course, the greens are hard and well manicured. The club has excellent practice facilities, including a driving range and chipping range. The policy is to accept golfers with a minimum 36 handicap. ⊠ *Alcsútdoboz, Mariavölgy* ☎ *22/594–200* ⊕ *www.pannonia-golf.hu* ✉ *Weekdays, 7,000 HUF for 9 holes, 12,000 HUF for 18 holes; weekends, 10,000 HUF for 9 holes, 16,500 HUF for 18 holes.*

Health Clubs

Health and fitness clubs are popular among Budapest's young professionals, and you can find work-out spaces all over the city. Many of the business hotels have upscale fitness facilities that can be used with a daily ticket even if you are not a guest.

A1 Fitness Center. The club has good weight-training and cardiovascular equipment and hourly aerobics classes in a renovated factory near the Danube. ✉ *District II, Árpád fejedelem útja 26–28, Óbuda* ☎ *1/346–3030.*
Michelle's Health & Fitness. This popular and well-equipped fitness center is in the Buda hills. ✉ *District II, Rózsakert Shopping Center, Gábor Áron u. 74, Buda Hills* ☎ *1/391–5808.*
World Class Fitness Centre. This place really does live up to its name, with a well-equipped gymnasium, aerobics classes, spinning classes, plus sauna and squash court. ✉ *District V, Marriott hotel, Apáczai Csere János u. 4, Around Váci u.* ☎ *1/266–4290.*

Horseback Riding

English saddle, not Western, is the standard in Hungary.

Budapesti Lovas Klub (Budapest Equestrian Club). Experienced riders can ride at the club for about 2,500 HUF per hour. Call about two weeks ahead to assure yourself a horse. ✉ *District VIII, Kerepesi út 7, Városliget* ☎ *1/313–5210.*
Petneházy Lovas Centrum (Petneházy Equestrian Center). In the verdant outskirts of Buda, the club offers horseback-riding lessons and trail rides for 2,500 HUF to 3,500 HUF per hour. ✉ *District II, Feketefej út 2, Adyliget* ☎ *1/397–5048.*

Swimming

Hungarians are enthusiastic about water sports and there's no shortage of swimming pools in Budapest. Most pools require swim caps.

Hajós Alfréd Nemzeti Sportuszoda. Margaret Island is home to the national swimming pool, which is named after the celebrated Hungarian swimming champ. The walls here testify to Hungarian prowess in the pool, with the names of Olympians etched in the walls. There are two outdoor pools with sunbathing terrace and one indoor pool. The national water polo team practices here. A daily ticket costs 800 HUF. ✉ *District XIII, Margitsziget, Margaret Island* ☎ *1/311–4046.*
Palatinus Strand. On summer days, you'll find half the city frolicking at the giant swimming complex on Margaret Island, drinking beer, eating hot dogs, and dipping into one of the seven swimming pools. It's a huge complex but it can get crowded. Entrance is 1,500 HUF, and you can rent everything, including swimsuits, towels, and swimcaps. ✉ *District XIII, Margitsziget, Margaret Island* ☎ *1/312–3069.*

Tennis & Squash

There are some 30 tennis clubs in Budapest, and some hotels also hire courts out to nonguests.

Hungarian Tennis Association. For those who can't travel without playing, the association produces a yearbook with a complete list of the country clubs with courts in Hungary. ✉ *District XIV, Dózsa György út 1–3* ☎ *1/252–6687.*

On-line Squash Club. On the near-outskirts of town, this trendy full-facility fitness club has five squash courts. Hourly rates run from 2,500 HUF to 4,000 HUF, depending on when you play. The club rents equipment and stays open until 11 PM on weekdays, 9 PM on weekends. ⊠ *Forrás u. 8, Budaörs* ☎ *23/501–2620.*

Városmajor Tennis Academy. The club has five outdoor courts (clay and hexapet) available daily from 7 AM to 10 PM. They are lit for night play and covered by a tent in winter. Court fees run around 2,000 HUF per hour in summer, 2,000 HUF to 4,000 HUF per hour in winter. Racket rentals and lessons are also offered. ⊠ *District VII, Városmajor u. 63–69, Around Moszkva tér* ☎ *1/202–5337.*

World Class Fitness Center. The health club has one excellent squash court available for 3,500 HUF to 5,000 HUF an hour, depending on when you play; be sure to reserve it a day or two in advance. ⊠ *District V, Marriott hotel, Apáczai Csere János u. 4, Around Váci u.* ☎ *1/266–4290.*

SHOPPING

By Betsy
Maury

STRICTLY SPEAKING, Budapest is not a shopping town. There are interesting things to buy, of course. However, a weekend in Budapest doesn't promise the same shopping thrill that, say, a weekend in Istanbul or Paris does. Major European and American retailers have outposts here and show the latest fashions, but prices are generally no cheaper than anywhere else in Europe and the selections can be limited.

That said, a day of shopping can have rich rewards in Budapest and you can leave the city with uniquely Hungarian treats if you look beyond the big high-street shops. In general, folk arts are high-quality and traditional crafts well-done here. The antiques shops clustered around Falk Miksa utca will also provide you an enjoyable half-day browse even though bargains are long gone for the most part. Interesting and reasonable bric-a-brac can be found in nearly all of Budapest's antiques shops and markets. Ever-changing Váci utca is worth a stroll as well for its vibrant downtown feel; there's a good mix of older shops and trendy new ones. Some of the big foreign fashion houses like Max Mara, Benetton, Escada, and Hugo Boss are in this neighborhood.

Meandering around District V can delight with unusual treasures, too, and perhaps the best shopping can be done in Pest's side streets and *udvars* (passage ways). In a nutshell, there are two types of shops to look for in Budapest: older shops selling classic goods such as leather gloves, wool hats, wooden toys, and antique silver, and newer shops run by artistic upstarts selling their own designs. Often, both kinds of shops are really unique. The areas around Király utca and Ferenciek tere are dotted with stylish design shops. The streets off Váci utca, toward Petőfi Sándor are good places to poke for both old-style shops and ateliers. Andrássy út—perhaps Budapest's most beautiful shopping street—is a must for strolling in any case, and serious shoppers will certainly enjoy the many upscale furniture and houseware shops lining the street between Oktogon and Ferenc Deák tér.

Shops are generally open until 5 or 6 on weekdays and 1 on Saturdays (only shops in the malls are open on Sundays, for the most part). Returning or exchanging items at most shops in Budapest is the exception, not the rule. If you are unsure of a purchase, or if it's a gift, inquire at the shop to find out whether an exchange or return is possible.

Major Shopping Districts

You'll find plenty of expensive boutiques, folk-art and souvenir shops, foreign-language bookstores, and high-end foreign fashion shops on or around touristy **Váci utca,** Budapest's famous, pedestrian-only promenade in District V. Some of the most interesting shops though, are tucked away on the side streets between Váci and **Petőfi Sandor utca.**

Although a stroll along Váci utca is integral to a Budapest visit, browsing among some of the smaller, less touristy, more typically Hungarian shops in Pest—on the **Kis körút** (Small Ring Road) and **Nagy körút** (Large Ring Road)—may prove more interesting and less pricey.

BUDAPEST BLITZ TOUR

BEGIN THE DAY IN BUDAPEST *bright and early by going to the* **Vasárcsarnok,** *which is at its liveliest in the mornings. Admire the building itself, but then stock up on paprika, salami, or tinned goose liver at one of the stalls downstairs. While upstairs, enjoy a coffee and lángos (fried dough with cheese and sour cream) at one of the büfé stands to fortify you for a full day of shopping. Then head north by walking on* **Váci utca.** *You'll pass* **Manier, V-50 Design Art Studio,** *and* **Folkart Centrum.** *Turn right on Irányi utca before you reach the underpass (you'll see the Erzsébet bridge to your left), and check out the whimsical designs at* **Naray Tamás** *before circling back towards Váci on Kigyó utca where you'll pass a branch of* **Herendi Porcelán.**

Once back on Váci, crisscross between there and Petőfi Sándor utca for the next few blocks and you'll come across the highly recommended design emporium **Magma,** *leather glove shop* **Balogh Kesztyű,** *bespoke shoe shop* **Vass,** *jewelry designer* **Varga Design,** *and the stationer* **BomoArt.** *Finish off your morning in the Váci utca area by having a coffee and light sandwich at* **Gerbeaud.** *From this point, you have two options. For antiques, head north to the largest concentration of antiques shops in the city, or if you want to look at a wider variety of stores, head off on foot to the Király utca neighborhood. Either way, you'll end up in the major square Deák Ferenc tér.*

If you choose antiques, go north by Tram No. 2 or 2A from Eötvös Tér (near the Danube in front of the Hotel InterContinental) toward Falk Miksa utca, get off on Szalay utca, and walk north to the antiques district. You'll pass **Pintér Antik Diskont, Studio Agram, Anna Antikvitás,** *and* **Nagyházi Galéria,** *as well as the interesting* **Wladis Galéria és**

Műterem *jewelry shop. Once you reach St. István Körút, turn right until you get to Nyugati Pályaudvar. To the left is* **West End City Center** *if you're up for more shopping. Otherwise, take Metro Line 3 back to centrally located Deák Ferenc tér.*

The other option is to walk through József Nádor tér and turn right onto József Attila utca, where you'll pass another branch of **Herendi Porcelán, Nádortex,** *and* **Ajka Kristály.** *Continue east on Jozsef Atilla, cross Bajcsy-Zsilinsky út and begin walking up lovely Andrássy út. Before long, you'll pass the high-end shoe shop* **La Boutique.** *Walk as far as Liszt Ferenc tér, turn right, and then turn right again on Paulay Ede utca. Work your way back towards Deák Ferenc tér on Paulay Ede. Along the way, you'll find a few ateliers such as* **Vasseva** *and* **Norma Fölöp.** *Cross over to Király utca on Nagymező, where you'll find housewares at* **Goa** *and* **Provence,** *groovy goods at* **Látmás** *and* **Psybaba,** *and flowers at* **Arioso.** *Király utca ends at Deák Ferenc tér.*

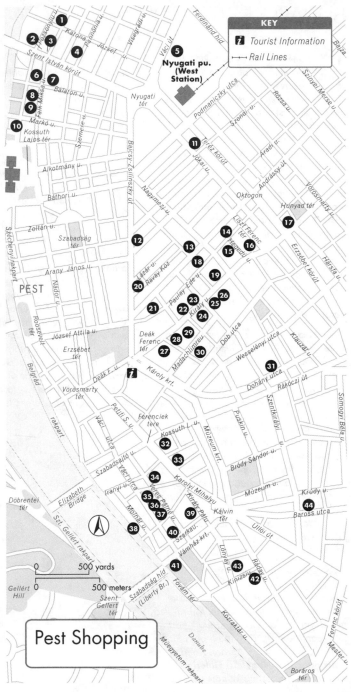

Pest Shopping

Budapest's luxury boulevard **Andrássy ut**, which runs from Ferenc Deák tér to Heroes Square, is lined with many high-end furniture stores. A spate of groovy interior design and houseware shops have sprung up in the section of District VI around **Király utca**. In District V, the areas **toward the Danube** and around **Kálvin tér** are good places to wander for unique, arty boutiques. **Falk Miksa utca**, also in District V, running south from Szent István körút, is one of the city's best antiques districts, lined on both sides with atmospheric little shops and galleries.

Department Stores & Malls

There are plenty of malls in Budapest and, by and large, they are busy and have a distinctly Hungarian feel. Winter weekends find both adults and children happily strolling the corridors of most Budapest malls, shopping, browsing, eating, and going to the movies. It's cold outside, after all. Although there are other downtown shopping areas, big branch stores of upscale chains are in just about every mall. If you're looking for a specific item, heading to a mall like West End City Center, which has nearly 400 shops, is a good way to maximize your effort.

Mammut. This cornerstone of Buda shopping, near Moszkva tér, is popular with young Hungarian women for its high-fashion shops. On the first floor alone, there are trendy Mexx and Promod, and preppy Jackpot & Cottonfield. Shoes are easy to find here as well, since there are over 10 shoe stores. The mall is referred to as Mammut 1 and Mammut 2, with the older section having a sports club and the newer one a multiplex. Although each section of the mall is relatively small, high-quality shops are the norm. A good fruit and vegetable market (known as the Fény utca piac) sets up behind the mall every morning except Sunday, selling top-notch produce. The mall is on the 4 and 6 tram lines. It is open from 10 to 9 Monday through Saturday, until 6 on Sunday. ✉ *District II, Lövőház 2, Around Moszkva tér* ☎ *1/345–8020* Ⓜ *M2: Moszkva tér.*

Mom Park. Spacious corridors and lots of light appeal to shoppers at this modern mall in affluent District XII. You'll find the overall shopping mood here remarkably relaxed. Take time to browse at boutiques like Kati Zoob—probably Hungary's most well-known fashion designer—for her unique haute couture pieces. Goa, run by the owners of Goa Cafe, sells Asian-inspired furniture and home accessories. The only local outlet of French children's clothing store Jacadi is here. Locals flock to the Paulaner Brauhaus after the movies for hearty German fare in a fun-loving Bavarian setting. The nine-screen cinema at the top is home to Budapest's only digital cinema. ✉ *District XII, Alkotás út 53, Around Déli Train Station* ☎ *1/487–5501.*

West End City Center. Central Europe's biggest shopping mall is home to many luxury retailers, including Italian handbag maker Mandarina Duck, Austrian lingerie purveyors Wolford and Palmer, high-end watchmaker Orex, and fashion-forward but relatively low-priced Mango (in the same league as Zara). There's a good offering of sports apparel here as well, with Nike, Champion, Puma, Adidas, and Quicksilver shops.

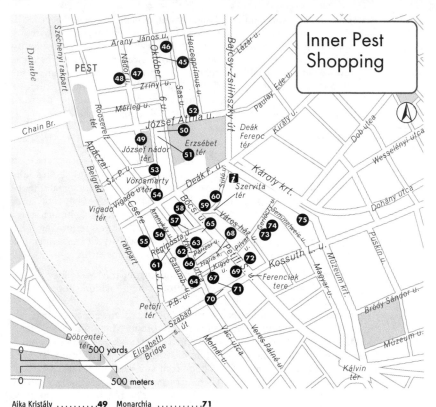

The rooftop of the mall is thoughtfully landscaped with benches and paths, providing welcome relief from the sometimes teeming floors below. The 14-screen cinema on the top floor is abuzz with activity most nights, with popular restaurants and bars right beside the box office. In addition to the Metro, the mall is served by the 4 and 6 trams. It is open until 11 PM nightly. ✉ *District VI, Váci út 1–3, Around Nyugati Train Station* ☎ *1/238–7777* Ⓜ *M3: Nyugati pu.*

Markets

Ecseri Piac. For true bargains and possibly an adventure, make an early morning trip to the vast and meandering flea market on the outskirts of the city. A colorful, chaotic market that shoppers have flocked to for decades, it is an arsenal of secondhand goods, where you can find everything from frayed Russian army fatigues to Herend and Zsolnay porcelain vases to antique silver chalices. Goods are sold at permanent tables set up in rows, from trunks of cars parked on the perimeter, and by lone, shady characters clutching just one or two items. As a foreigner, you may be overcharged, so prepare to haggle—it's part of the flea-market experience. Also, watch out for pickpockets. Ecseri is open weekdays from 6 AM to 1 PM, Saturday from 8 to 3. Although the best selection is on Saturday morning, when the market is generally livelier, prices are said to be 10% to 20% higher than on weekdays. Haggle hard. ✉ *District XIX, Nagykőrösi út 156, Kispest* ☎ *1/282–9563* Ⓜ *Bus 54 from Boráros tér.*

Petőfi Csarnok. A colorful outdoor flea market is held weekend mornings from 7 to 2 in this somewhat run-down group of buildings in City Park. The quantity and selection are smaller than at Ecseri Piac, but it's a fun flea-market experience closer to the city center. Red-star medals, Russian military watches, and other memorabilia from Communist days are popular buys here. East German postcards are worth looking at for their excellent kitsch value. Other more modern items, including car radios and mobile phones, often wind up here. ✉ *District XIV, Zichy Mihály út 14, City Park* ☎ *1/251–7266* Ⓜ *M1: Mexikói út.*

Vásárcsarnok. A trip to Budapest wouldn't be complete without a visit to this spectacularly renovated grand food hall. Pictures on the east wall show the history of this market, when it was Budapest's central location for meat and produce coming in from the countryside. Today, food stalls are still patronized by Hungarians, and like most markets in Hungary, seasonal products prevail. In summer tomatoes and peaches are abundant; in November celeriac and pumpkin. The stalls downstairs sell prepared food, and this is the place to buy Hungarian delicacies such as piquant salamis, robust paprika, and buttery goose or duck liver pâtés. Upstairs is filled with folk-art vendors and souvenir shops. Handmade tablecloths, painted boxes, and traditional embroidery are the best buys among the handcrafts. The market is open Monday from 6 AM to 5 PM, Tuesday through Friday from 6 AM to 6 PM, and Saturday from 6 AM to 2 PM. ✉ *District IX, Vámház krt. 1–3, South end of Váci utca* ☎ *1/217–6067.*

★ **Vörösmarty tér Christmas Market.** If you are lucky enough to be in Budapest in December, you may be able to get all your Christmas shopping done in one fell swoop at this old-fashioned market at Vörösmarty tér, in front of the famous Gerbeaud coffeehouse. The facade of Gerbeaud itself is blanketed with a colorful Advent calendar that counts the days to Christmas. The city of Budapest wisely restricted the goods sold at this market to include only handmade, traditional crafts so you won't find any tacky, plastic holiday kitsch here. Handmade paper diaries, wrought-iron candle sticks, fur hats, wooden toys, and an exquisite array of handmade ornaments are for sale. Many Hungarian ceramic artists have stalls here as well. Concerts take place most evenings, when shoppers are keeping warm with hot mulled wine and Christmas sweets. The market is open from 9 AM to 7 PM every day beginning the first weekend in December. ⊠ *District V, Vörösmarty tér, Around Deák Ferenc tér* Ⓜ *M1: Vörösmarty tér.*

Specialty Stores

Arts & Antiques

Antique stores are clustered around **Falk Miksa utca,** a leafy street north of the Parliament that's a browser's delight. A few auction houses and artisan's boutiques can be found on side streets as well as **St. István körút.** The side streets off **Váci utca** are a good place to hunt for antique decorative items such as vases, tablecloths, and silver.

Anna Antikvitás. The shelves and tables at this tiny shop are stacked with exquisite antique textiles—from heavily embroidered wall hangings to dainty lace gloves. The ceiling is dressed with a canopy of antique cotton umbrellas. The store also carries assorted antique objets d'art. ⊠ *District V, Falk Miksa u. 18–20, Parliament* ☎ *1/302–5461.*
BÁV Műtárgy. The State Commission Trading House has antiques of all shapes, sizes, kinds, and prices at its several branches around the city. All the stores are worth a visit for bric-a-brac, sets of sterling silver, old crystal vases, paintings, and furniture. Porcelain is the specialty at the branch on Kossuth Lajos utca, and paintings at the Szent István körút store. The Párizsi utca branch off Váci utca has a large selection of vintage jewelry and antique watches. ⊠ *District V, Ferenciek tere 12, Around Ferenciek tere* ☎ *1/318–3381* ⊠ *District V, Kossuth Lajos u. 1–3, Around Deák Ferenc tér* ☎ *1/318–6934* ⊠ *District V, Szent István krt. 3, Parliament* ☎ *1/331–4534* ⊠ *District V, Párizsi u. 2, Around Váci utca* ☎ *1/318–6217.*
Ernst Galéria. This small, elegant antique shop a few blocks from Váci utca is worth visiting for its first-rate painting collection as well as its furniture. Paintings are more beautifully framed and displayed here than anywhere else in Budapest. ⊠ *District V, Irányi u. 27, Around Ferenciek tere* ☎ *1/266–4016.*
Godot Galéria. A well-chosen selection of contemporary Hungarian artists' work is exhibited here. ⊠ *District VII, Madách Imre út, Around Deák Ferenc tér* ☎ *1/322–5272.*
Móró Régiség. If antique weapons are your thing, then check out this esoteric shop, which specializes in 18th-century weaponry. A curious

array of militaria and firearms and even torture devices will keep even the casual browser interested. ☒ *District V, Szent István krt. 1, Parliament* ☎ *1/312–7877.*

Nagyházi Galéria. A side street off Falk Miksa is home to one of Hungary's most prestigious auction houses. An impressive array of old masters paintings, antique furniture, and carpets line the aisles here, with a small corner of the shop dedicated to nude paintings. ☒ *District V, Balaton u. 8, Parliament* ☎ *1/331–9908.*

Pintér Antik Diskont. Take a deep breath before you head into this cavernous antiques store. Just when you think you've seen everything, you enter yet another basement room filled with a dining room set for twenty, or a Bohemian chandelier. The specialty here is furniture, everything from Biedermeier to art deco, with a good selection of antique pine armoires. Pieces are well-restored and reasonably priced. ☒ *District V, Falk Miksa u. 10, Parliament* ☎ *1/311–3030.*

Polgár Galéria és Aukciósház. Auctions are held once or twice a year at this well-established auction house. You can find everything from jewelry and furniture to antique porcelain. ☒ *District V, Kossuth Lajos u. 3, Ferenciek tere* ☎ *1/318–6954.*

Fodor's Choice ★ **Studio Agram.** If urban art deco is your aesthetic, head straight to where you'll find the most refined collection in Budapest. Vintage club chairs as well as silver coffee sets are exquisitely restored. ☒ *District V, Falk Miksa u. 10, Parliament* ☎ *1/428–0653.*

Style Antique. This French-Hungarian partnership has been working wonders with pine since the early 1990s, expertly restoring and selling antique pine furniture. Custom-made furniture can be made from either new or old wood and chosen from an expansive computerized catalog. ☒ *District V, Király u. 25, Király utca* ☎ *1/321–3473.*

V.A.M. Design. Step into this vast showroom to see the latest furniture creations by Hungarian and European designers. ☒ *District VI, Király u. 26, Around Király utca* ☎ *1/267–9540.*

Books

English-language newspapers can be found in most bookstores in Budapest. The bookstores listed here cater particularly well to English speakers.

Bamako. Planning a trip to Azerbaijan? Make your way downstairs from the Vista Travel Center to this comprehensive travel bookshop. It's one of Budapest's best sources for English-language travel guides. ☒ *District VI, Andrássy út 1, Around Andrássy út* ☎ *1/429–9706.*

★ **Bestsellers.** This stock at this popular bookshop consists almost entirely of English-language books and periodicals, including Hungarian classics translated into English, popular British and American best-sellers, and newspapers. There's a French-language section as well. ☒ *District V, Október 6 u. 11, St. István Bazilika* ☎ *1/312–1295.*

Central European University Bookshop. The two-floor bookshop housed in the Central European University building should be your first stop for books concerned with Central European politics and history. There's a decent collection of classics and travel books here, too. ☒ *District V, Nádor u. 9, St. István Basilika* ☎ *1/327–3096.*

Király Books. French cookbooks as well as English-language newspapers are available at this large bookshop in lower Buda, not far from the French Institute. ⊠ *District I, Fö u. 79, Around Batthyány tér* ☎ *1/214–0972.*

Párisi Udvar Könyvesbolt. To find this bookstore, tuck into one of Budapest's most beautiful arcades behind Váci utca. The shop specializes in foreign-language books, especially maps and travel-related writing. ⊠ *District V, Petőfi Sándor u. 2, Around Ferenciek tere* ☎ *1/235–0380.*

Pen Dragon. A friendly staff keeps expats happy at this English-language bookstore off St. István körút, not far from Falk Miksa utca. There's a big selection of coffee-table books and cookbooks; the latest New Age bestseller is also usually available. ⊠ *District XIII, Pozsonyi út 21–23, Parliament* ☎ *1/340–4426.*

Red Bus Bookstore. Although the shop seems small from the outside, you'll find thousands of English-language used books waiting to be discovered inside. Fiction, history, and classics are usually well-stocked. The store buys used books as well. ⊠ *District V, Semmelweis u. 14, Around Deák Ferenc tér* ☎ *1/337–7453.*

Crystal & Porcelain

Hungary is famous for its age-old Herend porcelain, which is hand-painted in the village of Herend near Lake Balaton. High-quality, hand-cut crystal is considerably less expensive here than in the United States. Crystal and porcelain dealers also sell their wares at the Ecseri Piac flea market, often at discount prices, but those looking for authentic Herend and Zsolnay should beware of imitations.

★ **Ajka Kristály.** Hand-cut lead crystal isn't as cheap as it once was in Hungary, but for a uniquely Central European gift, head to this leading Hungarian manufacturer for fine crystal. The huge selection of colored glasses—martini to cognac—comes in rich reds and blues, as well as pastel pinks and yellows. All can be packed for a long trip home. There are several outlets around town. ⊠ *District V, Jószef Atilla u. 7, St. István Bazilika* ☎ *1/317–8133.*

Aqua Múhely. If you want some pretty, old-fashioned ceramic goods to take back with you, check out this shop selling hand-painted floral plates, vases, and tiles. There's quite a range of ceramic items here including everything from salt and pepper shakers and pitchers to sinks and bidets. The styles are all quite sweet and the dining pieces can be bought in complete sets; there are 35 patterns in all. ⊠ *District V, Pesti Barnabás u. 4 (in the Millennium Center shopping center), Váci utca* ☎ *1/468–1288.*

Haas & Czjzek. This professional shop has been in business for more than 100 years, selling porcelain, glass, and ceramic pieces in traditional and contemporary styles. Today, you can find the best names in Hungarian porcelain as well as Villeroy & Boch from Germany, and the top companies from Limoges. If you're looking for a one-off piece (without a set), check upstairs, where among other odd pieces, there are marvelous soup tureens. ⊠ *District VI, Bajcsy-Zsilinszky út 23, St. István Bazilika* ☎ *1/311–4094.*

Herend Village Pottery. For the Herend name and quality without the steep price tag, visit this small shop where you can choose from Herend's practical line of informal ceramic cups, dishes, and table settings, all hand painted. The colorful pasta bowls are perfect for outdoor summer entertaining. ⊠ *District II, Bem rakpart 37, Around Batthyány tér* ☎ *1/ 356–7899.*

Herendi Porcelán. You can get a glimpse of the world famous Herend porcelain that has graced the tables of royal houses for centuries at one of two prominent stores in Budapest. Carefully hold a saucer up to the light and see how nearly transparent the finely worked porcelain is. All the brightly hand-painted animal figurines as well as most patterns can be picked up directly or ordered here. Sadly, prices are competitive with prices abroad. The multilingual staff is at the ready with calculators, though, for easy currency conversion. ⊠ *District V, József Nádor tér 11, St. István Bazilika* ☎ *1/317–2622* ⊠ *District V, Kigyó u. 5, Around Váci utca* ☎ *1/318–3439.*

Zsolnay Porcelain Shop. If you're unfamiliar with Zsolnay, Hungary's second most famous porcelain manufacturer, have a look at the tile roof of the Applied Arts Museum in downtown Pest to see the exquisite weatherproof mosaics. The hand-painted tile and porcelain are still made today in Pécs. Unfortunately, the company is not what it was in its heyday, when its art deco designs were internationally celebrated. Nevertheless, you can get an unusual hand-painted plate or vase that evokes the memory. ⊠ *District V, Kígyó u. 4, Around Váci utca* ☎ *1/ 318–3712.*

Clothing

Budapest is not Milan, though many of the big European and American brand names are represented in shopping centers like the West End City Centre. High-fashion favorites like Diesel and Mango (a distant cousin of Zara) are good places to look for trendy, younger styles. Women will find several good stores, though men's options are somewhat narrower.

Aqua-tick. You may encounter a steady stream of groovy students from neighboring CEU (Central European University) at this German retailer. Bright colors and mod prints are the look, with very retro accessories to match. ⊠ *District V, Zrínyi u. 12, St. Stephen's Basilica* ☎ *No phone.*

Glamour. Owner Brigitte Berdefy has done a brisk business since the early 1990s in what can only be called funwear. Inside this tiny shop you'll find the best collection of brightly colored feather boas this side of Greenwich Village. There's also a good selection of sequined things, including halter tops and briefs, not to mention humorous underwear. ⊠ *District VI, Nagymező u. 6, Around Andrássy út* ☎ *1/ 321–5161.*

Látmás. At the front of this shop you'll find quirky hand-knit accessories like scarves, hats, and backpacks. The back room has some really good vintage clothes, especially mod 1970s-style polyester prints. ⊠ *District VII, Király u. 11, Around Király utca* ☎ *1/266–2882.*

Manier. This popular atelier run by talented Hungarian designer Anikó Németh sells women's clothing, with designs ranging from quirky to totally outrageous. Though sometimes wacky, most shoppers find the clothes very wearable. The haute-couture salon and personal shopping department is just down the street, off Váci utca. ⊠ *District V, Váci u. 68, Around Váci utca* ☎ *1/411–0852* ⊠ *District V, Nyári Pál u. 4, Around Váci utca* ☎ *1/318–1292.*

Monarchia. Several Hungarian designers have banded together to create this showroom with a refreshingly broad selection of elegant evening gowns. Dresses for special occasions can be made to order. ⊠ *District V, Szabad sajtó út 6, Ferenciek tere* ☎ *1/318–3146.*

FodorśChoice **Naray Tamás.** A walk through Tamás Naray's colorful corner shop is
★ a feast for the eyes. Rich fabrics, whimsical accessories, and seamless tailoring characterize these exciting designs. No one would quarrel with the idea that Naray has an eye for dressing women with a "wow." Black polka dot skirts offset by lacy lingerie blouses get a giant red flower belt to hold them together. These clothes are not for the off-the-rack crowd. ⊠ *District V, Károlyi Mihály u. 12, Around Ferenciek tere* ☎ *1/266–2473.*

Norma Fölöp. Tucked away on Hegedű utca, around the corner from lively Liszt Ferenc tér, is this tiny atelier owned by upstart women's fashion designer Norma Fölöp. Beautiful silk and linen dresses are accented by ornate buttons and belts that evoke the Far East. It's hard to keep your hands off the richly textured scarves and pashminas. Some silk outfits are sold with matching evening bags. ⊠ *District VI, Hegedű u. 6, Around Liszt Ferenc tér* ☎ *1/322–9265.*

Pastell Studio. This Italian chain is a good bet for runway knockoffs at reasonable prices. ⊠ *District VII, Madách Imre tér 3, Around Deák Ferenc tér* ☎ *1/321–5739* ⊠ *District XIII, Szent László u. 31, North of Városliget* ☎ *1/239–7160.*

Springfield. Saturdays are crowded at this popular men's store, where you will find a good selection of basics like cotton sweaters, khaki pants, and colorful plaid shirts. The clean designs aren't too staid, and you can get fashion-forward club gear here as well. ⊠ *District VI, West End City Center, Váci u. 1–3, Around Nyugati Train Station* ☎ *1/ 238–7480.*

Terranova. The clubbing set gives this Italian chain high marks for its hip casual wear. Everything from trendy vests for men to miniskirts for women is a fairly good value, even considering that, for true hipsters, they're good for only one season. Accessories are excellent. ⊠ *District XIII, Szent István krt. 8, Parliament* ☎ *1/340–4456.*

V-50 Design Art Studio. If you've got a thing for hats, don't miss this shop carrying the unusual designs of Valéria Fazekas. Her brightly colored cloth hats range from elegant to pixyish, but all of them are functionally constructed. ⊠ *District V, Váci u. 50, Around Váci utca* ☎ *1/337–5320* ⊠ *Belgrád Rakpart 16* ☎ *1/337–0327.*

Van Laack. If you're looking for a really top-notch men's dress shirt, check out this German purveyor of pinpoint, broadcloth, and linen shirts. The impeccable details around the cuffs and collars are worlds better than what you'll find in almost any department store shirt, with prices that reflect the workmanship. ⊠ *District V, Váci u. 19–21, In the Millennium Center on Váci utca* ☎ *1/267–3294.*

Vasseva. Eva Vass is a Hungarian designer who's been bringing her clean lines and contemporary style to women's fashion since the early 1990s. Her shop, which is not far from Liszt Ferenc tér, has her own clothing designs as well as unique accessories. ⊠ *District VI, Paulay Ede u. 67, Around Liszt Ferenc tér* ☎ *1/342–8159.*

Flowers

Budapest isn't especially known for its flowers or flower shops, but all of these florist shops are professionally run and can create pleasing arrangements. If you plan to use the flowers in a vase somewhere, simply ask for paper to wrap them. If you plan to give flowers as a gift, for a nominal charge the florist will wrap them in pretty ribbon and cellophane.

★ **Arioso.** Stark bouquets of calla lilies, beautifully full topiary plants, or simple cactus arrangements are the kinds of things you're likely to find in this sophisticated flower shop on Király utca. The Swiss owners have found high-quality suppliers in Budapest to support their innovative and classy designs. This is the place to go for an impressive gift bouquet. ⊠ *District VII, Király u. 9, Around Király utca* ☎ *1/266–3555.*

Moha és Páfrány. This flower-cum-gift shop across the street from Buda's Déli train station displays potted plants and arrangements all over the sidewalk outside, so it's hard to pass by and not be tempted by something, including big cut sunflowers or a potted azalea. They do lovely gift packaging here, even for a single rose. ⊠ *District XII, Magyar jakobinusok tere 1, Around Déli Train Station* ☎ *1/356–7328.*

Viragneked.hu. A young and attentive staff puts together pretty arrangements at this well-stocked flower shop not far from the Parliament. Even in the winter, the store has a better stock than many other florists in Budapest. ⊠ *District V, Kossuth Lajos tér 18, Parliament* ☎ *06–30/ 954–4200.*

Folk Art

There are many folk art vendors along Váci utca, selling hand-painted wooden eggs and embroidered fabrics. For tablecloths and traditional Hungarian costumes, head to the second floor of the Vasárcsárnok.

Blue Bird. If you like the color blue, you'll notice this shop on Váci utca right away because the doors and windows are swung wide open every day to display the one-color inventory. Traditional folk crafts, such as blue-painted wooden eggs, blue-and-white painted ceramics, and hand-dyed blue tablecloths and napkins all seem appealing in the monochromatic scheme. ⊠ *District V, Váci u. 13, Around Váci utca* ☎ *1/313–4690.*

Folkart Centrum. If you are looking for an embroidered vest fit for a Hussar, this is the place to stop and browse. Beautifully embroidered fabrics in traditional motifs make handsome souvenirs from any trip to Hungary. Decorative wooden eggs and hand-painted ceramics are equally pleasing. ⊠ *District V, Váci u. 58, Around Váci utca* ☎ *1/318–5840.*

Folkart Kézműsesház. All the best Hungarian handicrafts are on display in this two-room shop off Váci utca. Heavily embroidered pillow cases and tablecloths, hand-painted ceramics, and traditional peasant clothing for children are just a few of the things you'll find. Nativity crèches made of corn husks have a holiday appeal. ⊠ *District V, Régiposta u. 12, Around Váci utca* ☎ *1/318–5143.*

★ **Holló Műhely.** László Holló is a master wood craftsman who has resurrected traditional motifs and styles of earlier centuries and sells beautiful handicrafts in his shop not far from Váci utca. You'll find lovely hope chests, chairs, jewelry boxes, candlesticks, and more, all hand-carved and hand-painted with cheery folk motifs—a predominance of birds and flowers in reds, blues, and greens. ⊠ *District V, Vitkovics Mihály u. 12, Around Váci utca* ☎ *1/317–8103.*

Food & Wine

Most supermarket chains in Budapest carry a good selection of Hungarian wines and Hungarian epicurian specialties like paprika, Pick-brand salami, and tinned goose liver. If you're looking for something special, several gourmet shops have a good selection of imported delicacies.

Bor Tár. You can find better wines here than are available in Budapest supermarkets. There's not a huge selection, but the Sas utca branch is in the heart of the downtown sightseeing district. ⊠ *District V, Sas u. 10–12, St. Stephen's Basilica* ☎ *1/301–8760* ⊠ *District III, Gellért Hotel, Bartók Béla út. 8, Gellért Hill and the Tabán* ☎ *1/361–4954.*

Fodor'sChoice **Budapest Bortársaság** (Budapest Wine Society). A good place to start
★ looking for Hungarian wines is in this cellar shop at the base of Castle Hill. There's an excellent selection of Hungarian vintners represented here, and the shop is open all day on Saturdays. The knowledgeable staff is always available to guide you on Hungary's wines, like this year's tokaji or kékoporto, and they'll deliver orders of a case or more free of charge anywhere in Budapest. There's a good selection of wine accessories as well, from oak wine racks to high-tech bottle openers. ⊠ *District I, Batthyány u. 59, Castle Hill* ☎ *1/212–2569 or 1/212–0262* 🖷 *1/212–5285.*

Culinaris. The traffic in and out of this modest shop moves briskly, as customers snatch up Hungarian-made goat cheeses just in from the countryside or pick up exotic Sri Lankan cinnamon. The shelves are lined with a selective array of gourmet foods and wines. Fresh-baked breads and garden herbs are highlights. The friendly owner, Zoltán Bogáthy, is often on hand to advise you of a porcini delivery or just what to do with ginger paste, handily serving customers in both Hungarian and English. ⊠ *District VI, Hunyadi tér 3, Around Andrássy út* ☎ *1/341–7001.*

Francia Borok Háza. There are over 1,000 wines in this wine shop near Váci utca, including the best selection of French vintages in Budapest, as well as a good range of champagne and Armagnac. You can even organize a personalized wine and cheese tasting here. ⊠ *District V, Szarka u. 4, Around Váci utca* ☎ *1/266–8054.*

In Vino Veritas. This shop is a bit off the beaten path, but it has a good stock of high-quality Hungarian wines. ✉ *District VII, Dohány u. 58–62, Around Király utca* ☎ *1/341–3174 or 1/341–0646* 🖷 *1/321–1953.*

Monarchia Wine Shop. One of the best distributors of wine in Hungary, Monarchia stocks an excellent selection of Hungarian and international wines. A very knowledgeable staff and long hours on Saturday (when it's open until 6) make this shop a favorite of local wine enthusiasts. ✉ *District IX, Kinizsi u. 30–36, Around Kálvin tér* ☎ *1/456–9898.*

Nagy Tamás Sajtüzlete. The oldest seller of imported cheese in Budapest, "Big Tom" now has a nascent selection of Hungarian cheeses to celebrate. Be sure to try one of the very fresh goat cheeses from the Molnár farm. All the things you need for a smart cocktail party or sumptuous picnic can be found here, including fresh-baked olive focaccia. ✉ *District V, Gerlóczy u. 3, Deák Ferenc tér* ☎ *1/317–4268.*

Szega Sajtszaküzlet (Szega Cheese Shop). This cheese and salami importer, one of Budapest's best, has outlets in all the tony shopping centers. It's worth the trip if you can't put down that craving for Parma ham or French Muenster cheese. There are lots of other goodies here, including homemade duck and goose liver pâtés, and hot Hungarian peppers stuffed with goat cheese. ✉ *District II, Budagyöngye Shopping Center, Szilágyi Erzsébet fasor 121, North Buda* ☎ *1/200–6777* ✉ *District II, Fény u. piac, behind Mammut I shopping center, Around Moszkva tér* ✉ *District II, Rózsakert shopping center, Gábor Áron u. 74–78, Buda Hills.*

Furs & Leather Goods

Balogh Kesztyű. Although leather gloves are widely available in most American retail stores, this store specializes in handmade and hand-dyed leather gloves made in Hungary. Some of the men's gloves have shearling lining and will keep you warm in near-Arctic temperatures. The buttery ladies models are lined with cashmere or wool. ✉ *District V, Haris Köz 2, Around Váci utca* ☎ *1/266–1942.*

Clara Liska. The furs in this first-class Viennese shop are on the right side of the store. There's a good choice of skins and colors, with beautiful tailoring to match. This is the place to walk away with a truly luxurious fur coat. The left side of the store sells upmarket Italian brand Malo cashmere sweaters and handbags. ✉ *District V, Váci u. 12, Around Váci utca* ☎ *1/318–6416.*

Klein Furs. A well-known name for fur in Budapest. You can look through styles and have a fur coat custom made. ✉ *District V, Millennium Center, Váci u. 19–21, Around Váci utca* ☎ *1/266–1332.*

La Boutique. A wide range of designer shoes is sold here, including Ferragamo, Dolce & Gabbana, and Prada. There are a few Hungarian knockoffs as well, for about half the price. Thankfully, they have two blowout sales a year, usually in summer and winter. ✉ *District VI, Andrássy u. 16, Around Andrássy út* ☎ *1/302–5646* ✉ *District V, Le Méridien Hotel, Deák Ferenc utca, Deák Ferenc tér* ☎ *1/266–7585.*

Fodor'sChoice **Mandarina Duck.** This small, first-rate Italian handbag maker has made ★ a name for itself by designing stylish yet incredibly durable leather goods. The leather quality can't be matched for easy upkeep and resistance to all kinds of wear and tear, making the pricey bags well worth the investment. There are wallets and small leather goods for sale here, as well as a range of non-leather handbags and luggage. ⊠ *District VI, West End City Center, Váci utca 1–3, Around Nyugati Train Station* ☎ *1/ 238–7579.*

Scandic Retail. Some very high-end fur brands such as Marina Rinaldi and Gianfranco Ferre can be found in this shop, which also sells designer leather jackets. ⊠ *District V, Galamb u. 6, Around Váci utca* ☎ *1/318– 4866.*

Szűcs Mester. If fur is what you need to face the Central European winter, take a step back in time into this alcove shop where Gábor Dán can address your needs. This is the kind of fur shop where you'll find only hanging pelts and the furrier himself. Elegant accessories like scarves and collars can be made here as well as mink muffs. ⊠ *District V, Régisposta u. 7–9, Around Váci utca* ☎ *1/337–2563.*

Vass. If you are looking for a really luxurious indulgence, why not consider a pair of handmade leather shoes, specifically measured to your feet? You can choose from a variety of traditional styles, from cordovan to nubuck. Though wildly expensive when compared to the cost of ready-made shoes—a pair of custom-made shoes will cost you anywhere from HUF 60,000 to HUF 100,000—prices are still very competitive with those in Europe and the U.S. There's a small selection of ready-to-wear shoes available in the window for those with limited time in Budapest. ⊠ *District V, Haris Köz 2, Around Váci utca* ☎ *1/318–2375.*

Home Decor & Gifts

Aita Studio. Imported Italian pewter decanters, silver picture frames, and wrought-iron andirons are just a few of the things you'll find in this warehouse-cum-shop on low-rent Lónyay utca. You're spoiled for choice in decorative table accessories; handsome caviar bowls and tasteful salt and pepper shakers can be had at almost garage-sale prices. It's hard to leave empty-handed. ⊠ *District IX, Lónyay u. 24, Around Kálvin tér* ☎ *1/ 216–1673.*

Arabeszk. Handmade silk lampshades—and mosaic tables and mirrors—are the things to seek out in this tiny shop off the beaten path a few blocks behind Váci utca. A few other handicrafts dot the place, and one or two of the responsible artists can usually be found nearby. ⊠ *District V, Királyi Pál u. 9, Around Kálvin tér* ☎ *1/317–9577.*

Fodor'sChoice   **BomoArt.** When walking in the Váci utca area, it's well worth your
   ★   while to step into this closet-size shop selling hand-made paper diaries, address books, and stationery. There are old-fashioned letter-writing accessories here, too, including bottled ink, quills, and sealing wax. The diaries are so nice that even if you're not a writer you'll be tempted to start one. ⊠ *District V, Régiposta u. 14, Around Váci utca* ☎ *1/318– 7280* ⊠ *District VI, West End City Center, Váci u. 1–3, 1st floor, Around Nyugati Train Station* ☎ *1/238–9701.*

Demko Feder. Natural-fiber housewares, rattan serving trays, and sheared wool blankets are just a few of the things you'll find in this eco-friendly shop. ⊠ *District V, József Atilla u. 20, St. Stephen's Basilica* ☎ *1/266– 1505* ⊠ *District II, Margit krt.* ☎ *1/212–4408.*

Goa. All the furniture and housewares in this large showroom have an Asian aesthetic. There are big wooden beds from Indonesia, tin alms bowls, rattan placemats, lovely Chinese silk pillow covers, and lots of votive candleholders. One part of the shop is devoted to indoor gardening with lush plants, clay pots, and the makings for a rock garden. ⊠ *District VII, Király u. 19–21, Arond Király utca* ☎ *1/352–8442* ⊠ *District XII, Mom Park shopping center, Alkotás u. 53, Around Déli Train Station* ☎ *1/487–5416.*

Hephaistos. Esther Gál's wrought-iron designs are a far cry from the staid stuff of traditional blacksmiths. Her loopy candlesticks and tables are playful and modern, not to mention one of a kind. Gorgeously upholstered furniture and silk textiles are another attraction in this two-floor emporium behind Váci utca. If the colorful table runners and placemats don't make you want to throw a lavish dinner party, then the hand-dripped candles, available in every possible color, will. ⊠ *District V, Mólnar u. 27, Around Váci utca* ☎ *1/266–1550.*

Impresszió. This little boutique is packed with home furnishings, baskets, picture frames, and decorative packaging, all made of natural materials and reasonably priced. The courtyard it calls home includes similar shops and a pleasant café. ⊠ *District V, Károly krt. 10, Ferenciek tere* ☎ *1/337–2772.*

Interieur Stúdió. Just down the street from the Holló Műhely, this old-fashioned shop sells wooden brushes, bookmarks, and even birdcages; candles of all shapes and sizes; and sundry other objects for the home. There's a good selection of dried flowers and pretty hat boxes as well. ⊠ *District V, Vitkovics Mihály u. 6, Deák Ferenc tér* ☎ *1/266–1666.*

Fodor'sChoice ★ **Magma.** To understand who's who in Hungarian applied arts, step into this professionally run collective of the best textile, jewelry, and furniture designers working in Hungary today. There are silk throw pillows and gorgeous satin and linen tablecloths, as well as sleek oak card tables and ceramic figurines. Stop in and chat with the owners, who are happy to talk about any of the artists. ⊠ *District V, Petőfi Sándor u. 11, Around Váci utca* ☎ *1/235–0277.*

Nádortex. Hungarian goose down is prized the world over for its featherweight warmth. Pillows and duvets made in factories in Szeged are sold at this old-fashioned but friendly textile store. Duvets come in winter, spring, and summer weights, offering varying degrees of warmth. Sizes are made to fit Hungarian standard beds, but with a little imagination you can find one that suits your needs. The veteran staff tries to speak a bit of English, but it's best to do some homework on what you need in advance. ⊠ *District V, József Nádor tér, St. Stephen's Basilica* ☎ *1/317–0030.*

Provence. Just next door to Goa and run by the same owners, this shop sells high-quality Provence-inspired housewares. There are beautiful tiles and textiles as well as table settings and dried flowers. ⊠ *District VII, Király u. 19–21, Around Király utca* ☎ *1/352–8442.*

Jewelry

M. Frey Wille. This Viennese jeweler has a world-class name for beautifully enamelled gold jewelry. Some of the designs are geometric, while others evoke art nouveau paintings. Although the style is not for every-one, bright colors and unusual materials set these pieces apart from other more traditional jewelry. ⊠ *District V, Régiposta u. 19, Around Váci utca* ☎ *1/318–7665.*

O'Mama Biszuja. Garnet rings in art deco settings and pendants in the shape of birds are among the many delightful things you'll find in this antique jewelry shop. Budapesters know O'Mama for her excellent taste and fair prices. ⊠ *District V, Szent István krt. 1, Parliament* ☎ *1/ 312–6812.*

Varga Design. Miklos Varga's work has won prizes in jewelry-design com-petitions, but that doesn't keep his modest shop from being accessible to the average shopper. Tahitian pearls and platinum seem to be his pre-ferred media, but there are lots of exciting combinations using other gems as well. Some of the rings you can imagine wearing everyday. ⊠ *Dis-trict V, Haris Köz 1, Around Váci utca* ☎ *1/318–4089.*

★ **Wladis Galéria és Műterem.** Striking sterling silver is the medium of Péter Vladimir, a jewelry designer par excellence. His distinct pieces are one-of-a-kind or limited issues. Big, clunky rings with cut-crystal stones or amethysts make a dramatic modern statement. Some of the necklaces harken back to ancient, primitive decorative jewelry. This store is not to be missed if you're looking for a unique bespoke silver adornment. ⊠ *District V, Falk Miksa u. 13, Parliament* ☎ *1/354–0834.*

Music

Recordings of Hungarian folk music or of pieces played by Hungarian artists are widely available on compact discs throughout Budapest.

Darius Music. This well-established shop doesn't sell recordings. Rather, they deal in fine and rare violins. ⊠ *District VI, Paulay Ede u. 58, Around Liszt Ferenc tér* ☎ *1/352–6159 or 06–20/944–1938.*

FOTEX Records. This well-stocked music and DVD store has strong con-temporary pop selections. There is a good selection of music DVDs here as well, including live concert recordings and long-play music videos. Classical and world music are well represented, as are the latest Hun-garian pop artists. There are many locations in downtown Pest, as well as in the major shopping malls. ⊠ *District V, Szervita tér 2, Deák Fer-enc tér* ☎ *1/318–3395* ⊠ *District V, Váci u. 13, Around Váci utca* ☎ *1/ 318–3128* ⊠ *District VI, Teréz krt. 27, Around Nyugati Pályaudvar* ☎ *1/332–7175* ⊠ *District XII, Alkotás út 11, Around Déli Pályaud-var* ☎ *1/355–6886.*

Psybaba. Music recordings can be found in the back of this shop, but the selection is limited to hippie-era pop music and reggae. The front section has all the gear you'll need to perform in a street fair, including such items as juggling pins and wooden noisemakers. ⊠ *District VI, Király u. 28, Around Király utca* ☎ *No phone.*

Rózsavölgyi Zenebolt. This is an old, established music store carrying the best selection of Hungarian composers on CD, as well as a good selec-tion of sheet music. There's a small number of recordings by the best Hungarian classical performers as well, including brilliant pianist Zoltán Koscis, who spends more time conducting these days than performing. ⊠ *District V, Szervita tér 5, Deák Ferenc tér* ☎ *1/318–3500.*

Trance Wave Records. There's an alternative vibe at this tiny store not far from St. Stephen's Basilica. The shop is separated into two sections, Wave and Trance. One sells underground dance music (Trance) and one sells indie guitar rock (Wave). The Web site—in Hungarian only—has listings of concerts in Budapest. ⊠ *District VI, Revay köz 2, St. Stephen's Basilica* ☎ *1/269–3135* ⊕ *www.trancewave.hu.*

Virgin Megastore. It's a bit out of town, but this well-known music store in the Duna Plaza shopping center has the large selection of CDs you'd expect. The metro will get you there in 10 minutes from downtown Pest. ⊠ *District XIII, Váci u. 178, Duna Plaza* ☎ *1/239–4409* Ⓜ *M3: Gyöngyösi út.*

Pastries & Sweets

While it's fun to participate in the local kávéház (coffeehouse) culture in Budapest—drinking coffee and eating cake in the late afternoon—most cukrázsdas will pack up a piece of cake to go (often beautifully) if you'd like to save it for dinner.

Artigiana Gelati Fagylaltozó. The line outside this popular ice cream shop can easily be 20 deep on a hot summer weekend. There's real Italian gelato here in loads of flavors, and you can also get containers to go. Tropical fruit flavors—particularly mango, coconut, papaya, and pineapple—are nearly as refreshing as a dip in the pool. ⊠ *District XII, Csaba u. 8, Around Moszkva tér* ☎ *1/212–2439.*

★ **Daubner Cukrászda.** It's with good reason that this popular confectioner has lines outside the door each morning. Every pastry here is delicate and light. Even a novice can taste the real butter cream in the famous Eszterhazy torta, which is a truly magnificent cake. Locals say the Sacher torte is every bit as good as it is in the famous Sacher Hotel in Vienna. It's usually crowded on weekends with families eating ice cream. ⊠ *District II, Szépvölgyi út 50, Buda Hills* ☎ *1/335–2253.*

Gerbeaud Ház. Around the corner from the famous Gerbeaud coffeeshop is the Gerbeaud Ház, where you can buy cakes to take away. There's a full selection of sweets, including chocolates, and everything can be packed up to travel. The Gerbeaud cake, only available here, is a moist chocolate and apricot creation that lasts for 3 to 4 weeks. There's a delivery service (cleverly called "Gerboy") that can get a cake anywhere in Budapest for a fee. ⊠ *District V, Vörösmarty tér 7–8, Around Váci utca* ☎ *1/429–9026.*

Godiva Boutique. The discreet staff will help you hand-pick candies to make a lovely gift box at this small branch of the famous Belgian chocolatier, but they won't mind if you take a few pralines or nut creams home yourself. ⊠ *District V, Budapest Marriott, Apaczai Csere János u. 4, Around Váci utca* ☎ *1/266–7000.*

Szamos Marzipán. Marzipan has always been a favorite in Central Europe, and this well-loved confectioner has turned out marzipan cookies, cakes, and candies since right after World War II. The store has always been most famous for its edible marzipan roses, but today, just as many people come for the ice cream as for the marzipan. ⊠ *District V, Párizsi u. 3, Around Váci utca* ☎ *1/317–3643.*

Toys

Fakopáncs. There's a big selection of Hungarian-made wooden toys as well as puzzles here. You can find wooden chess and backgammon replacement pieces, too. ✉ *District VIII, Baross u. 46, Around Kálvin tér* ☎ *1/337–8448.*

Játékszerek Anno (Toys Anno). For a look back into the world before Pokémon cards and action figures, stop in at this tiny store, where fabulous reproductions of antique European toys are sold. From simple paper puzzles to lovely stone building blocks to the 1940s wind-up metal monkeys on bicycles, these "nostalgia toys" are beautifully simple and exceptionally clever. Even if you're not a collector, it's worth a stop just to browse. ✉ *District VI, Teréz krt. 54, Around Nyugati Pályaudvar* ☎ *1/302–6234.*

THE DANUBE BEND

By Paul
Olchvary

ABOUT 40 KM (25 MI) NORTH OF BUDAPEST, the Danube abandons its eastward course and turns abruptly south toward the capital, cutting through the Börzsöny and Visegrád hills. This area is called the Danube Bend and includes the baroque town of Szentendre, the hilltop castle ruins and town of Visegrád, and the cathedral town of Esztergom, all on the Danube's west bank. The most scenically varied part of Hungary, the region is best known for a chain of riverside spas and beaches, bare volcanic mountains, and limestone hills. Here, in the heartland, are the traces of the country's history—the remains of the Roman Empire's frontier, the battlefields of the Middle Ages, and the relics of the Hungarian Renaissance.

The district can be covered by car in one day, the total round-trip no more than 112 km (70 mi), although this affords only a cursory look around. A day-trip to Szentendre from Budapest plus two days for Visegrád and Esztergom, with a night in either (both have lovely hotels small and large), would be best.

On the Danube's eastern bank, Vác is the prime cultural-commercial center. No bridges span the river in the Danube Bend until Esztergom, where a new bridge opened in 2001; the previous one, parts of which remained for 57 years as a visible testament to war, had been destroyed by German forces in 1944. So if you go to Esztergom, you can cross the Mária Valéria Bridge to Slovakia and head back into Hungary (a few miles to the east) on the opposite bank. But throughout the Danube Bend there are also numerous ferries (between Visegrád and Nagymaros, Basaharc and Szob, Szentendre Island and Vác), making it possible to combine a visit to both sides of the Danube on the same excursion, even if you don't wish to go as far as Esztergom.

Though the Danube Bend's west bank contains the bulk of historical sights, the less-traveled east bank has the excellent hiking trails of the Börzsöny mountain range, which extends along the Danube from Vác to Zebegény before curving toward the Slovak border. The Pilis and Visegrád hills on the Danube's western side and the Börzsöny Hills on the east are popular nature escapes.

About the Hotels & Restaurants
The Danube Bend offers a broad range of accommodations, but most are relatively small (and affordable), pension-like hotels that often exude a charm hard to find these days in Budapest. The only serious rival (in both quality and price) to Budapest's large, luxury venues is the Danubus Spa & Conference Center Hotel Visegrád, which opened in April 2004. But with market pressures being what they are, the future may see some now-quiet hotels lose some of their charm as they strive to keep from losing guests to their larger rivals.

Rates may be up to 20 percent lower in the colder months—between October and April, which roughly corresponds to the region's low season. Only a few hotels in this region set and advertise their rates in euros. That said, even these places will do a quick conversion for you and accept your forints. As for air-conditioning, most hotels in this region, as elsewhere outside of Budapest, are apt to offer just a few rooms with a/c.

The pressures of Hungary's burgeoning tourist industry in the past decade have seen some once "authentic" little restaurants expand into tourist mills, with tour groups passing through in assembly-line fashion; this is particularly the case in Szentendre; to a lesser extent in Visegrád and Esztergom; and least of all in Vác, which has been relatively unscathed by the tackiest side of tourism. Prices are often between 10 and 20 percent lower than those in Budapest for equivalent quality.

While the menus are much the same as in the capital, the Danube theme inevitably yields a relatively high number of restaurants that offer fish specialties; and, since the Bend is, after all, situated in the "countryside" (i.e., beyond Budapest), you will won't have to look far to find restaurants of the *csárda*, or country tavern, variety—where you can generally be assured of a bowl of *gulyás, halászlé* (fisherman's soup), or, say, *pacalpörkölt* (tripe stew), often for under 1,000 HUF or not much more.

WHAT IT COSTS In Euros & Forints					
	$$$$	**$$$**	**$$**	**$**	**¢**
HOTELS IN EUROS	over €225	€175–€225	€125–€175	€75–€125	under €75
HOTELS IN FORINTS	over 56,000	44,000–56,000	31,000–44,000	18,500–31,000	under 18,500
RESTAURANTS IN FORINTS	over 3,500	2,500–3,500	1,500–2,500	800–1,500	under 800

Hotel prices are for two people in a standard double room with a private bath and breakfast during peak season (June through August). Restaurant prices are per person for a main course at dinner and include 15% tax but not service.

Numbers in the margin correspond to numbers on the Szentendre and Danube Bend maps.

SZENTENDRE

21 km (13 mi) north of Budapest.

A romantic, lively little town with a long history as a haven for artists—a somewhat touristy haven, in recent years—Szentendre is the highlight of the Danube Bend. With its church steeples, colorful baroque houses, and winding, narrow cobblestone streets, it's no wonder Szentendre attracts swarms of visitors, tripling its population in peak season. Perhaps the only drawback of a visit here is the prospect of finding yourself shoulder to shoulder with people speaking all languages but Hungarian.

Szentendre was first settled by Serbs and Greeks fleeing the advancing Turks in the 16th and 17th centuries. They built houses and churches in their own style—rich in reds and blues seldom seen elsewhere in Hungary. To truly savor Szentendre, duck into any and every cobblestone side street that appeals to you. (Indeed, you may have to do so simply to escape the crowds.) Baroque houses with shingle roofs (often with an arched eye-of-God upstairs window) and colorful stone walls will enchant your eye and pique your curiosity.

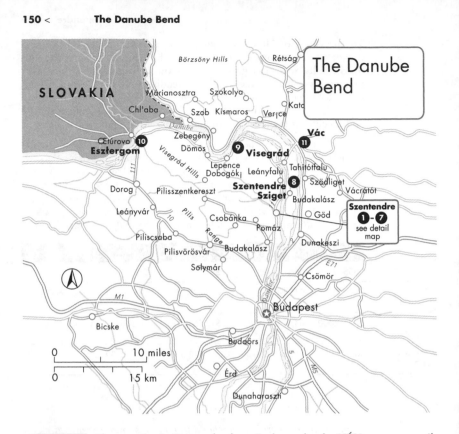

Börzsöny Hills   Rétság   **The Danube Bend**

SLOVAKIA   Mārianosztra   Szokolya
Chl'aba   Szob   Kismaros   Verjce   Kata

Čtúrovo ⑩   Zebegény   **Vác** ⑪
Esztergom   Dömös   ⑨ **Visegrád**

Lepence   Leányfalu   Tahitótfalu
Dobogókj   Szödliget
Dorog   Pilisszentkereszt   **Szentendre** ⑧   Vácrátót
Sziget   Budakalász
Leányvár   Csobánka   Göd   **Szentendre** ①-⑦ see detail map
Pomáz
Piliscsaba   Budakalász   Dunakeszi
Pilisvörösvár
Sólymár   E71

Csömör

M1   **Budapest**

Bicske   Budaörs

0 —— 10 miles
0 —— 15 km   Érd

Dunaharaszti

a good walk If you arrive in Szentendre from Budapest by the HÉV commuter railway—the most convenient way of traveling there short of driving—go straight ahead at the HÉV station in the direction the train was going and cross the busy road ahead of you by going through the underpass. Then, keep going straight, along Kossuth utca. Within five minutes you'll cross tiny Bükkös-*patak* (stream), where the road continues as Dumtsa Jenő utca. By this point you have entered the historic district, and in a couple minutes you'll reach the main square, **Fő tér** ①, the compact hub of this small town. At the far right of the square you'll see the **Görög templom** ②; a right here, into Görög utca, will take you to the **Kovács Margit Múzeum** ③. Tour the museum, then go back to Fő tér, from where a steep walk up Váralja lejtő to the top of Vár-domb (Castle Hill) will get you to the **Római Katolikus plébánia templom** ④; from the church, it's a short walk to the **Szerb Ortodox Egyházi Gyűjtemény** ⑤ and the adjacent **Szerb Ortodox Bazilika** ⑥. If you are inspired to do some more walking on the relatively quiet residential hillside before heading back toward tourist-filled Fő tér, you can wind your way north along streets such as Hunyadi utca and then Bartók Béla utca, which, here and there, provide splendid views of the town and river below. Head back down anywhere, all the way to the river, and saunter north a bit, as far as (or beyond) the dock of the Szentendre Island ferry, before walking back to the town center along the lovely Duna korzó (Danube promenade). If you have a couple hours to spare after taking in the heart of Szentendre, you may want to head out of town a tad to the **Szabadtéri Néprajzi Múzeum ❼** by catching a bus back at the HÉV station.

TIMING Szentendre is compact enough to allow you to cover it in half a day, unless you choose to take an additional side trip and cross by ferry to Szentendre sziget (Szentendre Island), though you'd best have a bicycle for that unless you're fine with walking a couple of miles down lush green, uninhabited roads into the sleepy village of Szigetmonostor (see ⇨ Szentendre Sziget, *below*). Plan to leave Budapest via HÉV in the late morning for the 45-minute trip so that you get there by lunch, then you can spend the afternoon looking around; or else, go sometime in the afternoon and stay for dinner. Or, of course, you can make more of a day of it and have both lunch and dinner in this charming but sometimes crowded town. Either way, plan on an excursion of six hours or more.

What to See

❶ **Fő tér** is Szentendre's main square, the centerpiece of which is an ornate **Memorial Cross** erected by Serbs in gratitude because the town was spared from a plague. The cross has a crucifixion painted on it and stands atop a triangular pillar adorned with a dozen icon paintings.

Every house on Fő tér is a designated landmark, and three of them are open to the public. The **Ferenczy Múzeum** (Ferenczy Museum; ⊠ Fő tér 6) has paintings of Szentendre landscapes. The **Kmetty Múzeum** (Kmetty Museum; ⊠ Fő út 21) displays the work of János Kmetty, a pioneer of Hungarian avant-garde painting. The **Szentendrei Képtár** (Municipal Gallery; ⊠ Fő út 2–5) has an excellent collection of local contemporary art and changing exhibits of international art. Each museum has a 400 HUF admission fee and the same hours: Tuesday through Sunday, from 10 to 6.

❷ Gracing the corner of Görög utca (Greek Street) and Szentendre's main square, Fő tér, the so-called **Görög templom** (Greek Church, or Blagovestenska Church) is actually a Serbian Orthodox church that takes its name from the Greek inscription on a red-marble gravestone set in its wall. This elegant edifice was built between 1752 and 1754 by a rococo master, Andreas Mayerhoffer, on the site of a wooden church dating to the Great Serbian Migration (around AD 690). Its greatest glory—a symmetrical floor-to-ceiling panoply of stunning icons—was painted between 1802 and 1804 by Mihailo Zivkovic, a Serbian painter from Buda. ⊠ *Görög utca, at Fő tér* ☏ *26/310–554* 💳 *100 HUF* ☉ *Mar.–Oct., Tues.–Sun. 10–5.*

★ ❸ If you have time for only one of Szentendre's myriad museums, don't miss the **Kovács Margit Múzeum,** which displays the collected works of Budapest ceramics artist Margit Kovács, who died in 1977. She left behind a wealth of richly textured work that ranges from ceramics to life-size sculptures. Admission to the museum is limited to 15 persons at a time, so it is wise to line up early or at lunchtime, when the herds of tour groups are occupied elsewhere. ⊠ *Vastagh György u. 1, off Görög u.* ☏ *26/310–244 Ext. 112* 💳 *600 HUF* ☉ *Mid-Mar.–early Oct., daily 10–6; early Oct.–mid-Mar., Tues.–Sun. 10–5.*

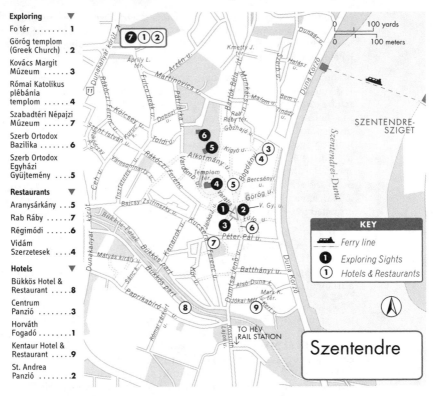

Szentendre

KEY

Ferry line
❶ Exploring Sights
① Hotels & Restaurants

④ Perched atop Vár-domb (Castle Hill) is Szentendre's oldest surviving monument, the **Római Katolikus plébánia templom** (Roman Catholic Parish Church). According to some sources, there was a church here dating to the 13th century, but church or no church, it was apparently destroyed in some conflict in 1294. What's certain is that between 1332 and 1337 a new church was built here, though this was heavily damaged during the Turkish occupation in the 16th and 17th centuries. After many reconstructions, the church's oldest visible part is a 15th-century sundial in the doorway. The church's small cobblestone yard hosts an arts-and-crafts market and, often on weekends in summer, street entertainment. From here, views over Szentendre's angular tile rooftops and steeples and of the Danube beyond are superb. ⊠ *Templom tér (enter from Alkotmány u.), Vár-domb* ☎*26/312–545* ⚐*Free* ⊙ *Daily, with sporadic hours.*

⑦ Szentendre's farthest-flung museum is the **Szabadtéri Néprajzi Múzeum** (Open-Air Ethnographic Museum), the largest open-air museum in the country. It is a living re-creation of 18th- and 19th-century village life from different regions of Hungary—the sort of place where blacksmith shops and a horse-powered mill compete with wooden houses and folk handicrafts for your attention. During regular crafts demonstrations, you can sit back and watch or give it a try yourself. Five kilometers (3 mi) northwest of the city center, the museum is reachable by bus from the

Szentendre terminus of the HÉV suburban railway; as of this writing, the bus leaves from stand No. 7 (ask for a ticket to the *Skanzen,* as this museum is also called). Throughout the year, the museum has regularly scheduled activity days on Thursday through Sunday as well as special festivals. ⊠ *Sztaravodai út* ☎ *26/502–500, 26/317–965, or 26/317–966* ⊕ *www.sznm.hu* ▦ *Open-Air Exhibits: Apr.–Oct., free Tues. and Wed., 600 HUF Thurs.–Sun., 1,000 HUF on festival days. Gallery: Apr.–Oct., free; early Jan.–Mar. and Nov.–mid-Dec., 300 HUF* ۞ *Apr.–Oct., Tues.–Sun. 9–5; Nov.–mid-Dec. and early Jan.–Mar., Tues.–Sun. 9–4 (special exhibition gallery only).*

❻ The crimson steeple of the handsome **Szerb Ortodox Bazilika** (Serbian Orthodox Cathedral) presides over a restful tree-shaded yard crowning the hill just north of Vár-domb (Castle Hill). It was built in the 1740s with a much more lavish but arguably less beautiful iconostasis than is found in the Greek Church below it. ⊠ *Pátriárka u. 5* ☎ *26/314–456* ▦ *Free* ۞ *Tues.–Sun. 10–4.*

★ ❺ The **Szerb Ortodox Egyházi Gyüjtemény** (Serbian Orthodox Collection of Religious Art) displays exquisite artifacts relating to the history of the Serbian Orthodox Church in Hungary. Icons, altars, robes, 16th-century prayer books, and a 17th-century cross with (legend has it) a bullet hole through it were collected from all over the country, after being sold or stolen from Serbian churches that were abandoned when most Serbs returned to their homeland at the turn of the 20th century and following World War I. The museum shares a tranquil yard with the imposing Serbian Orthodox Cathedral. ⊠ *Pátriárka u. 5* ☎ *26/312–399* ▦ *200 HUF* ۞ *May–Sept., Tues.–Sun. 10–6; Oct.–Dec. and Mar.–Apr., Tues.–Sun. 10–4; Jan.–Feb., Fri.–Sun. 10–4.*

> **need a break?**
>
> On your right above the stream, just before you cross a little bridge to enter Szentendre's historical center, is the **Adria Kaffeteria** (⊠ Kossuth Lajos u. 4). This café-cum-bistro is an awfully pleasant place to have a cappucino, a soft drink, a hot chocolate, or, say, a Greek salad before or after exploring the heart of the town. It offers light Mediterranean fare with a corresponding atmosphere, accentuated by colorful fish paintings on the wall and a decidedly sea-blue motif.
>
> For a quick cholesterol boost, grab a floppy, freshly fried *lángos* (flat, salty fried dough) drizzled with sour cream or brushed with garlic at **Piknik Büfé** (⊠ Dumtsa Jenő u. 22), right next door to the Tourinform office.
>
> A bit beyond the Piknic Büfé, farther into town toward the main square, is the **Múzeum cukrászda** (⊠ Dumtsa Jenő u. 12 ☎ No phone), renovated in 2003 to recapture its elegance as a traditional café. Featuring glazed-tile artwork on the walls plus regular photo exhibits and musical performances, here you can choose from a wide selection of scrumptious pastries—not least, the Múzeum torta, rum-soaked sponge cake topped off with sour-cherry-flavored whipped-cream icing.

Where to Stay & Eat

$$-$$$ ✕ **Aranysárkány.** A favorite of early-20th-century Hungarian writer
Fodor'sChoice Frigyes Karinthy, more recent high-profile guests have included Laura
★ Bush. The food is all prepared in an open kitchen. Since there are only
eight tables, be prepared to share on a busy night. Begin with *sárkány
erőleves* (dragon's bouillon) with quail eggs and sesame seeds. Main-
course specialties include trout fillets steamed in campari, and venison
steak in an almond crust. If you can still face dessert, try the poppy-seed-
spiked "opium" pudding or the cottage cheese pudding with cranber-
ries. A wine list with 60 varieties will tempt the inquisitive palate.
Reservations are a must in the summer. This is, by the way, one of Hungary's few air-conditioned restaurants. ⊠ *Alkotmány u. 1/a* ☎ *26/301–
479 or 26/311–670* ▭ *AE, DC, MC, V.*

$-$$$ ✕ **Régimódi.** This restaurant which has a very good wine list and spe-
cializes in fish and game dishes is practically on Fő tér. Lace curtains,
antique knickknacks, and lovely old paintings give the small upstairs
dining room a homey intimacy—and, perhaps, the restaurant its name:
Old-Fashioned (in the best sense, mind you). The downstairs dining room
and outside seating in front pale in comparison; what's more, the up-
stairs is nonsmoking and air-conditioned. The summer terrace, likewise
upstairs, is a delightful place to dine alfresco and look out over the red-
tile rooftops. ⊠ *Dumtsa Jenő u. 2* ☎ *26/311–105* ▭ *MC, V.*

★ **$-$$** ✕ **Rab Ráby.** Hungarian home-style cooking with an emphasis on freshwater fish is the mark of this hospitable and often busy restaurant. Old
lanterns, cowbells, and musical instruments decorate the walls of this
converted 18th-century blacksmith's workshop. Reservations are a must
during the busy summer months. ⊠ *Péter Pál u. 1* ☎ *26/310–819*
▭ *MC, V.*

$-$$ ✕ **Vidám Szerzetesek.** A former U.S. ambassador was a regular here. Laura
Bush even stopped by for a coffee, though apparently she ate at the
Aranysárkány. The Happy Monks (which has paintings of happy monks
on the walls) is well-touristed, but it's also popular with locals. The reasonably priced menu (in 17 languages) includes game dishes and hearty,
heavy Hungarian favorites such as "red winey lamb stew with ewe-cheese
noodles." Try the *suhajda* (literally, "monk's pleasure"), a savory brew
of smoked meat with a tasty dough cap baked over an earthenware pot.
⊠ *Bogdányi út 3–5* ☎ *26/310–544* ▭ *AE, MC, V* ⊘ *Closed Mon.*

$ ⊡ **Horváth Fogadó.** This pension is on a quiet hillside conveniently
within a 10-minute walk of Fő tér but refreshingly removed from the
throngs of tourists in the center of town. The clean, simply furnished
rooms are modern and reasonably priced. Combine that with friendly
service and lovely views of the town and the river below, and you've
got a good place to stay. Bathrooms have showers only. ⊠ *Darupiac 2,
H-2000* ☎☎ *26/313–950* ⊕ *www.option.hu/horvath* ⊭ *7 rooms*
△ *Restaurant, a/c in some rooms, free parking* ▭ *MC, V* ⍥ *EP.*

$ ⊡ **St. Andrea Panzió.** This remodeled *panzió* (pension) atop a grassy in-
cline has all the makings of a Swiss chalet. Attic space has been converted into clean, simply furnished rooms with full baths. On a warm
day you can eat breakfast on the outside patio. The owners are very
friendly; they've even been known to specially cook meals for guests ar-

riving late at night. The only drawback is that the small hotel is fairly far from the center of things in Szentendre. ⊠ *Egres u. 22, H-2000* ☎ *26/301–800, 26/311–989, or 06–30/900–2871* 🖥 *26/500–804* 🛏 *9 rooms, 1 suite* ⚐ *Restaurant, room service, cable TV, no a/c, bar, meeting room, parking* ⊟ *No credit cards* ¶⊙¶ *BP.*

¢ 🏨 **Bükkös Hotel & Restaurant.** Just west of the main square and across the bridge over tiny Bükkös Brook, this neat, well-run establishment is one of Szentendre's most conveniently located hotels. The narrow staircase and small rooms give it a genuinely homey feel. ⊠ *Bükkös part 16, H-2000* ☎ *26/312–021 or 26/310–772* 🖥 *26/310–782* ⊕ *www.hotels.hu/bukkos* 🛏 *16 rooms* ⚐ *Restaurant, minibars, cable TV, minibars, laundry service, free parking; no a/c* ⊟ *MC, V* ¶⊙¶ *BP.*

★ ¢ 🏨 **Centrum Panzió.** Szentendre's newest and most pristine B&B has only six rooms, but two are family-size, and all are pleasantly furnished in shades of blue and gray. Just a short step from Szerb utca, the Centrum has pleasant Danube views and an attentive and genuinely friendly English-speaking management. The rooms are spotless and bright. ⊠ *Bogdányi u. 15, H-2000* ☎ *26/302–500* ⊕ *www.szvsz.hu/centrum* 🛏 *6 rooms* ⚐ *Cable TV, laundry service, some pets allowed, free parking* ⊟ *No credit cards* ¶⊙¶ *BP.*

¢ 🏨 **Kentaur Hotel & Restaurant.** This handsome, modern, chalet-style hotel is less than a one-minute walk from the Danube and two minutes from Fő tér, on what may be Hungary's last surviving square still to bear Karl Marx's name. (As the manager explained, Fő tér, Szentendre's main square, used to be Marx tér, but on being renamed Main Square, this end of Kert utca inherited the dubious honor of the Marx moniker.) Rooms are clean and simple, with unfinished-wood paneling, and pastel-pink, yellow, or blue walls hung with original paintings by local artists. The bathrooms were remodeled and new carpeting was added in 2004, and plans call for 10 more rooms to be added. Children under 10 stay for free. ⊠ *Marx tér 3–5, H-2000* ☎ *26/318–184* 🖥 *26/312–125* ⊕ *www.hotels.hu/kentaur* 🛏 *16 rooms* ⚐ *Restaurant, café, room service, minibars, cable TV, bar, meeting room, free parking, some pets allowed, no a/c* ⊟ *No credit cards* ¶⊙¶ *BP.*

Sports & the Outdoors

BICYCLING The waterfront and streets beyond Szentendre's main square are perfect for a bike ride—free of jostling cobblestones and relatively calm and quiet. (Take the ferry across the river to the island, Szentendre Sziget, and there you'll find a largely undiscovered, sleepy, bicyclist's paradise.) Check with Tourinform for local rental outfits. Rentals are possible in Budapest; bicycles are permitted in a designated car of each HÉV suburban railway train for an extra, 120 HUF ticket. Many people make the trip between Budapest and Szentendre on bicycle along the designated bike path, which runs on busy roads in some places but is pleasant and separate from the road for the stretch between Békásmegyer and Szentendre.

Nightlife & the Arts

Most of Szentendre's concerts and entertainment events occur during the spring and summer. The annual **Spring Festival,** usually held from mid-March through early April, offers classical concerts in some of Szentendre's churches, as well as jazz, folk, and rock performances in the cultural center and other venues about town. In July, the **Szentendre Summer Days** festival brings open-air theater performances and jazz and classical concerts to Fő tér and the cobblestone courtyard fronting the town hall. Although the plays are usually in Hungarian, the setting alone can make it an enjoyable experience.

Bohemia. On a short side street, a two-minute walk from either Fő tér or the Danube, this pub lives up to its name as a popular, easygoing, intellectual, bohemian drinking-cum-cultural-political club. The large main room, characterized by comfy armchairs and couches, intimate lighting, a fair amount of smoke, worn wooden floors, and a couple of stuffed pheasants perched on a wall, is certainly a splendid place to have a beer and to discuss the meaning of life. As an added plus, three computers are available near the bar for free Internet use; just sit down and log on. Hungarian luminaries from politicians to the national police chief regularly hold talks in the adjoining room. ⊠ *Bercsényi utca, near Duna korzó* ☎ *26/314–771.*

Shopping
Flooded with tourists in summer, Szentendre is saturated with the requisite souvenir shops. Among the attractive but overpriced goods sold in every store are dolls dressed in traditional folk costumes, wooden trinkets, pottery, and colorful hand-embroidered tablecloths, doilies, and blouses. The best bargains are the hand-embroidered blankets and bags sold by dozens of elderly women in traditional folk attire, who stand for hours on the town's crowded streets. (Because of high weekend traffic, most Szentendre stores stay open all day on weekends, unlike those in Budapest. Galleries are closed Monday and accept major credit cards, although other stores may not.)

Art-éria Galéria. One tiny room is crammed with paintings, graphics, and sculptures by 21 of Szentendre's best contemporary artists. ⊠ *Városház tér 1* ☎ *26/310–111.*

Erdész Galéria. This sophisticated gallery on Szentendre's main square (not to be confused with the similarly named Gallery Erdész), displays paintings, statues, and other works by some 30 local artists. ⊠ *Fő tér 20* ☎ *26/310–139.*

Gallery Erdész. The gallery displays an impressive selection of contemporary Hungarian art, as well as gifts such as leather bags, colored-glass vases, and handmade paper—not to mention some unique, curvaceous silver pieces made by a famous local jeweler. ⊠ *Bercsényi u. 4* ☎ *26/317–925.*

Herend. For an impressive selection of Hungary's finest, most famous porcelain, check out the company shop, on the same side of the street as and near the Vidám Szerzetesek restaurant. ⊠ *Bogdányi út 1* ☎ *26/505–288.*

László Vincze Paper Mill. Beautiful stationery, booklets, and other handmade paper products are displayed and sold at this small workshop at the top of a broken cobblestone street. Mr. Vincze lovingly creates his thick, watermarked paper, using traditional, 2,000-year old bleaching methods. ⊠ *Angyal u. 5* ☏ *26/314–328.*

Palmetta Design Galéria. Traditional crafts take a back seat to refreshingly contemporary designs, including textiles, ceramics, lamps, jewelry, and artwork by Hungarian and international artists and designers. ⊠ *Bogdányi u. 14* ☏☏ *26/313–649.*

SZENTENDRE SZIGET

❽ *6 km (4 mi) north of Szentendre to bridge at Tahi; 27 km (17 mi) north of Budapest to the bridge at Tahi.*

Looking for some tranquility after a couple of hours of squeezing through the crowds in downtown Szentendre? The answer is Szentendre Sziget (Szentendre Island), the lush green oasis right across the river. At the time of the Hungarian conquest of the Carpathian Basin in AD 896, the flat island—33 km (21 mi) long and 3.8 km (2.4 mi) wide at its widest point—was used as pasture land. It subsequently became a key agricultural, ship-building, and fishing center that helped link the otherwise hilly Danube Bend with Buda to the south. Only after the end of the 120-year Turkish occupation of Hungary in the late 17th century did a loose-knit web of settlements develop; and from the mid-19th century on, resort districts began to spring up here and there for city-weary Budapesters. Beginning in the 1890s, agriculture was forced in toward the island center as the Budapest waterworks acquired much of the land on the island's perimeter to preserve as a natural aquifer, and by the 1970s Szentendre Island had become the prime source of water for the capital's two-million-plus residents. As a result, in stark contrast with other flat areas near Budapest, development here has been tightly restricted.

Though much of Szentendre Island comprises nature preserves and lush green countryside—this is a rich habitat and stopping off point for waterfowl—it also contains four villages, each separated by a few miles, and several distinct, sweeping districts of summer homes small and large. From quaint Kisoroszi on its northern tip to the larger but lovely Szigetmonostor on the southern end, the island is a real gem that is relatively, refreshingly untouched and ripe for exploration.

Although you can access the island farther down the Danube Bend by crossing the bridge at Tahi or at one of several car-carrying ferries, it's easier to make a little excursion from Szentendre on foot, and outright perfect by bicycle. Walk past downtown Szentendre along the Danube a few hundred yards to the second set of docks. (The first docks are for boats that run regularly between Szentendre and Budapest, though at a much more leisurely pace than the HEV railway.) Here, a small, noisy little boat takes pedestrians and bicyclists across for 200 HUF a person (double if you have a bicycle); pay as you board. The ferry embarks to the island at 35 minutes past every hour from 8:35 AM until 7:35 PM and returns at half-past, with the last trip leaving from the island at 7:30 PM. Again, do bear in mind that getting to the island's inhabited areas is far easier by bicycle; if you're on foot, you will see mostly lush young forests and open meadows unless you walk 3 mi or so into the lovely, quiet village of Szigetmonostor. There's only one way to go from the ferry landing; after several hundred yards the main road curves to the right and, before long, you'll reach a little four-way intersection. If you wish to encounter more people, go left.

Where to Stay & Eat

¢–$$ ✕ **Meteor Étterem.** Turn right (east) at the café if you're approaching from the Rosinante Lodge and continue about 5 minutes by car (10 minutes by bicycle) to the opposite bank of the Danube. There, you'll find a quintessential example of the sort of simple, unpretentious restaurant that sprang up in great numbers around Hungarian tourist resorts during Communism. In many of these places, including this one, the food is pretty darn good. Be adventurous and try the *pacalpörkölt* (tripe stew) with boiled potatoes; the tripe melts like butter in your mouth—heavenly. If you're not game for tripe, then try some game or a bowl of *gulyás.* ⊠ *Nagyduna sétány 83, Szigetmonostor* ☎ *26/394–043* ⊟ *No credit cards.*

¢ ✕ **Sarokház Cukrászda.** A bit more than a mile down the road from the Rosinante Lodge, this café is easy to find and well worthwhile to visit. Opened in 2004, it lies at the southern edge of Szigetmonostor and appears to be the village's only café of note (which helps explain its popularity). Here you'll find a good selection of scrumptious-looking pastries, combined with a bright, airy atmosphere and wood tables and floors. ⊠ *Fő út 66, Szigetmonostor* ☎ 26/393–625.

★ ¢ ▦ **Rosinante Fogadó.** This cloistered gem—also called the Rosinante Lodge—opened in 1999 in the middle of a vast natural area over a mile from the nearest town. Rooms, which have showers only, and have bright, modern furnishings, wood floors, checkered-quilt bedspreads, and a decidedly homey atmosphere. The restaurant menu (printed on parchment-like paper) offers delicious fare ($–$$$), including vegetarian and fish specialties. A 10-minute walk from the landing for the Szentendre ferry, the lodge can be reached by car if you cross over by ferry at Leányfalu or by the bridge a bit farther north, at Tahi. Drive south past Szigetmonostor; the hotel will be on your left. Reserve at least one month in advance. ⊠ *Szigetmonostor* ☎ *26/722–000 or 20/961–1843* 🖷 *26/722–010* ⊕ *www.rosinante.hu* ➳ *19 rooms, 2 suites* ⟐ *Restaurant, pool, sauna, minibars, meeting room; no a/c* ⊟ *AE, MC, V* ⎮⍉⎮ *BP.*

Sports & the Outdoors

FESTIVALS **Eperfeszivál** (Strawberry Festival). If you're around during the first weekend in June, when the island's many strawberries are at their peak, don't miss this two-day annual tradition, which was begun only in the late 1990s. The festival is held by the bridge that spans the mainland village Tahi with the island's largest village, Tahitótfalu. There is something for all: music and shows, a flea market, an amusement park, a classic tug-of-war on the bridge between the two villages, and a "super party" of concerts on Saturday night.

GOLF **Budapest Golf Park & Country Club.** Opened in 1984, the course—while not actually in Budapest—is in a magnificent setting just outside of Kisoroszi, on the northern tip of Szentendre Sziget. It was one of Hun-

INSPIRATION IN THE BEND

LONG AFTER HUNGARY'S KINGS *made their homes in Esztergom and Visegrád, the Danube Bend was to become a haven of rest and relaxation—and of inspiration—for Hungarian painters and writers. For example, the hopeless romantic Sindbad, immortalized in a story by Gyula Krudy (1878–1933) called "By the Danube," rested, "healing his broken-down brain and his hammering heart" on the shores of the great river.*

Though Hungarian painters these days are more apt to escape to retreats farther from Budapest and the crowds, Szentendre has a century-plus history as an artists' haven. Károly Ferenczy, Hungary's foremost master of plein air impressionism, lived and worked there from 1889 to 1892. The Danube Bend's most famous 20th-century painter was István Szőnyi (1894–1960), a former student of Ferenczy who spent much of life in Zebegény, a picturesque village set against the Börzsöny Hills across the river from Pilismarót (midway between Visegrád and Esztergom). His works include "The Danube Bend at Zebegény" (1927). Szőnyi's former home is today a museum in Zebegény.

The Szentendre Painters Association was formed in 1928 as a colony for Hungarian painters displaced from the influential school of painting in Nagybánya, which had been annexed along with the rest of Transylvania to Romania in 1920. The colony, whose artists managed to preserve a general bent toward "post-Nagybánya modernism" even after its nationalization in the 1950s by the Communist regime, functions to this day, albeit in a more eclectic form, attracting not only painters but other visual artists and even performance artists.

Whether or not you choose to dine at Szentendre's Rab Ráby restaurant, you should know its name comes from one of Hungary's most famous historical novels, *Rab Ráby (Ráby the Prisoner)*, by Mór Jókai (1825–1904), which is set in Szentendre. The profound impact on Hungarian letters of this romanticized account of Mátyás Ráby, a civil servant in Szentendre jailed in 1786 for opposing corrupt local officials, prompted another Hungarian writer to remark that all Hungarians should have two books by their bedside, the Bible and *Rab Ráby*. But this was hardly the only literary work focused on this region of Hungary.

Zsigmond Móricz (1879–1942), a novelist known mostly for his realistic portrayal of peasant life, moved to Leányfalu, just north of Szentendre, and his home there became a quasi-retreat for many other literary luminaries. Another Leányfalu resident was Ferenc Karinthy (1921–1992), whose one-act play "Danube Bend" is set not on the river but in a bar.

Visegrád, meanwhile, was home to the famous poet Lajos Áprily (1887–1967) beginning in 1937; like Móricz's home, Áprily's functioned as a haven for other poets and writers.

The great poet Mihály Babits (1883–1941) was so inspired by Hungary's largest Roman Catholic church that he wrote "Dal az esztergomi bazilikáról" ("Song about the Esztergom Basilica").

Beyond the matter of its rich history and breathtaking scenery, perhaps the ubiquitous idea among Hungarians that their nation is a cultural crossroads between East and West helps explain why the Danube's turn of course here—as it proceeds from Western Europe toward the Balkans—has resounded with such symbolic significance for painters and writers alike.

gary's first golf courses. From 8 to sunset between April and October, you can golf away on this 18-hole course for about 8,000 HUF per round. Call for reservations. ⊠ *Kisoroszi* ☎ *26/392–463* 🖹 *26/392–465.*

HORSEBACK **Zablakert lovarda.** One of many stables on the island, this one is 2½ km
RIDING (1½ mi) north of Tahitótfalu, on the main road to Kisoroszi. Here you
ⓒ can ride for about 2,200 HUF an hour. This part of the island is readily accessible by bus. ⊠ *Kisoroszi országút, Tahitótfalu* ☎ *30/961–5797.*

VISEGRÁD

❾ *23 km (14 mi) north of Szentendre, 44 km (27 mi) north of Budapest.*

Visegrád was the seat of the Hungarian kings during the 14th century, when a fortress built here by the Angevin kings became the royal residence. Today, the imposing fortress at the top of the hill towers over the peaceful little town of quiet, tree-lined streets and solid old houses. The forested hills rising just behind the town offer popular hiking possibilities. For a taste of Visegrád's best, climb to the Fellegvár, and then wander and take in the views of the Danube curving through the countryside; but make time to stroll around the village center a bit—on Fő utca and other streets that pique your interest.

★ Crowning the top of a 1,148-foot hill, the dramatic **Fellegvár** (Citadel) was built in the 13th century and served as the seat of Hungarian kings in the early 14th century. In the Middle Ages, the citadel was where the Holy Crown and other royal regalia were kept, until they were stolen by a dishonorable maid of honor in 1440; 23 years later, King Matthias had to pay 80,000 HUF to retrieve them from Austria. (For the time being, the crown is safe in the Parliament building in Budapest.) A *panoptikum* (akin to slide projection) show portraying the era of the kings is included with admission. The breathtaking views of the Danube Bend below are ample reward for the strenuous 40-minute hike up. ⊠ *Fellegvár Nagyvillám* ☎ *26/ 398–101* 🎟 *750 HUF* ☉ *Daily 10–4, closed in snowy conditions.*

In the 13th through 14th centuries, King Matthias Corvinus had a separate palace built on the banks of the Danube below the citadel. It was eventually razed by the Turks, and not until 1934 were the ruins finally excavated. Nowadays you can see the disheveled remnants of the Királyi palota (Royal Palace) and its Salamon torony (Salamon Tower), which are part of the **Mátyás Király Múzeum** (King Matthias Museum). The Salomon Tower has two small exhibits displaying ancient statues and well structures from the age of King Matthias. Especially worth seeing is the red-marble well, built by a 15th-century Italian architect. Above a ceremonial courtyard rise the palace's various halls; on the left you can still see a few fine original carvings, which give an idea of how magnificent the palace must once have been. Inside the palace is a small exhibit on its history, as well as a collection of gravestones dating from Roman times to the 19th century. Fridays in May, the museum hosts medieval-crafts demonstrations. ⊠ *Fő utca 29* ☎ *26/398–026* ⊕ *www. visegrad.hu/muzeum* 🎟 *Free* ☉ *Royal Palace Tues.–Sun. 9–4:30. Salomon Tower May–Sept., Tues.–Sun. 9–4:30.*

Like a tiny, precious gem, the miniature **Millennial Chapel** sits in a small clearing, tucked away on a corner down Fő utca, Visegrád's main street. The bite-size, powder-yellow church was built in 1896 to celebrate the Magyar Millennium and is open only on Pentecost and a few other holidays. ⊠ *Fő u. 113.*

Where to Stay & Eat

$$ ✕ **Sirály Restaurant.** Opposite the ferry pier, this restaurant, which operates jointly with the nearby Renaissance Restaurant, is well known for its rolled fillet of venison and its many vegetarian dishes, including fried soy steak in mayonnaise sauce with vegetables. In summer, when cooking is often done on the terrace overlooking the Danube, expect barbecued meats and stews, soups, and gulyás served in old-fashioned pots. ⊠ *Rév u. 15* ☎ *26/398–376* ⊟ *AE, MC, V.*

$–$$ ✕ **Fekete Holló.** The popular "Black Raven" restaurant (which has a stuffed black raven on the wall) has an elegant yet comfortable atmosphere— a great place for a full meal or just a beer. Try the chef's creative specialties, such as coconut chicken leg with pineapple, or stick to such regional staples as fresh, grilled fish. Whatever you do, save room for the *palacsinta*, which are filled with ground walnuts and smothered in chocolate sauce. ⊠ *Rév út 12* ☎ *26/397–289* ⊟ *MC, V.*

★ $–$$ ✕ **Gulyás Csárda.** This cozy little restaurant, decorated with antique folk art and memorabilia, complements its eight indoor tables with additional seating outside during the warmer months. The cuisine is typical home-style Hungarian, with a limited selection of tasty traditional dishes. Try the *halászlé* (spicy fish soup), served in a pot and kept warm on a small spirit burner; or, if you're adventurous, *pacalpörkölt* (tripe stew) with boiled parsley potatoes. ⊠ *Nagy Lajos király u. 4* ☎ *26/398–329* ⊟ *No credit cards.*

★ $–$$ ⬚ **Danubius Spa & Conference Hotel Visegrád.** The Danube Bend's newest, priciest, and largest hotel, the Visegrád Superior, as it's also called, has in pomp, luxury, and breathtaking views what it lacks in charm. Opened in April 2004, it's actually 3 km (2 mi) north of Visegrád on Route 11, facing the Danube and right beside a lovely outdoor swimming complex (under the same ownership). One might be tempted to call it a big, ultra-modern blight on an otherwise idyllic landscape if it weren't so nice in every other way. Most rooms, which are impeccably modern, have full baths. Rates vary depending on whether the rooms face the Danube and the Börzsöny hills beyond or the forested hillside behind the hotel. Suites are about twice the price of a regular room. ⊠ *Lepence-völgy, H-2025* ☎ *26/801–900* 🖶 *26/801–918* ⊕ *www.danubiusgroup.com* ⤳ *164 rooms, 10 suites* ⚅ *2 restaurants, café, minibars, refrigerators, cable TV, 1 indoor and 1 outdoor pool, hair salon, massage, sauna, Turkish bath, Ping-Pong, squash, 2 bars, shop, meeting rooms, car rental, free parking* ⊟ *AE, MC, DC, V* ⦿| *BP.*

$ ⬚ **Beta Hotel Silvanus.** Ideally situated high up on Fekete Hill, with commanding forest and Danube views, this is certainly Visegrád's highest-altitude hotel and one of the finest. The expanded amenities also include a wellness center with tepidarium (salt therapy). Because of the location, it's best to have a car if you stay here (although a bus does stop nearby three times daily). Hikers and bikers will find linking trails in the forest behind. Only suites are air-conditioned. ✉ *Fekete-hegy, H-2025* ☎☎ *26/398–311* ⊕ *www.hotels.hu/silvanus* ⤳ *96 rooms, 10 suites* ⚐ *Restaurant, café, room service, minibars, cable TV with movies, indoor pool, hair salon, massage, sauna, steam room, bowling, bar, playground, dry cleaning, laundry service, meeting rooms, free parking, some pets allowed; no a/c in some rooms* ▭ *AE, DC, MC, V* ⦿ *BP.*

¢ 🖭 **Hotel Honti.** This 23-room hotel and an older, alpine-style pension (where the rooms are on the lower end of the price scale) share the same yard in a quiet residential area, a three-minute walk from the town center. Apple trees and a gurgling brook create a peaceful, rustic ambience. The pension has seven tiny, clean rooms tucked under sloping ceilings with balconies, some with lovely Danube views; the rooms in the hotel are more spacious and more expensive, some with balconies affording a splendid view of the Citadel in the distance. Only two rooms in the hotel have a/c. ✉ *Fő u. 66, H-2025* ☎ *26/398–120* ⤳ *28 rooms* ⚐ *Restaurant, minibars, cable TV, meeting room, free parking, some pets allowed, no-smoking rooms; no a/c in some rooms* ▭ *No credit cards* ⦿ *BP.*

¢ 🖭 **Hotel Visegrád.** This centrally located hotel, built in the late 1990s, also has an in-house travel agency that organizes local excursions in the area for both groups and individuals. Every room has a balcony with views of the Danube or the Citadel, and all are pristine yet comfortable, many in warm lemony and ochre hues. The suites are suitable for a family with three children. The hotel's Renaissance Restaurant is a slightly tacky but likable medieval-theme restaurant. ✉ *Rév út 15, H-2025* ☎ *26/397–034* 🖨 *26/597–088* ⊕ *www.visegradtours.hu* ⤳ *33 rooms, 7 suites* ⚐ *2 restaurants, in-room safes, minibars, cable TV, meeting room, free parking, travel services* ▭ *AE, DC, MC, V* ⦿ *BP.*

¢ 🖭 **Patak Fogadó.** At a shaded bend in the road on the right, just beyond Visegrád's center leading up the hill to the Citadel, this former wine bar was reborn in 2000 as a friendly, reasonably priced pension. Occupying a forested hillside and overlooking a babbling brook, it has four bright, modern rooms with wood floors and ceilings; each room has a shower. If the owners' plans to add 36 new rooms, a pool, and a fitness room starting in 2005 bear fruit, the place may lose a bit of its charm, but the combination of location, tranquility, and affordable rates make this a good place to stay. ✉ *Mátýs Király u. 92, H-2025* ☎ *26/397–486* 🖨 *26/397–102* ⊕ *www.patakfogado.hu* ⤳ *4 rooms* ⚐ *Restaurant, bar; no a/c* ▭ *AE, MC, V* ⦿ *EP.*

Nightlife & the Arts

The **Visegrád International Palace Games,** held annually on the second weekend in July, take the castle complex back to its medieval heyday, with horseback jousting tournaments, archery games, a medieval music and crafts fair, and other festivities.

Sports & the Outdoors

HIKING Visegrád makes a great base for exploring the trails of the Visegrád and Pilis hills. A hiking map is posted on the corner of Fő utca and Rév utca, just above the pale-green Roman Catholic Parish Church. A well-trodden, well-marked hiking trail (posted with red signs) leads from the edge of Visegrád to the town of Pilisszentlászló, a wonderful 8½-km (5⅓-mi) journey that takes about three hours, through the oak and beech forests of the Visegrád Hills into the Pilis conservation region. Deer, wild boars, and mouflons (a type of wild sheep) roam freely here, and there are fields of yellow-blooming spring pheasant's eye and black pulsatilla.

SWIMMING   The outdoor thermal pools at **Lepence,** 3 km (2 mi) southwest of Visegrád on Route 11, combine good soaking with splendorous Danube Bend views. Those able to get there by 6 AM can get in for an early-morning swim that ends at 8 for just 500 HUF (less than half-price); the same price applies if you go after 4 PM. ⊠ *Lepence-völgyi Termál és Strandfürdő, Lepence* ☎ *26/398–208* ⊜ *1,100 HUF* ⊘ *May–mid-Sept., daily 9–6:30.*

TOBOGGAN SLIDE   Winding through the trees on Nagy-Villám Hill is the **Wiegand Toboggan Run,** one of the longest slides you've ever seen. You ride on a small cart that is pulled uphill by trolley, then careen down the slope in a small, steel trough that resembles a bobsled run. ⊠ *Panoráma út, ½ km (¼ mi) from Fellegvár* ☎ *26/397–397* ⊜ *280 HUF weekdays, 320 HUF weekends and holidays; 1,400 HUF for six runs weekdays, 1,600 HUF weekends and holidays* ⊘ *May–Aug., daily 10–7; Apr. and Sep.–Oct., daily 11–4; Nov.–Mar. (weather permitting), weekends 11–4.*

ESZTERGOM

⑩   *21 km (13 mi) north of Visegrád, 65 km (40 mi) northeast of Budapest.*

Esztergom stands on the site of a Roman fortress, at the westernmost curve of the heart-shaped Danube Bend, where the Danube marks the border between Hungary and Slovakia. (In 2001, a new bridge opened here to replace one destroyed 57 years earlier by German forces near the end of World War II.) St. Stephen, the first Christian king of Hungary and founder of the nation, was crowned here in AD 1000, establishing Esztergom as Hungary's first capital, which it remained for the next 250 years. The majestic Bazilika, Hungary's largest, is Esztergom's main draw, followed by the fine-art collection of the Primate's Palace. If you like strolling, leave yourself a little time to explore the narrow streets of Viziváros (Watertown) below the Bazilika, lined with brightly painted baroque buildings.

To the south of the cathedral, on **Szent Tamás Hill,** is a small church dedicated to St. Thomas à Becket of Canterbury. From here you can look down on the town and see how the Danube temporarily splits, forming an island, **Prímás-sziget,** that locals use as a base for waterskiing and swimming, in spite of the pollution. To reach it, cross the Kossuth Bridge.

★   Esztergom's **Bazilika** (cathedral), the largest in Hungary, stands on a hill overlooking the town; it is now the seat of the cardinal primate of Hungary. Completed in 1856—after decades of work—on the site of a medieval cathedral that had been largely destroyed during the wars against the Turks centuries before, this was where the famous anti-Communist cleric, Cardinal József Mindszenty, was finally reburied in 1991 (he was originally buried in Austria when he died in 1975), ending decades of religious intolerance and persecution of Catholics by the Communists. Its most interesting features are the Bakócz Chapel (1506), named for a primate of Hungary who only narrowly missed becoming pope; the sacristy, which contains a valuable collection of medieval ecclesiastical art; the vast crypt, where the cathedral's builders and its key priests are buried; and, for a great view of Esztergom and environs after a steep climb up a long, winding staircase, the observation platform in the cathedral's cupola. The bell tower is also open to the public. If your timing is lucky, you could attend a concert during one of the various classical music festivals held here in summer. ⊠ *Szent István tér* ☎ *33/311–895* 🖃 *Church free, crypt 100 HUF, sacristy 400 HUF, cupola 200 HUF, bell tower 200 HUF* ☉ *Church Mar.–Oct., daily 6–6; Nov.–Feb., daily 6–4. Crypt Mar.–Oct., daily 9–4:30; Nov.–Feb., daily 10–3. Sacristy Mar.–Oct., daily 9–4:30; Nov.–Dec., Tues.–Fri. 11–3:30; weekends 10–5:30. Cupola Apr.–Oct., daily 9–4:30.*

Considered by many to be Hungary's finest art gallery, the **Keresztény Múzeum** (Museum of Christian Art), in the Primate's Palace, has a thorough collection of early Hungarian and Italian paintings (the 14th- and 15th-century Italian collection is unusually large for a museum outside Italy). Unique holdings include the *Coffin of Our Lord* from Garamszentbenedek (today Hronský Beňadik, Slovakia); the wooden statues of the Apostles and of the Roman soldiers guarding the coffin are masterpieces of Hungarian baroque sculpture. The building also holds the Primate's Archives, which contain 20,000 volumes, including several medieval codices. Permission to visit the archives must be obtained in advance. ⊠ *Primate's Palace, Mindszenty tér 2* ☎ *33/413–880* 🖃 *200 HUF* ☉ *Mid-Mar.–Sept., Tues.–Sun. 10–6; Jan.–mid-Mar., Tues.–Sun. 10–5.*

Where to Stay & Eat

★ **$–$$** ✕ **Csülök Csárda.** With its delicious, hearty Hungarian fare, cozy atmosphere, and unbeatable location in view of the cathedral (just as you enter downtown Esztergom from the direction of Visegrád), the Ham Knuckle Tavern is enormously popular with both locals and Budapesters. So why shouldn't meat-eating visitors from farther away give it a try? Bean soup with knuckle is quite enough for a small meal. To fill up some more, try the "Craftsman Knuckle," a scrumptious mix of fried knuckle slices smothered with a hot, spicy sauce including diced ox tongue, chili beans, sweet corn, and pearl onions. ⊠ *Batthyány u. 9* ☎ *33/412–420* 🖃 *DC, MC, V.*

$–$$ ✕ **Prímás Pince.** Arched ceilings and exposed brick walls make a charming setting for refined Hungarian fare at this touristy—but good—restaurant built right into the imposing, 30-foot brick wall below the cathedral. Try the tenderloin steak baked with mushrooms and green-pea sauce, or perhaps the turkey strips cooked in a brew of marjoram-laced white wine with potato croquettes and almonds. Beware: what is translated as "trout" on the menu is actually walleye (pike-perch). ⊠ *Szent István tér 4* ☎ *33/313–495* 🖃 *AE, DC, MC, V* ☉ *No dinner Jan.–Feb.*

¢ ✕⊡ **Szalma Csárda & Panzió.** This restaurant and pension is on a tranquil, fairly undeveloped stretch of the Danube—even if it is beyond the more striking scenery just to the west of Esztergom. The 20-room pension, which from the outside resembles a ranch house, has small, double rooms that are clean and bright and furnished simply with low, summer-camp-style pine beds. An 80-bed hostel opened next door recently under the same management; beds there are just 2,000 HUF per night, but you share a room with three to five other guests. Also next door is a "Golf Youth Hostel," where even non-guests can play a round of miniature golf for 400 HUF (children 200 HUF). The restaurant ($–$$) is splendidly rustic, complete with a large earthenware stove in the main room. Listen to live Gypsy music while enjoying "long-forgotten peasant dishes"—such as chicken paprikash with wax beans and dill-spiced dumplings on the side. ✉ *Prímás-sziget, Nagyduna sétány 2, H-2500* ☎☎ *33/315–336 or 33/403–838* ⊕ *www.col.hu/szalmacsarda* ⇖ *20 rooms* ⚏ *No a/c, no room TVs* ☰ *AE, MC, V* ❏ *BP.*

¢ ⊡ **Alabárdos Panzió.** Conveniently downhill from the cathedral, this cozy, remodeled home provides excellent views from upstairs. Rooms (doubles and quads) are small but less cramped than at other small pensions. ✉ *Bajcsy-Zsilinszky u. 49, H-2500* ☎☎ *33/312–640* ⇖ *24 rooms* ⚏ *Cable TV, laundry facilities, meeting room; no a/c* ☰ *No credit cards* ❏ *BP.*

¢ ⊡ **Hotel Esztergom.** The otherwise presentable furnishings may be a bit old, but this hotel has an unbeatable setting on Primás-szíget, what with the Danube on one side, the cathedral on another, and a modern watersports complex under construction on yet another side (as of this writing, it was due to be completed by early 2005). Tennis, bowling, and horseback riding facilities are also nearby. All rooms have balconies, though the largest—and nicest—rooms face away from the river. However, four rooms that do face the Danube were blessed in 2003 with new furniture and mobile a/c units. ✉ *Primás-szíget, Nagyduna sétány, H-2500* ☎ *33/412–883 or 33/412–555* ☎ *33/412–853* ⊕ *www.hotel-esztergom.hu* ⇖ *34 rooms, 2 suites* ⚏ *Restaurant, cable TV, meeting room; no a/c in some rooms* ☰ *AE, DC, MC, V.*

Nightlife & the Arts

Every two years Esztergom hosts the **Nemzetközi Gitár Fesztivál** (International Guitar Festival), during which renowned classical guitarists from around the world hold master classes and workshops for participants. Recitals are held nearly every night in Esztergom's **Zöldház Művelődési Központ** (Green House Cultural Center) or the **Tanítóképző Főiskola** (Teachers College), where the festival is based, or elsewhere in Budapest and neighboring towns. The climax of it all is the glorious closing concert, held in the basilica, in which the hundreds of participants join together and perform as a guitar orchestra. The festival runs for two weeks, usually beginning in early August in odd-numbered years. Tickets and information are available at the tourist offices. ⊕ *www. guitarfestival.hu.*

VÁC

⓫ *34 km (21 mi) north of Budapest; 20 km (12 mi) south of Nagymaros, which is accessed by ferry from Visegrád.*

With its lovely riverfront promenade, a cathedral, an attractive main square, and a less delightful triumphal arch, the small city of Vác, on the Danube's east bank, is well worth a short visit if only to watch the sun slowly set from the promenade. It is certainly a more relaxing place to saunter than Szentendre, as you probably won't find yourself shoulder-to-shoulder with other tourists. While Vác's historic town center is not as compact as Szentendre's—nor quite as overflowing in historic sites—and while it may lack the scenic hill that serves to make Szentendre that much more of a tourist attraction, it is nonetheless replete with pretty baroque buildings in matte yellows and reds, offering many visual rewards and photo opportunities for those who wander onto a few of its narrow cobblestone side streets heading in toward the river. If you arrive by train in late April or early May, you'll be greeted outside the station by a lovely pink promenade of cherry blossoms.

Vác's 18th-century **Székesegyház** (Cathedral) on Konstantin tér is an outstanding example of Hungarian neoclassicism. It was built between 1763 and 1777 by Archbishop Kristóf Migazzi to the designs of the Italian architect Isidor Carnevale; the most interesting features are the murals by the Austrian Franz Anton Maulbertsch, both on the dome and behind the altar. Exquisite frescoes decorate the walls inside. Due to break-ins, you can view the interior only through a locked gate, except during Mass (daily 8–9 AM and 6–7 PM). Across the street, by the way, is the building that houses the local Bishop's headquarters, with a lovely park behind it. ⊠ *Konstantin tér 11* ☎ *27/317–010* ✆ *Free* ⊙ *Daily 8–7.*

The pale yellow baroque facade of the **Fehérek temploma** (Church of the White Friars) towers over one corner of the main square, Március 15 tér. Built by the Dominican order between 1699 and 1755, the inside is a mix of baroque and rococo styles. ⊠ *Március 15 tér 20–24.*

A fascinating if somewhat macabre discovery of the **Memento Mori,** which adjoins the Fehérek temploma, was made in 1994 during renovation work on the Church of the White Friars, and the result is this unusual museum. Workers happened upon the largely forgotten, sealed entrance to a crypt that had been used by the Dominicans (who built and formerly owned the church) to bury clergy and local burghers from 1731 to 1801. Inside were numerous ornately decorated coffins with surprisingly well-preserved, still-clothed mummies and burial accessories inside. The coffins (mostly closed) were moved to a nearby cellar on the same square. A steep staircase leads downstairs to the cold exhibit room. ⊠ *Március 15 tér 19* ☎ *27/313–463 or 27/500–750* ⊕ *www.muzeum.vac.hu* ⊙ *Mar.–Oct., Tues.–Sun. 10–6.*

On the spacious main square, **Noztalgia Cukrászda** (✉ Március 15 tér ☎ 27/313–539) is an elegant café with historic photos on the walls. Reasonably priced pastries include some notables it would be a shame to leave Vác without sampling: several types of absolutely scrumptious *pite* (pie), including *almás* (apple) and *meggyes* (sour cherry); and the cream-filled Rákózi túrótorta with its crispy, slightly burnt top.

In 1764, when Archbishop Migazzi heard that Queen Maria Theresa planned to visit his humble town, he hurriedly arranged the construction of a **triumphal arch**. The queen came and left, but the awkwardly situated arch remains, at the edge of the city's historic core next to a cement-and-barbed-wire prison complex. ✉ *Köztársaság út just past Barabás u.*

The **promenade** along the Danube is a wonderful place to stroll or picnic, looking out at the glistening river or back toward the pretty historic town. The main entrance to the riverfront area is from Petróczy utca, which begins at the cathedral on Konstantin tér and feeds straight into the promenade.

Vácrátóti Arborétum (4 km [2½ mi] from Vác) is Hungary's biggest and best botanical garden, with more than 12,000 plant species. The arboretum's top priority is botanical research, and the collection falls under the auspices of the Hungarian Academy of Sciences. You're welcome to stroll along the paths and sit on benches in the leafy shade. The greenhouse opens a bit later and closes earlier than the surrounding garden. If you're driving from Vác, follow the signs toward Gödöllő, then toward Vácrátóti. ✉ *Alkotmány u. 2–4* ☎ *28/360–122 Ext. 120* 💷 *500 HUF* ☉ *Apr.–Oct., daily 8–6; Nov.–Mar., daily 8–4. Greenhouse daily 9–4.*

Where to Eat

$–$$ ✕ **Halászkert Étterem.** The large terrace of this contemporary riverfront restaurant some 100 yards from the ferry landing is a popular place for a hearty lunch or dinner in warmer months. The menu includes some 250 dishes, including an unusually large selection of Hungarian fish specialties. ✉ *Liszt Ferenc sétány 9* ☎ *27/315–985* 🖃 *AE, DC, MC, V.*

Nightlife & the Arts

In July and August, a series of outdoor classical concerts are held in the verdant **Vácrátóti Arborétum.** The last weekend in July brings the **Váci Világi Vígalom** (Vác World Jamboree) festival, with folk dancing, music, crafts fairs, and other festivities throughout town.

Sports & the Outdoors

Vác is the gateway to hiking in the forests of the Börzsöny Hills, rich in natural springs, castle ruins, and splendid Danube Bend vistas. Consult the Börzsöny hiking map, available at Tourinform offices, for planning a walk on the well-marked trails. The **Börzsöny Természetjáró Kör** (Börzsöny Hiking Club; ✉ Március 15 tér 16–18 ☎ 27/316–160) organizes free guided nature walks every other Sunday all year round. Naturally, Hungarian is the official language, but chances are good that younger group members will speak English—however, even without understanding what is spoken, the trips afford a nice opportunity to be guided through the area. The Vác Tourinform office can give you further information on hikes.

Shopping

Duna-pArt Galéria. On the riverfront promenade across from the ferry landing and near the Halászkert Étterem, this art gallery has four exhibit rooms that display a wide variety of paintings and other works by more than 100 artists. (The capital "A" in the name, by the way, is a play on words, as *part* means "bank" in this context in Hungarian; and so "bank" melds with "art.") ⊠ *Liszt Ferenc sétány 3* ☎ *06–20/ 415–6776.*

Danube Bend Essentials

BICYCLE TRAVEL

The Danube Bend is a great place to explore by bike since most towns are relatively close together. Some routes have separate bike paths, while others run along the roads. Consult the "Danube Bend Cyclists' Map" (available at local Tourinform offices) for exact information. A perfect option is to rent a bicycle in Budapest and take it by the HÉV commuter railway—on the car that allows bikes, that is—to Szentendre, and ride from there.

BOAT & FERRY TRAVEL

If you have enough time, you can travel to the west-bank towns by cruise boat or jet foil from Budapest, a leisurely and pleasant journey, especially in summer and spring. Boating from Budapest to Esztergom takes five-and-a-half hours, to Visegrád three-and-a-half hours; the return trips are an hour or more shorter. Boats leave from the main Pest dock at Vigadó tér. The disadvantage of boat travel is that a round-trip by slow boat doesn't allow much time for sightseeing; the Esztergom route, for example, allows only under two hours before it's time to head back. Many people head upriver by boat in the morning and back down by bus or train as it's getting dark. There is daily service from Budapest to Visegrád, stopping in Szentendre. Less frequent boats go to Vác, on the east bank, as well.

Crossing the bridge between Esztergom and Stúrovo, on the Slovak side of the river, is a convenient way of accessing the opposite side of the Danube Bend in Hungary. (The Hungarian town of Szob, on the Slovak border along the east bank, is a five-minute drive from Stúrovo.) A scenic option is the regular daily passenger-and-car ferry service between several points on opposite sides of the Danube (except in winter when the river is too icy and the bridge is the only way to go). The crossing generally takes about 10 minutes and costs 1,000 HUF per car and driver, 270 HUF per additional passenger. The crossing between Nagymaros and Visegrád is recommended, as it affords gorgeous views of Visegrád's Citadel and includes a beautiful drive through rolling hills on Route 12 south and then west of Nagymaros. Mahart operates all these ferry services.

🖪 **Mahart Tours** ✉ District V, Vigadó tér, Budapest ☎ 1/318-1223 ⊕ www.maharttours. com.

BUS TRAVEL

Buses, which are relatively inexpensive and fairly comfortable—if you get a seat and don't have to stand—run regularly between Budapest's Árpád híd bus station and most towns along both sides of the Danube. The ride to Szentendre takes about half an hour. (For an extra 10 minutes or so, the HÉV commuter train offers a more scenic ride.) If you don't have a car, this is the only way to get beyond Szentendre toward points along the Danube on the same side of the river, as there is no train service there.

CAR TRAVEL

Route 11 runs along the western shore of the Danube, connecting Budapest to Szentendre, Visegrád, and Esztergom. Route 2 runs along the eastern shore for driving between Budapest and Vác.

TOURS

Cityrama runs its popular "Danube Tour" (16,000 HUF) daily during the high season (May through September) from Wednesday to Sunday; from October to May, the tour is offered only once a week, so call ahead for exact dates and times. Departing from Budapest, the full-day tour begins with sightseeing in Visegrád, then Esztergom. After lunch, the tour moves on to Szentendre for a guided walk and makes a scenic return to Budapest down the Danube. (The tour returns by bus when the water level is low.) The company also offers half-day tours of Szentendre alone, for 10,000 HUF. IBUSZ Travel organizes day-long bus trips from Budapest along the Danube (from May to October on Tuesday, Wednesday, Friday, and Saturday; from November to April on Saturday only), stopping in Esztergom, Visegrád, and Szentendre. There's commentary in English; the cost per person, including lunch and admission fees, is €73 (around 18,000 HUF)

🖪 **Cityrama** ☎ 1/302-4382 in Budapest ⊕ www.cityrama.hu. **IBUSZ Travel** ☎ 1/485-2700 in Budapest ⊕ www.ibusz.hu.

TRAIN TRAVEL

Vác and Esztergom have frequent daily express and local train service to and from Budapest's Nyugati (West) Station, but there is no service between Szentendre and Esztergom. Trains do not run to Visegrád, either. The HÉV suburban railway runs between Batthyány tér (or Margaret Island, one stop north) in Budapest and Szentendre about every 10 to 20 minutes daily; the trip takes 40 minutes, and a *kiegészítő* (supplementary) ticket—which you need in addition to a Budapest public transport pass or ticket—costs 312 HUF one-way. Bicycles cost an extra 140 HUF ticket. Bear in mind that not all trains go all the way to Szentendre; some go only as far as Békásmegyer, the last stop in the Budapest city limits, where you have to transfer to the next train that goes all the way (but you can do so with the same ticket). On a hot summer day, one advantage of this HÉV journey is the opportunity to take a break in Csillaghegy to go for a swim at the beautiful outdoor swimming facility there, just a block from the HÉV station.

VISITOR INFORMATION
🚺 **Esztergom Grantours** ✉ Széchenyi tér 25, Esztergom 📠📠 33/417–052. **IBUSZ** ✉ Kossuth L. u. 5, Esztergom 📞 33/411–643 ⊕ www.ibusz.hu. **Komtourist** ✉ Lőrinc u. 6, Esztergom 📞 33/414–152. **Tourinform** ✉ Dumtsa Jenő u. 22, Szentendre 📞 26/317–965 or 26/317–966 ⊕ www.tourinform.hu/ ✉ Március 15 tér 16–18, Vác 📞 27/316–160. **Visegrád Tours** ✉ Sirály Restaurant, Rév u. 15, Visegrád 📞 26/398–160.

LAKE BALATON

BEST HISTORICAL SIGHT
Bencés Apátság, *Tihany Peninsula* ⇨*p.180*

BEST SMALL RESORT
Club Hotel Badacsony, *Badacsony* ⇨*p.184*

BEST SMALL HOTEL
Club Imola, *Balatonfüred* ⇨*p.178*

MOST ELEGANT LODGING ON THE LAKE
Kastély Hotel, *Tihany Peninsula* ⇨*p.181*

MOST CONVIVIAL PENSION
Oliva Panzió, *Veszprém* ⇨*p.175*

BALATON'S MOST CHARMING TOWN
Veszprém ⇨*p.173*

By Kristen
Schweizer

LAKE BALATON, THE LARGEST LAKE IN CENTRAL EUROPE, stretches 80 km (50 mi) across Hungary. Its vast surface area today contrasts dramatically with its modest depths: averaging only 9¾ feet in depth, the lake is just 52½ feet at its deepest point in the center of the lake along the northern shore at the Tihany Félsziget (Tihany Peninsula). The Balaton—the most popular playground of this landlocked nation—lies just 90 km (56 mi) to the southwest of Budapest, so it's within easy reach of the capital by car, train, bus, and even bicycle. On a hot day in July or August, it seems the entire country and half of Germany are packed towel to towel on the lake's grassy public beaches, paddling about in the warm water, and consuming fried meats and beer at the omnipresent snack bars. The Balaton is also a major wine-producing region, and scores of vineyards and wine-tasting cellars can be found in many villages.

Called the "Hungarian Sea" by locals, Balaton was formed millions of years ago following volcanic eruptions and tectonic sagging. Today, freshwater flows in from several creeks and a river to feed the lake, and scientists estimate that the water in the lake is completely refreshed every two years.

On the lake's hilly northern shore, where you'll also find most of the region's wineries, is Balatonfüred, Hungary's oldest spa town, famed for natural springs that bubble out curative waters. The national park on the Tihany Peninsula lies just to the south, and regular boat service links Tihany and Balatonfüred with Siófok on the southern shore. Flatter and more crowded with resorts, cottages, and trade-union rest houses, the southern shore (beginning with Balatonszentgyörgy) has fewer sights and is not as attractive as the northern one: north-shore locals say the only redeeming quality of the southern shore is its views back across the lake to the north. Families with small children prefer the southern shore for its shallower, warmer waters—you can walk for almost 2 km (1 mi) before it deepens. The water warms up to 25°C (77°F) in summer.

Every town along both shores has at least one *strand* (beach). The typical Balaton strand is a complex of blocky wooden changing cabanas and snack bars, fronted by a grassy, flat stretch along the water for sitting and sunbathing. Most have paddleboat and other simple boat rentals. A small entrance fee is usually charged.

If you're interested in exploring beyond the beach, you can set out by car or bicycle along numerous well-groomed bike paths that follow the shores on beautiful village-to-village tours—stopping to view lovely old baroque churches, photograph a stork family perched high in its chimney-top nest, or climb a vineyard-covered hill for sweeping vistas. Since most vacationers keep close to the shore, a small amount of exploring into the roads and countryside heading away from the lake will reward you with a break from the summer crowds.

About the Hotels & Restaurants

The high season for hotels in the Lake Balaton region generally runs from June through September, and while off-season means lower rates, many hotels in the area close during winter months, from November to April, as Balaton is quite barren during colder months. Most hotels are large, resort-style complexes with their own pools and saunas, a short distance from the lake's shore. Hévíz, with its own thermal lake and spas, is one of the most-visited spa resorts in all of Europe. The majority of Balaton hotels quote rates in euros.

Menus in Balaton restaurants are heavily weighted toward freshwater fish, and a trip to Balaton is not complete without sampling fish from its waters. The most popular is the *Balatoni fogas* (pike-perch); also popular is *harcsa* (catfish). Hungarian *halászlé* (fish soup) is usually served in large bowls with *ponty* (carp), pasta, and spicy red paprika. Aside from fresh fish, the selection of food in Balaton is typically traditional Hungarian: lots of meat, battered vegetables, and salads laden with mayonnaise. Dress is casual at most restaurants.

WHAT IT COSTS In Euros & Forints				
$$$$	$$$	$$	$	¢
HOTELS IN EUROS				
over €225	€175–€225	€125–€175	€75–€125	under €75
HOTELS IN FORINTS				
over 56,000	44,000–56,000	31,000–44,000	18,500–31,000	under 18,500
RESTAURANTS IN FORINTS				
over 3,500	2,500–3,500	1,500–2,500	800–1,500	under 800

Hotel prices are for two people in a standard double room with a private bath and breakfast during peak season (June through September). Restaurant prices are per person for a main course at dinner and include 15% tax but not service.

Numbers in the margin correspond to numbers on the Lake Balaton map

VESZPRÉM

❶ *116 km (72 mi) southwest of Budapest.*

Fodor'sChoice
★ Hilly Veszprém is the center of cultural life in the Balaton region and often serves as the starting point for trips around Balaton. The city was established by Episcopalians during the first century AD under Hungary's King St. Stephen, but it was destroyed by the Turks during their occupation and again through Hungarian-Austrian independence battles. Veszprém was rebuilt in the early 18th century, but its castle was never reconstructed. This charming small city has several lovely pedestrian squares with cafés and outdoor seating in the summer months.

★ **Várhegy** (Castle Hill) is the most picturesque part of town, north of Szabadság tér. It's where you'll find all the sights that are worth seeing. The Hősök kapuja (Heroes' Gate), at the entrance to the castle, commemorates those who died during World War I and also houses a small exhibit on Hungary's history. Vár utca is the only street in the castle area, and it's off this street that all the sights can be found, including the cathedral and bishop's palace. The cathedral has been destroyed and rebuilt a handful of times since the 11th century, with its current

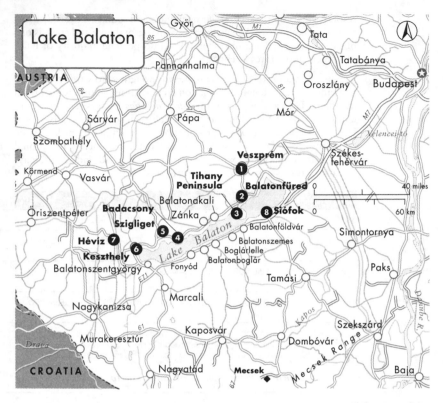

structure dating to the early 1900s. Vár utca continues past the square up to a terrace erected on the north staircase of the castle.

During the reconstruction of the cathedral in the early part of the 20th century, workers unearthed a vaulted chamber believed to part of a palace, which had stood on the site until the 14th century and which had once belonged to St. Stephen's queen, Gizella. The baroque chapel, called the **Gizella kápolna** (Gizella Chapel) was reconstructed in 1938, on the 900th anniversary of St. Stephen's death; its Byzantine-style frescoes of the apostles, which date to the 13th century, were restored. ⊠ *Vár utca* ☎ *88/ 426–088* 🎫 *100 HUF* ☉ *May–Oct., daily 9–5.*

Just past the Heroes' Gate and down a little alley to the left is the **Tűztorony** (Fire Tower). You'll see that lower level is medieval, although the upper stories are baroque. There is a good view of the town and surrounding area from the balcony. ⊠ *Vár utca 17* ☎ *88/425–204* 🎫 *300 HUF* ☉ *Apr.–mid-Oct., daily 10–6.*

off the beaten path

HEREND PORCELAIN FACTORY – Hungary's reputation for creating fine pieces of porcelain began with a purchase by England's Queen Victoria in 1851, when Windsor Castle ordered a dinner set from Herend. Following the celebrated purchase, the chosen pattern of colorful and detailed butterflies and flowers was coined the "Victoria" collection. Some 600 mold-makers, potters, and painters arc still trained at the company's headquarters to craft numerous patterns associated with Herend's high-quality dinnerware, decorative items, and figurines. The factory, founded in 1839, displays many valuable pieces in its Museum of Porcelain Arts. You can tour the factory as well as the museum. In the adjoining Apicius Restaurant, you can even dine off their collection of porcelain, worth several million forint. The town of Herend lies 16 km (10 mi) northwest of Veszprém on Road 8. ⊠ *Kossuth Lajos u. 144, Herend* 🕾 *88/523–197* ⊕ *www.museum.herend.com* 🕾 *Factory and museum 1,000 HUF; museum only, 300 HUF* ⊙ *Apr.–Oct., daily 9–5:30; Nov.–Mar., Mon.–Sat. 9–4:30.*

Where to Eat

★ ¢–$ ╳ **Cafe Piazza.** This quaint eatery has arched ceilings inside and a terrace filled with umbrella-shaded tables outside. The menu includes pizzas, pastas, and salads, all with celebrity-inspired or other creative titles, including "James Bond" fried Camembert cheese, a *"9-lyuk palacsinta"* (nine-hole pancake), and "'A' Pollo 13" chicken breast. There is a vast drinks and coffee menu as well. ⊠ *Óváros tér 4* 🕾 *88/444–445* ▬ *AE, MC, V.*

¢–$ ╳ **Elefánt Bisztró.** Next door to Cafe Piazza, the Elefánt offers a wider variety of pastas and pizzas at slightly higher prices; there is also a large selection of grilled poultry dishes, all loaded with vegetables. In nice weather, you can sit outdoors; indoors is a large, built-in aquarium housing tropical fish. ⊠ *Óváros tér 5* 🕾 *70/339–1217* ▬ *AE, MC, V.*

¢–$ ╳ **Szürkebarát Borozó.** The plain off-white walls of the Gray Monk Tavern may be less than inspiring, but the hearty Hungarian fare at this cellar restaurant in the city center more than compensates. For an unusual (but very Hungarian) appetizer, try the paprika-spiced *velős piritós* (marrow on toast; not listed on the English menu and sometimes unavailable); or for a main course, gnaw away at "Ms. Baker's pork hoofs." ⊠ *Szabadság tér 12* 🕾 *88/406–902* ▬ *No credit cards.*

¢ 🎁 **Éllő Panzió.** In this 18-room pension just southwest of the town center, you'll find ubiquitous golden lamp shades coupled with no lack of red—the carpeting, the velvety chairs, and the curtains. Rooms in the newer annex are more spacious than those in the chalet-like main house. Service is uniformly friendly. ⊠ *József Attila utca 25, H-8200* 🕾 *88/ 420–097 or 88/424–118* 🖷 *88/329–711* ⊕ *www.hotels.hu/ello* 🛏 *18 rooms* ♻ *Cable TV, dry cleaning, laundry service, some pets allowed, free parking* ▬ *DC, MC, V* ⊙ *Closed Christmas–New Year's* ⦿ *BP.*

¢ 🎁 **Oliva Panzió.** In the heart of downtown Veszprém, the Oliva pension, restaurant, and garden pub is a bit tricky to find, but it's as charming as they come, with dim lighting, clean, cozy rooms, and a friendly staff. The interior of the establishment is decorated in soft Mediterranean colors to relaxing effect. The outside garden has live jazz several nights a week, and the restaurant serves Mediterranean-inspired cuisine. ⊠ *Buhim utca 14–16, H-8200* 🕾 *88/561–900* 🖷 *88/403–875* ⊕ *www.oliva.hu* 🛏 *11 rooms* ♻ *Restaurant, pub, cable TV* ▬ *DC, MC, V* ⦿ *BP.*

FodorśChoice ★

BALATONFÜRED

❷ *18 km (11 mi) south of Veszprém, 115 km (71 mi) southwest of Budapest.*

Fed by 11 medicinal springs, Balatonfüred first gained popularity as a health resort (the lake's oldest) where people with heart conditions and fatigue would come to take or, more accurately, to drink a cure. The waters, said to have stimulating and beneficial effects on the heart and nerves, are still an integral part of the town's identity and consumed voraciously, but only the internationally renowned cardiac hospital has actual bathing facilities.

Today Balatonfüred, also known simply as Füred, is probably the Balaton's most popular destination, with every amenity to match. Above its busy boat landing, beaches, and promenade lined with great plane and poplar trees, the twisting streets of the Old Town climb hillsides thickly planted with vines. The climate and landscape also make this one of the best wine-growing districts in Hungary. Every year in July, the most elaborate of Lake Balaton's debutante cotillions, the Anna Ball, is held here.

The center of town is **Gyógy tér** (Spa Square), where the bubbling waters from five volcanic springs rise beneath a slim, colonnaded pavilion. In the square's centerpiece, the neoclassical **Well House** of the Kossuth Spring, you can sample the water, which has a pleasant, surprisingly refreshing taste despite the sulfurous aroma; for those who can't get enough, a 30-liter-per-person limit is posted. All the buildings on the square are pillared like Greek temples. At No. 3 is the **Horváth Ház** (Horváth House), a former sanatorium that housed uranium miners in the Communist era. The house is also where the Szentgyörgyi-Horváth family arranged the first of what was to become the Anna Ball in 1825 in honor of their daughter Anna.

The Anna Ball now takes place every July in another colonnaded building on the square, also a former sanatorium, the **Árkad Hotel** (1802). The day after the ball, the elected queen is paraded around town in a horse-drawn carriage. Under the Árkad Hotel's arcades is the **Balatoni Pantheon** (Balaton Pantheon): aesthetically interesting tablets and reliefs honoring Hungarian and foreign notables who either worked for Lake Balaton or spread the word about it. Among them is Jaroslav Hašek, the Czech author of the *Good Soldier Schweik,* who also wrote tales about Balaton.

On the eastern side of the square is the **Állami Kórház** (State Hospital), where hundreds of patients from all over the world are treated. Here, too, Rabindranath Tagore, the Indian author and Nobel prize winner, recovered from a heart attack in 1926. The tree that he planted to commemorate his stay stands in a little grove at the western end of the paths leading from the square down to the lakeside. Tagore also wrote a poem for the planting, which is memorialized beneath the tree on his strikingly animated bust: WHEN I AM NO LONGER ON EARTH, MY TREE,/LET THE EVER-RENEWED LEAVES OF THY SPRING/MURMUR TO THE WAYFARER:/THE POET DID LOVE WHILE

AN ARTS FESTIVAL NORTH OF BALATON

HUNGARY'S VALLEY OF THE ARTS FESTIVAL, *the largest summer arts event in the country, is hosted annually by six villages spread across the Eger Creek Valley, north of Lake Balaton between Balatonfüred and Badacsony. The two-week event, beginning the last week of July, features works from an estimated 3,500 local and foreign artists. Another 800 dance, theater, and concert performances are held at makeshift stages in meadows, churches, caves, and even along streets. There are also musical walks through the forest and numerous puppet shows for children. Villages hosting the event— Kapolcs, Monostorapáti, Öcs, Pula, Taliándörögd, and Vigántpetend—are literally transformed into outdoor walking art shows, and booths and vendors abound. What began in 1989 as a three-day event has turned into a major draw for Hungarians and visitors alike, with total attendance today around 150,000 people.*

One of the festival's aims is to showcase local craftsmanship in the hosting villages, which have histories steeped in pottery and weaving. Additionally, one city elsewhere in Hungary is invited to invite its artists, dance troupes, and musicians. Past years have included groups from Szolnok, Debrecen, and Szeged. Some of the proceeds from Valley of the Arts have gone to rehabilitating closed and run-down historic properties in the Eger Valley, including a former ceramics gallery, a water mill, and an 18th-century smithy. For a list of events and programming, contact: **Kapolcsi Kultrális és Természetvédelmi Egylet** *(Kapolcs Cultural and Environment Protection Association;* ☏ *20/347–0511 (mobile)* ⊕ *www.kapolcs.hu).*

HE LIVED. In the same grove are trees honoring visits by another Nobel laureate, the Italian poet Salvatore Quasimodo, in 1961, and Indian prime minister Indira Gandhi, in 1972. An adjoining grove honors Soviet cosmonauts and their Hungarian partner-in-space, Bertalan Farkas.

Trees, restaurants, and shops line the **Tagore sétány** (Tagore Promenade), named after the Nobel prize-winning poet Rabindranath Tagore, which begins near the boat landing and runs for nearly a kilometer (almost ½ mi).

A stroll up **Blaha Lujza utca** from Gyógy tér will take you past several landmarks, such as the **Blaha Lujza Ház** (Lujza Blaha House), a neo-classical villa built in 1867 and, later, the summer home of this famous turn-of-the-20th-century actress, humanist, and singer (today, it's a hotel). The sweet little **Kerek templom** (Round Church), consecrated in 1846, was built in a classical style and has a truly rounded interior.

need a break? The plush **Kedves Café** (✉ Blaha Lujza u. 7 ☏ 87/343–229), built in 1795, was once the favorite summer haunt of well-known Hungarian writers and artists. Now more touristy than literary, it is still one of Lake Balaton's most popular and famous pastry shops.

Where to Stay & Eat

$$–$$$$ ✕ **Baricska Csárda.** This rambling, reed-thatched inn has wood-beamed rooms, vaulted cellars, terraces, and views of both vineyards and the lake. The food is hearty yet ambitious: roasted trout, fish paprikás with gnocchi to soak up the creamy sauce, and desserts mixing pumpkin and poppy seeds. In summer, Gypsy wedding shows are held nightly under the grape arbors. ⊠ *Baricska dülő, off Rte. 71 (Széchenyi út) behind the Shell station* ☎ *87/580–095* ⚲ *Reservations essential* ⊟ *AE, DC, MC, V* ☉ *Closed Nov.–mid-Mar.*

$–$$$ ✕ **Tölgyfa Csárda.** Perched high on a hilltop, the Oak Tree Tavern has breathtaking views over the steeples and rooftops of Balatonfüred and the Tihany Peninsula. The dining room and menu are worthy of a first-class Budapest restaurant, and nightly live Gypsy music keeps things festive. ⊠ *Meleghegy, up the hill at the end of Csárda u.* ☎ *87/343–036* ⊟ *No credit cards* ☉ *Closed late Nov.–Apr.*

★ ¢ ⊞ **Annabella.** The cool, spacious guest quarters in this large, Miami-style high-rise are especially pleasant in the summer heat. The resort overlooks the lake and Tagore Promenade and has access to excellent swimming and water-sports facilities. All rooms have balconies; for the best views, request a room on a high floor with a view of the Tihany Peninsula. ⊠ *Deák Ferenc u. 25, H-8231* ☎ *87/342–222* 🖷 *87/483–029* ⊕ *www.danubiusgroup.com* ↪ *383 rooms, 5 suites* ⚮ *Restaurant, café, indoor pool, pool, hair salon, massage, sauna, bicycles, bar, nightclub, baby-sitting, laundry service, travel services* ⊟ *AE, DC, MC, V* ☉ *Closed late Oct.–mid-Apr.* ❢❘ *BP.*

¢ ⊞ **Blaha Lujza Ház.** Hungary's fin-de-siècle songbird and actress Lujza Blaha spent her summers at this neoclassical villa, which has been converted into a hotel. The rooms are a bit cramped, and there's not much room to negotiate your way around the bed sometimes. However, the front-desk staff is helpful, and the breakfast room, which functions as a restaurant on summer evenings, is a pleasant place to begin the day with a buffet or cooked breakfast. ⊠ *Blaha u. 4, H-8230* ☎ *87/581–210* 🖷 *87/581–219* ⊕ *www.hotelblaha.hu* ↪ *22 rooms* ⚮ *Restaurant, cable TV, minibars, in-room safes, gym, bar, free parking, no-smoking rooms* ⊟ *AE, DC, MC, V* ☉ *Closed late Dec.–Mar.* ❢❘ *BP.*

¢ ⊞ **Club Imola.** Drive through a metal archway etched with the name
FodorśChoice "Imola" overhead to find a large square of various buildings surrounded
★ by lush green trees, vines, and plenty of outdoor seating terraces and small gardens. The Imola is a quiet break from the hustle of the nearby Balatonfüred strand. The main hotel features clean and wooden-furnished rooms. Inside the hotel is a huge, new indoor pool with a brand-new Jacuzzi. For longer stays, you can also rent a gorgeous duplex apartment with a small balcony, skylights, and loft bedroom. ⊠ *Petőfi Sándor u. 22, H-8230* ☎ *87/341–722* 🖷 *87/342–602* ⊕ *www.imolanet.hu* ↪ *10 rooms, 8 apartments* ⚮ *Restaurant, 2 tennis courts, indoor pool, sauna, table tennis, bar, laundry service, meeting rooms, free parking* ⊟ *MC, V* ❢❘ *BP.*

¢ ⊞ **Hotel Park.** Hidden on a side street in town—but close to the lakeshore—the Park is noticeably calmer than Füred's bustling main hotels. Rooms are large and bright, with high ceilings and tall windows. Suites have large, breezy balconies but small bathrooms. ⊠ *Jókai u. 24, H-8230*

🖳 *87/343–203 or 87/342–005* ⊕ *www.balaton.hu/parkhotel* ⤴ *27 rooms, 5 suites* ⟊ *Restaurant, gym, sauna, bar, meeting room, free parking* ▭ *No credit cards* ⭕ *BP.*

¢ 🖃 **Marina.** A central beachfront location is the Marina's main draw. Rooms in the homey 12-story building range from snug to small; suites have balconies but suffer from tiny bathrooms and dark bedrooms. Your safest bet is to get a high-floor "Superior" room with a lake view. Or better yet, stay in the "Lido" wing, which opens directly onto the water and where rooms (suites only) get plenty of sun. ✉ *Széchenyi út 26, H-8230* ☎ *87/889–536* 🖶 *87/889–535* ⊕ *www.danubiusgroup.com* ⤴ *349 rooms, 34 suites, 34 apartments* ⟊ *Restaurant, indoor pool, hair salon, massage, sauna, beach, boating, bowling, bar, pub, nightclub, laundry service, travel services* ▭ *AE, DC, MC, V* ⊗ *Closed Oct.–late Apr.* ⭕ *BP.*

Sports & the Outdoors

BEACHES Most hotels have their own private beaches, with water-sports facilities
ⓒ and equipment or special access to these nearby. Balatonfüred has three public beaches, where you can rent sailboards, paddleboats, and other water toys. **Füred Camping** (✉ Széchenyi u. 24, next to the Marina hotel ☎ 87/343–823), Hungary's largest campground, rents non-motorized boats as well as water toys. Although motorboats are banned from the lake, if you're desperate to water-ski you can try the campground's electric water-ski machine, which tows enthusiasts around a 1-km (½-mi) circle. A two-tow ticket runs around 900 HUF.

BICYCLING In season you can rent bicycles from temporary, private outfits set up
ⓒ in central locations around town and near the beaches. You can also usually rent mopeds in front of the Halászkert restaurant, at Széchenyi út 2, for around 1,300 HUF per hour and 5,000 HUF per day.

Rent-a-Ride. The company offers hourly, daily, and weekly bicycle rentals. The office is open during the summer season from 9 AM to 4 PM. Bicycle rentals are 350 HUF per hour, 2,400 HUF per day, 12,000 HUF per week. ✉ *Hotel Tagore, Deák Ferenc utca* ☎ *30/630–4767 (mobile).*

HORSEBACK **Diana Lovasudvar** (Diana Riding Center). Trail rides and horseback-rid-
RIDING ing lessons are conducted from mid-May to the end of September for
ⓒ about 2,500 HUF an hour. The center is just southwest of the town center; turn right at the sign about 100 yards beyond the giant campground on the lake. ✉ *Rte. 71* ☎ *87/703–076.*

TIHANY & PENINSULA

★ ❸ *11 km (7 mi) southwest of Balatonfüred, 126 km (78 mi) from Budapest.*

The famed town of Tihany, with its twisting, narrow cobblestone streets and hilltop abbey, is on top of the Tihany Félsziget (Tihany Peninsula), which is joined to the mainland by a narrow neck and juts 5 km (3 mi) into the lake. Only 12 square km (less than 5 square mi), the peninsula is not only a major tourist resort but perhaps the most historic part of the Balaton area. In 1952 the entire peninsula was declared a national park, and because of its geological rarities, it became Hungary's first nature-conservation zone. As a result of volcanic activity in the area, there are more than 110 geyser craters, remains of former hot springs that are reminiscent of those found in Iceland, Siberia, and Wyoming's Yellowstone Park.

The smooth Belső Tó (Inner Lake), 82 feet higher than Lake Balaton, is one of the peninsula's own two lakes; around it are barren yellowish-white rocks and volcanic cones rising against the sky. Though the hills surrounding the lake are known for their white wines, this area produces a notable Hungarian red, Tihany cabernet.

FodorsChoice On a hilltop overlooking the old town is the **Bencés Apátság** (Benedic-
★ tine Abbey), with foundations laid by King András I (whose body lies in the abbey crypt) in 1055. Parts of the abbey were rebuilt in baroque style between 1719 and 1784. The abbey's charter—containing some 100 Hungarian words in its Latin text, making it the oldest written source of the Hungarian language—is kept in Pannonhalma, but a replica is on display in the 11th-century crypt. The contrast between the simple crypt, where a small black crucifix hangs over the tomb of King András, and the abbey's lavish baroque interior—all gold, gilded silver, and salmon—could scarcely be more marked. The altar, abbot's throne, choir parapet, organ case, and pulpit were all the work of Sebestyén Stuhloff. Local tradition says he immortalized the features of his doomed sweetheart in the face of the angel kneeling on the right-hand side of the altar to the Virgin Mary. A magnificent baroque organ, adorned by stucco cherubs, can be heard during evening concerts in summer.

In a baroque house adjoining and entered through the abbey is the **Bencés Apátsági Múzeum** (Benedictine Abbey Museum). The best exhibits are in the basement lapidarium: relics from Roman colonization, including mosaic floors; a relief of David from the second or third century; and 1,200-year-old carved stones—all labeled in English as well as Hungarian. Three of the upstairs rooms were lived in for five days in 1921 by the last emperor of the dissolved Austro-Hungarian monarchy, Karl IV, in a futile foray to regain the throne of Hungary. Banished to Madeira, he died of pneumonia there a year later. The rooms are preserved with nostalgic relish for Emperor Franz Joseph's doomed successor. The museum is closed from November through March. ⊠ *Első András tér 1* ☎ *87/ 448–405 abbey, 87/448–650 museum* ⊠ *400 HUF for abbey and museum* ☉ *May–Sept., daily 9–5:30; Oct.–Mar., Mon.–Sat. 10–3, Sun. 11–3; Apr., daily 10–4:30. Nov.–Mar. (church and lapidarium only).*

The **Szabadtéri Múzeum** (Open-air Museum), Tihany's outdoor museum of ethnography, assembles a group of old structures, including an unplastered dwelling house with basalt walls, a thatched roof, verandas, and white-framed windows dating back to the 18th century. Another building is the former house of the Fishermen's Guild, with all kinds of fishing tools on display, including an ancient boat—used until 1934— parked inside. ⊠ *Pisky István sétány 12* ☎ *87/714–960* ⊠ *330 HUF* ☉ *Apr. 11–June, Tues.–Sun. 10–6; July–Aug., Tues.–Sun. 10–8; Sept.–Oct. 15, Tues.–Sun. 10–6.*

It's said that from **Visszhang domb** (Echo Hill), just a brief stroll from the Benedictine Abbey, as many as 16 syllables can be bounced off the abbey wall. With noise from builders and traffic, these days you may have to settle for a two-second echo. ⊠ *Piski István sétány, at the end of the street.*

need a break?

You can practice projecting from the terraces of the **Echo Restaurant** (⊠ Visszhang út 23 ☎ 87/448–460), an inn atop Echo Hill. While you're at it, try some fogas, carp, and catfish specialties.

Where to Stay & Eat

★ **$–$$** ✗ **Ferenc Pince.** This restaurant and wine cellar atop the Tihany Peninsula has splendid views of the Balaton and surrounding vineyards. The menu is heavy on Balaton fish but also includes poultry, salads, and other Hungarian specialities. The real draw, however, are wine tastings in the cellar just below the restaurant, where you can sample numerous wines produced by Ferenc Pince. Wine tastings cost 1,400 HUF to 2,800 HUF per person, depending on how much you try, and include cheese, sausage, and various breads. White varietals, for which Balaton is known, are the best choices. More than 30 different local wines are sold ⊠ *Cserhegy* ☎ *87/448–575 or 20/942–3987 (mobile)* ⊕ *www.ferencpince.hu* ⌂ *Reservations required for tastings* ▤ *No credit cards* ⊘ *Closed Oct.–Apr.*

$–$$ ✗ **Pál Csárda.** Two thatch cottages house this simple restaurant, where cold fruit soup and fish stew are the specialties. You can eat in the garden, which is decorated with gourds and strands of dried peppers. ⊠ *Visszhang u. 19* ☎ *87/448–605* ⌂ *Reservations not accepted* ▤ *AE, DC, MC, V* ⊘ *Closed Oct.–Apr.*

$ ▥ **Club Tihany.** Picture Club Med transposed to late-1980s central Europe, and you'll have some idea of what to expect at Club Tihany. This 32-acre lakeside resort stays busy year-round. Accommodations are standard hotel rooms, or individual bungalows with kitchens. The list of activities is impressive—from fishing to thermal bathing at the spa. In summer, when the hotel is filled to capacity, the scramble for the breakfast buffet can be a little unnerving. MAP is included in the hotel, optional for bungalows. ⊠ *Rév u. 3, H-8237* ☎ *87/538–564* ▤ *87/448–083* ⊕ *www.clubtihany.hu* ↘ *330 rooms, 160 bungalows* ⌂ *3 restaurants, café, pub, in-room data ports, some kitchens, minibars, cable TV with movies, miniature golf, tennis court, pool, hair salon, health club, spa, beach, boating, fishing, bicycles, billiards, bowling, Ping-Pong, squash, 2 bars, dance club, children's programs (ages 3–17), Internet, meeting rooms* ▤ *AE, DC, MC, V* ⫶〇⫶ *MAP.*

¢–$ ▥ **Kastély Hotel.** Lush landscaped lawns surround this stately neobaroque mansion, which was built on the water's edge in the early 1930s for Archduke József Hapsburg, then taken over by the Communist state in the 1940s (it is still owned by the government). Inside, it's all understated elegance; rooms have soaring ceilings and crisp sheets. Rooms with lake-facing windows and/or balconies are worth the extra cost. ⊠ *Fürdő telepi út 1, H-8237* ☎ *87/448–611* ▤ *87/448–409* ⊕ *www.hotelfured.hu* ↘ *25 rooms, 1 suite* ⌂ *Restaurant, café, minibars, cable TV, miniature golf, 2 tennis courts, sauna, beach, boating, bicycles, bar* ▤ *AE, DC, MC, V* ⊘ *Closed mid-Oct.–mid-Apr.* ⫶〇⫶ *BP.*

Fodor'sChoice ★

★ ¢ ▦ **Adler Inn.** This cozy inn 500 meters from the Balaton shore has a friendly staff and small, clean rooms, each with an outdoor terrace. Outside the inn is a lovely dining area and outdoor pizzeria. The resident hotel basset hound named Salami can usually be found soaking up the sun outside, and he enjoys attention. Rooms are air-conditioned, but there is an extra charge. ⊠ *Felsőkopazhegyi út 1/a, H-8237* ☎ *87/538–000* ⊟ *87/448–755* ⊕ *www.adler-tihany.hu* ⊅ *13 rooms, 2 apartments* ⌂ *Restaurant, pizzeria, pool, hot tub, sauna* ⊟ *No credit cards* ⊙ *Nov.–mid-Mar.* ⊺◎⊺ *BP.*

Nightlife & the Arts

Well-known musicians perform on the Benedictine Abbey's magnificent organ during the popular summer **organ-concert series** (☎ 87/448–405 for information and tickets), which runs from July to August 20. Concerts are generally held on weekends at 8:30 PM.

Sports & the Outdoors

HIKING Footpaths crisscross the entire peninsula, allowing you to climb the small
ⓒ hills on its west side for splendid views of the area or hike down Belső-tó (Inner Lake). If in midsummer you climb the area's highest hill, the Csúcshegy (761 feet, approximately a two-hour hike), you'll find the land below carpeted with purple lavender. Introduced from France into Hungary, lavender thrives on the lime-rich soil and strong sunshine of Tihany. The State Lavender and Medicinal Herb Farm here supplies the Hungarian pharmaceutical and cosmetics industries.

off the beaten path — **ÖRVÉNYES** – The miniature town, which is about 7 km (4½ mi) west of Tihany, has the only working *vízi malom* (water mill) in the Balaton region. Built in the 18th century, it still grinds grain into flour while also serving as a tiny museum. In the miller's room is a collection of folk art, wood carvings, pottery, furniture, and pipes. On a nearby hill stand the ruins of a Romanesque church; only its chancel has survived. On Templom utca, a few steps from the bridge, is the baroque St. Imre templom (St. Imre Church), built in the late 18th century. *Water mill* ⊠ *Szent Imre u. 1, Örvényes* ☎ *87/449–360* ⊠ *100 HUF* ⊙ *May–Sept., Tues.–Sun. 9–4.*

BALATONUDVARI – About 1 km (½ mi) west of Örvényes is a pleasant beach resort famous for its cemetery, which was declared a national shrine because of its beautiful, unique heart-shape tombstones carved from white limestone at the turn of the 18th century. The cemetery is essentially on the highway, at the eastern end of town; it is easily visible from the road. Balatonudvari's beach itself is at **Kiliántelep,** 2 km (1 mi) to the west.

BADACSONY

★ ❹ *41 km (25 mi) southwest of Tihany, 167 km (104 mi) from Budapest.*

One of the northern shore's most treasured images is the slopes of Mt. Badacsony (1,437 feet), simply called the Badacsony, rising from the lake. The mysterious, coffinlike basalt peak of the Balaton Highlands is actually an extinct volcano flanked by smaller cone-shape hills. The masses of lava that coagulated here created bizarre and beautiful rock formations. At the upper edge, salt columns tower 180 to 200 feet like organ pipes in a huge semicircle. In 1965 Hungarian conservationists won a major victory that ended the quarrying of basalt from Mt. Badacsony, which is now a nature preserve. Badacsony is really an administrative name for the entire area and includes not just the mountain but also five settlements at its foot.

The land below Mt. Badacsony has been tilled painfully and lovingly for centuries. There are vineyards everywhere and splendid wine in every inn and tavern. In descending order of dryness, the best-loved Badacsony white wines are rizlingszilváni, kéknyelű, and szürkebarát. Their proud producers claim that "no vine will produce good wine unless it can see its own reflection in the Balaton." They believe it is not enough for the sun simply to shine on a vine; the undersides of the leaves also need light, which is reflected from the lake's mirrorlike surface. Others claim the wine draws its strength from the fire of old volcanoes.

Many restaurants and inns have their own wine tastings, as do the numerous smaller, private cellars dotting the hill. Look for signs saying *bor* or *Wein* (wine, in Hungarian and German, respectively) to point the way. Most places are open from mid-May to mid-September daily from around noon until 9 or 10.

A good starting point for Badacsony sightseeing is the **Egry József Múzeum** (József Egry Museum), formerly the home and studio of a famous painter of Balaton landscapes. His evocative paintings depict the lake's constantly changing hues, from its angry bright green during storms to its tranquil deep blues. ⊠ *Egry sétány 12* ☎ *87/431–044* 🖅 *300 HUF* ☉ *May–mid-Oct., Tues.–Sun. 10–6.*

Szegedy Róza út, the steep main street climbing the mountain, is flanked by vineyards and villas. This is the place to get acquainted with the writer Sándor Kisfaludy and his beloved bride from Badacsony, Róza Szegedy, to whom he dedicated his love poems. At the summit of her street is **Szegedy Róza Ház** (Róza Szegedy House), a baroque winepress house built in 1790 on a grand scale—with thatched roof, gabled wall, six semicircular arcades, and an arched and pillared balcony running the length of the four raftered upstairs rooms. It was here that the hometown girl met the visiting bard from Budapest. The house now serves as a memorial museum to both of them, furnished much the way it was when Kisfaludy was doing his best work immortalizing his two true loves, the Badacsony and his wife. Szegedy, meanwhile, was heavily involved with wine-making, and her homemade vermouth was famous throughout Hungary. ⊠ *Szegedy Róza út 87* ☎ *87/701–906* 🖅 *240 HUF* ☉ *May–Sept., Tues.–Sun. 10–6.*

The steep climb to the **Kisfaludy kilátó** (Kisfaludy Lookout Tower) on Mt. Badacsony's summit is an integral part of the Badacsony experience and a rewarding bit of exercise. Serious summitry begins behind the Kisfaludy-ház (Kisfaludy House), a restaurant just above the Rózsa Szegedy House, which was once owned by the family of Hungarian poet Sándor Kisfaludy. The trek to the Kisfaludy Lookout Tower begins at the Rózsakő (Rose Stone), a flat, smooth basalt slab with many carved inscriptions. Local legend has it that if a boy and a girl sit on it with their backs to Lake Balaton, they will marry within a year. From here, a trail marked in yellow leads up to the foot of the columns that stretch to the top. Steep flights of stone steps take you through a narrow gap between rocks and basalt walls until you reach a tree-lined plateau. You are now at the 1,391-foot level. Follow the blue triangular markings along a path to the lookout tower. Even with time out for rests and views, the ascent from Rózsakő should take less than an hour.

Just outside of town, **Rizapuszta** (✉ Káptalantóti út, Rizapuszta, Badacsonytomaj ☎ 87/471–243) is a wine cellar and restaurant that has regular tastings.

Where to Stay & Eat

$–$$$ ✕ **Halászkert.** The festive Fish Garden has won numerous international awards for its fine Hungarian cuisine. Inside are wooden rafters and tables draped with cheerful traditional blue-and-white *kékfestő* tablecloths; outside is a large terrace with umbrella-shaded tables. The extensive menu has such fresh-from-the-lake dishes as the house halászlé, and *párolt* (steamed) harcsa drenched with a paprika-caper sauce. There's live gypsy music several nights a week. ✉ *Park u. 5* ☎ *87/431–113* ▭ *AE, DC, MC, V* ⊙ *Closed Nov.–Apr.*

$–$$$ ✕ **Kisfaludy-ház.** Perched above the Szegedy Róza House is this Badacsony institution, once a winepress house owned by the poet Sándor Kisfaludy's family. Its wine cellar lies directly over a spring, but the main draw is a vast two-tier terrace that affords a breathtaking view of virtually the entire lake. Naturally, the wines are excellent and are incorporated into some of the cooking, such as creamy cold white-wine soup with dried grapes. ✉ *Szegedy Róza u. 87* ☎ *87/431–016* ▭ *AE, DC, MC, V* ⊙ *Closed Oct.–Apr.*

★ ¢–$ ✕ **Szent Orbán Borház.** Part of the illustrious Szent Orbán winery, this restaurant overlooks some of the vineyard's 30 acres. On summer days golden light bathes the 19th-century former farmhouse. There are written menus, but charming servers also recite the dishes (in English and other languages), and they'll steer you toward sampling two unique house wines, Budai zöld and Kéknyelű—both based on legendary varietals from Roman times. Smoked goose liver pâté is frequently available as an appetizer, as is fresh fish from Lake Balaton, including fogas. ✉ *Szegedy Róza u. 22* ☎ *87/431–382* ▭ *AE, DC, MC, V.*

¢–$ **Club Hotel Badacsony.** A private beach is just a step away from this hotel right on the shore of Lake Balaton. The Club Hotel is the largest in the area. Rooms are bright and clean, the staff extremely helpful, and a brand new outdoor swimming pool—heated in cool weather—opened in June 2004. ✉ *Balatoni út 14, Badacsonytomaj H-8258* ☎ *87/471–040* 🖷 *87/471–059* 🌐 *www.hotels.hu/club_hotel_badacsony* ⇨ *52 rooms, 4 suites* ♁ *Restaurant, café, cable TV, tennis court, hair salon, massage, sauna, beach, bowling, bar, playground, meeting rooms; no a/c* ▭ *DC, MC, V* ⊙ *Closed Nov.–Apr.* 🍴 *BP.*

Fodor'sChoice ★

🕑 ¢ ⊞ **Hotel Volán.** This bright yellow, restored 19th-century mansion is a cheerful, family-oriented inn with a manicured yard for sunning and relaxing. Well-kept rooms are in the main house and in four modern additions behind it. There's a massive outdoor sandbox for children, as well as a playground. ⊠ *Római út 184, H-8261* 🖂 *87/431–013* ⊕ *www.vhotel.hu* ⤴ *23 rooms* ⚭ *Restaurant, minibars, cable TV, pool, bar; no a/c* ⊟ *No credit cards* ⊙ *Closed Nov.–mid-Feb.* †⊙† *BP.*

Sports & the Outdoors

The upper paths and roads along the slopes of Mt. Badacsony are excellent for scenic walking. Well-marked trails lead to the summit of Mt. Badacsony. For beach activities, you can go to one of Badacsony's several beaches or head 6 km (4 mi) northeast, to those at Balatonrendes and Ábrahámhegy, combined communities forming quiet resorts.

SZIGLIGET

★ ❺ *11 km (7 mi) west of Badacsony, 178 km (110 mi) from Budapest.*

The village of Szigliget is a tranquil, picturesque town with fine thatchroof winepress houses and a small beach. Towering over the town is the ruin of the 13th-century **Óvár** (Old Castle), a fortress so well protected that it was never taken by the Turks; it was demolished in the early 18th century by Hapsburgs fearful of rebellions. A steep path starting from Kisfaludy utca brings you to the top of the hill, where you can explore the ruins, under ongoing archaeological restoration (a sign maps out the restoration plan), and take in the breathtaking views.

Down in the village, the Romanesque remains of the **Avas templom** (Avas Church) (⊠ Iharos út, at the intersection with the road to Badacsony), from the Arpad dynasty, still contain a 12th-century basalt tower with a stone spire. The **Eszterházy summer mansion** (⊠ Fő tér), on the main square, was built in the 18th century and rebuilt in neoclassical style in the 19th. In recent decades a retreat for writers, it is closed to the public—but just as well, for the bland inside has little to do with its former self. The mansion has a 25-acre park with yews, willows, walnuts, pines, and more than 500 kinds of ornamental trees and shrubs.

KESZTHELY

❻ *18 km (10 mi) west of Szigliget, 196 km (122 mi) from Budapest.*

With a beautifully preserved pedestrian avenue (Kossuth Lajos utca) in the historic center of town, the spectacular baroque Festetics Kastély, and a relative absence of honky-tonk, Keszthely is far more classically attractive and sophisticated than other large Balaton towns. Continuing the cultural and arts tradition begun by Count György Festetics two centuries ago, Keszthely hosts numerous cultural events, including an annual summer arts festival. Just south of town is the vast swamp called Kis-Balaton (Little Balaton), formerly part of Lake Balaton and now a nature preserve filled with birds. Water flowing into Lake Balaton from its little sibling frequently churns up sediment, making the water around

Keszthely's beaches disconcertingly cloudy. Keszthely is a good place to spend the afternoon, either walking around town or wading in the Balaton shore, but we do not recommend spending the night, as accommodation is typically run-down and over-priced.

The **Pethő Ház** (Pethő House), a striking town house of medieval origin, was rebuilt in baroque style with a handsome arcaded gallery above its courtyard. Hidden deep inside its courtyard is the restored 18th-century **synagogue**, in front of which stands a small memorial honoring the 829 Jewish people from the neighborhood, turned into a ghetto in 1944, who were killed during the Holocaust. ⊠ *Kossuth Lajos u. 22.*

★ Keszthely's magnificent **Festetics Kastély** (Festetics Palace) is one of the finest baroque complexes in Hungary. Begun around 1745, it was the seat of the enlightened and philanthropic Festetics dynasty, which had acquired Keszthely six years earlier. The palace's distinctive churchlike tower and more than 100 rooms were added between 1883 and 1887; the interior is lush. The **Helikon Könyvtár** (Helikon Library) in the south wing contains some 52,000 volumes, with precious codices and documents of Festetics family history. Chamber and orchestral concerts are held in the Mirror Gallery ballroom or, in summer, in the courtyard. The palace opens onto a splendid park lined with rare plants and fine sculptures. You'll pay a supplementary fee of 500 HUF to take photos (nonflash), 1,200 HUF to bring in your video camera. ⊠ *Kastély u. 1* ☎ *83/ 312–191* 📠 *1,400 HUF* ☉ *June, Tues.–Sun. 9–5; July–Aug., daily 9–6; Sept.–May, Tues.–Sun. 10–5.*

Supposedly the largest of its kind in Central Europe, Keszthely's **Babamúzeum** (Doll Museum) exhibits some 450 porcelain figurines dressed in 240 types of colorful folk dress. The building has a pastoral look, created not only by the figurines—which convey the multifarious beauty of village garb—but also by the ceiling's huge, handcrafted wooden beams. On the two upper floors are wooden models of typical homes, churches, and ornate wooden gates representative of all regions in and near present-day Hungary that Magyars have inhabited since conquering the Carpathian basin in 896. The museum's pièce de résistance is the lifework of an elderly peasant woman from northern Hungary: a 9-yard-long **model** of Budapest's Parliament building, patched together over 14 years from almost 4 million snail shells (which are 28 million years old, no less) originating from the Pannon Sea, which once covered much of Hungary. ⊠ *Kossuth u. 11* ☎ *83/318–855* 📠 *300 HUF, model of Parliament 200 HUF* ☉ *May–Sept., daily 10–5; Oct.–Apr., daily 9–5.*

need a break? **Hungária Gösser Söröző.** This beer garden keeps long hours and plenty of beer on tap. The food is better than you might guess judging just from the touristy atmosphere. Aside from barroom snacks, highlights of the huge menu include *ropogós libacomb hagymás törtburgonyával* (crunchy goose drumstick with mashed potatoes and onions) and *töltött paprika* (stuffed peppers). ⊠ *Kossuth Lajos u. 35, north of Fő tér* ☎ *83/312–265* 🚭 *AE, DC, MC, V.*

HÉVÍZ

❼ *6 km (4 mi) northwest of Keszthely, 202 km (126 mi) from Budapest.*

Hévíz is one of Hungary's biggest and most famous spa resorts, with the largest natural curative thermal lake in Europe. Lake Hévíz covers nearly 60,000 square yards, with warm water that never grows cooler than 33°C to 35°C (91.4°F–95°F) in summer and 30°C to 32°C (86°F–89.6°F) in winter, thus allowing year-round bathing, particularly where the lake is covered by a roof and looks like a racetrack grandstand. Richly endowed with sulfur, alkali, calcium salts, and other curative components, the Hévíz water is recommended for spinal, rheumatic, gynecological, and articular disorders and is drunk to help digestive problems and receding gums. Fed by a spring producing 86 million liters (22.7 million gallons) of water a day, the lake cycles through a complete water change every 28 hours. Squeamish bathers, however, should be forewarned that along with its photogenic lily pads, the lake naturally contains assorted sludgy mud and plant material. It's all supposed to be good for you, though—even the mud, which is full of iodine and is claimed to stimulate estrogen production in the body. The vast spa park has hospitals, sanatoriums, expensive hotels, and a casino.

The public bath facilities are in the **Szent András Kórház** (St. Andrew Hospital), a large, turreted medicinal bathing complex on the lakeshore with a large staff on hand to treat rheumatological complaints. Bathing for more than three hours at a time is not recommended. ⊠ *Dr. Schulhof Vilmos sétány 1* ☎ *83/340–587* ⌨ *500 HUF* ☉ *May–Sept., daily 8:30–5:30; Oct.–Apr., daily 9–4:30.*

The beautifully furnished **Talpasház** (House on Soles) takes its name from an interesting architectural detail: its upright beams are encased in thick foundation boards. Exquisite antique peasant furniture, textiles, and pottery fill the house along with the work of contemporary local folk artists. Some of their work is for sale on the premises, and you can also create your own works on a pottery wheel. Contact the caretaker, Csaba Rezes, who lives next door at No. 15, if the door happens to be closed. ⊠ *Dózsa György u. 17* ☎ *85/377–364 caretaker* ⌨ *200 HUF* ☉ *Late May–Sept., Tues.–Sun. hours vary (call the caretaker to let you in).*

off the beaten path

CSILLAGVÁR (Star Castle) – It's worth stopping in Balatonszentgyörgy to see this castle, hidden away at the end of a dirt road past a gaping quarry. The house was built in the 1820s as a hunting lodge for László, the Festetics family's most eccentric member. Though it's not star-shape inside, wedge-shape projections on the ground floor give the outside this effect. Today the castle houses a museum of 16th- and 17th-century life in the border fortresses of the Balaton. ⊠ *Irtási dűlő* ☎ *85/377–532* ⌨ *100 HUF* ☉ *Mar.–Sept., daily 9–5; Dec.–Feb., daily 9–1; Oct.–Nov., closed.*

Where to Stay

$–$$ ▦ **Rogner Hévíz Hotel Lotus Therme.** No expense has been spared at this spa and "wellness" hotel promoting relaxation and invigoration. In addition to enjoying thermal baths, a fitness center, and various purification and detoxification therapies, you can join in golf and tennis excursions. There are even in-house dieticians. The hotel itself is a large, crescent-shaped building just off the E71. ⊠ *Lótuszvirág u. 80, H-8380* ☎ *83/500–500* 🖹 *83/500–591* ⊕ *www.lotustherme.com* 📞 *231 rooms* ᗜ *Restaurant, café, cable TV with movies, indoor pool, health club, hair salon, massage, sauna, driving range, miniature golf, putting green, 4 tennis courts, bar, shops, Internet, no-smoking rooms* ▤ *AE, DC, MC, V* ¶⦿¶ *BP.*

$ 🖼 **Danubius Thermal Hotel Aqua.** This large, luxurious spa-hotel in the city center has its own thermal baths and physiotherapy unit (plus a full dental service). The rooms are fairly small and therefore not suited to families who intend to share a single room. Numerous cure packages are available. ⊠ *Kossuth Lajos u. 13–15, H-8380* ☎ *83/889–500* 🖹 *83/889–509* ⊕ *www.danubiusgroup.com/aqua* 📞 *227 rooms* ᗜ *Restaurant, pub, cable TV, minibars, pool, hair salon, massage, sauna, spa, dry cleaning, laundry service, bar, free parking; no a/c* ▤ *AE, DC, MC, V* ¶⦿¶ *BP.*

$ 🖼 **Hotel Palace Hévíz.** The art-deco exterior and atrium of the Hévíz might convey a hint of 1930s glamor, but all those gleaming white surfaces are new, as the hotel is a relatively recent construction. The hotel has thermal baths, various treatments, and its own dental center. Rooms are pretty conventional and standard, with a tiled entryway and carpeted sleeping area. ⊠ *Rákóczi u. 1–3, H-8380* ☎ *83/540–458* 🖹 *83/540–459* ⊕ *www.palace-heviz.hu* 📞 *160 rooms* ᗜ *Restaurant, café, indoor pool, hair salon, massage, sauna, bar, some pets allowed* ▤ *AE, DC, MC, V* ¶⦿¶ *BP.*

SIÓFOK

❽   *110 km (68 mi) east of Hévíz, 105 km (65 mi) southwest of Budapest.*

Siófok is the largest city on Balaton's southern shore and a major tourist and holiday center for Hungarians. It is also, arguably, the least beautiful. In 1863 a railway station was built for the city, paving the way for its "golden age" at the turn of the 20th century. In the closing stages of World War II the city sustained heavy damage; to boost tourism during the 1960s, the Pannonia Hotel Company built four of what many consider to be the ugliest hotels in the area. If, however, these were Siófok's *only* ugly buildings, there would still be hope for a ray of aesthetic redemption. With the exception of the twin-tower train station and the adjacent business district stretching a few blocks to the *Víztorony* (water tower), dating from 1912, the city is overrun by drab modern structures. Its shoreline is now a long, honky-tonk strip crammed with concrete-bunker hotels, discos, go-go bars, and tacky restaurants. So while Siófok is not for those seeking a peaceful lakeside getaway, it is exactly what hordes of action-seeking young people want—an all-in-one playground.

One worthwhile attraction is the **Kálmán Imre Múzeum** (Imre Kálmán Museum), housed in the birthplace of composer Kálmán (1882–1953), known internationally as the Prince of Operetta. Inside this small house-cum-museum are his first piano, original scores, his smoking jacket, and lots of old pictures. ⊠ *Kálmán Imre sétány 5* ☎ *84/311–287* 🎟 *200 HUF* ⊗ *Apr.–Oct., Tues.–Sun. 9–5; Nov.–Mar., Tues.–Sun. 9–4.*

Where to Stay & Eat

$$–$$$ ✕ **Millennium Étterem.** Imre Makovecz, one of Hungary's preeminent architects, oversaw renovation of this elegant restaurant, once an old villa, in the early 1990s. The menu includes several Hungarian specialties as well as fresh, local fish, including whole trout and pike perch. ⊠ *Fő utca 93–95* ☎ *84/312–546* ⊟ *AE, DC, MC, V.*

★ **$–$$**   ✕ **Csárdás Étterem.** The oldest and one of the best restaurants in Siófok, the Csárdás Étterem consistently wins awards for its hearty, never-bland Hungarian cuisine. House specialties include a breaded and fried pork fillet stuffed with cheese, ham, and smoked bacon. ⊠ *Fő utca 105* ☎ *84/310–642* ⊟ *AE, MC, V.*

$–$$ 🏨 **Hotel Atrium Janus Siófok.** Every room in this bright luxury hotel is clean and comfortably contemporary. The "relaxation center" downstairs has a swimming pool, sauna, and whirlpool. ⊠ *Fő u. 93–95, H-8600* ☎ *84/ 312–546* ☎ *84/312–432* ⊕ *www.janushotel.hu* ➿ *22 rooms, 7 suites* �ዼ *Restaurant, café, in-room safes, minibars, cable TV, indoor pool, gym, sauna, bar, meeting rooms, free parking* ⊟ *AE, DC, MC, V* ❢❍❢ *BP.*

¢   🏨 **Hotel Fortuna.** This three-story, bright-yellow rectangular block has the advantage of being somewhat removed from the multilane traffic of the city's main street and about 100 yards from the lakeshore. The rooms are modern and, like the building's facade, awash in a soothing yellow; all have balconies. ⊠ *Erkel Ferenc u. 51, H-8600* ☎☎ *84/311– 087 or 84/313–476* ➿ *41 rooms, 5 suites* ⍭ *Restaurant, bar, playground, meeting rooms; no a/c* ⊟ *AE, DC, MC, V* ❢❍❢ *BP.*

Nightlife & the Arts

Siófok is an important destination in the summer for Hungarian youth, who come to party here. Several outdoor raves and musical festivals are usually held between May and August. These outdoor events are advertised by posters plastered across Budapest.

The town remains loyal to Siófok-born operetta composer Imre Kálmán and hosts popular operetta concerts regularly in the summer at the **Kulturális Központ** (Cultural Center; ⊠ Fő tér 2 ☎ 84/311–855).

Sports & the Outdoors

GO-CARTS   Speed demons can whiz around the **Go-Cart Track** (⊠ Rte. 70, by the railroad crossing ☎ 84/311–917 or 06/209–512–510), which is open from mid-May through September; a five-minute drive costs 1,700 HUF and 10 minutes runs 2,600 HUF.

Lake Balaton Essentials

BUS TRAVEL

Frequent bus service links Budapest with Lake Balaton's major resorts. Arrive at the bus station early. You can buy a reserved-seat ticket at the station up to 20 minutes prior to departure, but you can only do so in person; otherwise, buy your ticket directly from the driver. Contact the tourist offices or Volánbusz for schedule and fare information. Buses leave Budapest's Népliget Bus Station.

🚩 **Volánbusz** ⊠ District X, Népliget Bus Station, Üllői út 131, Budapest ☎ 1/382–4900 ⊕ www.volanbusz.hu.

CAR TRAVEL

Driving is the most convenient way to explore the area, but keep in mind that traffic can be heavy during summer weekends. Expressway E71/ M7 is the main artery between Budapest and Lake Balaton, which runs through southwestern Hungary. From Budapest the E71 traverses the lake's southern shore to Siófok and towns farther west. Route 71 joins E71 at Balaton's eastern shore and travels up along the northern shore to Balatonfüred and lakeside towns southwest. The drive from Budapest to Siófok takes about 1½ hours, except on weekends, when traffic can be severe. From Budapest to Balatonfüred is about the same.

FERRY TRAVEL

The slowest but most scenic way to travel among Lake Balaton's major resorts is by ferry, for about 340 HUF per person. Schedules for MA-HART Tours, the national ferry company, are available from most of the tourist offices in the region.

🚣 **MAHART Tours** ☎ 84/310-050 in Siófok, 1/484-4000 in Budapest ⊕ www.balatonihajozas.hu.

TOURS

You can arrange tours directly with the hotels in the Balaton area and with the help of Tourinform offices; these can include boat trips to vineyards, folk-music evenings, and overnight trips to local inns.

FROM BUDAPEST Cityrama takes groups twice a week from April to October from Budapest to Balatonfüred for a walk along the promenade and then over to Tihany for a tour of the abbey. After lunch, you take a ferry across the Balaton and then head back to Budapest, with a wine-tasting stop on the way.

IBUSZ Travel has several day-long tours to Hévíz, Balatonfüred, and Siófok from Budapest; inquire at the office in Budapest.

🚣 **Cityrama** ☎ 1/302-4382 in Budapest ⊕ www.cityrama.hu. **IBUSZ Travel** ✉ District V, Ferenciek tere 10, Around Ferenciek tere, Budapest ☎ 1/485-2700 ⊕ www.ibusz.hu.

BOAT TOURS MAHART arranges several sailing excursions on Lake Balaton. From Balatonfüred, the *Csongor* sets out several times daily in July and August for an hour-long jaunt around the Tihany Peninsula. Most other summer tours depart from Siófok, including the "Tihany Tour" on Saturday at 10 AM, which stops for guided sightseeing in Balatonfüred and Tihany; the "Sunset Tour" is a daily 1½-hour cruise at 7:30 PM, during which you can sip a glass of champagne while watching the sun set. The "Badacsony Tour" departs from Keszthely and goes to Badacsony at 10:30 AM each Thursday.

🚣 **MAHART** ☎ 84/310-050 in Siófok ⊕ www.balatonihajozas.hu.

TRAIN TRAVEL

Daily express trains run from Budapest's Déli (South) Station to Siófok and Balatonfüred. The roughly two-hour trip costs about 1,100 HUF to Siófok and 1,300 HUF to Balatonfüred, each way.

Trains from Budapest serve the resorts on the northern shore; a separate line links resorts on the southern shore. There is no train service to

Tihany. While most towns are on a rail line, it's inconvenient to decipher the train schedules; trains don't run very frequently, so planning connections can be tricky. Since many towns are just a few miles apart, getting stuck on a local train can feel like an endless stop-start cycle. Also bear in mind that, apart from some trains between Budapest and Veszprém, you cannot reserve seats on the Balaton trains—it's first come, first seated.

Balatonfüred train station ⊠ Castricum tér, Balatonfüred ☎ 87/343-652. **Siófok train station** ⊠ Millenium tér, Siófok ☎ 84/310-061. **Veszprém train station** ⊠ Jutasi út 34, Veszprém, 2 km [1 mi] outside of town ☎ 88/329-999.

VISITOR INFORMATION

The Balaton Communication and Information Hotline is an excellent source of travel information for the region (in Hungarian only), with a comprehensive Web site (with some English information).

Tourist Information Balaton Communication & Information Hotline ☎ 88/406-963 ⊕ www.balaton.hu. **Balatontourist** ⊠ Tagore sétány 1, Balatonfüred ☎ 87/342-822 or 87/343-471. **Hévíz Tourist** ⊠ Rákóczi u. 4, Hévíz ☎ 83/341-348. **IBUSZ** ⊠ Fő u. 174, Siófok ☎ 84/315-213.

Tourinform ⊠ Park u. 6, Badacsony ☎🖷 87/531-013 ⊠ Petőfi u. 68, Balatonfüred ☎ 87/580-480 ⊠ Kossuth u. 28, Keszthely ☎🖷 83/314-144 ⊠ Víztorony, Siófok ☎ 84/315-355 ⊠ Kossuth u. 20, Tihany ☎🖷 87/438-016 ⊠.

SOPRON

9

By Kristen
Schweizer

SOPRON, WHICH LIES ON THE AUSTRIAN FRONTIER, between Lake Fertő (Neusiedlersee in German) and the Sopron Hills, is one of the most picturesque cities in Hungary. Nowhere else in the country are there so many monuments in such a small area; literally every other building in the Sopron city center seems to be a historic marker or landmark of some sort. Barely an hour away from Vienna by car, it is a bargain-shopping center for many Austrians who often come for the day. The joke in Sopron is that every day at noon, "We play the Austrian national hymn so that the Austrians have to stand still for two minutes while we Hungarians shop." German-speakers also come to Sopron for another reason: dental care. Calling itself the world's dental capital, Sopron claims to have one dentist for every 80 inhabitants. Most signs and menus are in both Hungarian and German, and most people here speak German as a second language. Don't be discouraged, however, if you don't speak German. Employees at Sopron's two Tourinform offices speak English, and information for museums and other places of interest is almost always in English as well.

There is much more to Sopron, however, than conspicuous consumption by foreigners. Behind the narrow storefronts along the City Ring Várkerület (called Lenin Boulevard until 1989) and within the city walls (one set built by Romans, the other by medieval Magyars) lies a horseshoe-shaped inner city that is a wondrous mix of Gothic, baroque, and Renaissance, mostly set in and around Fő tér, the main square of perfectly proportioned Italianate architecture. Sopron's inspired restoration won a 1975 Europe Prize Gold Medal for Protection of Monuments, and the work continues slowly and carefully.

Sopron is often called Hungary's most faithful town, as its residents voted to remain part of Hungary after the 1921 Trianon Peace Treaty following World War I shrunk Hungary's size by more than half. Today's city of 60,000 was a small Celtic settlement more than 2,300 years ago. During Roman times, as Scarabantia, it stood on the main European north–south trade route, the Amber Road; it also happened to be near the junction with the east–west route used by Byzantine merchants. In AD 896 the Magyars conquered the Carpathian basin and later named the city Suprun, after a medieval Hungarian warrior. After the Hapsburgs took over the territory during the Turkish wars of the 16th and 17th centuries, they renamed the city Ödenburg (Castle on the Ruins) and made it the capital of the rich and fertile Austrian Burgenland. Ferdinand III, later the Holy Roman Emperor, was crowned king of Hungary here in 1625, and at a special session of the Hungarian parliament in 1681, Prince Paul Esterházy was elected palatine (ruling deputy) of Hungary. And always, under any name or regime, Sopron was a fine and prosperous place in which to live.

About the Hotels & Restaurants

Despite throngs of tourists from neighboring Austria and Germany, the selection of quality hotels in Sopron is weak, and many hotels lie well outside the city center. The best places to stay are located either in the Old Town or along the Várkerület, and from either of these areas the city can easily be navigated by foot. Hotel rates may be quoted in either forints or euros.

Dining tends to be casual, and many restaurants have outdoor seating terraces during warmer months, usually from May through September. In addition to several cozy cafés and small eateries offering Hungarian food, Sopron has numerous pizzerias. Food prices are cheaper than in Budapest but more expensive than in eastern or southern Hungary.

WHAT IT COSTS In Euros & Forints				
$$$$	**$$$**	**$$**	**$**	**¢**
HOTELS IN EUROS	over €225	€175–€225	€125–€175	€75–€125	under €75
HOTELS IN FORINTS	over 56,000	44,000–56,000	31,000–44,000	18,500–31,000	under 18,500
RESTAURANTS IN FORINTS	over 3,500	2,500–3,500	1,500–2,500	800–1,500	under 800

Hotel prices are for two people in a standard double room with a private bath and breakfast during peak season (June through August). Restaurant prices are per person for a main course at dinner and include 15% tax but not service.

EXPLORING SOPRON

For those who plan to visit as many museums as they can, one collective ticket covering most of Sopron's museums may be purchased at the Storno Ház for 2,000 HUF

Numbers in the text correspond to numbers in the margin and on the Sopron map.

a good walk

Sopron is best navigated on foot as nearly every building in the city center has some historic importance attached to it. Starting from the train station, walk straight out the front door, which will lead you directly to Mátyás Király utca. Continue for about ten minutes until you reach Széchenyi tér, the city's largest square. From here, Mátyás Kiraly utca now turns into **Várkerület ❶**, Sopron's main boulevard, which is lined with shops, cafés, and dental offices. Continue along this street for about 10 minutes more until you reach the tall **Mária szobor ❷**, which juts into the sky and marks the beginning of Sopron's Old Town.

Keep to the left, past the statue and down the cobblestone Előkapu utca, which leads to Sopron's Old Town. Pass under the archways, where the Tourinform office will be on your right, as well as a huge bronze key to the city just beyond, also on the right. Directly above the key is the towering **Tűztorony ❸**. Pass through the wooden door under the Tűztorony, and you enter Fő tér, the main square of the Old Town.

The first building to your right is the grandest building in all of Sopron, the **Storno ház ❹**. Across the square, at No. 2, sits the **Angyal Patika Múzeum ❺**. In the center of Fő tér is the **Szentháromság szobor ❻**. Continue walking on the right side of the square, and you will come across the **Rómaikori Kőtár ❼**. Just after the museum, Fő tér turns into Templom utca, and at this junction is the Gothic **Kecske templom ❽**, which according

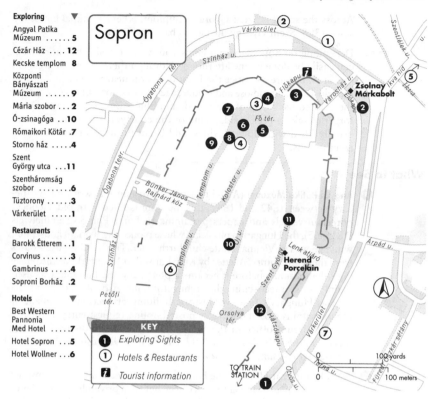

KEY

① Exploring Sights

① Hotels & Restaurants

🛈 Tourist information

to legend was constructed with treasure unearthed by a goat. Inside the church visit the Középkori Káptalan, a former burial chapel. The ceiling fresco inside the room depicts Franciscan saints and dates back to 1779. A few feet farther along Templom utca, at No. 2, is the **Központi Bányászati Múzeum** ⑨, which displays several centuries of Hungarian mining artifacts in a blue baroque building

From here you can continue down Templom utca, admiring the rows of quaint, colored houses, or you can backtrack to far-right corner of Fő tér, past the Angyal Patika Múzeum, and take a right down Új utca. At No. 22, is the **Ó-zsinagóga** ⑩. Continue down Új utca, whose name means "new street" in Hungarian but which is actually one of the Sopron's oldest streets. Prior to 1440, it was called Zsidó utca (Jew Street) and was mainly a Jewish neighborhood. Új utca ends at the small Orsolya tér, where a tall Gothic building houses the Római Katolikus Egyházművészeti Gyűjtemény; though interesting, the collection is rarely open.

As you approach the square, go left across it and take another left onto **Szent György utca** (St. George street) ⑪. A few feet up the street, at the first corner is the **Cézár Ház** ⑫. If you continue along Szent György utca, you'll see several other interesting buildings, including Sopron's richest rococo structure at No. 16 and the Eggenberg Ház two doors down.

Across the street is Szent György Templom, where a chapel has stood since 1398. Szent György utca leads back to Fő tér.

TIMING Depending on how many museums you want to visit, the entire walk can easily be done in one afternoon. Although there are many sights in this area, be sure to notice the front doors on nearly every building in the Old Town. Grandiose and unique, each set of doors stands out against the colored backdrop of green, red, and blue-painted buildings. Don't forget to take a peek inside many of the courtyards as well. They are usually filled with flowers, vines, and beautiful light streaming down from the sky.

What to See

❺ **Angyal Patika Múzeum** (Angel Pharmacy Museum). A working apothecary between 1642 and 1647, this museum is filled with old Viennese porcelain vessels and papers pertaining to Ignaz Philipp Semmelweis (1815–65), the Hungarian physician whose pioneering work in antiseptics, while he was in Vienna, made childbirth safer. The building itself dates from the 16th century. A letter by King Lajos II in 1525 forbade the building's demolition—before it became a pharmacy, the building was used mainly for storage—citing the architectural integrity of Fő tér. This letter was Hungary's first ever historic building protection document. If the museum is closed during its posted hours, request entry at the Soproni Múzeum office in the Storno Ház (➪ see the listing, *below*). ⊠ *Fő tér 2* ☎ *99/311–327* ⬛ *300 HUF* ⊘ *Apr.–Oct., usually Tues.–Sun. 9:30–2; Nov.–Mar., Tues.–Sun. 10–2.*

⓬ **Cézár Ház** (Cézár House). The Hungarian parliament met in the upstairs rooms here in 1681; the same space now houses a privately endowed museum, created by the widow of József Soproni-Horváth (1891–1961), a remarkable artist who prefixed his hometown's name to his own so he wouldn't be just another "Joe Croat" (*Horváth* means "Croat," in Hungarian). Famous for the wonders he worked with watercolors, Soproni-Horváth used the fragile medium to bring large surfaces to life in a density usually associated with oil paintings while depicting realistic scenes, such as a girl grieving over her drowned sister's body. A wine cellar offers the opportunity to sit with a glass of wine. ⊠ *Hátsókapú u. 2* ☎ *99/312–326* ⬛ *200 HUF* ⊘ *Thurs., Fri., and Sun. 10–1, Sat. 10–1 and 3–6.*

❽ **Kecske templom** (Goat Church). Legend has it that the early Gothic (1280–1300) church takes its name from a medieval billy goat that scratched up a treasure, enabling the Franciscans to build a church on the site (the Benedictines took over in 1802). More likely, however, the name comes from the figures of goats carved into its crests: the coat of arms of the Gutsch family, who financed the church. The Goat Church has a soaring, pointed, 14th-century steeple, three naves, and its original Gothic choir (betraying French influence). After several rebuildings, there are also a Hungarian Gothic-baroque red-marble pulpit, a rococo main altar, baroque altars, and a painting of St. Stephen by one of the Stornos. The church stands before the Holy Trinity Column in Fő tér. ⊠ *Templom u. 1* ⬛ *Free (donations accepted)* ⊘ *Daily 10–noon and 2–5.*

⑨ Központi Bányászati Múzeum (Central Museum of Mining). Hungarian mining dates back to the 10th century AD; indeed, gold and silver mining played a vital role in the country's trade in precious metals and mining up until the discovery of the so-called New World, when gold was more often imported. The museum features murals showing the first mine blast in Slovakia in 1627 and the discovery of Hungary's first coal mine near Sopron. Also on hand are the ornamental pieces created by silversmiths that decorated noblemen's tables in jewel-studded splendor, as well as paintings and statues. Tour a nobleman's baroque townhouse and view various antiquities and works of art, including samples of hundreds of minerals found in the Carpathian basin. ⊠ *Templom u. 2* ☎ *99/312–667* ⊕ *www.kbm.hu* ⊠ *300 HUF* ⊗ *Apr.–Oct., Tues.–Sun. 10–6; Nov.–Mar., Tues.–Sun. 10–4.*

② Mária szobor (St. Mary's Column). With its finely sculpted Biblical reliefs, the column is a superb specimen of baroque design. It was built in 1745 to mark the former site of the medieval Church of Our Lady, which was destroyed by Sopron citizens in 1632 because they feared the Turks would use its steeple as a strategic firing tower. ⊠ *At the Előkapu (Front Gate).*

need a break? | Red-velvety chairs, an ornate chandelier, a semi-spiraling wooden staircase, and scrumptious pastry are the hallmarks of the cozy little **Dömötöri cukrászda** (⊠ Széchenyi tér, at the corner of Erszébet u. ☎ 99/506–623) on Sopron's second-most famous—and largest—square. In summer, there are plenty of tables with umbrellas on an outside terrace. Be sure to notice footwear on the waitresses: open-toed and open-heeled white boots laced halfway up the calves, a popular shoe under Communism.

⑩ Ó-zsinagóga (Old Synagogue). The medieval synagogue, complete with a stone *mikva*, a ritual bath for women, is now a religious museum with old Torahs on display and an exhibit about the World War II deportation of the Jews. Built around 1300, it endured several incarnations over the centuries, including a stint as a hospital (in the 1400s) and a residential building (in the 1700s). Restored in 1973, the existing facade dates from 1734. A plaque honors the 1,640 Jews of Sopron who were murdered by the Nazis—the quiet street that is home to this and another old synagogue a few doors away, at No. 11, became the city's Jewish ghetto in May 1944. Only 274 of Sopron's Jews survived, and today there are scarcely enough to muster a *minyan* (quorum of 10), let alone a congregation. ⊠ *Új u. 22* ☎ *99/311–327* ⊠ *400 HUF* ⊗ *May–Sept., Wed.–Mon. 10–6; Oct., Wed.–Mon. 10–2.*

⑦ Rómaikori Kőtár (Roman Archaeology Museum). A fine Renaissance courtyard leads to the churchlike vaulted medieval cellar—a perfect setting for the gigantic statues of Jupiter, Juno, and Minerva unearthed beneath the main square during the digging of foundations for the city hall in the late 19th century. On the second floor a separate museum (with identical hours and admission prices) re-creates the living environment of 17th- and 18th-century Sopron apartments. ⊠ *Fő tér 6* ☎ *99/311–*

DENTAL TOURISM?

IN ADDITION TO BEING THE MUSEUM HUB OF HUNGARY, *Sopron calls itself the world's dental capital, with an estimated one dentist to every 80 residents. Along Sopron city streets, especially the main boulevard, Várkerület, are many dental practices specializing in implants and prostheses. Thousands of Austrians and Germans cross into Sopron on a regular basis for a day at the dentist—at prices 40 to 60 percent cheaper than in their native countries— usually to be combined with shopping or a trip to one of Hungary's thermal spas.*

An estimated 1,000 dentists can be found in Sopron and in the nearby border towns of Szombathely and Mosonmagyaróvár. But for the average Hungarian, such a dental trip is out of the question, since most Sopron dentists charge, at the very least, Budapest-style prices for dentistry, which are out of reach of the average Hungarian.

Austrian and German dentists have reported major drops in business. The Austrian Dental Association has even campaigned to ban Hungarian dentists from advertising across the border, while dentists in Austria and Germany publicly rail against Hungarian dentists for poor workmanship, but this hasn't slowed down dental tourism in Sopron. More and more dentists are migrating to the city to set up an office, according to tourism officials. This is good news for Sopron since the average dental tourist spends several days in Sopron while having their teeth fixed, spending money in local shops, attractions, restaurants, and hotels, most of which have a dentist on staff, or at least one they recommend.

327 ✉ 500 HUF for each museum ⊙ Apr.–Oct., Tues.–Sun. 10–6; Nov.–Mar., Tues.–Sun. 10–2.

❹ Storno Ház (Storno House). Right on the exquisite main square, the turFodor'sChoice reted house is the city's finest Renaissance-era building. Inside its two-★ story loggia is the restaurant Corvinus (see ⇨ Where to Stay & Eat), which is downstairs; upstairs, a museum houses a remarkable family collection of furniture, porcelain, sculptures, and paintings. The Stornos were a rags-to-riches dynasty of chimney sweeps who, over several generations, bought or just relieved grateful owners of unwanted treasures and evolved into a family of painters and sculptors themselves. The dynasty died out in Hungary in the late 1990s but a few remaining distant relatives agreed with the Hungarian state that nothing should be removed from the Storno House. On an exterior wall hangs a plaque commemorating visits by King Matthias Corvinus (winter 1482–83) and Liszt Ferenc (1840 and 1881). The museum can be visited by guided tour only, given every half hour (the last tour begins ½ hr before closing). ⊠ Fő tér 8 ☎ 99/311–327 ✉ 800 HUF ⊙ Apr.–Oct., Tues.–Sun. 10–6; Nov.–Mar., Tues.–Sun. 10–2, with tours every ½ hr.

⑪ Szent György utca (St. George Street). Numerous dragons of religion and architecture coexist in a somewhat harmonious fashion. The **Erdődy Vár** (Erdődy Palace), at No. 16, is Sopron's richest rococo building. Two doors down, at No. 12, stands the **Eggenberg Ház** (Eggenberg House), where the widow of Prince Johann Eggenberg held Protestant services during the harshest days of the Counter-Reformation and beyond. But the street takes its name from **Szent György templom** (St. George's Church), a 14th-century Catholic church so sensitively "baroqued" some 300 years later that its interior is still as soft as whipped cream. The church is generally open daily from 9 to 5; the other buildings are not open to the public.

⑥ Szentháromság szobor (Holy Trinity Column). The centerpiece of Fő tér is a sparkling, spiraling three-tiered monument aswirl with gilded angels. It represents the earliest (1701) and loveliest baroque monument to a plague in all of Hungary—in this case, the country's great plague, which lasted from 1695 to 1701. Kneeling figures carved in the pedestal represent the married couple who ordered the statue's work from the sculptor.

③ Tűztorony (Fire Tower). The symbol of the Sopron's endurance—and entranceway to the Old City—is 200 feet high, with foundations dating to the days of the Árpád dynasty (9th–13th centuries) and perhaps back to the Romans. The tower is remarkable for its uniquely harmonious blend of architectural styles: it has a Romanesque base rising to a circular balcony of Renaissance loggias topped by an octagonal clock tower that is itself capped by a brass baroque onion dome and belfry. The upper portions were rebuilt after most of the earlier Fire Tower was, ironically, destroyed by the Great Fire of 1676, which was started by students roasting chestnuts in a high wind. Throughout the centuries the tower bell tolled the alarm for fire or the death of a prominent citizen, and from the loggias musicians trumpeted the approach of an enemy or serenaded the citizenry. Both warning concerts were accompanied by flags (red for fire, blue for enemy) pointing in the direction of danger. Today you can take in good views of the town and surrounding countryside from the top of the tower. ⊠ *Fő tér* ☎ *99/311–327* 💴 *500 HUF* ☺ *Apr.–Oct., Tues.–Sun. 10–5.*

FodorśChoice
★

① Várkerület. Strolling along the circular boulevard that embraces Sopron's inner core allows you to take in the vibrant harmony of beautifully preserved baroque and rococo architecture and the fashionable shops and cafés of Sopron's thriving downtown business district.

off the beaten path

ESZTERHÁZY PALACE – The magnificent yellow baroque palace, built between 1720 and 1760 as a residence for the Hungarian noble family, is prized as one of the country's most exquisite palaces. Though badly damaged in World War II, it has been painstakingly restored, making it clear why in its day the palace was referred to as the Hungarian Versailles. Its 126 rooms include a lavish Hall of Mirrors and a three-story-high concert hall, where classical concerts are held in summer (usually Saturday at 6 PM). Joseph Haydn, court conductor to the Eszterházy family here for 30 years, is the subject of a small museum inside. Slippers—mandatory, to preserve the palace floors—are provided at the entrance. The palace lies 27 km (17 mi) southeast of Sopron, in Fertőd. ✉ *Bartók Béla u. 2, just off Rte. 85, Fertőd* ☎ *99/537–640* ✍ *1,000 HUF* ⊙ *Mid-Mar.–mid-Oct., Tues.–Sun. 9–5; mid-Oct.–mid-Mar., Tues.–Sun. 9–4.*

WHERE TO STAY & EAT

$–$$ ✕ **Barokk Étterem.** Specialties include meat fondue for two, trout, and veal with chicken-liver stuffing. Entrance to the restaurant is through a lovely courtyard, which is crammed by day with racks of merchandise from the neighboring boutiques. Pastels and modern fixtures fill the dining room, which has an arched ceiling. ✉ *Várkerület 25* ☎ *99/312–227* ▭ *AE, MC, V* ⊙ *Closed Sun.*

$–$$ ✕ **Corvinus.** The location, in the 700-year-old Storno House off So-
Fodor'sChoice pron's delightful cobblestone main square—the city's historic heart—
★ couldn't be better. The Corvinus itself combines a café, pub, pizzeria, and restaurant all in one. Among the Hungarian specialties are a meaty soup with a baked-on pastry cap, and roasted goose liver. Service is formal yet friendly, whether you dine inside under vaulted ceilings or at an outdoor table. ✉ *Fő tér 7–8* ☎ *99/505–035* ▭ *AE, DC, MC, V.*

$–$$ ✕ **Gambrinus.** This comfortable, simply furnished restaurant serves up Hungarian fare and grilled meats with few frills and is especially popular at lunchtime, when crowds of Austrian shoppers from across the border often fill its tables. Gambrinus and its attached hotel sit in a 700-year-old building on Sopron's main square. ✉ *Fő tér 3* ☎ *99/339–966* ▭ *No credit cards.*

$ ✕ **Soproni Borház.** This 300-year-old wine cellar just off the city's main
Fodor'sChoice shopping boulevard offers tastings of 300 different Hungarian wines,
★ including some made in Sopron. Your wine is ordered with a plate of accompanying light fare, which might include goose liver, salami, pork, sausage, and several types of vegetables. Servers are extremely friendly and will give you an earful on every wine you try. Try the Hungarian *almapaprika* (apple pepper), which is a round yellow pepper soaked in vinegar and spices and marinated for several days. The dish can be quite hot if you get a good batch. ✉ *Várkerület u. 15* ☎ *99/510–022* ▭ *No credit cards.*

$–$$ 🏨 **Best Western Pannonia Med Hotel.** There has been a hotel here since the 17th century, when the Golden Hind first welcomed stagecoaches traveling between Budapest and Vienna. It was destroyed in a fire but rebuilt in neoclassical style in 1893. With soaring ceilings, dripping chandeliers, and a breakfast room with gilt-edge mirrors and little golden chairs, the hotel is now quite elegant. Standard rooms are comfortable and smart, but they pale in comparison to the handsome suites, which have huge wooden beds and are furnished with antiques. Some services are noteworthy: it's not every hotel that has its own cosmetic-surgery consultant. In keeping with the Sopron spirit, there's also an on-site dentist offering free screenings. ✉ *Várkerület 75, H-9400* ☎ *99/312–180* 🖷 *99/340–766* ⊕ *www.pannoniahotel.com* ⇌ *48 rooms, 14 suites* ⚿ *Restaurant, in-room data ports, pool, gym, hair salon, sauna, spa, bar, meeting rooms, free parking* ▭ *AE, DC, MC, V* ⧖ *BP.*

★ $ ⌂ **Hotel Sopron.** There's no getting around the Hotel Sopron's outdated 1980s-era appearance, so the management wisely emphasizes the panoramic city views and services and amenities. Many, but not all, of the brown and beige rooms do have great views of Sopron's Old Town. As for services, the hotel can organize everything from wine-tasting tours to scenic train trips, as well as the ubiquitous dental services. ✉ *Fövényverem u. 7, H-9400* ☎ *99/512–261* 🖷 *99/311–090* ⊕ *www. hotelsopron.hu* ⟲ *106 rooms, 6 suites* ⚴ *Restaurant, minibars, cable TV, 2 tennis courts, pool, gym, sauna, bicycles, bar, playground, meeting room; no a/c in some rooms* ☰ *AE, DC, MC, V* ⎆ *BP.*

¢–$ ⌂ **Hotel Wollner.** Tucked inside the city center, this quiet and charming

Fodor's Choice

★ 18th-century hotel has been restored to its original splendor, as the proud staff will attest. Aside from the exquisite baroque interior, the best thing about the Wollner is a courtyard within the hotel, where there is plenty of outdoor seating in a amid flowers and greenery. On the wall of the courtyard is a cenotaph from the Roman age brought to the hotel by a former owner in 1756. ✉ *Templom u. 20, H-9400* ☎ *99/524–400* 🖷 *99/524–401* ⊕ *www.wollner.hu* ⟲ *18 rooms* ⚴ *Restaurant, in-room data ports, minibars, cable TV, gym, massage, sauna, bar, wine bar, conference room, parking (fee), no-smoking rooms* ☰ *AE, DC. MC, V* ⎆ *BP.*

NIGHTLIFE & THE ARTS

From mid- to late March, Sopron's cultural life warms up during the annual **Tavaszi Fesztivál** (Spring Festival), which coincides with Budapest's famous Spring Festival. On hand are classical concerts, folk-dance performances, and other events. Get details from Tourinform (see ⇨ Visitor Information, *in* Sopron Essentials). The peak season for cultural events is from mid-June through mid-July, when the **Sopron Ünnepi Hetek** (Sopron Festival Weeks) brings music, dance, and theater performances and art exhibits to churches and venues around town. ☎ *99/511–730 for Theater & Festival Office.*

SPORTS & THE OUTDOORS

The forested hills of the Fertő-Hanság National Park around Sopron have many well-marked hiking trails. Ask for a map and advice at Tourinform (see ⇨ Visitor Information, *in* Sopron Essentials).

☺ **Bobtrack.** Several miles outside Sopron on the Bécsi Hill (Vienna Hill), the Bobtrack is an outdoor luge of sorts that winds down the hill. Special sleds are used to navigate the Bobtrack throughout the summer and winter months. To reach the Bobtrack, take Route 84 about 4 mi from Sopron's city center to the Tercia Hubertusz Restaurant; there's a small admission booth in the hotel's parking lot. ✉ *Bécsi Hill* ☎ *99/334–266* 🎫 *280 HUF* ⊙ *Apr.–Oct., daily 10–4, Nov.–Mar., daily 11–4.*

SHOPPING

Várkerület is Sopron's main shopping street, where you'll find loads of shops both along the street and in courtyards, where vendors and booths hawk spices, clothing, shoes, and Hungarian wines.

Herend Porcelain Manufactory. Next door to the Herend Village Pottery is a small shop devoted to the famous Herend porcelain, whose history began with a purchase by England's Queen Victoria in 1851, when Windsor Castle ordered a dinner set from the company. ⊠ *Szent György u. 11* ☎ *99/508–712.*

Herend Village Pottery. This shop sells highly colorful patterns bearing a more relaxed style and lower prices than traditional Herend porcelain. It's next door to the Herend Porcelain Manufactory store. ⊠ *Szent György u. 11* ☎ *99/329–681.*

Zsolnay Márkabolt. If you can't make it to the less expensive factory outlet in Pécs, you can purchase exquisite Zsolnay porcelain here. A tiny room lined with glass cabinets displays the delicate wares. ⊠ *Előkapu u. 11* ☎ *99/311–367.*

A STOP IN GYŐR

The largest city in western Hungary, Győr, is often called the "Town of Rivers," sitting at the confluence of the Raba, Rabca, and Mosoni-Danube rivers. Győr is positioned in the middle of Hungary's *Kisalföld* (Little Plain) and dates back some 2,000 years. With a population of 130,000, it's in the middle of the direct route between Budapest and Vienna and is an automatic train stop along the way to Sopron.

The city has seen occupations by Romans, Tatars, Teutons, and Huns. And even though a former city fortress was built by Italian engineers, it was not strong enough to hold back the Turks, who took Győr in 1594. The fortress was later destroyed by Napoléon Bonaparte.

Although downtown Győr, where the three rivers meet, is packed with baroque buildings and museums, the outskirts of the town are mainly industrial, much of it owing to the city's geographical location at the rivers' confluence. Highlights include a 12th-century cathedral and several art museums with renowned collections. If your timing is right, you could also catch a performance by the Győr Ballet, the country's most renowned ballet company.

What to See

The ancient heart of Győr is at the confluence of the three rivers, called *Káptalan Domb* (Chapter Hill). Here you can see the **Püspöki vár** (Bishop's Palace), the residence of Győr bishops whose oldest section dates back to the 13th century. Unfortunately, it's not open to the public. Káptalan Domb is a good place to wander around, however, through a maze of fences and wonderfully curved gates surrounding baroque-style homes.

Fodor'sChoice
★

Next to the Püspöki vár is the **Püspöki katedra** (Bishop's Cathedral), which has Romanesque, Gothic, and baroque features. Inside, special ornaments and frescoes of the black altar were painted by A. F. Maulbertsch, who decorated many Hungarian churches in the 18th century. The bishop's throne was a gift from Empress Maria Theresa. The frame of a painting depicting the Blessed Virgin and baby Jesus is considered a rococo masterpiece. Just inside the entrance is **Szent László Chapel** (St. Leslie Chapel), devoted to the canonized monarch who ruled Győr rom 1077 to 1095. Beautifully moulded, a 15th-century bust of the saint is an excellent example of medieval Hungarian goldsmithing. ⊠ *Apor Vilmos Püspök tere* 🕾 *No phone* ▣ *Free* ☉ *Daily 9:15–12 and 2–6.*

Directly behind the cathedral is the former home of a bishop that is now the **Miklós Borsos Múzeum.** A prominent 20th-century sculptor, Borsos was a self-taught artist who designed several important Hungarian statues. In the courtyard of the building are several bronze and stone figures. ⊠ *Apor Vilmos Püspök tere 2* 🕾 *96/316–329* ⊕ *www.gyor-muzeum.hu* ▣ *300 HUF* ☉ *Mar.–Oct., Tues.–Sun. 10–6; Nov.–Feb., Tues.–Sun. 10–5.*

Walk down Káptalan Domb to reach the **Dunakapu tér** (Danube Gate square), a waterfront area where grain ships once docked and where open-air markets are still held on Wednesdays and Saturdays. At the square you will also see an iron weathercock, the symbol of Győr, created by the Turkish army after it took the fortress in 1594.

From Dunakapu tér, Jedlik Ányos utca runs along the western side of the square, ending at **Széchenyi tér** (Szechenyi Square), Győr's main square. Monuments adorning this square are the setting for the annual recreation of a "Baroque Marriage," a traditional ceremony where baroque music is played and participants dress up in ornate wedding outfits and perform for viewers in the square. The marriage is held every summer during the Győr Summer Festival.

A former 19th-century spice house, the Iron Stump House now houses the **Patkó Imre Gyűjtemény** (Imre Patko Collection), named in honor of an art historian who collected African and Oceanic applied arts. The museum also has an impressive display of Hungarian and European fine art from the 20th century. A log spiked with nails stands in the corner of the house; it was marked by travelers passing through who noted their journeys on it. ⊠ *Széchenyi tér 4* 🕾 *96/310–588* ▣ *300 HUF* ☉ *Apr.–Sept., Tues.–Sun. 10–6, Oct.–Nov., by appointment only.*

North of Széchenyi tér, the **Váczy Péter Gyűjtemény** (Peter Vaczy Collection) is on a small roundabout in a former retirement home. The collection of 17th- and 18th-century paintings, sculptures, and furniture comes from Hungary and all over Europe. Among the most important works in the collection are a 15th-century painting of Mary and Jesus, a biblical scene by Sebastian Bourdon, some 16th-century leather-and-velvet armchairs, a Giacomo Piazetta table, and a richly carved Italian dish holder. ⊠ *Nefeljcs köz 3* 🕾 *96/318–141* ⊕ *www.gyor-muzeum.hu* ▣ *300 HUF* ☉ *Mar.–Oct., Tues.–Sun. 10–6; Nov.–Feb., Tues.–Sun. 10–5.*

Where to Eat

★ **\$\$–\$\$\$\$** ✕ **Fonte.** Expensive by Győr standards, this restaurant is in the Hotel Fonte, in the downtown historic district, and has a great reputation among locals as a special-occasion spot. The menu includes a wide range of Hungarian classics plus international dishes, and there is a long wine list to boot. A large outdoor garden offers seating in the summer months. ✉ *Schweidel u. 17* ☎ *96/513–810* ▤ *AE, DC, MC, V.*

\$–\$\$ ✕ **Várkapu Vendéglő.** Set on a lovely square on Káptalan Domb, close to the Bishop's Palace, Várkapu has a wide selection of meat dishes, particularly steak, and a range of Hungarian salads. ✉ *Bécsi kapu tér 7* ☎ *96/328–685* ▤ *No credit cards.*

Nightlife & Arts

Győri Balett (Győr Ballet). Hungary's most famous and acclaimed ballet company performs regularly at Győr's Nemzeti Színház (National Theater). ✉ *Czuczor Gergely u. 7* ☎ *96/312–044.*

Győr Nemzetközi Fesztivál (Győr International Festival). The festival takes place in June and July with a series of events, including ballet, theater, folk dancing, folk music, classical music, and a massive handicraft fair. For information contact the local Tourinform office (see ⇨ Visitor Information *in* Sopron Essentials).

off the beaten path

PANNONHALMA APÁTSÁG (Pannonhalma Abbey) – Perched proudly above the countryside on top of a high hill roughly 20 km (12 mi) southeast of Győr and 135 km (84 mi) west of Budapest— the vast, 1,000-some-year-old Benedictine abbey still gleams like a gift from heaven. During the Middle Ages, it was an important ecclesiastical center and also wielded considerable political influence. It housed Hungary's first school and is said to be the first place the Holy Scriptures were read on Hungarian soil. It's still a working monastery and school; 60 monks and 320 students live here. A late-Gothic cloister and a 180-foot neoclassical tower are the two stylistic exceptions to the predominantly baroque architecture. A library of more than 300,000 volumes houses some priceless medieval documents, including one of the first known examples of written Hungarian: the 11th-century deed to the abbey of Tihany. Visits are permitted only with a guide, which is included in the admission price. Tours begin every hour on the hour; the last one of the day begins at the closing hour listed below. There are regularly scheduled English- and other foreign-language tours at 11 and 1 from late March to mid-November. Occasional organ recitals are held in the basilica in summer. ✉ *Off Rte. 82, south of Győr, Pannonhalma* ☎ *96/570–191* 🖷 *96/570–192* ⊕ *www.osb.hu* 🎟 *500 HUF (800 HUF for a foreign-language guide)* ☉ *Late Mar.–May and Oct.–mid-Nov., Tues.–Sun. 9–4; June–Sept., daily 9–5; mid-Nov.–late Mar., Tues.–Sun. 10–3. Monastery closed Sun. mornings except for those wishing to attend mass; library and yard remain open to tours.*

Sopron Essentials

BUS TRAVEL

Buses running between Budapest and Sopron, and Budapest and Győr travel regularly throughout the day. Prices are calculated by mileage and the type of bus, with newer, more comfortable buses costing more. Although bus and train travel times and costs are roughly equivalent, trains tend to be much more comfortable.

🚌 **Volánbusz** ✉ District XI, Etele tér, South Buda, Budapest ☎ 1/382-4900 ⊕ www.volanbusz.hu.

CAR TRAVEL

By car from Budapest, Győr is approximately 123 km (76 mi) west, along Motor Way 1 (E75). Hungary has five toll motorways, referred to as M0, M1, M7, M5, and M3. To drive on these toll roads, you must first stop at a gasoline station and buy a *matrica* (toll pass), affixing it to the lower left inside of your car's windshield. A matrica generally costs about HUF 1,000 and is valid for four days. The distance from Győr to Sopron is 87 km (54 mi) along Highway 85, a local road that does not require the toll pass.

TRAIN TRAVEL

The easiest way to get to Sopron is by train, as the entire three-hour trip, with a connection in Győr, offers a lovely view of the western Hungarian countryside and time to enjoy it. Trains running between Sopron and Budapest depart from Budapest's Keleti Pályaudvar (Eastern Train Station) about every 30 minutes throughout the day, with the last train to Budapest returning approximately 8 PM from Sopron, about 9 PM from Győr. For train timetables and prices check out : ⊕ www.elivira.hu. Tickets can be bought at any of Budapest's three train stations or at many travel agencies in town.

VISITOR INFORMATION

Tourinform offices have loads of information and brochures on Sopron, Győr, and the surrounding areas. They can also help arrange excursions outside the cities, including trips to Eszterházy Palace and Pannonhalma Abbey. The main Tourinform office in Sopron is conveniently just inside Sopron's Old Town, just past the archway on the right; a smaller branch office is inside the Liszt Ferenc Kultura Center, just off Széchenyi tér.

🏛 **Tourinform** ✉ Előkapu u. 11, Sopron ☎ 99/338-892 ⊕ www.tourinform.sopron.hu ✉ Liszt Ferenc u. 1, Sopron ☎ 99/517-500 ✉ Árpád u. 32, Győr ☎ 96/316-329.

PÉCS
WITH VILLÁNY

10

By Botsy
Maury

WESTERN HUNGARY, OFTEN REFERRED TO AS TRANSDANUBIA (*Dunántúl* in Hungarian), is the area south and west of the Danube, stretching to the Slovak and Austrian borders in the west and north and to Slovenia and Croatia in the south. It presents a highly picturesque landscape, including several ranges of hills and small mountains. Most of its surface is covered with farmland, vineyards, and orchards—all nurtured and made verdant by a climate that is noticeably more humid than in the rest of the country.

Pécs (pronounced *paytch*), the southern capital of Transdanubia, dates back to the Roman period, when the city was known as Sopianae and the southern Transdanubia region known as Pannonia. For centuries it was a frontier province and an important stop along the trade route; today it is far richer in Roman ruins than the rest of Hungary. The city played an important role during the Middle Ages as well; in 1009, St. Stephen set up a diocese in Pécs to help cement Christianity among the Magyar tribes. It was a thriving city up until the Turkish Conquest in 1543, and their 143-year rule left a distinct imprint on the city as well. While the Hapsburgs later destroyed or converted many of the Ottoman buildings, Pécs is home to many of Hungary's most important remaining Turkish-era sites. The latter half of the 19th century was important in Pécs, for it saw the rise of local hero, Vilmos Zsolnay, whose Secession-style ceramics company would go on to define the city and become one of Hungary's national treasures.

Today Pécs is a vibrant and dynamic university town, rich with historic sites. There are early Christian burial tombs, a magnificent basilica, two mosques dating back to the Turkish occupation, and a handsome synagogue. One can hardly walk a few blocks in Pécs and not see some fanciful Zsolnay tiles adorning a building or roof. On top of that, this small city is home to seven museums. Three of them—the Zsolnay, Vasarely, and Csontváry—justify a two- or three-day stay in this sparkling, eclectic city in the Mecsek Hills. Once in Pécs a detour to the nearby town of Villány, which is in one of Hungary's most fertile wine-producing regions, is a pleasant overnight excursion, particularly if you can sit under the stars and taste some of Hungary's prize vintages.

About the Hotels & Restaurants

There's a good cross-section of hotels available in Pécs to meet any budget, everything from full-service hotels to modest panzios catering to visiting students. Most hotels quote prices in euros, while some of the smaller panzios use forints for their prices. Although there's no real high season in Pécs—the city is popular year-round—summer does bring many small festivals. The city is also a favorite for Hungarian weddings from April through October, when hotels can get booked solid.

Dining in Pécs can be a much more laid-back affair than in Budapest, and you can expect prices to be significantly lower for a good meal. Although there are a few white-glove restaurants in the city, by and large you'll find dining more informal. The dress code everywhere seems to be smart and casual. Pécs is in the heart of southern Transdanubia, known for its honey, chestnut, and peach production, so don't miss a chance to try one of the many rich desserts made from these local products.

WHAT IT COSTS In Euros & Forints				
$$$$	$$$	$$	$	¢
HOTELS IN EUROS	over €225	€175–€225	€125–€175	€75–€125	under €75
HOTELS IN FORINTS	over 56,000	44,000–56,000	31,000–44,000	18,500–31,000	under 18,500
RESTAURANTS IN FORINTS	over 3,500	2,500–3,500	1,500–2,500	800–1,500	under 800

Hotel prices are for two people in a standard double room with a private bath and breakfast during peak season (June through August). Restaurant prices are per person for a main course at dinner and include 15% tax but not service.

EXPLORING PÉCS

Pécs is best explored on foot as some of the downtown area is blocked off to cars. The city is small enough to tour in a day but rich enough with attractions that you could spend a leisurely weekend exploring the area. Take time to meander through the side streets for glimpses of the Zsolnay tiles that adorn random buildings throughout the city.

Numbers in the margin correspond to numbers on the Pécs map.

a good walk

Begin at the base of Széchényi tér, where you can admire the distinctive eosin tile of the **Zsolnay Fountain ❶**. Walk up the hill past the *Nádor Szálló*, once the most famous hotel in Pécs but now shuttered, though under renovation at this writing. Across from the hotel is the **Belvárosi plébánia templom ❷**, a former 15th-century mosque that still retains its distinctive form. Walk up the hill on Hunyadi út, where you will pass a small park at the corner of Papnövelde utca. The Ezsperanto Park, built in 1966, is perhaps the only reminder in Hungary of the former enthusiasm for a single European language (esperanto).

Turn right on Káptalan utca, where you will find most of the city's important museums. On the right is the **Zsolnay Múzeum ❸**; to the left, are the **Vasarely Múzeum ❹** and the **Endre Nemes Múzeum ❺**. Walk to the end of the street and turn left; down the hill toward Janus Pannonius utca, where you'll find the **Csontváry Múzeum ❻**. From there, go right (left if you're exiting the museum) to **Dóm tér ❼** and the **Pécs Bazilika ❽**. A ticket to the basilica will get you into the tiny Peter & Paul Catacombs (to the right side of the basilica) where you can see Christian frescoes from the fourth century. To the left of the basilica is the diocese residence, and on the left balcony there's a metal statue of a somewhat wobbly-looking Franz Liszt, the great composer. Liszt became a devout Catholic in his later days after a rabble-rousing youth and paid frequent visits to the bishop of Pécs; however, the statue reminds us that it's far from certain that Liszt's Catholicism went hand in hand with a sober and austere life. Given that the statue is known locally as *a hányás* (the barf), it's likely that he didn't suddenly become a teetotaller.

Exit Dóm tér and walk back toward Janus Pannonius utca and enter Szent István tér. You will be walking among the early Christian cemetery chapels and tombs from the fourth century that are in the long process of excavation. Here is where you'll find the World Heritage Site of the **Ókeresztény mauzóleum** ❾. Bear to the right to leave the burial grounds by walking down the hill on St. István tér until you get to Ferencesek utca. Stay on the right side until you reach the intersection with Korház tér, and then continue to walk down Rákóczi út. You can get a good look of Pécs's Roman walls from here. If you continue down Rákóczi út, you will see on your right the **Jákovali Hászan Múzeum** ❿ on the site of a Turkish mosque. Walk around to the back, and you can still see at the original minaret. Backtrack to Ferencesek utca and walk back to Szechényi tér.

TIMING Pécs can get hot in the summer months, but the city will be less crowded because of the depleted student population. However, autumn is the most pleasant time to visit Pécs and neighboring Villány, when both towns have wine festivals.

What to See

❷ **Belvárosi plébánia templom** (Inner City Parish Church). Széchenyi tér is crowned by a delightful 16th-century former Turkish mosque. Dating from the years of Turkish occupation (1543–1686), the mosque is now a Catholic church, which you might infer from the cross that surmounts the gilded crescent atop the dome. Despite the fierce religious war raging on its walls—Christian statuary and frescoes beneath Turkish arcades and *mihrabs* (prayer niches)—this church, also known as the Gazi Khassim Pasha Jammi, remains the largest and finest relic of Turkish architecture in Hungary. ⊠ *Széchenyi tér* 🎟 *Free* ☉ *Mid-Apr.–mid-Oct., Mon.–Sat. 10–4, Sun. 11:30–4; mid-Oct.–mid-Apr., Mon.–Sat. 11–noon, Sun. 11:30–2.*

need a break? If you need something warm to keep you going stop by **Aranygaluska Gyorsetterem** (⊠ Irgalmasok utcaja 23–27 ☏ No phone), just off Széchenyi tér, for cheap, Hungarian comfort food served cafeteria-style

★❻ **Csontváry Múzeum** (Csontváry Museum). Mihály Tivadar Csontváry Kosztka (1853–1919) was a pharmacist who worked, as he put it, to "catch up with, let alone surpass, the great masters." An early expressionist and forerunner of surrealism, Csontváry's work even influenced Picasso. His paintings can be seen today almost exclusively here and in a room of the Hungarian National Gallery in Budapest.

The paintings in the five rooms of this museum are arranged in chronological order, to show Csontváry's progression from soulful portraits to seemingly conventional landscapes executed with decidedly unconventional colors to his 1904 *Temple of Zeus in Athens*—about which Csontváry said, "This is the first painting in which the canvas can no longer be seen." After a 1905 tryout in Budapest, Csontváry was ready for a 1907 exhibition in Paris, which turned out to be a huge critical success. Not long after finishing his last great epic painting, *Mary at the Well in Nazareth* (1908), his ego got the best of him. Though his canvases grew ever larger, Csontváry finished nothing that he started after 1909 except a patriotic drawing of Emperor Franz Joseph, completed at the start of World War I in 1914. Indeed, the final room is filled only

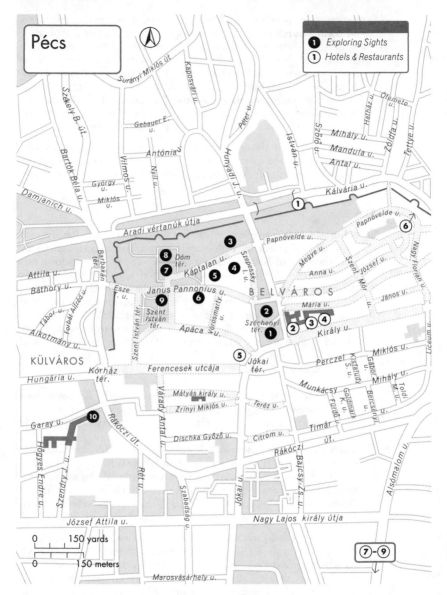

Pécs

❶ Exploring Sights
① Hotels & Restaurants

0 — 150 yards
0 — 150 meters

with sketches. After he died in Budapest in 1919, his canvases were about to be reused as furniture covers when a collector from Pécs named Gedeon Gerlóczy rescued them for 10,000 HUF.

The museum, which is considered to be one of the three major galleries in Pécs, sits just around the corner from its peers. If you've just left the Vasarely, it's probably best to wait a day and bring a fresh eye here if you have the time. ✉ *Janus Pannonius u. 11* ☎ *72/310–544* 🎟 *600 HUF* ☉ *Tues.–Sun. 10–6.*

⑤ Endre Nemes Múzeum (Endre Nemes Museum). The big draw at this museum, which displays the porcelain collection of Endre Nemes, is the chance to see the ceramics of Vilmos Zsolnay and his followers, with English texts describing their works. Another section of the museum contains a street scene titled *Utca*, constructed entirely of white plastic foam by the sculptor Erzsébet Schaár; the people on the street are made of gypsum, simple in body structure but with finely drawn heads and the faces of historical figures such as Karl Marx and Sándor Petőfi, the famous Hungarian poet. ✉ *Káptalan u. 5* ☎ *72/324–822* 🎟 *400 HUF* ☉ *Apr.–Oct., Tues.–Sun. 10–6; Nov.–Mar., Tues.–Sun. 2–6.*

★ ⑩ Jákovali Hászan Múzeum. Just beyond the ancient city wall to the west, this 16th-century Turkish mosque is the only Ottoman-era religious building in Hungary with its original minaret and architecture intact. (Another mosque of the same period became the Belvárosi plébánia templom, a Catholic church.) The museum itself has a few artifacts from the Turkish period plus a few Iznik ceramics. The mosque is still active, used today by Muslim students living in Pécs. ✉ *Rákoczi út* ☎ *No phone* 🎟 *240 HUF* ☉ *Tues.–Sun. 10–6.*

⑨ Ókeresztény mauzóleum (Early Christian Mausoleum). In front of Pécs Basilica is a serene little park, and just beyond is the fourth-century tomb, Hungary's largest and most important early Christian mausoleum and a World Heritage Site. Some of the subterranean crypts and chapels date to its earliest days; the murals on the walls (Adam and Eve, Daniel in the lion's den, the Resurrection) are in remarkably good condition. ✉ *Szent István tér* ☎ *No phone* 🎟 *300 HUF* ☉ *Tues.–Sun. 10–6.*

⑧ Pécs Bazilika (Pécs Basilica). One of Europe's most magnificent cathedrals was promoted from mere cathedral to basilica rank after Pope John Paul II's visit in 1991. At the beginning of the 19th century, Mihály Pollack directed the transformation of the exterior, changing it from baroque to neoclassical; its interior remained Gothic. Near the end of the 19th century, Bishop Nándor Dulánszky decided to restore the cathedral to its original, Árpád-period style—the result is a four-spired monument that has an utterly breathtaking interior frescoed in shimmering golds, silvers, and blues. Entry to the basilica includes the Peter & Paul Catacombs, next door. ✉ *Szent István tér* 🎟 *500 HUF; 1,000 HUF for English-language tour* ☉ *Apr.–Oct., weekdays 9–5, Sat. 9–2, Sun. 1–5; Nov.–Mar., Mon.–Sat. 10–4, Sat. 10–1, Sun. 1–4.*

Fodor'sChoice ★

④ Vasarely Múzeum (Vasarely Museum). The pioneer of Op Art (who later settled in France) was born Győző Vásárhelyi in 1908 in this house, which has been turned into something wild, as much a funhouse as a museum.

The first hall is a corridor of visual tricks devised by his disciples, at the end of which hangs a hypnotic canvas of shifting cubes by Jean-Pierre Yvaral. Upstairs, the illusions grow profound: a zebra gallops by while chess pieces and blood cells seem to come at you. ⊠ *Káptalan u. 3* ☎ *72/ 324–822* 🎟 *400 HUF* ⊙ *Tues.–Sun. 10–6.*

① **Zsolnay Fountain.** At the foot of Széchenyi tér, the grand sloping monumental thoroughfare that is the pride of the city, stands the dainty, petite art nouveau majolica temple. The fountain is guarded by shiny ox-head gargoyles made of green eosin porcelain that gush pure drinking water piped into Pécs via Roman aqueducts. It was built in 1912 by the famous Zsolnay family, who pioneered and developed their unique porcelain art here in Pécs.

need a break?

A short walk down pedestrians-only Király utca, opening from Széchenyi tér, is the **Caflisch Cukrászda** (⊠ Király u. 32 ☎ 72/310– 391), a cozy, informal café established in 1869—in a building dating to 1789—with tiny round, marble-top tables and small chandeliers. It's open until 10 PM.

③ **Zsolnay Múzeum** (Zsolnay Museum). Occupying the upper floor of the oldest surviving building in Pécs, the building housing the museum dates from 1324; it has been built and rebuilt over the years in Romanesque, Renaissance, and baroque styles during its checkered history. A stroll through the rooms is a merry show-and-tell waltz through a revolution in pottery that started in 1851, when Miklós Zsolnay, a local merchant, bought the site of an old kiln and set up a stoneware factory for his son Ignác to run. Ignác's brother, Vilmos, a shopkeeper with an artistic bent, bought the factory from him in 1863, imported experts from Germany, and, with the help of a Pécs pharmacist for chemical-glaze experiments and his daughters for hand-painting, created the distinctive namesake porcelain.

Fodor'sChoice ★

Among the museum's exhibits are Vilmos's early efforts at Delft-blue handmade vases, cups, and saucers; his two-layer ceramics; examples of the gold-brocade rims that became a Zsolnay trademark; and table settings for royal families. Be sure to look up and notice the unusual Zsolnay chandeliers lighting your way. The Zsolnay store in the center of Pécs, at Jokai tér 2, sells a wide selection of contemporary ceramics. ⊠ *Káptalan u. 2* ☎ *72/310–172* 🎟 *400 HUF* ⊙ *Tues.–Sun. 10–6.*

Zsolnay porcelán gyár (Zsolnay Porcelain Factory). If you haven't had enough Zsolnay after visiting the Zsolnay Museum, join the groups of tourists (usually German or Hungarian) braving heavily trafficked Zsolnay Vilmos utca to visit the company's factory, where gleaming monumental towers and statuary of seemingly pollution-proof porcelain hold their own among giant smokestacks. On a hill behind the factory stands the ultimate monument to the dynasty's founder, who died in 1900: the **Zsolnay Mausoleum** (☎ 06/309–297–803), with the bones of Vilmos and his wife in a blue ceramic well and, over the doorway, a relief of Vilmos, with disciples resembling his wife, daughters, and son kneeling before him. The mausoleum is open by appointment only; there's a number listed on its front door for a guided tour (it's the cell phone for the enterprising tour guide, who will ask for a 500 HUF donation).

The factory can be visited by guided tour only—groups must number between 10 to 30—but you can tag along on an already scheduled group tour even if you're just an individual or a smaller group. Contact either the factory or Tourinform (see ⇨ Visitor Information *in* Pécs Essentials) to determine if a tour is scheduled during your visit to Pécs. ⊠ *Zsolnay Vilmos u. 69* ☎ *72/325–266 factory tour information* 📧 *Factory 400 HUF; English-language tour 500 HUF.*

AN EXCURSION TO VILLÁNY

30 km (19 mi) south of Pécs.

The town of Villány, which is south of Pécs and nestled in the low, verdant Villányi Hills, is the center of one of Hungary's most famous wine regions. Roman ruins uncovered in the surrounding area attest to a long history of wine-production in this region. Today, the Villány-Siklos wine region covers over 2,000 hectares. Villány's exceptional and unique red wines are heralded both here and abroad; its merlots, cabernets, and ports are said to give the best of their French, Italian, and Portuguese peers a run for the money. Many wine cellars offer regular wine tastings, and an overnight trip to Villány is a worthwhile way to sample a few of the best vintages. The town is clustered with friendly *pincek* (cellars) and *panziók* (pensions), and most owners will be happy to tell you about winemaking in the region as you taste. The Villány vineyards are best known for rich red wines such as kékoportó, kékfrankos, cabernet franc, and merlot. You can get a list of Villány wine cellars from the Pécs Tourinform office (see ⇨ Visitor Information *in* Pécs Essentials).

If you wish to learn about the wine before imbibing, stop in at the **Bor Múzeum** (Wine Museum) for a look at the history of the region's viticulture, which dates back some 2,000 years. ⊠ *Bem u. 8* ☎ *72/492–130* 📧 *Free* ☉ *Tues.–Sun. 9–5.*

WHERE TO STAY & EAT

★ **$–$$** ✕ **Fülemüle Csárda.** A *csárda* is a rustic inn, usually found on a highway or crossroads in the Hungarian countryside. As you make your way from Pécs south to Villány, you'll pass this brown and white restaurant next to a stream on a hilly terrain covered with vineyards. It's a good place to get old-fashioned, Hungarian peasant food, like *bográcsgulyás* (stew cooked in kettle on an open fire). ⊠ *Villány külterület* ☎ *72/492–939* 🍴 *AE, MC, V.*

$–$$ ✕ **Replay Cafe.** Hip students as well as visiting art historians can be found at this popular downtown bar and restaurant not far from Széchenyi tér. They come for the first-rate pizzas, American-style bacon cheeseburgers, and draft beer. Tables are filled late into the evening on the weekends with a lively crowd. ⊠ *Király u. 4* ☎ *72/210–531* 🍴 *AE, MC, V.*

$–$$ ✕ **Tettye Vendéglő.** For a country-style lunch or dinner a bit out of the heart of downtown, try this rustic vendéglő (restaurant serving home

CloseUp
VILLÁNY WINE CELLARS

MOST WINE CELLARS are open for tastings all day on Saturday, although some close at midday, so it's best to make your way to Villány during the week or Saturday morning. If there's a particular cellar you want to visit, consider calling ahead. Most places offer simple fare like cheese or pogácsa (savory scones) and, with advanced notice of a few hours, can arrange a dinner to complement a wine tasting. The town has a well-marked wine route and it's easy to make your way to most establishments on foot.

Bock Pince (⊠ Batthyány u. 15, Villány ☎ 72/492-919) offers a wide range of Villány wines in its celebrated cellar. The wine bar is a sophisticated step up from some of the other tasting rooms in town.

Some of the finest cabernet sauvignon being made in Hungary comes from **Gere Attila Pince** (⊠ Erkel F. u. 2/a, Villány ☎ 72/492-839). Once here, don't miss a chance to taste the local kékoportó, a versatile dry table wine.

Gu:u:nzer Tamás Pince Borozó (⊠ Baross Gábor u. 79, Villány ☎ 72/493-163) is turning out some exciting wines, including a crisp Mont Blanc cuvée, blended from chardonnay and irsai oliver grapes, and a first-rate cabernet franc. The wine cellar offers tastings in a cozy country room.

You'll recognize the friendly **Szende Pince** (⊠ Baross Gábor u. 87, Villány ☎ 72/492-396) in the center of the wine route by its charming wooden tables and flower boxes spilling over with geraniums.

At **Tiffán Ede és Zsolt Pince** (⊠ Erkel F. u., Villány ☎ 72/592-000), one of the best wines to taste is Jammertal Cuvée, a blend of kékfrankos and kékoportó.

---

cooking) just north of the historic center, up Tettye utca. Aside from the hilly views, you'll find traditional Hungarian food as well as some Swabian specialties like *fladle uberbacken* (almond and raisin pancakes) and *maultaschen* (stuffed pasta parcels). ⊠ *Tettye tér 4* ☎ *72/532–788* ⊟ *AE, MC, V.*

¢–$ ✕ **All'Elefante Ristorante & Pizzeria.** This bustling Italian pizzeria opens onto a main square in downtown Pécs. The menu includes some 20 kinds of pizza and a wide range of inventive salads. ⊠ *Jókai tér 6* ☎ *72/216–055 or 72/532–189* ⊟ *MC, V.*

¢–$ 🏨 **Hotel Palatinus.** While art nouveau prevails throughout Hungary, for some pure art deco, check out this hotel in downtown Pécs. The grand public areas—lobby, sweeping staircases, restaurant, and ballroom—are all stunning; the detail of the peacock mosaic in the breakfast room is particularly breathtaking. Rooms are somewhat disappointing after the public areas but are reasonably well equipped. The hotel is a popular wedding venue, and the action in the ballroom can get noisy, so ask if a wedding is taking place when you plan to visit and request a room on an upper floor. ⊠ *Király u. 5, H-7621* ☎ *72/889–400* 🖷 *72/889–438* ⊕ *www.danubiusgroup.com* ⊅ *88 rooms, 6 suites* ♨ *2 restaurants, minibars, massage, sauna* ⊟ *AE, DC, MC, V* ⋈ *EP.*

¢ ▣ **Aranyhajó Fogadó.** The Golden Ship Inn is a hotel housed in a pretty yellow medieval building in the heart of pedestrian Király utca and just next door to the Palatinus hotel. The modern rooms are traditionally furnished and well equipped. The location can't be beat for sightseeing near Széchenyi tér. The restaurant has a popular terrace that spills out onto the street and is shaded under a big awning in the summer. ⊠ *Király u. 3, H-7621* ☎ *72/310–263* 🖶 *72/212–733* 🛏 *18 rooms* 🗘 *Restaurant, minibars, cable TV; no a/c in some rooms* ☰ *AE, MC, V.*

¢ ▣ **Bock Pince Panzió.** Bock is one of Villány's most celebrated vineyards
Fodor's Choice and indeed, you will find Bock *kékoportó* and royal cuvée in many of
★ Hungary's best restaurants. The pension arranges wine tastings and dinners in an elegant attached restaurant, and you can buy a case quite reasonably when you leave. Rooms are tastefully decorated and well equipped. ⊠ *Batthyány u. 15, Villány H-7773* ☎ *72/492–919* 🖶 *72/592–010* 🛏 *15 rooms* 🗘 *Restaurant, sauna, wine bar* ☰ *MC, V, AE* ⦿ *BP.*

¢ ▣ **Gere Attila Panzió.** Big wooden tables set up in the wine-tasting room of this rustic guesthouse give the place a proper wine-country feel. If the weather's nice, sit out on the lush terrace or borrow bikes to ride around the scenic vineyards. Gere is a top producer of red wines in the Villány region, and regularly turns out memorable bottles of cabernet sauvignon. Rooms are comfortable and decorated with traditional folk art. ⊠ *Diófás tér 4, Villány H-7773* ☎ *72/492–195* 🖶 *72/492–952* 🛏 *14 rooms* 🗘 *Restaurant, wine bar* ☰ *AE, MC, V* ⦿ *BP.*

★ ¢ ▣ **Hotel Millennium Szálló.** Renowned Hungarian architect Sándor Dévényi designed this chintzy suburban castle on Kálvária hill, amidst a nature reserve and just outside the old city wall. The rooms are pleasantly low-key, and four of them look out onto the four spires of the Pécs Basilica. It's a quick five-minute walk to downtown from here. ⊠ *Kálvária u. 58, H-7625* ☎ *72/512–222 or 72/512–223* ⦿ *www.hotels.hu/hotelmillennium* 🛏 *25 rooms* 🗘 *Restaurant, minibars, pool, laundry service, Internet, free parking, no-smoking rooms, some pets allowed* ☰ *AE, DC, MC, V* ⦿ *EP.*

NIGHTLIFE & THE ARTS

September brings harvest-related festivities such as classical concerts, folk-music and dance performances, and a parade or two to venues in and around Pécs. Inquire at the local Tourinform office (see ⇨ Visitor Information *in* Pécs Essentials) for specifics. Tourinform publishes a monthly arts and events calendar in English and can help with further schedule and ticket information.

Fregatt Arizona Pub. This pub has low, vaulted ceilings and Guinness on tap. ⊠ *Király u. 21* ☎ *72/210–486.*

Murphy's Pub. Accented by dark wood and polished brass, this Irish pub keeps an ample supply of Guinness on tap. ⊠ *Király u. 2* ☎ *72/325–439.*

Pécsi Nemzeti Színház (Pécs National Theater). This theater is the main venue for regular performances by the Pécs Symphony Orchestra and the theater's own opera and modern ballet companies. It is closed from late May until September. ⊠ *Színház tér 1* ☎ *72/211–965.*

SPORTS & THE OUTDOORS

The Mecsek Hills rise up just behind Pécs, with abundant well-marked hiking trails through the forests and fresh air. Guided walks are often organized on weekends by local nature clubs; contact Tourinform for dates and times (see ⇨ Visitor Information *in* Pécs Essentials).

SHOPPING

Kirakodóvásár (Flea Market). Pécs's large fleá market provides great browsing and bargain-hunting among its eclectic mix of goods—from used clothing and handcrafted folk art to antiques and fresh vegetables. It's held every day (from 5 AM until 2 PM), but weekends draw many more sellers, and the first Sunday of every month is the best for quantity and variety, especially in terms of antiques. ⊠ *Vásár tér, at Megyeri út* ☎ *72/516–160.*

Király utca, a vibrant, pedestrian-only street lined with beautifully preserved romantic and baroque facades, is Pécs's main shopping zone, full of colorful boutiques and outdoor cafés.

Zsolnay Márkabolt. The best place in the whole country to buy exquisite Zsolnay porcelain is in Pécs. At the Zsolnay factory's own outlet, the company offers guaranteed authenticity and the best prices on the full spectrum of pieces—from tea sets profusely painted with colorful, gold-winged butterflies to white-and-night-blue dinner services. ⊠ *Jókai tér 2* ☎ *72/310–220.*

PÉCS ESSENTIALS

BUS TRAVEL

There's regular bus service from Budapest to Pécs several times a day from Népliget station. Buses to Villány usually stop in Pécs first.

CAR TRAVEL

Traveling around Transdanubia is most easily done by car. Pécs and Budapest are directly connected by Route 6, which continues on to the Croatian border. Villány is a short excursion by car, about 19 mi southeast of Pécs, and is a beautiful drive through the wine country.

TRAIN TRAVEL

There are good rail connections from Budapest to Pécs and Villány. The trip—by InterCity (IC) trains, which run several times daily—takes 3 hours to Pécs and another 1½ hours to Villány. 🚆 Pécs train station ⊠ Indóhász tér ☎ 72/312–443

VISITOR INFORMATION
🚆 Tourinform ⊠ Széchenyi tér 9 ☎ 72/213–315

THE GREAT PLAIN

By Kristen
Schweizer

HUNGARY'S GREAT PLAIN—the Nagyalföld—stretches south from Budapest to the borders of Croatia and Yugoslavia and as far east as Ukraine and Romania. It covers an area of 51,800 square km (20,000 square mi) and is what most people think of as the typical Hungarian landscape. Almost completely flat, it is the home of shepherds and their flocks and, above all, of splendid horses and the *csikósok,* their riders. The plain has a wild, almost alien air; its sprawling villages consist mostly of one-story houses, though there are many large farms. Divided into two almost equal parts by Hungary's second-largest river, the Tisza, the Plain also contains several of Hungary's most historic cities. Because much of the region was never occupied by the Turks, it contains a wealth of medieval remnants; it's also the least developed area of Hungary.

As you near the region, you will soon find yourself driving in a hypnotically straight line from Budapest through the dream landscape of the Hortobágy, a grassy *puszta* (prairie), Hungary's answer to the U.S. wild west. Here, the land flattens out like a palacsinta, opening into vast stretches of dusty grassland interrupted only by stands of trees and distant thatch-roof *tanyák* (ranch homes). The only detectable movement here comes from the herds of *racka* (a breed of sheep) or cattle drifting lazily across the horizon, guided by shepherds and their trusty *puli* (herd dogs). Covering more than 250,000 acres, the Hortobágy became the first of Hungary's four national parks, in 1973. Its flora and fauna—including primeval breeds of longhorn cattle and racka sheep, prairie dogs, and *nóniusz* (horses)—are all under strict protection.

Numbers in the margin correspond to numbers on the Great Plain map

About the Hotels & Restaurants

Hotels in the Great Plain region tend to be more rustic than in other parts of Hungary and often have "Wild West" interiors; you're likely to see many pictures of horses and the puszta scattered across the walls. Most hotels, which usually quote rates in forints, are open year-round and can also help arrange horseback riding and hiking trips in the area.

Restaurants in the region serve typical Hungarian food: fried vegetables, meats, and basic salads. Menus will usually be translated into both English and German. Dress is casual. Restaurants also tend to open and close earlier along the Great Plain than in Budapest; most every place will be closed by 11 PM. Prices are typically cheaper in this region than anywhere else in Hungary, but that does not mean the quality of the food is lower; indeed, it is often prepared with much care and skill. Make sure to try traditional Hungarian goulash and *halaszlé* (fish soup), a Szeged speciality made with carp that is famous across Hungary.

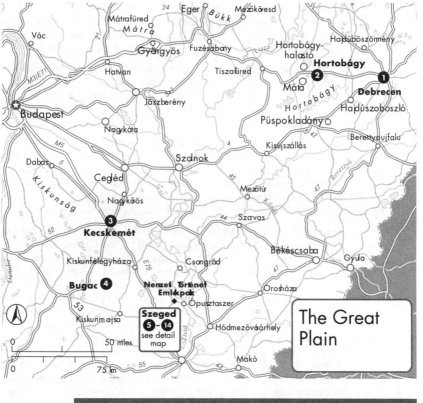

WHAT IT COSTS In Euros & Forints				
	$$$$	**$$$**	**$$**	**$**	**¢**
HOTELS IN EUROS	over €225	€175–€225	€125–€175	€75–€125	under €75
HOTELS IN FORINTS	over 56,000	44,000–56,000	31,000–44,000	18,500–31,000	under 18,500
RESTAURANTS IN FORINTS	over 3,500	2,500–3,500	1,500–2,500	800–1,500	under 800

Hotel prices are for two people in a standard double room with a private bath and breakfast during peak season (June through August). Restaurant prices are per person for a main course at dinner and include 15% tax but not service.

DEBRECEN

❶ *226 km (140 mi) east of Budapest.*

With a population approaching a quarter of a million, Debrecen is Hungary's second-largest city. Though it has considerably less clout than

Budapest, Debrecen was Hungary's capital twice. In 1849 it was here that Lajos Kossuth declared Hungarian independence from the Hapsburgs; in 1944, the Red Army liberated Debrecen from the Nazis and made the city the provisional capital until Budapest was taken.

Debrecen has been inhabited since the Stone Age. It was already a sizable village by the end of the 12th century and, by the 14th, an important market town. It takes its name from a Slavonic term for "good earth," and, indeed, much of the country's wheat, produce, meat, and poultry has been produced in this area for centuries.

Today, Debrecen is a vibrant, friendly city, with a sizable population of young people attending its several esteemed universities. There's only one tram line (appropriately numbered 1), but it runs fast and frequently in a nearly straight line from the railroad station along Piac utca and out to the Nagyerdő (Great Forest), a giant city park. All in all, it's a good place to spend a day before heading out to the puszta.

For almost 500 years, Debrecen has been the stronghold of Hungarian Protestantism—its inhabitants have called it "the Calvinist Rome." In 1536 Calvinism began to replace Roman Catholicism in Debrecen, and two years later the **Református Kollégium** (Reformed College) was founded on what is now Kálvin tér (Calvin Square). Early in the 19th century, the college's medieval building was replaced by a pillared structure that provides a vivid lesson in Hungarian religious and political history: the facade's busts honor prominent students and educators as well as religious reformers John Calvin and Huldrych Zwingli. Inside, the main staircase is lined with frescoes of student life and significant moments in the college's history (all painted during the 1930s in honor of the school's 400th anniversary). At the top of the stairs is the **Oratory,** which has twice been the setting for provisional parliaments. In 1849 Lajos Kossuth first proclaimed Hungarian sovereignty here, and the new National Assembly's Chamber of Deputies met here during the last stages of the doomed revolution. Kossuth's pulpit and pew are marked, and two rare surviving flags of his revolution hang on the front wall. Some relics from 1944 line the back wall. Also worth seeing are the college's **library,** which rotates exhibitions of illuminated manuscripts and rare Bibles, and two **museums.** The first museum, the Student History Museum, commemorates Hungarian intellectuals who studied at the college, while the Religious History Museum showcases jewelry, embroidered clothes, and painted furniture. ✉ *Kálvin tér 16* ☏ *52/414–744* 💲 *200 HUF* ⊙ *Tues.–Sat. 9–6:30, Sun. 9–1.*

Because the Oratory in the Reformed College was too small for a large crowd, Lajos Kossuth reread his declaration of independence by popular demand to a cheering public in 1849 in the twin-turreted, strikingly yellow **Nagytemplom** (Great Church). The most famous building in Debrecen, the Great Church opened its doors in 1821 after more than a decade of construction on the design of Mihály Pécsi; it was built on the site of a 14th-century church that had burned down in 1802. As befits the austerity of Calvinism, the church is devoid of decoration—but with all the baroque architecture throughout Hungary, you may welcome the contrast. The church's massive organ was made in Vienna in 1838, and the sanctuary is the site of frequent concerts ⊠ *Kálvin tér 4* 🕾 *52/412–459* 🕮 *Church 70 HUF, tower 100 HUF* ۞ *Jan.–Mar., Mon.–Sat. 10–noon, Sun. 11–1; Apr.–Oct., weekdays 9–4, Sat. 9–noon, Sun. 10–4; Nov.–Dec., Mon.–Sat. 10–noon, Sun. 11–1.*

need a break?

Bright and modern it may be, but the **Kismandula Cukrászda** (Little Almond Pastry Shop; ⊠ Liszt Ferenc u. 10 🕾 52/310–873) has age-old favorites aplenty—not least, fresh, well-packed rétes and *madártej* (literally, bird's milk), a vanilla-flavored liquid custard with a meringue of sorts floating inside. On summer evenings, a large terrace—shared by the pastry shop with a restaurant under the same ownership—is sometimes the scene of mime and other performances.

The **Déri Múzeum** (Déri Museum) was founded in the 1920s to house the art and antiquities of a wealthy Hungarian silk manufacturer living in Vienna. Its two floors are devoted to local history, archaeology, and weapons as well as to Egyptian, Greek, Roman, Etruscan, and Far Eastern art. On the top floor are Hungarian and foreign fine art from the 15th to the 20th century, including the striking (and huge) *Ecce Homo* by Mihály Munkácsy and, on loan since 2000, two similar scenes from the life of Christ by the same famous 19th-century artist. In front of the museum are allegorical bronze statues by Ferenc Medgyessy, grand prize winner at the 1937 Paris World Exhibition. ⊠ *Déri tér 1* 🕾 *52/416–950* 🕮 *580 HUF* ۞ *Apr.–Oct., Tues.–Sun. 10–6; Nov.–Mar., Tues.–Sun. 10–4.*

Debrecen's main artery, **Piac utca** (Market Street), is a wide and long boulevard that runs from the Great Forest to the railroad station. Its history goes back to the Middle Ages, when handfuls of outdoor vegetable and meat markets lined the road here. However, its architectural face began to take shape only in the first decades of the 19th century, under the impact of classicism. The majority of the existing buildings date to the beginning of 20th century, and you'll see several examples of the influence of secession and eclecticism.

At the corner of Széchenyi utca, the **Kistemplom** (Small Church)—Debrecen's oldest surviving church, which was built in 1720—looks like a rococo chess-piece castle. This Calvinist venue is known to the locals as the "truncated church" because early in the 20th century, its onion dome was blown down in a gale. The church is kept closed, except during services, but the ministers and caretakers next door at the church office are happy to open it for you. ⊠ *Révész tér 2* 🕾 *52/342–872* ۞ *Weekdays 9 AM–noon, Sun. 8:30 AM–11 AM.*

Across the street from the Kistemplom is the **Megyeház** (County Hall), built between 1911 and 1912 in Transylvanian art nouveau style, a darker and heavier version than what was popular in Paris, Munich, and Vienna. The ceramic ornaments on the façade are of Zsolnay majolica. Inside, brass chandeliers illuminate the stairs and halls, spotlighting the symmetry and delicate restraint of the interior. In the Council Hall upstairs, stained-glass windows by Károly Kernstock depict seven leaders of the tribes that conquered Hungary in AD 896. ⊠ *Piac u. 54* ☎ *52/ 507–550* ⊘ *Mon.–Thurs. 8–4, Fri. 8–1.*

★ The **Tímárház** (Tanner House), in a restored 19th-century building, is the center for preserving and maintaining the ancient folk-arts-and-crafts traditions of Hajdú-Bihar county. In its delightful, small complex you can wander into the artisans' workshops and watch them creating exquisite pieces—from impossibly fine, intricately handmade lacework to colorful hand-loomed wool rugs. The artisans—among the best in the country—encourage visitors of all ages to try their hand at the crafts. The complex's showroom displays magnificent leather whips, heavy wool shepherd robes, and other examples of the county's traditional folk art; the embroidered textiles are some of the best you'll see anywhere. Although the displayed pieces are not for sale, the staff can help you contact the artists to custom-order something. A tiny gift shop, however, does sell a small selection of representative goods at great prices. ⊠ *Nagy Gál István u. 6* ☎ *52/368–827* 💰 *200 HUF* ⊘ *June–Oct., Tues.–Fri. 10–6, Sat. 10–2; Nov.–May., Tues.–Fri. 10–5, Sat. 10–2.*

The 19th-century **Vörös templom** (Red Church) is as remarkable a Calvinist church as you'll find anywhere in Europe. On the outside it seems to be an undistinguished redbrick house of worship, built with the usual unadorned interior, but the church celebrated its 50th anniversary at the zenith of the applied-arts movement in Hungary. Its worshipers commissioned artist Jenő Haranghy to paint the walls with biblical allegories using no human bodies or faces (just an occasional limb) but rather plenty of grapes, trees, and symbols. Giant frescoes covering the walls, ceilings, niches, and crannies represent, among other subjects, a stag in fresh water, the Martin Luther anthem "A Mighty Fortress Is Our God," and the 23rd Psalm (with a dozen sheep representing the 12 Tribes of Israel and the 12 Apostles). The Red Church is open only during religious services (10 AM on Sunday and religious holidays), but you might try for a private church visit from the deaconage on Kossuth Lajos utca. The church is just a 10-minute walk from the county hall along Kossuth Lajos utca. ⊠ *Méliusz tér* ☎ *52/325–736.*

☺ Debrecen's one tram line runs out to the **Nagyerdő** (Great Forest), a huge city park with a zoo, a sports stadium, swimming pools, an artificial rowing lake, a thermal-spa-cum-luxury-hotel (the Termál Hotel Debrecen), an amusement park, restaurants, and an open-air theater. Also here is the photogenic Kossuth Lajos University, its handsome neobaroque facade fronted by a large pool and fountain around which six bronze nudes pose in the sun. The university is one of the few in Central Europe with a real campus, and every summer, from mid-July to mid-August, it hosts a world-renowned Hungarian-language program.

Where to Stay & Eat

★ **$–$$$** ✕**Városháza.** A visit begins with your descent down a grand staircase into a small foyer flanked by glass cases packed with liquor bottles from around the world. As you enter the fairly small dining room, your eye will probably next fall on two wax-doll 19th-century ladies taking tea.

This place has been long considered one of the best restaurants in Hungary; its reputation is still strong, but the longtime chef departed in the late 1990s. An illustrated wine list with explanations helps you match a Hungarian wine to your food. ⊠ *Piac u. 20* ☎ *52/444–767* 🖃 *AE, DC, MC, V.*

$ ✕ **Serpince a Flaskához.** When you walk into this completely unpretentious and very popular neighborhood pub, you may be surprised to be presented with a nicely bound menu in four languages. For a light meal, try a *palócleves,* a thick, piquantly sourish meat-and-potatoes soup with tarragon and caraway. For something heavier, try the "boiled hock strips covered with ewe cheese, Túróczi style." ⊠ *Miklós u. 4* ☎ *52/414–582* 🖃 *AE, DC, MC, V.*

$ 🏨 **Termál Hotel Debrecen.** Other hotels may be attached to spas, but this hotel is actually located within a medical spa. You can detect the (not unpleasant) smell of alkaline chloride as soon as you check in at the front desk. Amenities span the seasons: in summer, you can swim in a large outdoor pool; in winter, you can warm yourself by the library fire. The decorators have gone a bit wild with pinkish beige and paisley in the guest quarters, but with a balcony in each room overlooking the Great Forest, that's a minor quibble. ⊠ *Nagyerdei park 1, H-4032* ☎ *52/514–111* 🖷 *52/311–730* ⊕ *www.aquaticum.hu* ➭ *56 rooms, 40 suites* ♨ *Restaurant, snack bar, indoor pool, sauna, spa, bar, meeting rooms* ⦿ *BP* 🖃 *AE, DC, MC, V.*

★ **¢–$** 🏨 **Cívis Grand Hotel Aranybika.** Art nouveau classic on the outside, inside this hotel is a bit of a patchwork quilt. Designed by Hungary's first Olympic champion, Alfréd Hajós, it is the oldest hotel in Hungary (the original was built in the 17th century). Parts of the lobby, like the neobaroque doorway to the cocktail bar, are gorgeous, as is the airy and elegant restaurant. Brown and beige leftover renovations from the 1970s spoil the effect a bit, but the staff is extremely attentive and friendly, and the hotel's location in the center of Debrecen is excellent. The guest rooms in the old Grand section of the hotel are being spruced up, while those in the newer "tourist" wing are a bit on the institutional side. It also contains the Béla Bartók Concert Hall. ⊠ *Piac u. 11–15, H-4025* ☎ *52/508–600* 🖷 *52/421–834* ⊕ *www.civishotels.hu* ➭ *230 rooms, 4 suites* ♨ *Restaurant, café, indoor pool, gym, sauna, spa, casino, business services, meeting rooms; no a/c in some rooms* ⦿ *BP* 🖃 *AE, DC, MC, V.*

★ **¢** 🏨 **Korona Panzió.** This cheery little inn is just down the street from the Great Church. The immaculate rooms are a great value and have contemporary furnishings and terraces. Breakfast costs an extra 900 HUF, however. ⊠ *Péterfia u. 54, H-4026* ☎ *52/535–260* 🖷 *52/535–261* ⊕ *www.hotels.hu/koronapanzio1* ➭ *9 rooms* ♨ *Cable TV, in-room VCRs; no a/c, no smoking* ⦿ *EP* 🖃 *No credit cards.*

The Arts

Debrecen Tavaszi Fesztivál (Debrecen Spring Festival). The biggest annual event runs between mid- and late March, packing in two weeks full of concerts, dance, and theater performances, as well as special art exhibits. Main events are held at the Csokonai Theater and Bartók Hall. The biannual **Bartók Béla Nemzetközi Kórusverseny** (Béla Bartók International Choral Festival), scheduled next for July 2006, is a competition for choirs from around the world and provides choral-music aficionados with numerous full-scale concerts in Bartók Hall, which is in the **Cívis Grand Hotel Aranybika.** Jazz fans can hear local ensembles as well as groups from around Hungary and abroad during the **Debreceni Jazz Napok** (Debrecen Jazz Days) in late September. One of the city's favorite occasions is the **Debreceni Virágkarnevál** (Flower Carnival) on St. Stephen's Day (August 20), Hungary's national holiday, when a festive parade of flower-encrusted floats and carriages makes its way down Debrecen's main street along the tram line all the way to the Nagyerdő Stadium.

Csokonai Theater. One of Debrecen's main cultural venues is devoted to theater, opera, and dance productions (though none in English). ⊠ *Kossuth u. 10* ☎ *52/417–811* ⊕ *www.csokonaiszinhaz.hu.*

Debreceni Kulturális és Fesztivál Központ (Debrecen Culture and Festival Center). Call this agency for information on Debrecen's many festivals. ⊠ *Petőfi tér 10* ☎ *52/525–270* ⊕ *www.fesztivalkozpont.hu.*

Sports & the Outdoors

A visit to the Great Plain is hardly complete without at least some contact with horses. There are several horseback-riding outfits outside Debrecen on the puszta. Contact the Debrecen office of Tourinform (see ⇨ Great Plains A to Z, *below*) to arrange excursions.

Hortobágyi Nemzeti Park Igazgatóság (National Park's Headquarters). The headquarters for Hortobágy National Park is in Debrecen, even though the park itself is closer to the town of Horotágy, which is 39 km (24 mi) west. An access card costs 1,500 HUF (four people) or 900 HUF (one person). ⊠ *Sumen u. 2, H-4024 Debrecen* ☎ *52/349–922* ☎ *52/410–645* ⊕ *www.hnp.hu.*

☻ **Mediterrán Elményfürdő.** (Mediterranean Bath Experience). Next door to
Fodor'sChoice the Nagyerdei Lido, the Mediterrán is the newest addition to the Great
★ Forest park and opened for business in July 2003. A new take on thermal water fun, it is touted as Hungary's only covered thermal water theme park. ⊠ *Nagyerdei Park 1* ☎ *52/514–174* ⊕ *www.aquaticum.hu* ✉ *Weekdays 2,700 HUF, weekends 3,000 HUF* ⊙ *Daily 10–10.*

☻ **Nagyerdei Lido.** Debrecen's Nagyerdő (Great Forest) bubbles with thermal baths and pools. The main complex here has eight pools, including a large pool for actual swimming (most people soak idly in Hungary's public pools) and a wave pool. ⊠ *Nagyerdei Park 1* ☎ *52/514–100* ✉ *Weekdays 1,500 HUF, weekends 2,000 HUF* ⊙ *Daily 6:30 AM–7:30 PM.*

HORTOBÁGY

❷ *39 km (24 mi) west of Debrecen, 187 km (116 mi) east of Budapest.*

The main gateway and visitor center for the Hortobágy National Park is the Village of Hortobágy, the most famous settlement on the puszta.

WET & WILD—AND HOT

HUNGARY'S FIRST INDOOR THERMAL WATER PARK, the Mediterrán Elményfürdő (Mediterranean Bath Experience) opened its doors for business in Debrecen in July 2003, to the delight of children everywhere and the tune of $8.7 million in construction. The air temperature inside is a steamy 98.6 degrees Fahrenheit and, despite the fact that Debrecen lies in a flat and arid region, the interior attempts to look and feel like the Mediterranean. Beneath the large glass dome are whirlpool baths, spiraling water slides, an underground water cave, and a rock-climbing wall. Tropical plants and palm trees are everywhere and interior walls are painted in Egyptian-style murals.

The Debrecen government, capitalizing on Hungary's rich thermal traditions, hopes to make Hungary synonymous with water tourism. With an estimated 1,300 underground thermal springs—a third of which are employed at various spas across the country—Hungary is in a unique position to do this. Only Japan, Iceland, France, and Italy can boast similar thermal water capacity.

The Romans were the first to capitalize on Hungary's thermal waters in the first century, when they built baths on the banks of the Danube River. The tradition was continued under Turkish rule of the country during the 16th and 17th centuries. As development of thermal baths continued in Hungary, the United Nations took notice, and in the 1970s the "Thermal Project" institute was established in Budapest, charged with promoting development of the baths and planning programs to utilize the practice in other countries. Today there are more than 100 spas and bathhouses across Hungary.

Traveling from Debrecen, you'll reach this town just before you would cross the Hortobágy River. Before heading out to the prairie itself, you can take in Hortobágy's own sights: a prairie museum, its famous stone bridge, and the historic Hortobágyi Csárda inn.

At 196,800 acres, the **Hortobágy National Park** encompasses the largest continuous grassland in Europe. A major part of the area is formed by natural habitats, meadows, and small and large marshes. Natural wetlands occupy one-third of the park, while artificial wetlands, called fishponds, were created on 14,400 acres in the last century on the worst-quality grazing lands and former marshes. These fishponds are vital to the 342 types of birds registered in the Hortobágy National Park, of which 152 specifically nest there.

The park has three different types of terrain: forest, marshland, and grassland, and three trails are open to the public, one in each different type of terrain. **Halastó Nature Trail** (⊠ Rte. 33, between Km 64 & 65) passes through fishponds 5 km (3 mi) west of Hortobágy that were created in 1915. The ponds are now the habitat for pygmy cormorant, glossy ibis, and spoonbills. The marshes of **Egyek-Pusztakócs** (⊠ Rte. 33, at Km 55) can be traversed on a dirt bike path, a former salt road, that begins off at the parting of the Egyek. Among the birds you'll likely spot are ducks, grebes, and terns. Bikes can be borrowed at the Western Rest-House, which is the starting point of the trail. A day-long bike rental runs 1,000 HUF per person. **Szálkahalom Nature Trail** (⊠ Rte. 33, at Km 79) goes through the grassland grazing areas, and you are likely to spot herds of Nonius horses, Hungarian grey cattle, water buffalos, and Racka sheep. The Hortobágy Tourinform office is both an information resource and place to purchase tickets. *Tourinform* ⊠ *Petőfi tér 1* ☎ *52/ 589–321* ⊕ *www.hnp.hu.*

Crossing the Hortobágy River is one of the puszta's famous symbols: the curving, white-stone **Kilenc-lyukú híd** (Nine-holed Bridge). It was built in the early 19th century and is the longest stone bridge in Hungary. ⊠ *Rte. 33 at Petőfi tér.*

Built in 1699, the **Hortobágyi Csárda** (Hortobágy Inn) has been a regional institution for most of the last three centuries. Its construction is typical of the Great Plain: a long, white stone structure with arching windows, brown-wood details, and a stork nest—and occasionally storks—on its chimney. The restaurant is quite popular. ⊠ *Petőfi tér 2* ☎ *52/589– 339* ⊗ *Mid-Feb.–Sept., daily.*

For a glimpse into traditional Hortobágy pastoral life, visit the **Pásztormúzeum** (Shepherd Museum), across the street from the Hortobágy Inn. Exhibits focus on traditional costumes and tools, such as the shepherds' heavy embroidered cloaks and carved sticks. The area in front of the museum is the tourism center for the area, bustling with visitors and local touristic enterprises, including the helpful local Tourinform office. ⊠ *Petőfi tér 1* ☎ *52/589–321* 💷 *300 HUF* ⊗ *May–Sept., daily 9–6; Oct. and Apr., daily 10–4; mid-Mar. and Nov., daily 10–2; Dec.–mid-Mar., by appointment only.*

Where to Eat

★ **$–$$$** ✕ **Hortobágyi Csárda.** Old flasks and saddles, antlers, and dried corn-and-paprika wreaths hang from the walls and rafters of this traditional Hungarian roadside inn. This is the place to order the regional specialty, savory *Hortobágyi húsospalacsinta* (Hortobágy pancakes), which are filled with beef and braised with a tomato-and-sour-cream sauce. Follow the pancakes with *bográcsgulyás* (spicy goulash soup puszta-style, with meat and dumplings). Veal *paprikás* and solid beef and lamb *pörkölt* (thick stews with paprika and sour cream) are also recommended, as are the cheesecurd and apricot-jam dessert pancakes. ⊠ *Petőfi tér 2* ☎ *52/369–139* 🖃 *AE, DC, MC, V* ⊗ *Closed Oct.–mid-Feb.*

Local Festivals

The three-day **Hortobágyi híd vásár** (Hortobágy Bridge Fair), held annually in late August, brings horse shows, a folk-art fair, ox roasts, and festive crowds to the plot beneath the famous Nine-holed Bridge.

KECSKEMÉT

❸ *191 km (118 mi) southwest of Debrecen, 85 km (53 mi) east of Budapest.*

With a name roughly translating as "Goat Walk," this sprawling town smack in the middle of the country never fails to surprise unsuspecting first-time visitors with its elegant landmark buildings, interesting museums, and friendly, welcoming people. As far back as the 14th century, Kecskemét was a market town, and under Turkish rule in 1439 it was a *khas* (exclusive) city, which meant it received favorable treatment and was spared much of the devastation rendered on other Hungarian cities at the time. Thus, Kecskemét was able to flourish as other cities were destroyed and deserted.

The splendid main square, Szabadság tér (Liberty Square), is marred only by two faceless cement-block buildings, one of which houses the city's McDonald's (a true sign this is not just a dusty prairie town anymore). Home of the elite Kodály Institute, where famous composer and pedagogue Zoltán Kodály's methods are taught, the city also maintains a fairly active cultural life.

The Kecskemét area, fruit center of the Great Plain, produces *barack pálinka*, a smooth yet tangy apricot brandy that can warm the heart and blur the mind in just one shot. Ask for home-brewed *házi pálinka*, which is much better (and often stronger) than the commercial brews.

A short drive from town takes you into the expansive sandy grasslands of Kiskunság National Park, the smaller of the two protected areas (the other is Hortobágy National Park) of the Great Plain. You can watch a traditional horse show, do some riding, or immerse yourself in the experience by spending a night or two at one of the inns out on the prairie.

Fodor'sChoice The **Magyar Fotográfia Múzeum** (Hungarian Photography Museum) is
★ one of only a few museums in Hungary dedicated solely to photography. With a growing collection of more than 275,000 photos, documents, and pieces of equipment, it continues to be the most important photography center in the country. The main exhibits are fine works by such pioneers of Hungarian photography as André Kertész, Brassaï, and Martin Munkácsi, all of whom moved out of the country and gained their fame abroad. ⊠ *Katona József tér 12* ☏ *76/483–221* 🎫 *200 HUF* ⊘ *Wed.–Sun. 10–4.*

The handsome Moorish-style former synagogue anchoring one end of Liberty Square is beautifully restored but has been stripped of its original purpose. Today it is the headquarters of the **House of Science and Technology,** with offices and a convention center, but it also houses a small collection of Michelangelo sculpture reproductions from Budapest's Museum of Fine Arts. ⊠ *Rákóczi út 2* ☏ *76/487–611* 🎫 *Free* ⊘ *Weekdays 10–4.*

Kecskemét's most famous building is the **Cifrapalota** (Ornamental Palace), a unique and remarkable Hungarian-style art nouveau building built in

1902. A three-story cream-colored structure studded with folksy lilac, blue, red, and yellow Zsolnay majolica flowers and hearts, it stands on Liberty Square's corner like a cheerful cream pastry. Once a residential building, it now houses the **Kecskeméti képtár** (Kecskemét Gallery), displaying artwork by Hungarian fine artists as well as occasional international exhibits. ⊠ *Rákóczi u. 1* ☎ *76/480–776* 🖪 *300 HUF* ⏱ *Tues.–Sat. 10–5, Sun. 2–5.*

need a break?

You can treat yourself to fresh pastries or ice cream at a café that shares our name, the **Fodor Cukrászda** (Fodor Confectionery; ⊠ Szabadság tér 2 ☎ 76/497–545). It's right on the main square and is open from March through late December. We like more about this café than the name; try the *túrós rétes* (cottage cheese pastry), a famous Hungarian dessert with raisins mixed into the cheese, or the *csokis csiga* (chocolate snail), another popular dessert, which is a chocolate pastry rolled into the shape of a snail.

★ Built between 1893 and 1897 by Ödön Lechner in the Hungarian art nouveau style that he created, the **Városház** (Town Hall) is one of its finest examples. Window frames are arched here, pointed there, and the roof, covered with tiny copper- and gold-color tiles, looks as if it has been rained on by pennies from heaven. In typical Lechner style, the outlines of the central facade make a curving line to a pointed top, under which 37 little bells add the finishing visual and auditory touch: every hour from 7 AM to 8 PM, they flood the main square with ringing melodies from Kodály, Beethoven, Mozart, and other composers, as well as traditional Hungarian folk songs. The building's **Dísz Terem** (Ceremonial Hall) is a spectacular palace of glimmering gold-painted vaulted ceilings, exquisitely carved wooden pews, colorful frescoes by Bertalan Székely (who also painted the frescoes for Budapest's Matthiás Church), and a gorgeously ornate chandelier that floats above the room like an ethereal bouquet of lights and shining brass. The hall is open only to tour groups that have made prior arrangements; call in advance and ask for the reception desk. ⊠ *Kossuth tér 1* ☎ *76/483–683 Ext. 2153* 🖪 *Ceremonial hall 200 HUF* ⏱ *Mon.–Thurs. 8–4, Fri. 8–1. Ceremonial Hall by appointment only.*

The oldest building on Kossuth tér is the **Szent Miklós templom** (Church of St. Nicholas), known also as the Barátság templom (Friendship Church) because of St. Nick's role as the saint of friendship. The church, the oldest in the city, was built in Gothic style in either the 13th or 15th century (a subject of debate). What is not debated is that it was rebuilt in baroque style during the 18th century. ⊠ *Kossuth tér 5.*

🄲 The unusual, one-of-a-kind **Szórakoténusz Játékmúzeum és Műhely** (Szórakoténusz Toy Museum & Workshop) chronicles the history of Hungarian toys with more than 10,000 archaeological pieces such as stone figures and clay toys from medieval guilds. The museum also hosts changing international exhibits. In the workshop, artisans prepare traditional toys and invite you to try to make toys yourself. Next door to the toy museum (in the same building) is the small **Magyar Naív Mű-**

vészek Múzeum (Hungarian Naive Art Museum), where you can see a collection of this simple style of painting and sculpting created by Hungarian artists. ⊠ *Gáspár András u. 11* ☎ *76/481–469 Toy Museum, 76/324–767 Naive Art Museum* ☜ *300 HUF Toy Museum, 150 HUF Naive Art Museum* ☉ *Toy Museum Tues.–Sun. 10–12:30 and 1–5; Naive Art Museum Tues.–Sun. 10–5. Toy Workshop alternate Sat. 10–noon and 2:30–5, alternate Sun. 10–noon.*

off the beaten path

PIAC (Market) – Kecskemét is Hungary's fruit capital, and it's worth experiencing the region's riches firsthand by visiting the bustling market, where—depending on the season—you can indulge in freshly plucked apples, cherries, and the famous Kecskemét apricots. Provided there is no sudden spring freeze, apricot season is around June through August. It's about 2 km from the city center. ⊠ *Along Budai u., near corner of Nagykörösi út* ☉ *Tues.–Sat. 6–noon, Sun. 6 AM–11 AM.*

Where to Stay & Eat

$–$$$ ✕ **Kisbugaci Csárda.** This cozy eatery tucked away on a side street is warm and bright. The inner area has wood paneling and upholstered booths; the outer section has simple wooden tables covered with locally embroidered tablecloths and matching curtains. Food is heavy, ample, and tasty. Try the kitchen's goose specialties, such as the *Bugaci libatoros*— a sampling of goose liver, thigh, and breast with steamed cabbage and boiled potatoes. Request a plate of dried paprikas—usually crumbled into soup—if you really want to spice things up. ⊠ *Munkácsy u. 10* ☎ *76/ 322–722* ⊟ *MC, V* ☉ *No dinner Sun.*

$–$$
Fodor'sChoice
★
✕ **Liberté Kávéház.** The closest thing to a Viennese coffeehouse on the Great Plain—and pretty close at that—is this long art nouveau room with a restaurant-size menu. The menu runs the gamut from regional favorites such as Hortobágy pancakes to more adventurous dishes such as Hawaiian turkey breast fillet with pineapple. In front of you is Liberty Square, the center of Kecskemét; the windows at the back have a view through to the Reformed Church. ⊠ *Szabadság tér 2* ☎ *76/328– 636* ⊟ *AE, DC, MC, V.*

¢ 🏨 **Arany Homok Hotel.** The staff is cheerful and friendly, and Kecskemét is right on your doorstep at this hotel on a small square close to the city center. The design leaves much to be desired, however: it doesn't require an overheated imagination to envisage this concrete-bunker-style hotel as a resting place for Communist-era bureaucrats. And as the hotel brochure puts it, "the architecture suits the fashion of the '60s." Most rooms have pared-down blond-wood furnishings, generic gray wall-to-wall carpeting, and small bathrooms. All doubles have balconies. ⊠ *Kossuth tér 3, H-6000* ☎ *76/503–730* 🖷 *76/530–731* ⊕ *www.hotels.hu/ aranyhomok* ⇨ *111 rooms, 4 suites* ⚹ *Restaurant, minibars, gym, casino, laundry service, meeting rooms, travel services, some pets allowed* ⊟ *AE, DC, MC, V* ⦿I *BP.*

¢ 🏨 **Fábián Panzió.** It's hard to miss this very pink villa just off the main square. Once inside, the pink (though muted) continues, mixing with white, turquoise, and lavender. The friendly owners keep their pension immaculate: floors in the tiny entranceway are polished until they look wet, and even the paths through the blooming back garden are spotless. Rooms are in the main house and in a comely, one-story motel-like building in the garden. The largest and quietest rooms are in the back. A/C is available, but costs extra. ⊠ *Kápolna u. 14, H-6000* ☎ *76/477–677* 🖷 *76/477–175* ⊕ *www.hotels.hu/fabian* ⇗ *10 rooms* ⚲ *Minibars, cable TV, bicycles, laundry service* ⏝⊙⏝ *BP* ⊟ *No credit cards.*

¢ 🏨 **Hotel Centrál.** Facing a small park a few minutes walk away from Liberty Square, this hotel almost lives up to its name. The Central's contemporary furnishings and fittings adhere to an almost minimalistic aesthetic, with plain wooden chairs and simple white bed linens. The overall effect is pleasant. ⊠ *Kisfaludy u. 10, H-6000* ☎ *76/502–710* 🖷 *76/502–713* ⇗ *17 rooms* ⚲ *Cable TV, laundry facilities, meeting room, free parking; no a/c in some rooms* ⏝⊙⏝ *BP* ⊟ *AE, DC, MC, V.*

¢ 🏨 **Pongrácz Manor.** For total puszta immersion, spend a night or two at

FodorśChoice this Great Plain ranch, about 25 km (16 mi) outside of Kecskemét. The
★ manor, which sits adjacent to a complex of whitewashed buildings with reed roofs, has small, simple, comfortable rooms. The stables house some 70 horses; in addition to riding yourself you can watch resident champion csikósok perform daredevil stunts and stage mock 1848-revolution battles in full hussar dress. Anglers can try their luck in the nearby lake; the restaurant's kitchen will cook your catch (one fish per day). The ranch is popular, so reserve ahead. ⊠ *Kunpuszta 76, H-6041 Kerekegyháza* ☎ *76/710–093* 🖷 *76/371–240* ⊕ *www.hotels.hu/pongracz* ⇗ *31 rooms (26 with bath), 4 suites* ⚲ *Restaurant, 2 tennis courts, pool, sauna, fishing, bowling, horseback riding, squash* ⊟ *No credit cards* ⊙ *Closed Jan.–Mar.*

The Arts

Kecskemét's annual **Tavaszi Fesztivál.** (Spring Festival) is held from mid-March to early April and includes concerts, dance performances, theater productions, and art exhibits by local and special guest artists from around the country and abroad. Every two years in July, the city hosts a giant children's festival, **Európa Jövője Gyermektalálkozó.** (Future of Europe Children's Convention), during which children's groups from some 25 countries put on colorful folk-dance and singing performances outside on the main square; the next one will take place in 2006.

Katona József Theater. The beautiful theater is known for its excellent dramatic productions (in Hungarian) and also hosts classical concerts, operas, and dance performances during the Spring Festival and other celebrations. ⊠ *Katona József tér 5* ☎ *76/483–283.*

Kodály Zoltán Zenepedagógiai Intézet (Zoltán Kodály Music Pedagogy Institute). In a former Franciscan monastery, the school often holds student and faculty recitals, particularly during its international music seminar in mid- to late July, which is held in every odd-numbered year. ⊠ *Kéttemplom köz 1* ☎ *76/481–518.*

Sports & the Outdoors

The nearby puszta is the setting for traditional horse-stunt shows, carriage rides, guided horseback rides, and other horsey activities. Full-length shows and daylong excursions are bus tour–centric (because of the costs involved), although essentially anything can be arranged if a smaller group or individuals are willing to pay for it. Contact Tourinform (see ⇨ Visitor Information, *below*) for other possibilities and for help making arrangements.

Nyakvágó Kft. This company sometimes offers full- and half-day "Puszta Programs" for smaller groups of individuals who want to take part in the program on the same day. The program includes carriage rides, horse shows, a visit to a working farm, and folk dancing, all lubricated with wine and pálinka (brandy) and including typical puszta meals. A full-day program costs roughly 5,000 HUF, and a half day costs about 4,000 HUF. It's best to call a day or so in advance. ⊠ *Bösztörpuszta-Nagyállás, Kunszentmiklós* 🕿 *76/711–598* 🕿 *76/351–201.*

BUGAC

❹ *46 km (29 mi) south of Kecskemét, 120 km (74 mi) southeast of Budapest.*

The Bugac puszta, declared by UNESCO as a bioreserve for its unique flora and fauna, is the central and most-visited section of the 127,200-acre **Kiskunsági Nemzeti Park** (Kiskunság National Park)—the smaller sister of Hortobágy National Park (farther northeast); together they compose the entire Great Plain. Bugac puszta's expansive, sandy, impossibly flat grassland scenery has provided Hungarian poets and artists with inexhaustible material over the centuries. Although the dry, open stretches may seem numbingly uniform to the casual eye, the Bugac's fragile ecosystem is the most varied of the entire park; its primeval juniper trees, extremely rare in the region, are the area's most protected and treasured flora. Today, Bugac continues to inspire visitors with its strong equestrian traditions and the fun but touristy horse shows and tours offered in its boundaries. The park's half-hour traditional horse show, included in the entrance fee, takes place daily at 1:15 PM. You can also wander around the area and peek into the Kiskunság National Park Museum, which has exhibits about pastoral life on the prairie. ⊠ *Kiskunság National Park Management Center, House of Nature, Liszt Ferenc u. 19, Kecskemét* 🕿 *76/501–596* ⊕ *www.knp.hu* 🕿 *2,000 HUF per person, plus 1,000 HUF per car* 🕘 *May–Oct., Mon.–Fri. 8–4, Sat.–Sun. 8–1.*

Where to Eat

$–$$$ ✕ **Bugaci Csárda.** Bugac's most famous and popular restaurant is a tour-bus magnet but is still considered a mandatory part of a puszta visit. It's at the end of a dirt road just past the park's main entrance, in a traditional whitewashed, thatch-roof house decorated inside with cheerful red-and-white folk embroideries. Here you can feast on all the

Hungarian standards. ⊠ *Rte. 54, at the park entrance, Bugac* ☎ *76/ 372–522* ☵ *No credit cards* ☾ *Closed Nov.–Mar.*

Sports & the Outdoors

The region specializes in equestrian sports, and several companies offer horseback-riding lessons, trail rides, and horse-carriage rides.

☾ **Bugac Tours.** Through its office at the *Karikás Csárda* (Karikás Inn) inside Kiskunság National Park, Bugac Tours organizes horseback-riding trips, horse-show excursions, barbecue dinners, and visits to local ranch homes and farmhouses. ⊠ *Karikás Csárda, Bugac* ☎ *76/575–112* ☰ *76/ 575–114.*

☾ **Bugaci Ménes.** Also located inside Kiskunság National Park, Bugaci Ménes breeds sport horses, sheep, and grey cattle, but is most famous for horse shows it puts on for tourists. ⊠ *Off Rte. 54, Bugac* ☎☰ *76/ 575–028.*

☾ **Juhász és Társa.** The company regularly presents traditional horsemanship shows, including the "Puszta Five," a prestigious domestic and international equestrian team. Visitors can attend courses under the instruction of László Juhász, a world champion in equestrian stunts and driving. ⊠ *Móritz u. 5, Bugac* ☎ *76/372–583.*

SZEGED

❺ *87 km (54 mi) south of Kecskemét, 171 km (106 mi) southeast of Budapest.*

The city that lays at the junction of the Tisza and the Maros rivers is the largest in southern Hungary. Although Szeged owes its origin to the Tisza River, the river has also been its ruin. In 1879, a disastrous flood known by the residents simply as "the water," destroyed the old Szeged in just one night. It's ironic then, to say the least, that Szeged is called "The Sunshine Town," after its average 2,100 hours of sunshine a year. With international assistance the city was rebuilt, and out of gratitude Szeged's ring boulevards bear the names of the cities that helped (Vienna, Moscow, London, Paris, Berlin, Brussels, and Rome).

Historical excavations show the probability that Szeged was once the seat of Atilla, the king of the Huns, during the 5th century. The city later became a Turkish stronghold after it was conquered in 1543. Under Turkish rule, Szeged continued to develop and became a center for trade in southern Hungary, especially given its favorable location along the Tisza River. In 1686, with help from Austrian forces, Szeged was liberated from the Turks. But Hungarians were not happy with Austrian rule either, and in 1704 they tried to take back the city. However, they had poor weaponry, and their rebellion was easily put down. Under Austrian rule Szeged served as a military outpost.

Szeged's darkest hour, known as the Great Flood, came in 1879 when melting snow caused the Tisza and Maros rivers to burst with extra water and smash open a dyke near the outskirts of town. The entire

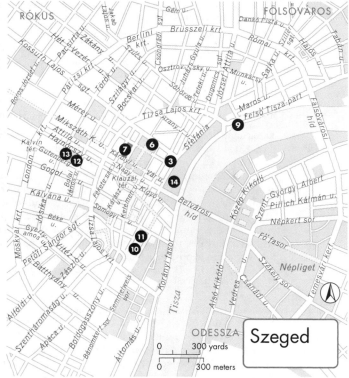

city was nearly washed away, and when it was over, 150 people had died and only 265 houses remained standing—5,458 were destroyed. Since 1931, Szeged has held its Open-Air Festival in memory of those lost in the Great Flood.

Aside from the flood, however, Szeged is famous for two other things: paprika and salami. Szeged's paprikas are useful not only in goulash kettles but also in test tubes. Local biochemist Albert Szentgyörgyi won the Nobel Prize in 1937 for his discoveries about vitamin C, extracted from his hometown spice. In late summer and early autumn, you can see rack after rack of red peppers drying in the open air all over town. World-famous Pick salami also comes from Szeged.

While Szeged does hold architectural delights, they are few compared to cities of similar size; it makes up for this, however, with a dynamic atmosphere that peaks during the school year, when students from the city's schools and universities liven up the streets, cafés, and bars.

Numbers in the margins correspond to numbers on the Szeged map.

6 The heart of the city center is the large **Széchenyi tér.** Szeged's inner park-like square is lined with trees and surrounded by imposing buildings.

② The most notable of Szeged's structures is the bright yellow, neo-baroque **Városház** (Town Hall; ✉ Széchenyi tér 10), built at the turn of the 19th century and, after suffering major damage during the flood of 1879, reconstructed by well-known eclectic art nouveau architect Ödön Lechner. Across Széchenyi tér from the Town Hall stands the pale-green **Hotel ③ Tisza** (✉ Wesselényi u. 4). Although the guest rooms and lobby look tired and worn, the hotel's lovely—and still quite active—concert hall was the site of many piano recitals by legendary composer Béla Bartók. Its restaurant was a favorite haunt of famous poet Mihály Babits.

⑨ The ground floor of the two-story **Pick Szalámi és Szegedi Paprika Múzeum**
Fodor'sChoice (Pick Salami and Szeged Paprika Museum) is devoted entirely to the his-
★ tory of the Pick company and its salami production. Knives and tools used in the process are on display—which could turn your stomach— as are videos showing the production of salami and audio recording from former workers at the Pick factory. Upstairs is loads of information on paprika, including information about the picking and planting of the peppers and the numerous health benefits. In return for the museum fee, visitors are treated to samples of salami and free postage anywhere in the world for a postcard from the company. ✉ *Felső Tiszapart 10* ☎ *62/421–814* ⊕ *www.museum.hu/szeged/pick* ☜ *240 HUF* ☉ *Tues.–Fri. 3–6, Sat. 1–4.*

> **need a break?** Grab a hot strudel stuffed with apple, poppy seed, or even peppery cabbage at the counter of **Hatos Rétes** (✉ Klauzal tér 6 ☎ 62/420–121). This bakery-cum-café is a popular spot, not only for a quick snack but also *óriás palacsinta* (giant stuffed crepes) that come either savory (ham, cheese) or sweet (plum, raspberry, chestnut). This is also among the few places in Hungary that serves decaffeinated coffee.

⑩ Beneath the archways surrounding **Dóm tér** (Cathedral Square), which was built in 1920, is a row of 90 statues of Hungary's most famous scientists, politicians and other noteworthy personalities.

★ **⑪** Szeged's most striking building is the **Fogadalmi templom**. (Votive Church), an imposing neo-Romanesque brick edifice that was built between 1912 and 1929 in fulfillment of a municipal promise made after the 1879 flood. One of Hungary's largest churches, it seats 6,000 and has a splendid organ with 12,000 pipes, one of the biggest in Europe; the church's bell is the second-largest in the country. The church forms the backdrop to the annual Szeged Open-Air Festival, held in the vast Dóm tér (Cathedral Square). A performance of a different sort takes place here daily at 12:15 PM, when the mechanical figures on the church's clock put on their five-minute show to music. During excavations for the Votive Church, Szeged's oldest building, the Dömötör Tower, was discovered; it's estimated to have been built between the 11th and 13th centuries. ✉ *Dóm tér* ☎ *62/420–157 church* ☎ *62/420–953* ☜ *Church free, crypt 300 HUF* ☉ *Church weekends 9–6, Sun. 12:30–6. Crypt Apr.–Oct., Tues.–Sun. 10–6; Nov.–Mar., Tues.–Sun. 10–4.*

⑫ Szeged's neoclassical **Régi Zsinagóga** (Old Synagogue) was built in 1839. On its outside wall a marker written in Hungarian and Hebrew shows the height of the floodwaters in 1879, an estimated 3.8 meters high. It took four months for water to recede and the town to dry up completely. It is open only rarely for special events. ⊠ *Hajnóczi u. 12* ⊘ *Apr.–Sept., Sun.–Fri. 9–noon and 1–6 (often closes earlier on Fri.).*

★ ⓭ The **Új Zsinagóga.** (New Synagogue), finished in 1905, is Szeged's purest and finest representation of the art nouveau style. Its wood and stone carvings, wrought iron, stained-glass windows, and spectacular dome are all the work of local craftspeople. A memorial in the entrance hall honors Szeged's victims of the Holocaust. The New Synagogue is not far from the smaller Old Synagogue. ⊠ *Gutenberg u. 20, at Jósika u.* ☎ *62/423–849* 🎟 *200 HUF* ⊘ *Apr.–Oct., Sun.–Mon. 9–noon and 1–5; Nov.–Mar., Sun.–Mon. 9–2.*

⓮ The eclectic **Móra Ferenc Múzeum** (Ferenc Mora Museum), named after one of Szeged's early-20th-century writers and museum curators, sits at the foot of the Tisza Bridge, which connects both sides of the city. The museum displays artifacts found during various excavations dating back to when Hungary was first settled. In addition to natural-science displays, you'll also see works by contemporary Hungarian sculptors. ⊠ *Roosevelt tér 1–3* ☎ *62/549–040* 🖨 *62/549–061* 🎟 *400 HUF* ⊘ *Oct.–June, Tues–Sun. 10–5; July–Sept., Tues.–Sun. 10–6.*

off the beaten path **NEMZETI TÖRTÉNETI EMLÉKPARK –** The ultimate in monuments to Hungarian history and pride is the enormous National Historic Memorial Park in Ópusztaszer, 29 km (18 mi) north of Szeged. It was built on the site of the first parliamentary congregation of the nomadic Magyar tribes, held in AD 895, in which they agreed to be ruled by mighty Árpád. Paths meander among an open-air museum of traditional village buildings. The main draw, however, is the **Feszty Körkép** (Feszty Cyclorama), an astounding 5,249-foot, 360-degree panoramic oil painting depicting the arrival of the Magyar tribes to the Carpathian basin in the 9th century AD—effectively, the birth of Hungary. It was painted between 1892 and 1894 by Árpád Feszti and exhibited in Budapest to celebrate the Magyar millennium. Sixty percent of it was destroyed during World War II, and it wasn't until 1991 that a group of art restorers brought it here and started a painstaking project to resurrect it in time for Hungary's millecentennial celebrations in 1996. Today, housed in its own giant rotunda, the painting is viewable as part of a multimedia experience: groups of up to 100 at a time are let in every half-hour for a 25-minute viewing of the painting, accompanied by a recorded explanation and, at the end, a special sound show in which different recordings are played near different parts of the painting—galloping horses, trumpeting horns, screaming virgins, rushing water—to the scene depicted. The attraction is so popular that on summer weekends it's a good idea to call ahead and reserve a spot (timed tickets are given for specific shows). The explanation is in Hungarian, but English-language versions on CD, available at the entrance, can be listened to on headphones before or after the viewing. The cyclorama is the only park attraction open in winter. ⊠ *Szoborkert 68, Ópusztaszer* ☎ *62/275–257 or 62/275–133* 🎟 *1,600 HUF* ⊘ *Apr.–Oct., daily 9–6; Nov.–Mar., daily 9–4.*

Where to Stay & Eat

\$\$–\$\$\$\$ ✕ **Alabárdos Étterem.** An 1810 landmark houses this elegant eatery, and its specialty is not just a meal but an experience: the lights are dimmed as waiters rush to your table with a flaming spear of skewered meats, which they then prepare in a spicy ragout at your table. The restaurant also does very well with fish if you're not into red meat. ⊠ *Oskola u. 13* ☎ *62/420–914* ☒ *MC, V* ☯ *Closed Sun.*

\$–\$\$\$ ✕ **Botond Restaurant.** Originally the location of Szeged's first printing press,
Fodor'sChoice this 1810 neoclassical building now houses a popular restaurant. Spe-
★ cialties include *Tenkes-hegyi szűzérmek* (Tenkes Hill pork tenderloin), which is served with bacon, mushrooms, and paprika. The outdoor terrace is a prime dining spot in good weather. Try the *halászlé* (fisherman's soup), a spicy fish soup made with hot paprika for which Szeged is famous for countrywide. There's Gypsy music nightly from 7. ⊠ *Széchenyi tér 13* ☎ *62/420–435* ☒ *AE, DC, MC, V.*

¢–\$\$ ✕ **Öreg Kőrössy Halászkert Vendéglő.** This thatch-roof fisherman's inn on the Tisza River first opened in 1930; decades later, this place mixes rustic charm and modern glitter. The menu still includes original house staples such as rich-red *Öreg Kőrössy halászlé* (Old Kőrös fish soup) and *kőrössy* (fish paprikás). It's not easy to find; take a car or bus, as it's a long walk from the city center. To reach the restaurant, head north along river on Felső-Tiszapart and turn left after about 2 km (1 mi), where the main road makes its first curve, at a sign pointing to a restaurant; follow the smaller road around several curves and go past a restaurant with a similar name. ⊠ *Sárga üdülőtelep 262* ☎ *62/495–481* ☒ *MC, V.*

¢–\$ 🏨 **Marika Panzió.** This friendly inn sits on a historic street in the Alsóváros (Lower Town), a five-minute drive from the city center. Cozy rooms have light-wood paneling and larger-hotel amenities, including color TVs, minibars, and air-conditioning. The back garden has a small swimming pool. ⊠ *Nyíl u. 45, H-6725* ☎ *62/443–861* ⊕ *www.hotels.hu/marika szeged* ⇆ *9 rooms* ⚭ *Minibars, cable TV, pool, laundry service, free parking* ⑩ *BP* ☒ *AE, DC, MC, V.*

The Arts

Szeged's own symphony orchestra, theater company, and famous contemporary dance troupe form the solid foundation for a rich cultural life. Chamber-music concerts are often held in the conservatory and in the historic recital hall of the Hotel Tisza. The city's concert season runs from September to May.

Szeged Nemzeti Színház (Szeged National Theater). The city's main theater stages Hungarian dramas, as well as classical concerts, operas, and ballets. Just to the left of the theater is a statue of Hungary's most famous gypsy musician, Pista Dankó. ⊠ *Deák Ferenc u. 12* ☎ *62/479–279.*

Szegedi Szabadtéri Játékok (Szeged Open-Air Festival). Szeged's most important annual event, drawing crowds from around the country, is the annual festival, a tradition established in 1931 in remembrance of the great flood. The festival lasts from mid-July through mid-September. The gala series of dramas, operas, operettas, classical concerts, and folk-dance performances by Hungarian and international artists is held outdoors on the vast cobblestone Cathedral Square. The line-up always includes outstanding performances of Hungary's great national drama, Imre Madách's *Tragedy of Man.* Classical music groups from the seven cities that assisted Szeged's rebuild are also on hand for performances. Tickets are always hot commodities, so plan far ahead. ✉ *Festival Ticket Office, Deák Ferenc u. 28–30* ☎ *62/554–710* ⊕ *nemzetiszinhaz.szeged.hu.*

Shopping

You'll have no trouble finding packages of authentic Szegedi paprika. in all sizes and degrees of spiciness in most of the city's shops. Szeged's other famous product is its excellent salami, which has been made by the local Pick salami factory since 1869.

Pick Factory Outlet. You'll find an extensive salami selection at the company store, which has two outlets in town. ✉ *Jókai u. 7, in Nagyárúház Passage* ☎ *62/425–021* ✉ *Maros u. 21, next to the factory* ☎ *62/421–879.*

THE GREAT PLAIN ESSENTIALS

BUS TRAVEL
Volánbusz operates service from Budapest's Népstadion terminal to towns throughout the Great Plain. Local buses connect most towns within the region.
🚍 **Volánbusz** ☎ 1/219–8080 in Budapest ⊕ www.volanbusz.hu.

CAR TRAVEL
From Budapest, Route 4 goes straight to Debrecen, but it's faster to take the M3 expressway and switch to Route 33 midway there; the M5 goes to Kecskemét and Szeged.

The flat expanses of this region make for easy, if eventually numbing, driving. Secondary route 47 runs along the eastern edge of the country, connecting Debrecen and Szeged. It's easy to drive between Debrecen and Kecskemét via Route 4 through Szolnok before you drop south in Cegléd. The puszta regions of Bugac and Hortobágy are accessible from Kecskemét and Debrecen by well-marked roads.

TRAIN TRAVEL
Service to the Great Plain from Budapest is quite good; daily service is available from the capital's Nyugati (West) and Keleti (East) stations. Intercity (IC) trains, the fastest choice, run between Budapest and Debrecen, Kecskemét, and Szeged; they require seat reservations.

The train ride to Debrecen from Budapest is around three hours, with the Debrecen train station about a 10-minute walk from the city center. The train from Budapest to Kecskemét is about one hour, while the trip to Szeged from Budapest by rail is 2½ hours.

Connections within the region are via the rail junctions in Szolnok and Cegléd, in the geometric center of the Great Plain. The Szeged train station is a 30-minute walk from the town center, but you can also take a tram. The train ride from Szolnok to Debrecen takes about 90 minutes. The trains for Kecskemét are on the Szeged line; the trip between the towns takes roughly an hour. From Kecskemét you can also take a narrow-gauge train service to Kiskunmajsa, another village on the puszta, aboard a "nostalgia" train with old engines and carriages.

🚆 Train Stations **Debrecen train station** ✉ Petőfi tér 12, Debrecen ☎ 52/346-777. **Kecskemét train station** ✉ Kodály Zoltán tér 7, Kecskemét ☎ 76/322-460. **Kecskemét narrow-gauge train station** ✉ Halasi út 19, Kecskemét ☎ 76/504-308. **Szeged train station** ✉ Tisza pályaudvar, Indóház tér, Szeged ☎ 62/420-136.

TOURS

Cityrama runs daylong tours several times a week to the Great Plain from Budapest. They begin with a sightseeing walk through Kecskemét, then head out to the prairie town of Lajosmizse for drinking, dining, Gypsy music, carriage rides, and a traditional csikós horse show. The cost is 17,000 HUF per person.

IBUSZ Travel also operates full-day tours out to the Great Plain, to Lajosmizse as well as to Bugac, both first taking in Kecskemét's sights. These tours cost approximately 21,000 HUF per person.

🚆 **Cityrama** ✉ District V, Báthory u. 22, St. Stephen's Basilica, Budapest ☎ 1/302-4382 in Budapest ⊕ www.cityrama.hu. **IBUSZ Travel** ✉ District V, Ferenciek tere 10, Around Ferenciek tere, Budapest ☎ 1/485-2700 in Budapest ⊕ www.ibusz.hu.

VISITOR INFORMATION

🚆 **Tourinform** ✉ Piac u. 20, Debrecen ☎ 52/412-250 🖶 52/535-323 ✉ Hortobágy Pusztainform ✉ Pásztormúzeum, Hortobágy ☎🖶 52/589-321 ✉ Kossuth tér 1, Kecskemét ☎ 76/481-065 ✉ Dugonics tér 2, Szeged ☎ 62/488-690.

NORTHERN HUNGARY

(12)

Paul Olchvary

NORTHERN HUNGARY STRETCHES FROM THE DANUBE BEND, north of Budapest, along the northeastern frontier with Slovakia as far west as Sátoraljaújhely. It is a clearly defined area, marked by several mountain ranges of no great height but of considerable scenic beauty. The highest peaks reach 3,000 feet and are thickly wooded almost to their summits. Grottoes and caves abound, as well as thermal baths. In the state game reserves, it's not uncommon to spot herds of dainty little roe deer, the much larger red deer (a European counterpart of the American elk), wild boars, and eagles.

Historically, the valleys of northern Hungary have always been of considerable strategic importance, as they provided the only access to the Carpathian Mountains. The city of Eger, renowned throughout Hungarian history as one of the guardians of these strategic routes, retains its splendor, with many ruins picturesquely dotting the surrounding hilltops. What's more, this is one of the great wine-growing districts of Hungary, with Eger contributing the "Magyar nectar" and Tokaj producing the "wine of kings."

Numbers in the margin correspond to numbers on the Northern Hungary map.

HOLLÓKŐ

★ ❶ *100 km (62 mi) northeast of Budapest.*

UNESCO lists this tiny mountain village close to the Slovakian border as one of its World Heritage Sites because of Hollókő's unique medieval structure and the age-old Palóc (ethnographic group indigenous to northern Hungary) cultural and handcrafting traditions still practiced today by the village's 400 inhabitants. The most famous of these traditions is its Easter celebration, when villagers dress in colorful embroidered costumes. During this time, thousands of visitors descend upon the village.

Pocket-size though it may be, Hollókő is authentically enchanting: old whitewashed houses, some of them built in the 17th century, cluster together on narrow cobblestone pathways; directly above them loom the hilltop ruins (restored in the mid-1990s) of a 13th-century castle. If you enter the village by car, which is the easiest way to get there unless you go by a bus tour from Budapest, you will probably be directed up to a parking area on the hillside a short walk from the village's historical center below; the village center is closed to most outside traffic. The parking fee, good for the entire day, is around 400 HUF. For information on Hollókő's Easter festivities and other events, contact the village's cultural foundation (see ⇨ Visitor Information *in* Northern Hungary Essentials).

Where to Stay & Eat

$–$$ ✕ **Muskátli Vendéglő.** Named for the bright red and pink flowers lining its windowsills, the Geranium Restaurant is a cozy little eatery on Hol-

lókő's main street. Specialties include *palócgulyás,* a rich local goulash thick with chunks of pork, potatoes, carrots, and wax beans that makes for a good, quick meal. You can also get *nógrádi palócpecsenye* (pork cutlets bathed in mustard-garlic sauce). ⊠ *Kossuth út 61* ☎ *32/379–262* ⊟ *AE, DC, MC, V* ✆ *Closed Mon. in Mar.–Dec. and Mon.–Wed. in Jan.–Feb.*

$ ⌂ **Kastély Szirák.** One of Hungary's best country-house hotels was built in 1748, on the foundations of a 13th-century knights' hostel, for Count József Teleki, an arts patron who created a vast library and covered the main hall with frescoes depicting Ovid's *Metamorphoses.* A newer wing houses the "tourist hotel," comprising relatively bland but recently spruced-up units that contribute little to the aura of this country house. You can also go horseback riding, even if you're not a guest. The hotel lies about 35 km (22 mi) along Route 21 and then some lovely side roads from Hollókő. A world away from the luxury of the hotel is the unassuming village center just down the road, where you may see local romas (gypsies) riding horse-drawn wagons. ⊠ *Petőfi út 26, H–3044 Szirák* ☎☎ *60/353–053* ⊕ *www.kastelyszirak.hu* ⭯ *21 rooms, 4 suites* ⌃ *Restaurant, cable TV, tennis court, sauna, horseback riding, meeting rooms; no a/c* ⊟ *AE, DC, MC, V* ⦿| *CP.*

EGER

80 km (50 mi) east of Budapest.

Surrounded by vineyards and with more than 175 of Hungary's historic monuments—a figure surpassed only by Budapest and Sopron—the picture-book baroque city of Eger is ripe for exploration. The city, which lies in a fertile valley between the Mátra Mountains and their eastern neighbor, the Bükk range, has borne witness to much history, heartbreak, and glory. It was settled quite early in the Hungarian conquest of the land, and it was one of five bishoprics created by King Stephen I when he Christianized the country almost a millennium ago.

In 1552 the city was attacked by the Turks, but the commander, István Dobó, and fewer than 2,000 men and women held out for 38 days against 80,000 Turkish soldiers and drove them away. One of Hungary's great legends tells of the women of Eger pouring hot pitch onto the heads of the Turks as they attempted to scale the castle walls (the event is depicted in a famous painting now in the National Gallery in Budapest). Despite such heroism, however, Eger fell to the Turks in 1596 and became one of the most important northern outposts of Muslim power until its reconquest in 1687.

Today, restored baroque and rococo buildings line Eger's cobblestone streets, making for excellent strolling and sightseeing. Dobó István utca, which runs right under the castle walls, is not to be missed. The spacious, lovely city park and the adjacent outdoor swimming complex make cooling off (or warming up, in a thermal pool) aesthetically as well as physically soothing. Wherever you wander, make a point of peeking into open courtyards, where you may happen upon otherwise hidden architectural gems.

Numbers in the margin correspond to numbers on the Eger map.

★ ❷ The grand, neoclassical **Bazilika,** the second-largest cathedral in Hungary, was built in the center of town early in the 19th century. It is approached by a stunning stairway flanked by statues of Sts. Stephen, László, Peter, and Paul—the work of Italian sculptor Marco Casagrande, who also carved 22 biblical reliefs inside and outside the building. Ironically, perhaps, a few yards to the left of the main steps leading up to the Bazilika—on what appears to be its property—is a popular wine bar built into the high brick wall that flanks each side of the steps. From May 15 through October 15, organ recitals are held Monday through Saturday at 11:30 AM and Sunday at 12:45 PM. It's best to visit when no masses are taking place—from 9 until 6. ✉ *Eszterházy tér* ☎ *36/515–725* 🎟 *Free* ☉ *Daily 5:45 AM–7:30 PM.*

☾ ❸ The baroque building opposite the basilica, which covers the entire block, is a former lyceum, now the **Eszterházy Károly főiskola** (Károly Eszterházy Teachers College). The handsome library has a fine trompel'oeil ceiling fresco that gives an intoxicating illusion of depth. High up in the structure's six-story observatory, now a museum, is a horizontal sundial with a tiny gold cannon, which, when filled with gunpowder,

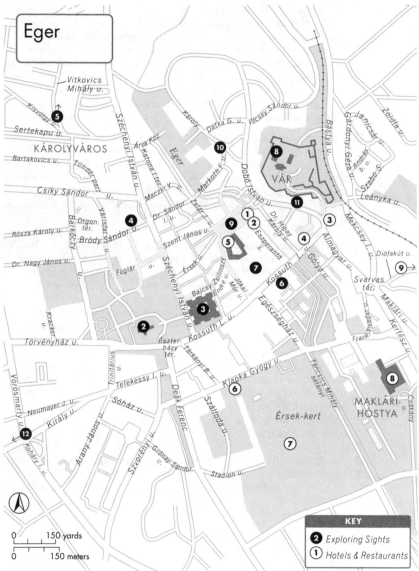

Eger

used to let out a burst at exactly high noon. Also here, the noonday sun, shining through a tiny aperture, makes a palm-size silvery spot on the meridian line on the marble floor. Climb higher to the grand finale, a "Specula Periscope": in a darkened room, a man manipulates three rods of a periscope—in operation since 1776—to project panoramic views of Eger onto a round table. Children squeal with delight as real people and cars hurry and scurry across the table like hyperactive Legos. ⊠ *Eszterházy tér 1* 🕾 *36/520–400* 🖼 *Library and museum 450 HUF each* ☉ *Apr.–Sept., Tues.–Sun. 9:30–3:30; Oct.–Mar., weekends 9:30–1:30.*

❹ Eger s rococo **Cistercia templom** (Cistercian Church) was built during the first half of the 18th century. A splendid statue of St. Francis Borgia kneeling beneath Christ on the cross dominates the main altar, which dates to 1770. The church can be visited only during mass; other times it can be viewed only through the locked gate. ⊠ *Széchenyi u. 15* 🕾 *36/313–496* 🖼 *Free* ☉ *Mass weekdays at 7:15 and 8 AM, Sun. at 8 and 10 AM and 7 PM.*

need a break?

Rádi Kávéház-Bisztró (⊠ Széchenyi u. 2 🕾 36/312–442), on Eger's central pedestrian street a few yards from the Basilica, is a spacious, irresistibly stylish self-service (i.e., no tips) café in which to revive after sightseeing if you don't mind the blinding red tabletops, counters, signs, and trays. Not only do they offer an appealing selection of coffee, ice cream, and pastry (plus champagne, wine, and beer) but their mayonnaise-based salads make for a quick, affordable bite to eat. Outdoor seating is right across the street from the tranquil garden of the Archbishop's Palace beside the Basilica.

Dobos Cukrászda (⊠ Széchenyi u. 6, 🕾 36/413–335), in the next block after the Rádi Kávéház, is a more traditional café with table service, where the focus is more strictly on coffee and pastries; try the *Eszterházy torta* (walnut-cream cake) or the *bécsi gesztenyés* (chestnut-cream roll).

❺ The light, lovely, dove-gray **Rác templom** (Serbian Orthodox Church) contains more than 100 icon paintings on wood that look as though they were fashioned from gold and marble. The church sits on a hilltop north of the city center. ⊠ *Vitkovits u. 30* 🕾 *36/320–129* 🖼 *300 HUF* ☉ *Tues.–Sun. 10–4, but often opens earlier and closes later.*

❻ The **Nagypréposti palota** (Provost's House) is a small rococo palace still considered one of Hungary's finest mansions despite abuse by the Red Army (soldiers ruined several frescoes by heating the building with oil). The building now serves as European headquarters of the International Committee of Historic Towns (ICOMOS). Alas, it is not open regularly to the public. ⊠ *Kossuth Lajos u. 4.*

During a brief stay in Eger (1758–61), German artist Henrik Fazola graced many buildings with his work but none so exquisitely as the wrought-iron twin gates that, facing each other just inside the entryway of the ❼ **Megye Ház** (County Council Hall), frame the inner entrances to the building's two wings. Sent to Paris in 1889 for the international exposition, the richly ornamented, mirror-image gates—which have not only numerous flowers and leaves but clusters of grapes and a stork with a snake in its beak—won a gold medal 130 years after their creation. On the wall to the right of the building's street entrance, a sign indicates the level of floodwaters during the flooding of the Eger stream on August 31, 1878. Similar signs can be seen throughout this area of the city. ⊠ *Kossuth Lajos u. 9* ⊙ *Weekdays 9–5, often later.*

Ⓒ ❽ **Eger Vár** (Eger Castle) was built after the devastating Tartar invasion of
Fodor'sChoice 1241–42. When Béla IV returned from exile in Italy, he ordered the erec-
★ tion of mighty fortresses like those he had seen in the West. Within the castle walls an imposing Romanesque cathedral was built and then, during the 15th century, rebuilt in Gothic style; today only its foundations remain. Inside the foundation area, a statue of Szent István (St. Stephen), erected in 1900, looks out benignly over the city. Nearby are catacombs that were built in the second half of the 16th century by Italian engineers. By racing back and forth through this labyrinth of underground tunnels and appearing at various ends of the castle, the hundreds of defenders tricked the attacking Turks into thinking there were thousands of them. The Gothic-style **Püspök Ház** (Bishop's House) contains the castle history museum and, in the basement, a numismatic museum where coins can be minted and certified (in English). Also here are an art gallery, displaying Italian and Dutch Renaissance works; a prison exhibit, near the main entrance; and a wax museum, depicting characters from the Hungarian historical novel *Eclipse of the Crescent Moon*, about Hungary's final expulsion of the Turks. Videotaping is not allowed anywhere in the castle, but you can take pictures (no flash) for a fee, except in the art gallery, where no photos are allowed at all. ⊠ *Dózsa György tér* ☎ *36/312–744* 🖭 *Castle with all museums 800 HUF; castle grounds only 300 HUF; photography fee 500 HUF* ⊙ *Castle grounds Apr.–Oct., daily 6 AM–8 PM; Nov.–Mar., daily 6–5. Museums Apr.–Sept., Tues.–Sun. 9–5; Oct.–Mar., Tues.–Sun. 9–3. Prison exhibit and catacombs Apr.–Sept., Tues.–Sun. 9–5 (catacombs remain open on Mon.). Wax museum daily 9–6.*

❾ Downtown, picturesque **Dobó tér** is marked by two intensely animated statues produced in the early 20th century by a father and son: *Dobó the Defender* is by Alajos Stróbl, and the sculpture of a Magyar battling two Turks is by Stróbl's son, Zsigmond Kisfaludi-Stróbl.

Dobó tér's famous statues flank the pale-pink **Minorita templom** (Minorite Church; ☎ *36/516–613* or *36/417–979*), which with its twin spires and finely carved pulpit, pews, and organ loft is considered one of the best baroque churches in Central Europe. It's open daily from 10 to 6.

Ⓒ The **Kisvonat,** a miniature train that actually runs on wheels, leaves from Dobó tér every hour on the hour for an approximately 40-minute tour of Eger's historical sights. ⊠ *Dobó tér* ☎ *34/487–381* or *20/388–6241* 🖭 *400 HUF* ⊙ *Apr.–Oct. and late Dec.–early Jan., daily 9–5 or later.*

❿ A bridge over the Eger stream—it's too small to be classified as a river—leads to an early-17th-century Turkish **minaret**, from the top of which Muslims were called to prayer. After the Turks were driven out of Hungary in the late 1600s, an effort was made to topple the minaret using no less than 400 oxen. The venture failed, and it became the northernmost surviving Turkish structure in Europe. ⊠ *Knézich K. u.* ▣ *200 HUF* ☉ *Apr.–Oct., daily 9–6.*

 In a tranquil courtyard right under the castle wall, the **Palóc Folk Art Exhibition** is a charming, three-room museum displaying traditional carvings, embroidery, folk costumes, furniture, pillows, and pottery of the Palóc region. You must pay a fee to use your camera and a larger one to use your video camera. ⊠ *Dobó u. 12* ☎ *36/312–744* ▣ *140 HUF; photography fee 500 HUF per camera; video fee 1,000 HUF per camera* ☉ *Apr.–Oct., Tues.–Sun. 9–5.*

Eger wine is renowned beyond Hungary. The best-known variety is *Egri Bikavér* (Bull's Blood of Eger), a full-bodied red wine. Other outstanding vintages are the Medoc Noir, a dark red dessert wine; Leányka, a delightful dry white; and the sweeter white Muskotály. The place to sample them is the **Szépasszony-völgy,** a vineyard area on the southwestern edge of Eger's city limits. More than 200 small wine cellars (some of them literally holes-in-the-wall) stand open and inviting in the warm weather, and a few are open in winter, too. You may be given a tour of the cellar, and wines will be tapped from the barrel into your glass by the vintners themselves at the tiniest cost (but it's prudent to inquire politely how much it will cost before imbibing).

off the beaten path

SZILVÁSVÁRAD – About 25 km (16 mi) from Eger up into the Bükk Mountains brings you to this village, one of Hungary's most important equestrian centers. For more than 500 years, the white Lipizzaner horses have been bred here, and every year on a weekend in early September they prance and pose in the Lipicai Lovasfesztivál, an international carriage-driving competition held in the equestrian stadium. At other times, you can see them grazing in the village fields.

The proud history of the Lipizzaner horses is covered at the **Lipicai Múzeum** (Lipizzaner Museum; ⊠ Park u. 8 ☎ 36/355–155). Admission is 80 HUF, and the museum is open from April through October, Tuesday to Sunday from 9 to noon and 2 to 5. Szilvásvárad is also a popular base for hiking and bicycling through the surrounding gentle green hills of Bükk National Park.

Where to Stay & Eat

$–$$$ ✕ **Excalibur Középkori Lovagétterem.** Eger's newest dining rage is well worth a try—if not necessarily for the slightly gimmicky medieval-period atmosphere—for the hearty fare and an excuse to visit the lovely city park. With candlelighted rustic wooden tables, benches, chairs, and plates, and waiters dressed in ostensibly authentic costumes, the spacious dining room and outdoor seating area are, on the whole, a pleasant setting in which to delight in the various poultry and wild game dishes; for example, the "Tasty Virgin Treat" (grilled goose wing with vegetables) or wild boar soup with tarragon. ⊠ *Érsekkert 1, in city park* ☎ *36/427–754* ▤ *AE, MC, V.*

★ **$–$$$** ✕ **Fehér Szarvas.** The name of this rustic cellar means "white stag," and game is the uncontested specialty. Favorites include venison fillet served in a pan sizzling with chicken liver, sausage, and herb butter, with a blanched pear as an added plus; leg of rabbit is braised in red wine and bathed in a sour-cream vegetable-mustard sauce with potato croquettes. The many antlers, skulls, skins, and mounted birds hanging from rafters and walls—not to mention the two little stuffed goats by the entrance— make the inn look like Archduke Franz Ferdinand's trophy room. ⊠ *Klapka György u. 8* ☎ *36/411–129* ☰ *AE, MC, V.*

★ **$–$$$** ✕ **HBH Bajor Sörház.** For substantial Hungarian (and, it seems, Bavarian) fare, it's impossible to beat the popular HBH Bavarian Beer Tavern, which has a great location on Dobó tér. Favorites include Bavarian pig's knuckle "baked in beer" and veal stew with cottage-cheese noodles. Any of these will go down smoothly with a glass of Bull's Blood— or perhaps a Munich Hofbräuhaus, the beer that gives the restaurant its initials. ⊠ *Bajcsy Zsilinszky u. 19, at Dobó tér* ☎ *36/515–516* ☰ *AE, MC, V.*

★ **$–$$** ✕ **Efendi Restaurant.** Excellent food makes this restaurant, in an arched basement room a few doors away from Eger's castle gate, a regional favorite. The interior is "modern-medieval-romantic"—candlelighted tables among floral landscape paintings interspersed with a bit of medieval weaponry. A hearty quick lunch is *legényfogó leves* (wedding soup or, literally, "catcher of young men"). Made with meat, vegetables, cream, and liver, this stew is one of the lures that Hungarian women have used for centuries to attract potential husbands. ⊠ *Kossuth Lajos u. 19* ☎ *36/410–323* ☰ *AE, DC, MC, V* ☉ *No lunch weekdays.*

$ ⌂ **Hungest Hotel Flóra.** Fully refurbished in 1999, Eger's largest hotel is right next to the city's spacious Strandfürdő (open-air baths) and roughly across the street from the city's beautiful indoor swimming complex, a few blocks from the main square. Though it's a bit removed from the charm of Eger's historic city center and its more intimate, smaller accommodations, the hotel is a good choice if you prefer a big, bright, modern, full-service lodging. Ask for a room facing the parklike view of the open-air baths. ⊠ *Fürdő u. 5, H-3300* ☎ *36/320–211* 🖨 *36/320–815* ⊕ *www.hunguesthotels.hu* ➔ *124 double rooms, 48 singles, 4 suites* ⌂ *Restaurant, a/c in rooms facing the open-air baths, minibars, cable TV, exercise equipment, sauna, thermal bath* ☰ *AE, DC, MC, V* ⧈ *BP.*

★ **$** ⌂ **Imola Udvarház.** Apartments at the most upmarket small hotel in Eger are pricey for this town, but the location, facilities, and pleasant, spacious self-catering quarters justify the tariff. Imola Udvarház practically sits on the steps up to the castle, and the oak and wicker furnished apartments are spotless yet homey. The hotel restaurant offers a hundred different wines. Breakfast is extra. ⊠ *Dózsa György tér 4, H-3300* 🖨 *36/516–180* ⊕ *www.imolanet.hu* ➔ *6 apartments* ⌂ *Restaurant, café, in-room data ports, kitchens, cable TV, bar, meeting room* ☰ *AE, DC, MC, V* ⧈ *EP.*

¢ ⌂ **Garten Vendégház.** This informal, family-run pension is named after its garden full of lilacs, geraniums, and acacias. It's on top of a rural hill, a 10-minute walk from Eger's main square. Rooms are furnished in pine. The suites, with eat-in kitchens, are great for families. The cheerful owners, Olga and Sanyi, can arrange tennis at the neighboring courts. If the main house is full, guests can be lodged in a separate, newer building (which also has quite a garden) a few blocks away, much closer to the town center. ✉ *Legányi u. 6, H-3300* ☎ *36/420–371* ⊕ *www. hotels.hu/garten* ⇩ *7 rooms, 2 suites* ⚸ *Some kitchens, cable TV; no room phones, no a/c* ⊟ *No credit cards* ⦿| *EP.*

★ ¢ ⊞ **Hotel Senator Ház.** This little inn, a lovely 18th-century town house, sits on Eger's main square. Whimsical paintings by Budapest artist András Győrffy hang in all the guest rooms, which are decidedly more modern than the small, elegant lobby might have you believe but are tastefully decorated in pale tans and whites. ✉ *Dobó tér 11, H-3300* ☎ *36/320– 466* ☎☎ *36/411–711* ⊕ *www.hotels.hu/senatorhaz* ⇩ *11 rooms* ⚸ *Restaurant, minibars, cable TV, free parking; no a/c* ⊟ *MC, V* ⦿| *BP.*

★ ¢ ⊞ **Offi Ház.** Picturesque Dobó tér has an equally picturesque inn, with a yellow-brick exterior and suites tastefully furnished with reproduction furniture. Upstairs there's a silver-service restaurant, decorated with a series of sugar sculptures, including a full-size grandfather clock that actually keeps the correct time. Downstairs you can eat a pub lunch in a somewhat smoky, far more basic dining room. At this writing, construction was being completed on a new, six-room pension a block away under the same ownership. ✉ *Dobó tér 5, H-3300* ☎ *36/ 311–005* ☎ *36/311–330* ⊕ *www.offihaz.hu* ⇩ *5 suites* ⚸ *2 restaurants, cable TV* ⊟ *AE, DC, MC, V* ⦿| *BP.*

Festivals & Nightlife

Festivals

From June to mid-September live bands sometimes play folk music for free out on Kis Dobó tér, part of Eger's main square.

Agria Nyári Játékok (Agria Summer Festival). The festival, which runs from July to early September, includes folk-dance and theater performances as well as concerts of everything from Renaissance to jazz to laser karaoke. Performances are held in various locations.

Szüreti Napok Egerben (Eger Harvest Festival). In early September, the three- to four-day festival celebrates the grape harvest with a traditional harvest parade through the town center, ample wine tastings in the main squares, appearances by the crowned Wine Queen, and an outdoor Harvest Ball on Dobó tér.

Ünnepi Hetek a Barokk Egerben (Festival Weeks in Baroque Eger). For two weeks every summer, beginning around late July, a cultural festival of classical concerts, dance programs, and more takes place in Eger's venues and streets and squares.

Nightlife

Hippolit Club & Restaurant. Eger's most popular upscale dance club is said to be a favorite, particularly among twenty- and thirty-something revelers. The dance floor is open on Friday and Saturday from midnight to 4 AM, while the adjoining restaurant, which serves a wide range of traditional fare, is open 7 days a week to midnight. It is conveniently located a couple of blocks from Dobó tér and right next door to Eger's outdoor food market. Just upstairs is a popular pizzeria. ⊠ *Katona tér 2* ☎ *36/412–452.*

Old Jack's Pub. The popular English-style pub is just outside the center of town. ⊠ *Rákóczi út 28* ☎ *36/425–050.*

Sports & the Outdoors

Bicycling

The forested hills of the Bükk National Park around the village of Szilvásvárad, north of Eger, comprise some of the country's most popular mountain-biking terrain.

Mountain Bike Kölcsönző. Rentals, maps, route advice, and tour guides are available at Csaba Tarnai's bike shop. As of this writing, only mountain bikes are available for rental, at 800 HUF per hour and 200 HUF more for each additional hour up to 2,000 HUF for 24 hours. Tarnai also has a bike shop in Eger. ⊠ *Szalajka-völgy út, Szilvásvárad, at entrance to Bükk National Park in the Szalajka Valley* ☎ *30/335–2695* ⊠ *Egészségház u. 11 Eger.*

Hiking

Bükk National Park, just north of Eger, has plenty of well-marked, well-used trails. The most popular excursions begin in the village of Szilvásvárad. The Tourinform in Eger (see ⇨ Visitor Information *in* Northern Hungary Essentials) can provide a hiking map and suggest routes according to the level of difficulty and duration.

Horseback Riding

A famous breeding center of the prized white Lipizzaner horses, the village of Szilvásvárad is the heart of the region's horse culture, but you needn't stray far from the heart of Eger to ride horses.

Állami Ménesgazdaság. At the State Stud-Farm, not only can you have a look at the approximately 250 Lipizzaner studs, but if you shell out 2,000 HUF or more, you can go on carriage rides, be instructed in how to lead a carriage yourself, and watch special Lipizzaner shows. ⊠ *Egri u. 16, Szilvásvárad* ☎ *36/355–155 or 36/564–002.*

Mátyus Udvarház. This convenient stable can accommodate your every equestrian need. Taking the reins into your own hands in the yard for 30 minutes costs 1,800 HUF; if an instructor guides the horse it's 2,000 HUF; and a ride out a bit farther out (holding your own reins) with a guide is 3,200 HUF per hour. Kids can ride a pony for 150 HUF per short round. A one-hour carriage ride for up to five people costs 6,000 HUF. ⊠ *Off Noszvaji út (about 2 km [1.5 mi] outside of downtown Eger in a conspicuously marked location on the right-hand side of the road to the town of Noszvaj)* ☎ *36/517–937 or 06–20/957–0806.*

Swimming

Bitskey Aladár Uszoda. Opened in 2000, what might look like a magnificent concert hall from the outside is Eger's first indoor, Olympic-size swimming pool. This imposing, modern facility is conveniently located in the city center a few blocks from Dobó tér and within 100 yards of the Strandfürdő—so you can now take a dip in downtown Eger no matter what the weather is like. By the way, what appears to be a historic clocktower benevolently preserved against one wall of the swimming complex is, on closer inspection, a merely modern little casino-cum-bar. Oh, well. Admission is 660 HUF, the sauna is 300 HUF extra, and a safe for your valuables is 300 HUF extra for every 30 minutes. The pool is open Tuesday through Sunday, from 6 AM to 8:30 PM, or sometimes 9:30, and Monday from 6 AM to 6:30 PM. ⊠ *Frank Tivadar út 5* ☎ *36/511-810.*

Termál fürdő. Eger's thermal baths are in a vast, shaded, lovely park in the center of town. You can pick where to plunge from among six outdoor pools of varying sizes, temperatures, and curative powers. All-day admission costs 800 HUF; it costs 500 HUF extra for two hours in the *élmény fürdő* (adventure baths), a combination open-air and closed facility that includes a Jacuzzi, underwater massage, and even a waterfall. The baths are open daily from 8:30 to 6:30. ⊠ *Petőfi Sándor tér 2* ☎ *36/314-142.*

Shopping

Bornivó. This is the place to stop for a huge variety of local and national wines, including a choice selection of reds, whites, and rosés from 12 of Eger's best wineries and some terrific wines from the Tokaj region. It's one storefront down from the Dobós Cukrászda café. ⊠ *Széchényi u. 8.*

Egri Galéria. In this bright, spacious gallery you'll find works by contemporary artists—paintings, ceramics, blown glass, and more—from all over Hungary. ⊠ *Érsek u. 8.*

AGGTELEK NATIONAL PARK

⓭ *75 km (47 mi) north of Eger, 155 km (97 mi) northeast of Budapest via the motorway and secondary roads, 200 km (125 mi) from Budapest via the motorway and major roads.*

One of the most extensive cave systems in Europe lies at Aggtelek, right on the Slovak border. Containing the largest stalactite system in Europe, the largest of the caves, Baradla, is 24 km (15 mi) long, extending well into Slovakia; its stalactite and stalagmite formations are of extraordinary size—some more than 49 feet high. In one of the chambers of the cave is a 600-seat concert hall, where classical concerts are held every summer. When the lights are left off for a brief period—and they will be during a tour—you experience the purest darkness there is; try holding your hand up to your face. No matter how hard you strain, you won't see it.

There are three entrances to Baradla Cave: in the town of Aggtelek, at Vörös-tó (Red Lake), and in the village of Jósvafő. Guided tours vary in length and difficulty, from the short, one-hour walks beginning at either Aggtelek or Jósvafő to the five- to eight-hour, 7-km (4½-mi) exploration from Aggtelek that ends at Jósvafő. One-hour tours are conducted several times daily.

The two-hour tour, which leaves from Jósvafő, is considered the best. The group meets at the Jósvafő ticket office, then takes a public bus (fare covered by tour admission) to the Vörös-tó entrance, from where you make your way back to Jósvafő underground.

Although all tours are conducted in Hungarian, written English translations are available at the ticket offices. Requests for the long (five- to eight-hour) tour must be sent in writing to the National Park headquarters at least two weeks ahead of time so the unmaintained sections can be rigged with proper lighting; a minimum of five adults must sign up for the long tour for it to be conducted. The caves are open year-round—they maintain a constant temperature, regardless of the weather. Keep in mind that it's chilly and damp underground—bring a sweater or light jacket and wear shoes with good traction. Tickets available at one of three ticket offices: in Aggtelek, Jóvafő, or at the Vörös-tó entrance, midway between the Aggtelek and Jósvafő (about 5 km [3 mi] from each) in a conspicuously marked location along a forested road (no street address or phone as of this writing for this ticket office). Those traveling by bus should note that the bus will stop at the Vörös-tó entrance if signalled to do so. It's not usually necessary to make tour reservations in advance, but you should call to confirm exact tour times, particularly if you are coming all the way from Budapest. ⊠ *Baradla oldal 1, Aggtelek* ☎ *48/503–003* ⊕ *www.anp.hu* ⊠ *Tengerszem oldal 3, Jósvafő* ☎ *48/506–009* ⊠ *1,300 HUF for 1-hr tour from Aggtelek, 900 HUF for 1-hr tour from Jósvafő, 1,500 HUF for 2-hr tour from Jósvafő, 4,500–5,500 for long tours from Aggtelek (5-person minimum)* ⊙ *Mid-Apr.–Sept., daily 10–6; Oct.–mid-Apr., daily 10–4; the last tour leaves 1 hr before closing.*

TOKAJ

⑭ *117 km (73 mi) east of Eger, 187 km (123 mi) northeast of Budapest.*

This enchanting village is the center of one of Hungary's most famous wine regions. It's home to the legendary Aszú wine, a dessert wine made from grapes allowed to shrivel on the vine. Aszú is produced to varying degrees of sweetness, based on how many bushels of sweet grape paste are added to the wine essence, the already highly sweet juice first pressed from them; the scale goes from two *puttonyos* (bushels) to nectar-rich six puttonyos.

The region's famed wines, dubbed (allegedly by Louis XV) the "wine of kings and king of wines," are typically golden yellow with slightly brownish tints and an almost oily texture. They've been admired outside of Hungary since Polish merchants first became hooked in the Middle Ages. In 1562, after a few sips of wine from the nearby village of Tállya, Pope Pius IV is said to have declared, "*Summum pontificem talia vina decent*" ("These wines are fit for a pope"). Other countries—France, Germany, and Russia included—have tried without much success to produce the wine from Tokaj grapes. (The secret apparently lies in the combination of volcanic soil and climate.) Still, this hasn't kept them from occasionally marketing their own "Tokaj" brands, something that riles Hungarians to no end. The branding of Tokaj wines was a major issue for Hungary as the country negotiated its entry into the EU in 2004.

The surrounding countryside is beautiful, especially in October, when the grapes hang from the vines in thick clusters. Before or after descending into the wine cellars for some epic tasting, be sure to pause while the bells toll at the lovely baroque Roman Catholic church (1770) on the main square and wend your way along some of the narrow side streets winding up into the vineyard-covered hills: views of the red-tile roofs and sloping vineyards are like sweet Aszú for the eyes. If you can still focus after a round of wine tasting, be sure to look up at the top of lampposts and chimneys, where giant white storks preside over the village from their big bushy nests. They usually return here to their nests in late April or May after wintering in warmer climes.

The third floor of the **Tokaj Múzeum** (Tokaj Museum), housed in a late-18th-century building, displays objects connected with the history of wine production in the region. The first room to your right as you enter, though, has an impressive collection of Tokaj wine and brandy bottles from the 18th and 19th centuries; also on the first floor is a film room where you can watch a video (in English or Hungarian) about Tokaj wine. All this is not to mention a special, third-floor attraction added in 2004, an exhibit of some 80 different "fake Tokaj" bottles from various countries. A wine cellar was added in 2003; and, yes, for a modest fee you can sample. If you could use a break from Tokaj's ubiquitous wine theme, the first and second floors contain exhibits of ecclesiastical art and the history of the country, respectively. The museum's tranquil courtyard hosts a summer concert series. ⊠ *Bethlen Gábor u. 7* ☎ *47/352–636* 🖅 *400 HUF* ☉ *Tues.–Sun. 11–4.*

need a break? **Halász Cukrászda** (⊠ Rákóczi út 16), also known as the Café Halász (Fisherman's Café), is a small but pleasant place to stop for coffee and a pastry before or after heading into the city center; for it is situated toward the head of the main street. The decent selection of pastries includes, notably, a scrumptious Eszterházy cake. Order at the counter.

Open daily until 10 pm, the **Integral Internet & LAN Club** (⊠ Bajcsy Zsilinszky u. 34. ☎ 47/352–137) is a couple of storefronts down from the Millennium Hotel and a convenient place to surf the Internet at affordable rates. If you arrive by train, it's about a ten-minute walk from the station, before you reach downtown.

Fodor'sChoice ★ Tokaj's most famous wine cellar, the nearly 700-year-old **Rákóczi-pince** (Rákóczi Cellar), is also Europe's largest, comprising some 1½ km (1 mi) of branching tunnels extending into the hills (today, about 1,312 feet are still in use). You can sample Tokaj's famed wines and purchase bottles of your favorites for the road (most major credit cards are accepted). Standard cellar tours, which include tasting of six different wines and some *pogácsa* (salty biscuits) are given every hour, on the hour (in English at no extra cost), and English-language pamphlets are also available. Off-season tours are by reservation only (you need to make the arrangement at least a week in advance), at varying costs, depending on the size of the group. ✉ *Kossuth tér 15* 🕾 *47/352–408, 47/352–009 for off-season reservations* 🕾 *2,000 HUF* ⊘ *Mid-Mar.–early Oct., daily 10–6, often until 8 in the summer; early Oct.–mid-Mar., by reservation only.*

The Várhelyi family offers wine tastings in the cool, damp cellar of their 16th-century house, called **Hímesudvar**. After the initial tasting, you can purchase bottles of your favorite wines and continue imbibing in their pleasant garden. A standard sampling includes six different wines. If you don't see anyone on arriving, don't hesitate to ring the bell. ✉ *Bem út 2* 🕾 *47/352–416* 🕾 *2,000 HUF and up* ⊘ *Daily 10–9.*

Where to Stay & Eat

The local Tourinform office (see ➪ Visitor Information *in* Northern Hungary Essentials) can book you a room in a private home as well as in other hotels and pensions in the area.

$$–$$$$
Fodor'sChoice
★

✕ **Ős Kaján.** It's not easy getting to one of Hungary's best little restaurants—but it's worth it. Frenchman Pascal Leeman and his wife Anne have created a homey peasant-house atmosphere decorated with traditional furniture and bric-a-brac. The cuisine is Hungarian, but uniquely so; an on-site garden provides a splendorous mix of herbs and fruits to lend the cuisine a special Mediterranean touch. Fish and game specialties characterize the small but unmistakably singular menu, which varies by season. The *Egri húsleves* (Eger meat soup) is rich with meat, vegetables, and herbs, of course, but, unlike practically anywhere else, it *seems* almost fat free. Main courses might include wild boar with Tokaj wine sauce. One delightful dessert is *almafeszitvál* (a dish of raw, baked, and breaded apple slices artfully arranged, delicately sweetened, and spiced with cinnamon). By car from Tokaj, the drive takes about 20 minutes. Go 9 km (5½ mi) west on Route 38, then some 13 km (8 mi) northeast on Route 37 toward Sárospatak. Watch for signs to Tolcsva, which is about 2 km to the left. ✉ *Kossuth u. 14–16, Tolcsva* 🕾 *47/384–195 or 47/584–036* 🕾 *Reservations essential* ▭ *No credit cards* ⊘ *Closed Mon. and Feb. 20–Dec. 20.*

$
Fodor'sChoice
★

✕🛏 **Count Degenfeld Castle Hotel.** With perhaps the exception of fake-marble plastic trash cans in the bathrooms, not a forint was spared in turning this once-neglected countryside mansion into one of Hungary's most elegant luxury hotels and best bargains. Countess Maria Degenfeld's personal, meticulous touch shows in every nook and cranny. During the Communist era, when the mansion housed a state-run agricultural cooperative, some rooms doubled as trash bins. That era is decidedly over. Immaculate rooms have period Italian, cherry-wood furnishings, Chagall prints adorn walls, beds are covered by hypoallergenic duvets, and silky red curtains carefully hide radiators. Rooms in the front have terraces that overlook the first-floor patio restaurant and the gardens. The first-floor salon has not only Venetian chandeliers but also one of two original paintings depicting Emperor Francz Joseph with Sissi (Elizabeth), Queen of Hungary, as newlyweds. The Gróf Degenfeld ($–$$$),

CloseUp
A NOBLE LINE AND A NOBLE WINE

THERE MAY BE ALMOST TOO MANY Degenfeld counts and countesses to count, but one thing is certain: Hungary—and Tokaj in particular—owes much to this legendary family. Originally from Switzerland, the Degenfelds fled in AD 850 when Leonárd Degenfeld murdered the Bishop of Lausanne. Over the next several hundred years its various branches established themselves in a territory ranging from present-day Germany to Transylvania. In present-day Hungary, one Degenfeld base was Szirák, where in the 19th century the family purchased an imposing country-house from the Teleki family (it is today a hotel, the Kastély Szirák). The other base was Tokaj.

In 2000 Count Sándor Degenfeld came to Tokaj to mark the opening of the one-time family palace (the Degenfeld Palota) as Tokaj's finest restaurant. He remarked that, although his great-great-grandparents had come from German-speaking lands, the Degenfelds became true Hungarian patriots and had done much to establish Tokaj's international reputation. Indeed, back in 1857, Count Imre Degenfeld cofounded the Tokaj-Hegyalja Viticultural Association and, around the 19th-century's end, helped establish a prominent school for vintners in the family mansion in Tarczal. This branch of the family fled back to Germany from Hungary at the end of World War II. Under Communism, the building housed a state-run agricultural cooperative and fell into disrepair. However, with a huge investment from the family—and under the watchful eye of Countess Maria Degenfeld, who lives near Munich—it reopened in 2003 as the lavish Count Degenfeld Castle Hotel. The house's vineyard has since been re-establishing itself as the producer of some of the Tokaj region's finest wines.

on the small square in the palace, is Tokaj's most elegant restaurant. The lavish interior tastefully evokes a Tokaj of centuries past—though with pop music in the background, typical of Hungarian restaurants. A multicourse meal might include an appetizer of mozzarella marinated in balsamic vinegar with tomatoes and pearl onions and a main course of fillet of "Zander" (pike perch) baked in ginger and seasoned with apple and served with mashed potatoes. Reservations are necessary for the restaurant. ⊠ Terézia kert 9, Tarczal 3915 ☎ 47/580–400 for hotel, 47/552–173 for restaurant 🖷 47/580–401 ⊕ www.hotelgrofdegenfeld.hu ➔ 20 rooms, 1 suite ⚐ Restaurant, minibars, cable TV, 2 tennis courts, pool, gym, hot tub, sauna, wine bar, meeting room, some pets allowed ⊟ AE, MC, V ⦿ BP.

¢ ✕🖾 **Hotel Tokaj.** What could well be the weirdest-looking building in the country is Tokaj's largest hotel. Giant red balls that resemble clown's noses protrude from each boxy cement balcony under a rainbow-striped facade. If the exterior doesn't put you off, you'll find adequately comfortable rooms inside, most of which have balconies that afford a better (if not quite spectacular) view of the Tisza River than does the nearby, newer Millennium Hotel. The bathrooms were remodeled in 2001, and if funding comes through, the hotel will undergo a more comprehensive sprucing up by spring 2005. The large, popular restaurant ($–$$) serves excellent fish specialties, including spicy halászlé with a swirl of sour cream. ✉ *Rákóczi u. 5, H-3910* ☎ *47/352–344 or 47/552–023* 🖷 *47/352–759* ☛ *42 rooms* ⚒ *Restaurant, cable TV, free parking; no a/c* ▤ *MC, V* ⦿ *EP.*

¢ ✕🖻 **Millennium Hotel.** One of many hotels and restaurants around Hungary named after the 1,000th anniversary of Hungarian statehood opened in the millennium year 2000. It's the first large building you'll see as you enter Tokaj on the main street from the direction of the train station. The most prominent feature is a round, bastionlike tower at one end. Rooms are bright and spacious, offering two simple beds and bathrooms with showers only. Some rooms afford a view of the Tisza River, although (unlike the older, more worn-looking Hotel Tokaj down the road) none have terraces. The suite, with a plush velvety sofa and armchairs to sink into as well as a lovely bathtub, is in the bastion. A classy little restaurant ($–$$$) has a menu of fish, poultry, and game dishes plus an extensive wine list. ✉ *Bajcsy-Zs. út 34, H-3910* ☎ *47/352–247* 🖷 *47/552–091* ⊕ *www.tokajmillennium.hu* ☛ *14 double rooms, 1 2-person suite, 1 4-person suite* ⚒ *Restaurant, cable TV, hot tub, massage, sauna, Internet, meeting room, free parking; no a/c* ▤ *AE, DC, MC, V* ⦿ *EP.*

★ ¢ 🖻 **Toldi Fogadó.** The historic building with a pleasantly rustic interior is right in the town center. A new, more modern-looking wing opened in 2003, adding six rooms plus a swimming pool with an opening roof. The rooms are clean and spacious, with pictures of Tokaj above the beds. ✉ *Hajdú köz 2, H-3910* 🖷 *47/353–403* ☛ *20 rooms* ⚒ *Restaurant, minibars, cable TV, swimming pool, hot tub, sauna* ▤ *DC, MC, V* ⦿ *CP.*

Festivals

Classical concerts by well-known artists are performed here during the **Zemplén Művészeti Napok** (Zemplén Art Days), a countywide classical music festival held annually in mid-August.

Naturally, Tokaj's best festival is the annual **Szüreti Napok** (Harvest Days) on the first weekend of October, celebrating the autumn grape harvest with a parade, a street ball, folk-art markets, and a plethora of wine tastings from the local vintners' stands erected on and around the main square.

Shopping

Tokaj Art Gallery & Salon. Near the main square, you'll find an impressive selection of contemporary paintings and other art not only from Hungary but from Germany, Russia, Poland, and Ukraine. ✉ *Rákóczi út 45* ☎ *No phone* ⊙ *Closed Mon.*

Tokaj Gobelin & Embroidery Salon. The name pretty much sums it up: this is the place to check out in Tokaj if you're looking for a wide selection of tapestry and embroidery. ✉ *Rákóczi út 60.* ☎ *No phone* ⊙ *Closed Sun. mid-Oct.–Mar.*

Northern Hungary Essentials

BUS TRAVEL

Most buses to northern Hungary depart from Budapest's Stadion station, which was rebuilt in recent years into an altogether modern, presentable-looking transport hub. Getting to Eger by bus is even easier than it is by train: beginning around 6:25 AM and then leaving every half-hour to 45 minutes until evening, buses depart from the Stadion station and take about two hours to reach Eger. The Eger–Budapest routes follow a similar schedule, but the last bus of the day leaves before 7 PM on weekdays and Saturday, around 8 PM on Sunday. As for Tokaj, going by bus is a bit of a hassle (relatively time-consuming and sometimes requiring more than one transfer); if you're not driving, go by train (one transfer, in Miskolc).

Getting to Aggtelek by bus from Budapest takes nearly five hours, but service begins around 6 AM or shortly after from Budapest's Stadion station; as long as you get a seat, it's a comfortable ride. That said, you will have just five hours to spend there, at most, as the last bus back to Budapest leaves shortly after 4 PM (an earlier bus leaves around 3 PM), though it somehow manages to reach Budapest in one hour less time than it takes to get to Aggtelek. If you're visiting Eger, though, Aggtelek is a much easier day-trip: a bus leaves around 8:45 AM and gets to Aggtelek 2½ hours later; though the return to Eger is a bit complicated, with a transfer either in Miskolc or Ózd; the last buses leave in the late afternoon or early evening, depending on the season.

🏛 **Stadion Bus Station** ✉ District XIV, Hungária krt. 48–52, Eastern Pest, Budapest ☎ 1/251–0125 Ⓜ M2: Stadion

CAR TRAVEL

The M3 expressway is the main link between Budapest and northern Hungary, cutting toward the northeast and Ukraine. Construction has been underway for years; it is, at this writing, already more than halfway to the border, somewhere beyond the Tisza River. There's an exit near Füzesabony, from where you can drive north about 20 km (13 mi) to Eger. Smaller roads through the Bükk mountains north of Eger are winding but in good shape and wonderfully scenic—this is the best way to see the region. You can go on toward Tokaj either by taking the M30 expressway, which soon hooks up with the smaller, older Route 3 north toward Miskolc, from where Route 37 branches eastward toward Tokaj and Sárospatak. Shorter on the map but perhaps a bit longer in fact: continue on the M3 past the Tisza River, then take secondary roads northeast toward Tokay.

The most convenient way to reach Aggtelek is by car. From Budapest, take the M3 motorway east, and then turn up toward Miskolc on the M30, which soon becomes Route 26. Route 26 will take you past Miskloc to Sajószentpéter, from where you continue north on Route 27 and turn west after about a half hour for the final leg of the journey. From Eger, rather than head initially east, toward Miskolc, you can take a shortcut by secondary roads due north toward Route 26, then other secondary roads the rest of the way.

TOURS

IBUSZ Travel offers its all-day "Eger Wine Region" tour leaving from Budapest on Tuesdays and Thursdays from May through October for €93. The excursion involves a thorough look at downtown Eger including the fortress, a hearty lunch, and wine-tasting in Szépasszonyok völgye on the city outskirts. An alternative is the combined all-day tour of both Eger and Tokaj offered by TGV Tours for €76 on Mondays and Sundays from April to October.

IBUSZ Travel ☎ 1/485-2700 in Budapest ⊕ www.ibusz.hu. **TGV Tours** ☎ 1/354-0755 ⊕ www.tgvtours.hu.

TRAIN TRAVEL

Trains between Eger and Budapest run several times daily from Keleti station. Trains run frequently all day between Budapest and Miskolc.

Several daily trains connect Miskolc with Sárospatak and with Tokaj. Szilvásvárad and Eger are easily accessible from each other by frequent trains.

The Eger train station lies about 1 km (½ mi) from the center of town (a 20-minute walk). Miskolc's station is about 15 minutes by bus or tram from the center of town.

Eger train station ✉ Állomás tér 1, Eger ☎ 36/314-264. **Miskolc train station** ✉ Tiszai pályaudvar, Miskolc ☎ 46/412-665.

VISITOR INFORMATION

Hollókőért közalapítvány ✉ Kossuth u. 68, Hollókő H-3176 ☎📠 32/579-010. **Tourinform** ✉ Bajcsy Zsilinszky út 9, Eger ☎📠 36/517-715 ✉ Serhaz u. 1, Tokaj ☎ 47/352-259.

UNDERSTANDING BUDAPEST

BUDAPEST AT A GLANCE

Fast Facts

Type of government: Democracy, with chief mayor, four deputy mayors, and a 67-member city council administering a metropolitan government, with each of the city's 23 districts electing its own mayors and representatives for district affairs
Population: 1.8 million
Population Density: 3,387 people per square km (8,758 people per square mi)

Median age: Female 43.7, male 39.0
Crime rate: Down 1.4% from 2001–02; 105,000 reported offenses
Language: Hungarian (official)
Ethnic groups: Hungarian 92%; other 6%; German 1%; gypsy 1%
Religion: Catholic 56%; unaffiliated 23%; Protestant 19%; Jewish 1%; other 1%

Geography & Environment

Latitude: 47.5° N (same as Seattle, Washington; Ulaanbaatar, Mongolia; Quebec City, Canada)
Longitude: 19° E (same as Stockholm, Sweden)
Elevation: 102 meters (337 feet); highest point: János Hill 527 meters (1,729 feet)
Land area: 525 square km (203 square mi) city; 2,250 square km (869 square mi) metro
Terrain: City split by the Danube River, with Buda on a series of hills on the right bank and Pest on the flatlands on the left bank
Natural hazards: Tornadoes
Environmental issues: Budapest and the rest of Hungary are cutting carbon-dioxide emissions in accordance with the Kyoto Treaty, air quality has been under close watch since 1994; wastewater treatment is slowly ending outlet of untreated sewage into Danube River

Economy

Per capita income: Average take-home pay 1.0 million HUF ($4,842)
Unemployment: 2.4%
Work force: 743,673; government 20%; manufacturing and processing 14%; trade and repairs 13%; real estate and business related services 11%; transport, warehousing, post, and telecommunications 10%; education 8%; health care and social services 8%; other 6%; financial activities 4%; construction 4%; accommodation and catering 3%
Major industries: Banking, electronics, farm machinery, food processing, pharmaceutical products, publishing, textiles, tourism, transportation

Did You Know?

• Eight bridges connect Buda and Pest. All but one were built before World War II.

• One-third of Hungary's gross national product is generated in the capital, and two-thirds of foreign investment in Hungary goes to Budapest.

• Budapest receives 1,853 hours of sunshine every year. London gets only 1,500 hours.

• Kristian Kristof of the Hungarian State Circus in Budapest is the only man in the world who has demonstrated that he can toss three cigar boxes in the air, spin around four times, and catch them.

• The Danube is the only major European river to flow from west to east.

After bisecting Budapest, it ends in Danube Delta at the Black Sea in Romania.

• The majority of Budapest's buildings were built before 1919.

• In the U.S., there is a Budapest, Missouri, and a Budapest, Georgia.

• Fifty-nine percent of people in Budapest use public transportation to get to work, 29% drive a car, and 11% walk. Three-quarters of the population ride the city's trams, buses, underground and suburban trains, which handle about 1.5 billion passengers each year.

HUNGARIAN WINE

WHEN ASKED TO NAME HUNGARY'S most famous export, people usually respond goulash or the Gabor sisters. A few might recall Hungarian actor Béla Lugosi who as Dracula chillingly intoned, "I never drink wine." Ironic, since nearly five decades of Communist mass production sucked the blood from Hungary's once flourishing wine industry. But since the bloc's 1989 collapse, no Eastern European nation has made greater strides in reclaiming top neglected vineyards and upgrading winemaking techniques and equipment. Given the right marketing, "Old World," post–Cold War Hungary may well become the hot new wine frontier.

The country boasts a distinguished wine history. The Romans planted vines extensively some two millennia ago. The Tokaj region discovered that grapes shriveled by botrytis mold, which concentrates sugar and flavor, produced exemplary dessert wine a century before France's Sauternes were even conceived. Tokaj also arguably established the earliest known appellation/vineyard classification system in the 17th century. Europe's royal courts demanded Hungarian wines, while leading cultural lights—Voltaire, Goethe, Schubert—lavished praise in poem and song. Napa as we know it might not exist: California's wine industry was jumpstarted by Hungarian immigrant, Ágoston Haraszthy, who brought 300 different vine cuttings with him when he came to America in 1861.

Despite its small size, Hungary embraces many microclimates, from sub-Mediterranean in the south to Germanic/Continental by the Danube and Carpathians, and varied soil types conducive to producing grapes combining intense flavor with great acidic structure. Its 22 official viticultural regions lie between the same latitudes as France's Champagne and Bordeaux regions. Yet Hungary's warmer, sunnier summers—not to mention less cloud cover and autumnal rain—provide even more consistent growing conditions, allowing the slow ripening that maximizes flavors and aromas.

Nonetheless, when the bulk wine market crashed after Communism ended, few Hungarians possessed the capital to renovate. Several enterprising locals (such as Tibor Gál, who won worldwide acclaim as winemaker of Marchese Ludovico Antinori's celebrated "Super Tuscan," Ornellaia; famed restaurateur George Lang; and recently, cable entrepreneur Nimród Kovács, whose Monarchia Wines both produces and distributes leading wines from several appellations) scrambled to fund modern vineyard plantings and facilities. Foreign investment poured in, including money from Italy's Nicolò Incisa della Rochetta (of Sassicaia fame) and Piero Antinori; cosmetics magnate Ron Perelman; British wine authority Hugh Johnson; Spain's illustrious Vega Sicilia; and French conglomerate AXA.

Most of the investment initially focused on Tokaj, whose rare, expensive sweet wines still retained cachet among connoisseurs. But savvy vintners knew that high-quality dry wines—especially reds—showed great promise throughout Hungary. The industry's major controversy is whether to emphasize the so-called international varietals (cabernet sauvignon, cabernet franc, merlot, pinot noir, chardonnay, et al.) or to resurrect the neglected Hungaricums (indigenous grapes), which the BorKombinát (State Farm) often suppressed. The latter are a tougher sell internationally due to their unfamiliarity and names that are difficult to pronounce. There's also bickering over Bikavér (Bull's Blood), a noble wine adulterated for export as cheap, if potent, plonk downed by undiscriminating collegians. Legally, only Eger and Szekszárd may produce bottles of Bull's Blood, from a combination of at least three of nine grapes (though many argue that specific regulations should be standardized); several winemakers have taken the "Bull" by the horns, crafting both superb traditional (from Hungaricums) and innovative (mostly syrah and merlot) examples they hope will erase the stigma.

Hungarian wines have already garnered prestigious awards from the likes of VinItaly, VinExpo Bordeaux, and London's IWSC. The infusion of capital and fresh blood of a new, peripatetic generation may start taking a bigger bite out of the global market.

Wine Labels

Some exceptional Hungarian wines are exported in minuscule amounts (distributors hope to create boutique buzz). Many export bottles sport catchy "fantasy names," especially for the unjustly tarnished Bikavérs, with the actual varietals and story relegated to the back label. Look for labels stating Minősegi (Quality), Különleges (Superior Quality) or Válogatás (Special Selection, similar to Reserve). You can easily confirm the appellation (an "i" is added to the end of the delimited area, as in Egri for Eger, Tokaji for Tokaj, etc.). Increasingly, you'll find single-estate wines (usually indicated by the word Szőlő), though many producers still favor blending from their best vineyard lots. Tokaji comes in several varieties, including still-dry, mono-varietal, and late-harvest bottlings. Aszú refers to the desiccated, botrytized grapes; the levels of sugar content (and presumably quality) are measured in 3, 4, 5, and 6 puttonyos (Aszú Esszencia, the rarest, is roughly equivalent to 8 puttonyos). Esszencia Natur is pure nectar: the syrup created by pressed Aszú berries, a legendary panacea, low in alcohol (rarely more than 4%), and fabulously expensive. Szamarodni is made from partially botry-

tized grapes bunches left after the main selection and can be dry or sweet.

Regions, Wineries & Varietals

Of course, visitors can sample a wide variety of wines at shops and restaurants in Budapest and by touring the regions themselves. The major wine appellations are lovely, historic, relatively unspoiled, and (mostly) remote. Although many regional organizations have created wine routes, roads are often bumpy; signage is poor or nonexistent; official maps might lack names, hours, and addresses; English skills of vintners might be minimal; and the quality of member wineries may vary wildly. A car, map, and fortitude are necessary to explore the farther-flung areas. Good highways and trains connect Budapest with the most famous regions, the northeast's Eger and Tokaj—both walkable villages, but whose actual wineries are scattered through several communities. Lake Balaton, "the Hungarian Sea" west of Budapest, is also geared toward intrepid viti-tourism. Villány (and Szekszárd somewhat) in the temperate southeast are the only towns where you can stroll from one pince (cellar) to the next. Call ahead to ensure wineries are open for tours.

Volcanic hills, including distinctive basalt "pipe organ" formations, ring the northern edge of Central Europe's largest freshwater lake, **Balaton.** Ancient monasteries and waterwheels adorn tiny villages, ruined fortresses command lonely craggy hills, and thermal waters sculpt miniature moonscapes woven with startling ribbons of green. The Badacsony Historical Wine Region (also known as the Valley of the Volcanoes Wine Route) intelligently combines all the area's attractions. Top producers include István Nemeth Cellars; articulate, opinionated Huba Szeremley's modernized 19th-century mountaintop Helvécia Estate vineyard/restaurant in Badacsony; and Mihály Figula's contemporary, beautifully situated "Fine Wines" winery in adjacent Balatonfüred-Csopak. The appellations surrounding Lake Balaton are most noted for steely, smoky, mineral-accented whites, from pinot gris (a. k.a. szürkebarát), sauvignon blanc, and welschriesling (a.k.a. olaszrizling; not related to the noble Riesling but planted extensively throughout Central Europe) to cserszegi fűszeres (a fragrant, spicy hybrid of irsai olivér, itself a cross, and gewürztraminer).

Eger is an utterly ravishing town near the Slovakian border, established in the 11th century and seat of the Hungary Bishopric since the 1300s. Parts of the castle/fortress crowning the town (with splendid panoramas) date to 1272; today the maze of catacombs often hosts impromptu discos. Magnificent late-Gothic and baroque churches serenely command tree-choked plazas. Ornately embellished buildings in hues from olive to ocher with cast-iron balconies, carved-stone gates, and elaborate interior courtyards tiptoe up and down hills. Stone bridges cross the tiny river. Pedestrian cobblestone streets overflow with sidewalk cafés; old ladies in babushkas sell fish, fruit, and flowers in markets that are scented with dried peppers and garlic braids. Several winemakers have won international awards for their reds (this is an up-and-coming area for pinot noir, merlot, and syrah), including Egri Bikavér. Look also for the indigenous peppery kékfrankos (a.k.a. blaufränkisch). In whites, you'll find chardonnay, muscat ottonel (the lightest of this grape family known for its apricot/peach notes), and királyleányka (translated as princess, this grape produces wines with a cross-producing muscat-like bouquet with full body and light acidity). Among the many superb vintners are Tibor Gál at GIA, Vilmos Thummerer, Béla Vincze, István Tóth, and Dr. Tamás Pók (Monarchia's head winemaker and co-owner of its subsidiary, Pók-Polónyi Pince). Monarchia's own state-of-the-art facility, crowning one of the region's prized hilltop vineyards in Noszvaj, is slated for completion late 2004, at this writing.

Tokaj-Hegyalja, in the northeast corner near the Slovakia and Ukraine borders, was declared a UNESCO World Heritage Site in 2002. The village of Tokaj is one of 27 within the fairy-tale appellation, with the Tisza and Bodrog rivers snaking around emerald rolling hills. Creeping vines adorn 18th-century houses painted orange and ocher with red barrel-tile roofs. Tokaj's labyrinthine cellars carved from solid volcanic rock are covered with a mold that helps maintain proper temperature and humidity; it also "cleanses" the air and retards development of harmful bacteria. The best, if most touristy, option is the grand original, Hétszőlő built in 1502, right off the main square. The exquisitely restored 18th-century Királyudvar (in neighboring Tarcal), which means royal estate, is co-owned and managed by innovative Tokaji producer, István Szepsy; its wines are made by wunderkind Zoltán Demeter. Disznókő and Oremus are architecturally stunning and state-of-the-art. Gróf Degenfeld also operates a historic castle-hotel and excellent gourmet restaurant in the town. Try not only the superlative sweet wines, but also fresh, crisp whites from the primary grapes: the fiery, floral furmint and the highly aromatic, spicy, acidic hárslevelű (linden leaf).

The sub-Mediterranean climate of **Villány,** Hungary's answer to Bordeaux, provides ideal conditions for cabernet and merlot, as well as kékfrankos, syrah, zweigelt, and pinot noir; the appellation includes Siklós, noted for highly acidic aromatic whites. Narrow-shingled whitewashed and brick Swabian houses with brightly painted shutters and doors contain small, mostly mom-and-pop cellars (many sporting gorgeous arcaded, barrel-and-groin vaulted ceilings and floors). The Villány-Siklós association (Hungary's first, officially formed in 1994) includes around 60 wineries, 30 accommodations, and 5 restaurants as members. The quaint villages, their homes and gardens a color wheel of flowers most of the year, are filled with baroque castles and hand-painted chapels, as well as small wine museums containing ancient equipment from presses to enormous vats. The most contemporary, state-of-the-art facility is the extensive Vylyan (in Kisharsány), though using the town's 15th-century name for its label clearly honors owners Pal and Monika Debreczeni's heritage. Father and son Ede and Zsolt Tiffán started their winery in 1990, but the family have passed their viticultural traditions on for generations. Jószef Bock, from another respected local wine family, was one of the first to bottle his own wines under Communism. Attila Gere also produces typically silken but virile reds and partners in a venture with Austrian master Franz Weninger. To the north lies Szekszárd, also ridiculously quaint, with grand churches and humble thatched, whitewashed cellar-houses dating back half a millennium situated among gently rolling forested hills. The area, also noted for its thermal waters, likewise produces excellent reds, including the Bordeaux varietals and kékfrankos. Ferenc Veszterombi honors a winemaking tradition dating to 1790. Takler Pince is celebrated for Bordeaux blends and cabernet franc, but the father-son team fervently, feverishly works to restore the reputation of Szekszárdi Bikavér and the native kadarka grape.

— Jordan Simon

BOOKS & MOVIES

Although Hungarians have played a central role in the intellectual life of the past century, their literary and cinematic masters are less well known abroad than their luminaries in other arts, such as Béla Bartók in music and André Kertész in photography.

When Imre Kertész won the 2003 Nobel Prize in Literature, for *Fateless* and other novels, he was the first Hungarian to achieve this distinction but certainly not the first regarded by his compatriots as worthy. Novelist and poet Dezső Kosztolányi was prominent in Europe after World War I and admired by Thomas Mann. Some years earlier, the great novelist Gyula Krudy created the most memorable character in modern Hungarian literature, the hopelessly romantic gentleman Szindbád. In his novel *Azarel*, Károly Pap, who perished in the Holocaust, wrote with piercing candor about growing up Jewish. In the 1960s and '70s, István Örkény penned his popular novellas and *One Minute Stories*. Later in the Communist era, novelist and dissident György Konrád reflected on intellectual life under totalitarianism in *The Loser*. In her 1987 novel *The Door*, Magda Szabó explores the relationship between a writer and her housekeeper.

The 1990s saw the extraordinary literary revival of Sándor Márai, whose many books—most of which he published by 1945—include the fictional memoir *Confessions of a Bourgeois* and the novella *Embers*. Márai fled Hungary after World War II; he died in California in 1989. Among Hungary's greatest contemporary novelists are Péter Nádas, whose magnum opus is the Proustian *Book of Memories*; Péter Eszterházy, whose inventive prose has inspired a generation of younger Hungarian writers while also earning him enormous popularity; and László Krasznahorkai, whose labyrinthine novels have likewise been critically acclaimed.

Writers of Hungarian descent abroad have certainly helped interpret Hungary for the outside world. The English novelist Tibor Fischer's *Under the Frog* is set in Hungary under Communism. In *Budapest 1900*, the American historian John Lukacs provides an elegant, illustrated look at Hungary's capital in a golden age. Austrian-Hungarian journalist Paul Lendvai's *The Hungarians* is a novel-like encapsulation of 1,000 years of nationhood.

Though hard to express its beauty in English, Hungary's poetry is really at the heart of its literature. Some 20th-century greats, whose work has appeared in fine translations, are Endre Ady, Attila József, Miklós Radnóti, János Pilinszky, Sándor Weöres, and Ágnes Nemes-Nagy.

Turning to film: István Szabó (*Mephisto*; Oscar, 1981) and Miklós Jancsó are best known abroad among Hungarian directors. Péter Bacsó's *The Witness* is a disarming satire of Communism made in the late 1960s but kept from the general public for years. The 1970s yielded Károly Makk's *Love* and Zoltán Huszárik's *Sindbad*, both masterpieces. Péter Gothár, who rose to fame in the 1980s, produced a moving treatment of the aftermath of the 1956 revolution in *Time Stands Still*. Márta Mészáros's films masterfully explore women's lives. Ildikó Enyedi gained international recognition beginning in the late 1980s with her cosmic-ironic fairy tales, including *My Twentieth Century*. One of several recent films that have garnered international prizes is György Pálfi's *Hukkle*, on the explosive undercurrent of village life.

Hungary may look small on a map, but it is a universe of great literary and cinematic art that is still expanding.

HUNGARIAN VOCABULARY

Tricky double consonants (with English equivalents as they appear in the pronunciation guide below):

gy = a one-syllable "dy" sound (a quick *dya*—indicated in the pronunciation guide below as *dy*)
ly = y (as in "yard")
ny = a one-syllable "ny" (a quick *nya*—indicated below as *ny*)
ty = a one-syllable "ty" (a quick *tya*—indicated below as *ty*)

Tricky vowels:

ö = the "i" in a short, snapped out "*Sir!*" (pronounced with slightly rounded lips)
ő = the "i" in a long "s*iiii*r" (pronounced with very rounded lips)
ü = no clear English equivalent; like the "ü" in the German expression "*über alles*" (pronounced with slightly rounded lips)
ű ř a longer form of the "ü" (pronounced with very rounded lips)

English	Hungarian	Pronunciation

Basics

English	Hungarian	Pronunciation
Yes/no	Igen/nem	**ee**-gen/nem
Please [when asking for something]	Kérem (szépen)	**kay**-rem (**say**-pen)
Please [to get the attention of someone; e.g., a waiter]	Legyen szives	le-dyen **see**-vesh
Thank you (kindly)	Köszöszöm (szépen)	**kuh**-suh-nuhm (**say**-pen)
Excuse me	Elnézést	**el**-nay-zaysht
Sorry [for doing something]	Bocsánat	**boh**-chah-nut
I'm sorry [about something]	Sajnálom	**shuy**-nah-lome
Hello [during the day]	Jó napot	**yo**-nup-ote
Good evening	Jó estét	**yo**-esh-tate
Goodbye [formal]	Viszontlátásra	**vees**-ohnt-lot-osh-ruh
Goodbye [informal]	Viszlát	vees-**lot**
Today/During the day	Ma/Nappal	**muh/nup-pawl**
Tonight	Ma este	**muh** eshte
Tomorrow	Holnap	**hole**-nup
Hello [not too formal]	Szervusz	**ser**-voose

Hi [informal, chummy; commonly used]	Szia	see-ya
Do you speak English?	Beszél angolul?	**bess**-ale un-goal-ool
I don't speak Hungarian.	Nem tudok magyarul.	**nem** tood-ook **mu**-dyur-ool
I don't understand.	Nem értem.	**nem** air-tem
Please speak slowly.	Kérem, beszéljen lassan.	**kay**-rem, **bess**-ale-yen lush-shun
Please write it down.	Kérem, írja fel.	**kay**-rem, **eer**-yuh fell
Please show me.	Kérem, mutassa meg.	**kay**-rem, **moo**-tush-shuh meg
I am American.	Amerikai vagyok.	**uh**-meh-ree-kuh-ee vuh-*d*yoke
I am English.	Angol vagyok.	**un**-goal vuh-*d*yoke
I am Australian.	Ausztrál vagyok.	**ouse**-trahl vuh-*d*yoke
I am Canadian.	Kanadai vagyok.	**cun**-uh-duh-ee vuh-*d*yoke
Right/left	bal/job	ball/yobe
Open/closed	nyitva/zárva	**nyeet**-vuh/**zahr**-vuh
Arrival/departure	érkezés/indulás	**air**-kez-ayshe/ **een**-dool-ahsh
Where is . . .?	Hol van . . .?	**hole** vun
. . . the train station?	. . . a pályaudvar?	uh **pah**-ya-ood-var
. . . the bus station?	. . . a buszállomás?	uh **boose**-ah-low-mahsh
. . . the bus stop?	. . . a buszmegalló?	uh **boose**-meg-ahl-low
. . . the airport?	. . . a reptér?	uh **rep**-tair
. . . a post office?	. . . a posta?	uh **pohsh**-tuh
. . . a bank?	. . . a bank?	uh **bunk**
. . . a hotel?	. . . egy szálloda?	e*d*y **sahl**-ode-uh
. . . an internet café?	. . . egy internet kávézó?	e*d*y **een**-tair-net kah-vay-zoe
. . . a restroom?	. . . egy vécé?	e*d*y **vay**-tsay
Stop here.	Álljon meg itt.	**ahl**-yone meg eet
I would like . . .	Szeretnék . . .	**ser**-et-nake
How much does it cost?	Mennyibe kerül?	**men**-yee-beh kair-uhl
Letter/postcard	level/képeslap	**lev**-ehl/**kay**-pesh-lup
By airmail	légi postával	**lay**-ghee pohsh-tah-vuhl
Help!	Segitség!	**sheh**-geet-shaig

Meeting people

My name is . . .	[stress on name] . . . a nevem.	uh ne-vem
What is your name? [literally]	Mi a neve?	**me** uh ne-ve
What is your name? [What are you called?]	Hogy hívnak?	**hodye** heev-nuk
Where are you from?	Honnan van?	**hone**-un-vun
What do you study?	Mit tanul?	**meet** tun-ool
What is your major?	Milyen szakos?	**me**-yen suck-oshe
What is your occupation?	Mi a foglalkozása?	**me** uh foge-lull-koze-ahsh-uh
What music do you like?	Milyen zenét szeret?	**me**-yen zen-ate ser-et
Let's have a coffee.	Kávézunk egyet.	**kah**-vaze-oonk e-*dy*et
You are beautiful.	Szép vagy.	**sape** vuh*dy*
You have lovely eyes.	Szép a szeme.	**sape** uh sem-e
I like you.	Tetszel.	**tet**-sell
I love you.	Szeretlek.	**ser**-et-lek
Stop harassing me!	Ne zaklasson!	**ne** zuk-lush-un
I've got to go.	Mennem kell.	**men**-nem kell

Numbers

One	egy	e*dy*
Two	kettő	**ket**-tuh
Three	három	**hah**-rome
Four	négy	nay*dy*
Five	öt	uht
Six	hat	hut
Seven	hét	hate
Eight	nyolc	*ny*olts
Nine	kilenc	**kee**-lents
Ten	tíz	teez
Eleven	tízenegy	**teez**-en-e*dy*
Twelve	tízenkettő	**teez**-en-ket-uh
Thirteen	tízenhárom	**teez**-en-hah-rom
Fourteen	tízennégy	**teez**-en-na*dy*e
Fifteen	tízenöt	**teez**-en-uht

Sixteen	tízenhat	**teez**-en-hut
Seventeen	tízenhét	**teez**-en-hate
Eighteen	tízennyolc	**teez**-en-nyoltse
Nineteen	tízenkilenc	**teez**-en-kee-lents
Twenty	húsz	hoose
Thirty	harminc	**hawr**-meents
Fourty	negyven	**nedy**-ven
Fifty	ötven	**uht**-ven
Sixty	hatvan	**hut**-vun
Seventy	hetven	**het**-ven
Eighty	nyolcvan	**nyoltse**-vun
Ninety	kilencven	**kee**-lents-ven
One hundred	száz	sahz
One thousand	ezer	**ez**-zer

Days of the Week

Sunday	vasárnap	**vuh**-shahr-nup
Monday	hétfő	**hate**-fuh
Tuesday	kedd	ked
Wednesday	szerda	**ser**-duh
Thursday	csütörtök	**chit**-ir-tik
Friday	péntek	**pain**-tek
Saturday	szombat	**soam**-but

Where to Sleep

A room	egy szoba	e*dy* soh-buh
The key	a kulcsot	uh **koolch**-oat
With a bath/a shower	fürdőszobával/ zuhannyal	**fuhr**-duh-soh-bah-vuhl/ **zoo**-hun-*n*yal

Food

A restaurant	az étterem	uhz **eht**-teh-rem
The menu	az étlap	uhz **ate**-lup
The check, please.	a számlát kérem.	uh **sahm**-lot **kay**-rem
I'd like to order this.	Ezt szeretném.	**est** ser-et-name
Breakfast	reggeli	**reg**-ell-ee
Lunch	ebéd	**eb**-ehd

Dinner	vacsora	**vutch**-oh-ruh
Bread	kenyér	**ke**-*ny*air
Butter	vaj	vuy
Salt/pepper	só/bors	show/borsh
Bottle	üveg	ew-veg
Red/white wine	vörös/fehér bor	**vuh**-ruhsh/ **feh**-hair boar
Beer	sör	shur
(Tap) water	sima víz	**shee**-muh veez
Sparkling water	szódavíz	**soda**-veez
Mineral water	ásványvíz	**ahsh**-vah*ny*-veez
Milk	tej	tey
Coffee (with milk)	kávé/tejeskávé	**kah**-vay/ **tey**-esh-kah-vay
Tea (with lemon)	tea (citrommal)	**tey**-yuh (**tseet**-rome-awl)
Chocolate	csokoládé	**chook**-kaw-lah-day

INDEX

NOTES

NOTES

NOTES

NOTES

NOTES

NOTES

NOTES

NOTES